Heinrich Brüning and the Dissolution of the Weimar Republic

Scholars have long debated whether Heinrich Brüning, head of the German government from 1930 to 1932, was the "last democratic chancellor" of the Weimar Republic or the trail-blazer of the Nazi dictatorship. His memoirs (published in 1970) damaged his reputation badly by terming the restoration of monarchy the "crux" of his policies. This book is the first scholarly biography of Brüning in any language and offers a systematic analysis of the economic, social, foreign, and military policies of his cabinet as it sought to cope with the Great Depression. With the help of newly available sources, it clarifies the peculiar distortions in the memoirs, showing that Chancellor Brüning intended to restore parliamentary democracy intact when the economic crisis passed. He was curbing the Nazi menace successfully when President Hindenburg, reactionary landowners, and army generals eager for massive rearmament made the disastrously misguided decision to topple him.

William L. Patch, Jr., is Associate Professor of History at Grinnell College and the author of *Christian Trade Unions in the Weimar Republic, 1918–1933*. While a student at the University of Göttingen, he observed the challenges to German democracy posed by Red Army terrorism, the second oil shock, and student radicalism. Patch was also educated at the University of California at Berkeley, Yale, and the University of Bochum. He has taught at Yale and Trinity College in Hartford, Connecticut, in addition to Grinnell.

An official portrait of Chancellor Brüning at his desk. (Bundesarchiv Koblenz-102-75/66/3)

Heinrich Brüning and the Dissolution of the Weimar Republic

William L. Patch, Jr.

CAMBRIDGE
UNIVERSITY PRESS

PUBLISHED BY THE PRESS SYNDICATE OF THE UNIVERSITY OF CAMBRIDGE
The Pitt Building, Trumpington Street, Cambridge CB2 1RP, United Kingdom

CAMBRIDGE UNIVERSITY PRESS
The Edinburgh Building, Cambridge CB2 2RU, UK   http://www.cup.cam.ac.uk
40 West 20th Street, New York, NY 10011-4211, USA   http://www.cup.org
10 Stamford Road, Oakleigh, Melbourne 3166, Australia

First published 1998

Printed in the United States of America

Typeset in Ehrhardt 10.25/12, in Macintosh

*A catalog record for this book is available from
the British Library*

Library of Congress Cataloging-in-Publication Data
Patch, William L., 1953–
Heinrich Brüning and the dissolution of the Weimar Republic/
William L. Patch, Jr.
p.   cm.
Includes bibliographical references and index.
ISBN 0-521-62422-3
1. Brüning, Heinrich, 1885–1970.   2. Statesmen – Germany –
Biography.   3. Germany – Politics and government – 1918–1933.
4. Political parties – Germany – History.   5. National socialism –
Germany.   I. Title.
DD247.B7P38   1998
943.085′092 – dc21
97-43388   CIP

ISBN 0 521 62422 3

Contents

Acknowledgments

This book is based largely on archival research undertaken during several summers from 1988 to 1994, and thanks are due therefore to the donors who have given generously to Grinnell College to support faculty research trips to Europe, especially Alf A. Johnsen and Helena and Ignacio Percas de Ponseti. My colleagues in the Grinnell History Department, Don Smith and Dan Kaiser, have read this manuscript, helped me to improve the reasoning, and provided much encouragement. I owe a special debt of gratitude to the distinguished experts on the Weimar Republic, Henry Turner and Gerald Feldman, who have offered many valuable suggestions for improving the manuscript and shared generously with me the fruits of their own research. I would also like to thank Hans Mommsen and the participants in his graduate seminar at the University of Bochum, who subjected an early (and, I fear, rather primitive) version of my argument to rigorous criticism in July 1989; they challenged me to delve more deeply into the topic. Finally, I would like to thank my wife Ingrid for her unfailing support and gracious acceptance of the postponement of numerous family projects for the sake of scholarship.

William L. Patch, Jr.

List of Abbreviations

BAK	Bundesarchiv Koblenz (German National Archive, Koblenz)
BAP	Bundesarchiv, Abteilung Potsdam (Potsdam branch of the German National Archive)
BVP	Bayerische Volkspartei (Bavarian People's Party)
CDU	Christlich-Demokratische Union (Christian Democratic Union)
DDP	Deutsche Demokratische Partei (German Democratic Party)
DGB	Deutscher Gewerkschaftsbund (German Labor Federation)
DHV	Deutschnationaler Handlungsgehilfen-Verband (German Nationalist Union of Commercial Employees)
DNVP	Deutschnationale Volkspartei (German Nationalist People's Party)
DVP	Deutsche Volkspartei (German People's Party)
HUG	Harvard University Archive
IfZ	Institut für Zeitgeschichte (Institute for Contemporary History, Munich)
KPD	Kommunistische Partei Deutschlands (Communist Party of Germany)
NL	Nachlass (collection of personal papers)
NSDAP	Nationalsozialistische Deutsche Arbeiterpartei (National Socialist German Workers' Party)
ÖSA	Österreichisches Staatsarchiv (Austrian State Archive)
RDI	Reichsverband der Deutschen Industrie (Reich Association of German Industry)
RLB	Reichslandbund (Reich Agrarian League)
SA	Sturmabteilung (Nazi Stormtroopers)
SPD	Sozialdemokratische Partei Deutschlands (Social Democratic Party of Germany)

Introduction
Brüning and the Prussian Tradition

Heinrich Brüning has long been praised by some as the "last democratic chancellor" of the Weimar Republic and attacked by others as the trail-blazer of dictatorship. In the seminal work on his chancellorship, Karl Dietrich Bracher depicted him as the largely unwitting agent of reactionaries around President Hindenburg who sought to abolish democracy by toppling the last majority coalition of the Weimar Republic in March 1930. Brüning was an "apolitical" technocrat, Bracher argued, obsessed with diplomacy and the details of ever more complex emergency decrees designed to cope with the Great Depression, and his aloof style of government contributed much to the growth of the Communist and Nazi parties. By the time that Hindenburg dismissed him in May 1932, Brüning's style of government had undermined democratic institutions so much that military dictatorship offered the only remaining alternative to a Nazi seizure of power.[1] Several historians defended Brüning by arguing that the Reichstag had succumbed to paralysis long before his appointment, that he distributed the unavoidable hardships of the Great Depression as fairly as possible and intended to restore parliamentary democracy when the economic crisis passed. Brüning had good reason, they maintained, to focus on diplomatic efforts to abolish war reparations as the prerequisite for economic recovery, and he was near success when Hindenburg foolishly dismissed him.[2] Keynesian economic historians soon developed a second line of criticism, however, that depicted Brüning as the stubborn adherent of an obsolete orthodoxy who inflicted needless hardship on the German people by ignoring all arguments in favor of deficit spending for public

---

1 Karl Dietrich Bracher, *Die Auflösung der Weimarer Republik. Eine Studie zum Problem des Machtverfalls in der Demokratie*, 5th ed. (1955; Villingen, Schwarzwald, 1971). For a summary in English, see Bracher, *The German Dictatorship* (New York, 1970), chapters 1 and 4.
2 Werner Conze, "Die Krise des Parteienstaates in Deutschland 1929/30," *Historische Zeitschrift*, 178 (1954): 47–83; Conze's review of Bracher in *Historische Zeitschrift*, 183 (1957): 378–82; Waldemar Besson, *Württemberg und die deutsche Staatskrise 1928–1933* (Stuttgart, 1959), esp. pp. 358–70; Wolfgang Helbich, *Die Reparationen in der Ära Brüning. Zur Bedeutung des Young-Plans für die deutsche Politik 1930 bis 1932* (Berlin, 1962); Werner Conze, "Die politischen Entscheidungen in Deutschland, 1929–1933," in Werner Conze and Hans Raupach, eds., *Die Staats- und Wirtschaftskrise des Deutschen Reichs 1929–1933* (Stuttgart, 1967), pp. 211–39.

works.[3] The debate has proved very difficult to resolve, in part because Brüning burned his personal papers before fleeing Germany in 1934. This book will seek nevertheless to demonstrate with the help of newly available sources that Brüning did intend to restore parliamentary democracy with relatively minor reforms when the economic crisis passed, and that his fall, not his appointment to office, marked the crucial turning point in the dissolution of the Weimar Republic.

Brüning himself did little to enlighten the historians. He published one article in a German magazine in 1947 on the causes of his fall but retreated from the limelight when other witnesses contradicted his assertion that President Hindenburg had suffered "a mental collapse lasting ten days" in September 1931 and a steady loss of intellectual capacity thereafter.[4] Brüning had written detailed memoirs of his chancellorship in 1934/5 but now decided not to publish them until they "serve a purpose for our fatherland and the public seems receptive," conditions that he never saw fulfilled.[5] His critics and defenders alike were nonplused when his memoirs finally appeared a few months after his death in 1970. Brüning portrayed himself as a staunch conservative in the spirit of Bismarck, indeed to the right of the Iron Chancellor, since he condemned Bismarck's introduction of equal suffrage in national elections as premature. The Weimar constitution had broken with German traditions by imposing a democracy based on foreign models. At critical junctures throughout his tenure, Brüning recalled, he had struggled to secure approval for a constitutional amendment to replace the elected President with a hereditary monarch. He supposedly discussed this plan with Hitler in October 1930 and then employed secret intermediaries to forge an alliance with the second most powerful Nazi leader, Gregor Strasser. He thought of making way for a Nazi chancellor at some point in 1932 in a coalition government dedicated to restoring monarchy, and he even revealed this plan in November 1931 to the Social Democrats Rudolf Hilferding, Carl Severing, and Otto Braun. They "intimated" (*liessen durchblicken*) that they could accept a restoration if Brüning concluded that this was the only way to prevent a Hitler dictatorship. The plan was thwarted by Hindenburg's legitimist devotion to the

---

3 See Gerhard Kroll, *Von der Weltwirtschaftskrise zur Staatskonjunktur* (Berlin, 1959), and Horst Sanmann, "Daten und Alternativen der deutschen Wirtschafts- und Finanzpolitik in der Ära Brüning," *Hamburger Jahrbuch für Wirtschafts- und Gesellschaftspolitik*, 10 (1965): 109–40.

4 Heinrich Brüning, "Ein Brief," *Deutsche Rundschau*, 70, #7 (1947): 1–22, reprinted in *Heinrich Brüning. Reden und Aufsätze eines deutschen Staatsmanns*, ed. Wilhelm Vernekohl (Münster, 1968) (hereafter cited as Brüning, *Reden*); original letter to Rudolf Pechel, written in English on 20 April 1947 (quotation on pp. 4–5), Nachlass (NL) Pechel/51. Contrast Otto Meissner, *Staatssekretär unter Ebert – Hindenburg – Hitler* (Hamburg, 1950), pp. 213–14, and Hans-Otto Meissner, *Junge Jahre im Reichspräsidentenpalais. Erinnerungen an Ebert und Hindenburg 1919–1934* (Munich, 1988), pp. 274–79.

5 Brüning to Helene Weber, 27 October 1947, in Claire Nix, ed., *Heinrich Brüning. Briefe 1946–1960* (Stuttgart, 1974) (hereafter cited as "*Briefe*, II"), p. 102; Rudolf Morsey, *Zur Entstehung, Authentizität und Kritik von Brünings "Memoiren 1918–1934"* (Opladen, 1975), pp. 10–12, 29–32; Frank Müller, *Die "Brüning Papers." Der letzte Zentrumskanzler im Spiegel seiner Selbstzeugnisse* (Frankfurt a.M., 1993), pp. 123–70.

hopelessly unpopular ex-kaiser and by hypocrites on the right who placed partisan advantage above monarchist principle.[6]

The publication of these memoirs damaged Brüning's reputation badly. Werner Conze still defended him as one who sought to preserve the substance of democracy by creating a British-style monarchy, but if the memoirist's description of his goals is accurate, then he should doubtless be considered either reactionary or terribly naive.[7] Careful readers soon questioned Brüning's vague account of a plan for restoration, however. The memoirist never identifies the potential monarch, glossing over the fact that the ex-kaiser and his oldest son could not agree on who should claim the throne. His assertion that he had initiated Hilferding, Severing, and Braun into this plan was indignantly denied by everyone who knew them. The memoirist also loses the reader's confidence with faulty chronology, a refusal to acknowledge any mistakes, and efforts to deny his colleagues any credit for his achievements. The few surviving associates of Chancellor Brüning agreed that he had pursued far more constructive goals and displayed a more appealing personality than the petulant and self-righteous memoirist. Rudolf Morsey soon concluded in a thoughtful study that the memoirs were seriously distorted by the trauma of dismissal, that Brüning had grossly exaggerated his enthusiasm for Bismarck and the Hohenzollern dynasty ever since June 1932 to prove that there was no foundation for the reproach of hostility toward the right that had persuaded Hindenburg to dismiss him.[8] Andreas Rödder has recently strengthened Morsey's case, moreover, by demonstrating several noteworthy contradictions between Brüning's memoirs and the contemporary documentary sources with regard to the chancellor's goals in both foreign policy and domestic politics.[9] If Morsey and Rödder are correct, then historians obviously should not rely on the memoirist's testimony about his long-term goals without corroborating evidence.

Yet many historians continue to cite the memoirs uncritically to establish that

---

6 Heinrich Brüning, *Memoiren 1918–1934* (Stuttgart, 1970), pp. 54–56, 145–47, 191–95, 209–10, 378, 453–54, 461–62, 512–13, 520–21 (quotation on p. 462).
7 Contrast Conze, "Die Reichsverfassungsreform als Ziel der Politik Brünings," *Der Staat*, 11 (1972): 209–17; with Karl Dietrich Bracher, "Brünings unpolitische Politik und die Auflösung der Weimarer Republik," *Vierteljahrshefte für Zeitgeschichte*, 19 (1971): 113–23, and Hans Mommsen, "Betrachtungen zu den Memoiren Heinrich Brünings," *Jahrbuch für die Geschichte Mittel- und Ostdeutschlands*, 22 (1973): 270–80.
8 See Friedrich Freiherr Hiller von Gaertringen, "Zur Beurteilung des 'Monarchismus' in der Weimarer Republik," in Gotthard Jasper, ed., *Tradition und Reform in der deutschen Politik. Gedenkschrift für Waldemar Besson* (Frankfurt a.M., 1976), pp. 138, 170–76; Ernest Hamburger, "Betrachtungen über Heinrich Brünings Memoiren," *Internationale wissenschaftliche Korrespondenz zur Geschichte der Arbeiterbewegung*, 8, #15 (1972): 18–39; Arnold Brecht, "Gedanken über Brünings Memoiren," *Politische Vierteljahresschrift*, 12 (1971): 607–40; Sir John Wheeler-Bennett, "The End of the Weimar Republic," *Foreign Affairs*, 50 (January 1972): 368–71; Tilman Koops, "Heinrich Brünings 'Politische Erfahrungen.' (Zum ersten Teil der Memoiren)," *Geschichte in Wissenschaft und Unterricht*, 24 (1973): 197–221; Morsey, *Zur Entstehung*, pp. 50–53; and Müller, *Brüning Papers*, pp. 72–73.
9 Andreas Rödder, "Dichtung und Wahrheit. Der Quellenwert von Heinrich Brünings Memoiren und seine Kanzlerschaft," *Historische Zeitschrift*, 265 (1997): 77–116.

Chancellor Brüning aimed at the restoration of monarchy, linking him with blatant reactionaries such as Franz von Papen. This premise colors some of the most recent textbooks on German history for undergraduates and has led to highly questionable deductions even in otherwise carefully researched monographs.[10] Most influential among scholars, however, has been the more subtle line of criticism based on the memoirs advanced by Hans Mommsen. He discounts the story about a restoration of monarchy but nevertheless finds in the memoirs "an unexpectedly frank depiction of the chancellor's motives and long-term goals," which were to divide and cripple the socialist labor movement while seeking constitutional amendments that would permanently liberate the executive power from any meaningful parliamentary control.[11] Mommsen has ample evidence for his incisive analysis of the practices of the Brüning cabinet, under which decision-making power was concentrated in the hands of an ever smaller circle of the chancellor's closest advisers. To reconstruct Brüning's goals, however, he relies almost entirely on the memoirs, attaching great weight in particular to Brüning's recollection that he had hoped to make "the position of the head of state stronger than in the Bismarckian constitution." Noting other statements in the memoirs that Brüning had formulated a bold plan for public works but delayed implementation until reparations were abolished, Mommsen argues that he deliberately prolonged a devastating rate of unemployment because it crippled laborite opposition to his antidemocratic political reforms. Thus Brüning sought to "instrumentalize" the Great Depression instead of overcoming it. One should note, however, that the passage in the memoirs about the position of the head of state is vague and confusing; Brüning also declares that no amendment of the Weimar constitution was needed to achieve this goal, and his language obscures the distinction between remembered wishes and actual events.[12]

10　See, for example, Holger Herwig, *Hammer or Anvil? Modern Germany 1648–Present* (Lexington, Mass., 1994), pp. 256–61; Detlev Peukert, *The Weimar Republic: The Crisis of Classical Modernity* (New York, 1989), pp. 258–63; Dietrich Orlow, *A History of Modern Germany 1871 to Present*, 2nd ed. (Englewood Cliffs, N.J., 1991), pp. 175–85; Dietrich Orlow, *Weimar Prussia 1925–1933: The Illusion of Strength* (Pittsburgh, 1991), p. 164; Reinhard Neebe, *Grossindustrie, Staat und NSDAP 1930–1933. Paul Silverberg und der Reichsverband der Deutschen Industrie in der Krise der Weimarer Republik* (Göttingen, 1981), pp. 58–59, 78–80; and Michael Grübler, *Die Spitzenverbände der Wirtschaft und das erste Kabinett Brüning* (Düsseldorf, 1982), pp. 219–25. For perhaps the best treatment of the Brüning cabinet in a general history, see Heinrich August Winkler, *Weimar 1918–1933. Die Geschichte der ersten deutschen Demokratie* (Munich, 1993), chaps. 13–15.
11　Mommsen, "Betrachtungen," pp. 271–74.
12　See Hans Mommsen, "Heinrich Brünings Politik als Reichskanzler. Das Scheitern eines politischen Alleinganges," in Karl Holl, ed., *Wirtschaftskrise und liberale Demokratie* (Göttingen, 1978), pp. 16–45 (quotation on p. 33, taken from Brüning, *Memoiren*, pp. 371–73); "Die Stellung der Beamtenschaft in Reich, Ländern und Gemeinden in der Ära Brüning," *Vierteljahrshefte für Zeitgeschichte*, 21 (1973): 151–65; and "Staat und Bürokratie in der Ära Brüning," in Jasper, ed., *Tradition und Reform*, pp. 82–121. The first and third articles are now available in English translation in Hans Mommsen, *From Weimar to Auschwitz: Essays in German History* (Cambridge, 1991); see also Mommsen's textbook account, *The Rise and Fall of Weimar Democracy* (Chapel Hill and London, 1996), chaps. 8–11.

Brüning's memoirs cannot simply be dismissed. At times his memory was remarkably accurate, and the fragmentary documentary record of his chancellorship cannot be shaped into a coherent narrative without careful consideration of his recollections. Only since 1992, however, have historians gained the opportunity to study the full range of those recollections in Brüning's voluminous correspondence from the years after 1934 housed in the Harvard University Archive, along with a photocopy of the first draft of his memoirs, typescripts of a dozen lectures on the true meaning of democracy, and a few other miscellaneous items. Historians have long felt stymied by the unscholarly editions of Brüning's memoirs and the two published volumes of his later correspondence, which omit most discussions of the Weimar years for inclusion in a third volume that never appeared. But the 7,000 letters by Brüning now accessible at Harvard make it possible to trace in detail the evolution of his recollections.[13] When writing letters Brüning often recalled specific events of his chancellorship in a way that is far more consistent than the memoirs with the other sources, doubtless because he was not engaged in a narrative thrusting toward the conclusion that Hindenburg had no reason to dismiss him. Nobody has written a scholarly biography of Brüning,[14] although Morsey has published a series of valuable articles on his career before and after the chancellorship, so the time has come to test the full range of Brüning's recollections against the other sources for German politics in the years 1930–2.

The best research into those other sources in the German archives has recently been summarized by Gerhard Schulz in a monumental political history of what he labels the "Brüning era." Schulz lacked access to the Brüning Papers, however, and made little effort to reconstruct the chancellor's background and world-view.[15] I have been able to consult a few sources in Germany, moreover, not utilized by Schulz. In the national archive in Koblenz, the voluminous correspondence from 1919 to 1921 between Brüning's "neo-conservative" friends Martin Spahn and Eduard Stadtler sheds new light on the obscure first phase of his political career,[16] and the partial collection of the personal papers of Brüning's interior minister, Joseph Wirth, supports his recollections in some key respects. The Wirth Papers include few documents written during Brüning's

---

13 See Rudolf Morsey, "Zur Problematik einer zeitgeschichtlichen Briefedition," *Historische Zeitschrift*, 221 (1975): 69–95, and Müller, *Brüning Papers*, pp. 22–30. The Brüning Papers found in the Harvard University Archive will hereafter be cited as HUG FP.

14 Much can be learned though from the two short biographies published by admirers during his chancellorship: Rüdiger Robert Beer, *Heinrich Brüning* (Berlin, 1931), and Alphons Nobel, *Brüning* (Leipzig, 1932). Beer's work appeared in four editions in 1931, and the third and fourth include some additions based on Brüning's comments on the first edition. Eilert Lohe relied heavily on Beer and Nobel in *Heinrich Brüning. Offizier – Staatsmann – Gelehrter* (Göttingen, 1969).

15 See *Von Brüning zu Hitler. Der Wandel des politischen Systems in Deutschland 1930–1933* (Berlin and New York, 1992), vol. 3 of *Zwischen Demokratie und Diktatur. Verfassungspolitik und Reichsreform in der Weimarer Republik*; and my review in *Central European History*, 26 (1993): 131–35.

16 In the Bundesarchiv Koblenz (German National Archive, Koblenz, hereafter cited as BAK), NL Martin Spahn/3; see also the correspondence with Adam Stegerwald in vol. 19 and the letters from Brüning himself (which are utilized by Schulz) in vol. 22.

chancellorship but at least one important attempt to write memoirs.[17] In the reorganized Potsdam branch of the national archive, moreover, historians now gain unrestricted access to the files of the Reich interior ministry and the office of the Reich President, which contain some previously neglected material on the presidential elections of 1932 and government surveillance of the Nazi Party.[18] My first book on the Christian trade unions, which employed Brüning from 1920 to 1929, also uncovered evidence on his early career and ties with trade unionists that has been neglected by historians of the Brüning cabinet. The press of the Christian unions is a valuable source for Brüning's early editorials and later speeches as a politician; I have also studied those speeches in the published transcript of the proceedings of the Reichstag and the Cologne organ of the Center Party, which reported in the greatest depth on the activities of Chancellor Brüning.[19]

How should one read Brüning's memoirs? As Morsey and Rödder argue, the assertion that he sought as chancellor to restore a monarchy is almost undoubtedly quite misleading. The minutes of Brüning's cabinet meetings contain no hint of any such plan, and in public the chancellor declared emphatically and repeatedly that the Weimar constitution was not to blame for any of Germany's problems. The most valuable confidential record of the thought processes of Brüning's inner circle, the voluminous daily diary of the state secretary of finance, Hans Schäffer, also contains no discussion about a restoration until the subject was raised by Brüning's successors. In June 1932 Brüning expressed contempt for their political judgment by telling Schäffer that General Kurt von Schleicher planned to make Crown Prince Wilhelm the next head of state. When Schäffer's friends in the entourage of Chancellor Franz von Papen later expressed the hope that Brüning might be persuaded to accept a restoration, Schäffer responded that Brüning had firmly rejected any such idea in conversations with him both before and after his fall from power.[20]

17 In his Swiss exile Wirth often began to write memoirs but broke off after a few pages. Fortunately for the historian, his fellow exile Wilhelm Hoegner induced him in August 1942 to answer a detailed list of questions about his political career: see NL Wirth/18, "Gespräche zweier deutschen Politiker am Vierwaldstädtersee," especially Part III, "Ereignisse und Gestalten, 1918–1933."

18 Bundesarchiv, Abteilungen Potsdam (the Potsdam branch of the German National Archive, hereafter cited as BAP), "Akten der Präsidialkanzlei" (R601) and "Reichsministerium des Innern" (R15.01).

19 Brüning contributed numerous editorials in 1922–24 to the daily newspaper for the Christian unions that he founded, *Der Deutsche*, which is available in the archive of today's *Deutscher Gewerkschaftsbund* in Düsseldorf. For his ties with it, with the leaders of the Christian unions, and with the editors of the *Kölnische Volkszeitung*, see William Patch, *Christian Trade Unions in the Weimar Republic, 1918–1933: The Failure of "Corporate Pluralism"* (New Haven and London, 1985); Nobel, *Brüning*, pp. 27–43; and Josef Hofmann, *Journalist in Republik, Diktatur und Besatzungszeit. Erinnerungen 1916–1947*, ed. Rudolf Morsey (Mainz, 1977), pp. 60–67.

20 See the transcription of Schäffer's shorthand diary in the Institut für Zeitgeschichte, Munich (hereafter cited as IfZ), conversation with Brüning, 7 June 1932, and with Erwin Planck, 28 October 1932, NL Schäffer/21/567 and 23/945. For Brüning's indignant public commentary on the Papen cabinet's lack of respect for the Weimar constitution, see the *Kölnische Volkszeitung*, 22 July 1932, #199, 31 July #208, 24 October #293, and 5 November 1932, #305.

Of course, Brüning might not have opened his heart to Schäffer, who never gained his complete confidence. Schäffer himself judged that there were only three people of whom that could be said, the conservative politician Gottfried Treviranus, Brüning's chief of staff Hermann Pünder, and Rudolf Hilferding.[21] The last two of these three at least were also ignorant of any plans for a restoration that the chancellor might have had. Hilferding's friend and party colleague, Hans Staudinger, later recalled attending tea at Hilferding's on a day when his host was deeply upset by a conversation that he had just had with Chancellor Brüning:

> He [Hilferding] reported that Brüning had spoken with him about his political program and sought his reaction to a new political idea. Shortly before his death, Stresemann had spoken with Brüning in the Reichstag about the question of the reelection of old Hindenburg and suggested the idea of naming a regent [*Reichsverweser*] to take his place; he (Stresemann) had suggested Crown Prince Wilhelm. Hilferding answered Brüning that it was easy to imagine Stresemann saying such a thing, because he never paid enough attention to the echo and the possible consequences of the things he said. But Hilferding was astounded to hear Brüning repeat it. That would mean leaving the foundation of democracy, indeed, the resurrection of monarchy. He told Brüning: "Just don't say anything more about it." ["*Schweigen Sie nur darüber!*"]

That was the last Staudinger heard of the idea. He noted on the basis of his own dealings with the chancellor that although Brüning obviously admired the British constitutional monarchy, he believed sincerely in "democratic ideals" and knew very well as an expert on foreign policy that "a democratic republic was the only form of state that could be trusted in the western world of democracies."[22] Schäffer also recalled vividly in later years an encounter in Paris in 1940 with the exiled Hilferding, who was shocked because Treviranus had just told him that Brüning had discussed a restoration with Hindenburg in the winter of 1931/2. Hilferding felt "disappointed on a personal level" that Brüning had deceived him about his goals. Schäffer replied shrewdly that such talk was probably just a gambit to overcome Hindenburg's reluctance to campaign for reelection.[23]

Hermann Pünder, the state secretary in the Reich chancellery, had been friendly with Brüning for years, was a Center Party colleague, and conferred at length with the chancellor almost every day. He later declared that he and Brüning had "often discussed the ideal of a parliamentary monarchy down through the years, which was a favorite concept of us both. Since it was then (1931/2) at least a decade too late to implement such plans, however, these ideals

---

21 Schäffer to Hans Luther, 28 September 1961, NL Schäffer/44/39–42; compare NL Wirth/18, "Ereignisse und Gestalten von 1918–1933," question #22, pp. 4–6.
22 Hans Staudinger, *Wirtschaftspolitik im Weimarer Staat. Lebenserinnerungen eines politischen Beamten im Reich und in Preussen, 1889 bis 1934*, ed. Hagen Schulze (Bonn, 1982), pp. 91, 108–09.
23 Schäffer to Werner Conze, 12 September 1964, NL Schäffer/45/56–57.

of ours did not find their way into any sort of formal proposals." Pünder was an eloquent defender of the Weimar constitution while in office, and his diary from 1929 to 1932 contains no discussion of a restoration. When King Alfonso XIII of Spain abdicated in April 1931, Pünder recorded the following observation: "A heavy blow for the idea of monarchy. Alfonso was a modern man. He never believed that the Spanish monarchy would last long." Thus Brüning's chief of staff did consider monarchy anachronistic by 1931.[24]

Treviranus stands therefore as the only knowledgeable witness who later corroborated the story that Brüning sought from the fall of 1931 to restore a monarchy. This fact is highly suggestive, because Treviranus stayed in such close touch with Brüning in exile that the two men forged a single memory of these events. Indeed, Treviranus served as a conduit in the 1950s and '60s through which Brüning sought to disseminate his version of history to sympathetic scholars in Germany.[25] Only after Hitler became chancellor, as we shall see in Chapter 6, is there any documentary evidence that Brüning and Treviranus sought to promote a restoration as the only alternative to a one-party dictatorship. Just after he began to write his memoirs in England, moreover, Brüning visited Winston Churchill in September 1934 and was fascinated to learn that his host explained the Nazi seizure of power as the result of the Allies' mistaken decision in 1918 to topple the Hohenzollern and Habsburg dynasties. Churchill had recently begun to propagate the view that the constitutional monarchy was the best form of government to save Europe from the twin threats of communism and fascism. Brüning found Churchill's company exhilarating and sought him out repeatedly thereafter. Treviranus also took part in these conversations, and it seems most likely that both expatriates reshaped their memories as they sought to persuade Tory friends that they had always shared Churchill's outlook. The first published version of Brüning's story about a restoration, in John Wheeler-Bennett's biography of Hindenburg, was also based on discussions with Brüning and Treviranus in 1934. That book obviously reflects hindsight when it declares that Brüning had arrived at the following conclusion in the fall of 1931: "Long hours of contemplation had convinced him that one course, and one course only, could prevent Hitler from ultimately obtaining supreme power – the restoration of the monarchy."[26] In fact Brüning pursued the unheroic policy during his last months

24 Pünder to Wilhelm Vernekohl, 2 April 1962, in Brüning, *Reden*, p. 329; Pünder's speech of 23 November 1929 on the Weimar constitution, BAK NL Pünder/3/113–15; Hermann Pünder, *Politik in der Reichskanzlei. Aufzeichnungen aus den Jahren 1929–1932*, ed. Thilo Vogelsang (Stuttgart, 1961), p. 95.

25 See the three folders of correspondence with Treviranus in HUG FP 93.10/Box 34, especially the report by Treviranus on 21 November 1963 (folder 2) about his efforts to influence the historians Repgen, Josef Becker, Morsey, and Conze; and Gottfried Treviranus, *Das Ende von Weimar. Heinrich Brüning und seine Zeit* (Düsseldorf and Vienna, 1968), pp. 166, 295–96.

26 See William Patch, "Heinrich Brüning's Recollections of Monarchism: The Birth of a Red Herring," *Journal of Modern History* (forthcoming June 1998); Sir John Wheeler-Bennett, *Wooden Titan: Hindenburg in Twenty Years of German History 1914–1934* (New York, 1936), p. 352; Wheeler-Bennett, *Knaves, Fools and Heroes: In Europe between the Wars* (New York, 1975), pp. 54–57; Gottfried Treviranus, *Für Deutschland im Exil* (Düsseldorf, 1973), pp. 34–38, 51–56; and

in office of waiting for diplomatic successes and the gradual recovery of the world economy to bring the German electorate back to its senses.

If we discount Brüning's later story about a restoration, then the related story that he forged an alliance with the "Strasser wing" of the Nazi Party in the fall of 1931 loses credibility as well. Brüning remembered these matters more clearly when he was not writing memoirs. He became furious, for example, when Hjalmar Schacht and Count Schwerin von Krosigk sought at Nuremberg to justify their roles in the Third Reich by testifying that even the distinguished statesman Brüning had wanted Hitler to succeed him as chancellor. Brüning denied indignantly that he had ever told anyone as chancellor that the Nazis should enter the Reich government; all his efforts had aimed at excluding them from any such role. The most he had ever considered was to admit them as junior partners into the Prussian state government after the democratic parties lost their majority there in April 1932.[27] All the other sources support this recollection, not the account in the memoirs. In August 1932, however, Brüning did become so angry with the arbitrary conduct of Chancellor Papen that he advocated making Hitler chancellor in a cabinet bound to a parliamentary coalition between the Nazi and Center parties. He did form an alliance with Gregor Strasser at that juncture, and the memoirs obviously project some of these later discussions back onto the events of his chancellorship.

Brüning's memoirs sometimes echo phrases employed by neo-conservative foes of the Weimar constitution in the 1920s, but we now have access to more detailed accounts of his attitude toward that constitution in the typescripts of his public lectures delivered in the United States from 1937 to 1943. These were thoughtful efforts to explain the collapse of so many democracies in the Great Depression and the preconditions for a revival of democracy in Germany.[28] The lecturer spoke often of the need to secure legitimate "authority" and "stability" for democratic government, but he always assumed that Germany's constitution should be based on the formal responsibility of cabinets to a parliament elected by universal and equal suffrage. His major criticism of the work of the National Assembly in Weimar was that it had undermined parliamentary democracy by

---

Brüning's memorandum of 17 September 1934 and Brüning to Churchill, 28 August 1937, in Claire Nix, ed., *Heinrich Brüning. Briefe und Gespräche 1934–1945* (Stuttgart, 1974) (hereafter cited as "*Briefe*, I"), pp. 29–31, 147–49.

27 See Brüning to Hans von Raumer, 1 May 1947, HUG FP 93.10/Box 26/Hans von Raumer; Brüning to Theodore Draper, 11 July 1947, HUG FP 93.10/Box 7/Theodore Draper; Brüning's affidavit of 15 December 1947, in Müller, *Brüning Papers*, pp. 200–01; and Brüning to Dr. Leutze, 6 December 1956, in Udo Kissenkoetter, *Gregor Strasser und die NSDAP* (Stuttgart, 1978), pp. 204–05.

28 HUG FP 93.45/Lectures in America: "Some Reflections on the Decay of European Democracy," lecture series delivered at Queen's College, Princeton, early in 1937; "The Essence of Democracy," three lectures delivered at Dartmouth College, 16–19 March 1937; "The Changing Background of Democracy," three Page-Barbour Lectures at the University of Virginia, January 1939; "Democratic Reorientation," Brookings Institute lecture of 6 March 1941; "Some Thoughts on the Spiritual Background of the Present Crisis," lecture at the University of Iowa School of Religion in 1941; untitled Detroit lecture of 7 December 1941; untitled Boston University lecture of 1 November 1943. Brief excerpts are published in Müller, *Brüning Papers*, pp. 203–12.

introducing redundant guarantees of popular sovereignty borrowed from the United States and Switzerland, a powerful presidency and the popular referendum. Thus his arguments anticipated the conclusions of the founders of the Federal Republic of Germany. The provisions of the Weimar constitution were nevertheless sufficiently flexible, Brüning argued, that a truly "healthy democracy" could be created within its framework. Any effort to amend the constitution in the years 1930–2 would have provoked explosive controversy and failed to win the necessary two-thirds majority in the Reichstag. Brüning praised the Weimar Republic warmly, moreover, for stimulating patriotism among the working class, for exemplary regulation of church–state relations, and for state labor arbitration and other social experiments that represented the most successful attempt ever to translate the ideals of Catholic social theory into practice.[29] These lectures strongly suggest that Brüning was a monarchist by sentiment but a "republican from reason," a *Vernunftrepublikaner* who went through a learning process in the early 1920s similar to that experienced by Friedrich Meinecke and Gustav Stresemann.

Brüning's memories of the Weimar Republic experienced further distortion at the end of the Second World War. After the saturation bombing of German cities, revelations about the Holocaust, and the harsh decisions of the Potsdam Conference, he became extremely pessimistic about historical trends. Only in 1947 did Brüning decide that Bismarck's conservative critics were right to oppose his introduction of universal suffrage, and the opening section of the published memoirs, the section closest in tone to the neo-conservatives, was not written until then.[30] The opportunity to visit Germany again upset his mental equilibrium further, as Brüning plunged into investigations of who had persuaded Hindenburg to dismiss him. His opinion of the obvious suspects in the presidential entourage kept fluctuating, and he developed several implausible conspiracy theories.[31]

With regard to economic policy, Brüning's memoirs undermined any defense of his actions based on the argument that he could not have been expected to understand the novel ideas of John Maynard Keynes. In the 1950s and '60s the view spread among economic historians that the Brüning cabinet could have lowered the unemployment rate substantially through deficit spending on public

29 See p. 6 of Lecture #1, "Some Reflections on the Decay of European Democracy," and the entire Detroit lecture of 7 December 1941. These passages are ignored in Frank Müller's excerpts and contradict his conclusion (*Brüning Papers*, pp. 76–80) that Brüning advocated an "authoritarian democracy" closer in spirit to Franz von Papen than to the Weimar constitution.

30 See Brüning to Fritz Kern, 4 February 1947, and Brüning to Rudolf Pechel, 9 February 1947, in *Briefe*, II:70–74; Brüning, *Memoiren*, pp. 52–56; and Müller, *Brüning Papers*, pp. 134–36. The first draft of the memoirs from 1934/5 in HUG FP 93.4 opens with a brief account of Brüning's relationship with President Hindenburg (compare pp. 107, 116, and 145 of the published *Memoiren*) and then on p. 3 takes up basically the same narrative of events from 1929 begun on p. 145 of the published version.

31 See Gerhard Schulz, "Die Suche nach dem Schuldigen. Heinrich Brüning und seine Demission als Reichskanzler," in Karl Dietrich Bracher et al., eds., *Staat und Parteien. Festschrift für Rudolf Morsey zum 65. Geburtstag* (Berlin, 1992), pp. 669–87, and Müller, *Brüning Papers*, pp. 84–111.

works, so that the kindest interpretation of his economic policy was that he clung to an obsolete orthodoxy. His memoirs declare, however, that he had prepared a bold plan to reduce unemployment through public works, which he intended to implement as soon as reparations were abolished. Thus Brüning implied that he had deliberately ignored the devastating consequences of unemployment to further his diplomatic agenda. In fact, however, the Brüning cabinet was largely fatalistic about world economic trends. It did formulate plans for public works in the spring of 1932, but they were modest in scope and presupposed conventional financing through foreign loans or a domestic bond issue, methods with little prospect for success.[32] Chancellor Brüning, as we shall see, always believed that bold experiments with an expansionist monetary policy could not succeed until the world economic crisis had "bottomed out," that is, until world commodities prices began to rise again, and this did not happen until after he left office.

To say that Brüning was fatalistic is no defense in itself, but recent research in economic history has discredited many premises of the early "Keynesian" critics of Brüning. Knut Borchardt sparked an epic debate in 1978/9 with the argument that the economy of the Weimar Republic was fundamentally "sick" and that the Brüning cabinet had almost no maneuvering room in economic policy. Some of Borchardt's arguments about the "real economy" have been challenged effectively, in particular the argument that Germany's system of state labor arbitration granted such excessive wage increases from 1925 to 1929 as to depress levels of investment, retard technological innovation, and weaken industry's ability to compete on the world market. Borchardt, Harold James, and Theo Balderston have all uncovered impressive evidence, however, that the "monetary economy" made it impossible for Brüning to adopt a bold counter-cyclical policy in 1930/1. The German government lacked any credit on the bond market, and the German currency remained so weak on the international money market that Brüning could not adopt any policy considered unsound by the financial community. Only in January 1932 did the German central bank acquire effective control over foreign exchange reserves through the "Second Standstill Agreement" with foreign bankers, and only then, the best recent research suggests, did Brüning acquire genuine maneuvering room in economic policy.[33]

---

32 Contrast Brüning, *Memoiren*, pp. 503–04, 572–75, with Henning Köhler, "Arbeitsbeschaffung, Siedlung und Reparationen in der Schlussphase der Regierung Brüning," *Vierteljahrshefte für Zeitgeschichte*, 17 (1969): 267–307.

33 See "Constraints and Room for Manoeuvre in the Great Depression of the Early Thirties" and "Economic Causes of the Collapse of the Weimar Republic," in Knut Borchardt, *Perspectives on Modern German Economic History and Policy* (Cambridge, 1991); Harold James, "Gab es eine Alternative zur Wirtschaftspolitik Brünings?" *Vierteljahresschrift für Sozial- und Wirtschaftsgeschichte*, 70 (1983): 523–41; Carl-Ludwig Holtfrerich, "Zu hohe Löhne in der Weimarer Republik? Bemerkungen zur Borchardt-These," *Geschichte und Gesellschaft*, 10 (1984): 122–41; Harold James, *The German Slump: Politics and Economics 1924–1936* (Oxford, 1986); Jürgen Baron von Kruedener, ed., *Economic Crisis and Political Collapse: The Weimar Republic 1924–1933* (New York and Oxford, 1990); Ian Kershaw, ed., *Weimar: Why Did German Democracy Fail?* (New York, 1990);

Some German "Keynesians" have recently vilified Brüning to the point that he almost seems a scapegoat for the failure of the Weimar Republic. They argue not only that a bold new monetary policy could have lowered unemployment substantially – a contentious yet defensible position – but also that a political consensus in favor of such a program was emerging by December 1931, a view that runs contrary to the evidence. In their opinion Brüning systematically defamed and harassed all who suggested alternatives to deflation. His rigid policies drove the German people to despair; he was the primary cause of the radicalization of the electorate.[34] This indictment neglects the fact that the three political parties which drafted the Weimar constitution and actively supported it lost their electoral majority already in June 1920 and never regained it thereafter. The best research into the causes of the steady decline of the moderate parties in their competition with extremists emphasizes not the emergency decrees of Brüning, but the mildly authoritarian values fostered by Germany's family structure and educational system, the old hostility toward the labor movement that permeated the middle classes, the hyper-inflation of 1923 and the failure of the mainstream parties to deal fairly with its victims, the failure of German governments since the 1880s to encourage farmers and businessmen to adjust rationally to price trends in the world market, frustration with the paralysis of parliamentary government in 1928/9, and the ossification of all the mainstream parties, their failure to recruit activists from the younger generation.[35] It would

Rainer Meister, *Die grosse Depression. Zwangslagen und Handlungsspielräume der Wirtschafts- und Finanzpolitik in Deutschland 1929–1932* (Regensburg, 1991); and Theo Balderston, *The Origins and Course of the German Economic Crisis, November 1923 to May 1932* (Berlin, 1993). The Second Standstill Agreement was largely neglected by historians until Brüning highlighted it in *Memoiren*, pp. 491–92; compare Harold James, *The Reichsbank and Public Finance in Germany, 1924–1933* (Frankfurt a.M., 1985), pp. 218–36, and Stephen Schuker, *American "Reparations" to Germany, 1919–1933: Implications for the Third-World Debt Crisis* (Princeton, 1988), pp. 59–81.

34 See Werner Jochmann, "Brünings Deflationspolitik und der Untergang der Weimarer Republik," in Dirk Stegmann et al., eds., *Industrielle Gesellschaft und politisches System* (Bonn, 1978), pp. 107–12; Carl-Ludwig Holtfrerich, *Alternativen zu Brünings Wirtschaftspolitik in der Weltwirtschaftskrise* (Wiesbaden, 1982); Carl-Ludwig Holtfrerich, "Was the Policy of Deflation in Germany Unavoidable?" in Kruedener, ed., *Economic Crisis*, pp. 63–70; and Ursula Büttner, "Politische Alternativen zum Brüningschen Deflationskurs," *Vierteljahrshefte für Zeitgeschichte*, 37 (1989): 209–51.

35 See Ralf Dahrendorf, *Society and Democracy in Germany* (New York, 1967); Herman Lebovics, *Social Conservatism and the Middle Classes in Germany, 1914–1933* (Princeton, 1969); Heinrich August Winkler, *Mittelstand, Demokratie und Nationalsozialismus. Die politische Entwicklung von Handwerk und Kleinhandel in der Weimarer Republik* (Cologne, 1972); Heinrich August Winkler, "From Social Protectionism to National Socialism: The German Small-Business Movement in Comparative Perspective," *Journal of Modern History*, 48 (1976): 1–18; Gerald Feldman, "The Weimar Republic: A Problem of Modernization?" *Archiv für Sozialgeschichte*, 26 (1986): 1–26; Larry Eugene Jones, "In the Shadow of Stabilization: German Liberalism and the Legitimacy Crisis of the Weimar Party System, 1924–1930," in Gerald Feldman, ed., *Die Nachwirkungen der Inflation auf die deutsche Geschichte 1924–1933* (Munich, 1985), pp. 21–41; Larry Eugene Jones, "Crisis and Realignment: Agrarian Splinter Parties in the Late Weimar Republic, 1928–1933," in Robert G. Moeller, ed., *Peasants and Lords in Modern Germany* (London, 1985); Larry Eugene Jones, *German Liberalism and the Dissolution of the Weimar Party System, 1918–1933* (Chapel Hill and London, 1988); Richard Hamilton, *Who Voted for Hitler?* (Princeton, 1982); Thomas Childers, *The Nazi Voter: The Social Foundations of Fascism in Germany, 1919–1933* (Chapel Hill and London, 1983); and Jürgen Falter, *Hitlers Wähler* (Munich, 1991).

be a giant step backward for historical understanding if a hostile portrait of Brüning distracted attention from these structural factors in the dissolution of the Weimar Republic.

Brüning's critics are correct to observe that he did not place the same emphasis on economic prosperity that is expected of democratic politicians today. The chancellor and his inner circle did not anticipate a future in which a steadily rising standard of living would legitimize government authority and social hierarchy, and they probably did not even desire "stability" on such terms.[36] They assumed that hard economic times would last for years, so that Germany's political crisis could not be overcome without reviving a sense of national community based on the teaching of the greatest statesmen of Prussian history that progress toward democracy must be linked with acceptance by the citizens of the "Prussian" values of diligence, self-denial, and devotion to the common good. This book will seek to recreate their idealistic vision of Prussia, which resembled the tradition of "classical republicanism" in France and the United States, and to show how it influenced specific policy decisions. Brüning enjoyed considerable success with his "Prussian" statecraft, much more than the newspaper polemics of that era would suggest, at promoting consensus among a wide range of politicians, lobbyists, and government officials. His relations with the presidential entourage deteriorated steadily after July 1931, however, and the most valuable element in Brüning's memoirs is the account of this estrangement from Hindenburg, which can now be substantiated by other sources.[37] Brüning based his political strategy on the premise that the most famous embodiment of the Prussian tradition, Field Marshal Paul von Hindenburg und Beneckendorff, would support centrist policies and defend the Weimar constitution, but here he definitely miscalculated.

36 Compare "The Two Postwar Eras and the Conditions for Stability in Twentieth-Century Western Europe," in Charles Maier, *In Search of Stability: Explorations in Historical Political Economy* (Cambridge, 1987).

37 See Reinhold Quaatz, *Die Deutschnationalen und die Zerstörung der Weimarer Republik. Aus dem Tagebuch von Reinhold Quaatz 1928–1933*, ed. Hermann Weiss and Paul Hoser (Munich, 1989); Joseph Goebbels, *Die Tagebücher von Joseph Goebbels. Sämtliche Fragmente: Teil I*, ed. Elke Fröhlich, 4 vols. (Munich, 1987); and Gerhard Granier, *Magnus von Levetzow: Seeoffizier, Monarchist und Wegbereiter Hitlers. Lebensweg und ausgewählte Dokumente* (Boppard am Rhein, 1982).

1

Brüning's Political Apprenticeship

In the very year of Heinrich Brüning's birth, 1885, Pope Leo XIII and Bismarck negotiated the end of the *Kulturkampf*, the bitter struggle over cultural policy between Prussia and the Catholic Church. Nobody greeted this development more enthusiastically than the Catholic populace of Brüning's home town, Münster in Westphalia. Ever since their involuntary incorporation into Prussia in 1815, the citizens of Münster had been notorious for passive resistance to the Protestant officials dispatched from Berlin. They opposed the anti-clerical legislation of the 1870s but yearned for reconciliation with the Prussian state nevertheless; the numerous clergymen, teachers, and civil servants of this administrative center shuddered when the *Kulturkampf* caused riots in other more industrialized cities. They cheered when Bismarck allowed the Bishop of Münster to return from exile in 1884, and when Kaiser Wilhelm I visited the city a few months later. As Brüning grew up, his priests and teachers emphasized the similarity between Catholic moral teachings and "Prussian" virtues, while praising the Hohenzollern dynasty's commitment to religious toleration. He therefore sought throughout his life to reconcile values that were considered antithetical in most other regions of Germany.[1] Brüning also learned from the *Kulturkampf* to regard the National Liberal Party as a movement "against religious freedom and tolerance" and for a "regime of the bureaucracy." The reluctance of German Conservatives to support the religious policy of the National Liberals persuaded him that they were the natural allies for Catholic politicians.[2]

---

1 See Jonathan Sperber, *Popular Catholicism in Nineteenth-Century Germany* (Princeton, 1984), pp. 155–59, 227–31; Erich Schmidt-Volkmar, *Der Kulturkampf in Deutschland, 1871–1890* (Göttingen, 1962); Rudolf Morsey, "Die deutschen Katholiken und der Nationalstaat zwischen Kulturkampf und dem ersten Weltkrieg," *Historisches Jahrbuch*, 90 (1970): 31–64; Rudolf Morsey, "Brünings politische Weltanschauung vor 1918," in Gerhard A. Ritter, ed., *Gesellschaft, Parlament und Regierung* (Düsseldorf, 1974), pp. 327–29; and Doris Kaufmann, *Katholisches Milieu in Münster 1928–1933* (Düsseldorf, 1984), pp. 39–44.
2 See Brüning to Raymond Buell, 21 September 1939, HUG FP 93.10/Box 2/Brie-Bürger (excerpted in *Briefe*, I:290).

14

1.1. The Education of a Prussian Patriot

Brüning's ancestors had worked as peasants and artisans around Münster since the seventeenth century at least. His paternal grandmother brought a small fortune into the family, which financed the construction of a vinegar factory. His father, Friedrich Wilhelm Brüning, added a wine dealership to the family business, leaving his wife and children well off when he died in 1887. Friedrich Wilhelm had not married until age forty-six and died when Heinrich was only nineteen months old. Three of Heinrich's siblings died in early childhood, but an older brother, Hermann, grew up to become a priest and exerted a powerful influence on the future statesman. An older sister, Maria, became a nurse and kept house for her mother while the two brothers went off to make their careers.[3]

Family stories about Heinrich Brüning's father exerted the first influence on his political outlook. Friedrich Wilhelm Brüning had just attained manhood when the revolution of 1848 broke out, and for twenty years thereafter he lived in Vienna. Young Heinrich was told that his father despised the misguided revolution but despised even more the subsequent violation of legal principles by the Prussian police in their persecution of revolutionaries, and that he had chosen two decades of self-imposed exile to protest the conduct of the authorities. This idealized portrait of the father he never knew helped to inspire Brüning's lifelong devotion to the *Rechtsstaat*, the rule of law.[4] This devotion was nurtured by a rigorous classical humanist education in Münster's thousand-year-old Gymnasium Paulinum, where Brüning learned Latin, Greek, French, and English, impressing his teachers with his broad knowledge of history and fondness for literature. A frail youth, he was excused from gymnastics on the advice of his family doctor. The Gymnasium Paulinum also taught reverence for the empire created by Bismarck, celebrating national unification on no fewer than five holidays a year. Upon graduating in 1904, Brüning received from the school's director a volume of Horace with an inscription to the effect that the "man of justice" would not allow his resolve to be swayed by the wrath of the people, the threats of the tyrant, or the intoxicating south wind from the Adriatic.[5] The political style of Chancellor Brüning can be glimpsed in this sentiment.

Brüning always took pride in Münster as a center of ecumenicism. He was taught that the people of Münster had never lost faith that Protestants and Catholics would someday reunite in a single church, so they had worked out peaceful arrangements to share power during periods of intense religious conflict in Germany at large. Their local traditions had taught the Prussian bureaucracy

---

3 Beer, *Heinrich Brüning* (4th ed.), pp. 7–8; family tree in Brüning, *Reden*, pp. 309–11.
4 Compare p. 7 of the first and fourth editions of Beer's *Heinrich Brüning* (for Brüning's addition to the original text), and see his outburst in September 1945 during a stressful interview with two American officers gathering evidence for the International Military Tribunal, on p. 13a of the transcript in HUG FP 93.10/Box 16/Interview.
5 Treviranus, *Ende von Weimar*, p. 17; Morsey, "Brünings politische Weltanschauung," pp. 327–28; teachers' evaluations in Brüning, *Reden*, pp. 311–12.

the value of religious tolerance.[6] Brüning ascribed the harmonious relations between local Catholics and Protestants to the influence of *The Imitation of Christ* by Thomas à Kempis. Brüning's own religious faith was molded by listening to his mother read this book, and he believed that the gentle Thomas had taught both Catholics and Protestants in northwestern Germany to treasure piety and humanity above dogma or loyalty to institutions.[7]

In 1904 Brüning went to study law at the University of Munich but left after one semester to study history, philosophy, and economics at Strasbourg. This university received special patronage from Kaiser Wilhelm II to uphold the Prussian heritage amid an Alsatian population all too fond of French ways. Brüning soon learned something about the ambiguity of the Prussian ideal, however, through the antagonism between his two favorite teachers, the liberal Protestant historian Friedrich Meinecke and the conservative Catholic Martin Spahn. Meinecke and Spahn had both studied in Berlin under Treitschke, who taught them to complete Bismarck's work of national unification by disseminating patriotic values, but Meinecke had become critical of the authoritarian features of the Wilhelmian Empire, while Spahn resolved to defend it against all subversives. Meinecke believed that Spahn was a poor scholar who had gained a chair at Strasbourg only because he was the son of the chairman of the Catholic Center Party and the first Catholic historian to evaluate Luther and Bismarck in positive terms. In Spahn's view, Meinecke embodied the old prejudice that Catholicism was incompatible with genuine scholarship. The two colleagues ignored each other, and most students felt compelled to choose between them.[8]

One who refused to make this choice was Brüning. Although he shared mutual friends with Spahn, he found Meinecke's lectures more stimulating and soon won permission to enter his seminar on Prussian history. Meinecke taught his Strasbourg students that Frederick the Great had developed Prussia into a Great Power by championing religious toleration and the impartial administration of the laws, but that his state could make no further progress because of its reliance on blind obedience. Baron Karl vom Stein, who became chancellor in 1807 after Prussia's catastrophic defeat by Napoleon, was the greatest of Prussian statesmen because he understood that further development required active participation in government by the citizens. To educate the citizenry in the virtues of patriotism, self-discipline, and service to the community, Stein abolished serfdom, created municipal self-government, and opened military careers to

---

6 Brüning to Detlev Schumann, 14 April 1955, *Briefe*, II:387–88.
7 Brüning to Mona Anderson, 23 May 1941, and to Hermann Ullmann, 18 December 1950, *Briefe*, I:358–60.
8 See Gabriele Clemens, *Martin Spahn und der Rechtskatholizismus in der Weimarer Republik* (Mainz, 1983), pp. 11–38; Friedrich Meinecke, *Freiburg, Strassburg, Berlin*, in *Werke*, ed. Hans Herzfeld et al., 9 vols. (Darmstadt, 1957–1979), VIII:124–27, 139–48; and Konrad Jarausch, *Students, Society, and Politics in Imperial Germany: The Rise of Academic Illiberalism* (Princeton, 1982), pp. 96–98, 166–73.

talent. He laid the foundations for Prussia's resurrection by "reuniting state, nation, and individual" in the spirit of Rousseau and the French Revolution, but with greater realism and "a more highly developed ethical sense." Meinecke praised Stein in particular for understanding that Prussia's mission did not end with its own borders, that it must teach all of Germany how to create a healthy political community, and this was the lesson that Brüning always remembered most vividly.[9] Meinecke acknowledged that Stein had suffered painful defeats by reactionary aristocrats but argued that his work had been vindicated by Prussia's triumph in the Wars of Liberation, which revealed a glowing new patriotism in the younger generation. Bismarck and the Reichstag had recently avenged many of Stein's defeats, Meinecke suggested, and healthy progress was being made toward parliamentary democracy.[10] To understand Brüning's statements later in life praising Bismarck's constitution, it is important to note that Meinecke taught his students to adopt a remarkably optimistic view of it. Brüning later echoed Meinecke, for example, when he asserted that the Imperial Reichstag would have gained the same influence as the British House of Commons if only the kaiser had been persuaded before 1918 to recruit his cabinet ministers from its ranks.[11]

Meinecke left Strasbourg in 1906, and Brüning gravitated toward Spahn, who took an active interest in his personal welfare. When Brüning agonized over his choice of research topic for a master's thesis, Spahn nudged him toward the history of political philosophy, and Brüning eventually wrote about the influence of Rousseau on Justus Möser. In 1911 Brüning passed his *Staatsexamen* (earning the equivalent of an American master's degree) after an episode that underscored his personal debt to Spahn; he apparently lost his nerve and tried to flee his oral examination but was fetched in person by his mentor.[12]

At Strasbourg Brüning developed from a mildly anticlerical youth into an active critic of the antimodernist Pope Pius X. Like Spahn he expressed anguish that the Vatican had introduced fatal divisions into the German nation by failing to discover a constructive response to the largely sound teachings of Martin Luther, and he feared a similar rigidity in the Church's response to contemporary social unrest.[13] Brüning greatly admired the efforts of the People's League for Catholic Germany (Volksverein für das katholische Deutschland) to combine

9 See the English translation of Meinecke's Strasbourg lectures of 1905, *The Age of German Liberation 1795–1815*, ed. Peter Paret (Berkeley and Los Angeles, 1977), pp. 50–52, 60–70, 108–11; Treviranus, *Ende von Weimar*, pp. 18–19; and Brüning to Meinecke, 30 June 1953, *Briefe*, II:332–33.

10 Meinecke noted for example that the Reichstag had recently closed a "profound gap" in Stein's reforms by transferring rural police powers from the squires to elected county councils (*Age of German Liberation*, p. 80).

11 Brüning to Raymond Buell, 21 September 1939, HUG FP 93.10/Box 2/Brie-Bürger; Brüning to James Reber, 7 January 1941, and Queen's College lecture of 1937, in Müller, *Brüning Papers*, pp. 198–99, 207–08.

12 Brüning to Martin Spahn, 20 September and 8 October 1908, NL Spahn/22; Morsey, "Brünings politische Weltanschauung vor 1918," pp. 321–22.

13 Treviranus, *Ende von Weimar*, pp. 256–57; diary entry of 31 October 1934, in Brüning, *Briefe*, I:36; Brüning to Hermann Ullmann, 18 December 1950, *Briefe*, II:247–48.

anti-Marxist apologetics with practical steps toward social reform in a movement independent of the Church hierarchy. In 1931 he told his biographer, R. R. Beer, that he had perceived the "seriousness of the social question" sooner than most because of the troubling contrast in Westphalia between tranquil, centuries-old peasant villages and the turbulent "modern world of the machine" in the Ruhr basin.[14]

After leaving Strasbourg in 1911, Brüning decided to pursue a doctorate in economics under Heinrich Dietzel at the University of Bonn. Brüning had studied economics at Strasbourg under an exponent of the historical school, G. F. Knapp, who devoted his life to archival research on the impact of Stein's emancipation of the serfs on German agriculture.[15] Dietzel was a more innovative scholar than Knapp – he embraced the new English and Austrian theory of marginal utility – but nevertheless encouraged Brüning to choose a historical dissertation topic comparing the development of England's privately owned railroad system with that of the Prussian state railway. For Brüning the topic's main attraction apparently lay in the opportunity for a lengthy sojourn in 1912/13 with his brother Hermann, now serving as a parish priest in Manchester. There Brüning developed an enduring fondness for English mores, political institutions, and literature. The Great War broke out as he was completing a dissertation on the superiority of the English system, which avoided the bureaucratic red tape that lowered productivity among Prussian railroad workers. Brüning tried to volunteer for the army but was rejected for his poor eyesight. Just after submitting the dissertation in February 1915, he found an army regiment willing to accept him; Brüning received his doctorate in economics cum laude shortly before arriving at the front in the Argonne Forest.[16]

Brüning had been a university student for an unusually long time, eleven years, taking advantage of his family's financial support to postpone difficult decisions about the future. For him, as for so many other middle-class students, the outbreak of the Great War ended a time of painful indecision, compounded of reluctance to choose a career, uncertainty over whether to start a family, anxiety over the chain of war scares since the turn of the century, and ambivalent feelings toward the Wilhelmian regime. Only with the outbreak of war did Brüning gain a sense of purpose in life.[17] The topic of Brüning's political attitude as a student has generated some controversy as to whether he displayed con-

14 Compare p. 9 of the first and fourth editions of Beer, *Heinrich Brüning* (which was revised on the basis of Brüning's comments on the first edition). See also Brüning to Johann Steffes, 17 May 1948, *Briefe*, II:477–78; R. R. Beer, "Rückschau nach dreissig Jahren," in Wilhelm Vernekohl, ed., *Heinrich Brüning. Ein deutscher Staatsmann im Urteil der Zeit* (Münster, 1961), p. 72; and Horstwalter Heitzer, *Der Volksverein für das katholische Deutschland im Kaiserreich 1890–1918* (Mainz, 1979).

15 See Georg Jahn, "Die Historische Schule der Nationalökonomie und ihr Ausklang," in Antonio Montaner, ed., *Geschichte der Volkswirtschaftslehre* (Cologne and Berlin, 1967), pp. 41–50.

16 Morsey, "Brünings politische Weltanschauung," pp. 323–24; Nobel, *Brüning*, pp. 9–13.

17 Compare Robert Wohl, *The Generation of 1914* (Cambridge, Mass., 1979), and Jarausch, *Students, Society, and Politics*, pp. 333–416.

formism or a critical spirit.[18] Both assertions are probably correct. In fact, Brüning's two mentors, Meinecke and Spahn, gained national prominence by 1913 as champions of opposing political philosophies; each formulated arguments well suited to appeal to Brüning, and he obviously found himself unable to choose clearly between them.

Martin Spahn gained notoriety as the sharpest critic within the Center Party of the democratic tendency associated with Matthias Erzberger, the populist from Württemberg who sought to parliamentarize the national government. In 1913 Spahn launched a vitriolic attack on Erzberger that represented the most reactionary of the formative influences on Brüning. "Parliamentary democracy is of all forms of government the worst imaginable," he declared. "Every king and every aristocracy must, in order to survive, have regard for the entire people," but every nation that pursued Rousseau's bewitching dream of popular sovereignty discovered that all power in a democracy gravitates toward the lower house of parliament, which never truly represents the people but only the plutocrats who finance election campaigns. Spahn reckoned that this calamity had already befallen "the whole New World," China, Portugal, France, Belgium, Denmark, Norway, Switzerland, and, most disappointing of all, Great Britain since the emasculation of the House of Peers in 1911. The only hope for the future lay in further development of the ideal of Karl vom Stein, "who has been so unjustly claimed by liberalism and democracy" – the combination of a powerful monarchy at the center with a gradual strengthening of local self-government. Spahn later softened this message by attacking "formal democracy" in contrast to the "healthy democracy" of Stein, but this was merely a rhetorical concession to the current of public opinion. In private he always used the term "democracy" as synonymous with demagoguery and mob rule, like many other academics reared on Plato and Aristotle, and he reverted to this usage in public in the late 1920s.[19]

Yet men whose judgment Brüning undoubtedly respected, Meinecke prominent among them, were arguing the opposite case in 1913. Meinecke became a political activist in support of Friedrich Naumann's campaign to rejuvenate German liberalism by synthesizing "national" and "social" values, and Brüning always displayed more respect for Naumann's social liberalism than for the national liberalism associated with the *Kulturkampf*. Like Max Weber, Meinecke repudiated the "democratic illusion" that the majority of the populace could actually rule but insisted that parliamentary government was the most effective method for a modern industrial society to select dynamic leaders whose authority would be acknowledged by the masses. The flourishing British Empire proved

18 Contrast Josef Becker, "Heinrich Brüning in den Krisenjahren der Weimarer Republik," *Geschichte in Wissenschaft und Unterricht*, 17 (1966): 201, with Morsey, "Brünings politische Weltanschauung," p. 335.
19 Martin Spahn, "Was ist Demokratie?" *Hochland*, 11, #1 (1913): esp. pp. 72–77, 82–85; Klaus Epstein, *Matthias Erzberger und das Dilemma der deutschen Demokratie* (Frankfurt a.M., 1976), pp. 85–109; Clemens, *Martin Spahn*, pp. 38–50, 59–62.

this beyond any doubt. Under modern conditions, so different from those in Plato's time, democracy promoted not a cultural leveling but rather government by the most energetic and talented citizens:

> *Everywhere a new aristocracy is emerging among us*. . . . Everywhere "the few" are at work to organize the labor of the many, creating syndicates, cartels, etc. to regulate it. And the managers and leaders retain their office, standing, and influence only as long as they justify the confidence that the many place in them – and always *must* place in a few, because otherwise there is no way to get anything done. Thus the *temporary dictatorship based on confidence [temporäre Vertrauensdiktatur]* is actually the specifically modern form of administration and government! In England it is already central to the state, because the majority parties of the lower house, which ostensibly govern, are today nothing more than electoral colleges for choosing the ministers who manage and do everything.[20]

For Meinecke the crucial lesson for the modern age of imperialist competition remained that discovered by Stein a century earlier, that domestic reform was the necessary precondition for effective participation in international power politics. Meinecke's reasoning later gained enormous influence among all those politicians who were monarchists at heart but decided to support the Weimar constitution, and he revived the phrase *temporäre Vertrauensdiktatur* specifically to defend the methods of Chancellor Brüning.[21]

Rudolf Morsey has succeeded best at tracking down the surviving letters by the youthful Brüning, and he concludes that Brüning supported Spahn in this debate over parliamentarism. In 1913 Brüning applauded Spahn's opposition to progressive tax reform, for example, and told student friends that he wanted "to contribute to a better theoretical foundation for what is called the nationalist world-view, 'conservative' in the broadest sense of the word."[22] Yet Brüning's definition of conservatism was shaped by the example of Disraeli and diverged widely from that of Spahn. He greatly admired the tone of British parliamentary debate, saw in the M.P. the type of politician that must emerge in Germany, and displayed no trace of Spahn's despair over the recent triumph of the Commons over the Peers. Brüning argued that the confrontation tactics of Erzberger actually weakened the Reichstag, and that the Center Party should work patiently with the experienced parliamentarians of the Conservative Party

---

20 Friedrich Meinecke, "Der Sinn unseres Wahlkampfes" (first published on 5 January 1912), *Werke*, II:50–51. See also Dieter Düding, *Der nationalsoziale Verein 1896–1903* (Munich and Vienna, 1972); Robert Pois, *Friedrich Meinecke and German Politics in the Twentieth Century* (Berkeley and Los Angeles, 1972), pp. 4–25; and Wolfgang J. Mommsen, *Max Weber and German Politics, 1890–1920* (Chicago, 1984).

21 Meinecke, "Sammlungspolitik und Liberalismus" and "1811–1911," in *Werke*, II:40–48; Harm Klueting, "'Vernunftrepublikanismus' und 'Vertrauensdiktatur': Friedrich Meinecke in der Weimarer Republik," *Historische Zeitschrift*, 242 (1986): 70–98.

22 Morsey, "Brünings politische Weltanschauung vor 1918," pp. 330–32.

to increase the influence of that body gradually.[23] In 1913 he spoke with greatest enthusiasm about writing a major study of the ethical philosophy of Walter Pater, his favorite writer. Brüning adored Pater's didactic novel set in the Roman Empire of Marcus Aurelius, *Marius the Epicurean*, and kept it on his desk throughout his political career. His fondness for Pater suggests a philosophical skepticism and distaste for the role of brute force in history alien to Spahn and most other German conservatives. In a revealing phrase, Brüning often told friends that the most important lesson he had learned in England was to suspend judgment, "not to commit himself."[24]

Brüning's attention was diverted from politics when he arrived at the Western Front in 1915. He discovered in himself a gratifying ability to control his fear in combat and a talent for soldiering. He became a corporal, was wounded, and then trained as an officer. Brüning returned to the front in an experimental machine gun detachment of heavily armed troops thrown in to hold the second or third line of trenches in case of an enemy breakthrough. He fought many bloody battles, mostly against the British, and became a company commander, receiving the Iron Cross First Class.[25] Brüning's later recollections of the war were mostly uncommunicative, focusing on the standard theme of the joys of comradeship. His memoirs emphasize his pleasant surprise over the human qualities of the common soldiers under his command, most of them skilled metalworkers from Berlin and members of the socialist Free Unions. He learned to admire trade unionism for instilling self-discipline and noted that "neither before nor after have I ever in my life encountered anything comparable in terms of mutual trust, independence of outlook, a cooperative attitude, sense of humor and self-sacrifice."[26] Brüning did not allow himself to dwell on the horrors of war, but a visit to the Dutch coast in 1935 generated an unusually vivid diary entry, as he recalled being detailed to chop wood in the Argonne two and a half kilometers behind the front lines. The beautiful forest engendered manic high spirits at first, as the men hurled themselves against the tallest trees to stretch their cramped muscles, but the very beauty of their surroundings soon made them despondent until they returned to their familiar trenches:

> The sight of mortal danger purified our souls. The excursion into the world of life stirred everything up. Now still again. Here was home. Here, where all hope for life was forgotten, was serene calm. How else could one begin to attempt to hit the stranger over there with a bullet through the slit in the parapet? He throws hand grenades. Now everything gets lively, with blows

23 See Brüning to Raymond Buell, 21 September 1939, HUG FP 93.10/Box 2/Brie-Bürger; Hermann Ullmann, *Publizist in der Zeitenwende* (Munich, 1965), pp. 117–18; and Beer, *Heinrich Brüning*, pp. 12–13.
24 Nobel, *Brüning*, pp. 11–13; Morsey, "Brünings politische Weltanschauung," p. 330; Brüning to Mona Anderson, 1 May 1938, *Briefe*, I:194.
25 Nobel, *Brüning*, pp. 13–15; Beer, *Heinrich Brüning*, pp. 15–26.
26 Brüning, *Memoiren*, p. 18.

and explosions. None of us are hurt. But why? Why? But such questions never occurred to us then. Men in action are different from men in reflection.[27]

Here is a rare acknowledgment that Brüning fought in the same war as Remarque and Robert Graves, a war that often spread bitter disillusionment.

Brüning retained his patriotic outlook nonetheless through a massive effort of will. In the spring of 1917 he rejoiced that the army commanders Hindenburg and Ludendorff had persuaded the kaiser to resume unrestricted submarine warfare against the objections of the civilian authorities. In July he applauded the resignation of the "weak" Bethmann Hollweg as chancellor and denounced Erzberger for conducting a resolution through the Reichstag that demanded immediate negotiations for a compromise peace. Brüning feared that the emerging "parliamentary regime" at home represented "the beginning of the end."[28] Yet Brüning also displayed reformist sentiments as the war entered its decisive phase. He later recalled that "contempt for the parliament" spread at the front only after the politicians in Berlin continued to debate how much foreign territory to annex long after the troops all knew that victory was impossible. Brüning opposed the army's seniority system and concluded that its system of patriotic instruction was utterly ineffective. His metalworkers understood immediately that the Bolsheviks were their enemies when Brüning explained that Lenin prohibited strikes in Russia. When the kaiser abdicated, Brüning's company sang "The International" and then unanimously elected him chairman of their "soviet." Strong trade unions obviously offered the best hope for political stability, Brüning concluded, but the kaiser and his advisers were blind to this fact.[29]

When Ludendorff resigned in October 1918, Brüning denounced the "loss of nerve" by the High Command, arguing that the army could still defend the borders of the Reich if it promptly evacuated all occupied territory. He also denounced the "Bolsheviks" within Germany – the units transferred from the Russian front that had been corrupted by Leninist propaganda, the small group of active revolutionaries in the Spartacus League, and the many deserters who, in Brüning's opinion, seized on political ideology to rationalize their cowardice. He rejoiced on 8 November when the High Command ordered reliable units including his company to secure the rail system from Aachen to Cologne in preparation for an offensive against the mutineers. He despaired when this plan was abandoned the next day, as the kaiser abdicated. Brüning then experienced humiliation as his unit was demobilized in Frankfurt an der Oder, where the local revolutionary authorities greeted them with red banners and a peremptory demand to surrender their weapons. The officers were even locked up briefly.

---

27 Diary entry of 17 February 1935, Brüning, *Briefe*, I:61–62; the original travel diary covering the period from 31 October 1934 to 10 September 1935 is now accessible in HUG FP 93.35/Box 1.
28 Morsey, "Brünings politische Weltanschauung vor 1918," pp. 334–35.
29 Brüning, *Memoiren*, pp. 22–23, 31–33, 39–40.

"That marked the beginning of a wave of resentment that must someday have consequences," Brüning later observed. "Neither the politicians, who spent the war years safely at home, nor the High Command had the faintest idea what political consequences this resentment would someday have."[30] Brüning struggled thereafter to attain a more balanced view of these events. "Every revolution is synonymous with disorganization," he wrote in 1920, but Germany's disorganization had begun with the onset of inflation in 1916 and "resulted from the incredible transformation of all personal, economic, social, and political relationships during wartime." Brüning nevertheless wrote in 1923 that any "true Christian democrat" must "hate" the revolution of November 1918 because of the dangerous illusions that had nearly plunged Germany into chaos.[31] He never actually blamed the radical left for Germany's defeat but was resolved that such elements must not come to power.

Brüning decided at war's end that it was his duty to serve the public. "I must go out among the people who are suffering," he replied when Professor Dietzel urged him to return to academia. He also felt obliged to postpone any thought of marriage, holding that "whoever dedicates himself to service to humanity and the public good should not be devoted to any one person, should not found a family."[32] This statement suggests a fairly typical Victorian response to ambivalent feelings about one's own sexuality, but such a response was distinctly old-fashioned by the 1920s. In despondent moments during his later exile, Brüning himself felt that there was something peculiar and very sad about his decision to forswear most pleasures after 1914, to storm through life worrying only about his country when he could have gotten happily married.[33] Before 1934 such questions apparently did not trouble him, however; he felt a special vocation to help rescue the fatherland from the material hardships and internal divisions caused by the Great War.

Brüning still had no political experience and no idea of how to translate ethical principles into government policies. He failed to win appointment as economic adviser to the German peace delegation at Versailles, offered his services to the municipal government of Münster but got no response, and then went to Berlin in March 1919 to work with the mission for Catholic university students founded by Carl Sonnenschein on behalf of the People's League for Catholic Germany. Brüning was excited by the intellectual ferment in the metropolis but repelled by the garbage in the streets and the luxurious lifestyle of the "war profiteers";

---

30 Brüning, *Memoiren*, pp. 25–37; see also Beer, *Brüning*, pp. 27–28, with excerpts from the war diary of Brüning's unit, and Brüning's Reichstag speech of 25 February 1932, in *Reden*, pp. 116–17.

31 Heinrich Brüning [unsigned], "Der Wiederaufbau des deutschen Finanzwesens," in *Jahrbuch der christlichen Gewerkschaften für 1921* (Cologne, n.d. [1920]), pp. 88–93; Brg., "Franz Wiebers 65. Geburtstag," *Der Deutsche*, 28 March 1923, #73. Compare Gerald Feldman, *The Great Disorder: Politics, Economics, and Society in the German Inflation 1914–1924* (New York and Oxford, 1993).

32 Treviranus, *Ende von Weimar*, pp. 11–12; Treviranus, *Exil*, p. 195.

33 See Brüning to Mona Anderson, 25–30 August 1935, *Briefe*, I:87.

he discerned "complete moral chaos" when friends took him on a tour of the beer gardens.[34] In Berlin Brüning again encountered Martin Spahn and a student friend from Strasbourg named Eduard Stadtler as prominent activists in the June Club, which sought to perpetuate the wartime spirit of national unity against the threats emanating from Moscow and Versailles. The June Club's discussion evenings and journalistic activities initially embraced a broad spectrum of opinion, but the core membership of neo-conservatives around Spahn and Stadtler became increasingly hostile toward parliamentary democracy in the summer of 1919, as the Versailles Treaty and Weimar constitution both took final shape. They accepted subsidies from Ruhr industrialists to agitate against the peace treaty and for the creation of a corporatist upper house of parliament to represent economic associations rather than individuals. Brüning apparently took no position on the second demand but actively supported their polemics against Versailles. In September 1919 he was finally rescued from political and vocational drift when mutual friends found him work that he could consider truly important as personal assistant to the Prussian minister of welfare and leader of the Christian trade unions, Adam Stegerwald.[35] He had now found a mentor well qualified to teach him about politics as the art of the possible.

1.2. The Trade Union Secretary

Eleven years older than Brüning, Stegerwald was the homely son of poor Catholic peasants in Franconia, a cabinetmaker who had led the League of Christian Trade Unions since 1903. He had received little formal education but learned from the social theorists of the People's League for Catholic Germany to base his agitation on a vision of Prussian history similar to Brüning's. Stegerwald and Brüning shared a fervent admiration for Karl vom Stein in particular, whose emancipation of the serfs set a great precedent for the integration of outcasts into civil society that they hoped to apply to the industrial proletariat.[36] Brüning also admired the anticlericalism of Stegerwald, who had gained national prominence before the war as the sharpest critic of efforts by some bishops to require Catholic workers to participate only in non-striking Catholic trade unions under clerical supervision. By 1914 Stegerwald had persuaded most bishops and Catholic politicians that his "interconfessional" trade unions, which

---

34 Brüning, *Memoiren*, p. 44 (source of quotation); job application to Münster in Brüning, *Reden*, pp. 317–18; Treviranus, *Ende von Weimar*, pp. 35–39; Dirk Müller, *Arbeiter, Katholizismus, Staat. Der Volksverein für das katholische Deutschland und die katholischen Arbeiterorganisationen in der Weimarer Republik* (Bonn, 1996), pp. 92–93.

35 Clemens, *Martin Spahn*, pp. 64–79; Klemens von Klemperer, *Germany's New Conservatism: Its History and Dilemma in the Twentieth Century* (Princeton, 1968), pp. 107–16; Yuji Ishida, *Jungkonservative in der Weimarer Republik. Der Ring-Kreis 1928–1933* (Frankfurt a.M., 1988), pp. 28–32; Stadtler to Martin Spahn, 10 January, 21 February, and 27 June 1919, NL Spahn/3; Brüning, *Memoiren*, pp. 41–43, 57–59; Treviranus, *Ende von Weimar*, pp. 39–40.

36 Patch, *Christian Trade Unions*, pp. 7–20; Helmut Schorr, *Adam Stegerwald: Politiker der 1. deutschen Republik* (Recklinghausen, 1966), pp. 17–50; Heitzer, *Volksverein*, pp. 24–43, 54–66, 113–23; Ronald Ross, *Beleaguered Tower: The Dilemma of Political Catholicism in Wilhelmine Germany* (Notre Dame, 1976), pp. 59–82.

carried out strikes and recruited Protestant colleagues in the workplace, offered the only hope for slowing the growth of the socialist labor movement.[37] Brüning first heard Stegerwald speak at a campaign rally in Münster in January 1919 and applauded his call for an interconfessional political formation uniting the Catholic Center Party with all Protestants who supported progressive social policies and Christian cultural values. Brüning had also heard of Stegerwald's prominent role in November 1918 as a mediator of the Stinnes–Legien Agreement, which established mandatory collective bargaining and an eight-hour day in all branches of industry, and as cofounder of the Central Association of Employers and Employees, through which labor and management jointly organized the transition to a peace economy. Brüning considered the Central Association a triumph for the campaign by Catholic social reformers to establish a healthy balance between capital and labor.[38]

Brüning sought to steer his new employer toward cooperation with Protestant conservatives in particular. Stegerwald had sharply opposed the Center Party's short-lived coalition with the Conservative Party in 1909, and in 1917/18 he worked closely with liberal democrats such as Naumann, Meinecke, Ernst Troeltsch, and Walther Rathenau to agitate for a compromise peace and democratic reforms. At the war's end Stegerwald and his closest ally in the Center Party, Heinrich Brauns of the People's League for Catholic Germany, looked first to these left liberals for support for an interconfessional party.[39] Stegerwald nevertheless attended some meetings of the June Club and encouraged Brüning to speak freely about conservative ideals. Their sometimes heated discussions initially focused on the issue of whether to include a guarantee of established tenure rights for civil servants in the new Weimar constitution. Stegerwald favored a purge of monarchist officials, but Brüning defended the Prussian bureaucracy's traditions of rigorous training, nonpartisanship, and security of tenure. Brüning confided to an old friend that he and his boss could almost always reach agreement, despite the fact that Stegerwald operated from different premises as "a Bavarian and a democrat." Stegerwald eventually endorsed the strong tenure provisions in Article 129 of the Weimar constitution.[40]

37 See Eric Dorn Brose, *Christian Labor and the Politics of Frustration in Imperial Germany* (Washington, D.C., 1985); Rudolf Brack, *Deutscher Episkopat und Gewerkschaftsstreit* (Cologne and Vienna, 1976); and Ross, *Beleaguered Tower*, pp. 83–127.

38 Brüning, *Memoiren*, pp. 40–43; Brüning's Detroit lecture of 7 December 1941, pp. 4–5, HUG FP 93.45. See also Feldman, *The Great Disorder*, pp. 85–131; Gerald Feldman and Irmgard Steinisch, *Industrie und Gewerkschaften 1918–1924. Die überforderte Zentralarbeitsgemeinschaft* (Stuttgart, 1985); and Patch, *Christian Trade Unions*, pp. 34–38.

39 Brose, *Christian Labor*, pp. 287–91; Patch, *Christian Trade Unions*, pp. 24–45; Rudolf Morsey, *Die Deutsche Zentrumspartei 1917–1923* (Düsseldorf, 1966), pp. 61–109; reminiscences by Stegerwald in Gesamtverband der christlichen Gewerkschaften Deutschlands, *25 Jahre christlicher Gewerkschaftsbewegung 1899–1924* (Berlin, 1924), pp. 37–39, 142; reminiscences by Stegerwald in *Niederschrift der Verhandlungen des 13. Kongresses der christlichen Gewerkschaften Deutschlands* (Berlin, 1932), pp. 175–76.

40 See Brüning to Hermann Platz, 28 August and 27 November 1919, quoted in Treviranus, *Ende von Weimar*, pp. 39–41, and Nobel, *Brüning*, pp. 24–25.

Brüning deferred to his employer, on the other hand, by arguing in public that the civil service must incorporate experienced trade union functionaries alongside those with a university education.[41] Brüning also firmly opposed the effort by monarchist troops to overthrow the Republic in April 1920, the Kapp Putsch. Some neo-conservatives applauded this venture, but Brüning perceived that the putschists lacked any popular support and discredited the very concept of monarchism. His first response to the news was to exclaim, "Now the idiots have ruined the old colors forever!" Brüning gained his first taste of political drama by assisting the efforts of the Christian railroad workers' union to shut down rail traffic in regions controlled by the rebels.[42]

In the tense weeks after the Kapp Putsch, Brüning persuaded Stegerwald to attempt to reconcile the neo-conservatives with the Center Party. Stegerwald himself was friendly with Martin Spahn; they had served together in the wartime administration of food rationing and shared a personal antipathy for Erzberger.[43] Urged on by Brüning, Stegerwald demanded in April 1920 that his party colleagues nominate Spahn to represent northern Westphalia in the Reichstag. Stegerwald argued that the Center Party needed Spahn to help it develop a clear alternative to the version of democracy advocated by the Social Democratic Party (SPD); it sought to centralize all power in the hands of the Reichstag, but Centrists should seek instead to encourage citizen participation in organs of local government and in corporate bodies such as the Central Association of Employers and Employees. Stegerwald warned that a rebuff to Spahn might drive him out of the party and alienate many young Catholic intellectuals, but these arguments failed to persuade his party colleagues.[44]

Spahn was indeed offended by this rebuff, and Brüning sought anxiously to mediate between his two mentors. He assured Stegerwald (apparently without foundation) that Spahn had opposed the Kapp Putsch and would remain loyal to the Center Party. When Spahn attacked the Weimar constitution in the press and attended meetings of Catholic noblemen in Westphalia who contemplated the formation of a monarchist party, Brüning rebuked him:

> I believe now as always that the greatest art in politics is to wait. The second greatest: to allow those things which one sees coming to ripen quietly, not to appeal to the public through programmatic declarations . . . but rather to win a group of strong, self-sacrificing individuals for your ideas and then wait patiently for the day when one can act.

41 Beer, *Heinrich Brüning*, pp. 32–3; Nobel, *Brüning*, p. 29.
42 Alphons Nobel, "Der letzte demokratische Kanzler," in Vernekohl, ed., *Heinrich Brüning*, p. 146; Brüning, *Memoiren*, pp. 63–66.
43 Stegerwald to Martin Spahn, 3 August 1917, 29 December 1918, and 22 April 1919, NL Spahn/19; Stegerwald's reminiscences in *Tremonia*, 19 November 1926 (NL Stegerwald/003/Band 1926/#431); Clemens, *Martin Spahn*, p. 63.
44 Stegerwald to Generalsekretär Brand, 29 April, and reply of 11 May 1920, NL Stegerwald/014/Nachtragsband/#1–2; Clemens, *Spahn*, pp. 95–97.

Brüning declared that the aristocratic landowners plotting secession from the Center Party "can never understand the burning problems of the urban populace. They are bloodless men, who have lost their energy under the leaden skies of the Münsterland, cobbling together a Romantic theory of the state based on Catholic ideas of the Restoration, cut off from all contact with reality." Brüning warned that Spahn would lose any support from the Christian trade unions if he associated with this faction, and that "I also am prepared, if the time comes, to combat it to the utmost in the public arena." Thus, even at the outset of his career when he felt closest to the neo-conservatives, Brüning sharply repudiated the rightist fringe of the Center Party associated with Franz von Papen. His warning apparently had some effect, because Spahn avoided an open break with the Center for another year.[45]

Stegerwald made a bid for the support of the neo-conservatives at the Essen Congress of the Christian trade unions in November 1920 with a speech calling for the coalescence of all "constructive forces" that was written largely by Brüning.[46] This speech reflected an atmosphere of crisis that resulted from inflation, shortages of food and coal, the weakness of the new government agencies designed to reconcile management and labor, and the excessive use of lethal force by troops defending the government. The combined vote of the three parties of the Weimar Coalition that wrote the new constitution (the SPD, German Democratic Party or DDP, and the Center) had plummeted from 72 percent in January 1919 to just 44 percent in June 1920; the parties of the far right were mushrooming, and the German Communist Party (KPD) had begun to grow into a genuine mass movement.[47] Stegerwald argued that Germany's dire problems could be mastered only if all moderate Catholics and Protestants banded together in a great new centrist party capable of forming coalitions with either the left or right. This party must be "Christian, German, democratic, and social." "Christian" meant "the rejection in principle of all views emanating from the rationalistic and mechanical thought of the French Enlightenment of the 18th century." "German" meant "that the form of our constitution and our legal precepts must be based on German history and not the paragraphs hastily assem-

---

45 Brüning to Martin Spahn, 30 April, 16 July (source of quotations), and 17 July 1920, NL Spahn/ 22. The faction attacked by Brüning was based on the Christian Peasants' Clubs of Westphalia and led by Clemens von Loë and the Freiherr von Kerkerinck zur Borg, who secured a seat in the Prussian Landtag for Papen in 1921. See Morsey, *Zentrumspartei 1917–1923*, pp. 277–324; Clemens, *Spahn*, pp. 90–96; and Joachim Petzold, *Franz von Papen. Ein deutsches Verhängnis* (Munich and Berlin, 1995), pp. 24–27.

46 Brüning later exaggerated by claiming sole authorship, but Stegerwald confirmed to R. R. Beer in 1930 that Brüning had a "decisive influence" on the speech. See Brüning, *Memoiren*, pp. 70–71; R. R. Beer, "Rückschau nach dreissig Jahren," in Vernekohl, ed., *Heinrich Brüning*, p. 77; Larry Eugene Jones, "Adam Stegerwald und die Krise des deutschen Parteiensystems," *Vierteljahrshefte für Zeitgeschichte*, 27 (1979): 1–29; Leo Schwering, "Stegerwalds und Brünings Vorstellungen über Parteireform und Parteisystem," in Hermens and Schieder, eds., *Staat, Wirtschaft und Politik*, pp. 23–40; and Hermann Ullmann, "Das Essener Programm, November 1920," *Deutsche Rundschau*, 76 (1950): 897–903.

47 See Feldman, *The Great Disorder*, pp. 211–54, and Patch, *Christian Trade Unions*, pp. 35–67.

bled from foreign constitutions in a provisional constitution [*Notverfassung*]."
"German" also implied a determination to campaign tirelessly for revision of
the Treaty of Versailles. "Democratic" meant commitment to "the democracy
of self-government" instead of "the formal democracy of French centralism"
with its all-powerful national parliament. Finally, "social" implied "the implementation of the organic view of state and society" as well as "recognition of the
principle that the employee is an equal partner in the production process."[48]

These theoretical remarks were intended to impress Martin Spahn, and Stegerwald sent him the speech in advance for comment. The historian condemned
it though on the grounds that Stein's principle of self-government must be
understood as the alternative to democracy, not a step toward genuine democracy. Beyond demanding more autonomy for local governing bodies, Spahn
implied, one must have the courage to insist that only property-owners be represented in them.[49] Stegerwald would never repudiate equal suffrage, however,
and soon lost interest in the neo-conservative critique of the Enlightenment.
Brüning, on the other hand, believed throughout his life that Germany must
develop its own form of democracy, and that the authors of the Weimar constitution had thrown together ideas borrowed from Swiss, French, and American
democracy that did not fit well with the provisions retained from Bismarck's constitution. Under Stegerwald's influence, however, Brüning soon decided that the
provisions of the Weimar constitution were sufficiently malleable that a truly
Germanic democracy could be created within its framework.[50]

With the Essen Program Stegerwald actually diverted Brüning away from
Spahn's divisive campaign to alter the constitution toward the more constructive
goal of simplifying the party constellation. The real core of Stegerwald's argument was that parliamentary government could never become effective with
seven major parties in the Reichstag. There was no justification in particular for
the ongoing rivalry on the middle of the political spectrum between a Catholic
Center and two different liberal parties (the DDP and the German People's
Party, or DVP), which owed their creation to special problems of the Bismarckian era that no longer appeared significant to the younger generation. The classic
English two-party system remained unattainable, but Germans should be able
to feel their way toward a three-party system.[51] To show moderate politicians
that this idea was popular, Stegerwald announced several initiatives by the
new umbrella organization, the German Labor Federation (Deutscher Gewerkschaftsbund, or DGB), recently established to unite the blue-collar Christian

---

48 Adam Stegerwald, "Die christlich-nationale Arbeiterschaft und die Lebensfragen des deutschen Volkes," *Niederschrift der Verhandlungen des 10. Kongresses der christlichen Gewerkschaften
Deutschlands, 20–23 November 1920* (Cologne, 1920), pp. 183–84, 191–94, 231.
49 Spahn to Stegerwald, 18 October 1920, NL Spahn/19.
50 See "Some Reflections on the Decay of European Democracy," Queen's College lecture #1 of
1937, esp. pp. 4–6 (partially excerpted in Müller, *Brüning Papers*, pp. 206–08); "The Essence of
Democracy," Dartmouth College lecture #2 of March 1937, pp. 6b–27; and the untitled Boston
University lecture of 1 November 1943, in HUG FP 93.45.
51 *10. Kongress der christlichen Gewerkschaften*, pp. 214–16.

trade unions with nationalist unions for white-collar workers and civil servants, with a total membership of two million. The DGB would establish a new daily newspaper dedicated to political affairs, *Der Deutsche*, and organize a committee to coordinate lobbying activities among its thirty-odd Reichstag delegates in several different parties. Brüning was assigned to supervise these initiatives with the new title of executive secretary (*Geschäftsführer*) of the DGB.[52]

When Stegerwald's Essen speech received widespread applause in the press, Brüning expected his employer to resign from the Center Party to found the new Christian democratic German social party. He learned to his dismay that it was up to him, the unknown, to conduct the exploratory talks, and he then exhausted himself in fruitless negotiations with politicians who did not take him seriously. Stegerwald meanwhile campaigned actively for the Prussian Center Party in the state elections of February 1921 and accepted office from it thereafter as prime minister. He knew that many Christian trade unionists still identified closely with the Center Party, and he was content to employ the threat of a new party to promote democratization within and cooperation among the existing moderate parties. So Brüning found to his dismay that the bold initiative announced at Essen resulted in little more than a series of patient efforts by DGB leaders to develop political *Querverbindungen*, that is, a network of contacts with a wide variety of party leaders.[53]

Brüning enjoyed more success for his efforts to develop consensus among the diverse elements within the DGB. The most important white-collar ally of the Christian unions was the German Nationalist Union of Commercial Employees (Deutschnationaler Handlungsgehilfen-Verband, or DHV), which emerged from a north German tradition of militant nationalism tinged with anti-Semitism that was alien to the outlook of the egalitarian Catholic industrial workers of western and southwestern Germany. Brüning assured the leaders of the DHV that Stegerwald respected higher education, free enterprise, and the need for special consideration for white-collar workers in welfare legislation. He also established an immediate bond of sympathy with the DHV's chief political strategist, Max Habermann.[54] Even within the blue-collar Christian unions, most members of the Protestant minority did not support the liberal parties congenial to Stegerwald but rather the fervently monarchist and sometimes anti-Semitic Christian Social Party founded by Adolf Stoecker in 1878. In December 1918 the Christian Socials merged with the remnants of the Conservative and Free Conservative Parties in the German Nationalist People's Party, the DNVP, which advocated a restoration of monarchy. As executive secretary of the DGB,

52 Michael Schneider, *Die Christlichen Gewerkschaften 1894–1933* (Bonn, 1982), pp. 486–94; Nobel, *Brüning*, p. 26.

53 Brüning, *Memoiren*, pp. 72–74; Brüning to Clara Bechly, 2 October 1954, HUG FP 93.10/Box 3/Hans Bechly; Ullmann, *Publizist*, pp. 102–05, 112–13; Patch, *Christian Trade Unions*, pp. 63–70.

54 Max Habermann, "Der DHV im Kampf um das Reich" (unpublished memoir of 1934, DHV Archive, Hamburg), pp. 15–17; for background, see Iris Hamel, *Völkischer Verband und nationale Gewerkschaft. Der Deutschnationale Handlungsgehilfen-Verband 1893–1933* (Frankfurt a.M., 1967).

Brüning worked tirelessly to acquaint blue-collar Catholic democrats with the sentiments of Protestant monarchists and nationalists; that he also won the confidence of most Catholic labor leaders showed that he was developing into a skillful politician. To friends he boasted that he could steer senior union colleagues in the right direction with such gentle nudges that they did not even notice the steering.[55]

The first test of Brüning's efforts to forge consensus in the DGB began on the eve of the Essen Congress when the Social Democrats launched a campaign to nationalize the coal industry. This goal was supported by the powerful chairman of the Christian miners' union, Heinrich Imbusch, but was opposed by the DHV on the grounds of liberal economic theory. Brüning agreed with the DHV and sought earnestly to persuade Stegerwald and Heinrich Brauns, who played a pivotal role as Reich labor minister from 1920 to 1928, to delay any government action.[56] After twelve months of parliamentary hearings and public debate about the coal industry, Brüning made a rare public appearance to address a convention of Christian miners in July 1921. He spoke at length of the recent decision by the Allied Powers at the London Conference to demand a total reparations bill of 132 billion gold marks, and he appealed for cooperation among all elements of organized labor to develop a responsible fiscal plan to shoulder this enormous burden. Imbusch, doubtless nudged discreetly by Brüning, then chose this forum to announce that he had decided to oppose nationalizing the coal mines because that would expose them to confiscation by foreign powers in lieu of reparations. Even the SPD dropped the issue soon thereafter, and Brüning had enjoyed a first victory for the strategy of focusing attention on foreign policy rather than domestic divisions that was to characterize his political career.[57]

Brüning opposed socialization plans in part because liberal economic theory offered the best foundation for criticism of the Treaty of Versailles. Germany, he argued, must demonstrate to world public opinion the importance of achieving an efficient international division of labor. The Great War had destroyed vast stocks of capital and stimulated vast investments that were irrational in economic terms, so the world economy could revive only if markets functioned to guide factors of production everywhere to the tasks where they could be employed most effectively. The Versailles Treaty created the potential for a host of future trade wars, however, and drew borders without regard for economics. Worse still

---

55 Beer, *Heinrich Brüning*, pp. 39–40; Emil Dofivat, "Erinnerungen an den Anfang," on p. 21 of "Der Deutsche 1921–1931," insert in *Der Deutsche*, 1 April 1931, #77; Patch, *Christian Trade Unions*, pp. 11–15, 41–54.

56 Brüning to Stegerwald, 30 July and 7 August 1920, NL Stegerwald/001/vol. 1919–1920/#78 & 80; Peter Wulf, "Die Auseinandersetzungen um die Sozialisierung der Kohle in Deutschland 1920–21," *Vierteljahrshefte für Zeitgeschichte*, 25 (1977): 53–89.

57 Gewerkverein christlicher Bergarbeiter, *Protokoll der 16. Generalversammlung, 3–7 Juli 1921* (Essen, n.d.), pp. 61–62, 236–44; Patch, *Christian Trade Unions*, pp. 59–62; Michael Schäfer, *Heinrich Imbusch. Christlicher Gewerkschaftsführer und Widerstandskämpfer* (Munich, 1990), pp. 114–18. For background, see Bruce Kent, *The Spoils of War: The Politics, Economics, and Diplomacy of Reparations 1918–1932* (Oxford, 1989), pp. 103–32.

was its requirement that Germany pay for the entire cost of the war. This requirement could never be fulfilled, but even partial fulfillment would compel Germany to adopt such desperate measures to achieve a trade surplus as to disrupt the entire European economy.[58] Brüning's arguments resembled those of John Maynard Keynes.

Brüning's economic training made him unusually far-sighted regarding the threat of hyper-inflation. In 1921 he called publicly for draconian measures to tax the wealth of war profiteers, increase rates of taxation on inheritance and capital gains, and alter methods of collection so that the value of taxes on business did not evaporate.[59] Brüning also played some role in devising the basic plan to stabilize the currency that guided both the Prussian cabinet formed by Stegerwald in April 1921 and the Reich cabinet formed by his party colleague Joseph Wirth a month later: to deregulate work hours as a concession to big business in exchange for massive increases in direct taxation on the propertied. Brüning did not understand the crucial importance of securing the SPD's support for this plan, however. Stegerwald and Wirth agreed that they must form "Great Coalition" cabinets to represent all parties from the SPD to the right-liberal DVP; only by uniting the foremost representatives of labor and big business could the currency be stabilized and the Weimar Republic placed on a secure foundation.[60] Eduard Stadtler pursued a very different agenda, however, when he resumed contact with Brüning in early 1921. He reported with dismay to Martin Spahn that Brüning "seems to have become completely middle-of-the-road in outlook [*ganz mittelparteilich eingestellt*], denounces the German Nationalists, . . . denounces the industrialists. . . . What an influence is exerted by one's milieu!"[61] Stadtler decided to rescue Brüning by winning Stegerwald over to the right, so he persuaded Brüning to support a plan to replace the SPD in the Prussian government coalition with the two "national" parties, the DVP and DNVP. When Stegerwald found in April 1921 that the SPD still rejected any coalition with the DVP, he presented the Landtag a minority cabinet of just the Center and Democratic parties, hoping to win toleration from the SPD. When the Social Democrats decided to oppose him, Stadtler and Brüning persuaded

---

58 Brüning, "Wiederaufbau des deutschen Finanzwesens," pp. 85–87, 104–06; Brüning, "Welt-Finanzwesen," *Deutsche Arbeit,* 7 (1922): 111–12.

59 Brüning, "Wiederaufbau des deutschen Finanzwesens," pp. 88–96; B.[rüning], "Die eigentlichen Aufgaben der neuen Steuerreform," *Der Deutsche,* 27 September 1921, #152; Brüning, *Memoiren,* pp. 43, 82–85, 367; Rudolf Morsey, "Brünings Kritik an der Reichsfinanzpolitik 1919–1929," in Erich Hassinger et al., eds., *Geschichte, Wirtschaft, Gesellschaft. Festschrift für Clemens Bauer* (Berlin, 1974), pp. 361–65.

60 See the remarks by Wirth in a discussion with party leaders on 13 September 1921, and by Brauns and President Ebert in the cabinet meeting of 15 November 1921, in Ingrid Schulze-Bidlingmaier, ed., *Akten der Reichskanzlei der Weimarer Republik. Die Kabinette Wirth I und II* (Boppard am Rhein, 1973), I:254–55, 406–07; Stegerwald to Francisco Mühlenkamp, 8 October 1921, NL Stegerwald/018; Stegerwald's editorial in *Zentralblatt der christlichen Gewerkschaften,* 26 September 1921, pp. 290–91; and the reminiscences in Wirth's letters to Heinrich Brüning on 5 February 1929 (NL Wirth/10) and to Josef Andre on 23 July 1948 (NL Wirth/7).

61 Stadtler to Spahn, 24 February 1921, NL Spahn/3.

the DVP and DNVP to save the new cabinet. Stegerwald's unexpected support from the right involved him in bitter polemics with the SPD, which accused him of sabotaging the effort to form a Great Coalition in the Reich.[62]

Stegerwald sought for several months to expand his minority cabinet to include the Great Coalition, but Brüning urged him to change course, arguing that the London Ultimatum on reparations would transform German politics:

> If our trade unions were resolved to base their agitation on a firmly nation-alist viewpoint, rejecting all bourgeois pacifist ideas, it would undoubtedly be possible to tear great chunks out of the edifice of the Social Democratic trade unions. A great many regimental associations of combat veterans have been founded in the last year. I know of many that already have 10,000 to 15,000 members, of whom 80 percent belong to the Free Unions. At heart 70 percent of German workers care nothing any more about Marxism or anti-Marxism, socialization or private enterprise. They are fed up with such things and recognize that the programs of almost all parties and all the rival trade unions contain the same things, while an ever heavier weight presses down on the German people from abroad, preventing any of the fair promises from being fulfilled. Here is where we must spring in. Our goal must be to cultivate the national ideal, i.e., to strengthen the determination to regain Germany's freedom at all costs.

Brüning appealed to Stegerwald to revive his call for a broad new party of the middle and to oppose Wirth openly, because the cooperation with the SPD advo-cated by him could only weaken the Christian unions. Brüning also promised to detach the Christian Socials from the DNVP in order to strengthen the new party.[63] This advice reflected the impetuosity of youth; Stegerwald would never endorse such a plan for simultaneous declarations of war against Chancellor Wirth, the Free Unions, and the DNVP. Brüning felt nevertheless that his sense of historic trends was vindicated by Lenin's adoption a few months later of the New Economic Policy. Brüning editorialized that all elements of the labor move-ment, even the Bolsheviks, now recognized Marxism as "the product of mis-guided theoreticians cut off from real life, who did not come from the working class, . . . an academic, hyper-intellectual fool's cap that has been pulled down over the clear-sighted eyes of the authentic labor movement."[64]

Brüning and Stegerwald both lost credibility, however, when right-wing extremists assassinated Erzberger in August 1921. Catholic laborites denounced the DNVP for inciting the deed and reproached Stegerwald for accepting

---

62 Stadtler to Albert Vögler, 10 September 1920, to Stegerwald on 24 March 1921, and to Martin Spahn, 21 October 1920, and 8 and 10 March and 11 April 1921, all in NL Spahn/3; Stadtler's memorandum "Zur politischen Lage," sent to Spahn, Stresemann, Vögler, and Hugenberg on 14 April 1921, NL Spahn/3; Herbert Hömig, *Das preussische Zentrum in der Weimarer Republik* (Mainz, 1979), pp. 99–111; Hagen Schulze, *Otto Braun oder Preussens demokratische Sendung* (Frankfurt a.M. and Berlin, 1977), pp. 329–38; Dietrich Orlow, *Weimar Prussia 1918–1925: The Unlikely Rock of Democracy* (Pittsburgh, 1986), pp. 77–82. Brüning later distorted this episode in *Memoiren*, pp. 74–76, by reporting that he had persuaded Stegerwald to seek a coalition with the DNVP.
63 Brüning to Stegerwald, 4 August 1921, NL Stegerwald/018.
64 B.[rüning], "Arbeiterbewegung und Nation," *Der Deutsche*, 10 November 1921, #190.

support from such chauvinists. When Martin Spahn defected to the DNVP and publicly invited Stegerwald to follow him, many Catholic workers canceled their subscriptions to *Der Deutsche*. Recriminations continued within the Christian unions even after Stegerwald was removed from the political firing line in October, when the SPD agreed to form a Great Coalition in Prussia under Otto Braun if Stegerwald resigned from the cabinet.[65] Brüning now discovered that the general secretary of the blue-collar League of Christian Trade Unions, Bernhard Otte, enjoyed more authority and a much larger budget than did he. In the fall of 1921 Brüning submitted elaborate plans for expanding the functions of his office, and he submitted his resignation when they were ignored. Stegerwald persuaded him to take a long vacation and then return to work, but the year 1922 marked the nadir of Brüning's career.[66] His only success came in April 1922, when he secured the appointment of a Protestant friend from the June Club, the Sudeten German Hermann Ullmann, as chief editor of *Der Deutsche* and then persuaded all factions of the DGB to resume cooperation with the paper.[67]

Brüning's morale and influence revived in January 1923 after the French army occupied the Ruhr Valley to compel Germany to pay reparations. The Christian trade unions immediately resolved to strike rather than work under French direction; the much larger Free Unions soon adopted a similar attitude, and a campaign of passive resistance gained widespread support from the Ruhr populace. Brüning felt that this display of working-class patriotism vindicated the work of the National Assembly in 1919, just as the victorious Wars of Liberation against Napoleon had vindicated the reforms of Karl vom Stein. "If the Weimar constitution had only this one merit," he later declared, "it would have rendered one of the greatest historical services to the German nation."[68] Brüning worked closely with Labor Minister Brauns to reinvigorate the Central Association of November 1918 by creating joint committees of employers and union leaders throughout the Ruhr to distribute strike support payments. This program was eventually expanded to provide covert financial support directly to the trade unions. Brüning later recalled frequent trips from Berlin to confer with strike leaders in Elberfeld, just outside French lines, and he probably served as one of the confidential agents of the labor ministry who carried suitcases full of cash to support their efforts.[69]

---

65 Brüning, *Memoiren*, p. 404; Patch, *Christian Trade Unions*, pp. 71–72; Orlow, *Prussia 1918–1925*, pp. 82–87.
66 Brüning to Stegerwald, 24 September 1921, NL Stegerwald/014/Nachtragsband/#4, and 23 November 1921, NL Stegerwald/018; Michael Schneider, *Die christlichen Gewerkschaften*, pp. 494–95; Morsey, "Brünings Kritik an der Reichsfinanzpolitik," p. 365, n. 28.
67 See Alphons Nobel, "10 Jahre 'Der Deutsche,'" and Emil Dovifat, "Erinnerungen an den Anfang," on pp. 21 and 25–28 of "Der Deutsche 1921–1931," insert into *Der Deutsche*, 1 April 1931, #77.
68 "Some Reflections on the Decay of European Democracy," Queen's College lecture #1, p. 6, HUG FP 93.45; see also Brüning, *Memoiren*, pp. 87–90, and Lothar Erdmann, *Die Gewerkschaften im Ruhrkampf* (Berlin, 1924).
69 Patch, *Christian Trade Unions*, pp. 78–81; Feldman, *Great Disorder*, pp. 631–58; Schäfer, *Heinrich Imbusch*, pp. 130–34; Brüning, *Memoiren*, p. 90.

Brüning also sought to promote cooperation between the trade unions and the army command. In March 1923 Ullmann reintroduced him to Major Friedrich Wilhelm Freiherr von Willisen, another June Club activist and a man Brüning considered the best sort of Prussian aristocrat. General Hans von Seeckt had assigned this intelligence officer to coordinate operations by the Free Corps along Germany's eastern borders in 1919, and Willisen enlisted several organizations like the June Club to funnel volunteers and supplies to the defense of the Baltic Republics against the Red Army, the agitation for *Anschluss* with Germany in Austria and the Sudetenland, and the defense of Upper Silesia against Polish troops. After the Allies enforced a strict ceiling of 100,000 troops on the German army in 1920, Willisen played some role in preparing covert mobilization plans for the defense of the "eastern march," and Brüning supported these efforts by seeking to arouse the interest of Christian trade unionists in western Germany.[70] Willisen was retired in 1923, but Seeckt apparently asked him to help coordinate resistance efforts in the Ruhr. By July 1923, as hyper-inflation and food shortages created a major political crisis, Brüning was making daily rounds from DGB headquarters to the home of Willisen and then to the labor ministry. He provided Willisen with intelligence on the strike movement from DGB contacts and considered himself a vital link between organized labor, the cabinet, and the Reichswehr (Armed Forces) in the desperate struggle to preserve national unity against French agents, Bavarian separatists, Communist revolutionaries, and right-wing putschists. Seeckt hoped to create a foundation for active resistance by organizing the remnants of the Free Corps into an illegal army reserve, but Brüning later insisted that he and Willisen opposed such ideas and helped the Prussian police to infiltrate the Free Corps and prevent them from doing harm. Brüning doubtless exaggerated his role (there is no documentary evidence that he or Willisen advised the army command in 1923), but in old age he recalled these activities as his fondest memory and greatest achievement.[71]

Brüning's experiences in the summer of 1923 strengthened his emotional identification with the Weimar Republic. When he editorialized against the putschists of left and right, he issued the following appeal to the SPD to rejoin the Reich government:

> We emphasize again: whoever truly respects the fatherland must appeal for an alliance of all the parties and groups that reject any violent alteration of the constitution in order to give the Reich government the broad foundation that it absolutely needs for its diplomatic negotiations. . . . The deeper

70 Ullmann, *Publizist*, pp. 93–99; Brüning, *Memoiren*, pp. 45–47; Ishida, *Jungkonservative*, pp. 31–32; Brüning to Martin Spahn, 30 April 1920, NL Spahn/22.
71 Brüning, *Memoiren*, pp. 91–99; Treviranus, *Ende von Weimar*, pp. 57–58; Brüning to Hermann Ullmann, 23 September 1947 and 7 December 1955, NL Ullmann/6/42–43, 265; Brüning to Walther Stennes, 11 August 1949, *Briefe*, II:193; Francis L. Carsten, *The Reichswehr and Politics, 1918 to 1933* (Oxford, 1966), pp. 118–22, 149–65; Robert Waite, *Vanguard of Nazism: The Free Corps Movement in Postwar Germany 1918–1923* (Cambridge, Mass., 1952), pp. 235–53; Heinz Hürten, ed., *Quellen zur Geschichte des Parlamentarismus und der politischen Parteien. 2. Reihe: Militär und Politik. Band 4: Das Krisenjahr 1923* (Düsseldorf, 1980), pp. xxiii–xxiv.

cause for the polarization of domestic politics lies essentially in the lack of concern for national security [*mangelnden nationalen Einstellung*] of many circles in Social Democracy and the complete lack of creative ideas in their ranks. If one seeks to make of the Republic a Caudinian yoke [for the humiliation of one's enemies], or to exploit it as a propaganda slogan, that would create the greatest danger for its survival in the long run. . . . If Social Democracy always slips away from responsibility in critical moments in order to burden the bourgeois parties with the odium for failed political gambits, then it must not be surprised if all responsible elements lose hope that Social Democracy will really develop into a responsible party with statesmanlike leaders.

Brüning's criticism of the SPD was doubtless unfair, but he displayed a spirit very different from that of the neo-conservatives when he attacked it not as the creator of the Weimar Republic but as a threat to its survival.[72]

Gustav Stresemann of the DVP finally assembled the first national Great Coalition cabinet in August 1923, which made the unpopular but unavoidable decision to capitulate to France. Unfortunately, Stresemann too proved unable to break the political deadlock between big business and organized labor. Brüning criticized the laborites who rejected any exceptions to the eight-hour day, but he considered the business community more to blame for the deadlock. His editorials denounced the price-gouging by cartels and syndicates, the absurdly loose credit policies of the Reichsbank (National Bank), and the belief among industrialists that inflation benefited exports even after it had obviously become so severe as to plunge the German people into misery. In October Brüning responded to an effort by Ruhr heavy industry to abolish the eight-hour day unilaterally by proclaiming that Germany's worst political problem was the effort by the syndicates and trusts to create a *"private Zwangswirtschaft,"* a bureaucratized economy under private ownership that would combine all the worst features of capitalism and socialism.[73] Brüning developed more sympathy in these weeks for the SPD, noting impressive intellects and admirable realism in his private discussions with the new finance minister, Rudolf Hilferding, and the leaders of the SPD Reichstag delegation. He also sensed a paralysis of will, however:

Many leaders of the SPD, Hilferding above all, clearly saw what could and should be done in order to save the people in its utmost distress. But if they had spoken clearly and openly about the limits of the possible, then they would have lost the greatest portion of their supporters to the extremists,

---

72 See the unsigned editorial, "Gegen das Verbrechen des Bürgerkriegs," *Der Deutsche*, 20 July 1923, #167, and Nobel, *Brüning*, pp. 30–32.
73 See the series on "Die Forderungen des Deutschen Gewerkschaftsbundes zur Lage," *Der Deutsche*, 2–8 August 1923; "Dollarkurs und Devisenpolitik," 5 October 1923, #233; "Gegen industrielle Wucherpolitik," 18 October 1923, #244; "Private Zwangswirtschaft. Zum Kampf gegen die Kartelle und Konventionen," 19 October 1923, #245; and Morsey, "Brünings Kritik an der Reichsfinanzpolitik," pp. 365–67.

who derived their strength from the fact that fanaticism is always easier in politics than realism.[74]

Brüning sought throughout the following years to persuade SPD leaders to draw a sharper line between themselves and the Communist competition.

By October 1923 most neo-conservatives openly demanded the replacement of parliamentary government by some form of dictatorship. Brüning sought a parliamentary resolution of the crisis, however, and persuaded Stegerwald and Heinrich Brauns to endorse the idea of replacing the SPD with the DNVP in a right-of-center majority coalition. When the SPD decided to withdraw from the Reich cabinet in November, President Ebert commissioned Stegerwald to form such a cabinet, but the attempt failed over the DNVP's demand for simultaneous admission into the Prussian state government.[75] Wilhelm Marx of the Center Party then became chancellor of a minority centrist cabinet and secured the necessary two-thirds majority in the Reichstag for an enabling act that delegated legislative powers to the cabinet for all measures needed to stabilize the currency. Using these powers, the Marx cabinet purged the economy of inflation through drastic austerity measures devised by Heinrich Brauns and Finance Minister Hans Luther, which included massive tax increases, wholesale layoffs of public employees, and the virtual deregulation of work hours. These measures proved extremely unpopular among workers, but Brüning agreed with most professional economists that they were unavoidable.[76]

President Ebert also set a precedent that Brüning studied carefully by employing dozens of presidential emergency decrees based on Article 48 of the constitution to implement stabilizing measures that fell outside the scope of the enabling act. Ebert invoked Article 48 frequently in 1923/4 to impose tax reforms, restrictions on currency speculation, reforms of the court system, and other measures with the force of enduring laws. Brüning acknowledged that the authors of the constitution had intended Article 48 to apply only in cases of invasion or insurrection, but he applauded Ebert's decision to expand its scope, arguing that riots would have spread quickly if the inflation had resumed.[77] The final lesson Brüning drew from the events of 1923 was that financial speculators

---

74 Brüning, *Memoiren*, p. 98.
75 Patch, *Christian Trade Unions*, pp. 83–87; Feldman, *Great Disorder*, pp. 736–80.
76 Feldman, *Great Disorder*, pp. 780–835; Charles Maier, *Recasting Bourgeois Europe: Stabilization in France, Germany, and Italy in the Decade after World War I* (Princeton, 1975), pp. 387–419; Claus-Dieter Krohn, *Stabilisierung und ökonomische Interessen. Die Finanzpolitik des Deutschen Reiches 1923–1927* (Düsseldorf, 1974), pp. 29–45; Karsten Ruppert, *Im Dienst am Staat von Weimar. Das Zentrum als regierende Partei in der Weimarer Demokratie 1923–1930* (Düsseldorf, 1992), pp. 40–49.
77 Ulrich Scheuner, "Die Anwendung des Art. 48 der Weimarer Reichsverfassung unter den Präsidentschaften von Ebert und Hindenburg," in Hermens and Schieder, eds., *Staat, Wirtschaft und Politik*, pp. 257–65; Hans Boldt, "Der Artikel 48 der Weimarer Reichsverfassung," in Michael Stürmer, ed., *Die Weimarer Republik. Belagerte Civitas*, 2nd ed. (Königstein/Ts., 1985), pp. 288–96; Ludwig Richter, "Das präsidiale Notverordnungsrecht in den ersten Jahren der Weimarer Republik. Friedrich Ebert und die Anwendung des Artikels 48 der Weimarer Reichsverfassung," in Eberhard Kolb, ed., *Friedrich Ebert als Reichspräsident. Amtsführung und Amtsverständnis* (Munich, 1997), pp. 207–57; Brüning to Philip Dessauer, 16 March 1956, in Müller, *Brüning Papers*, pp. 178–79.

possessed a disturbing new power to circumvent the decisions of parliament in times of great economic uncertainty:

> In the Reichstag people debated for weeks about radical tax increases without coming to prompt and resolute decisions. . . . Nothing was achieved in this way but a flight of capital and further inflation. The propertied were best able to evade the new tax measures through their sophisticated financial maneuvers. It then became clear to me that, in such times, the normal parliamentary conduct of such business can achieve nothing. Severe crises of public finance can only be overcome if a government knows what it wants, and proclaims carefully designed laws overnight, so that speculation cannot begin immediately the next day to undermine the newly created stability.

Brüning considered Marx's enabling act, whereby the cabinet issued laws in the name of the Reichstag and did not require presidential approval for its measures, the ideal device for reconciling constitutional government with the need for decisive action in such matters.[78]

Brüning parted company with most of his neo-conservative friends in 1923, dismayed by their sweeping attacks on parliamentarism that ignored the practical difficulties facing any government. Brüning also experienced disillusionment with the leaders of the German army, who revealed "an absolute lack of any constructive political ideas." In January 1924, Brüning later recalled, he conveyed an urgent appeal to Willisen to dissuade General Seeckt from any thought of seizing power.[79] Brüning later acknowledged to Hermann Ullmann that he had been impatient and unrealistic immediately after the Great War:

> My attitude changed in the critical months at the end of 1923, when I was in close collaboration with the trade unions, the Cabinet, and the Army. You remember that you yourself were then frequently angry with me for my reticence in speaking of final aims, for my silence on certain days, and even my inactivity on days when the nervous tension seemed unbearable. Those weeks were the finishing school of my political education.[80]

Brüning had finally matured, as the lessons of Meinecke about the importance of parliament supplanted the lessons of Martin Spahn. Meinecke was in fact invited to advise Christian trade unionists on how to achieve the ideals of the Essen Program in the newspaper supervised by Brüning in April 1921. All admirers of Karl vom Stein, the historian editorialized, must recognize that "today the republic is the constitutional form that divides us least." In December 1922 Meinecke coined the term *Vernunftrepublikaner* to describe his own development from a sentimental monarchist into a "republican from reason." The phrase accurately described the learning process experienced by Brüning and by Gustav

---

78 Brüning, *Memoiren*, pp. 86–87; compare his Page-Barbour Lecture #1 of January 1939, pp. 21–29, HUG FP 93.45.
79 Brüning, *Memoiren*, pp. 96, 107; compare Treviranus, *Ende von Weimar*, pp. 60–61, and Carsten, *Reichswehr*, pp. 186–98.
80 Brüning to Ullmann, 13 July 1946, NL Ullmann/6/282.

Stresemann as well, the leader of the DVP who also concluded by 1923 that any effort to alter the Weimar constitution would cause disastrous civil strife.[81] For Spahn and Stadtler, after 1923 there could be no doubt that Brüning had betrayed his neo-conservative ideals and sunk into the democratic swamp.[82]

1.3. The Parliamentarian

Brüning became acquainted with parliamentary government from the inside after the Reichstag election of May 1924, when Stegerwald secured him a seat representing the Center Party in Upper Silesia. He was assigned to the Reichstag taxation committee, and his tireless study of the arcane details of the budget and latest economic statistics won him selection as his party's chief spokesperson on tax policy in 1925. Most Reichstag delegates became glassy-eyed during prolonged discussion of such matters, but Brüning sensed in the crafting of the tax code the best opportunity to stabilize parliamentary government and promote a successful foreign policy.[83] The Weimar Republic's system of proportional representation did not encourage close ties between members of the Reichstag and their districts, but Brüning made an unusual effort to learn about his constituents. He visited Upper Silesia almost every week, consulting trade unionists, businessmen, and landowners alike, and his early speeches to the Reichstag focused on such problems as the housing shortage in the Waldenburg mining district and the lack of good railroad connections along the eastern border. In 1928 Brüning graduated from number 3 to number 1 on the Center Party's list of nominees in Upper Silesia, a sign that he was no longer a candidate imposed on a provincial party by its national leadership but rather genuinely popular in the region.[84]

Brüning continued to champion an idea that made many Christian trade unionists uncomfortable, a parliamentary coalition between the Center Party and DNVP. His role in the German Labor Federation brought him close to the Christian Social wing of the DNVP and to its liaison officer with the DHV, Walther Lambach, and in 1924 he befriended Gottfried Treviranus, a newly elected Nationalist Reichstag delegate from Westphalia, an agronomist and former naval officer. Treviranus, Ullmann, Brüning, and Lambach shared an enthusiasm for Karl vom Stein and Disraeli's version of "Tory democracy." The DHV provided modest funding for Ullmann to found a new magazine in the fall of 1924 as a mouthpiece for the left wing of the DNVP, and it articulated a creed of "popular

---

81 See Friedrich Meinecke, "Volksgemeinschaft" (first published in *Der Deutsche*, 8 April 1921) and "Das Ende der monarchischen Welt," *Werke*, II:320–24, 344–50; Pois, *Meinecke*, pp. 86–117; and Henry A. Turner, Jr., *Stresemann and the Politics of the Weimar Republic* (Princeton, 1963), pp. 98–160.

82 See Stadtler's reminiscences in *Werksgemeinschaft als soziologisches Problem* (Berlin, 1926), pp. 21, 35–36, and *Schafft es Brüning?* (Berlin, 1931), pp. 144–50.

83 Beer, *Heinrich Brüning*, p. 41; Morsey, "Brünings Kritik an der Reichsfinanzpolitik," pp. 367–68.

84 Beer, *Heinrich Brüning*, pp. 46–48; Nobel, *Brüning*, pp. 44–46.

conservatism" (*Volkskonservatismus*) that emphasized the shared interests of workers and peasants. Unlike the neo-conservatives, Brüning's new friends sought to reconcile the DNVP with parliamentary democracy.[85] Brüning supported the "popular conservatives" by promoting personal contacts between politicians in the Center and DNVP. In the process he seems to have perpetuated the student lifestyle, reading German, French, and English newspapers in the cafes of Berlin and then conversing far into the night with some wit and considerable learning about European economic conditions, points of agreement between Catholic and Protestant doctrine, and Germany's strategic errors in the Great War. His friends of the 1920s later recalled a congenial companion who relished good wine, beer, and cigars, often smiled though rarely laughed, and always had something interesting to say. He enjoyed conversation with the handful of women in the leadership of the Center Party and Christian unions, but nobody ever observed him in any romantic relationship.[86]

Brüning wrote misleadingly in his published memoirs that a new spirit of nonpartisanship arose among the combat veterans from all parties who streamed into the Reichstag in 1924. He accurately recalled forming cordial ties with all his colleagues on the Reichstag taxation committee from Hilferding of the SPD to Reinhold Quaatz of the DNVP, but he displayed wishful thinking when he sought to interpret political conflict as the result of division by generation, not social class:

> The younger delegates elected to the Reichstag in 1924 worried little about party politics and tactical advantage. . . . Confidential discussions between former soldiers were not exploited for party politics. The old men in all the parties, who had already served a generation long in parliaments before the war, welcomed this mutual confidence, knowing full well that no parliament can achieve lasting successes if it is not present. "The youngsters" were therefore promoted by them over the heads of the middle-aged. The suspicion of the middle generation and its attempts to disrupt contacts led to the idea of rigorous party discipline under a single leader within the various parties, above all the DNVP.[87]

The first draft of his memoirs reveals a more partisan spirit. Brüning rejoiced in January 1925 when the leaders of the DNVP swore to uphold the constitution in exchange for inclusion in a right-of-center cabinet under Hans Luther, and he became even more optimistic in April, when Field Marshal Paul von

85 Ullmann, *Publizist in der Zeitenwende*, pp. 112–18; Treviranus, *Ende von Weimar*, pp. 93–94; Erasmus Jonas, *Die Volkskonservativen 1928–1933* (Düsseldorf, 1965), pp. 15–21. See also Walther Lambach, *Die Herrschaft der 500. Ein Bild des parlamentarischen Lebens im neuen Deutschland* (Hamburg and Berlin, 1926), a highly informative and respectful account of the workings of the Reichstag, and the enthusiastic book reviews from the liberal and Social Democratic press collected in NL Lambach/18.

86 See Treviranus, *Ende von Weimar*, pp. 71–84; Nobel, "Der letzte demokratische Kanzler," in Vernekohl, ed., *Heinrich Brüning*, pp. 146–49; and Beer, *Heinrich Brüning*, pp. 39–44, 51–52.

87 Brüning, *Memoiren*, pp. 108–13; compare Wohl, *Generation of 1914*, pp. 25–40, 73–83.

Hindenburg defeated Wilhelm Marx for the presidency. Franz von Papen publicly denounced the Center Party's decision to nominate Marx as the candidate of the Weimar Coalition, and he campaigned actively for Hindenburg, as did the Bavarian People's Party (BVP), the Center's sister party in the south. Unlike Papen, Brüning always observed party discipline, but he dragged his feet during this campaign. "I can remember no election speeches that were so difficult for me," he later recalled, as to speak for Marx against Hindenburg. The election of the field marshal inspired him with bright hopes: "I concluded that it should be possible, with his support, for me and my friends on the right to erect a long-lasting conservative regime."[88]

Brüning's hopes soon dimmed when the Luther cabinet confirmed many of the worst fears of those who had opposed the admission of the DNVP into government. Many Christian trade unionists became angry when the government reimposed agricultural tariffs and favored the interests of big business in compensating inflation victims. Brüning secured some populist amendments to the government's income tax bill of August 1925, but public reaction to the final bill was mixed, and Joseph Wirth resigned from the Center Reichstag delegation to protest this "victory of the reactionaries."[89] Brüning experienced acute embarrassment when the signing of the European Security Pact at Locarno, an important gesture of reconciliation between Germany and France, provoked the DNVP into leaving the government in October 1925. He tried to persuade party colleagues that Count Kuno von Westarp and the other veterans of the old Conservative Party in the DNVP were selfless patriots, that its sometimes unreasonable behavior resulted from the influx of militant imperialists from a National Liberal background, such as Alfred Hugenberg. But Wirth gained new credibility for his argument that the DNVP was hopelessly authoritarian and chauvinistic, that only "dedicated republicans" should be admitted to cabinets in the future. In the year 1926, as weak minority cabinets looked to the left for support in foreign policy and to the right in domestic policy, Stegerwald and most other Center Party leaders decided to advocate a revival of the Great Coalition with the SPD.[90]

Yet Brüning insisted that a renewed coalition with the DNVP was essential

88 Brüning, manuscript memoirs, pp. 1–2, HUG FP 93.4. See also Brüning to Gessler, 31 January 1955, in Otto Gessler, *Reichswehrpolitik in der Weimarer Zeit*, ed. Kurt Sendtner (Stuttgart, 1958), pp. 507–08; Ruppert, *Dienst am Staat*, pp. 110–22; and Richard Rolfs, *The Sorcerer's Apprentice: The Life of Franz von Papen* (Lanham, Md., 1996), pp. 52–55.
89 Jakob Kaiser to Brüning, 4 September 1925, NL Kaiser/217; Heinrich Brüning, "Die Arbeit der Zentrumspartei auf finanzpolitischem Gebiete," in Karl Anton Schulte, ed., *Nationale Arbeit. Das Zentrum und sein Wirken in der deutschen Republik* (Leipzig, 1929), pp. 367–68; Patch, *Christian Trade Unions*, pp. 102–05; Ruppert, *Dienst am Staat*, pp. 147–49; Krohn, *Stabilisierung*, pp. 185–96.
90 Brüning, *Memoiren*, p. 123; Brüning to Ullmann, 25 July 1951, NL Ullmann/6/122–23; Deutsche Zentrumspartei, *Offizieller Bericht des vierten Reichsparteitages der Deutschen Zentrumspartei, 16–17 November 1925* (Berlin, n.d.), pp. 32–38, 70–76, 84–85; Michael Stürmer, *Koalition und Opposition in der Weimarer Republik 1924–1928* (Düsseldorf, 1967), pp. 107–27; Patch, *Christian Trade Unions*, pp. 105–14; Jon Jacobsen, *Locarno Diplomacy: Germany and the West 1925–1929* (Princeton, 1972), pp. 47–67.

for a sound fiscal policy. In March 1926 Finance Minister Peter Reinhold of the DDP responded to a recession by lowering tax rates to stimulate economic growth. In June he launched Germany's first experiment with a counter-cyclical program to borrow money for public works, and in September he publicly attacked the ruinous caution of previous finance ministers who had starved the economy of investment funds by accumulating a budget surplus. Reinhold's program is sometimes hailed as Germany's first "Keynesian" experiment, but Brüning was probably correct to condemn it as poorly administered and ineffective.[91] Brüning protested to Chancellor Marx that Reinhold was ruining a long-term fiscal plan that required a budget surplus for another year or two to replenish the reserves of social insurance funds ravaged by inflation, meet the rising cost of reparations (which would not reach their peak level under the Dawes Plan until 1929), and help municipal governments to reduce local property tax rates. Brüning prophesied that the Reich might find itself unable to borrow to cover a future deficit:

> The greatest worry caused me by the remarks of the Reich finance minister is that, if tax rates are now lowered to a level that cannot be sustained throughout the next years, then the parties will not be able to muster the resolve to increase them again when that becomes necessary, especially since we do not know if there will then be a government that commands a stable majority in parliament. . . . It is the historic duty of the Center Party to bear responsibility among all the shifting coalitions for the continuity of the Reich's foreign policy and for fiscal policy, which is closely connected with it and the precondition for its success.

Brüning's letter prompted a reprimand from the chancellor to his finance minister and a press release from Reinhold denying that he opposed the policies of his predecessors. The DNVP was the only party to attack Reinhold for dissipating the treasury surplus, however, so Brüning concluded that the government needed a healthy dose of Prussian conservatism.[92]

Brüning's sympathy for the DNVP left him isolated within the Center Party in the fall of 1926, but his position grew stronger because of clumsy tactics by the Social Democrats. On 16 December, just when Marx and Heinrich Brauns believed that they had reached agreement with the SPD to form a Great Coalition, the Social Democrat Philipp Scheidemann attacked Defense Minister Gessler in the Reichstag with sensational revelations about illegal cooperation

---

91 See Dieter Hertz-Eichenrode, *Wirtschaftskrise und Arbeitsbeschaffung. Konjunkturpolitik 1925/1926 und die Grundlagen der Krisenpolitik Brünings* (Frankfurt a.M. and New York, 1982); Krohn, *Stabilisierung*, pp. 199–222; Balderston, *German Economic Crisis*, pp. 224–34; and Gerald Feldman, "Industrialists, Bankers, and the Problem of Unemployment in the Weimar Republic," *Central European History*, 25 (1992): 79–80.

92 Brüning to Chancellor Marx, 7 September 1926, and State Secretary Pünder to Reinhold, 7 September 1926, *Akten der Reichskanzlei. Die Kabinette Marx III und IV*, ed. Günter Abramowski, 2 vols. (Boppard am Rhein, 1988), I:189–98; Brüning, "Arbeit der Zentrumspartei," pp. 365–66, 380–82; Brüning, *Memoiren*, pp. 117–19.

between the German military and the Soviet Union. The SPD thereby alienated even its best friends in the bourgeois parties and outraged President Hindenburg. Brüning thought (erroneously) that Scheidemann had acted in concert with foreign intelligence agencies, and even the cautious jurist Marx considered his speech nothing less than high treason.[93] Now Major Kurt von Schleicher, the liaison officer between the defense ministry and the Reichstag delegations, decided to intervene. At his urging, President Hindenburg had recently notified the cabinet that he opposed any law to define the circumstances under which he could invoke Article 48. Now the President also declared that he opposed any effort by the SPD to exclude Gessler from the cabinet and regarded the naming of the defense minister as his own exclusive prerogative.[94] Schleicher then decided that the struggle for Gessler required a coalition between the Center Party and DNVP, so he offered Hindenburg the following advice:

> All the figures involved must be informed that, after the last two cabinet crises, there can no longer be a government without a firm majority, since the President is no longer willing to tolerate the back and forth of these constant crises. If the parliament does not succeed in forming a government with a secure majority, then it would be the President's duty to appoint a government enjoying his confidence without regard for the wishes of the parties, and to give it all constitutional powers to secure a majority in parliament.
>
> Personally, I am convinced that such action will create a government on a broad basis or at least the necessary atmosphere for new elections. The people always sympathize with a clear course and a firm will.

Thus Schleicher intended to threaten the party leaders with government by presidential emergency decree, the threat that became reality under Brüning.[95]

There is no evidence that Brüning advocated such action at this juncture or had any contact with Schleicher. He again sought a parliamentary resolution of the crisis through negotiations with the DNVP, and he persuaded his party colleague, the chancellor's chief of staff Hermann Pünder, to collaborate with the President's top aide Otto Meissner to resolve the impasse. Hindenburg urged Chancellor Marx in an open letter on 20 January 1927 to form a coalition with the DNVP, the first effort by a President of the Weimar Republic to determine the outcome of coalition talks through an appeal to public opinion. Stegerwald told party colleagues that the President's letter "has created a different situa-

---

93 Stürmer, *Koalition*, pp. 169–81; Ruppert, *Dienst am Staat*, pp. 237–38; chancellor's reception for SPD leaders, 15 December 1926, *Die Kabinette Marx III und IV*, I:458; Brüning, *Memoiren*, p. 122; Wilhelm Marx, "Das Jahr 1926," NL Marx/71/4–5.

94 Otto Meissner to Gessler, 23 November 1926, BAP R601/Reel 112/vol. 763/141; Gessler to Reich interior minister, 12 November, Hindenburg to Marx, 22 November, and Meissner's remarks to the cabinet, 16 December 1926, *Kabinette Marx III und IV*, I:329–35, 350–55, 459–60.

95 Schleicher memorandum of late December 1926 and "Aktionsplan" of 1926/27, in Josef Becker, ed., "Dokumentation: Zur Politik der Wehrmachtabteilung in der Regierungskrise 1926/27," *Vierteljahrshefte für Zeitgeschichte*, 14 (1966): 76–78; see also the minutes of Schleicher's confidential remarks in Thilo Vogelsang, *Reichswehr, Staat und NSDAP* (Stuttgart, 1962), p. 411.

tion," and Marx felt absolved from honoring his promise to the Social Democrats not to work with the DNVP. Many of their followers expressed outrage that Hindenburg had coerced them in this way, but in fact Pünder and Meissner had written the letter together and amended it according to Marx's wishes. Thus Brüning helped to create an opportunity for his senior party colleagues to retreat honorably after their declarations of opposition to the DNVP had increased that party's willingness to offer concessions.[96]

After the Center Party "bowed to the President's will," it appointed Wirth to draft rigorous provisions in the government platform on foreign policy and defense of the constitution, while Brauns drafted extensive demands for welfare legislation. Brüning then persuaded the DNVP to accept this platform. The result was a solemn pledge by Nationalist leaders, published on 27 January, to accept all existing foreign treaties, defend the constitution and republican flag against all insults, and create national unemployment insurance and a new law to restrict work hours. The nearly unanimous verdict of the press was that the DNVP thereby repudiated its own past and forfeited its most successful themes for electoral agitation.[97] Brüning's skillful tactics won applause from all factions in his party, although Wirth eventually decided to oppose the new cabinet as a conciliatory gesture toward the SPD. The Baden Centrist Heinrich Köhler was amazed to discover when he arrived in Berlin to take office as finance minister under Marx that his party's course was now determined by two men virtually unknown to the public, Brüning and Monsignor Ludwig Kaas, a professor of canon law and the party's spokesperson on foreign policy. Köhler termed the formation of the fourth Marx cabinet Brüning's "first great victory behind the scenes."[98]

The new cabinet fulfilled its pledges to restrict work hours and create Germany's first national system of unemployment insurance, but extremists in the DNVP mobilized the rank and file against Count Westarp and the parliamentary leaders who had compromised so many principles in the party's platform. In September 1927 the influential Alfred Hugenberg, head of Germany's

---

96 Andreas Dorpalen, *Hindenburg and the Weimar Republic* (Princeton, 1964), pp. 125–26; Stürmer, *Koalition*, pp. 182–87, 299–303; Ruppert, *Dienst am Staat*, pp. 239–47; Rudolf Morsey, ed., *Die Protokolle der Reichstagsfraktion und des Fraktionsvorstands der Deutschen Zentrumspartei 1926–1933* (Mainz, 1969) (hereafter cited as *Zentrumsprotokolle*), 20 January 1927, pp. 89–90 (source of Stegerwald quotation); Franz Röhr to Wilhelm Marx, 21 January 1927, NL Marx/73/28; Meissner to Pünder, 18 January, and Hindenburg to Marx, 20 January 1927, *Kabinette Marx III und IV*, I:501–02, 507–08. Brüning had nominated Pünder for his promotion to state secretary, and Pünder relied heavily on his advice; see *Kabinette Marx III und IV*, I:198–99, n. 7, and Brüning, *Memoiren*, p. 121.

97 Pünder memorandum on coalition talks, 23–31 January 1927, *Kabinette Marx III und IV*, I:515–23; survey of press commentary in *Westdeutsche Arbeiterzeitung*, 5 February 1927, pp. 31–32; Stürmer, *Koalition*, pp. 188–90.

98 Heinrich Köhler, *Lebenserinnerungen des Politikers und Staatsmannes 1878–1949*, ed. Josef Becker (Stuttgart, 1964), pp. 190–91; Josef Becker, "Joseph Wirth und die Krise des Zentrums während des IV. Kabinetts Marx (1927–1928). Darstellung und Dokumente," *Zeitschrift für die Geschichte des Oberrheins*, 109 (1961): 373–77.

largest newspaper chain, boycotted a party congress and wrote Westarp that the DNVP rested on a world-view that was "anti-parliamentary in its innermost essence." The DNVP would lose all support from the younger generation unless it took up the crusade for "a completely new state, molded according to the German character." Westarp felt compelled to promise Hugenberg a moratorium on all welfare legislation, and the position of Brüning's "popular conservative" and Christian Social allies began to weaken.[99]

All of Brüning's plans began to unravel in September 1927 when Finance Minister Köhler unveiled before a convention of civil servants a generous plan to increase government salaries by an average of 18 percent for senior officials, 21 percent for middle-, and 25 percent for lower-ranking civil servants. The DNVP, both liberal parties, and the SPD quickly endorsed the plan, since the minister charged with exercising fiscal restraint promised that these presents could be distributed without tax increases. Brüning was appalled. He thought when he departed in August for a conference of parliamentarians in Rio de Janeiro that he had secured a promise from Köhler not to increase government salaries by more than 10 percent. Brüning learned of Köhler's initiative while steaming homeward in the company of Hilferding, and both men were shocked. They strongly suspected that Köhler's budget projections were faulty; even if the Reich could afford these salary increases, moreover, they would spark imitation on the state and local level, causing painful tax increases there, and inspire a wave of job actions in the private sector that would undermine the ability of German export industry to compete on the world market. Brüning returned to Berlin to encounter furious polemics between trade unionists and civil servants in the Center Party that reflected a sudden revival of hostile class stereotypes from the Wilhelmian era. Brüning confined his opposition to narrowly fiscal arguments, but Stegerwald and Heinrich Imbusch denounced Köhler for an effort to restore the old Wilhelmian class hierarchy by restoring old pay differentials. In December 1927 Brüning, Stegerwald, and nine other Catholic laborites abstained in the final vote on the law, while Imbusch voted No.[100]

The flare-up of class tensions during the civil service controversy crippled the government coalition, and Chancellor Marx soon called for new elections. Brüning sensed abysmal morale in the bourgeois parties during the election campaign and was not surprised when the voting share of the SPD grew from 26 to 30 percent in May 1928, while the DNVP and both liberal parties suffered painful losses. He felt so depressed that he considered retirement from politics. His memoirs confuse the issue by denouncing Schleicher for unconstitutional maneuvers to supplant the Marx cabinet with a Great Coalition, but this development was considered inevitable by most observers in Berlin. The real cause of

99 Hugenberg to Westarp, 17 September 1927, published in Jonas, *Die Volkskonservativen*, pp. 180–82; Patch, *Christian Trade Unions*, pp. 115–19.
100 See Brüning, *Memoiren*, pp. 126–28, and William Patch, "Class Prejudice and the Failure of the Weimar Republic," *German Studies Review*, 12 (1989): 35–54.

his depression was doubtless the indifference of most Centrists toward Brüning's campaign to transform the DNVP into a moderate conservative party. Brüning had good reason to believe that the survival of parliamentary democracy depended on the emergence of a viable right-of-center option for majority coalitions with which left-of-center governments could alternate. With their eloquent attacks on all who were not "dedicated republicans," however, Wirth and his admirers had imposed a series of humiliations on the moderate Nationalists that played into the hands of the radicals.[101] Brüning saw his worst fears confirmed when the election returns prompted Hugenberg to launch a press campaign arguing that the DNVP would never be able to persuade an electoral majority to endorse the constitutional reforms needed for Germany's survival. Hugenberg and his allies proclaimed that Count Westarp had been wrong to seek a "large right" – the goal should be an ideologically pure "strong right" prepared to offer vigorous leadership when the next economic crisis swept the parliamentary system away. By October 1928 Hugenberg had mustered such widespread support in the provincial associations of the DNVP that Westarp surrendered the party chairmanship to him without a fight, and the new chairman soon excluded Brüning's "popular conservative" friends from positions of influence.[102]

Brüning had few friends in the SPD and feared political isolation when the Social Democrat Hermann Müller formed a cabinet of the Great Coalition in June 1928. Brüning had a bright political future nevertheless because he had earned the respect of all factions in the Center Party. Catholic civil servants considered him the only official of the Christian trade unions accessible to rational argument, and he proved effective at restoring party unity during the election campaign.[103] Brüning was asked by his party's leaders to add service in the Prussian Landtag delegation (which generally leaned more to the left than did the party at large) to his duties in the Reichstag delegation to improve communication between those two bodies. He served in this double capacity from May 1928 until July 1929 and apparently succeeded at promoting consensus.[104] He also played a pivotal role as peacemaker at the Center Party congress of December 1928. The parliamentary leadership of the party had recommended that Stegerwald succeed Marx as party chairman, but when the civil servants organized

---

101 Brüning, *Memoiren*, pp. 131–32; Nobel, *Brüning*, pp. 47–50; Becker, "Joseph Wirth," pp. 419–21; Josef Becker, "Heinrich Brüning und das Scheitern der konservativen Alternative," *Aus Politik und Zeitgeschichte*, 80 (31 May 1980): 4–6; Stürmer, *Koalition*, pp. 238–47; Ruppert, *Dienst am Staat*, pp. 296–305; Childers, *Nazi Voter*, pp. 124–34.

102 Axel von Freytagh-Loringhoven, "Nicht grosse, sondern starke Rechte," and Hugenberg, "Block oder Brei?" from *Der Tag*, 25 July and 28 August 1928, reprinted in Manfred Dörr, "Die Deutschnationale Volkspartei, 1925–1928" (Ph.D. diss., University of Marburg, 1964), pp. 579–81, 588–89; Patch, *Christian Trade Unions*, pp. 127–33; Jonas, *Volkskonservativen*, pp. 36–41.

103 Deutscher Philologenverband, circular of 1 November 1927, NL Stegerwald/010/ "Beamtenfragen"/#1143; speech by Brüning to the "Beamtenbeirat der westfälischen Zentrumspartei," *Tremonia*, 5 March 1928, #65; Becker, "Joseph Wirth," pp. 408–18.

104 Brüning, *Memoiren*, pp. 134–35; Hömig, *Das preussische Zentrum*, p. 298.

opposition among the delegates, Brüning devised a proposal for a troika that was acceptable to all party leaders. The delegates insisted on a single chairman, however, electing the cleric Ludwig Kaas because he was not identified with any interest group. When Stegerwald's laborite supporters walked out of the convention in protest, Kaas secured Brüning's services as his deputy, and Brüning soon persuaded Stegerwald to accept office under Kaas as chairman of the Center Reichstag delegation. Kaas said of Brüning in 1930 that "I have always advanced him to the foremost rank because I discovered in him a synthesis of thought and action that probably has no parallel except among the ancient Greeks."[105]

Brüning was by no means isolated, moreover, in his initial wariness toward the Great Coalition in 1928. The biggest gains in the May elections were scored by a melange of two dozen special interest parties whose combined voting strength of 14 percent now surpassed that of both historic liberal parties combined. The "Business Party" (Wirtschaftspartei) increased its share of the national vote to an impressive 4.5 percent by focusing narrowly on the grievances of small businessmen and landlords, while a new "Christian Nationalist Peasants' Party" won over 1.1 million votes in response to a wave of bankruptcies in the countryside that resulted from falling world market prices for farm commodities.[106] For most bourgeois politicians these returns suggested that middle-class voters insisted on the uncompromising defense of their material interests. The liberal parties had also become financially dependent on subsidies from big business, while most leaders of the Center Party responded to their modest losses by seeking to revive that party's distinctive Roman Catholic religious identity. Party leaders saw no alternative to the Great Coalition but felt that they must hold the SPD at arm's length to avoid disintegration. The parliamentary leader of the DVP, Ernst Scholz, raised so many difficulties when Hermann Müller opened coalition talks that the two ministers from the DVP in the old cabinet, Stresemann and Julius Curtius, felt compelled in late June to volunteer to join Müller in a *Kabinett der Persönlichkeiten*, a cabinet of notable individuals not bound to a formal coalition of parties. The DVP Reichstag delegation accepted Stresemann's decision only on the condition that it was not obliged to support the policies of the new cabinet. After observing the DVP's stance, the Center Party decided to send just one "observer" into the government, and Adam Stegerwald announced to the press that, like the DVP, his party was "not bound

---

105 Beer, *Heinrich Brüning*, pp. 55–56 (source of quotation); Patch, *Christian Trade Unions*, pp. 137–41; Jakob Kaiser memorandum of 12 January 1929, NL Kaiser/247; Marx's unpublished memoirs, NL Marx/74/48–49.

106 See J. Falter, T. Lindenberger, and S. Schumann, *Wahlen und Abstimmungen in der Weimarer Republik* (Munich, 1986), pp. 41–44; Childers, *Nazi Voter*, pp. 142–50; Martin Schumacher, *Mittelstandsfront und Republik. Die Wirtschaftspartei–Reichspartei des deutschen Mittelstandes 1919–1933* (Düsseldorf, 1972); Larry Jones, "In the Shadow of Stabilization," pp. 21–34; Jones, "Crisis and Realignment," pp. 198–207; Dieter Gessner, *Agrarverbände in der Weimarer Republik* (Düsseldorf, 1976), pp. 97–119; and Gerhard Schulz, *Deutschland am Vorabend der grossen Krise. Zwischen Demokratie und Diktatur, Band II*, 2nd ed. (Berlin and New York, 1987), pp. 149–66.

to the cabinet."[107] This decision compelled the SPD to shoulder primary responsibility for domestic policy.

Hugenberg's election as chairman of the DNVP persuaded Brüning nevertheless that the SPD was far more reasonable than the DNVP, and he therefore supported a new initiative by Chancellor Müller in November 1928 to transform his "cabinet of notables" into a formal coalition government. Scholz refused to consider such action, however, until the parties reached agreement on a budget for the coming fiscal year.[108] Because there were now three million unemployed, which necessitated government borrowing to keep the new unemployment insurance fund solvent, Finance Minister Hilferding felt compelled to propose an additional RM 379 million in taxes on beer, brandy, and capital gains. The cabinet approved this plan in January 1929, but the Reichstag delegations of the SPD, DVP, and BVP all rejected it. An exasperated Stresemann then called a meeting of the DVP central committee for 26 February but found to his dismay that influential representatives of Ruhr heavy industry raised several demands that would break the coalition, such as the abolition of state labor arbitration.[109] Stresemann responded with an impassioned plea that his party resist permeation by the business lobbyists, warning that Germany had developed a "caricature of parliamentarism" because the Reichstag delegations of the bourgeois parties concerned themselves with little but the expenditure of public funds to benefit the interest groups from which they received campaign contributions. He argued that chancellors had become dangerously weak in their dealings with the Reichstag delegations because of the passivity of President Hindenburg. The authors of the Weimar constitution, he asserted, had intended the President to function as a "counter-weight" to the Reichstag, but for years he had signed whatever laws were passed by the majority of the moment. Only when the President made more vigorous use of his constitutional prerogatives would the chancellor gain the authority needed to reject short-sighted demands by the parties in the name of the public good. Stresemann foresaw the day when the Reichstag would prove incapable of forming any majority; he hoped that Hindenburg would then ignore the parties and assemble a team of courageous individuals willing to provide vigorous leadership. He eventually persuaded the men from the Ruhr to withdraw their resolution designed to break the Great Coalition, but only after agreeing to

107 Larry Jones, *German Liberalism*, pp. 295–316; Lothar Döhn, *Politik und Interesse. Die Interessenstruktur der Deutschen Volkspartei* (Meisenheim am Glan, 1970), pp. 71–80, 343–68; Werner Schneider, *Die Deutsche Demokratische Partei in der Weimarer Republik 1924–1930* (Munich, 1978), pp. 35–51, 70–72, 163–73; Winkler, *Schein der Normalität*, pp. 529–36; *Zentrumsprotokolle*, meetings of 25–28 June 1928, pp. 219–25; Stegerwald's press release in *Germania*, 29 June 1928, #297.

108 Chancellor's meeting with party leaders, 27 November 1928, in Martin Vogt, ed., *Akten der Reichskanzlei der Weimarer Republik. Das Kabinett Müller II*, 2 vols. (Boppard am Rhein, 1970), I:245–50.

109 Ilse Maurer, *Reichsfinanzen und Grosse Koalition. Zur Geschichte des Reichskabinetts Müller (1928–1930)* (Bern and Frankfurt a.M., 1973), pp. 49–54; Wilhelm Keil, *Erlebnisse eines Sozialdemokraten*, 2 vols. (Stuttgart, 1948), II:353–54; Ewald Hecker to Stresemann, 24 February, and memorandum of 27 February 1929, in NL Stresemann, Reel 3164/vol. 103/174567–71, 174694–97.

present the SPD with a tough ultimatum on social policy himself if given a free hand for a few months at least to conduct diplomatic talks over a reduction of Germany's reparations burden.[110] Stresemann's view that the President must support his chancellors more vigorously to lower the Weimar Republic's dangerously high rate of cabinet turnover exerted considerable influence on Brüning.

Brüning returned to the center of the political stage in March 1929 when Chancellor Müller appealed to the taxation experts of the government parties to draft their own budget to break the deadlock. Brüning quickly wrote a new budget with Carl Cremer of the DVP and Paul Hertz of the SPD that trimmed spending by RM 200 million and replaced Hilferding's proposed beer tax with a recalculation of anticipated revenue. Cremer secured approval from the Reich Association of Industry (Reichsverband der Deutschen Industrie, or RDI), while Brüning won over the Bavarian People's Party.[111] The result was a popular but unrealistic budget. Brüning himself later admitted that most of its savings came merely from postponing necessary purchases by government agencies. Hilferding gloomily informed the cabinet that this budget would not really balance, but he urged acceptance nevertheless as the only way to preserve the Great Coalition. When the cabinet agreed to this compromise, the Center Party entered it with three ministers, Theodor von Guérard, Stegerwald, and Wirth, in a sign of renewed support for the government. The Brüning–Cremer budget limped through to final parliamentary approval in June, but a downcast Stresemann gained the impression in these weeks that a majority of his party colleagues rejected his support for the Great Coalition even though it represented the only hope for democracy. Indeed, when the party's executive committee in the district of southern Westphalia was told "that Dr. Scholz urges agreement to the [budget] compromise as essential for the salvation of parliamentarism, the view generally expressed was that it would not be a bad thing if this parliamentarism died [_dass dieser Parlamentarismus ruhig zugrundegehen solle_]." Stresemann was probably correct that the only thing keeping his party in the Great Coalition was the hope that a government led by Social Democrats could secure lucrative concessions from the Western powers over reparations.[112]

1.4. Physician and Heir to the Great Coalition

Brüning's memoirs indicate that Kurt von Schleicher began a campaign to replace the Great Coalition with some kind of "Hindenburg cabinet" during this

110 DVP Zentralvorstand, 26 February 1929, BAK R45II/43/103–13, 219–21, 323–89; Jones, _German Liberalism_, pp. 319–22; Döhn, _Politik und Interesse_, pp. 380–94.
111 Cremer to Stresemann, 23 and 28 March 1929, NL Stresemann/Reel 3164/vol. 104/174823–29, 174891–95; Brüning, _Memoiren_, p. 140.
112 _Kabinett Müller II_, meeting of 7 April 1929, I:524–26; Brüning, "Arbeit der Zentrumspartei," pp. 385–86; Stresemann to Wilhelm Kahl, 13 March 1929, NL Stresemann/Reel 3164/vol. 104/174726–30; Trucksäss to Stresemann, 23 April 1929, reporting on a meeting in Westphalia chaired by the Reichstag delegate Adolf Hueck on 18 April (source of quotation), NL Stresemann/3164/105/174980–82; Maurer, _Reichsfinanzen_, pp. 59–63.

budget crisis in the spring of 1929. Brüning misremembered important details of his conversations with the President's advisers, but his memoirs do shed new light on their calculations.[113] After drafting his budget with Carl Cremer, Brüning approached his old friend, the Freiherr von Willisen, to argue that the defense ministry should accept slight reductions in military outlay for the sake of political stability. Willisen agreed but warned that, in return, the Reichswehr would expect Brüning to support "a major constructive policy initiative that would commence at the end of the year. This was the only way to overcome the resistance of the field marshal." Schleicher wanted to discuss this project with Brüning in person. Brüning found this description of the President's attitude plausible because Treviranus had already told him that Hindenburg "was resolved to put an end to the wasting disease [*Marasmus*] in politics." The invitation to join the circle of the President's friends left Brüning in a peculiar frame of mind. During the war he had revered the commander-in-chief but later came to suspect that Hindenburg was only a figurehead. He had refused several invitations to socialize at the presidential palace, "because I did not want the last glimmer of my shining image of Hindenburg to be extinguished." Now he was excited by Schleicher's invitation: "At first skeptical, I became more eager, doubtless primarily from the impulses that are always at work when a person again has hope of regaining a faith that has been lost."[114]

Schleicher's motives for this initiative can be reconstructed with some precision. For years he had sought to discredit both pacifism on the left and sentimental monarchism on the right, striving to promote a broad consensus among politicians from the SPD to the DNVP in favor of the army's clandestine mobilization programs to secure trained manpower in case of war beyond the 100,000 troops permitted by the Treaty of Versailles. The Prussian state government of Otto Braun suspected counter-revolutionary plots behind these programs, however, and the Prussian police sometimes confiscated their arms caches.[115] Schleicher hoped that the Prussian authorities would accept covert mobilization programs if they were authorized by a Social Democratic chancellor, and in January 1928 he prepared for the coming of the Great Coalition by securing the appointment as defense minister of his old mentor, Wilhelm Groener, who had earned the SPD's respect by cooperating with organized labor during and after the Great War. Schleicher, Groener, and President Hindenburg were all

---

113 Brüning's account in *Memoiren*, pp. 139–61, is almost identical with pp. 3–20 of his first draft of 1934 (HUG FP 93.4). He plausibly reports a first talk with Schleicher around Easter 1929 and a second on 26 December, but problems arise when he recalls a private conversation with President Hindenburg in mid-December 1929 and a lengthy conversation with Wilhelm Groener in mid-March. The account below will follow the chronology suggested by Treviranus, *Ende von Weimar*, pp. 114–16; Rudolf Morsey, "Neue Quellen zur Vorgeschichte der Reichskanzlerschaft Brünings," in Hermens and Schieder, eds., *Staat, Wirtschaft und Politik*, pp. 212–19; Koops, "Heinrich Brünings 'Politische Erfahrungen,'" pp. 206–15; and Rödder, "Dichtung und Wahrheit," pp. 85–90.

114 Brüning, *Memoiren*, pp. 140–41, 145.

115 See Carsten, *Reichswehr*, pp. 8–17, 118–24, 149–52, 212–23; Peter Hayes, "'A Question Mark with Epaulettes'? Kurt von Schleicher and Weimar Politics," *Journal of Modern History*, 52 (1980): 35–43; and Otto Braun, *Von Weimar zu Hitler*, 2nd ed. (New York, 1940), pp. 105–06, 265–69.

dismayed, however, when the SPD included in its electoral platform a pledge to repeal a bill recently adopted by the Reichstag to construct the Weimar Republic's first armored cruiser. Hindenburg anticipated that the Great Coalition would neglect the vital interests of the armed forces and farmers, and he solemnly promised Count Westarp in June 1928 to protect both groups. Hermann Müller nevertheless persuaded the President and defense ministry of his patriotism, and the Müller cabinet agreed on 10 August to proceed with construction of the cruiser. Ordinary Social Democrats were outraged by this violation of their electoral platform, however, and when the KPD launched a referendum campaign against the ship, the SPD decided that it must support this initiative. Schleicher was so dismayed by the strength of the pacifist current in the SPD that he inquired among friends in the DNVP in late August about the prospects for reviving a right-of-center coalition, but Treviranus replied that the Nationalists would require much time in opposition to reorganize their party. The DNVP eventually joined the moderate parties in November to save the ship on the floor of the Reichstag, but party discipline required Müller and the other Social Democratic ministers to vote against the bill of their own cabinet, an unprecedented embarrassment.[116]

Schleicher and Groener made a last effort to reach an understanding with the leaders of the SPD in April 1929, when the Reich cabinet secretly adopted formal guidelines authorizing "frontier defense" (*Grenzschutz*), that is, the stockpiling of weapons and enrollment of volunteers, in the provinces east of the Oder River vulnerable to Polish invasion. No covert programs were permitted on the western frontier, but Schleicher and Groener found this compromise acceptable. Otto Braun repudiated the new guidelines, however, and the skirmishes between garrison commanders and the Prussian state police continued.[117] The ersatz general staff of the army (the *Truppenamt*) had meanwhile drafted an ultra-secret armaments plan to be implemented in the years 1930–3, designed to secure enough arms and trained manpower to expand the army from ten to twenty-one divisions in case of war. In March 1929 it concluded that some form of conscription must be introduced soon to achieve this goal, perhaps under the cover of a year of compulsory labor service for all young men.[118] Any cabinet led by Social Democrats would be most unlikely to approve such a plan. The head of the

---

116 Memorandum on Westarp's audience with Hindenburg, 9 June 1928, BAP R601/19721/vol. 45/28; *Kabinett Müller II*, meetings of 10 August and 14–15 November 1928, I:61–2, 224–28; Schleicher to Groener, 18 and 25 August and 3 September 1928, NL Groener/25/#224; Johannes Hürter, *Wilhelm Groener. Reichswehrminister am Ende der Weimarer Republik (1928–1932)* (Munich, 1993), pp. 65–77; Donna Harsch, *German Social Democracy and the Rise of Nazism* (Chapel Hill and London, 1993), pp. 46–51; Winkler, *Schein der Normalität*, pp. 542–55, 629–39.

117 *Kabinett Müller II*, meeting of 26 April 1929, I:583–84; Pünder memorandum of 20 March 1930, in Vogelsang, *Reichswehr*, pp. 413–14; Hürter, *Wilhelm Groener*, pp. 111–22, 128–36; Schulze, *Otto Braun*, pp. 612–13.

118 See Gaines Post, Jr., *The Civil-Military Fabric of Weimar Foreign Policy* (Princeton, 1973), pp. 195–201; Edward W. Bennett, *German Rearmament and the West, 1932–1933* (Princeton, 1979), pp. 36–38; and Michael Geyer, ed., "Dokumentation: Das Zweite Rüstungsprogramm (1930–1934)," *Militärgeschichtliche Mitteilungen*, 16 (1975): 125–30.

general staff, General Werner von Blomberg, also urged the extension of frontier defense to the western provinces. In April 1929 Schleicher firmly rejected this idea, and soon thereafter a telegram summoned Blomberg from an inspection tour to the Reich chancellery to answer charges that he had attended illegal maneuvers by volunteers in Westphalia. He expected Schleicher to join him in the army's traditional policy of denying everything before civilians, but instead Schleicher urged his dismissal for insubordination. The government contented itself with transferring Blomberg to the East Prussian divisional command, but Schleicher had made an enemy of the man who would later become Hitler's defense minister. For months thereafter Groener continued, much to his irritation, to receive skeptical inquiries from garrison commanders as to whether he really desired adherence to the Müller cabinet's guidelines for frontier defense. Many officers were further alienated by Schleicher's unusually rapid promotion to major general in early 1929, and he must have been feeling great pressure from army colleagues to neutralize Social Democratic opposition to rearmament when he contacted Brüning.[119]

Brüning later recalled that his first meeting with Schleicher took place over breakfast at Schleicher's apartment shortly after Easter, that is, just after Schleicher's conflict with Blomberg came to a head. Hindenburg, Schleicher declared, feared that Germany's "whole domestic and foreign policy would sink in the mud" and had decided "to put things in order before he died, together with the Reichswehr and the younger forces in parliament." Pressed for details, Schleicher explained that Hindenburg intended "to send parliament home" for a while and undertake needed reforms through presidential decrees based on Article 48 of the constitution. Pressed for an estimate of the time required for these reforms, Schleicher answered six months, ignoring the fact that Articles 23 and 25 required elections within sixty days of any dissolution of the Reichstag and a meeting of the new Reichstag within thirty days of elections. According to Brüning's memoirs, Schleicher denied any plan to restore monarchy immediately but indicated that "the field marshal does not want to die without solving this question." Brüning recalled warning that any restoration would require a constitutional amendment approved by a two-thirds majority in the Reichstag, but Schleicher supposedly replied that Article 48 could be used even to rewrite the constitution, asserting that the state secretaries of justice and the interior had just written legal opinions to this effect.[120]

Brüning's memory must have distorted this conversation. There is no evidence of research into the scope of Article 48 by high officials before December 1929, and Schleicher had long campaigned to persuade his brother officers to renounce any talk of restoring monarchy as hopelessly impractical. The general did maintain social ties with the heir to the imperial throne, but Crown Prince

119 Post, *Civil-Military Fabric*, pp. 152–57; Carsten, *Reichswehr*, pp. 297–302; "Notizen für die Kommandeurbesprechung," October-December 1929, NL Schleicher/44/109.
120 Brüning, *Memoiren*, pp. 145–47.

Wilhelm deprived himself of political influence through relentless womanizing and ill-tempered attacks on Hindenburg.[121] Brüning's real disagreement with Schleicher almost undoubtedly focused on the controversial views of the legal scholar Carl Schmitt. The first paragraph of Article 48 clearly authorized the President to depose state governments that defied federal laws, while the third clearly required that all emergency decrees be submitted promptly to the Reichstag, which could vote to rescind them by a simple majority. But there was some debate among the experts about the meaning of the following second paragraph:

> The Reich President can, if the public security and order of the German Reich are significantly disrupted or endangered, adopt the measures needed to restore public security and order, if necessary with the help of armed force. For this purpose he can temporarily suspend, partly or wholly, the fundamental rights guaranteed in Articles 114, 115, 117, 118, 123, 124, and 153.

The seven listed articles involved civil liberties such as free speech, freedom of the press, and freedom from arbitrary detention. Most jurists held that the President must respect all other provisions of the constitution, but Carl Schmitt maintained that circumstances might require the President to suspend any article temporarily, that Article 48 implied unlimited freedom for the President to define a "state of emergency" and choose whatever methods were needed to overcome it. The only limitation on his powers was that he must restore the constitution intact after the state of emergency ended. Thus Schmitt's interpretation, the broadest offered by any jurist, denied that Article 48 could be invoked to restore monarchy, but it did imply that the President could dissolve the Reichstag and postpone new elections beyond sixty days.[122] Schmitt came into direct contact with the presidential entourage when he accepted a chair at the University of Berlin in 1928. In March 1929 he published an essay arguing that Germany's supreme court was too weak to check unconstitutional actions by the Reichstag; in the modern age of mass democracy, only the popularly elected President could serve as the "guardian of the constitution." This article won enthusiastic praise from Schleicher, Otto Meissner, and other high officials, and the presidential entourage relied heavily on Schmitt's legal opinions throughout the subsequent years of crisis.[123] Schleicher must have echoed Schmitt's recent article when he first met Brüning.

Brüning had long condemned Schmitt's position, however. Treviranus wit-

121 See Schleicher's memorandum of December 1926 in Vogelsang, *Reichswehr*, pp. 409–13; Müldner von Müllnheim to Schleicher, 23 November 1928, NL Schleicher/27/11–12; and Brüning to Norman Ebbutt, 11 June 1946, in Müller, *Brüning Papers*, pp. 181–82.
122 Hermann Mosler, ed., *Die Verfassung des Deutschen Reichs vom 11.8.1919* (Stuttgart, 1968), pp. 18–19; Joseph Bendersky, *Carl Schmitt: Theorist for the Reich* (Princeton, 1983), pp. 74–84; Dan Diner, "Constitutional Theory and 'State of Emergency' in the Weimar Republic: The Case of Carl Schmitt," *Tel Aviver Jahrbuch für deutsche Geschichte*, 17 (1988): 303–21; Gerhard Schulz, *Vorabend*, pp. 264–72.
123 Carl Schmitt, "Der Hüter der Verfassung," *Archiv des öffentlichen Rechts*, Neue Folge, 16 (1929): 161–237; Bendersky, *Carl Schmitt*, pp. 112–19; Dorpalen, *Hindenburg*, pp. 169–70; Reinhard Schiffer, *Elemente direkter Demokratie im Weimarer Regierungssystem* (Düsseldorf, 1971), pp. 189–90.

nessed an angry debate between them at a scholarly conference in 1928, when Brüning attacked Schmitt for a "relativistic" attitude that undermined the rule of law and severed any connection between politics and morality. Brüning himself later recalled in a somewhat muddled fashion that ever since 1923 he had opposed Schmitt's tendency to ascribe "dictatorial" powers to the President: "I was convinced that the . . . true interpretation of the spirit and letter of the Weimar constitution . . . gave to the President and to the government enough power to master all difficult situations without need of any permanent dictatorial power."[124] Brüning had no qualms about applying Article 48 to a fiscal emergency, since rioting would doubtless spread if the government failed to pay salaries or welfare benefits, but he always endorsed the mainstream view that presidential emergency decrees must respect every article of the Reich constitution except the seven listed in Article 48, Paragraph 2. This implied that no more than ninety days could pass between the dissolution of a Reichstag and the first meeting of its successor, so that the Reichstag must retain the power to review presidential decrees frequently. As Brüning later summarized their disagreement, Schleicher believed that he could "recapitulate exactly the plan of the fall of 1923," when it had been possible briefly to issue emergency decrees without any regard for parliamentary review, but Brüning insisted that a slow-acting deflationary crisis demanded methods quite different from those employed to bring a sudden end to an inflationary crisis.[125]

Brüning wrote Schleicher a letter in May 1929, whose contents confirm his recollection that they had established personal contact by then but also suggest that their first meeting did not have quite such a sterile outcome as the memoirs imply. Brüning requested Schleicher's support against a plan by the interior ministry to disburse an appropriation of 8.6 million marks for subsidized housing, which Brüning thought had been targeted for his own Reichstag district in Silesia, to projects all over East Elbia. The politician sought to persuade the general that this issue was "very closely linked with the name of the Reich President," since Hindenburg had been deeply moved by the poverty of the miners of Waldenburg during a visit to Brüning's district six months earlier and had promised to help. "After the population of Waldenburg has placed such high hopes for the alleviation of their distress on the intervention of the Reich President, I would be very sorry to see them experience a bitter disappointment." This lobbying gambit suggests that Brüning may have had an understanding with Schleicher to enhance the personal reputation of Hindenburg as a valuable resource in any future political crisis.[126]

---

124 Treviranus, *Ende von Weimar*, pp. 85–86; Brüning, "The Essence of Democracy," Dartmouth College lecture #2 of March 1937, pp. 6–8, HUG FP 93.45.

125 Brüning to Philipp Dessauer, 16 March 1956, in Müller, *Brüning Papers*, pp. 178–79; Brüning to Graf Brünneck, 19 August 1949, HUG FP 93.10/Box 5/Manfred von Brünneck (source of quotation); Scheuner, "Anwendung des Art. 48," pp. 250–84; Becker, "Scheitern der konservativen Alternative," p. 7. Contrast Hans Boldt, "Artikel 48," pp. 288–309, which associates Brüning with Schmitt's standpoint.

126 Brüning to Schleicher, 16 May 1929, NL Schleicher/52/33–35.

It is unclear whether President Hindenburg had directly authorized Schleicher's overtures to Brüning, but he did tell Westarp in March 1929 that Schleicher was his favorite candidate to become chancellor if Hermann Müller fell. Hindenburg worried, however, that the appointment of any general would nourish fears of "a violent dictatorship" and did not see how he could turn the SPD out of office as long as the rigid Hugenberg led the DNVP. He seemed quite relieved when Brüning and Cremer resolved the budget crisis and absolved him from any duty to act.[127] Schleicher continued nevertheless to encourage a wide variety of efforts to prepare public opinion for some kind of "Hindenburg cabinet" or "presidential government." His friends in the leadership of the Stahlhelm, the nationalistic league of 300,000 combat veterans, had sought since October 1928 to organize a referendum campaign to strengthen the presidency by repealing Article 54 of the Weimar constitution, which required cabinets to enjoy the confidence of the Reichstag. The Stahlhelm felt compelled, however, to seek the support of the still tiny Nazi Party for this campaign, to avoid partisan identification with the DNVP, and Hitler eventually vetoed the plan in April 1929.[128] The frankly elitist Herrenklub (Gentlemen's Club) of Berlin, founded in 1924/5 by upper-class veterans of the old June Club, then took up the banner of "presidential government," urging Hindenburg to appoint a chancellor who would remove the SPD from power in both Prussia and the Reich, reject any negotiations with the Reichstag delegations, and rule by emergency decree if parliament did not accept his program. The adoption of this line followed consultations with Schleicher by the club leaders Heinrich von Gleichen and Werner von Alvensleben. A similar position was taken by the neo-conservative Hans Zehrer, who began in the summer of 1928 to proclaim the death of parliamentarism in the magazine *Die Tat* and acquired some influence when he became its chief editor in October 1929.[129] The idea of a stronger presidency proved especially popular with the farm lobby, which knew that Hindenburg's instinctive sympathy for agriculture had been strengthened in 1927 when a group of industrialists and agrarians presented him with the old family estate of Neudeck in East Prussia. In February 1929 all agrarian organizations united in a "Green Front" to protest the indifference to the farm crisis displayed by the Great Coalition, and Hindenburg supported its calls for new protective tariffs and debt relief with unprecedented activism.[130]

Schleicher's plans encountered an obstacle when the debate over reparations

---

127 Westarp memorandum of 18 March 1929, in Jonas, *Volkskonservativen*, pp. 186–88; Dorpalen, *Hindenburg*, pp. 152–53.
128 Volker Berghahn, *Der Stahlhelm. Bund der Frontsoldaten 1918–1935* (Düsseldorf, 1966), pp. 119–29.
129 Ishida, *Jungkonservative*, pp. 136–38; Klaus Fritzsche, *Politische Romantik und Gegenrevolution. Fluchtwege in der Krise der bürgerlichen Gesellschaft: Das Beispiel des "Tat"-Kreises* (Frankfurt a.M., 1976), pp. 50–65, 112–27.
130 Gerhard Schulz, *Vorabend*, pp. 167–92; Dorpalen, *Hindenburg*, pp. 135–36; Gessner, *Agrarverbände*, pp. 154–76; Jones, "Crisis and Realignment," pp. 202–11; Braun, *Von Weimar zu Hitler*, pp. 295–96.

opened a gulf between the friends and foes of the President on the right. In June 1929 Stresemann felt that he had achieved a great diplomatic victory when the Paris conference of financial experts chaired by the American banker Owen Young proposed a "final settlement" of reparations that would initially cost Germany only 1.8 billion marks per year (although in later years the bill would rise to a level close to the 2.5 billion currently being paid).[131] The publication of this plan prompted Hugenberg to undertake his first bold initiative as leader of the DNVP. On 9 July 1929 a monster rally greeted the formation of a national committee to organize a referendum campaign to condemn all reparations. Adolf Hitler gained new prestige by joining Hugenberg as a cofounder of this committee, alongside the leaders of the Christian Nationalist Peasants' Party, the Reichslandbund (Agrarian League), and the Stahlhelm. Hugenberg was obsessed with the need to show the younger generation that free-market Nationalists could be no less militant in their resistance to foreign oppressors than were the anti-capitalist Nazis, so he agreed with Hitler to draft their "Freedom Law" in the most provocative terms with a fourth paragraph threatening any government official who signed the Young Plan with imprisonment for treason. President Hindenburg still hesitated to pronounce his judgment on the Young Plan but immediately condemned Paragraph 4 as an insult to his cabinet ministers, and pragmatic farm lobbyists felt that Hugenberg had blundered badly.[132] While the Nationalists and Nazis gathered signatures on their petitions, the Weimar Republic suffered a great loss with the death of Stresemann, who was succeeded as foreign minister by his admirer Julius Curtius. An overwhelming Reichstag majority honored Stresemann's memory by rejecting the "Freedom Law" on 29 November – even within the DNVP only 55 of 78 Reichstag delegates voted for Paragraph 4 – and in the referendum ballot on 22 December, only 5.8 million citizens voted Yes when the approval of 21 million was required. Hugenberg had succeeded only in antagonizing moderate politicians while he helped the Nazi Party to gain a new audience in the respectable middle class.[133]

Gottfried Treviranus began in October 1929 to foment rebellion in the DNVP by telling his "popular conservative" friends that the Center Party would form a new government with them if they broke cleanly with Hugenberg. Schleicher,

131 Maurer, *Reichsfinanzen*, pp. 68–77; Peter Krüger, *Die Aussenpolitik der Republik von Weimar* (Darmstadt, 1985), pp. 414–92; Jacobsen, *Locarno Diplomacy*, pp. 250–76; Kent, *Spoils of War*, pp. 287–303.

132 Otto Schmidt-Hannover, "Kriegsgeneration und Jugend im Freiheitskampf gegen den Marxismus," speech of 23 November 1929, NL Hugenberg/86/53–60; Elisabeth Friedenthal, "Volksbegehren und Volksentscheid über den Young-Plan und die Deutschnationale Sezession" (Ph.D. diss., University of Tübingen, 1957), pp. 38–52, 65–72; Dieter Gessner, "Dokumentation: 'Grüne Front' oder 'Harzburger Front,'" *Vierteljahrshefte für Zeitgeschichte*, 29 (1981): 110–23; Volker Berghahn, "Das Volksbegehren gegen den Young-Plan und die Ursprünge des Präsidial-regimes, 1928–1930," in Dirk Stegmann et al., eds., *Industrielle Gesellschaft und politisches System. Festschrift für Fritz Fischer* (Bonn, 1978), pp. 437–45.

133 Jonas, *Volkskonservativen*, pp. 52–60; Falter, *Hitlers Wähler*, pp. 123–25; Jones, *German Liberalism*, pp. 339–51.

who regarded Hugenberg as the chief obstacle to replacement of the Great Coalition, spurred them on and arranged financial backing through Werner von Alvensleben, who secured at least one contribution of 20,000 marks from Carl Duisberg of I. G. Farben by promising explicitly that the schism of the DNVP would pave the way for rule through presidential decree.[134] Treviranus appealed to Count Westarp to lead a secession, promising that a new "popular conservative formation" would receive lavish funding, an enthusiastic reception in the press, and the support of at least thirty DNVP Reichstag delegates. Westarp replied that the prospects for a new party were dim because Hugenberg firmly controlled the DNVP party machine and nationalist press. Treviranus was left with no choice, however, when Hugenberg initiated expulsion proceedings against his three most vocal critics in the party; twelve "popular conservative" and Christian Social Reichstag delegates therefore resigned from the DNVP at the beginning of December. Schleicher offered Treviranus further subsidies and arranged a cordial reception for him by President Hindenburg, where prospects for a non-socialist cabinet were discussed. In return Treviranus promised to arrange a second meeting between Schleicher and Brüning.[135]

Brüning had meanwhile become one of the most energetic supporters of the Müller cabinet as the slowly rising unemployment rate made the wrangling between the coalition parties over fiscal policy more and more bitter. In November 1929 the state secretary of finance, Johannes Popitz, persuaded Hilferding to embrace a bold plan to stimulate economic growth in the budget for 1930. They agreed to devote the anticipated savings from the Young Plan and additional revenue from indirect taxes to achieve a dramatic reduction of RM 910 million in taxes on property and the higher income brackets, designed to promote investment. Brüning applauded the concept, and the cabinet approved the plan on 25 November.[136] The president of the Reichsbank, Hjalmar Schacht, considered this plan a formula for disaster, however, and refused on 4 December to help the cabinet borrow to meet its 250 million marks in immediate obligations. He demanded instead that it administer shock treatment to the public by invoking Article 48 to delay the payment of government salaries. When the cabinet refused, Schacht published a plan for a sinking fund to retire the national debt and a scathing attack on the government's fiscal policy. Angered by this attack, the cabinet opened direct negotiations with American bankers for a dollar loan

---

134 Treviranus to Ahlefeld, 1 November 1929, in DNVP "Mitteilungen," #53, 10 December 1929, Anlage 2; von Alvensleben to Duisberg, 28 November 1929, and reply, in Ilse Maurer and Udo Wengst, eds., *Politik und Wirtschaft in der Krise, 1930–1932. Quellen zur Ära Brüning*, 2 vols. (Düsseldorf, 1980) (cited hereafter as *Quellen: Politik und Wirtschaft*), I:11–12; Henry A. Turner, "The *Ruhrlade*, Secret Cabinet of Heavy Industry in the Weimar Republic," *Central European History*, 3 (1970): 203–08; Jonas, *Volkskonservativen*, pp. 63–64; Ishida, *Jungkonservative*, pp. 130–35.

135 "Niederschrift des Grafen Westarp über Entstehung und Verlauf der Parteikrise Ende November/Anfang Dezember 1929," NL Westarp; Patch, *Christian Trade Unions*, pp. 149–53; Treviranus, "Kurt von Schleicher," p. 371.

136 Maurer, *Reichsfinanzen*, pp. 89–93; *Kabinett Müller II*, meeting of 25 November 1929, II:1188–94; Brüning, "Arbeit der Zentrumspartei," pp. 387–88.

and linked its program for tax reductions next spring with an "immediate program" to raise the tobacco tax and increase the unemployment insurance premiums paid by both employers and workers by 0.5 percent of the hourly wage. The cabinet resolved on 9 December to present both the long-term and immediate programs to the government parties in the form of an ultimatum.[137] Brüning had just been elected unanimously to chair the Center Reichstag delegation at the exceptionally young age of forty-four (Stegerwald having laid that office down when he entered the cabinet), and he had therefore resigned as executive secretary of the DGB to devote himself full time to party business. He was the only party leader to accept Müller's program without reservation. The SPD and BVP supported the "immediate program" but objected to the idea of reductions in direct tax rates next year, while the DVP opposed the immediate tax hikes without binding guarantees that the promised reductions would be implemented. Müller grimly informed the cabinet that he would resign "in peaceful times" if the coalition parties adopted such attitudes; now, however, the cabinet must continue to fight for its program to avoid a "crisis of state."[138] Brüning agreed with the SPD that the crucial point was to implement the "immediate program" and that the promised tax reductions might well prove impractical. The Center Party leadership considered the DVP the villain in this confrontation and feared that those who sought to abolish parliamentary democracy had gained the upper hand in that party since Stresemann's death.[139]

The crisis came to a head on 13 December when the DVP threatened to withdraw its ministers from the cabinet. President Hindenburg arranged an emergency meeting between the cabinet and the leaders of the government parties that night, following a state dinner where Brüning was first introduced to him. Brüning again supported Müller's fiscal program without qualification, and Hermann Pünder then won approval from the other party leaders for a Reichstag motion endorsing it.[140] The next morning a narrow majority of the DVP Reichstag delegation agreed to support the government. Hindenburg himself, Pünder noted gratefully in his diary, exerted "a certain pressure" on the DVP, and the senior officials Hans Schäffer and Ernst Trendelenburg mobilized their many friends in the banking world to inform DVP leaders that a cabinet crisis would destroy political stability and thus ruin German credit abroad. The government won support from twenty-one DVP delegates in the decisive confidence vote on 14 December, while fourteen voted No and three abstained. The Munich leadership of the BVP opposed Hilferding's fiscal plan, but Brüning persuaded its Reichstag delegation to abstain as well. The cabinet's supporters interpreted

---

137 *Kabinett Müller II*, II:1210–29, 1238–44; Hans Schäffer diary, 9 December 1929, NL Schäffer/7/501–19; James, *Reichsbank*, pp. 113–17.

138 *Kabinett Müller II*, meetings of 11 December 1929, II:1246–48; for Brüning's elevation, see *Zentrumsprotokolle*, 5 December 1929, pp. 348–49, and the Christian miners' union Hauptvorstand meeting of 7 December 1929, pp. 2–3, NL Imbusch/2 (DGB Archive).

139 *Zentrumsprotokolle*, 2 October and 11 December 1929, pp. 334, 353.

140 *Kabinett Müller II*, meetings of 13 December 1929, II:1254–58; Brüning, *Memoiren*, p. 148.

this vote as a decisive victory in the campaign to defend the Weimar Republic against its enemies.[141]

Yet within just two days the chancellor stunned party leaders with the news that the fiscal outlook was much worse than they had realized. Popitz had concealed from the cabinet a precipitous decline in monthly tax receipts that called all of his projections into question, and he had just confessed that he could not meet the Reich's immediate obligations. Chancellor Müller saw no alternative but to submit to the demands of the Reichsbank, so the cabinet agreed on 19 December to drop any plan for tax reductions and retire 500 million marks in public debt, while Popitz and Hilferding resigned from office. Paul Moldenhauer of the DVP became finance minister and appointed Hans Schäffer, who had always urged cooperation with the Reichsbank, as his state secretary. Schacht then proved able to raise all the cash that the government needed, and the Reichstag quickly passed his debt reduction law.[142]

Some commentators have linked Chancellor Brüning's policy of fiscal austerity with authoritarian values, asserting that any good democrat should be willing to incur a budget deficit for the sake of full employment.[143] In December 1929, however, the most emphatic support for a balanced budget came from the SPD. All factions of that party agreed that direct tax rates should be increased to guarantee funding for welfare programs, and Friedrich Stampfer published the following editorial on the fall of Hilferding in the SPD's official organ:

> The government and the Reichstag should have done on their own initiative everything that they are now doing under pressure from Schacht and the financiers who stand behind him, and they should continue these measures on their own initiative! Reduce the debt, assure an adequate cash flow, balance the Reich budget! Every other consideration must be subordinated to these vital interests of the state! If we don't achieve these goals, we will choke with anxiety on the first day of each quarter, and we will be forced to change all our laws, including those on social policy, according to the dictates of those who help pay government salaries.[144]

Thus Stampfer reminded his readers of the German Reich's continuing poor credit rating that resulted from the hyper-inflation of 1923. Hilferding had

141 Pünder, *Politik in der Reichskanzlei*, entry of 15 December 1929, pp. 31–32; Schäffer diary, 14 December 1929, NL Schäffer/7/533–34; Maurer, *Reichsfinanzen*, pp. 100–101; Otto Altendorfer, *Fritz Schäffer als Politiker der Bayerischen Volkspartei 1888–1945*, 2 vols. (Munich, 1993), II:534–40.

142 *Kabinett Müller II*, meeting of 16 December 1929, II:1272–74; Schäffer diary, 16 December 1929, NL Schäffer/7/536; Pünder, *Politik*, 20 December 1929, pp. 32–37; Maurer, *Reichsfinanzen*, pp. 102–07.

143 See, for example, Maurer, *Reichsfinanzen*, p. 144.

144 *Vorwärts*, 22 December 1929, quoted in Winkler, *Schein der Normalität*, pp. 752–53. See also Wilhelm Keil, *Erlebnisse*, II:360–65, and Keil's speech of 16 December 1929 and the left-wing "Positive Vorschläge zur Finanzreform" of 1 February 1930, in Wolfgang Luthardt, ed., *Sozialdemokratische Arbeiterbewegung und Weimarer Republik, 1927–1933*, 2 vols. (Frankfurt a.M., 1978), I:125–29, 141–44.

sought in May 1929 to float a tax-free bond issue, but it never found subscribers for more than 177 of an offered 500 million marks. Government bodies were therefore compelled to rely on foreign lenders or short-term loans from German banks at very high interest rates, and even these sources of credit were drying up. Popitz's subordinates in the finance ministry had always considered his plan for tax reductions utopian and urged revenue enhancers instead. By year's end the leaders of the SPD, all officials in the finance ministry, and most knowledgeable observers agreed with Brüning that any deficit in the budget for the fiscal year 1930 would lead to a cash-flow crisis and to delays in the payment of government salaries, pensions, and welfare benefits that would probably cause rioting in the streets.[145]

This renewed fiscal crisis and the schism of the DNVP persuaded General Schleicher that the time was ripe for a change of government, and he almost undoubtedly encouraged the right wing of the DVP to topple Hermann Müller. In a closed meeting of the DVP central committee, the Ruhr lobbyist Otto Hugo justified his opposition to the cabinet in the confidence vote of 14 December by declaring mysteriously that it would soon be possible to form a government based on a "bourgeois majority" through methods he could not yet reveal. The pro-government majority in the DVP Reichstag delegation blamed Schleicher for the obstreperous behavior of dissidents like Hugo, and one of them (Rudolf Schneider of Dresden) even approached Chancellor Müller that same day to report rumors that Schleicher was planning a putsch. The chancellor did not take this report seriously, and Defense Minister Groener indignantly demanded that the parliamentary leadership of the DVP should discipline its wayward colleague. Adolf Kempkes defended Schneider stoutly, however, telling Groener that a great many Reichstag delegates had heard "that General von Schleicher was somehow engaged in an effort to exert a strong influence on politics in the direction of altering the current coalition or in the direction of employing Article 48 of the constitution to circumvent the Reichstag." Nobody knew for certain whether the army contemplated legal or illegal methods in this campaign, but any parliamentary delegate had the right and probably the duty to pass such reports along to the head of government.[146]

Unlike Schleicher, Brüning did not attach much significance to the schism of the DNVP. He had advised the "popular conservatives" to work patiently to

---

145 James, *The German Slump*, pp. 53–61; Theo Balderston, "The Origins of Economic Instability in Germany 1924–1930: Market Forces versus Economic Policy," *Vierteljahresschrift für Sozial- und Wirtschaftsgeschichte*, 69 (1982): 488–514; Balderston, *German Economic Crisis*, pp. 200–214, 266–87; Peter-Christian Witt, "Die Auswirkungen der Inflation auf die Finanzpolitik des Deutschen Reiches 1924–1933," in Feldman, ed., *Nachwirkungen der Inflation*, pp. 54–67; Eckhard Wandel, *Hans Schäffer: Steuermann in wirtschaftlichen und politischen Krisen* (Stuttgart, 1974), pp. 133–40; Lutz Graf Schwerin von Krosigk, *Staatsbankrott. Die Geschichte der Finanzpolitik des Deutschen Reiches von 1920 bis 1945* (Göttingen, 1974), pp. 53–56.

146 DVP Zentralvorstand, 14 December 1929, BAK R45II/44/293–301; Wilhelm Groener to Dr. Zapf, 31 December 1929, and Adolf Kempkes to Groener, 14 and 27 January 1930, NL Schleicher/5.

regain control of that party from the bottom up, and he was dismayed when the open breach occurred. He later recalled telling Treviranus that a handful of individuals could never win a battle against a party machine and would seem like "traitors and deserters" even to their friends. He saw his forebodings confirmed when Westarp, Martin Schiele as president of the Reichslandbund, and every provincial association of the DNVP pledged loyalty to Hugenberg, while the secessionists could not even agree on a single program. The Christian Socials joined with Pietists from southwestern Germany to found the Christian Social People's Service, while the more worldly friends of Treviranus eventually founded the Conservative People's Party. None of these developments offered any real hope for the emergence of a right-of-center parliamentary majority in the near future.[147] Joseph Wirth has also testified that Brüning was skeptical about the prospects of the popular conservatives and sought to avoid any political crisis. Brüning told his party colleagues repeatedly that many people around the President upon whose support Treviranus counted were prejudiced against Roman Catholics, and that "many mistakes have been made for the past fifty years in the construction of our nationalist and conservative right." To correct these mistakes would require much time.[148]

Brüning therefore defended the Great Coalition during his second meeting with Schleicher on 26 December. Willisen played host, while Treviranus and Otto Meissner also participated. Schleicher and Meissner announced that Hindenburg would appoint Brüning chancellor as soon as the Young Plan was ratified. Brüning objected that the use of Article 48 would not eliminate the need for close consultation with the Reichstag delegations. The constitution required that a newly elected Reichstag must convene within ninety days of the dissolution of its predecessor, and it would then have the power to rescind emergency decrees. The current economic crisis would last much longer than three months, however, and antagonizing the SPD would intensify the risk of popular unrest. Brüning concluded that the Müller cabinet should retain office at least until the autumn of 1930, by which time the DNVP might be ready to cooperate with the moderate parties again. When the discussion became most heated, Treviranus later recalled, Brüning exclaimed that "one thing is for certain: the Reichstag cannot be shut out." Schleicher left the meeting with grave doubts as to whether Brüning would prove useful, while Brüning was deeply alarmed by Schleicher's frivolous attitude toward the constitution.[149]

---

147 Brüning to Mona Anderson, 30 December 1938, *Briefe*, I:223; Brüning to Hermann Ullmann, 25 July 1951 and 13 March 1954, NL Ullmann/6/56, 122–23; Patch, *Christian Trade Unions*, pp. 152–53.

148 Wirth memoir of August 1942, "Ereignisse und Gestalten von 1918–1933," question #22, p. 3, NL Wirth/18.

149 Brüning, *Memoiren*, pp. 150–51; Treviranus, "Kurt von Schleicher," pp. 371–72; Treviranus, *Ende von Weimar*, p. 115; Brüning to Hans von Raumer, 4 July 1954, HUG FP 93.10/Box 22/Hans von Raumer; Wheeler-Bennett, *Knaves, Fools and Heroes*, pp. 38–39.

Wilhelm Groener proved far more skillful than Schleicher at courting Brüning. As the new year 1930 dawned, Groener wrote an old friend that he had forged close ties with the best of moderate politicians, including Treviranus, Brüning, Kaas, Moldenhauer, Scholz, and Hermann Dietrich and Erich Koch-Weser of the DDP; they had all agreed to cooperate in case Hermann Müller lost control of the SPD. Groener's goal was to restore the ability of the DNVP "to conclude alliances and participate in government" through patient coopera-tion with all conservatives who were not "blind followers of Hugenberg."[150] Thus Groener was somewhat more cautious than Schleicher, more in tune with Brüning's approach, and he established genuine rapport with Brüning during a stroll through Berlin's Grunewald Park a few weeks after the stressful discussion of 26 December. Arguing that Hermann Müller was too ill to rally support from the SPD for the fiscal reforms Germany needed, Groener explained that Hin-denburg had decided to make Brüning his "last chancellor" to end his political career with a partner who shared his own conservative ideals. Brüning tested the waters by suggesting that a general, perhaps Schleicher, should be entrusted with this mission, but Groener insisted that the army must be "held out of politics." He, Groener, would never serve as chancellor, because his highest ambition was to promote the "military training of our youth, in order to replace the twelve-year soldier with a people's army on the Swiss model." Thus the defense min-ister revealed that one of the goals of the next cabinet would be to restore mili-tary conscription, and Brüning apparently found this reasonable.[151]

Oddly enough, Brüning was most interested in questioning Groener, the last quartermaster-general of the Imperial army, about the end of the Great War. Brüning confessed that he had blamed Groener alone for the hasty capitulation in November 1918, but "I have gradually come to the conviction that the Reich President himself bears a large measure of the responsibility for the disaster. I have never forgiven him for abandoning the kaiser. Is the old man really reliable?" Groener answered that Hindenburg was not to blame for Germany's defeat, but that he owed Groener a great personal debt for having shielded him from direct responsibility for the abdication of the kaiser and accep-tance of the Versailles Treaty. As Brüning later recalled, the defense minister went on to say:

> The old man is so obliged to be grateful to me that I will always be able to gain his support for your course if difficulties should arise. I will stand behind you through thick and thin. After my conduct toward him in the last twelve years, the old man can do nothing else but follow my advice. It would

---

150 Groener to Alarich von Gleich, 4 January 1930, in Dorothea Groener-Geyer, *General Groener, Soldat und Staatsmann* (Frankfurt a.M., 1955), p. 262; Hürter, *Wilhelm Groener*, pp. 242–43.

151 Brüning, *Memoiren*, pp. 158–60, dates this conversation in mid-March 1930, but Treviranus, *Ende von Weimar*, p. 114, is emphatic and more plausible in dating it on 16 January; Brüning called Treviranus after the walk to boast of having persuaded Groener to renounce Schleicher's wild plans.

be inhuman for him to behave otherwise. I give you my word as an officer that I will use my influence to the utmost to support you.[152]

This conversation was indecisive in that the two men still disagreed about the prognosis for the Great Coalition, but Groener had won Brüning's trust. Throughout his term as chancellor, Brüning believed that he and Hindenburg were linked by a special bond of personal loyalty forged by Groener. Brüning later confided to friends that this conversation had also focused on Hindenburg's medical condition. The defense minister had just commissioned a thorough examination by a team of Germany's best doctors, who expressed confidence that the President would retain his faculties for another three or four years at least. Such a medical opinion could have been little more than guesswork, but Brüning and Groener felt encouraged to base their political hopes on the octogenarian president.[153]

Brüning's inside information about the threats to the Great Coalition impelled him to redouble his efforts to prolong its life. When the Hague Conference of heads of government reached final agreement on the Young Plan, Brüning notified Chancellor Müller at the end of January 1930 that the Center Party would not ratify this treaty until the government parties agreed on a tax program that guaranteed a balanced budget. Müller and his party colleague, Interior Minister Carl Severing, expressed revulsion against any such effort to subordinate foreign to domestic policy, but Stegerwald explained that "there are currents in the Reichstag that intend to dissolve the Reichstag and implement financial and tax reform on the basis of Article 48 of the constitution as soon as the Hague Accord is ratified."[154] Indeed, the right wing of the DVP had just caucused to press for a non-socialist minority cabinet that would reduce government outlay drastically, and the dissidents extracted a promise from Ernst Scholz that he would present the SPD with an ultimatum on tax reform as soon as the Young Plan was ratified. "Scholz told us confidentially," the lobbyist Erich von Gilsa reported to the industrialist Paul Reusch, "that he was thereby deliberately seeking to break with Social Democracy. To prepare for this break he has already formed contacts with Schiele, Treviranus, and Brüning."[155] Brüning seems, however, to have responded to this overture by seeking to thwart Scholz's plan.

Social Democrats were wary of Brüning's linkage between the Young Plan and taxation because the Reich Association of Industry endorsed it. Indeed,

152 Brüning, *Memoiren*, p. 160. For background see Dorpalen, *Hindenburg*, pp. 16–43; Walther Hubatsch, *Hindenburg und der Staat. Aus den Papieren des Generalfeldmarschalls und Reichspräsidenten von 1878 bis 1934* (Göttingen, 1966), pp. 25–43, 183–87; Groener-Geyer, *General Groener*, pp. 73–111, 151–89; and Carsten, *Reichswehr*, pp. 5–44.

153 Brüning to Jakob Goldschmidt, 29 November 1945, HUG FP 93.10/Box 12/Jakob Goldschmidt; Brüning to Hans von Raumer, 18 September 1957, HUG FP 93.10/Box 26/Hans von Raumer.

154 *Kabinett Müller II*, meeting of 30 January 1930, II:1402–05; Winkler, *Schein der Normalität*, pp. 774–76.

155 Von Gilsa to Reusch, 25 and 29 January and 5 February 1930 (source of quotation), *Quellen: Politik und Wirtschaft*, I:23–24, 32–34, 41–42.

many industrialists thought at first that Brüning intended to compel the SPD to accept a drastic reduction in government expenditure, but they soon noted with dismay that the Center Party actually shared the priorities of the SPD, seeking above all to secure the revenue needed to fund existing welfare programs.[156] On 1 February Brüning promised the parliamentary leader of the SPD, Rudolf Breitscheid, that the Center Party was not trying to sabotage the Young Plan but to generate the revenue needed to restore government credit. Brüning also told his own Reichstag delegation that the demand for linkage "has the goal of holding the current government parties together for later parliamentary work and removing the danger of a break-up in the coalition as much as possible."[157] When the leaders of the government parties conferred on 7 February, Brüning argued again that linkage between the Young Plan and taxes offered the best chance of "guaranteeing the continuation of the present coalition for the long term." Breitscheid and Scholz both demanded the immediate ratification of the Young Plan, but Chancellor Müller now endorsed Brüning's position.[158]

Stegerwald then took one step further toward the position of the SPD than Brüning considered prudent by proposing a direct tax to help fund unemployment insurance, an "emergency contribution" (*Notopfer*) of 2 percent of the salaries of civil servants. Brüning reproached him for strengthening the resistance of Social Democrats to the indirect taxes that had the best chance of securing a Reichstag majority, but the idea proved so popular that the Center Party soon embraced it.[159] On 27 February Moldenhauer glumly informed the cabinet that most of the government parties rejected his idea to raise indirect taxes, while the DVP would never accept the emergency contribution. A straw poll then revealed a cabinet majority of 7 to 5 in favor of the *Notopfer*, comprised of the ministers of the SPD and Center Party.[160] When the cabinet resumed debate the next day, the most enthusiastic endorsement for the emergency contribution came from Hindenburg's representative Meissner: "For the Reich President, the *Notopfer* symbolizes the concept of the national community [*Volksgemeinschaft*]. The economically secure must come to the aid of those segments of the populace who fall into need." This was a fairly bold gesture of support for Chancellor Müller, but it had no effect on the DVP.[161]

---

156 Fritz Schäffer to Paul Reusch, 4 February, Kastl to Moldenhauer, 8 February, and von Gilsa to Reusch, 11 February 1930, *Quellen: Politik und Wirtschaft*, I:38–39, 43–44, 47–50. See also Brüning's sharp criticism of the idea of balancing the budget through a rollback of entitlements in "Arbeit der Zentrumspartei" (published in December 1929), pp. 384–85.

157 Breitscheid memorandum of 1 February 1930, in Morsey, "Neue Quellen," pp. 209–12; *Zentrumsprotokolle*, 10 February 1930, pp. 383–84.

158 *Kabinett Müller II*, II:1438–42.

159 Stegerwald memorandum of 11 February 1930, *Kabinett Müller II*, II:1449–52; *Zentrumsprotokolle*, 13 February 1930, pp. 387–88; Wilhelm Fonk to Rudolf ten Hompel, 25 February 1930, NL ten Hompel/11.

160 *Kabinett Müller II*, II:1502–09; Winkler, *Schein der Normalität*, pp. 778–80.

161 *Kabinett Müller II*, meeting of 28 February 1930, II:1512–16 (source of quotation); Schäffer diary, 28 February 1930, *Quellen: Politik und Wirtschaft*, I:56–60.

On 1 March Brüning tried to shore up the President's support for the Great Coalition. Hindenburg received Scholz that morning, ostensibly to urge acceptance of the emergency contribution, but they obviously discussed the outlook for a non-socialist cabinet as well. When he received Brüning a few hours later, Hindenburg sought to extract a promise that the Center Party would support whatever cabinet he might appoint. Brüning responded with the following declaration, formulated in advance with the Center Party leadership:

> The present coalition should be maintained as long as possible and should enact a whole series of social, economic, and financial reforms after the Young Plan that are vitally important for the German people. Implementing these reforms without Social Democracy would lead to great political unrest, not to mention the fact that it is most uncertain whether any majorities could be formed on these questions outside of Social Democracy.[162]

Hindenburg brushed this declaration aside to ask whether the Center Party would support a coalition with the DNVP. Brüning termed this impossible as long as Hugenberg led it, and the President agreed sadly that Hugenberg refused to listen to reason. Hindenburg declared that he would be in an "extraordinarily difficult position" if the coalition parties failed to reach agreement soon on fiscal reform, and Brüning replied that the Center Party "would not reject any appeal that his patriotic convictions might lead him to make." This was a crucial concession, because Hindenburg now had reason to believe that Brüning would agree to succeed Müller. Some critics of Brüning hold that he had succumbed to personal ambition and now sought to come to power by any means, but he was probably swept along by his feelings. According to Brüning's memoirs, Hindenburg raised himself up at his desk, clutched Brüning's hand between his hands, and delivered the following appeal with tears in his eyes: "Everyone has abandoned me in my life; you must promise that your party will not leave me in the lurch at the end of my life." Brüning was overwhelmed by "a feeling of the deepest sympathy." Hindenburg displayed a similar talent for seduction two years later, when tearful appeals to soldierly duty and pity for an old man recruited several reluctant volunteers for the Papen cabinet.[163]

The thesis that Brüning had succumbed to personal ambition cannot be reconciled easily with his actions during the next four weeks, when he displayed more energy and skill than any other politician in the effort to preserve the Great Coalition. He visited Moldenhauer just after this presidential audience to secure the finance minister's support for some kind of direct tax to appease the SPD. After this conversation he warned the chancellor through Pünder that the DVP now favored a non-socialist minority cabinet as the best way to promote the for-

---

162　Brüning memorandum of 4 March 1930, Morsey, "Neue Quellen," pp. 212–14 (source of quotation); *Zentrumsprotokolle*, 28 February 1930, p. 398; Pünder, *Politik*, 3 March 1930, pp. 40–41.

163　Morsey, "Neue Quellen," pp. 213–15; Brüning, *Memoiren*, pp. 148–49; entries of 16–22 March 1930, in Quaatz, *Tagebuch*, pp. 105–06; Gerhard Schulz, *Vorabend*, pp. 484–86; Dorpalen, *Hindenburg*, pp. 333–35.

mation of a "State Party" uniting all factions from the DDP to the "popular conservatives." Although this project never quite materialized, Brüning had correctly identified a powerful yearning in the liberal camp for a "bourgeois union" (*bürgerliche Sammlung*) that distracted attention from efforts to preserve the Great Coalition.[164]

By now the yearning for stronger leadership by Hindenburg had become so widespread that, when the cabinet met on 3 March, the Social Democrat Severing proposed dissolving the Reichstag so that the government could enact tax increases by presidential emergency decree. Hermann Müller, Stegerwald, and Brüning all endorsed the idea. Severing's plan presupposed an improbable alliance between the field marshal and the SPD, but by now the Social Democratic ministers could see no other way for the cabinet to survive. Hindenburg was still prepared, moreover, to grant the cabinet at least one more gesture of support. Hjalmar Schacht chose this moment for a last effort to turn Hindenburg against the Young Plan by resigning as president of the Reichsbank, but Hindenburg followed the chancellor's advice by promptly appointing Hans Luther to succeed him. Luther enjoyed such prestige in the business community as the vanquisher of inflation that Schacht's gesture lost any political significance.[165]

Brüning tried to cement an alliance between Hindenburg and the Social Democrats when he concluded that the DVP was unreasonable. On 5 March Moldenhauer restored unanimity within the cabinet by proposing a nearly painless form of sacrifice by the propertied, a tax increase of 50 million marks on industrial exports, alongside an increase in unemployment insurance dues from 3.5 to 4 percent, with no reduction in benefits for the time being. Brüning told his party colleagues that this plan was "a great political success for the SPD" and a source of satisfaction for the Center as well; the Center, DDP, and BVP quickly endorsed it. The Reich Association of Industry rejected the plan on 7 March, however, and its firmness encouraged Scholz to do likewise.[166] Scholz isolated himself with this cavalier rejection of the budget of his own finance minister, and Brüning revived his threat to obstruct ratification of the Young Plan. Pünder then huddled with Brüning and Meissner to arrange another presidential intervention designed to influence the DVP. After a new audience with the President on 11 March, Brüning announced that the Center Party would ratify the Young Plan in exchange for Hindenburg's pledge to employ "all of his constitutional prerogatives" to secure a balanced budget by the end of the month. This press release was intended to signal a promise of decree powers for

---

164 Pünder memorandum of 1 March 1930, in Morsey, "Neue Quellen," pp. 216–17; Jones, *German Liberalism*, pp. 345–56.

165 *Kabinett Müller II*, II:1516–21; Schacht to Hindenburg, 3 March 1930, and Moldenhauer memoirs in *Quellen: Politik und Wirtschaft*, I:71–75.

166 *Kabinett Müller II*, meetings of 4–8 March 1930, II:1525–39, 1554–59; *Zentrumsprotokolle*, 5 March 1930, p. 403; Winkler, *Schein der Normalität*, p. 788; Jones, *German Liberalism*, pp. 354–56.

Chancellor Müller, who soon confirmed to the party leaders that Hindenburg had made this promise directly to him.[167]

Hindenburg was most anxious for the debate over the Young Plan to end. After some hesitation, he had committed himself to its support despite a painful social boycott by his aristocratic friends, and he became much less concerned about the wishes of the Center Party when the treaty was finally ratified on 12 March.[168] Schleicher and Groener also intervened with the President to argue that, if he granted decree powers to Müller, he would "again take an official stand for the SPD and against the DVP and the whole right." Reichstag elections would inevitably result, with "boundless agitation by the right against the R[eich] P[resident]" and a "great strengthening of the SPD." The President should instead encourage the DVP to topple Müller and then appoint "Brüning or Scholz, in case Br[üning] refuses for some reason, as chancellor with the mission of forming a cabinet of notable individuals prepared to put our economy and finances in order without regard for the parties and state governments, without asking the party delegations or forming any coalition." This initiative would gain the support of the Green Front, big business, and the Stahlhelm, indeed of everyone on the right except a few supporters of Hugenberg. Groener and Schleicher reminded Hindenburg of the "sabotage of frontier defense by Prussia" and the SPD's opposition to armored cruisers, and Groener apparently threatened to resign when he presented these arguments to the President orally on 11 or 12 March.[169]

Schleicher capped his efforts to win over the President by embracing the interests of big landowners. The general knew that Hindenburg was attracted to the ideas of the Rhenish industrialist Paul Silverberg, who sought ways to assist German agriculture without resort to protective tariffs. At the annual congress of the RDI in December 1929, Silverberg had proposed raising RM 200 million per year from a levy on industrial exports to provide debt relief for East Elbian agriculture, and Hindenburg's agrarian friends called this statesmanlike plan to his attention.[170] In February 1930 Hindenburg had also received an appeal from Nikodem Caro of the potash syndicate to implement the Silverberg plan and other measures urgently required by agriculture. Caro urged the President to suspend parliamentary government for the duration of the economic crisis, "to create a governing body that can work quickly, without friction and without long speeches, to do the necessary work for a certain time to achieve certain goals." Schleicher now seconded this appeal with the dubious argument that bankrupt-

167 Pünder, *Politik*, 9–14 March 1930, pp. 41–44; *Kabinett Müller II*, meeting of 11 March 1930, II:1565.
168 Hindenburg to Admiral von Schröder, 4 November 1929, in Hubatsch, *Hindenburg*, pp. 294–99; Dorpalen, *Hindenburg*, pp. 156–63; Julius Curtius, *Sechs Jahre Minister der Deutschen Republik* (Heidelberg, 1948), pp. 143–45; Moldenhauer memoirs, NL Moldenhauer/3/85.
169 Undated notes by Schleicher's aide Noeldechen for a report to the President, in Vogelsang, *Reichswehr*, pp. 414–15; Carsten, *Reichswehr*, p. 307; Hürter, *Wilhelm Groener*, pp. 244–47.
170 Neebe, *Grossindustrie, Staat und NSDAP*, pp. 51–53; Schulz, *Von Brüning zu Hitler*, pp. 76–78; memorandum of 26 January 1930 by Magnus von Braun, *Quellen: Politik und Wirtschaft*, I:24–29.

cies among old landed families on the "eastern march" would undermine national security, and he told the President that no government including Social Democrats would ever support agriculture adequately.[171] Hindenburg invited Caro, Silverberg, Ludwig Kastl of the RDI, and Martin Schiele for confidential discussions on 17/18 March and adopted their plan for Eastern Aid as his own. He declared that "you have demanded decisive leadership. I am prepared to offer that leadership, and I count on industry's support." Hindenburg then instructed Chancellor Müller to adopt the Silverberg plan in an open letter whose peremptory tone created the impression that the cabinet had lost the President's support. Meissner explained to Schleicher that "this is the first stage and the bridge toward your solution! This is also the foundation for the best that we can have, for the leadership of 'Hindenburg.'" The oddly placed quotation marks almost suggested that the man Hindenburg was merely a figurehead. Also on 17 March, Treviranus warned Brüning privately that he would be appointed chancellor soon and should draw up a list of ministers, so this seems to be the date on which Hindenburg abandoned any thought of granting decree powers to Müller.[172]

Brüning meanwhile sought a parliamentary solution to the crisis by transforming the Great Coalition into a more compact Weimar Coalition, which would retain a small majority if supported by the Bavarian People's Party. He gathered the tax experts of all government parties except the DVP to hammer out a new budget compromise on 9/10 March, and they agreed to drop any hike in direct taxes or the beer tax in favor of an increase in the sales tax.[173] The Weimar Coalition was revealed to be unviable, however, when the Bavarians broke ranks to oppose the Young Plan in the final ratification votes of 11/12 March. The BVP Reichstag delegation had agreed to Brüning's tax program, but the Bavarian Prime Minister Held and party chairman Fritz Schäffer stormed into Berlin from Munich at the last moment to demand a written guarantee from the chancellor that the beer tax would not be raised in future. They also ignored a personal appeal from the President, maintaining that they had been deceived so often by Reich cabinets in the past that they could not rely on informal agreements now. Their behavior angered the leaders of the Center Party, who concluded sadly that the BVP was even less willing than the DVP to subordinate particular interests to the public good.[174]

In mid-March Brüning tried again to reach agreement with the DVP but remained suspicious of its motives. He told party colleagues that "if the DVP

---

171 Caro memorandum of 22 February 1930, and Schleicher to Meissner, 18 March 1930, *Quellen: Politik und Wirtschaft*, I:91–93.

172 Von Gilsa to Reusch, 18 March 1930, Meissner memorandum of 18 March and Meissner to Schleicher, 19 March 1930, in *Quellen: Politik und Wirtschaft*, I:87–91, 94; Hindenburg to Hermann Müller, 18 March 1930, *Kabinett Müller II*, II:1580–82; Treviranus, *Ende von Weimar*, pp. 115–16.

173 Report by Brüning in *Zentrumsprotokolle*, 10 March 1930, pp. 409–10.

174 *Kabinett Müller II*, meeting of 11 March 1930, II:1561–64; *Zentrumsprotokolle*, 13 March 1930, pp. 417–18; Klaus Schönhoven, *Die Bayerische Volkspartei 1924–1932* (Düsseldorf, 1972), pp. 241–44; Altendorfer, *Fritz Schäffer*, II:545–50.

and BVP really intend to do the unpopular things with the SPD and then shove it aside, then we must give the SPD a sign as soon as we notice this. For we could not permit that."[175] On 21 March Brüning publicly censured the DVP as a threat to the survival of democracy:

> The viability of every cabinet must be determined according to whether it is in a position to formulate a budget and secure its passage. . . . Even though we now have a very strong form of democracy anchored in the constitution, today we still have many views in the parliaments and among the voters that are not compatible with a truly responsible democracy. If a party that provides the finance minister refuses out of hand to support the fiscal program of its own finance minister, preferring instead to conduct electoral propaganda, then that is the *end of all political responsibility, that is also the end of democracy* [emphasis in original].

Brüning concluded with a promise that President Hindenburg was still determined to invoke Article 48 if the DVP obstructed passage of a budget. Three days later, Brüning's party colleague and ally Eugen Bolz, head of the state government of Württemberg, went a step further by declaring publicly that the "failure of the parliament and parties" made "dictatorship" all but inevitable. The only question was whether this dictatorship would be "constitutional, legally regulated, and temporary" or "unconstitutional, revolutionary, led by the radical left or right." Brüning always avoided such provocative terminology but may have agreed with Bolz in substance.[176]

On 25 March, when the cabinet met again with the party leaders, Brüning declared that agreement must be reached quickly because the political crisis was undermining investor confidence. Chancellor Müller agreed that a final decision must be reached within forty-eight hours, but Moldenhauer murmured to Hans Schäffer that there would be no agreement, "because the People's Party has learned that the Reich President will grant this government neither the powers of Article 48 nor the right to dissolve [the Reichstag]." Scholz nevertheless softened his position slightly, intimating that he could accept an increase in unemployment insurance dues from 3.5 to 3.75 percent and would not insist on a large reduction in benefits. The Social Democrat Breitscheid adopted the more rigid stance by refusing to accept any modification in Moldenhauer's plan of 5 March.[177] Brüning reported with surprise to his party colleagues that the DVP now behaved more reasonably than the SPD; he blamed the "clumsy tactics of Labor Minister Wissell," a veteran trade unionist who opposed any reduction of welfare benefits. There was a real chance to secure a reasonable compromise

175 *Zentrumsprotokolle*, 17 March 1930, p. 420; see also Moldenhauer to Duisberg, 15 March 1930, *Quellen: Politik und Wirtschaft*, I:86, and Moldenhauer memoirs, NL Moldenhauer/3/90–93.

176 Brüning, *Reden*, pp. 28–30; Bolz speech to a Stuttgart rally of the Center Party on 24 March 1930, quoted in Joachim Sailer, *Eugen Bolz und die Krise des politischen Katholizismus in der Weimarer Republik* (Tübingen, 1994), p. 106.

177 *Kabinett Müller II*, II:1594–98 (quotation from n. 4).

pegging insurance dues at 3.75 percent, Brüning concluded, but the Center Party must prepare itself to demand Müller's resignation if he could not persuade the SPD to reach agreement with Scholz.[178]

On the evening of 26 March Brüning undertook the last effort to preserve the coalition, urging the leaders of the government parties to postpone any decision on unemployment insurance until a deficit actually arose that required new loans from the Reich. In its final form, his resolution entailed a political risk for the SPD by mentioning a reduction in benefits as one of the possible solutions that might then be adopted to repay the loan. This provision has given rise to assertions that Brüning sought to drive the SPD out of the government, but the proposal drafted by him mentioned only an increase in dues or in general tax revenue as two possible solutions, the alternatives preferred by the SPD. Breitscheid refused to participate, however, when the party leaders discussed this proposal, because he clung to Moldenhauer's plan of 5 March, and his passivity enabled the representatives of the liberal parties to tilt the draft toward their point of view. When the party leaders withdrew, Wissell told the cabinet that he too could never accept a bill whose provisions were worse than those of 5 March, but Chancellor Müller and all the other ministers supported Brüning's compromise resolution.[179]

The Reichstag delegations of the Center Party, DDP, and DVP promptly endorsed Brüning's compromise. The Ruhr industrial lobbyists mounted sharp opposition within the DVP, but Scholz persuaded a majority of 25 to 16 that the formula on unemployment insurance represented enough of a victory for their party to justify prolonging the coalition's life.[180] So the decision lay with the SPD. Müller and Severing urged their delegation to accept Brüning's compromise, but the trade unionists and the Marxist left wing both insisted that the SPD must never give the impression that it would accept any reduction in jobless benefits. After one speaker threatened that the Free Unions would openly attack the party leadership if it accepted the compromise, the ailing Müller lapsed into gloomy silence, and no more than five delegates backed him in the final vote. Thus the Free Unions adhered rigidly to the standpoint adopted by most of their leaders in the summer of 1929 that, to avoid membership losses in the face of Communist agitation, they must sacrifice the Great Coalition before accepting any loss of ground in social policy.[181] The cabinet resigned that evening. The ministers of the SPD and Center Party briefly hoped that Hindenburg might intervene

---

178 *Zentrumsprotokolle*, 26 March 1930, pp. 423–24.

179 *Kabinett Müller II*, meeting of 27 March 1930, II:1602–07 (see esp. Anlagen I and II); Winkler, *Schein der Normalität*, pp. 803–04. Contrast Maurer, *Reichsfinanzen*, pp. 134–45; Koops, "Brünings 'Politische Erfahrungen,'" p. 220; and Mommsen, *Rise and Fall*, p. 291.

180 Moldenhauer memoirs, *Quellen: Politik und Wirtschaft*, I:98–99; Winkler, *Schein der Normalität*, p. 807.

181 See Winkler, *Schein der Normalität*, pp. 621–25, 805–07; Friedrich Stampfer, *Die ersten 14 Jahre der Deutschen Republik* (Offenbach a.M., 1947), pp. 561–62; and Ursula Hüllbüsch, "Die deutschen Gewerkschaften in der Weltwirtschaftskrise," in Conze and Raupach, eds., *Staats- und Wirtschaftskrise*, pp. 137–45.

if Moldenhauer would defy the DVP and insist on his tax bill of 5 March, but Meissner signaled that the President would not grant this cabinet decree powers because it had already suffered too many defeats. Brüning endorsed the President's decision on the grounds that government by emergency decree had no chance of success if implemented by a chancellor who had been disavowed by his own party.[182]

The SPD's decision on 27 March has been criticized as a triumph of material interest over political principle, but that judgment is too harsh. Rumors then swirled through Berlin that President Hindenburg had fallen under the sway of reactionary generals, landowners, and industrialists determined to banish the Social Democrats forever from the corridors of power, so the final version of Brüning's compromise formula naturally reinforced suspicions that the SPD would be saddled with responsibility for unpopular measures and then expelled from government anyway. Even Social Democrats who undoubtedly considered the preservation of democracy more important than the material interests of the trade unions concluded that this cause would best be served if the SPD revived its popularity in opposition, while defending its bastion of power in the Prussian state government.[183] But the SPD had not really been asked to concede anything on 27 March, only to postpone a decision, and its refusal blurred the distinction between the friends and foes of democracy. Even the most sympathetic observers in the bourgeois parties concluded that the Social Democrats would not become reasonable again until shown that Germany could be governed without them. Brüning himself at first considered it self-evident that the SPD was responsible for Müller's fall.[184]

Looking back on these events after his own fall from power, Brüning came to ascribe more significance to the DVP's refusal to support Moldenhauer's reasonable tax bill of 5 March. Brüning had heard rumors at the time that Hindenburg was encouraging Scholz to reject this bill, so he asked Pünder to inquire about this of Meissner, who denied it. Brüning later concluded that Schleicher must have approached Scholz on his own initiative to ask him in the President's name to obstruct the compromise, but that Hindenburg failed to clear up this

182 *Kabinett Müller II*, meeting of 27 March 1930, II:1608–10; *Zentrumsprotokolle*, 27 March 1930, p. 426; Brüning to Kunrat Hammerstein, 23 September 1946, HUG FP 93.10/Box 14/ Hammerstein; Brüning to Franz Greiser, 24 July 1953, HUG FP 93.10/Box 11/Grabein-Guttenberg.

183 See Carl Severing, *Mein Lebensweg*, 2 vols. (Cologne, 1950), II:239–40; Keil, *Erlebnisse*, II:370–72, 383–85; Braun, *Von Weimar zu Hitler*, p. 292; and Dieter Schiffmann, "Die Freien Gewerkschaften und das Scheitern der Regierung Müller 1930," in Erich Matthias and Klaus Schönhoven, eds., *Solidarität und Menschenwürde. Etappen der deutschen Gewerkschaftsgeschichte von den Anfängen bis zur Gegenwart* (Bonn, 1984), pp. 203–07.

184 See the remarks by Koch-Weser in the DDP leadership conferences of 5 and 25 May 1930, *Linksliberalismus in der Weimarer Republik. Die Führungsgremien der Deutschen Demokratischen Partei und der Deutschen Staatspartei 1918–1933*, ed. Lothar Albertin and Konstanze Wegner (Düsseldorf, 1980) (hereafter cited as *Quellen: Linksliberalismus*), pp. 530, 535; Oswald Wachtling, *Joseph Joos. Journalist, Arbeiterführer, Zentrumspolitiker* (Mainz, 1974), pp. 152–54; *Zentrumsprotokolle*, 27 March 1930, p. 427; "Reichsausschuss der Zentrumspartei," speech by Brüning on 6 April 1930, *Der Deutsche*, 8 April 1930, #83; and Brüning, *Memoiren*, pp. 156–57.

misunderstanding when it was called to his attention. Brüning discerned a pattern of passive aggression in Hindenburg's treatment of Müller that resembled his treatment of Ludendorff and the kaiser in 1918.[185] Despite Schleicher's intrigues, however, Hindenburg had treated Chancellor Müller correctly before March 1930; indeed, he had risked his own prestige to defend the Young Plan, to appeal to the DVP for a vote of confidence in Müller on 14 December, to urge Schacht to help the government borrow money, and to support the "emergency contribution" by civil servants. Parliamentary government remained paralyzed, unfortunately, for reasons that lay outside the President's control – primarily because of the refusal by middle-class supporters of the DVP and BVP to accept compromises with the Social Democrats. If this deadlock was to be resolved by threatening to govern through presidential decree, the solution recommended even by Hermann Müller and Carl Severing, then it was inevitable that Hindenburg would insist on the formation of a cabinet that was congenial to him personally.

185 Brüning, *Memoiren*, p. 156, tells this story about the vote of 27 March, but the DVP supported the government then. In a conversation with Hans Schäffer on 7 June 1932 (NL Schäffer/21/565–66), Brüning raised the more intriguing suggestion that Schleicher's misrepresentations began on 5 March. Compare Schäffer's memoir, "Müller-Brüning," NL Schäffer/29/60.

2

The Establishment of
Semi-Parliamentary Government

Within an hour or two of Chancellor Müller's resignation on 27 March 1930, Otto Meissner telephoned Brüning with a commission from the President to form a new cabinet "without any fixed ties to parties." He invited Brüning to meet with Hindenburg that very evening, but a wary Brüning postponed the meeting until the next day so that he could consult the Center Reichstag delegation.[1] Although Ernst Scholz was the logical candidate to succeed Müller, Brüning told them, "Hindenburg does not want that, but rather desires for psychological reasons to spend the last years of his life working, not on a liberal, but on a conservative solution for the state. He wants to create order on the right; that is to be the purpose of a Brüning cabinet." His party colleagues all urged Brüning to accept the commission. The two most prominent left-wing republicans among them, Joseph Wirth and Joseph Joos, did the most to overcome his reservations; they expressed great personal confidence in him and feared a military dictatorship if he did not become chancellor. Wirth advised shrewdly that Brüning should not encourage talk of a fundamental political transformation (*"nicht von einem Übergang reden!"*); instead he should emphasize the "socially progressive" to balance the "Christian-conservative." Stegerwald glumly agreed that Hindenburg's offer could not be refused, although he feared "the radicalization of the SPD and Free Unions."[2]

While Brüning formed his cabinet, persistent rumors identified his friend Treviranus as the prime mover in a plot to replace parliamentary democracy with authoritarian government by decree. Wilhelm Keil of the SPD publicly accused Brüning of bad faith in his last efforts to mediate between the parties of the Great Coalition, and some historians have repeated this charge.[3] The documentary record nevertheless supports Brüning's emphatic declarations at the time

---

1 Meissner, *Staatssekretär*, p. 188; Brüning, *Memoiren*, pp. 157–58.
2 *Zentrumsprotokolle*, 27 March 1930, pp. 427–28; see also Treviranus, *Ende von Weimar*, pp. 116–17, and Brüning, *Memoiren*, p. 161.
3 See Pünder, *Politik*, 30 March 1930, p. 46; Keil, *Erlebnisse*, II:370–72, 383–85; and Koops, "Brünings 'Politische Erfahrungen,'" pp. 217–21.

and in all his later correspondence that he had done everything he could to prolong the life of the Great Coalition. His goal when he took office, he always insisted, remained that of Hermann Müller – to secure parliamentary approval for a genuinely balanced budget, if necessary by threatening to invoke Article 48, so that the Reich would not suffer a disastrous cash-flow crisis.[4] Looking back on these events years later, Joseph Wirth also testified that Brüning had sought to keep Müller in office:

> Brüning approached this question cautiously. He had gradually accustomed himself to the thought that he would be called someday, but in accordance with the mood of everyone on the middle and most of those on the right [of the Center Reichstag delegation] he held the view: Just don't push! It would be irrational for bourgeois elements in a period of rising unemployment to press to take responsibility away from the Social Democrats, who should instead be allowed to show what they could accomplish. But they just showed what they could not accomplish.[5]

Brüning wavered between two conflicting strategies to attain the goal of a balanced budget. The first, urged by Treviranus and the friends of the President, was to protect agriculture with measures designed to isolate Alfred Hugenberg and forge a right-of-center parliamentary majority. The second, urged by Brüning's colleagues in the Center Party and German Labor Federation, was to revive something like the Central Association of November 1918 between management and labor, so that his budget could be supported by the parties of the Great Coalition even if the SPD was not represented in the cabinet. Only after both these strategies failed did Brüning seek confrontation with the Reichstag, and even with hindsight it is very difficult to discern any third alternative for a parliamentary solution of Germany's fiscal problems.

2.1. In Search of a Parliamentary Solution

Brüning took office determined first and foremost to base government policy on a realistic assessment of economic trends. Big business and many academic economists argued that the recession would end quickly if tax rates and real wages were slashed, while the Free Unions argued no less confidently that full employment would return if wages rose so as to strengthen the "purchasing power" of

---

4 "Reichsausschuss der Zentrumspartei," *Der Deutsche*, 8 April 1930, #83; "Brünings Programm," *Der Deutsche*, 7 May 1930, #106; Brüning to Arnold Brecht, 6 August 1944, in Brecht, *Kraft des Geistes*, pp. 416–17; Brüning to Gerhard Ritter, 24 September 1952, HUG FP 93.10/Box 26/Gerhard Ritter; Brüning to Franz Greiser, 24 July 1953, HUG FP 93.10/Box 11/Grabein-Guttenberg; Morsey, "Neue Quellen," pp. 207–31; Hans Schäffer to Max Warburg, 2 August 1930, *Quellen: Politik und Wirtschaft*, I:355; Conze, "Die politischen Entscheidungen in Deutschland," pp. 193–213; Winkler, *Schein der Normalität*, pp. 816–18; Ruppert, *Dienst am Staat*, pp. 404–07; Gerhard Schulz, *Von Brüning zu Hitler*, pp. 8–18.
5 Wirth memoir of August 1942, "Ereignisse und Gestalten von 1918–1933," question #22, pp. 3–4, NL Wirth/18.

the masses. Neither viewpoint was based on careful research.[6] The wage issue caused political turmoil because of the Weimar Republic's system of state labor arbitration, under which the Reich labor minister could declare legally binding any wage decree by a district arbitrator. The steel industrialists of the Ruhr challenged this system in November 1928 when they locked out 230,000 workers rather than accept a binding decree that increased wages by 7 percent. Public opinion condemned this defiance of the state, but most businessmen deduced from a growing trade deficit that real wages were rising so fast as to undermine the ability of German industry to compete on the world market. The cabinet therefore undertook a partial retreat with a new arbitration decree that trimmed the original wage increase in half.[7] Recent research confirms that Germany experienced an extraordinary upsurge of real wages from 1927 to 1929, when wages definitely rose faster than did productivity per work hour. The real causes of this wage surge remain subject to debate, and businessmen certainly exaggerated its impact on their ability to compete on the world market. But the evidence seems inescapable that these wage increases did contribute to the onset of recession by making businessmen pessimistic about the long-term profit outlook; this pessimism caused a dramatic decline in private investment in 1928/9.[8] The Social Democratic cabinet ministers Hilferding, Hermann Müller, and Carl Severing soon concluded that the "purchasing power" theory of the Free Unions was misguided, and in December 1928 the chancellor instructed Labor Minister Wissell not to impose any wage increase in the Saxon textile industry on the grounds that "preserving our real wages would already be a success now that the business cycle is turning downward." Hilferding in particular combined support for Marxist theory with a sense of obligation to serve as a conscientious physician for the capitalist economy at this stage in Germany's historical development, and he sought to persuade his party that the costs of production must be lowered.

6 See Claus-Dieter Krohn, *Wirtschaftstheorien als politische Interessen. Die akademische Nationalökonomie in Deutschland, 1918–1933* (Frankfurt a.M., 1981), pp. 19–45; James, *German Slump*, pp. 324–28; and Michael Schneider, *Das Arbeitsbeschaffungsprogramm des ADGB. Zur gewerkschaftlichen Politik in der Endphase der Weimarer Republik* (Bonn-Bad Godesberg, 1975), pp. 34–50.
7 Patch, *Christian Trade Unions*, pp. 141–45; Gerald Feldman and Irmgard Steinisch, "Notwendigkeit und Grenzen sozialstaatlicher Intervention. Eine vergleichende Fallstudie des Ruhreisenstreits in Deutschland und des Generalstreiks in England," *Archiv für Sozialgeschichte*, 20 (1980): 99–113; Bernd Weisbrod, *Schwerindustrie in der Weimarer Republik. Interessenpolitik zwischen Stabilisierung und Krise* (Wuppertal, 1978), pp. 420–43; Winkler, *Schein der Normalität*, pp. 559–70. For a good summary of contemporary business arguments, see the petition from the Deutsche Industrie- und Handelstag to Chancellor Müller of 10 January 1929, *Kabinett Müller II*, I:339–55.
8 For the best analysis, see James, *German Slump*, pp. 190–221, and Balderston, *German Economic Crisis*, pp. 18–42, 54–121, 365–89. See also Borchardt, *Perspectives*, pp. 176–83; Claus-Dieter Krohn, "'Ökonomische Zwangslagen' und das Scheitern der Weimarer Republik. Zu Knut Borchardts Analyse der deutschen Wirtschaft in den zwanziger Jahren," *Geschichte und Gesellschaft*, 8 (1982): 415–26; Holtfrerich, "Zu hohe Löhne in der Weimarer Republik?"; Albrecht Ritschl, "Zu hohe Löhne in der Weimarer Republik? Eine Auseinandersetzung mit Holtfrerichs Berechnungen zur Lohnposition der Arbeiterschaft 1925–1932," *Geschichte und Gesellschaft*, 16 (1990): 375–402; and Hans-Joachim Voth, "Wages, Investment, and the Fate of the Weimar Republic: A Long-term Perspective," *German History*, 11 (1993): 265–92.

This view remained anathema to most trade unionists, however, which helps to explain why Hilferding lost support from his own Reichstag delegation in December 1929.[9]

Brüning and Adam Stegerwald had long campaigned to persuade the Christian trade unions to base their collective bargaining strategy on a realistic analysis of economic trends, and in 1929 they formed a gloomy assessment of those trends in consultation with the party colleagues whom they trusted to combine practical economic experience with commitment to the ideal of social partnership. In December 1928 Brüning and Stegerwald organized monthly summit conferences between Catholic labor leaders and the Center Party's Business Advisory Council to alleviate the class tensions resulting from the Ruhr steel lockout. The regular participants included Bernhard Letterhaus of the Catholic Workers' Clubs, the Christian trade unionists Bernhard Otte and Heinrich Fahrenbrach, the cement industrialist Rudolf ten Hompel, the corporate lawyer Clemens Lammers (an influential advocate of the Central Association of November 1918 within the RDI), and Friedrich Dessauer, an inventor and manufacturer of X-ray equipment and the Center's chief parliamentary spokesperson on economic policy. Brüning considered Letterhaus and Dessauer two of his closest friends.[10] The industrialists in these summit conferences imparted to the laborites their sense of alarm over the dramatic decline of business investment, the tendency of hourly wages to rise faster than productivity, and the growing trade deficit.[11] These discussions inspired an incisive report on economic policy for the Twelfth Congress of the Christian Trade Unions in September 1929. The delegates heard a somber assessment of the "price scissors" – the precipitous decline in world market prices of raw materials relative to those of manufactured goods – that had already devastated economies throughout the southern hemisphere and impoverished many German farmers. Rising unemployment was Germany's most urgent problem, they were told, and the second most urgent was the agricultural depression, which robbed industry of a vital market. To

9 *Kabinett Müller II*, meeting of 14 December 1928, I:302 (source of quotation); Maurer, *Reichsfinanzen und Grosse Koalition*, pp. 48–50; Winkler, *Schein der Normalität*, pp. 647–51, 743–44, 821–23; Harold James, "Rudolf Hilferding and the Application of the Political Economy of the Second International," *Historical Journal*, 24 (1981): 847–69.

10 Rudolf ten Hompel to Wilhelm Fonk, 3 November 1928, NL ten Hompel/29; "Mitteilungen der Handels- und Industrie-Beiräte der Deutschen Zentrumspartei," 22 December 1928, NL ten Hompel/38; Lammers speech of 23 April 1929, "Mitteilungen der Handels- und Industriebeiräte der Deutschen Zentrumspartei," 15 May 1929, pp. 9–11, NL ten Hompel/38; Lammers to Wilhelm Fonk, 17 March 1930, NL ten Hompel/33; Brüning, *Memoiren*, pp. 176–77, 615; Brüning, *Briefe*, I:65, II:163; Treviranus, *Ende von Weimar*, pp. 84–85; Rudolf Morsey, "Zentrumspartei und Zentrumspolitiker im rückblickenden Urteil Heinrich Brünings," in Jürgen Heideking et al., eds., *Wege in die Zeitgeschichte. Festschrift zum 65. Geburtstag von Gerhard Schulz* (Berlin and New York, 1989), pp. 60–62.

11 See ten Hompel to Konermann, 21 May 1929, NL ten Hompel/34; memorandum on economic problems of 18 June 1929, NL ten Hompel/35; minutes of the conference of 19 December 1929, NL ten Hompel/33; and Brüning to Heinrich Krone, 5 September 1957, HUG FP 93.10/Box 19/Heinrich Krone.

increase the real income of industrial workers came third on the list, and this goal must be pursued "by way of reduced prices" instead of higher nominal wages so as to preserve competitiveness for German exports on the world market. German workers could best hope to improve their living standard by campaigning for the abolition of reparations. The government should build up a major surplus in the balance of trade, ostensibly to finance reparations but also to inflict pain on business and farming interests in the countries that had won the Great War. This trade surplus would generate political pressure for a comprehensive bargain in which the United States would forgive its war loans to France and Great Britain in exchange for the cancellation of German reparations.[12] This report accurately summarized Brüning's views when he took office.

Alfred Hugenberg and Hjalmar Schacht gained notoriety in 1929 by predicting a disastrous economic crisis, but most senior government experts derided them as "prophets of doom" (*Katastrophenpolitiker*) when Brüning took office. State Secretary Hans Schäffer in the finance ministry clung until 1931 to the belief that there was no real economic crisis, just nervousness on the financial markets, and Ernst Wagemann of the Reich Statistical Office hoped for a "Young boom" in the fall of 1930. Wagemann's first report to Chancellor Brüning argued that the current recession might last longer than that of 1926 but would not get any worse; since unemployment had peaked at three million in 1926 and had just reached three million again, then three million was doubtless its natural ceiling at this stage of German economic development.[13] Within eighteen months that number had doubled. Brüning was nearly as pessimistic as Hugenberg and Schacht, however, and one source of his growing authority in government circles was that he came to seem more and more like a genuine prophet with each passing month. He sensed that the economic crisis and the polarization of the political parties had created a vicious circle: "I felt just as I had so often in the war when, sometimes without even having any maps, we suddenly received orders out of the blue to secure some section of the front where the enemy had broken through, to defend it to the utmost without knowing whether any of our troops remained in front of us, or to our right or left." The new chancellor anticipated a world economic crisis of unprecedented scope and duration.[14]

The one prospect that kindled Brüning's enthusiasm was that the coming economic crisis would strengthen the case against war reparations. He had always criticized Stresemann's decision to open negotiations over a revision of repara-

---

12 Karl Schmitz, "Gewerkschaften und Wirtschaftspolitik," *Niederschrift der Verhandlungen des 12. Kongresses der christlichen Gewerkschaften Deutschlands* (Berlin, 1929), pp. 233–45. Compare Charles Kindleberger, *The World in Depression, 1929–1939*, rev. ed. (Berkeley and Los Angeles, 1986), pp. 70–94.

13 Brüning, *Memoiren*, p. 172; Schäffer memoranda of 1 March and 12 September 1930, *Quellen: Politik und Wirtschaft*, I:64–65, 380; Schäffer to Hermann Dietrich, 11 August 1930, NL Schäffer/29/111–12; Ernst Wagemann to Hermann Pünder, 17 April 1930, NL Pünder/135/174–90.

14 Brüning, *Memoiren*, p. 164. Compare Brüning's remarks in *Zentrumsprotokolle*, 26 May 1930, pp. 451–52, and his speech of 15 July 1930 in *Stenographische Berichte der Verhandlungen des Deutschen Reichstags* (Berlin, 1920–33), vol. 428, pp. 6373–75.

tions in February 1929 as premature; world public opinion did not yet understand the harmful consequences of reparations, he argued, and voluntary acceptance now of a "final settlement" involving only modest reductions would gravely complicate the task of meaningful revision later.[15] Brüning revealed his most cherished goal shortly before taking office in his public commentary on the final ratification vote for the Young Plan. The Müller cabinet's "plan of attack" had been faulty because negotiations should not have begun "until the moment comes when economic reasons alone guide the determination of the reparations burden." After opening these talks, however, Germany had been compelled to accept whatever agreement emerged because the reckless policies of Finance Ministers Reinhold and Köhler in 1926/7 had left the treasury and Reichsbank vulnerable; a failure of the talks would cause a disastrous run on the mark. All combat veterans knew that one must not exchange recriminations after an attack was broken off. The unit must begin "that very evening" to formulate a better plan, so that a successful assault could be launched the next day. Germany must seek to meet its obligations under the Young Plan, but it must also demonstrate to world public opinion that its capacity to pay had been grossly exaggerated, and that reparations damaged the entire world economy. Germany must above all put its fiscal house in order so that it could undertake the next round of diplomatic negotiations from a position of strength.[16] According to Max Habermann, Brüning spoke even more frankly to his closest associates in the German Labor Federation, warning that his chief aim as chancellor would be to liberate the German economy from the burden of reparations and foreign debt. This goal required an unpopular policy of tight credit and a rollback of all wage and salary increases since 1927 to enhance the ability of German exports to compete on the world market. "He would not be able to shield the trade unions from this time of trial." They replied that "no sacrifice was too great to liberate the nation from the chains of Versailles. . . . As long as the sacrifices of the liberation struggle were distributed justly among all classes of the German people, then the trade unions too must support unpopular measures. . . ." Brüning did not take office with any plan for specific diplomatic initiatives, but a passionate determination to regain for Germany the autonomy of a Great Power inspired all his efforts to balance the budget.[17]

Unfortunately for Brüning, the advisers closest to President Hindenburg did not care much about reparations and balanced budgets; they were preoccupied instead with rearmament, subsidies for agrarians, and the removal of Social

15 See Hertz-Eichenrode, *Wirtschaftskrise*, pp. 238–42, and Morsey, "Brünings Kritik an der Reichsfinanzpolitik," pp. 370–73.
16 Brüning's speech to a Cologne party rally, 21 March 1930, *Reden*, pp. 21–25, 49; compare his Reichstag speech of 12 March, *Verhandlungen des Reichstags*, 427/4371–73.
17 Max Habermann, "Der DHV im Kampf um das Reich," unpublished memoir from 1934, pp. 70–71, DHV Archive; Franz Knipping, *Deutschland, Frankreich und das Ende der Locarno Ära, 1928–1931* (Munich, 1987), pp. 162–66; Hans Mommsen, "Brünings Politik," pp. 23–26. Contrast Winfried Glashagen, "Die Reparationspolitik Heinrich Brünings 1930–1932," 2 vols. (Ph.D. diss., University of Bonn, 1980), I:91–98.

Democrats from all positions of power.[18] Hindenburg himself did not discuss policy matters when he received the new chancellor designate on 28 March, but he set narrow parameters for the Brüning cabinet by insisting that it retain his friends Wilhelm Groener as defense minister and Georg Schätzel of the BVP as postal minister, add Martin Schiele of the Reichslandbund as minister of agriculture, and include Treviranus in some capacity. Hindenburg laid special emphasis on the participation of the last two in order to shield himself from attacks by the right. Brüning retained seven ministers from the Müller cabinet, including three who were respected by the SPD, Stegerwald as labor minister, Joseph Wirth as interior minister, and Hermann Dietrich of the DDP as minister of economics and vice-chancellor. Social Democrats regarded Wirth in particular as a guarantee of adherence to the republican constitution. He later recalled that he had accepted this office only because Brüning promised to maintain friendly contacts with the leaders of the SPD and adopt policies which they could tolerate; Wirth believed that Brüning had always lived up to this bargain.[19]

To secure the services of the friends of the President nevertheless required Brüning to make commitments that drew him away from the SPD. Groener extracted a pledge that the military would be exempt from the budget cuts that loomed ahead, and he soon wrote his oldest friend that Brüning, "as an old combat veteran, has a very warm heart for the young *Wehrmacht*."[20] Groener doubtless secured a further promise that the state of Prussia would be pressured to support covert mobilization programs on the eastern frontier, because the new chancellor sent a detailed critique of the SPD's sins against military preparedness to the head of the Center delegation in the Prussian Landtag, Joseph Hess. Brüning refused, however, to seek to topple the Prussian government led by Otto Braun, which Hugenberg demanded as the price of DNVP support for the new cabinet. Hess was a firm supporter of the Weimar Coalition in Prussia, and he persuaded the chancellor that the threat to topple Braun offered the Center Party invaluable leverage in all future dealings with the SPD in the Reichstag.[21]

Brüning's toughest negotiations involved Martin Schiele, who was encouraged by Hindenburg to demand drastic action on behalf of farmers. Dreading an open break with the DNVP, Schiele obtained Westarp's help to draft demands

---

18 See the advice for Hindenburg in Westarp's memorandum of 15 January 1930, and Alvensleben to Schleicher, 12 March 1930, *Quellen: Politik und Wirtschaft*, I:15–18, 84–85.

19 *Zentrumsprotokolle*, 31 March 1930, pp. 429–30; Brüning, *Memoiren*, pp. 162–66; Treviranus, *Ende von Weimar*, pp. 118–21; Severing, *Lebensweg*, II:241; Wirth memoir, "Ereignisse und Gestalten von 1918–1933," question #22, pp. 4–6, NL Wirth/18.

20 Groener to Gleich, 21 July 1930, NL Groener/7/#27. Hans Schäffer learned to his horror of Brüning's pact with Groener as soon as he attempted to pare military outlay; see his diary entries of 25 June and 28 July 1930, NL Schäffer/9/163–64, 194–95, and Hürter, *Wilhelm Groener*, pp. 158–59.

21 Brüning to Hess, 7 May 1930, BAK R43I/2663/96–97; Moldenhauer memoirs, *Quellen: Politik und Wirtschaft*, I:121–22; Quaatz, *Tagebuch*, 22 March–14 April 1930, pp. 105–10; Hömig, *Das preussische Zentrum*, pp. 232–36; Morsey, "Die Deutsche Zentrumspartei," pp. 294–96; Hagen Schulze, *Otto Braun*, pp. 627–28; Eric D. Kohler, "The Successful German Center-Left: Joseph Hess and the Prussian Center Party, 1908–32," *Central European History*, 23 (1990): 313–48.

intended to drive a wedge between Brüning and the Social Democrats. Schiele demanded sweeping powers to raise tariffs on meat and grain, the commitment of 200 million marks per year for the next five years to debt relief in East Elbia, and a pledge that the government would not raise unemployment insurance dues. He also demanded that his program be implemented through emergency decree if it could not win a Reichstag majority.[22] Dismayed by these demands, Brüning approached Rudolf Breitscheid on the morning of 29 March to ask whether the SPD would tolerate his cabinet if he dispensed with the services of Schiele and Treviranus. Breitscheid replied that his colleagues still objected to Brüning's position on unemployment insurance, but their conversation was quite cordial. Brüning persuaded Breitscheid of his innocence in Müller's fall and promised to retain Julius Curtius as foreign minister to guarantee continuity with Stresemann's pro-western policy. The two men agreed heartily that "the Great Coalition was still the best solution." Brüning promised that "his person would never be an obstacle" to its revival but warned that the DVP's attitude made this impossible for the time being. Brüning obviously did not wish to lead an antisocialist crusade but rather a centrist cabinet that could seek support from either the left or right.[23]

Breitscheid's rebuff left Brüning no option but to secure the support of the farm lobby and the Business Party. The new cabinet's program therefore promised lavish subsidies for agriculture that conflicted with its basic commitment to fiscal austerity and a lower cost of living. Big business and the SPD both denounced this protectionism.[24] The BVP compelled Brüning to scale back his planned increase of beer tax rates from 100 to 43 percent in exchange for the services of Schätzel, and the Business Party insisted on a measure long cherished by shopkeepers, a sales tax surcharge on large department stores and consumer cooperatives, in exchange for the services of Johann Viktor Bredt as minister of justice. Wilhelm Keil observed sardonically that, despite all the rhetoric about "presidential" government, Brüning was more tightly bound by specific commitments to special interests than any previous chancellor.[25]

---

22 Westarp memorandum of 3 April 1930, *Quellen: Politik und Wirtschaft*, I:112–13; Schiele to Brüning, 29 March 1930, in *Akten der Reichskanzlei. Die Kabinette Brüning I und II*, ed. Tilman Koops, 3 vols. (Boppard am Rhein, 1982–90), I:1–4; Schiele to President Hindenburg, 29 March 1930 (enclosing his letter to Brüning), BAP R601/19721/vol. 46/8–14; Schulz, *Von Brüning zu Hitler*, pp. 28–32.

23 Breitscheid memorandum, 29 March 1930, in Morsey, "Neue Quellen," pp. 227–28. Meissner, *Staatssekretär*, p. 188, accurately describes the centrist strategy but misleadingly attributes it to Hindenburg.

24 Otto Braun, *Von Weimar zu Hitler*, pp. 295–98; Kastl circular to RDI presidium, 9 April 1930, *Quellen: Politik und Wirtschaft*, I:119–21; Deutscher Industrie- und Handelstag to Hermann Dietrich, 9 April 1930, NL Dietrich/320/57–59.

25 *Kabinette Brüning*, meetings of 9 April 1930, I:40–45; *Zentrumsprotokolle*, 11–14 April 1930, pp. 439–43; Moldenhauer memoirs, *Quellen: Politik und Wirtschaft*, I:122–24; Schönhoven, *Bayerische Volkspartei*, pp. 245–48; Altendorfer, *Fritz Schäffer*, II:556–58; Martin Schumacher, ed., *Erinnerungen und Dokumente von Johann Victor Bredt, 1914 bis 1933* (Düsseldorf, 1970), pp. 222–28; Keil, *Erlebnisse*, II:386.

Brüning could gain the support of only four dozen Reichstag delegates on the moderate right in exchange for the 150 Social Democrats lost to the government camp, so he emphasized his special relationship with the President when he first stepped before the Reichstag on 1 April. At first he issued only the conventional threat, uttered by several chancellors in the past, to hold new elections if his budget was rejected:

> The new Reich cabinet is bound to no coalition, in accordance with the commission given me by the Reich President. Yet the political forces of this high house naturally could not be ignored during its formation. The cabinet was formed for the purpose of solving those problems generally considered most vital to the Reich in the shortest possible time. This will be the last effort to achieve the solution with this Reichstag. Nobody can accept responsibility for further postponement of the essential tasks.[26]

The Reichstag gained more insight into Brüning's thinking when Breitscheid declared that the government would violate the constitution if it invoked Article 48, which was intended solely to deal with the threat of civil war, to impose tax increases. Brüning replied that the central task of every parliamentary government was to pass a realistic budget: "The constitution's last resort, Article 48, can only be employed if the government has no more hope that parliament and the parties will fulfill their mission." Brüning considered Breitscheid's speech sheer demagoguery, because Hermann Müller had sought decree powers from the President to raise taxes just three weeks earlier. Two dozen moderate Social Democrats apparently agreed, including Müller, Hilferding, and Otto Braun; they boycotted their own party's vote of no confidence, holding that the SPD's decision to topple the previous government implied a responsibility to give the new one a chance.[27]

Brüning's first parliamentary victory resulted from the popularity of Schiele's agricultural program in the DNVP. Hugenberg curtly announced to the Reichstag on 3 April that his party would oppose the votes of no confidence by the leftist parties. He had urged his Reichstag delegation to topple Brüning but was compelled to retreat when Count Westarp and the Reichslandbund declared their support for Schiele. A jubilant Treviranus told his cabinet colleagues that Hugenberg would soon disappear from the political scene.[28] Brüning intensified the pressure on the DNVP by linking the consumption tax increases needed to balance the budget with Schiele's program for agricultural tariffs in a single

---

26 *Verhandlungen des Reichstags*, 427/4728.
27 Ibid., 427/4737–38, 4769; Brüning to Wilhelm Sollmann, 20 September 1940, IfZ/F206/14–16; Brüning, "Ein Brief," in *Reden*, p. 246; Otto Braun, *Von Weimar zu Hitler*, p. 295; Heinrich August Winkler, *Der Weg in die Katastrophe. Arbeiter und Arbeiterbewegung in der Weimarer Republik, 1930 bis 1933* (Berlin and Bonn, 1987), p. 127.
28 DNVP Reichstagsfraktion, 2 April, and Westarp memorandum of 3 April 1930, *Quellen: Politik und Wirtschaft*, I:108–14; Quaatz, *Tagebuch*, 1–3 April 1930, p. 107; *Kabinette Brüning*, meeting of 3 April 1930, I:14; John A. Leopold, *Alfred Hugenberg: The Radical Nationalist Campaign against the Weimar Republic* (New Haven and London, 1977), pp. 73–75.

legislative package. Hugenberg opposed the tax increases, but on 12 April the DNVP Reichstag delegation voted 28 to 22 to support the government program. This decision gave Brüning his first legislative victory two days later, by a thin margin of five votes made possible only because twenty-four Social Democrats absented themselves again.[29]

Schleicher and the Reich Association of Industry urged Brüning to drive home the campaign against Hugenberg by drawing two more DNVP leaders into the cabinet and excluding the Prussian state government from the administration of the Eastern Aid program for debt relief.[30] Instead Brüning sought to make Eastern Aid more palatable to the SPD. He first rejected Schiele's demand for a moratorium on farm foreclosures and reserved to the Prussian courts the authority to balance the rights of creditors and debtors. The cabinet then decided in mid-May to appropriate 50 million marks for debt relief in East Elbia (one-fourth the sum demanded by Schiele) on the condition that the Prussian state bank raise a similar amount, with the funds to be administered jointly by Treviranus as Reich Commissar for Eastern Aid and the Prussian welfare ministry. The Reich appropriated another 50 million to finance peasant homesteads as a form of unemployment relief and 25 million to construct housing for poor farm workers. Hermann Dietrich rejoiced that Prussia's administrative role would prevent Schiele from pursuing "a crazy policy of subsidies to benefit bankrupt agrarians." Brüning agreed that it was irrational to subsidize large rye-growing estates that were incapable of making a profit; his memoirs conclude that Hindenburg just wanted to preserve the old landed families as a reservoir of future army officers.[31]

Otto Braun distrusted the new chancellor initially but recognized that the Prussian Center Party would topple him if Brüning fell. On 8 May Braun repaid the Center for its support in the budget debate in the Prussian Landtag by publicly reproaching the Social Democratic press for its attacks on Brüning.[32] The role that Brüning granted Prussia in Eastern Aid cemented this alliance. In late June Brüning's chief of staff Hermann Pünder wrote Robert Weismann, his opposite number in Prussia and an old friend, that "you know how hard I have worked these many years for the closest cooperation with you and the Prussian cabinet; fortunately the present Reich chancellor in particular is of exactly the same opinion." Weismann replied with a pledge of unconditional support for

---

29 *Kabinette Brüning*, meetings of 11 April 1930, I:47–51; Schmidt-Hannover diary, April 1930, *Quellen: Politik und Wirtschaft*, I:131–38; Winkler, *Katastrophe*, pp. 131–32.

30 Graf von der Schulenberg to Schleicher, 6 May, reply of 13 May, and Crown Prince Wilhelm to Schleicher, 16 June 1930, NL Schleicher/21/4–9; RDI petition of 17 May 1930, *Quellen: Politik und Wirtschaft*, I:162–63.

31 *Kabinette Brüning*, meetings of 1–15 May 1930, I:76–78, 97–114, 128–31; "Brünings Programm," *Der Deutsche*, 7 May 1930, #106; Landeshauptmann Caspari to Otto Braun, 15 May 1930, *Quellen: Politik und Wirtschaft*, I:159–60; Dietrich to Oberforstrat Zircher, 16 May 1930, NL Dietrich/126/594–98 (source of quotation); Brüning, *Memoiren*, pp. 172–73; Schulz, *Von Brüning zu Hitler*, pp. 33–38, 62–73.

32 Schulze, *Otto Braun*, pp. 627–31.

Brüning in the federal upper house of parliament, the Reichsrat: "My heart is so closely bound to the Reich government that I consider its problems to be much greater still [than those of Prussia] and will do everything in my power to help solve them." Indeed, Brüning soon gained powerful support by the leaders of most state governments, who shared with him an overriding concern to balance the budget and defend the authority of the state against the special interests and political extremists.[33]

Many rightists who had initially greeted the formation of the Brüning cabinet soon complained sharply about his reluctance to offend Otto Braun.[34] Hugenberg rallied support from DNVP party locals against the "materialistic" parliamentarians willing to sacrifice their principles for participation in government, and Westarp's line was condemned by an overwhelming majority of the DNVP national committee on 25 April. Brüning's former teacher Martin Spahn launched the sharpest attack on him, arguing that he had opened the final phase of a campaign to destroy any "truly nationalist right" which had begun with the formation of the fourth Marx cabinet in January 1927. "Brüning is anything but a rightist politician," warned Spahn, because he would always hold the door open for the Great Coalition and continue the fiscal policies of Hilferding. It was futile to seek an understanding with the Center Party, Spahn concluded; the DNVP must smash it instead by actively recruiting Catholic voters. Westarp's following shrank steadily in the following weeks as the price of rye continued to fall, and old rivals of Schiele in the Reichslandbund soon challenged his leadership. By late May it was obvious that no right-of-center majority would coalesce in this Reichstag.[35]

Brüning had meanwhile shifted his political strategy toward an effort to revive something like the Central Association of November 1918. He first hoped to promote consensus between big business and organized labor in favor of a bold program to create jobs. Brüning is widely regarded as a dogmatic foe of government borrowing for public works, and it is true that all the major business associations in 1930 opposed any such program as a harmful diversion of investment capital away from productive enterprise in the private sector. Brüning and his colleagues in the Christian trade unions had long argued, however, that the state must finance public works during recessions because construction workers were so vulnerable to cyclical fluctuations in the economy. The Free Unions also began to agitate for public works in January 1930, and the idea seemed

33 Pünder to Weismann, 25 June, and reply of 30 June 1930, NL Pünder/658/20–21; Pünder, *Politik*, entry of 28 May 1930, p. 52; Besson, *Württemberg*, pp. 119–29, 139–58.

34 See von Gilsa to Reusch, 21 May, and Blank to Reusch, 24 May 1930, *Quellen: Politik und Wirtschaft*, I:168, 174–75; and Berghahn, *Der Stahlhelm*, pp. 143–49.

35 Schmidt-Hannover diary, April 1930, *Quellen: Politik und Wirtschaft*, I:146–47 (source of quotation); Spahn to Hugenberg, 23 April 1930, NL Spahn/86; Pünder note of 30 April, Gilsa to Reusch, 17 May, and Blank to Reusch, 24 May 1930, *Quellen: Politik und Wirtschaft*, I:150, 164, 175–76; Gessner, *Agrarverbände*, pp. 223–30; Leopold, *Hugenberg*, pp. 74–77.

popular.[36] Brüning warned the cabinet on 30 April that the SPD and DNVP would probably both reject its budget. Both the need to prepare for an election campaign and the grim long-term economic outlook obliged the cabinet to formulate a "five-year plan" designed "to bolster the economy" through lower production costs and large-scale public works. "Public confidence in the economy and in our fiscal policy will be strengthened by a comprehensive legislative program of this sort," Brüning argued, and it would make an excellent campaign platform if the Reichstag was dissolved. "To accelerate the return of the unemployed to the process of production," the chancellor concluded, "is one of the most important tasks of the government." Stegerwald then suggested the formation of an "economic general staff" to be composed of enlightened economists, the leading representatives of management and labor, and senior government officials.[37] After this meeting Dietrich and Stegerwald wanted to submit a bill to the Reichstag requiring all local government agencies and publicly owned corporations to support a counter-cyclical economic strategy with their purchasing practices, but Finance Minister Moldenhauer persuaded them to rely instead on persuasion. The transportation, labor, and postal ministries then developed plans to invest a total of 1.5 billion marks, to be raised on foreign bond markets, in the purchase of railroad and telecommunications equipment and the construction of highways, canals, and public housing.[38] Brüning's talk of a five-year plan suggests that he was impressed by the propaganda value of Stalin's grandiose projects for industrial development, and he displayed a glimmer of Keynesian insight when he argued that public works would help to restore "confidence in the economy" among private investors.

As bad economic news continued to arrive in the following weeks, Brüning spurred the planning of public works forward through appeals to the cabinet ministers and personal contacts with industrialists. On 19 May he warned the cabinet of a disastrous decline in tax receipts, stagnation in the construction industry, and the failure of unemployment to follow its normal seasonal decrease in the spring. If the government did not undertake extensive public works, he

---

36 Grübler, *Spitzenverbände der Wirtschaft*, pp. 181–84; Meister, *Grosse Depression*, pp. 193–96; *Zentralblatt der christlichen Gewerkschaften*, 25 May 1925, pp. 152–53; *Niederschrift der Verhandlungen des 11. Kongresses der christlichen Gewerkschaften Deutschlands* (Berlin, 1926), pp. 532–33; Zentralverband christlicher Bauarbeiter, *Bericht über die Verhandlungen der 15. Generalversammlung, August 1928* (Berlin, n.d.), p. 129, and *Geschäftsbericht des Vorstandes für die Jahre 1928–30* (Berlin, n.d.), pp. 44–45, 63–65; Michael Schneider, *Arbeitsbeschaffungsprogramm*, pp. 167–70; Schiffmann, "Die Freien Gewerkschaften," pp. 193–95, 203–04. Contrast Hertz-Eichenrode, *Wirtschaftskrise*, pp. 238–40, and Mommsen, *Rise and Fall*, pp. 293–94.

37 *Kabinette Brüning*, I:66–67, 71.

38 Dietrich memorandum, "Konjunktur- und Saisonausgleich durch öffentliche Aufträge," 5 May 1930, BAK R43I/898/94–97; Grübler, *Spitzenverbände*, pp. 179–83; Meister, *Grosse Depression*, pp. 194–96; Michael Wolffsohn, *Industrie und Handwerk im Konflikt mit staatlicher Wirtschaftspolitik? Studien zur Politik der Arbeitsbeschaffung in Deutschland 1930–1934* (Berlin, 1977), pp. 45–56.

concluded, it would face devastating criticism from the SPD.[39] On 22 May the cabinet learned that it faced a projected deficit of 436 million marks in the coming budget year even if it raised unemployment insurance dues by another 1 percent, and five days later the projected deficit had climbed to a stunning 900 million. The national railway also faced an operating deficit of 600 million. Brüning told his party colleagues that they were witnessing "the first truly world-wide economic crisis" since the Great War. World market prices for raw materials were collapsing, while those of manufactured goods continued to rise despite rising unemployment; this price scissors indicated a fundamental sickness of the world economy. Things would get much worse before they got better. "Price reductions, wage reductions, reduction in the standard of living of all classes of the people are necessary. Here there will have to be intervention through laws." Brüning promised nevertheless to combine this program for deflation to promote competitiveness on the world market with massive public works for the jobless, beginning with a major highway construction bill.[40]

Brüning hoped that a formal agreement between the trade unions and big business about the outlines of economic policy would help to balance the budget. This plan was formulated by Catholic industrialists and labor leaders on 22 May, when Bernhard Otte privately conceded a thesis that no trade unionist dared as yet to espouse in public, that reductions in nominal wages were necessary to combat unemployment. He emphasized, however, that "one must begin the reform with government and the civil servants; then workers would gradually come to understand" what was necessary. Rudolf ten Hompel agreed enthusiastically that Brüning's budget should impose major sacrifices on the civil servants to create the proper atmosphere for reductions in wages and prices.[41] The chancellor hoped to broker a similar agreement between the Free Unions and the RDI. Discussions between them began soon after the fall of the Great Coalition, when the industrial lobbyists Ludwig Kastl (the executive secretary of the RDI) and Hans von Raumer began discussing ways to defuse the political crisis with the labor leaders Theodor Leipart and Peter Grassmann. Von Raumer, an architect of the original Central Association and advocate of the Great Coalition within the DVP, informed the cabinet that union leaders hoped to avoid reproaches from their membership over the inevitable wage losses that lay ahead if they could respond to an appeal from the President to cooperate with the simultaneous reduction of prices and wages.[42] In late May he arranged a dinner

---

39 *Kabinette Brüning*, 19 May 1930, I:138–43; see also G. Zapf to Brüning, 20 May, and Brüning to Schätzel, 4 June 1930, BAK R43I/898/115–16.

40 *Kabinette Brüning*, I:152, 165–67; *Zentrumsprotokolle*, 26 May 1930, pp. 451–52.

41 Conference of 22 May 1930, NL ten Hompel/36.

42 Schäffer diary, 26 May 1930, conversation with von Raumer, NL Schäffer/8/135–36; Hans Staudinger to Otto Braun, 14 June 1930, *Quellen: Politik und Wirtschaft*, I:232–33; Grassmann's circular to the Free Unions of 26 June 1930, in Peter Jahn, ed., *Quellen zur Geschichte der deutschen Gewerkschaftsbewegung im 20. Jahrhundert. Band 4: Die Gewerkschaften in der Endphase der Republik, 1930–1933* (Cologne, 1988) (hereafter cited as *Quellen: Gewerkschaften*), pp. 100–101; Udo

party where Stegerwald, Brüning, and the leaders of the RDI agreed on the outlines of a speech by President Hindenburg to greet a joint deputation from management and labor. After gaining the approval of the labor leaders, Brüning sent the industrialists a draft declaration that prices and the costs of production must both be lowered, that all of Germany's welfare programs should be retained but with cost-cutting reforms, and that the unemployment insurance fund would require a special "crisis contribution" from everyone with an annual salary over 2,400 marks.[43]

For the cabinet the crucial point was the "crisis contribution," which it needed to balance the budget. Prodded by Brüning, Moldenhauer decided on 3 June to revive this proposal, which had been repudiated by the DVP and business associations in March. He was encouraged by Kastl and Paul Silverberg, who told the cabinet that the RDI now considered a balanced budget more important than tax reductions. Silverberg won Brüning's enduring respect with the declaration that, "if you promise that the budget for 1930 is balanced, then we will support any demand you make to achieve this end."[44] Moldenhauer hoped that business support for the emergency contribution would overcome objections in the DVP. Brüning too believed on 3 June that management and labor would reach agreement within a day or two, and that such agreement represented "the essential precondition for the success of our national policy."[45]

That same day, however, the executive committees of the major industrial associations rejected the draft agreement with labor. Reactionary industrialists led by Fritz Thyssen demanded that the President's speech call for the abolition of state labor arbitration. Most business leaders considered this demand too extreme, but many agreed with Thyssen that they should wait for the trade unions to become weaker as a result of rising unemployment before they struck a bargain. Silverberg then conceded that the draft agreement should be renegotiated to include specific endorsement of wage reductions where the original referred vaguely to lowering the costs of production.[46] This new demand made the trade unionists fear an effort to discredit them in the eyes of workers, and on 4 June they demanded a guarantee that the cost of living would be reduced even more than nominal wages. All industrialists agreed that this demand was absurd. The next day President Hindenburg waited two hours in vain for the joint deputation to appear and then left on vacation; the negotiators decided to

---

Wengst, "Unternehmerverbände und Gewerkschaften in Deutschland im Jahre 1930," *Vierteljahrshefte für Zeitgeschichte*, 25 (1977): 102–09; Reinhard Neebe, "Unternehmerverbände und Gewerkschaften in den Jahren der Grossen Krise, 1929–33," *Geschichte und Gesellschaft*, 9 (1983): 302–10.

43 Draft declaration of 30 May and Pietrkowski's report to business leaders of 3 June 1930, *Quellen: Politik und Wirtschaft*, I:189–91.

44 Schäffer diary, 20 May 1930, NL Schäffer/8/127–28.

45 *Kabinette Brüning*, 3 June 1930, I:176–83 (quotation on p. 183); Kastl to Blohm, 27 May 1930, NL Silverberg/263/105–06; Moldenhauer memoirs, *Quellen: Politik und Wirtschaft*, I:205–10.

46 Conference of RDI Präsidium and the League of German Employers' Associations, 3 June 1930, *Quellen: Politik und Wirtschaft*, I:191–93.

recess to consult their followings. The cabinet could not wait to present its budget to parliament, however, so on 6 June the public learned of the proposed "crisis contribution" without any supportive declaration by management and labor.[47]

Stegerwald agreed that same day to impose the first compulsory arbitration decree lowering wages since 1924. A district labor arbitrator had reduced piece-rate wages in the Ruhr steel industry by 7.5 percent in the "Oeynhausen Decree," and the labor minister declared it binding after the steel lobbyist Ernst Poensgen promised him that such action would persuade Ruhr industrialists to endorse the joint declaration with the trade unions. The steel industry also promised to pass its savings along to consumers in the form of price reductions of 3 percent. Stegerwald was doubtless correct that the system of state labor arbitration could survive only if it ratified the downward trend in wages suggested by all the economic indicators. He remained determined to preserve that system in order to defend collective bargaining, which many employers might have renounced without the threat of arbitration decrees, and to guarantee that the downward slide of wages proceeded more gradually than it would have in the free labor market of the nineteenth century.[48] The timing of the Oeynhausen Decree was unfortunate, however. The Communist Party leadership concluded that "the whole wage reduction offensive of the bosses is taking place with the full deployment of the capitalist state apparatus." It denounced the leaders of the Free Unions as "social fascists" who had joined with the government and monopoly capital in a campaign for the "fascistization of Germany." This thesis was implausible, but many union members obviously felt that any cooperation by labor leaders with a program for wage reductions was a form of betrayal.[49] Even moderate industrialists lost interest in an agreement with the trade unions, moreover, after the labor ministry gave them what they most desired, wage reductions. On 13 June the next round of talks between the umbrella organizations of management and labor went badly after the nervous union leaders presented a manifesto that blamed the recession on "under-consumption by the broad masses of the population," demanding that the cost of living be reduced more than

---

47 Rival draft agreements of 3/4 June and reports on the talks by Herle, Martin Blank, and Pünder in *Quellen: Politik und Wirtschaft,* I:193–96, 202–04, 235–36; Grassmann's circular of 26 June 1930, *Quellen: Gewerkschaften,* pp. 102–07; cabinet meeting of 5 June 1930, *Kabinette Brüning,* I:186–88.

48 Conference between Stegerwald and Poensgen, 6 June 1930, *Quellen: Politik und Wirtschaft,* I:197–201; "Sitzung des A-Produkte- und Stabeisenverbandes," 11 June 1930, BAK R13I/ 401/31–42; Schorr, *Adam Stegerwald,* pp. 162–75; Grübler, *Spitzenverbände,* pp. 157–60; Hans-Hermann Hartwich, *Arbeitsmarkt, Verbände und Staat 1918–1933* (Berlin, 1967), pp. 160–62; Bernd Weisbrod, "Die Befreiung von den 'Tariffesseln.' Deflationspolitik als Krisenstrategie der Unternehmer in der Ära Brüning," *Geschichte und Gesellschaft,* 11 (1985): 295–325; Balderston, *German Economic Crisis,* pp. 32–48.

49 KPD leadership circular of 21 June 1930, in Hermann Weber, ed., *Die Generallinie. Rundschreiben des Zentralkomitees der KPD an die Bezirke 1929–1933* (Düsseldorf, 1981) (hereafter cited as *Quellen: Generallinie*), pp. 158–64; KPD Polbüro resolution of 15 June 1930 in Hermann Weber, ed., *Der deutsche Kommunismus. Dokumente* (Cologne and Berlin, 1963), pp. 150–51; Winkler, *Katastrophe,* pp. 144–55; Freya Eisner, *Das Verhältnis der KPD zu den Gewerkschaften in der Weimarer Republik* (Cologne and Frankfurt a.M., 1977), pp. 232–39.

nominal wages. The talks were again suspended, and the Free Unions announced publicly on 25 June that they had broken off negotiations because the labor ministry had joined employers in a brutal offensive to slash wages. Hostility toward Brüning spread among workers because the cost-of-living index actually rose slightly in June and July as a result of Schiele's food tariffs.[50]

As the talks between management and labor bogged down, the DVP Reichstag delegation repudiated its own finance minister. On 16 June it echoed the arguments of Fritz Thyssen by rejecting any new tax on civil servants unless employers faced with bankruptcy won the right to reduce unilaterally the wages guaranteed by collective labor contracts. The next day the DVP revived its old demand that the budget be balanced through "ruthless reduction of expenditure" instead of tax increases, and on 18 June it demanded that Moldenhauer resign from the cabinet. He meekly agreed despite appeals from cabinet colleagues to defy his party. Brüning blamed the heavy industrialists of the Ruhr for this development and denounced them to party colleagues for having toppled Hermann Müller, sabotaged all efforts to revive the Central Association, and obstructed any balanced budget. He feared that they backed Hugenberg's program for dictatorship.[51]

The collapse of negotiations between management and labor also doomed the government's efforts to finance public works. The national railway enjoyed much better credit on the bond markets than did the Reich, but its autonomous administrative council resisted any new investment program, arguing that it must first balance its operating budget through major wage reductions. The council president, the powerful industrialist Carl Friedrich von Siemens, maintained that the national railway's legal obligation to serve the interests of the economy as a whole merely required it to keep fares as low as possible. In mid-June the council offered to authorize a bond issue of 150 million marks for investments only if the Reich forgave it 130 million marks in debt owed the government. Transport Minister von Guérard offered to forgive the 130 million if the railway issued 500 million in bonds, but Siemens emphatically rejected this suggestion. The growing firmness displayed by big business in its dealings with organized labor encouraged the railway officials to take this stand.[52] Von Guérard also sought a foreign loan of RM 300 million for highway construction. The law now required, however, that any foreign bond issue receive certification from the Reichsbank that it served a "productive" purpose, that is, would generate enough revenue to

50 Declarations of 13 and 25 June 1930, *Quellen: Politik und Wirtschaft*, I:212–30, 237–38, 257–60; ADGB circular of 26 June 1930, *Quellen: Gewerkschaften*, pp. 110–15; Meister, *Grosse Depression*, p. 204.

51 Von Gilsa to Reusch, 17 June 1930, Blank to Reusch, 17 June 1930, and the Moldenhauer memoirs, in *Quellen: Politik und Wirtschaft*, I:238–46; *Kabinette Brüning*, 18 June 1930, I:209–14; remarks by Brüning and Esser in *Zentrumsprotokolle*, 20–24 June 1930, pp. 456–57; Brüning, *Memoiren*, pp. 176–77.

52 *Kabinette Brüning*, meeting of 5 June 1930, I:188–90; Siemens to von Guérard, 25 June, von Guérard to Brüning, 26 June, and Karl Steuernagel to Erwin Planck, 28 June 1930, in BAK R43I/898/169–80; Grübler, *Spitzenverbände*, pp. 180–81; James, *German Slump*, pp. 60–61.

service the debt, and Hans Luther warned the cabinet on 13 June that his board of governors would not approve any grandiose highway program. When the transport minister received a definite promise of foreign funding in July, Luther vetoed his plan on the grounds that the scarce loan funds available must go to projects more urgent than highway construction; the Reichsbank then ignored further communications from the transport ministry on the subject. Like Siemens, Luther was obviously influenced by the failure of the talks between big business and organized labor. When Stegerwald could secure financing only for 100 million marks' worth of subsidized housing construction, the government's budget for public works was pared down to a total of just 250 million marks, which could have no impact on the labor market.[53]

Brüning sensed by mid-June that the government's lack of credit doomed his initial plans. He told party colleagues that "there is no money to be had for the consolidation of communal debt, public works for the unemployed [*wertschaffende Arbeitslosenfürsorge*], the railroad, etc., if the finances of the Reich and unemployment insurance are not in order." The only hope for economic recovery lay in cooperation between big business and organized labor to lower the niveau of both wages and prices, which should enable German industry to capture new export markets.[54] The open rupture of the talks between management and labor a week later suggested that the government would need to implement this program on its own authority.

Free trade unionists and most industrialists discussed the possibility of reviving the Central Association solely in terms of enlightened self-interest, but to Brüning it represented a moral imperative. He felt ashamed that Fritz Thyssen, a pious Catholic, cited the authority of the Vatican for his crusade against the trade unions. Thyssen told business leaders in June 1930, Brüning later recalled, that the trade unions "had lost all importance, as the encyclical *Quadragesimo anno*, which was then in preparation, would impose a Fascist corporative ideal upon all Catholics." Thyssen adhered to the hierarchical social theory developed by the Austrian Catholic Othmar Spann, which called for economic "corporations" dominated by employers to supplant the democratically elected parliament, and he argued that the Lateran Treaties of 1929 demonstrated the Vatican's sympathy for Italian Fascism. Brüning adhered to the social theory developed by the People's League for Catholic Germany that labeled itself "solidarism" in opposition to Spann's "universalism." Solidarists taught that government should encourage reconciliation between the classes by delegating some of its regulatory powers to the voluntary associations of management and labor, but that political control must always reside in a parliament based on universal suffrage. The solidarists eventually gained dominant influence over the drafting

53 *Kabinette Brüning*, meetings of 5 and 13 June 1930, I:191–92, 195; Luther to von Guérard, 26 July, reply of 16 August, and chancellery memorandum of 9 September 1930, BAK R43I/898/266–69, 360–64; Grübler, *Spitzenverbände*, pp. 182–83; Balderston, *German Economic Crisis*, pp. 296–98.
54 *Zentrumsprotokolle*, 16 June 1930, p. 453; compare Schwerin von Krosigk, *Staatsbankrott*, pp. 65–66.

of *Quadragesimo anno* (issued in May 1931), but in his American exile Brüning later reproached Pope Pius XI bitterly for having criticized the Italian Fascist syndicates in language so subtle and ambiguous as to encourage Thyssen's sinister caricature of Catholic social teaching.[55]

2.2. Brüning's Test of Strength with the SPD

Although Brüning maintained a studied silence on the point, a revival of the Great Coalition was a natural corollary of his efforts to promote consensus between management and labor, and Silverberg and Hans von Raumer certainly hoped for such a revival. Silverberg told the RDI leadership on 25 June that it had been "the worst of mistakes to release Social Democracy from responsibility by toppling Hilferding," but he feared that the SPD would now refuse any invitation to reenter the cabinet because the fiscal crisis had become so acute.[56] Brüning apparently responded to the resignation of Moldenhauer with a discreet query to Breitscheid about the prospects for an understanding with the SPD. His every feeler to Social Democrats was immediately reported to the President in an unfavorable light, however, and Brüning concluded that Schleicher's agents in military intelligence kept him under constant surveillance. The chancellor's belief that his phone was tapped and mail opened struck some colleagues as paranoid, but he did have at least one aide, Erwin Planck (son of the physicist Max), who reported to Schleicher regularly behind his back.[57] The hostile attitude of Schleicher and Hindenburg certainly limited Brüning's contacts with the SPD.

Otto Braun encouraged Brüning nevertheless to hope that the Social Democrats might approve an enabling act to grant the cabinet legislative powers to deal with the fiscal crisis, similar to those granted Chancellor Marx in 1923/4, so

---

55 Brüning, Detroit lecture of 7 December 1941, p. 8, HUG FP 93.45; Brüning, *Memoiren*, p. 136; lecture by Bernhard Otte in Josef van der Velden, ed., *Die berufsständische Ordnung. Idee und praktische Möglichkeiten* (Cologne, 1932), pp. 89–102; Heinrich Busshoff, "Berufsständisches Gedankengut zu Beginn der 30er Jahre in Österreich und Deutschland," *Zeitschrift für Politik*, 13 (1966): 451–63; Emil Ritter, *Die katholisch-soziale Bewegung Deutschlands im neunzehnten Jahrhundert und der Volksverein* (Cologne, 1954), pp. 396–97, 421–35, 468–70; Gotthard Klein, *Der Volksverein für das katholische Deutschland 1890–1933. Geschichte, Bedeutung, Untergang* (Paderborn, 1996), pp. 285–94; Klaus-Peter Hoepke, *Die deutsche Rechte und der italienische Faschismus* (Düsseldorf, 1968), pp. 79–95; Oswald Nell-Breuning, "Octogesimo anno," in *Wie sozial ist die Kirche? Leistung und Versagen der katholischen Soziallehre* (Düsseldorf, 1972), pp. 116–36; Pope Pius XI, *After Forty Years* (New York, 1931), esp. pp. 37–38.

56 RDI Präsidum und Vorstand, 25 June 1930, NL Silverberg/230/98–99 (partially published in *Quellen: Politik und Wirtschaft*, I:255–56); Silverberg to Duisberg, 16 June 1930, NL Silverberg/268/179–81; Neebe, *Grossindustrie*, pp. 68–72.

57 See Gattineau to Carl Duisberg, 18 June, and Blank to Reusch, 19 June 1930, *Quellen: Politik und Wirtschaft*, I:242; Regierungsrat Hesse to Hermann Dietrich, 10 June 1930, NL Dietrich/320/187–89; exchange between Marx and Brüning, *Zentrumsprotokolle*, 24 June 1930, p. 458; and Brüning, *Memoiren*, pp. 396–98. Hans Schäffer believed Brüning's story about the phone taps, but Planck vehemently denied it (conversation of 2 September 1932, NL Schäffer/22/830–31); see also Arnold Brecht, "Gedanken über Brünings Memoiren," pp. 624–27, and Schwerin von Krosigk, *Staatsbankrott*, p. 64.

Brüning sought a new finance minister congenial to the left. He first offered the job to the Prussian finance minister, Höpker-Aschoff of the DDP, but was compelled to withdraw the offer when he demanded major reductions in the military budget. Brüning then decided to appoint Hermann Dietrich, and they agreed to appease the SPD by imposing a levy of 3 percent on civil service salaries (later reduced to 2.5%) and an income tax surcharge of 5 percent on annual incomes above 8,400 marks. They also proposed some restrictions on entitlements, mainly the elimination of unemployment insurance benefits for sixteen-year-olds, but Dietrich promised the Social Democrats not to reduce jobless benefits through emergency decree.[58] Stegerwald, Wirth, and Hilferding then warned the chancellor that the SPD would oppose any enabling act as a "declaration of bankruptcy by parliamentarism" but might well vote for the budget itself with slight modifications. Brüning therefore decided to present his budget in the normal course of legislation with the threat to implement it by presidential decree if it was rejected. Stegerwald and Wirth requested time for further negotiations with the SPD, but Brüning and all other leaders of the Center Party agreed that they must act promptly to prevent a cash-flow crisis and the collapse of government authority. The cabinet approved this plan on 25 June in a major step toward confrontation with the Reichstag.[59]

Brüning's resolve was strengthened on 28 June by an impressive victory in the Reichsrat. Brüning imbued its proceedings with unaccustomed drama when he appeared in person to plead that his tax increases offered the only chance to restore the credit of the Reich and finance public works or farm aid. Vigorous support came from Otto Braun and Brüning's party colleague, Eugen Bolz of Württemberg, and the government budget passed by the impressive margin of 56 to 9. This vote increased the cabinet's prestige and reassured Brüning that his policy was objectively correct. He told party colleagues soon thereafter that "he would not consider another program. One must not be distracted by reports of the decisions of other parties. He held fast to his program and would see it through."[60] The chancellor was reverting to the personal qualities essential for success as a company commander in the Great War.

Brüning did modify his program in one unfortunate respect under pressure from the liberal parties. In the Saxon state elections of 22 June, the Nazis increased their share of the vote dramatically from 5 percent in 1929 to 14 percent at the expense of the DDP, DVP, and DNVP. This result offered the first solid evidence that Hitler posed a major threat to democracy, although the

58 Otto Meissner's reports to the vacationing President Hindenburg, 21 and 23 June 1930, BAP R601/19721/vol. 46/105–08; *Kabinette Brüning*, 24 June 1930, I:219–24; Schäffer diary, 24 June 1930, in *Quellen: Politik und Wirtschaft*, I:249–52; Pünder, *Politik*, 1 July 1930, p. 56.

59 Schäffer diary, 24–25 June 1930, *Quellen: Politik und Wirtschaft*, I:251–54; cabinet meetings of 24–25 June 1930, *Kabinette Brüning*, I:225–31, 235–39; *Zentrumsprotokolle*, 24 June 1930, p. 458; Schulz, *Von Brüning zu Hitler*, p. 104.

60 "Appell des Reichskanzlers," *Der Deutsche*, 29 June 1930, #150; report by Württemberg's ambassador to the Reich, 28 June 1930, *Quellen: Politik und Wirtschaft*, I:264–70; Pünder, *Politik*, 3 July 1930, p. 56; *Zentrumsprotokolle*, 3 July 1930, pp. 461–62 (source of quotation).

lesson was obscured by the fact that the party of Hugenberg lost the most ground.[61] Ernst Scholz saw all his old fears confirmed that the DVP would collapse if it abandoned its categorical opposition to tax increases, and he denounced Brüning to the DVP central committee for abandoning his original "bourgeois economic and fiscal policy." Many veterans of the Democratic Party concluded that it was no longer viable and must merge with the DVP in a united liberal front, so on 4 July both liberal Reichstag delegations rejected Dietrich's levy on civil servants, demanding ruthless budget cuts instead. The only new tax Scholz would accept was a poll tax (*Kopfsteuer*) for balancing municipal budgets, an assessment of an equal amount on each citizen designed to inflict such pain on the voters that city councils would slash their outlay (similar to the "community charge" that later caused the fall of Margaret Thatcher).[62] Brüning agreed that something must be done eventually to impose more fiscal discipline on the cities but understood that this harshly regressive tax would antagonize the SPD. He could hardly invoke Article 48 in favor of a budget supported only by the Center Party, however, so the chancellor reluctantly endorsed the poll tax on 8 July, reserving the right to graduate it slightly in proportion to income.[63]

Schleicher, Treviranus, and Martin Schiele exhorted Brüning to look to the right for parliamentary support, arguing that the poll tax would help Westarp to rally a majority against Hugenberg in the DNVP. Stegerwald, Wirth, Dietrich, and Curtius were no less emphatic in urging accommodation with the SPD. Stegerwald even threatened to resign over the poll tax.[64] On 9 July Brüning restored consensus within the cabinet by predicting that the mere threat to invoke Article 48 would secure a Reichstag majority with at least thirty votes from the DNVP, a reckoning that apparently assumed numerous abstentions by moderate Social Democrats. Brüning concluded with the following appeal:

> The current cabinet was not formed in order to pursue normal political maneuvers under all circumstances, but has assumed the task of using all legal means to implement the measures it perceived to be necessary. . . . The whole cabinet is doomed to failure even if just one single cabinet member should seek to avoid following through with all the steps necessary to this end.

The chancellor asked whether anyone present refused to follow him into the decisive battle, and a deep silence filled the room.[65]

61 Falter et al., *Wahlen*, p. 108; Jones, *German Liberalism*, pp. 362–65; Harsch, *Social Democracy*, p. 76.
62 DVP Zentralvorstand, 4 July 1930, BAK R45II/46/49–59; *Kabinette Brüning*, meeting with party leaders, 4 July 1930, I:255–58; Werner Schneider, *Deutsche Demokratische Partei*, pp. 199–200, 250–55.
63 Brüning, "Arbeit der Zentrumspartei," pp. 377–78, 386–87; *Kabinette Brüning*, meeting with party leaders, 8 July 1930, I:275–79; Schäffer diary, 8 July 1930, NL Schäffer/9/176–82.
64 Schleicher to Groener, 7 July 1930, NL Schleicher/77/105; *Kabinette Brüning*, 9 July 1930, I:284–86; Bredt, *Erinnerungen*, p. 228; Keil, *Erlebnisse*, II:388; Curtius, *Sechs Jahre*, pp. 164–65.
65 *Kabinette Brüning*, I:289–93; Schäffer diary, 9 July 1930, NL Schäffer/9/182–83.

Brüning then decided to ignore a fairly promising overture from the SPD. Breitscheid and Hermann Müller told him on 11 July that their party could never tolerate the poll tax but would accept Dietrich's original budget if the reform of unemployment insurance was postponed until the fall. Breitscheid sought out Dietrich the next day to emphasize his flexibility, promising "that agreement with the Social Democratic delegation can doubtless be reached even if it does not enter the government."[66] Wirth renewed his call for more negotiations with the SPD, but Brüning and all the other ministers believed that the Social Democrats were bound to insist on at least one concession that would drive the DVP and moderate conservatives into opposition. On 14 July the cabinet therefore authorized the chancellor to issue his budget as an emergency decree if the Reichstag rejected it, and to dissolve the Reichstag and hold new elections if it voted to rescind that decree. Brüning later acknowledged that Breitscheid had been reasonable, but he feared that further negotiations would anger Hindenburg and that "the majority of the SPD would in the end leave me in the lurch just as they had their own chancellor" on 27 March.[67] Brüning kept alive a chance for compromise nevertheless by notifying the cabinet that evening that the Center Party demanded a version of the poll tax including some graduation by income level. He reserved the right to introduce this amendment on the floor of the Reichstag the next day, and Wilhelm Keil later judged that the amended version might well have won the approval of the SPD. Brüning apparently exaggerated the opposition to the poll tax by his party colleagues as a pretext for a concession to the SPD, since the Center Reichstag delegation had just voted to endorse his budget without reservation.[68]

President Hindenburg ruined any chance of compromise with the SPD, unfortunately, by publishing a letter to Otto Braun on the morning of 15 July that denounced a long-standing police ban on Stahlhelm rallies in the Rhineland as "unjustified and contrary to the sense of the law." Hindenburg threatened not to attend the ceremonies to celebrate the end of French occupation in the Rhineland unless the Prussian government reversed itself. Brüning and Wirth had persuaded Braun to open negotiations with the Stahlhelm to avoid conflict with Hindenburg, but this letter took them by surprise. Protests by friends in the Stahlhelm had persuaded the President's son and adjutant, Oskar von Hindenburg, that the Prussian government was not negotiating in good faith, and he persuaded his father to publish this letter without consulting the cabinet.[69]

66 Pünder memorandum of 12 July 1930, *Kabinette Brüning*, I:302–03.
67 *Kabinette Brüning*, 14 July 1930, I:311–18; *Zentrumsprotokolle*, 14 July 1930, p. 468; Brüning to Andreas Dorpalen, 12 May 1957, HUG FP 93.10/Box 7/Andreas Dorpalen (source of quotation); Keil, *Erlebnisse*, II:393; Stampfer, *14 Jahre*, pp. 574–76.
68 *Kabinette Brüning*, I:311; Keil, *Erlebnisse*, II:393; *Zentrumsprotokolle*, 14 July 1930, p. 468.
69 Hindenburg to Otto Braun, 15 July 1930, *Ursachen und Folgen. Vom deutschen Zusammenbruch 1918 und 1945 bis zur staatlichen Neuordnung Deutschlands in der Gegenwart*, ed. Herbert Michaelis and Ernst Schraepler, 9 vols. (Berlin, n.d. [1958]), VIII:224–25; *Kabinette Brüning*, meeting of 15 July 1930, I:320–22; Pünder memorandum of July 1930, NL Pünder/30/64–66; Brüning, *Memoiren*, pp. 177–78; Wirth to Otto Braun, 22 July 1941, in Hagen Schulze, ed., "Dokumentation: Rückblick

This action probably resulted from a clever gambit by Oskar's friend Schleicher to drive a wedge between Brüning and the SPD. Someone started a rumor on the morning of 15 July that Brüning had written Hindenburg's letter and intended to form a new government in Prussia with the DNVP. Assuming that the chancellor must have co-authored such an important presidential declaration, Otto Braun agreed to lift the Stahlhelm ban but showered Hindenburg and Brüning with reproaches when he conferred with them that afternoon. Breitscheid meanwhile notified the Center Party that Hindenburg's letter and the rumors about Brüning's complicity had angered his Reichstag delegation. He wanted the SPD to abstain in the budget vote but requested an adjournment of the Reichstag so that he could reason with his followers. Brüning refused, insisting on a prompt resolution of the crisis.[70]

Brüning quarreled sharply with the Social Democrats when the Reichstag reconvened in the late afternoon of 15 July. The chancellor threatened to invoke Article 48, arguing that the German people demanded swift action to eliminate the "stifling feeling of uncertainty." Keil replied sternly that Article 48 was never intended "for the salvation of a government that has miscalculated." Employing it to enact laws rejected by the Reichstag would amount to "suspending the constitution." Breitscheid even echoed the Communist Party line the next morning; if the government carried out its threat, he declared, this would represent "a step toward a German version of fascism."[71] On 16 July the Reichstag rejected the budget by a vote of 193 to 256, with the entire SPD delegation and a majority of the Nationalists in opposition. Within the cabinet Wirth agreed with the SPD that Article 48 could not be invoked to issue a law rejected by the Reichstag, but Brüning and Pünder discerned no such prohibition in the constitution. The government avoided a clear stand on this point by modifying the budget slightly before it was issued as an emergency decree. When the SPD promptly introduced a bill to rescind that decree, a dangerous test of strength had begun.[72]

Negotiations with the DNVP offered the last opportunity to avoid dissolving the Reichstag. Brüning thought that Nationalists would admire his decision to invoke Article 48, and he assumed that their heavy losses in Saxony would make them reluctant to face national elections. Hugenberg felt strangely

auf Weimar. Ein Briefwechsel zwischen Otto Braun und Joseph Wirth im Exil," *Vierteljahrshefte für Zeitgeschichte*, 26 (1978): 169–70; Berghahn, *Der Stahlhelm*, pp. 147–52; Schulze, *Otto Braun*, pp. 631–33; Schulz, *Von Brüning zu Hitler*, pp. 110–14.

70 *Zentrumsprotokolle*, 15 July 1930, pp. 469–70; Otto Braun, *Von Weimar zu Hitler*, pp. 300–303; Brüning, *Memoiren*, pp. 178–79; Schulze, *Otto Braun*, pp. 633–35; Winkler, *Katastrophe*, pp. 165–69. Schleicher knew that the President's letter would strike a raw nerve in the SPD because Breitscheid had sent Brüning a sharp complaint against performances by army bands at Stahlhelm rallies, which the chancellor had just forwarded to the defense ministry for investigation: see Breitscheid to Brüning, 7 July, and Groener to Pünder, 25 July 1930, BAK R43I/688/13–14, 44.

71 *Verhandlungen des Reichstags*, 428/6373–75; Keil, *Erlebnisse*, II:391.

72 Winkler, *Katastrophe*, pp. 169–70; cabinet minutes of 24 June and 14 and 16 July 1930, and Pünder memorandum of 12 July, *Kabinette Brüning*, I:225–26, 303–04, 313–16, 322–25.

confident, however, because his predictions of economic catastrophe were coming true.[73] On 17 July Hugenberg approached Brüning with an offer to adjourn the Reichstag until the fall, postponing all difficult decisions, if the Center Party immediately toppled Otto Braun. The chancellor replied that he had no authority to negotiate the fate of the Prussian coalition. When Hugenberg reported this answer to party colleagues, Otto Schmidt-Hannover denounced Brüning as the "Kerensky" of the right who must be toppled in "the second revolution." Hugenberg then won a majority of 30 to 25 in favor of supporting the SPD's bill, a decision that drove the Westarp group out of the party but doomed the government to defeat. Brüning lost by seven votes on 18 July because Hugenberg retained the support of a narrow majority in his delegation, while Otto Braun and most other SPD moderates voted against the government. The chancellor dissolved the Reichstag and scheduled new elections for 14 September.[74]

Brüning's actions in July 1930 have been widely criticized. Despite Breitscheid's heated rhetoric, most historians agree that the chancellor's application of Article 48 was constitutional, and it won endorsement at the time from all the most prominent legal scholars. The most serious criticism questions the wisdom of Brüning's decision to abandon efforts to reach a budget compromise with the SPD.[75] The critics tend, however, to neglect the crucial political problem facing the government. By now any concessions to the SPD would almost undoubtedly drive the DVP, Business Party, Christian Nationalist Peasants' Party, and the BVP into the opposition. The leaders of all parties to the right of the Center believed that they faced extinction if they compromised the material interests of their constituents, and they did not care enough about the principle of parliamentary democracy to make sacrifices for its sake. Only tangible evidence that political instability harmed the economy, such as a run on the mark or a sharp increase of interest rates, could still impel these parties to compromise. Unfortunately, July 1930 happened to be a moment of calm on international financial

---

73 *Kabinette Brüning,* 14 July 1930, I:312; DNVP circular by Hans Brosius, "Die politische Lage," 25 June 1930, BAP/DNVP/16/97–99; DNVP Reichstagsfraktion, 2 July 1930, *Quellen: Politik und Wirtschaft,* I:272–73; Leopold, *Alfred Hugenberg,* pp. 75–79.

74 DNVP Reichstagsfraktion, 17 July 1930, *Quellen: Politik und Wirtschaft,* I:286–99; Pünder memorandum of 19 July 1930, Hugenberg's open letter to Brüning of October 1930, and cabinet meeting of 14 October to discuss Hugenberg's charges, *Kabinette Brüning,* I:326–29, 536–39; Brüning, *Memoiren,* pp. 180–81; Schulz, *Von Brüning zu Hitler,* pp. 115–17; Winkler, *Katastrophe,* pp. 173–78. To emphasize Hugenberg's stubbornness, Brüning later asserted that he had offered to create a rightist coalition in Prussia if the DNVP joined the Reich cabinet, but the contemporary accounts of Pünder and Hugenberg agree that the chancellor refused to discuss this demand. Contrast Orlow, *Weimar Prussia 1925–1933,* pp. 197–99.

75 See Scheuner, "Anwendung des Art. 48," pp. 262–64, 274–79; Achim Kurz, "Zur Interpretation des Artikels 48 Abs. 2 WRV 1930–33," and Thomas Wisser, "Die Diktaturmassnahmen im Juli 1930 – Autoritäre Umwandlung der Demokratie?" in Rolf Grawert et al., eds., *Offene Staatlichkeit. Festschrift für Ernst-Wolfgang Böckenförde zum 65. Geburtstag* (Berlin, 1995), pp. 398–402, 415–34; Bracher, *Auflösung,* pp. 299–303; Mommsen, "Staat und Bürokratie," pp. 101–02; and Winkler, *Katastrophe,* pp. 160–78.

markets and falling interest rates in Germany. Thus the dissolution of this Reichstag was probably inevitable.[76]

Finance Minister Dietrich set the altruistic tone for the campaign by Brüning's supporters in his last speech to the old Reichstag. He could tolerate no more negotiations with the party leaders, Dietrich declared, because "everyone is just trying to cook his own soup and make sure he doesn't lose any voters":

> It is of decisive importance that we accept the necessary measures demanded of us by the state. A people like the German, which still spends many billions on tobacco and beer, must be able to close such a gap in its finances. . . . We must make an end to the politics of the special interests, which make it impossible to preserve the state. The question comes down to this: Are we Germans just a heap of special interests or a true nation [*ein Interessenhaufen oder ein Staatsvolk*]?[77]

Dietrich soon emerged as the most dynamic campaigner among left liberals. His campaign speeches defended the Weimar constitution, unemployment insurance, and free enterprise unhampered by trusts and cartels, coming closer to Brüning in spirit than those of any other party leader. Dietrich also achieved the only practical step toward liberal unity in 1930 by arranging with his cabinet colleague, Julius Curtius, for joint tickets uniting the remnants of the DDP and DVP in Baden and Württemberg.[78]

Despite this altruistic rhetoric, the cabinet modified its budget substantially to give the government parties a better campaign platform. The budget finally issued by decree on 26 July included a reduction of 5 percent in civil service salaries, cuts in government pensions, a version of the poll tax that was only mildly regressive, and authorization for the economics ministry to dissolve cartels that did not lower their prices. Dietrich wanted to dissolve all cartels immediately, but Hans Schäffer persuaded him that this would be too drastic. Schätzel of the BVP opposed the new budget for its concessions to the left, but Wilhelm Groener replied that now "the primary task of the government is to conduct the elections." The cabinet also proclaimed that it would carry out public works on a grand scale, and Brüning spoke of a billion-mark program on the campaign trail. The government could raise only about 180 million marks in new credits, however, beyond the 250 million raised in June.[79] To maximize the impact of this modest expenditure on the labor market, the cabinet required that firms utilize domestic materials whenever possible and not resort to overtime to fill these

---

76 See Conze, "Die politischen Entscheidungen," pp. 214–17; Schulz, *Von Brüning zu Hitler*, pp. 117–18; Jones, *German Liberalism*, pp. 358–67; Döhn, *Politik und Interesse*, pp. 362–94; Schönhoven, *BVP*, pp. 240–50, 272–77; and Balderston, *German Economic Crisis*, pp. 302–09.

77 *Verhandlungen des Reichstags*, 18 July 1930, 428/6514–15.

78 See the "Aufruf der Deutschen Staatspartei!" and Dietrich's Karlsruhe campaign speech of 4 August 1930, NL Dietrich/222/29–36; Adelheid von Saldern, *Hermann Dietrich. Ein Staatsmann der Weimarer Republik* (Boppard am Rhein, 1966), p. 110; and Jones, *German Liberalism*, pp. 399–401.

79 Decree published in *Ursachen und Folgen*, VIII:54–70; Schäffer diary, 19 July 1930, NL Schäffer/9/190–91; *Kabinette Brüning*, 24 July 1930, I:334–36 (source of quotation); Grübler, *Spitzenverbände*, pp. 179–83; Meister, *Grosse Depression*, p. 205.

contracts, and Brüning himself actually took time on the campaign trail to investigate rumors that these guidelines were being ignored.[80] The cabinet also angered big business in August by requiring substantial price reductions from any firm that accepted a government contract, regardless of its obligations under cartel agreements. The RDI opposed any effort to undermine cartels, but the Christian trade unions had long attacked them for raising prices during every boom without lowering them during recessions. Brüning, Dietrich, and Stegerwald always agreed that the government must pressure cartels and syndicates to lower their prices, if necessary with the threat of dissolution. This first blow against "bound prices" achieved little economic benefit – indeed, it may have slowed business activity somewhat by nurturing deflationary expectations – but they hoped mainly for political gains by demonstrating that the government was independent of the special interests.[81]

The cabinet's last-minute tinkering with the budget reflected fear above all of the SPD. In the election campaign that party denounced the Brüning cabinet as the "government of social reaction," the "most reactionary cabinet" since the fall of the monarchy; indeed, the SPD seems to have attacked Brüning more frequently and in harsher language than any other foe, even the Nazi Party. In part this stance was forced upon it by Communist attacks on the Social Democrats as collaborators with Brüning's "program to plunder the workers," but the SPD also nurtured misguided hopes for electoral gains among Catholic workers.[82] In response, the Christian trade unions and Catholic Workers' Clubs lumped the SPD together with the extremists in the Nationalist, Nazi, and Communist parties who demanded an impossible fiscal policy: "In the election of 1928 the majority of the German people chose parliamentarians who may not have slaughtered democracy but certainly allowed it to starve to death." Brüning's defenders also revived stale accusations from the 1890s against atheist propaganda in the Free Unions.[83] Thus the best defenders of democracy were locked in a fratricidal struggle as the Nazi propaganda machine entered high gear.

Brüning himself avoided polemics but campaigned tirelessly in dozens of rallies. He was not an inspiring orator but offered Centrist voters an eminently

---

80 Stegerwald's summary of the rules governing public works, 21 June 1930, BAK R43I/898/146–48; Pünder to the ministries of labor, transport, and post, 12 August, and replies of 14 and 16 August 1930, BAK R43I/898/344–45, 357–58.
81 See *Konzentration, Rationalisierung und Sozialpolitik. Berichte und Entschliessungen des 4. Kongresses des Internationalen Bundes der christlichen Gewerkschaften, München, September 1928* (Utrecht, 1928), pp. 8–21; Michael Schneider, *Christliche Gewerkschaften,* p. 683; RDI Kartellstelle circulars of 29 July and 14 August 1930, NL Silverberg/346/148–55, 165–89; chancellor's reception for RDI leaders, 4 August 1930, *Kabinette Brüning,* I:355–59; RDI to Brüning, 1 September 1930, NL Silverberg/346/208–13; Grübler, *Spitzenverbände,* pp. 175–78, 183–85; James, *German Slump,* pp. 154–56.
82 Keil, *Erlebnisse,* II:393–94; KPD circular to party locals, 17 July 1930, *Quellen: Generallinie,* pp. 193–95; ADGB election manifesto of 16 August 1930, *Quellen: Gewerkschaften,* pp. 120–22; Harsch, *Social Democracy,* pp. 79–85; Winkler, *Katastrophe,* pp. 179–83.
83 *Zentralblatt der christlichen Gewerkschaften,* 1 August 1930, p. 233 (source of quotation); *Westdeutsche Arbeiter-Zeitung,* 27 September 1930, p. 236; Bernhard Otte circular to the Christian trade unions, 20 August 1930, BAK Kleine Erwerbung 461/2/108–10.

reasonable case, designed primarily to refute the charges of the SPD. The Reich budget must be balanced because any deficit would prevent the government from borrowing money for public works, undermine the credit of private enterprise as well, and jeopardize the funding of welfare benefits. Every war for the past century had been followed by a major economic crisis, so recriminations over which party, interest group, or provision of the Weimar constitution should be blamed for the depression were ridiculous. The constitution did not require any amendment, Brüning declared, but German politicians must renounce their habit of making vital decisions in small, secret conferences among the leaders of the Reichstag delegations:

> Just one thing is necessary: the cabinet must take the lead and not the parties. That is what we have lacked in recent years. The cabinet must accept responsibility and then submit to decisions made in open debate on the floor of the Reichstag. Only in this way can we define responsibility clearly as the foundation of democracy. The time has come to make the last effort to save a genuinely responsible democracy and make it viable on the basis of the present constitution.

Thus Brüning wanted to make German parliamentary practice conform more closely to British precedent, but the only institutional reform he proposed was an amendment to the Reichstag's rules of order, which could be changed by a simple majority, to require that any proposal for new expenditure specify the source of funding, an idea proposed already by Finance Minister Hilferding in 1929. "I want to say clearly and emphatically," Brüning concluded in a Cologne rally, "that this is no struggle against parliament but rather a struggle for the salvation of parliament!"[84] On 11 August the chancellor interrupted his campaign to preside over the official ceremony commemorating the anniversary of the Weimar constitution; here he could not match the eloquence of Interior Minister Wirth, but he did praise the constitution for having contributed greatly to the spread of patriotism through all classes.[85]

Brüning has gained the reputation of a bloodless technocrat, but he proved an effective campaigner. He forged unprecedented unity among all factions of the Center Party, achieved close cooperation with the BVP as well, and enjoyed unprecedented success as a fund-raiser. Even Ruhr heavy industry, which had always given its largest contributions to the DVP and DNVP in the past, decided in July 1930 that the Center Party should receive as large a subsidy as any other.[86]

---

84 "Der Kanzler rechnet mit der Sozialdemokratie ab," *Der Deutsche*, 31 July 1930, #177; Cologne speech of 8 August 1930, Brüning, *Reden*, pp. 54–64. For Hilferding's reform program of March 1929, see *Kabinett Müller II*, I:496–97, and Schwerin von Krosigk, *Staatsbankrott*, pp. 51–52.
85 "Verfassungsfeier der Reichsregierung," *Der Deutsche*, 12 August 1930, #187.
86 Pünder memorandum of 14 August 1930 and petitions to the chancellor from industrial associations, NL Pünder/158/174–81; Brüning, *Memoiren*, pp. 134–45; Morsey, "Deutsche Zentrumspartei," pp. 295–96, 420–21; Hömig, *Das preussische Zentrum*, pp. 234–36; Schönhoven, *Bayerische Volkspartei*, pp. 249–55; Altendorfer, *Fritz Schäffer*, pp. 560–61; Martin Blank to Fritz Springorum, 29 July 1930, *Quellen: Politik und Wirtschaft*, I:339–40; Neebe, *Grossindustrie*, pp. 73–76; Henry A. Turner, *German Big Business and the Rise of Hitler* (Oxford and New York, 1985), pp. 105–07.

During this campaign Brüning also began to achieve genuine popularity among Catholic voters, who were impressed by reports of his ascetic lifestyle, donation of large portions of his salary to charity, and refusal to use his official limousine for anything but government business (he took a taxi to go shopping). Many Catholics regarded Brüning as the epitome of the "Christian statesman," not because he invoked religion in his speeches, but because he had mastered all selfish impulses and thought only of the problems facing the people.[87] Brüning cultivated this image through extraordinarily grim poses for photographers; he was usually seen working at his desk with jaw clenched in a grimace of patriotic resolve. The Center Party waged its campaign entirely on the platform of defending Brüning, and this platform generated unprecedented enthusiasm. The party held far more rallies with larger audiences than it had in any election since 1919; in Düsseldorf, for example, it held 46 rallies with a total attendance of 28,000 in 1928, but 128 rallies for 127,000 supporters in 1930. The Center and BVP won 528,000 more votes in September 1930 than they had in 1928. Because of a massive upsurge in voter participation, their share of the national vote dipped slightly from 15.2 to 14.8 percent, but this was a remarkable achievement when every other party between the Nazis and Communists suffered massive defections. Despite its sharp attacks on the government, the SPD lost 580,000 votes.[88] Thus Brüning won his test of strength with the Social Democrats.

Brüning obviously could not win the election, however, without a strong showing by the new parties of the moderate right, and here the campaign developed into a comedy of errors. Some of Brüning's Protestant admirers hoped that he would resign from the Center Party to found a new "State Party" for both Catholics and Protestants, reviving the Essen Program of 1920. Unfortunately, the same personality traits that won admiration for Brüning among pious Catholics struck agnostics and casual Protestants as peculiar – Friedrich Stampfer later recalled that "every cheerful conversation ceased when he entered the room, as if a strict young priest had encountered a group of high-spirited boys."[89] Devout Protestants, moreover, often displayed virulent distrust of ultramontane influences. In Siegen, for example, a Protestant group very close to the chancellor in its social program listed "the power of the Roman Church" alongside "godless Bolshevism," "mammonistic capitalism," and "power-hungry

---

87 Morsey, "Deutsche Zentrumspartei," pp. 291–95; Beer, *Heinrich Brüning*, pp. 68–71; Nobel, *Brüning*, pp. 83–84; Theoderich Kampmann, "Brüning, oder die deutsche Mitte," in Vernekohl, ed., *Brüning*, pp. 41–55 (first published in June 1932); Josef Hofmann, *Erinnerungen*, pp. 60–63.

88 See Falter et al., *Wahlen*, pp. 41, 71–72; Wolfgang Stump, *Geschichte und Organisation der Zentrumspartei in Düsseldorf, 1917–1933* (Düsseldorf, 1971), pp. 75–85; Kaufmann, *Münster*, pp. 123–25; Herbert Kühr, *Parteien und Wahlen im Stadt- und Landkreis Essen in der Zeit der Weimarer Republik* (Düsseldorf, 1973), pp. 68–71, 87; Günter Plum, *Gesellschaftsstruktur und politisches Bewusstsein in einer katholischen Region 1928–1933. Untersuchung am Beispiel des Regierungsbezirks Aachen* (Stuttgart, 1972), pp. 124–33; and Jürgen Aretz, *Katholische Arbeiterbewegung und Nationalsozialismus. Der Verband katholischer Arbeiter- und Knappenvereine Westdeutschlands, 1923–1945* (Mainz, 1978), pp. 49–58.

89 Ullmann, *Publizist*, pp. 133–34; R. R. Beer, "Rückschau," in Vernekohl, ed., *Brüning*, pp. 101–02; Stampfer, *14 Jahre*, pp. 567–68.

fascism" as the four sinister forces that threatened to overwhelm the German people. President Hindenburg enjoyed far more influence among such Protestants than Brüning, but he wanted "to stand above the parties," so the DNVP could argue without contradiction that it was the party closest to Hindenburg's ideals.[90]

Efforts to promote consolidation among the parties of the moderate right failed miserably. By May 1930 three new parties had emerged that each included a few hundred activists among Brüning's Protestant trade union colleagues – the Christian Social People's Service, the Popular Conservative Federation founded by Treviranus and Walther Lambach, and the Popular Nationalist Federation, the political arm of the paramilitary Young German Order. Brüning and the leaders of the DGB hoped to promote the fusion of these parties with the Westarp group from the DNVP into "a broad-based conservative party in which Protestant workers can find a home just as Catholic workers have found a home in the Center Party."[91] Westarp did join Treviranus at the end of July to found the Conservative People's Party, but most of the twenty-nine Reichstag delegates who followed him out of the DNVP joined the Christian Nationalist Peasants' Party instead, which subordinated all other considerations to the material interests of farmers. Agriculture Minister Schiele and the "Tory democrat" Hans von Schlange-Schöningen, the former provincial chairman of the DNVP in Pomerania, accepted Reichstag mandates from this party and tried to persuade it to support Brüning, but the swelling popularity of the Nazi Party in the countryside made it very difficult for Christian Nationalists to do so. Schiele also undermined the coherence of the government parties' campaign by attacking the constitution that Brüning defended.[92]

Germany's leading industrialists meanwhile threatened to withhold all campaign contributions in order to promote a merger of the two liberal parties with the Business Party, but this project also failed because of personal rivalries and the growing unpopularity of big business. The leaders of these three parties devoted much of their energy during the campaign to denouncing each other for the failure to achieve "bourgeois union."[93] The Christian Social People's Service ignored these fusion talks, urging true Christians to champion morally correct policies without concern for the political consequences. Its leaders supported Brüning's ideal of social partnership enthusiastically, but their biblical fundamentalism enjoyed limited appeal in Germany.[94] The only real step toward con-

---

90 Campaign leaflet of the "Evangelische Volksdienst" (the Westphalian branch of the Christian Social People's Service), BAK Kleine Erwerbung 461/6/228–29; Brüning, *Memoiren*, pp. 183–84; Conze, "Die politischen Entscheidungen," pp. 218–19; Dorpalen, *Hindenburg*, pp. 190–94.

91 *Der Deutsche*, 25 July 1930, #172; Patch, *Christian Trade Unions*, pp. 147–53, 164–66.

92 Jones, "Agrarian Splinter Parties," pp. 208–15; Gessner, *Agrarverbände*, pp. 235–46; Jonas, *Volkskonservativen*, pp. 84–86; Dorpalen, *Hindenburg*, pp. 194–96.

93 Jones, *German Liberalism*, pp. 366–91; Turner, *Big Business*, pp. 107–10; Werner Schneider, *Deutsche Demokratische Partei*, pp. 126–41; Schumacher, *Mittelstandsfront*, pp. 140–55.

94 Günter Opitz, *Der Christlich-soziale Volksdienst* (Düsseldorf, 1969), pp. 149–64; Beer, "Rückschau," in Vernekohl, ed., *Brüning*, pp. 117–18.

solidation occurred in May 1930 when the leaders of the Democratic Party and the Young German Order merged their organizations in a new "State Party." DDP activists soon noted with dismay, however, that the Young Germans displayed the monarchist flag, excluded Jews from their order, and employed ancient Teutonic names for the months of the year. The State Party polled a disappointing 3.8 percent of the national vote in September and soon lost its Young German component amid a welter of recriminations over this defeat.[95]

The result of all this maneuvering was that Brüning's allies campaigned in no fewer than eight different parties that often attacked each other. Brüning and Hindenburg pinned their greatest hopes on the Conservative People's Party, but it never developed inner cohesion or popular appeal. Westarp even resented the "people's party" label as implicit criticism of the old Conservative Party. Treviranus and Lambach insisted that the party platform endorse trade unionism and Germany's existing welfare programs, but this decision cost them financial support from the business community. The party's leaders made little effort to found party locals and apparently assumed that the goodwill of Hindenburg and the defense ministry guaranteed a respectable measure of success.[96] At the eleventh hour friends alerted Hermann Pünder to the crucial importance of defending the government's record against the vicious distortions of the Nazi Party, and they persuaded him that it would be proper to expend the taxpayers' money for this purpose. But little was done by the chancellery or interior ministry to influence this campaign.[97] On 14 September the parties supporting Brüning together captured only 193 of 577 Reichstag seats. The Nazis emerged as the spectacular winners, with over 18 percent of the vote and 107 seats, while the Communist share rose from 10.6 to 13.1 percent. The SPD sank from 29 to 24.5 percent, and the Conservative People's Party scored a miserable 291,000 votes and three seats. The only bright spot from the government's perspective was an unexpected success by the Christian Social People's Service with fourteen seats.[98]

Some analysts have argued that Brüning must have anticipated the Nazi landslide when he dissolved the Reichstag and must have desired it to intimidate the SPD. In retrospect it seems obvious, if one extrapolates from the results of the five state elections of 1929/30, that the Nazis would win about 18 percent in September.[99] Such calculations apparently did influence Groener, Schleicher, and Treviranus. They supported Brüning's effort to seek a parliamentary majority ranging from the Reichslandbund to the Democrats but anticipated its failure.

95 Jones, *German Liberalism*, pp. 369–72, 379–83; Klaus Hornung, *Der Jungdeutsche Orden* (Düsseldorf, 1958), pp. 92–109.
96 Bernhard Leopold to Westarp, 21 July 1930, and reply of 16 August, NL Westarp; Martin Blank memorandum of 21 July 1930, *Quellen: Politik und Wirtschaft*, I:305–06; Jonas, *Volkskonservativen*, pp. 79–86, 137–38.
97 See Adolf Kempkes to Pünder, 29 August, reply of 3 September, and Pünder to Wirth, 3 September 1930, BAP/R15.01/13129.3/164–69.
98 Childers, *Nazi Voter*, pp. 140–42; Falter et al., *Wahlen*, pp. 44–60.
99 Bracher, *Auflösung*, p. 307; Falter, *Hitlers Wähler*, pp. 33–36.

They consoled themselves with the thought that an influx of radicals into the Reichstag would compel Brüning to stop negotiating with the party leaders and simply dissolve parliament if it opposed him. The election returns left Treviranus and Schleicher strangely cheerful because they anticipated a pure form of "presidential" government in future.[100] Brüning himself, on the other hand, probably believed what he told journalists during the campaign, that the clear-sighted German people would reward the government for its unprecedented honesty and realism. He also told party colleagues in private that the goal of their campaign was "the creation of a parliament that is conscious of its responsibilities."[101] These hopes gain some plausibility when one recalls that the only impressive successes by the Nazis to date had come in two states famous for unpredictable voter behavior, Saxony and Thuringia. Brüning and his closest advisers worried about the combined vote for Hitler and Hugenberg, moreover, not the Nazi vote in isolation, and the state elections gave them every reason to anticipate a major defeat for the DNVP. Even Hans Schäffer, who was more pessimistic than Brüning about Nazi prospects, predicted that the Nazis and the Conservative People's Party would each win thirty to forty seats, a result that would have left the combined strength of the Nazis and DNVP significantly weaker than it had been in 1929.[102]

In later years Brüning did sometimes claim to have foreseen the Nazi landslide, taking credit for an election brilliantly timed soon enough to preserve a fairly moderate Reichstag but late enough to avoid any need for further elections until 1934, by which time the economic crisis would have ended.[103] But his memoirs are more illuminating as they describe vividly his dismay when the moderate parties failed to coalesce, his indignation when employers and labor leaders poisoned the atmosphere through aggressive job actions, and his frustration on election eve when he could only issue a vague appeal for all Germans to vote because the feuding government parties watched jealously to see whether he supported one more than the others. Only on election day, when Brüning saw Nazi Stormtrooper (SA) detachments at every polling station, did he sense what was coming, and he stayed up all night to hear the disastrous results.[104] Brüning almost certainly did not engage in a cynical maneuver to place the revolver of

---

100 Groener to Gleich, 21 July 1930, NL Groener/7/#27; Martin Blank's report on a talk with Treviranus, 21 July 1930, *Quellen: Politik und Wirtschaft*, I:306–07; Schleicher to von der Schulenberg, 26 September 1930, in Vogelsang, *Reichswehr*, p. 415; Treviranus, *Exil*, p. 76.

101 *Zentrumsprotokolle*, 18 July 1930, p. 475; interview with Brüning in *Der Deutsche*, 6 September 1930, #209. Compare Ambassador Rumbold's report on a talk with Prussian State Secretary Weismann, 18 September 1930, *Documents on British Foreign Policy 1919–1939: Series II* (London, 1946–1957) (hereafter cited as *DBFP*), I:510.

102 Schäffer diary, 2 August 1930, *Quellen: Politik und Wirtschaft*, I:356–57; Besson, *Württemberg*, pp. 159–61; Conze, "Die politischen Entscheidungen," pp. 214–17; Schulz, *Von Brüning zu Hitler*, pp. 161–63.

103 Brüning to Arnold Brecht, 6 August 1944, in Brecht, *Kraft des Geistes*, p. 416; Brüning's Lowell Institute lecture of 1937/8 in Müller, *Brüning Papers*, pp. 208–10.

104 Brüning, *Memoiren*, pp. 183–86; compare Köhler, *Lebenserinnerungen*, pp. 300–301, and Pünder, *Politik in der Reichskanzlei*, 14 September 1930, pp. 58–59.

political radicalism at the SPD's temple; instead he over-estimated his ability to influence the voters.

Brüning has often been reproached for adopting policies that caused the radicalization of the electorate, but those policies played very little role in Nazi propaganda in 1930. The National Socialist German Workers' Party (NSDAP) actually supported Brüning's tax and tariff bill of April 1930, and Joseph Goebbels, who coordinated Nazi propaganda throughout Germany, instructed all party speakers during this election campaign to focus on the single question, "For or against Young?" Hitler too concentrated in his enormously popular campaign speeches on foreign enemies and the German politicians who had collaborated with them by advocating the Young Plan. Nazi leaders consistently avoided any mention of Chancellor Brüning or the specific measures recently adopted by the government.[105] Goebbels's strategy provides good insight into the actual motives of Nazi voters, because the NSDAP had developed sophisticated marketing techniques to adjust its message to consumer choices about which pamphlets to buy and which rallies to attend. Numerous local studies also indicate that the Nazi takeoff toward mass popularity began before Brüning took office, and that the NSDAP prospered most where it exploited nationalist sentiment among the middle classes with rallies linking all of Germany's problems to the "stab in the back" of November 1918, the "chains of Versailles," and alleged corruption in the socialist labor movement.[106]

The Communists focused much more than the Nazis on attacking Brüning but did not prosper nearly as well. The KPD generated the most powerful electoral appeal to the unemployed of any party through relentless attacks on Brüning's austerity measures.[107] KPD gains in the September vote came almost

---

105 Childers, *Nazi Voter*, pp. 137–59 (quotation on p. 138); Viktor Reimann, *Goebbels* (Garden City, N.Y., 1976), pp. 102–21; Ralf Georg Reuth, *Goebbels* (San Diego and New York, 1994), pp. 98–120; Peter Stachura, *Gregor Strasser and the Rise of Nazism* (London, 1983), pp. 73–83; Dietrich Orlow, *The History of the Nazi Party: 1919–1933* (Pittsburgh, 1969), pp. 174–87; Horst Gies, "NSDAP und landwirtschaftliche Organisationen in der Endphase der Weimarer Republik," *Vierteljahrshefte für Zeitgeschichte*, 15 (1967): 347–53; Joachim C. Fest, *Hitler. Eine Biographie* (Frankfurt a.M., 1973), pp. 374–400; Christian Hartmann, ed., *Hitler. Reden, Schriften, Anordnungen. Band III, Teil 3, Januar–September 1930* (Munich, 1995), esp. pp. 278–81, 323–26; confidential police reports on Hitler's Munich rally of 18 July and Essen rally of 15 August 1930, BAP R15.01/25790/118–19, 300–307.

106 William S. Allen, *The Nazi Seizure of Power: The Experience of a Single German Town 1922–1945*, rev. ed. (New York, 1984), pp. 34–52, 130–32, 142–44; Wilfried Böhnke, *Die NSDAP im Ruhrgebiet 1920–1933* (Bonn-Bad Godesberg, 1974), pp. 130–54, 210–15; Ellsworth Faris, "Takeoff Point for the National Socialist Party: The Landtag Election in Baden, 1929," *Central European History*, 8 (1975): 140–71; Johnpeter Horst Grill, *The Nazi Movement in Baden, 1920–1945* (Chapel Hill, 1983), pp. 181–94; Rudy Koshar, *Social Life, Local Politics, and Nazism: Marburg, 1880–1935* (Chapel Hill and London, 1986), pp. 188–205; Sigurd Plesse, *Die nationalsozialistische Machtergreifung im Oberharz. Clausthal-Zellerfeld 1929–1933* (Clausthal-Zellerfeld, 1970), pp. 44–48; Geoffrey Pridham, *Hitler's Rise to Power: The Nazi Movement in Bavaria, 1923–1933* (New York, 1973), pp. 136–45; Eberhart Schön, *Die Entstehung des Nationalsozialismus in Hessen* (Meisenheim am Glan, 1972), pp. 155–79.

107 See Jürgen Falter, "Unemployment and the Radicalization of the German Electorate 1928–33," in Peter Stachura, ed., *Unemployment and the Great Depression in Weimar Germany* (London, 1986), pp. 187–207.

entirely at the expense of the SPD, however, not of the government parties, and its voting share of 13 percent was not very impressive now that the unemployment rate had risen since May 1928 from under 9 to over 20 percent. KPD leaders also found that their ultra-leftist party line, which denounced almost all political opponents as "fascists" of one sort or another, tended to confuse their followers.[108] Late in the campaign they too decided to place primary emphasis on nationalism, seeking to outdo Goebbels with the following manifesto:

> The Social Democratic leaders . . . are not just the paid executioners of the German bourgeoisie but also at the same time the conscious agents of French and Polish imperialism. All the actions of the treacherous, corrupt Social Democracy represent high treason against the vital interests of the laboring masses in Germany.
>
> Only we Communists struggle both against the Young Plan and the Versailles plunderers' peace [*Raubfrieden*], and also against all the international treaties, agreements, and plans that are based on the Versailles Treaty. . . . We Communists are against every payment of reparations and against every payment of international debts.

The level of activism within the KPD apparently increased after this change of course, and the party leadership concluded that its blue-collar base was affected by the rising tide of francophobia.[109] Thus not even the growth of the Communist vote can be attributed solely to anger against the Brüning government.

2.3. The SPD as Brüning's Silent Partner

Hermann Pünder and Hans Schäffer perceived well before election day that the government parties could not win a majority, and they sought to persuade Brüning to revive the Great Coalition. Schäffer wrote for the cabinet a detailed refutation of the charge that the SPD was fiscally irresponsible, showing that it had offered more support for a balanced budget since the spring of 1929 than had the DVP. He also promoted a Great Coalition in conferences with Moldenhauer and Hilferding, although Moldenhauer warned that the DVP remained hostile to the idea. In late August Pünder told the chancellor repeatedly "that only a coalition from Breitscheid to Treviranus can master the situation," and Brüning seemed to agree.[110] This idea was supported by Otto Braun, who

---

108 See Siegfried Bahne, *Die KPD und das Ende von Weimar. Das Scheitern einer Politik, 1932–1935* (Frankfurt a.M. and New York, 1976), pp. 15–19; Hermann Weber, *Die Wandlung des deutschen Kommunismus. Die Stalinisierung der KPD in der Weimarer Republik*, 2 vols. (Frankfurt a.M., 1969), I:186–241, 362–66; and Eve Rosenhaft, *Beating the Fascists? The German Communists and Political Violence 1929–1933* (Cambridge, 1983), pp. 57–71.

109 "Programmerklärung zur nationalen und sozialen Befreiung des Deutschen Volkes," 24 August 1930, in Weber, ed., *Der deutsche Kommunismus*, pp. 58–65; *Quellen: Generallinie*, pp. xxvi–xxix, and circular to party locals of 18 September 1930, pp. 204–06; Winkler, *Katastrophe*, pp. 181–84; Conan Fischer, *The German Communists and the Rise of Nazism* (New York, 1991), pp. 104–09, 121–23.

110 Schäffer to Max Warburg, 2 August 1930, *Quellen: Politik und Wirtschaft*, I:353–60; Schäffer diary, entries of 23–26 August and 2 September 1930, NL Schäffer/9/137–46, 216; "Gegen Legendenbildung," 21 August 1930, NL Schäffer/29/137–46.

deplored his party's ad hominem attacks on the chancellor and appealed on 8 September for a "Great Coalition of all reasonable persons," urging the chancellor to declare himself ready to take the SPD back into government after the election. "It is vital," Brüning replied cautiously in a speech the next day, "to assemble all constructive forces in the service of the fatherland. We open our arms wide to all who are willing to share our heavy labors."[111]

On election day, 14 September, Pünder and Brüning decided to bring one Social Democrat into the cabinet in exchange for approval by the SPD of an enabling act similar to that granted Chancellor Marx in December 1923. They apparently hoped to recruit Braun as vice-chancellor in a step toward *Reichsreform*, that is, to combine the opening toward the SPD with an effort to satisfy the business community's desire for a money-saving fusion of the governments of Prussia and the Reich. Meissner told them that President Hindenburg opposed any revival of the Great Coalition but might accept this procedure. Hopes for an enabling act were dashed, however, when the radical opposition parties won more than one-third of the vote.[112] Hindenburg lifted Brüning's spirits the next morning with a phone call to pledge continued support for the existing cabinet, but the chancellor felt constrained by the knowledge that the President expected him to look only to the right for additional support. "This was a chess game in which one player was not allowed to use his pawns and could not attack the other side's king. Thus it remained throughout the future." Otto Braun continued to advocate a revival of the Great Coalition, but Brüning saw no point in trying to persuade Hindenburg to accept the idea when the DVP emphatically rejected it. The dominant tendency in that party after the election was to blame its precipitous decline from 8.7 to 4.7 percent of the national vote on past collaboration with the SPD, and to insist more emphatically than ever on the need for "bourgeois union."[113]

Brüning also refused to consider suggestions by some of his rightist supporters that he form a coalition with the NSDAP (see Section 3.2). On the afternoon of 15 September he agreed instead with President Hindenburg that the existing cabinet should remain in office to implement a comprehensive fiscal and economic program, and the cabinet approved this course the next day. Joseph Wirth, chosen to cushion the blow to the SPD, announced the cabinet's decision over the radio on 17 September. This speech could be interpreted as a bold

---

111 Schulze, *Otto Braun*, pp. 635–36; Brüning speech of 9 September 1930, *Ursachen und Folgen*, VIII:88–89.

112 Pünder, *Politik*, entry of 14 September 1930, pp. 58–59; Bavarian Ambassador von Preger to Held, 19 September 1930, *Quellen: Politik und Wirtschaft*, I:390–91; Winkler, *Katastrophe*, pp. 207–09. Compare Brüning to Wilhelm Sollmann, 29 September 1940, in Thomas Knapp, ed., "Dokumentation: Heinrich Brüning im Exil. Briefe an Wilhelm Sollmann, 1940–1946," *Vierteljahrshefte für Zeitgeschichte*, 22 (1974): 99 and 107, and Staudinger, *Wirtschaftspolitik*, pp. 90–91.

113 Brüning, *Memoiren*, pp. 186–87 (source of quotation); Schulze, *Otto Braun*, pp. 636–40; Jones, *German Liberalism*, pp. 385–88; Larry Eugene Jones, "Sammlung oder Zersplitterung? Die Bestrebungen zur Bildung einer neuen Mittelpartei in der Endphase der Weimarer Republik," *Vierteljahrshefte für Zeitgeschichte*, 25 (1977): 265–304; Döhn, *Politik und Interesse*, pp. 185–93.

affirmation of "presidential" government independent of the parties, but Brüning and Pünder agreed from the outset that success for this experiment would depend on what Pünder called "objective cooperation" (*sachliche Zusammenarbeit*) with the Social Democrats, that is, regular confidential meetings with SPD leaders to seek consensus on the substance of the government's program.[114] Some historians have been misled by Brüning's memoirs into believing that he now insisted on "presidential" government even if a parliamentary majority could be formed, but Hilferding correctly identified the real problem in his public commentary on the election results. The effort to create a "constitutional right" had failed, he noted, and the parties that supported the Weimar constitution, the SPD, State Party, and Center, together commanded just 43 percent of the vote. The Nazi electoral success generated tremendous pressure on all parties to the right of the Center to seek detente with Hitler. No parliamentary majority could be formed any longer without the support of at least two of those parties that were indifferent to democratic principles and hostile toward the SPD. Under these circumstances the Center Party had no alternative but to renounce any formal alliance with the Social Democrats in order to prevent the slide of the small parties toward the radical right.[115]

Brüning's plan for "objective cooperation" with the SPD received support from big business because the Nazi electoral victory gave a dangerous shock to financial markets. Nervous German savers and foreign investors converted 700 million German marks into foreign currencies in the six weeks after the September election. German interest rates had fallen steadily in the past year, as one would expect during a recession, but dwindling gold reserves compelled the Reichsbank to raise its discount rate from 4 to 5 percent on 9 October, and the rate did not go as low as 4 percent again for the next two years.[116] Anticipating this development, Ludwig Kastl telephoned Pünder on 15 September to declare that the cabinet should pay no attention to press reports that big business desired the entry of the Nazis into government. On the contrary, the RDI believed that the government should secure a parliamentary foundation for its reform program through cooperation with the SPD; only this could restore investor confidence and calm the financial markets. Pünder replied that a Great Coalition was not feasible but explained Brüning's plan for "objective cooperation." Kastl endorsed it enthusiastically and won approval from all the members of his executive council. The RDI also promoted cooperation with the SPD by supporting further salary reductions for the civil service. Kastl declared, obviously referring to the DVP, that the cabinet must ignore those who whined, "if we do that, then

114 Pünder, *Politik*, entry of 16 September 1930, pp. 59–60; *Kabinette Brüning*, meeting of 16 September 1930, I:429–31; Brüning, *Memoiren*, p. 187.
115 Hilferding, "In der Gefahrenzone," *Die Gesellschaft*, 7, #2 (1930): 289–95; compare Brüning's erratic recollections in *Memoiren*, pp. 187–91.
116 Karl Erich Born, *Die deutsche Bankenkrise 1931. Finanzen und Politik* (Munich, 1967), pp. 57–58; Borchardt, *Perspectives*, pp. 145–46; James, *German Slump*, pp. 295–302; Balderston, *Economic Crisis*, pp. 142, 148 (chart on discount rates), 171–73.

our party will disappear altogether. . . . It makes no difference whether this or that organization, this or that party survives. Everything depends on drawing the appropriate conclusions about what is necessary to preserve the state and nation, and then acting on those conclusions." Thus the executive secretary of the RDI, himself formerly a high official in the finance ministry, began to echo the speeches of Chancellor Brüning, and he always supported Brüning thereafter. Kastl's line received powerful backing from Silverberg and RDI chairman Carl Duisberg of I. G. Farben, who regarded Brüning as the best chancellor since Bismarck.[117]

Brüning's plan for "objective cooperation" also won support from the leadership of the SPD. Hilferding told Hans Schäffer on 18 September that the Social Democrats would prefer a covert alliance with the government to any formal coalition. In this way, he explained, the SPD would "not compromise itself among the workers to the point where the masses all run away afterward. Then the last bastion [of democracy] would fall. The best course would be to help solve the problems outside of government."[118] Hilferding arranged a confidential meeting between Brüning and Hermann Müller on 23 September, where the ex-chancellor criticized some measures contemplated by the government but agreed to further talks. In the next few days Müller, Otto Braun, Keil, Breitscheid, and Paul Hertz all decided that the SPD could not afford to topple Brüning because the most likely alternative was a "fascist" government under Hugenberg and Hitler. They all exhorted the SPD Reichstag delegation to tolerate the existing cabinet. "Toleration" struck most ordinary party members as a form of vacillation, however, and the debate among Social Democrats in the provinces focused on the polar alternatives of a Great Coalition or vigorous opposition to the government.[119] After the leadership of the Free Unions endorsed toleration nevertheless, a senior adviser to Otto Braun, State Secretary Hans Staudinger of the Prussian ministry of commerce, requested Schäffer on 29 September to notify Brüning that the Social Democrats would cooperate with him as long as they believed that he really intended to restore parliamentary government after the emergency. The SPD would be happy to conduct its business with him surreptitiously, "but everything depends on the Center Party's showing us that it stands by our side as a guardian of democracy." The tests of the chancellor's good faith were that he cooperate with the existing Prussian government and refuse to admit Nazis into the Reich cabinet. Wilhelm Eggert defined the same two litmus tests before the national committee of the Free Unions, and

---

117 Pünder memorandum, 15 September, and Kastl to Silverberg, 19 September 1930, *Kabinette Brüning*, I:427–28; RDI Vorstand, 19 September 1930, *Quellen: Politik und Wirtschaft*, I:393–97 (source of quotation); reminiscences in Kastl to Hans Schäffer, 8 December 1965, NL Schäffer/43/102a–02b; speeches by Duisberg, Kastl, and Silverberg at the RDI *Hauptausschuss*, 27 November 1930, "Veröffentlichungen des RDI," Nr. 55, in NL Silverberg/274/46–64. Contrast Neebe, *Grossindustrie*, pp. 76–77, 81–87.
118 Schäffer diary, 18 September 1930, NL Schäffer/9/225.
119 Pünder, *Politik*, 25 September 1930, p. 61; Brüning, *Memoiren*, p. 187; Otto Braun, *Von Weimar zu Hitler*, pp. 308–10; Keil, *Erlebnisse*, II:397–98; Stampfer, *14 Jahre*, pp. 580–81; Harsch, *Social Democracy*, pp. 86–98; Winkler, *Katastrophe*, pp. 207–11.

Brüning adhered to both these conditions throughout his tenure in office. By now, it would appear, most SPD leaders had concluded that Brüning's intentions were good, although few defended him in public.[120]

On 30 September the cabinet tested the SPD's patience by publishing its fiscal plan for the year 1931, designed to counteract the run on the mark. The government proposed to raise unemployment insurance dues from 4.5 to 6.5 percent, reduce the salaries of all federal, state, and municipal officials by 6 percent (with a 20% cut for the President, chancellor, and cabinet ministers), raise the tobacco tax, reduce subsidies to the state governments, and offer tax breaks for farmers and small business. The SPD considered the last provision a disturbing sign of reactionary influence but could win no concessions from Brüning. In fact, this program was tailored to meet the demands of American bankers, not German rightists, and the chancellor had no room to maneuver. The finance ministry and Reichsbank were engaged in frantic efforts to secure a life-saving loan of $125 million from the Boston firm of Lee, Higginson and Co., which was granted on 11 October, and the Americans insisted on "sound" budget practices. The German government could not ignore such pressure under the circumstances of 1930.[121]

Pünder arranged meetings to discuss this fiscal plan between Brüning and the SPD cochairmen, Müller and Otto Wels, on 30 September and 2 October. Pünder himself conferred with Otto Braun and summarized the results of these conversations with the formula that the cabinet would not be expanded leftward, "since this would not be tolerated by the right and is not requested by the left." The Social Democrats sympathized, however, with the chancellor's request that they oppose all motions of no confidence and renounce any bill to suspend the entire emergency decree of July 1930. The chancellor would have no objection, on the other hand, if the SPD introduced specific bills in the Reichstag to amend the most painful features of the decree. Pünder hoped that these discussions would inaugurate a new form of government by emergency decree, "not in conflict with the Reichstag, but in silent agreement with a majority." Brüning later recalled deciding immediately after the defeat of 18 July never to employ emergency decrees again unless he knew in advance that a parliamentary majority would tolerate them.[122]

120 Schäffer diary, 29 September 1930, NL Schäffer/9/233; Schäffer to Pünder, 29 September 1930 (source of quotation), NL Schäffer/29/210–12; ADGB Bundesausschuss, 12/13 October 1930, *Quellen: Gewerkschaften*, pp. 158–61; Hermann Müller to Otto Braun, 25 September 1930, in Braun, *Von Weimar zu Hitler*, pp. 308–09; Staudinger, *Wirtschaftspolitik*, pp. 91, 94–95; Rainer Schaefer, *SPD in der Ära Brüning: Tolerierung oder Mobilisierung?* (Frankfurt a.M., 1990), pp. 65–74; Winkler, *Katastrophe*, pp. 210–15.

121 Cabinet meeting, 29 September, and response of 2 October 1930 to a questionnaire from Lee, Higginson, *Kabinette Brüning*, I:469–75, 480–84; Winkler, *Katastrophe*, pp. 217–18; Schulz, *Von Brüning zu Hitler*, pp. 186–87, 197–98; James, *Reichsbank*, pp. 119–37; Harold James, "Economic Reasons for the Collapse of the Weimar Republic," in Kershaw, ed., *Weimar*, pp. 40–42; Balderston, *German Economic Crisis*, pp. 302–15.

122 Pünder, *Politik*, entries of 30 September and 3 October 1930, pp. 62–64; Brüning, *Memoiren*, p. 190.

As the newly elected Reichstag delegates caucused in the first days of October, the Social Democrats adopted a public stance far more constructive from Brüning's standpoint than that of many so-called government parties. The Christian Social, Business, and Christian Nationalist Peasants' parties all introduced resolutions that echoed the demand by Nazis and Communists for an immediate moratorium on reparations. The SPD, on the other hand, issued a restrained declaration emphasizing the need to defend constitutional government against fascism; it promised to seek amendment of the worst features of the emergency decree of July 1930 but said nothing about rescinding it.[123] The SPD helped the government to defeat all motions of no confidence in the Reichstag session of 13–19 October, to secure approval for the terms of the American loan, and then to adjourn the Reichstag for six weeks. The press was astonished by the strength of the government's parliamentary support, despite all efforts to disrupt the proceedings by the Nazi delegates, who marched into the chamber in SA uniform singing battle songs.[124]

Brüning tested the SPD's patience again by harnessing the system of state labor arbitration to further his plan for an "export offensive" through lowered production costs. He told the cabinet on 24 September that its long-term goal must be to return wages to the level of early 1927, which implied reductions of 15 percent in most trades. The government declaration of 30 September urged the private sector to imitate the government's example when it lowered salaries for civil servants, and Stegerwald told the press that wage policy had been "lost in a maze" ever since Heinrich Köhler's overly generous reform of government salaries in 1927.[125] Bernhard Otte concluded grimly that the working class would suffer because Brüning could do little to lower rents and food prices, which accounted for three-quarters of the household budget of most workers, so the Christian unions joined the Free in attacking this program.[126] On 15 October a binding arbitration decree nevertheless imposed wage reductions of 6–8 percent on Berlin metalworkers, provoking a strike by 126,000. Strikes had little hope of success under conditions of high unemployment, however, and Free Union leaders themselves became alarmed when the Nazi and Communist parties incited the strikers to riot. Stegerwald persuaded the unions to submit to new arbitration by a three-man panel under the former labor minister Heinrich

123 SPD resolution of 3 October 1930, *Ursachen und Folgen*, VIII:96; *Kabinette Brüning*, meeting of 4 October 1930, I:495–98; Schulz, *Von Brüning zu Hitler*, pp. 193–97; Jones, "Agrarian Splinter Parties," pp. 216–17; Schumacher, *Mittelstandsfront*, pp. 144–55.

124 Pünder, *Politik*, 26 October 1930, p. 68; Winkler, *Katastrophe*, pp. 237–44.

125 *Kabinette Brüning*, I:443–45; Stegerwald interview in *Kölnische Volkszeitung*, 1 October 1930, #501B; Hartwich, *Arbeitsmarkt*, pp. 163–69; Johannes Bähr, *Staatliche Schlichtung in der Weimarer Republik. Tarifpolitik, Korporatismus und industrieller Konflikt zwischen Inflation und Deflation 1919–1932* (Berlin, 1989), pp. 298–304.

126 Otte circular of 2 October 1930, BAK Kleine Erwerbung 461/2/119–21; *Zentralblatt der christlichen Gewerkschaften*, 15 October and 1 November 1930, pp. 305, 333–34; *Kabinette Brüning*, Christian union resolution of 10 October and Free Union resolution of 13 October 1930, I:515–17, 531–32.

Brauns, which reissued the original decree with only minor changes on 8 November. Similar decrees were issued by arbitrators wherever a collective labor contract expired in the following weeks, on the basis of confidential instructions from the labor minister to seek wage reductions of 15 percent in two installments. Applauding the labor ministry in a speech to fellow industrialists, Silverberg declared that, whereas almost every previous cabinet of the Weimar Republic had been obsessed with "mass psychology," Brüning appeared to understand the "psychology of the entrepreneurs," that is, the profound pessimism about the future that discouraged private investment. Brüning and Stegerwald were also hailed by the League of German Employers' Associations as the most reasonable government leaders of the last decade.[127]

This enthusiasm in the business community ebbed as the cabinet displayed the resolve to lower prices as much as wages. State Secretary Trendelenburg now had the legal authority as acting minister of economics to dissolve cartels and syndicates, and the non-cartellized metalworking industry complained sharply to the cabinet that German prices for coal and raw steel were not following the world market's downward trend.[128] In mid-October Trendelenburg browbeat the Rhenish-Westphalian Coal Syndicate into an immediate price reduction of 6 percent, even though its collective labor contract did not expire until the end of the year, so that Brüning could trumpet the news on the floor of the Reichstag. The National Economic Council (Reichswirtschaftsrat) then published a report demanding substantial reductions in domestic iron and steel prices to revive German industry. After Trendelenburg told leaders of the steel industry that they should lower their prices by 10 percent, even the political moderate Peter Klöckner, a member of the Center Party, burst out to business colleagues that it was "absolute insanity" to hear such talk from an economics minister, "who is supposed to protect business and care for it."[129] The Ruhr coal mine operators resented Trendelenburg's pressure tactics, and they denounced the government in December when it rejected demands for a 10 percent wage cut. Forming the first cell of opposition to Brüning in the business community, they threatened at year's end to secede from the Reich Association of Industry unless it withdrew support from Brüning. The steel industry, closely tied to coal financially, blocked

---

127 Bähr, *Staatliche Schlichtung*, pp. 304–11; Hartwich, *Arbeitsmarkt*, pp. 169–81; Winkler, *Katastrophe*, pp. 222–25; Silverberg speech to the RDI Hauptausschuss, 27 November 1930, "Veröffentlichungen des RDI," Nr. 55, p. 28, NL Silverberg/274/46–64; report by Carl Köttgen to the Vereinigung deutscher Arbeitgeberverbände Hauptausschuss, 11 December 1930, NL Silverberg/231/6–24.

128 "Besprechung bei den Vereinigten Stahlwerken," 6 October 1930, and "Besprechung zwischen Eisen schaffender und Eisen verarbeitender Industrie," 6 October 1930, BAK R13I/402/53–81; J. W. Reichert to Ernst Poensgen, 27 November 1930, BAK R13I/403/68–70; Grübler, *Spitzenverbände der Wirtschaft*, pp. 175–79; Balderston, *German Economic Crisis*, pp. 366–72; Harold James, *German Slump*, pp. 146–60, 173–74.

129 Lübsen to Paul Reusch, 16 October 1930, *Quellen: Politik und Wirtschaft*, I:421–25; Brüning, *Memoiren*, p. 199; Reichswirtschaftsrat resolution of 6 November 1930, BAK R43I/1158/274–76; Peter Klöckner to Ernst Poensgen, 10 November 1930, BAK R13I/403/178–80 (source of quotation).

this initiative, but the mine operators allowed their collective labor contract to expire in an effort to impose massive wage reductions.[130]

Brüning also decided to confront the leaders of the farm lobby with a campaign to lower food prices. The Christian Nationalist Peasants' Party appealed to Hindenburg over the chancellor's head after the election to dismiss the free trader Curtius as foreign minister and embrace the principle that "we must not import any food from abroad." It also demanded a tax moratorium for farmers and the removal of Prussia's administrative influence over Eastern Aid.[131] The collapse of grain prices did persuade the cabinet to endorse an increase in the wheat tariff, but it rejected any further agrarian demands. Pünder was much relieved to find that President Hindenburg endorsed this decision. Brüning then told a deputation from the Reichslandbund bluntly that its political radicalism aggravated the economic crisis; it must lower food prices by forging direct links with consumer cooperatives or else forfeit all sympathy among the urban populace. Brüning's attitude cost him the support of most Christian Nationalist Reichstag delegates, although he retained cordial ties with party leaders like Günther Gereke and Schlange-Schöningen.[132]

Brüning's campaign to lower the cost of living also led to conflict with the Business Party. Traumatized by Nazi electoral gains, it declared on 26 September that it could support "no government on which the Social Democrats exert direct or indirect influence, which they actively support or passively tolerate." On 13 October it demanded Johann Viktor Bredt's resignation as justice minister, but he persuaded his colleagues to drop this demand when the President appealed to their patriotism.[133] Bredt's position weakened, however, as the cabinet increased its pressure for a reduction in retail prices. On 11 November Stegerwald secured cabinet approval for the abolition of the sales tax surcharge on consumer cooperatives, the Business Party's great achievement of April 1930; the cabinet agreed that its survival depended on a dramatic reduction in the cost of living, even if that meant bankruptcy for thousands in the "over-populated" retail sector. Brüning intervened personally that same day to persuade the grocers of Berlin to announce a reduction of 8 percent in the price of bread and meat.[134] On 12 November Stegerwald and Trendelenburg convened another summit conference between big business and organized labor, where the labor

130 J. W. Reichert to Max Schlenker, 4 December 1930, *Quellen: Politik und Wirtschaft*, I:478–80; RDI Fachgruppe Bergbau, Vorstandssitzung of 16 January 1931, NL Silverberg/382/10–12; Neebe, *Grossindustrie*, pp. 82–89; Turner, *Big Business*, pp. 162–63; Rudolf Tschirbs, *Tarifpolitik im Ruhrbergbau 1918–1933* (Berlin and New York, 1986), pp. 382–91.

131 Presidential audience of 23 October 1930, *Kabinette Brüning*, I:548–49; Gessner, *Agrarverbände*, pp. 239–42.

132 *Kabinette Brüning*, meetings of 24–25 October and chancellor's reception of 20 November 1930, I:554–60, 561–64, 638–39; Pünder, *Politik*, 13 November 1930, p. 73; Günther Gereke, *Ich war königlich-preussischer Landrat* (Berlin, 1970), p. 169.

133 Bredt, *Erinnerungen und Dokumente*, pp. 229–32, 253–54, 359–61; Hermann Drewitz to Chancellor Brüning, 13 October 1930, *Kabinette Brüning*, I:535–36; Schumacher, *Mittelstandsfront*, pp. 155–60.

134 *Kabinette Brüning*, meeting of 11 November 1930, I:618–23; Brüning, *Memoiren*, pp. 207–08. Compare Trendelenburg's remarks on 8 July in *Kabinette Brüning*, I:270–71.

minister appealed to the trade unionists not to argue about inevitable wage reductions but to focus instead on cooperation with employers to lower the cost of living and avoid layoffs. The trade unionists were impressed by the cooperative attitude of the industrialists, and they soon agreed on proposals to strengthen consumer cooperatives, monitor price-gouging by retailers, and promote more economical government. The labor leaders declared publicly that, since wage reductions sometimes proved unavoidable, union members should concentrate on the struggle to lower retail prices: "The present weakness versus employers must not be followed by weakness versus shopkeepers and other groups."[135] The cost of living did fall rapidly in the autumn of 1930, and by January 1931 real wages for employed workers were higher than they had ever been. Bredt could secure no concessions from the cabinet and felt compelled to resign on 25 November, when open mutiny in his party seemed imminent.[136]

The cabinet completed its legislative proposals in late October so that they could be discussed with state governments before the Reichstag convened on 3 December. The Prussian cabinet quickly endorsed them; Otto Braun's only objection was that the Prussian police must be exempt from salary cuts because they faced such hazardous street duty. Groener replied that soldiers could not be treated worse than policemen, but Brüning arranged a compromise whereby the 6 percent cut applied equally to all, but the police would receive generous overtime bonuses.[137] The southern German states expressed stronger opposition, fearing that Brüning intended to undermine their autonomy by starving them of revenue. The chancellor therefore took great pains to secure a solid majority in the Reichsrat. He agreed to some enhancement of the states' share of revenues in a meeting with the southern prime ministers in Stuttgart, paid a state visit to Dresden to win Saxony's support, and appeared in person before the Reichsrat to defend his program. Brüning also agreed to a face-saving compromise with Bolz of Württemberg whereby the Reich did not require but rather "authorized" state governments to impose salary reductions, delegating presidential decree powers to them. These maneuvers left Bavaria isolated in denying the legal authority of the Reich to impose fiscal measures on the states, and even its representatives joined the overwhelming majority in the Reichsrat that approved the government's fiscal program on 20 November.[138]

135 Labor–management conference of 12 November and Christian union circular of 13 November 1930, *Quellen: Politik und Wirtschaft*, I:461–65; ADGB summary of the proceedings in *Quellen: Gewerkschaften*, pp. 171–73; joint declaration by the Free, Christian, and Hirsch-Duncker unions, *Zentralblatt der christlichen Gewerkschaften*, 1 December 1930, pp. 353–55 (source of quotation).
136 Balderston, *German Economic Crisis*, pp. 44–48; Bredt, *Erinnerungen*, pp. 255–63; Bredt to Chancellor Brüning, 25 November 1930, and related documents in *Kabinette Brüning*, I:626–33, 651, 684–86, 729–35.
137 *Kabinette Brüning*, meeting of 27 October 1930, I:566–68.
138 Protest letters to the chancellor of 11–29 October 1930 from Baden, Bavaria, and Hesse, *Kabinette Brüning*, I:517–30, 540–46, 581–84; Pünder, *Politik*, entries of 3–8 November 1930, pp. 70–72; Besson, *Württemberg*, pp. 166–69, 379–81, 391–93; Altendorfer, *Fritz Schäffer*, pp. 562–65; Manfred Peter Heimers, *Unitarismus und süddeutsches Selbstbewusstsein. Weimarer Koalition und SPD in Baden in der Reichsreformdiskussion 1918–1933* (Düsseldorf, 1992), pp. 300–304; Mommsen, "Brünings Politik," pp. 35–36.

This victory set the stage for the final discussions with the Reichstag delegations. The path still seemed rocky on 15 November, when Paul Hertz of the SPD
urged the chancellor to postpone all painful austerity measures indefinitely.
Pünder confided to his diary that he and Brüning then had a gloomy conversation about "the worst case scenarios, where adhering to the constitution is like
walking on the razor's edge." They agreed that, if the Reichstag voted to suspend
their next emergency decree, then the government could stay in power only by
dissolving it and postponing new elections indefinitely. "I am just about persuaded," Pünder wrote, "but the Reich chancellor – I must record that here to
his credit – is not; I think he would rather resign." This diary entry confirms
the sincerity of Brüning's commitment to constitutional government. Pünder
approached Wilhelm Groener without Brüning's knowledge to ask whether the
army would support such bold action and received a hearty affirmative.[139] Pünder
obviously did not know that Schleicher had urged this course on Brüning unsuccessfully ever since the spring of 1929.

Hopes for rightist parliamentary support revived briefly on 18 November,
when Albert Vögler of the United Steelworks told the chancellor that eight
leading industrialists had corralled Hugenberg for a day-long discussion of the
many ways in which the DNVP's intransigence aggravated the economic crisis.
If Brüning would arrange another meeting with Hugenberg, Vögler predicted,
he would find the DNVP chairman amenable to reason. Brüning agreed to
make the attempt but warned that he could not sacrifice the Weimar Coalition
in Prussia.[140] The chancellor promoted detente with the DNVP by seeking out
Elard von Oldenburg-Januschau, an old friend of Hindenburg from East Prussia
who had recently joined its Reichstag delegation. Brüning apparently revealed
his monarchist sympathies to the elderly Junker and spoke vaguely of trying to
persuade the SPD to support some kind of restoration in a few years if the
DNVP supported him now. Oldenburg-Januschau made no promises but later
told Hindenburg and others that Brüning was the best chancellor since Bismarck.[141] Hugenberg felt confident, however, that Brüning would soon forfeit all
support from the President and moderate conservatives if he continued to cooperate with Otto Braun. When Brüning met with him on 26 November, four hours
of persuasion and cajolery had no effect; Hugenberg simply reiterated his
demand for Otto Braun's head. Brüning later recalled that his frank explanation
of Germany's diplomatic and fiscal problems had the following result:

> After another half hour Hugenberg suddenly looked at his watch, stood up,
> and concluded the conversation with a stereotypically ice-cold manner: "I
> am more convinced than ever that I was always right. Germany stands in

---

139 Pünder, *Politik*, 15 November and 4 December 1930, pp. 73–74, 79.
140 Pünder, *Politik*, entry of 19 November 1930, p. 75.
141 Brüning, *Memoiren*, pp. 209, 273; compare Ambassador Rumbold to Henderson, 13 February 1931,
      DBFP, I:559, and Otto Schmidt-Hannover, *Umdenken oder Anarchie. Männer – Schicksale – Lehren*
      (Göttingen, 1959), p. 259.

the middle of the collapse that I predicted. Your detailed remarks make that more clear to me than ever. Therefore I must combat you and the whole system."

Brüning replied that he had long agreed with Hugenberg on the likelihood of economic disaster, but that his sense of duty would not permit him to stand aside until everything lay in ruins.[142]

The Social Democrats proved far more reasonable than Hugenberg. Breitscheid, Hilferding, and Hertz told the chancellor that same day that they would support his program if he alleviated the three worst hardships imposed on workers by the emergency decree of July 1930. They then huddled with Stegerwald to draft specific proposals to exempt the unemployed from user fees in the medical insurance system and from the municipal poll tax, and to restore the right of sixteen-year-olds to jobless benefits. Brüning accepted these amendments and summoned Otto Braun on 29 November to ask whether the SPD could accept this modified program if it was issued as an emergency decree just before the Reichstag convened. Braun noted that the form of the government's action might be considered "a certain affront to parliament," but that the content was "acceptable to Social Democracy." He promised to persuade the SPD Reichstag delegation to accept this decree.[143] Much relieved, Brüning told his cabinet the next day that the government program enjoyed the support of a parliamentary majority but must be issued as an emergency decree so that the special interests could not mobilize. Stegerwald explained that "there is a weak majority in the Reichstag for all the laws, but if the laws were submitted for normal parliamentary treatment, this majority could not withstand the artillery barrage from the opposition." Brüning turned directly to the Prussian State Secretary Weismann, a regular observer at cabinet meetings, to make sure that Otto Braun understood that the Center Party would topple him if the SPD toppled the chancellor, and Weismann replied that this was perfectly clear.[144]

The government's conservative supporters found this decree more difficult to accept than did the SPD. At the last minute, Schiele demanded sweeping new decree provisions to assist family farmers and threatened to resign when they were rejected by the chancellor and other ministers. The BVP attacked the government's plan to standardize local property tax rates throughout Germany, but Brüning ignored them too.[145] Thus the right wing of the cabinet was on the verge of revolt when Brüning persuaded President Hindenburg to sign his first com-

---

142 Pünder memorandum of 26 November 1930, *Kabinette Brüning*, I:652–54; Brüning, *Memoiren*, pp. 210–11. See also Martin Spahn to Hugenberg, 17 September 1930, and reply in NL Spahn/86; Hugenberg's open letter of October 1930, *Kabinette Brüning*, I:536–38; and Leopold, *Hugenberg*, pp. 80–87.

143 Pünder memoranda of 26 and 29 November 1930, *Kabinette Brüning*, I:654–55; 661–62; Pünder, *Politik*, 28 November 1930, p. 77; Winkler, *Katastrophe*, pp. 260–66.

144 *Kabinette Brüning*, 30 November 1930, I:663–67.

145 Ibid., meeting of 30 November and Schiele to Brüning, 1 December 1930, I:676–82; Schönhoven, *BVP*, pp. 252–56.

prehensive "Emergency Decree to Secure the Economy and Public Finances" on the evening of 1 December. Hindenburg cut the tension as he signed by intoning, "May the Lord God give his blessing to this – and the Devil take anyone who kicks up a fuss!" Pünder confided to his diary that the cabinet might be swept away if the public knew how fragile was its facade of unity: "Three ministers whose hearts are not in it [i.e., Bredt, Schiele, and Schätzel]. But we strive to preserve the facade. That is the main thing. Behind this facade there operates the all-dominating energy of Chancellor Brüning, who for some time now has developed into a leading statesman in the noblest sense of the word."[146]

Brüning told the Reichstag on 5 December that his decree satisfied 90 percent of the wishes expressed by the parties, and that no government on earth could satisfy the remaining 10 percent. The next day the Social Democrats gave him a majority of thirty-eight against a bill to rescind the decree supported by the KPD, DNVP, Nazi Party, Business Party, and most Christian Nationalists. The Reichstag then followed the government's wishes by adjourning itself until February 1931. Pünder concluded that "the only way to work with this Reichstag is for the government to employ Article 48, then permit the debate prescribed by the constitution over whether to rescind the decrees, and then have the Reichstag disappear again. I would like to think that it is not impossible to govern in this fashion for a long time." He noted with surprise that the Social Democratic press had begun to adopt the same viewpoint.[147] Indeed, the SPD's leader in the Prussian parliament, Ernst Heilmann, now joined Hilferding in arguing publicly that Brüning offered the closest thing to democracy that anyone could expect. "A people that chooses such a Reichstag," he declared, "thereby renounces self-government, and its right to legislate is automatically replaced by Article 48. This fact, although most disturbing for every friend of democracy, must be accepted until the German people is capable of a wiser choice."[148]

As Pünder hoped, the emergency decree of 1 December established an enduring form of semi-parliamentary government. Brüning had adopted the somewhat controversial view that Article 48 empowered the President to impose fiscal measures on state governments, but he always defended the Reichstag's right to review emergency decrees and adhered to the mainstream view that decrees must respect all articles of the Reich constitution except for the seven listed as suspendable in Article 48, Paragraph 2. Bavaria pressed a lawsuit against the standardization of local property tax rates before the Supreme Court but eventually dropped it in June 1931, after Brüning and Hindenburg promised Fritz Schäffer never to issue a decree altering the powers of state governments. Thereafter

146 Pünder, *Politik*, 2 December 1930, pp. 77–78.
147 Brüning's speech in *Verhandlungen des Reichstags*, 444/307–11; Pünder, *Politik*, 14 December 1930, p. 81; Schulz, *Von Brüning zu Hitler*, pp. 230–36.
148 Quoted in Winkler, *Katastrophe*, p. 271; compare Braun, *Von Weimar zu Hitler*, p. 362.

most legal experts and all relevant court verdicts supported the Brüning cabinet's interpretation of Article 48; indeed, the community of legal scholars displayed a striking tendency to defend all of Chancellor Brüning's initiatives but soon fell into discord under his successor Franz von Papen.[149] Brüning exaggerated, to be sure, when he argued in later years that his resort to government by decree did not suspend parliamentary control but merely changed its form. His practice of convening the Reichstag only for brief sessions at long intervals promoted a steady deterioration in the Reichstag delegations' access to information and sense of responsibility for the public welfare; this form of therapy for parliamentary democracy could not be administered indefinitely without making the patient sicker.[150] Brüning nevertheless won a majority of at least twenty votes in every subsequent test of the government's authority in the Reichstag, a success based on dozens of confidential meetings with the leaders of the SPD, in which the chancellor's need to appear independent from the left in the eyes of Hindenburg and the officer corps was carefully balanced against the Social Democrats' need to respond to Communist attacks. Brüning became so anxious to retain the appearance of independence despite the fact of cooperation that his memory later obliterated all trace of the simple bargain with the SPD on 29 November 1930 that created the foundation for government by decree. In the memoirs he decides on his own initiative to exempt the unemployed from the poll tax and boasts that "I rejected virtually all other demands, no matter what their origin."[151]

Brüning failed, however, to secure a stable foundation for his government by promoting any formal agreement between big business and organized labor. The negotiators summoned by Stegerwald hammered out a draft agreement on 9 December, proclaiming a shared determination to lower the cost of living, oppose agrarian protectionism, reduce the length of the work week to stretch out job opportunities, and renegotiate wage levels in firms threatened with bankruptcy.[152] The Christian trade unions and industrial associations promptly ratified this agreement. The executive committee of the socialist labor federation failed, however, to persuade the delegates of its member unions to accept it; they rejected anything that might give the impression that they endorsed wage reductions. One delegate noted that the Free Unions could survive almost any wage cut imposed by government fiat but not those to which it agreed: "We live in a

149 Cabinet memoranda of 18 and 21 November 1930, and reception for Fritz Schäffer by the President and chancellor, 27 April 1931, *Kabinette Brüning*, I:633–34, 639–41, and II:1031–32; Schulz, *Von Brüning zu Hitler*, pp. 241–63, 269–75, 372–77; Besson, *Württemberg*, pp. 169–74; Altendorfer, *Fritz Schäffer*, pp. 566–83; Scheuner, "Artikel 48," pp. 279–81; Kurz, "Artikel 48," pp. 402–13.
150 Contrast Brüning's Page-Barbour lecture #1 of January 1939, pp. 21–22, HUG FP 93.45, and Brüning to Philipp Dessauer, 16 March 1956, in Müller, *Brüning Papers*, pp. 178–79, with Mommsen, "Brünings Politik," pp. 19–22, 35–38.
151 Brüning, *Memoiren*, p. 211.
152 Circular to the Christian trade unions, 10 December 1930, BAK Kleine Erwerbung 461/2/141–47; ADGB Bundesausschuss, 14/15 December 1930, *Quellen: Politik und Wirtschaft*, I:494–95.

time of hardship, but we will not voluntarily renounce anything that has been achieved." Bernhard Otte noted with alarm that reactionary industrialists rejoiced over this decision.[153]

The failure of these negotiations weakened the government in its dealings with heavy industry. After further study of the issue of steel prices, Trendelenburg reported to the cabinet that the ideal solution would probably be to dissolve all trusts and marketing associations. Hans Luther stoutly defended the status quo, however, in line with the position of the RDI, and the cabinet did not feel strong enough to take any action.[154] There could be no bold economic reforms without a revival of something like the Central Association of November 1918. The most Brüning could do was to reassert the government's authority over labor arbitration. After wage negotiations in the Ruhr mining industry deadlocked at the end of the year, management served notice of a general lockout to begin on 15 January 1931 and insisted that the state had no legal authority to issue an arbitration decree without the support of at least one of the parties in the dispute. On 8 January the government issued a presidential emergency decree affirming the right of state arbitrators to issue a wage decree without the support of either party. Stegerwald secured this measure by conceding to his fellow ministers the right to decide as a body whether any such arbitration decree should be declared binding. Never before had the cabinet assumed such direct responsibility for establishing wage levels, and Ruhr heavy industry denounced this decree for subordinating economics to politics.[155]

Brüning found that many labor leaders privately endorsed his policies but implored him to take all responsibility for wage reductions. Leaders of the SPD, Business Party, and DVP told him that they wanted his program to succeed but did not want to vote for it in the Reichstag; they preferred to accept emergency decrees passively. Brüning saw himself becoming a scapegoat, asked to bear responsibility for all the painful measures considered necessary by the entire political and economic elite.[156] Brüning had taken office pessimistic about world economic trends but optimistic about his chances to implement public works, boost German exports, revive the Central Association of November 1918, and rally support from the voters. As each of these positive goals was thwarted, he began to develop the martyr complex that makes his memoirs such grim reading. Stegerwald actually told a rally of the Christian trade unions on 7 December that

153 ADGB Bundesausschuss, 14/15 December 1930, *Quellen: Politik und Wirtschaft*, I:493–507 (quotation on p. 499); ADGB Bundesvorstand, 14 January 1931, *Quellen: Gewerkschaften*, pp. 225–30; Otte circular to the Christian unions, 29 December 1930, BAK Kleine Erwerbung 461/2/149–50; Wengst, "Unternehmerverbände und Gewerkschaften," pp. 111–16.

154 Cabinet subcommittee discussion, 16 December 1930, *Kabinette Brüning*, I:729–35; J. W. Reichert to Ernst Poensgen, 27 November and 17 December 1930, BAK R131/403/10–11, 68–70.

155 Cabinet meeting of 8 January 1931, *Kabinette Brüning*, I:771–76; Tschirbs, *Tarifpolitik*, pp. 391–98; Bähr, *Staatliche Schlichtung*, pp. 311–18.

156 *Zentrumsprotokolle*, 12 December 1930, p. 501; Brüning, *Memoiren*, pp. 235–37; Brüning, "The Essence of Democracy," Dartmouth College lecture #2 of March 1937, pp. 33–35, HUG FP 93.45; Brüning to Gerhard Ritter, 24 September 1952, HUG FP 93.10/Box 26/Gerhard Ritter.

"to be labor minister at this time is a martyrdom."[157] Embittered by the irrationality and selfishness displayed by many lobbyists and politicians, Brüning confined himself more and more to discussions within the small circle of colleagues whose patriotism and judgment he trusted. By December 1930 foreign policy seemed to offer the only hope for positive initiatives.

157 *Zentralblatt der christlichen Gewerkschaften*, 15 December 1930, p. 371.

3

Foreign Policy and the "National Opposition"

After the Reichstag election of September 1930, Brüning firmly resisted suggestions by some rightist supporters that he bring the Nazi Party into his cabinet or dissolve the Reichstag indefinitely. Indeed, he always sought to deny the Nazis any share of power in the national government. The chancellor and his inner circle were determined to revise the Treaty of Versailles eventually, however, and believed that the German electorate was being swept by a tidal wave of nationalist sentiment. For months therefore they agonized over the question of how to appease public opinion without doing anything premature or counter-productive in the realm of foreign policy.

3.1. The Meaning of "Prussia" for Brüning's Inner Circle

Brüning measured public figures against a very high standard of self-sacrificing patriotism and found most of them deficient. He unmasked many real hypocrites who mouthed patriotic slogans while pursuing selfish interests, but his judgments were sometimes overly harsh; this confirmed bachelor could display scathing contempt for a politician who seemed to have an ambitious wife or to worry too much about his children's future. Gradually Brüning established close ties with a dozen trusted colleagues who shared his vision of "Prussia" as a political community based on civic virtue, a virtue nourished by universal military conscription, a dedicated professional civil service, and a determination to help less fortunate members of the community. This vision of Prussia discouraged any appreciation of the viewpoint of feminists, youthful pleasure-seekers, or pacifists, but it encouraged genuine dedication to the impartial mediation of class conflict.

Brüning's small inner circle first included three long-time associates, Adam Stegerwald (1874–1945), Ludwig Kaas (1881–1952), and Gottfried Treviranus (1891–1971). There was some personal tension between Chancellor Brüning and his first political mentor, but Stegerwald accepted his subordinate status as labor minister with fairly good grace. He pursued Brüning's goal of a balanced budget and deflation for the sake of an "export offensive" with single-minded dedica-

The first Brüning Cabinet, spring 1930. Sitting, from left: Wilhelm Groener, Hermann Dietrich, Heinrich Brüning, Julius Curtius, Georg Schätzel (postal minister). Standing, from left: Gottfried Treviranus, Johann Viktor Bredt, Adam Stegerwald, Paul Molden-hauer, Theodor von Guérard (minister of transport). (Bundesarchiv Koblenz 82/166/15A)

tion, and Brüning relied heavily on him to maintain faith in the government's fairness among workers without alienating the business community. The chancellor believed that he could easily dispense with the services of Joseph Wirth or Transport Minister von Guérard, but that Stegerwald's resignation from the cabinet would spell political disaster.[1] Cabinet colleagues sometimes rolled their eyes when the autodidact Stegerwald discoursed on world historical trends, but he was the pioneer of the brand of populist nationalism that Chancellor Brüning hoped to persuade the SPD and Free Unions to adopt. He had demanded "adequate *Lebensraum* [living space] for the German people" as early as 1927,

1 Hans Schäffer to Max Warburg, 2 August 1930, *Quellen: Politik und Wirtschaft*, I:356; Pünder, *Politik*, entry of 25 February 1931, p. 90. Heinrich Köhler, *Lebenserinnerungen*, p. 223, depicts Stegerwald as consumed with envy of his successful protegé, but contrast Hans Schäffer to Josef Becker, 10 May 1961, NL Schäffer/45/3–6. In 1944 Brüning recommended Stegerwald to the U.S. military as a reliable anti-fascist but concluded from his utterances at the war's end that Stegerwald had come to hate him. See Brüning to Ullmann, 6 December 1949, NL Ullmann/6/197; Brüning to Otto Friedrich, 30 August 1954, HUG FP 93.4.5/Folder 2; and Müller, *Brüning Papers*, pp. 110–11.

although he emphasized that this campaign must be linked with efforts to promote international reconciliation. Stegerwald had also long demanded that Germany's neighbors must either disarm or permit Germany to rearm, and he depicted reparations as an intolerable burden that made German workers "slaves of international capitalism." During a tense cabinet debate over food tariffs in February 1931, Stegerwald exclaimed that "he had carried out the wage reductions in order to undermine the system of reparations. Further support for domestic agriculture is not consistent with that goal."[2] Only the thought that he would go down in history as the right-hand man to another architect of national liberation like Karl vom Stein sustained Stegerwald in his thankless duties as the labor minister charged with implementing an austerity program.

Brüning quarreled bitterly with Ludwig Kaas over Hitler's Enabling Act in March 1933, and his memoirs offer a somewhat unsympathetic portrait of the professor of canon law and Center Party chairman. Kaas had nevertheless done everything he could to further Brüning's career, and he was Chancellor Brüning's most frequently consulted adviser.[3] As his party's spokesman on foreign policy in the 1920s, Kaas enjoyed the special confidence of the foreign office and supported Stresemann's long-term strategy to undermine the Treaty of Versailles. Although Stresemann sincerely favored reconciliation with France, he always planned to employ diplomacy and economic pressure to reduce or eliminate reparations, achieve military parity with France, recover some of the territory lost to Poland, and achieve union with Austria. Kaas began in 1926 to consult Brüning about the fiscal ramifications of Stresemann's initiatives, introducing him to the complex debate within government circles over the order in which these goals should be pursued and the proper tempo for the revisionist campaign.[4]

Gottfried Treviranus was Brüning's closest friend. He later recalled Brüning as an older brother in whom he could always confide, although the confidences might not be returned: "Even I could expect no entry into his inner sanctum, which lived its own secret life."[5] Treviranus inspired Brüning's initial effort to carve out a right-of-center majority in the Reichstag, and he depicted the new cabinet as the first to represent the "generation of 1914" (he had translated the war memoirs of Robert Graves for Rowohlt just before taking office). This stance offended some admirers of the Great Coalition like Hans Schäffer, who felt that he insulted the many combat veterans in the SPD, but Treviranus did support

2 Zentralverband christlicher Lederarbeiter, *Niederschrift über die Verhandlungen der 11. Verbandsgeneralversammlung* (Frankfurt a.M., 1927), p. 97; Christlicher Metallarbeiterverband, *Protokoll über die Verhandlungen der 12. General-Versammlung, 16–20 September 1928* (n.p., n.d.), pp. 39–40; *Kabinette Brüning*, meeting of 17 February 1931, I:874–76; Patch, *Christian Trade Unions*, pp. 188–96.

3 See George May, *Ludwig Kaas. Der Priester, der Politiker und der Gelehrte aus der Schule von Ulrich Stutz*, 3 vols. (Amsterdam, 1981), III:127–70; Morsey, *Zur Entstehung*, p. 48; and Morsey, *Der Untergang des politischen Katholizismus. Die Zentrumspartei zwischen christlichem Selbstverständnis und "Nationaler Erhebung" 1932/33* (Stuttgart and Zürich, 1977), pp. 30–31.

4 Brüning, *Memoiren*, pp. 121–22; Brüning to Otto Friedrich, 30 August 1954, p. 12, HUG FP 93.4.5/Folder 2; May, *Kaas*, I:489–99; Jacobsen, *Locarno Diplomacy*, pp. 3–12, 76–119, 223–35; Post, *Civil-Military Fabric*, pp. 13–84, 160–89; Krüger, *Aussenpolitik*, pp. 207–364.

5 Treviranus, *Exil*, p. 201.

Brüning's efforts to maintain friendly contacts with SPD leaders. He agreed with Brüning that the Social Democrats should not be attacked but rather encouraged to renounce Marxism and evolve along the lines of the British labor movement.[6] Treviranus was the cabinet's most impetuous revisionist in foreign policy and sought from the outset to commit his colleagues explicitly to "the goal of regaining for the German Reich the normal position of a European Great Power in political, military, and economic terms."[7]

The political influence of Treviranus diminished after his party's electoral defeat in September 1930, and Hermann Dietrich (1879–1954) emerged as the most powerful minister beside Stegerwald. Brüning, Dietrich, and Stegerwald often set the agenda for cabinet meetings, and knowledgeable observers spoke of them as the "triumvirate."[8] As the son of a Lutheran pastor serving in a village in the Black Forest, Dietrich might seem far removed from the Prussian tradition, but his father was a champion of national unification and taught him to revere Frederick the Great, Karl vom Stein, and Bismarck. As a long-time Reichstag delegate from the Black Forest, Dietrich nevertheless maintained close ties with his rural constituents (he bought a farm in 1919 and called himself *ein Bauer*), and he was the one member of Brüning's inner circle who displayed overt anti-Semitism. Throughout his career he expressed intense suspicion of the influence of cosmopolitan Jews over the big banks and the ministerial bureaucracy in Berlin.[9] Brüning and General Schleicher both greatly admired the "objectivity" displayed by Dietrich as agriculture minister under the Great Coalition, when he sought to maintain grain price levels despite ample evidence that this policy cost the DDP votes, and as finance minister in June 1930, when he ignored the wishes of party colleagues while drafting his budget. After the election defeat in September, Dietrich threatened to secede from the State Party with his followers in Baden if it criticized the government. His party colleagues nevertheless elected the powerful finance minister as their chairman in November 1930, and he cemented his alliance with Brüning and Hindenburg by expelling the small pacifist wing of the old DDP that opposed any standing army. Brüning later eulogized Dietrich as an exemplary statesman who always followed the great Prussian motto, *patriae in serviendo consumor* ("I am consumed in service to the fatherland").[10]

---

6 Schäffer memoir, "Müller-Brüning," NL Schäffer/29/61; Wirth memoir, "Ereignisse und Gestalten von 1918–1933," question #21, p. 5, and question #22, p. 2; Treviranus, *Ende von Weimar*, p. 115; Treviranus, *Exil*, p. 38.

7 Memorandum of 24 June 1930, *Kabinette Brüning*, I:232.

8 Brüning to Otto Friedrich, 16 December 1951, *Briefe*, II:290–91; "Zustand der Regierung," DNVP memorandum of November 1930, BAP/DNVP/18/24–25; Pünder, *Politik*, 29 May 1931, p. 98; Luther, *Vor dem Abgrund*, p. 147; Schwerin von Krosigk, *Staatsbankrott*, pp. 61–62.

9 Von Saldern, *Hermann Dietrich*, pp. 3–5, 36–39, 82; Schwerin von Krosigk, *Staatsbankrott*, pp. 61–62.

10 Von Saldern, *Hermann Dietrich*, pp. 62–82, 100–113; Schleicher to Gessler, 28 August 1929, in Gessler, *Reichswehrpolitik*, pp. 491–92; eulogy for Dietrich, 9 March 1954, in Brüning, *Reden*, pp. 275–81; Staatspartei Vorstand, 16 October 1930, *Quellen: Linksliberalismus*, p. 604; Dietrich to Meissner, 15 November 1930, NL Dietrich/122/159; Werner Schneider, *Deutsche Demokratische Partei*, pp. 195–200; Jones, *German Liberalism*, pp. 399–402.

Thus Dietrich earned great influence in the cabinet but could not prevent the collapse of democratic liberalism at the polls. Like Stegerwald he sustained himself with the vision of national liberation. Dietrich had long urged the DDP to oppose the Versailles Treaty more vigorously, and he promoted *Anschluss* (union with Austria) and cultural ties with ethnic Germans throughout eastern Europe. He was inspired by Friedrich Naumann's concept of *Mitteleuropa*, that is, a natural symbiotic relationship between Germany and the lands to its south and east.[11] During a gloomy hour on 20 July 1930 when Dietrich concluded that the coming Reichstag election would greatly strengthen the radical parties, he drafted a memorandum arguing that Germany should adopt "the constitution of George Washington, which Bismarck praised." This reform would solve the immediate problem of strengthening the President's authority, but more important, it should promote a diplomatic breakthrough. The United States would surely champion the cause of its "sister republic," and the new constitution would facilitate the grant of German statehood to Austria and someday perhaps to Hungary and the Baltic Republics as well. Dietrich apparently decided not to show this fanciful document to Brüning or the President, but it illustrates the strength of his revisionist impulse.[12]

Brüning did not pay a great deal of attention to the rest of his cabinet ministers but often worked directly with their subordinates. Most senior officials in the ministerial bureaucracy were, as Count Schwerin von Krosigk later recalled, animated by "the 'idea of Prussia' as the epitome of . . . incorruptible and tireless dedication to public service." Such diplomats and civil servants felt anguish throughout the 1920s whenever the squabbling political parties toppled yet another cabinet and thereby disrupted the long-term planning which, in their view, Germany so badly needed.[13] Brüning encountered many kindred spirits in these circles and forged especially close ties with the state secretaries in the chancellery, foreign office, and economics and finance ministries, Hermann Pünder, Bernhard Wilhelm von Bülow, Ernst Trendelenburg, and Hans Schäffer.

Pünder (1888–1976) had worked closely with Hans Luther, Wilhelm Marx, and Hermann Müller, but he considered Brüning his first boss "with really profound knowledge of policy matters, who pursues large aims and does not allow himself to be deflected."[14] Himself a decorated combat veteran and Center Party member, Pünder developed some expertise in foreign policy because Chancellor Marx had often sent his chief of staff to represent him at international confer-

11 Von Saldern, *Hermann Dietrich*, pp. 33–35; Werner Schneider, *Deutsche Demokratische Partei*, pp. 200–212. See also Dietrich's correspondence with Richard Bahr over measures to influence the Austrian press in NL Dietrich/204.
12 "Zur Lage," 20 July 1930, NL Dietrich/254/5–11.
13 Schwerin von Krosigk, *Staatsbankrott*, pp. 44–45; compare the scathing criticism of the politicians in the correspondence of Ernst von Weizsäcker from 1929/30, in Leonidas Hill, ed., *Die Weizsäcker-Papiere 1900–1932* (Berlin, Frankfurt a.M., and Vienna, 1982), pp. 389–401.
14 Pünder, *Politik*, entry of 28 May 1930, p. 51.

ences. Pünder articulated the self-image of all members of Brüning's inner circle when he offered German newspaper editors some reflections on the tenth anniversary of the signing of the Versailles Treaty. This was no "peace treaty" but rather a "shameful and humiliating document." Signing it had been necessary, however, just as it had been necessary to sign the Peace of Tilsit after defeat by Napoleon. Ebert, Erzberger, Wirth, Rathenau, Stresemann, and Hermann Müller had all displayed heroism with their "policy of fulfillment":

> Men whose patriotic resolve and value for the salvation of Germany from the upheavals of that time are no longer doubted – I cite Freiherr vom Stein, Hardenberg, Scharnhorst, and Gneisenau – took exactly the same political line back then that has been rewarded with physical assault, murder, and defamation in speeches and print in the years after the Versailles Treaty. They too accepted conditions that could not be fulfilled even with the best of will; but through this wise moderation they saw to it that this chained and oppressed little Prussia again became a significant political factor in the Wars of Liberation.

In March 1933 Ludwig Kaas made exactly the same argument, placing Brüning's name at the top of the list, to defend the statesmen of the Weimar Republic against Nazi slanders during the Center Party's last election campaign.[15]

The professional diplomat Bernhard Wilhelm von Bülow (1885–1936), the nephew of an imperial chancellor, was also a decorated combat veteran and remained a bachelor after the war, sharing Brüning's single-minded devotion to the task of rescuing the fatherland. In the mid-1920s he championed participation in the League of Nations as the best way to revise the Treaty of Versailles. He agreed with the broad outlines of Stresemann's foreign policy but was impatient to regain at least part of the territory lost to Poland and skeptical about the prospects for genuine reconciliation with France.[16] Peter Krüger has suggested that Brüning signaled a new policy of isolating France diplomatically when he promoted Bülow to the rank of state secretary in May 1930, and it is true that Brüning's friends Ullmann and von Willisen had introduced him to Bülow as the most energetic revisionist at the foreign office.[17] Brüning probably did not intend any change of course with this appointment, however. He had insisted to Hindenburg that Stresemann's disciple Curtius remain foreign minister, and he promised the leaders of the SPD to walk in Stresemann's path; Curtius then supported Bülow's promotion enthusiastically, as did most officials in the foreign office. Brüning regarded Stresemann as a brilliant statesman who had been impelled by personal vanity to adopt needlessly divisive rhetoric when attacked

---

15 Pünder speech of 21 November 1929, NL Pünder/3/107–12; Kaas speech in *Kölnische Volkszeitung*, 2 March 1933, #61.

16 See Peter Krüger and Erich Hahn, "Der Loyalitätskonflikt des Staatssekretärs Bernhard Wilhelm von Bülow im Frühjahr 1933," *Vierteljahrshefte für Zeitgeschichte*, 20 (1972): 377–79; Krüger, *Aussenpolitik*, pp. 89, 261–62, 345–56, 391–93; and Lutz Graf Schwerin von Krosigk, *Es geschah in Deutschland. Menschenbilder unseres Jahrhunderts* (Tübingen and Stuttgart, 1951), pp. 307–09.

17 Krüger, *Aussenpolitik*, pp. 512–15; Ullmann, *Publizist*, p. 135; Treviranus, *Ende von Weimar*, p. 147.

by the DNVP. He apparently expected Curtius and Bülow to carry on the same basic policy as Stresemann but to display more tact with nationalist critics. Brüning valued (and perhaps over-rated) Bülow's sober judgment, skeptical temperament, and dry wit, granting him unrestricted access to the chancellor's office and private apartment.[18] Krüger is doubtless correct, however, that neither Brüning, Bülow, nor Curtius understood the French point of view as well as Stresemann had.

Ernst Trendelenburg (1882–1945) was Brüning's most experienced economic adviser. He had supervised the wartime rationing of fats and chemical products and rose to become state secretary in the ministry of economics by 1923. His influence was strengthened at the end of the war when he recruited as his aide a brilliant young Jewish lawyer and decorated combat veteran, Hans Schäffer (1886–1967), the son of a factory-owner in Breslau. Trendelenburg and Schäffer struggled against the advocates of a swift return to free enterprise, seeking to prolong the government's wartime economic controls for the sake of national reconstruction. They soon lost that battle but collaborated successfully with Foreign Minister Rathenau in 1921/2 to develop the "policy of fulfillment" referred to by Pünder, the strategy concerning war reparations that also guided Stresemann and Brüning. A weak Germany, they reasoned, must give every appearance of striving to fulfill its treaty obligations, but it must also demonstrate to world public opinion and the international banking community that reparations harmed debtor and creditor alike. Trendelenburg and Schäffer helped to negotiate the Dawes and Young plans, and reparations were still Schäffer's field of expertise when he became state secretary of finance in December 1929.[19]

Schäffer was by all accounts the most brilliant of Germany's senior officials, and he performed an invaluable service for historians by maintaining an exhaustive daily record of his political conversations. Some colleagues complained about his practice of taking short-hand notes during cabinet meetings, but he was gripped by a presentiment that right-wing demagogues would someday distort the historical record.[20] Schäffer located himself between the DDP and SPD on the political spectrum and was married to the daughter of a famous pacifist, but in December 1929 he accepted the chairmanship of the secret oversight com-

---

18 Brüning, *Memoiren*, pp. 111–12, 121–23, 167; Brüning to Dr. Goldschmidt, 29 June 1954, HUG FP 93.10/Box 12/Theo Goldschmidt; Brüning to Otto Friedrich, 30 August 1954, p. 12, HUG FP 93.4.5/Folder 2; Brüning to Hans Berger, 16 April 1957, HUG FP 93.10/Box 3/Hans Berger; Breitscheid memorandum, 29 March 1930, in Morsey, "Neue Quellen," pp. 227–28; Curtius, *Sechs Jahre*, pp. 146–47; Andreas Rödder, *Stresemanns Erbe: Julius Curtius und die deutsche Aussenpolitik 1929–1931* (Paderborn, 1996), pp. 27–31, 70–71, 80–83; Michael Salewski, "Zur deutschen Sicherheitspolitik in der Spätzeit der Weimarer Republik," *Vierteljahrshefte für Zeitgeschichte*, 22 (1974): 125–30; Post, *Civil-Military Fabric*, pp. 267–69.

19 Wandel, *Hans Schäffer*, pp. 15–129; Erna Danzl, ed., "Dokumentation: Erinnerungen Hans Schäffers an Ernst Trendelenburg," *Vierteljahrshefte für Zeitgeschichte*, 25 (1977): 865–88.

20 Luther, *Vor dem Abgrund*, p. 55; Wandel, *Hans Schäffer*, pp. 291–97; Schwerin von Krosigk, *Staatsbankrott*, pp. 59–60.

mittee that disbursed funds for covert rearmament. His predecessor Popitz described the goal of these efforts as "not preparation of a war, but adequate defense against an attack, especially from the east, and suppression of possibly rebellious organizations at home." Schäffer preferred to deputize his subordinate Schwerin von Krosigk to represent him on this committee, but he established a cordial working relationship with General Schleicher and helped the military to expand beyond the limits prescribed at Versailles.[21] Schäffer initially distrusted Chancellor Brüning but agreed with him about the urgent need to balance the budget and reduce "excessive" welfare benefits. The two men had a long conversation in May 1930 that cleared the air, and Schäffer became one of Brüning's most loyal supporters, a sometime confidant, and a highly influential participant at cabinet meetings. He later recalled Brüning as "one of the most responsible and courageous of German statesmen," terming the day of his fall "one of the blackest days in German history."[22]

Brüning's inner circle also included the military planners Wilhelm Groener (1867–1939) and Kurt von Schleicher (1882–1934). Groener was the son of a humble sergeant in Württemberg, but he too shared Brüning's devotion to the study of Prussian statecraft and became the first officer of the army of Württemberg to join the Prussian general staff.[23] Groener was also the first "revisionist" of the Weimar Republic. As quartermaster-general of the army in 1918/19, he focused attention on patient, long-term planning to restore the authority of the national government and revive the economy in order to lay the foundations for eventual rearmament and the recovery of lost provinces. Groener worked tenaciously to further this master plan as minister of transport from 1920 to 1923, then as a military historian appealing to world public opinion, and finally as defense minister since January 1928.[24] Groener termed Chancellor Brüning the best statesman he had ever known and the first worthy successor to Bismarck. "What a pity," he wrote his closest friend, "that we did not have such a man as Reich chancellor during the war." Schäffer felt that most of Groener's infrequent interventions in cabinet debates about non-military issues occurred, through prior arrangement with Brüning, to advance a point of view that the chancellor favored.[25]

---

21 Schäffer diary, 29 December 1929, NL Schäffer/8/1 (source of quotation); Luther, *Vor dem Abgrund*, pp. 53–54; Schwerin von Krosigk, *Staatsbankrott*, pp. 58–59.
22 "Reportorium," p. 5, NL Schäffer; memoir "Müller-Brüning," NL Schäffer/29/61–64; diary entry of 10 May 1930, NL Schäffer/8/118–20; Schwerin von Krosigk, *Staatsbankrott*, pp. 60–61.
23 See Dorothea Groener-Geyer, *General Groener. Soldat und Staatsmann* (Frankfurt a.M., 1955), pp. 15–26. This book by his daughter, the only biography of Groener, is erratic in judgment but includes valuable documents. For the years 1928–32 it has been superseded by Johannes Hürter's *Wilhelm Groener*.
24 Groener-Geyer, *General Groener*, pp. 143–46, 211–56, 379–86; Carsten, *Reichswehr*, pp. 33–48.
25 Groener to Gleich, 26 April 1931, in Groener-Geyer, *Groener*, p. 279; Theodor Eschenburg, "Die Rolle der Persönlichkeit in der Krise der Weimarer Republik: Hindenburg, Brüning, Groener, Schleicher," in Theodor Eschenburg, *Republik von Weimar* (Munich, 1984), pp. 249–67; Schäffer to Werner Conze, 5 February 1965, NL Schäffer/45/73–80.

Groener's top aide in the defense ministry, Schleicher, embodied the Prussian tradition as an offspring of the warrior nobility raised in military academies since early childhood. Charming, vivacious, and credited with numerous romantic conquests before he finally married in August 1931, Schleicher displayed a warmer personality than Brüning, but his understanding of Prussian statecraft was more authoritarian. The general praised King Frederick William I to Schäffer for understanding "that the German must obey a little, that he fouls up when granted too much independence. That can be seen again now." Schleicher also told Brüning with a smile that he worried too much about material problems; the masses yearned for circuses as well as bread, so the chancellor should ride up and down the boulevard Unter den Linden at least once a day in a coach-and-four with cavalry escort.[26] During his tenure as chancellor, Brüning regarded Schleicher as a trusted adviser. After his fall Brüning became convinced that the general had treacherously sought to undermine him ever since October 1930, but he eventually concluded that Schleicher had probably tried to defend him until Hindenburg himself became implacably hostile.[27] As Brüning finally began to perceive in old age, Schleicher had always acted from a rather weak position; he lacked prestige in the army because he had served just two months at the front (in Galicia in the summer of 1917) and never exercised a field command. Schleicher's role as political representative of the army came to him by default as the only senior officer with any interest in party politics, and he could not retain that role without demonstrating his usefulness to the officer corps in the question of rearmament.[28]

On the outer fringe of the inner circle stood the former chancellor Hans Luther (1879–1962). At first Brüning regarded the Reichsbank president as a dangerous rival. Luther had founded a League for the Renovation of the Reich in 1927/8 to promote *Reichsreform*, the subdivision of the huge state of Prussia to avoid the wasteful duplication of functions between it and the federal government. There was an objective rationale for such reform, but the "Luther League" gained financial backing primarily from conservative industrialists such as Paul Reusch who were eager to expel the Social Democrats from their Prussian bastion of power. Luther sought Hindenburg's support for his league from the outset, and when his program for *Reichsreform* failed to win the support of any political party, he shifted his focus in 1929 to agitation for a stronger presidency, exalting the role played by Hindenburg as "guardian of the constitution."

---

26 Schäffer diary, 29 January 1932, *Quellen: Politik und Wirtschaft*, I:1250–51; Schwerin von Krosigk, *Es geschah in Deutschland*, p. 119. For Schleicher's background, see Friedrich-Karl von Plehwe, *Reichskanzler Kurt von Schleicher. Weimars letzte Chance gegen Hitler* (Esslingen, 1983), pp. 14–29.

27 Brüning, *Memoiren*, pp. 199–201, 649; Brüning to Ullmann, 13 July 1946, NL Ullmann/6/282; Brüning to Johannes Dettmer, 13 August 1950, HUG FP 93.10/Box 6/Dale-Deym; Müller, *Brüning Papers*, pp. 98–101.

28 See Carsten, *Reichswehr*, pp. 297–304; Post, *Civil-Military Fabric*, pp. 293–330; Hayes, "Question Mark," pp. 41–45; von Plehwe, *Kurt von Schleicher*, pp. 17–20, 86, 212; and Schwerin von Krosigk's interview of 24 April 1952, pp. 4–5, IfZ/ZS 145/Schwerin von Krosigk.

Many of Luther's admirers in the business community hoped that Chancellor Brüning would soon discredit himself so that Luther could replace him and impose massive reductions in welfare expenditure and tax rates.[29] Luther joined Brüning's circle of admirers within a few months, however, discovering a "shared conviction that political problems must be solved with the greatest objectivity, to the exclusion of all partisan interests." He became the cabinet's most vigorous defender in the business community and rejoiced when Treviranus told him in June 1931 that Brüning had finally come to trust him.[30] Luther's reverence for the Prussian tradition facilitated entry into the inner circle. After attending the dedication of a new war memorial in Berlin, he recorded the following sensations in his diary: "Many recollections of past times, also the feeling that these Reichswehr and police troops marching by could mean much for us again. Think what a loss it will be that the next Reich President will not come in uniform with a field marshal's baton."[31]

One more surprising name should be included among Brüning's closest advisers, Rudolf Hilferding (1877–1941). The chief theoretician of the SPD (a Viennese Jew by birth) was no great admirer of Prussia, but Brüning came to trust his judgment during their joint service on the Reichstag taxation committee and often praised his selfless character and thorough grasp of fiscal and economic problems. Hans Schäffer, a close friend of Hilferding, first heard of Brüning when the Social Democrat sang his praises. Schäffer later judged that Pünder, Treviranus, and Hilferding were the only three people in Berlin whom Chancellor Brüning really trusted. Joseph Wirth has offered similar testimony, and Hilferding's party colleague, Hans Staudinger, jibed in February 1931 that he had become Brüning's "court jester."[32] Hilferding opposed any large-scale rearmament, but he supported Brüning's diplomatic campaign against reparations and agreed that the Weimar Republic needed some kind of success in foreign policy to acquire legitimacy. In private he sternly lectured party colleagues about their tendency to sacrifice long-term foreign policy goals to short-term domestic political considerations.[33] Brüning often dined alone with

29 Hans Luther, *Vor dem Abgrund*, pp. 33–47; Luther to President Hindenburg, 8 October, and reply of 10 October 1928, BAP R601/Reel 6/vol. 7/24–25; James, *Reichsbank*, pp. 161–63; Scheuner, "Artikel 48," pp. 270–71; Dorpalen, *Hindenburg*, pp. 169–70; Gerhard Schulz, *Vorabend*, pp. 307–09; memorandum by Walther Jänecke on a conversation with Luther, 9 March 1930, *Quellen: Politik und Wirtschaft*, I:78–81.
30 Luther, *Vor dem Abgrund*, pp. 114, 129–30 (source of quotation); Luther's speech to the RDI, 27 November 1930, NL Silverberg/274/37–44; Schäffer diary, 16 January 1931, NL Schäffer/10/18.
31 Entry of 2 June 1931, NL Luther/425/57.
32 Brüning, *Memoiren*, pp. 113–16; Schäffer memorandum, "Müller–Brüning," NL Schäffer/29/61; Schäffer to Hans Luther, 28 September 1961, NL Schäffer/44/39–42; Wirth memoir, "Ereignisse und Gestalten von 1918–1933," question #22, pp. 4–6, NL Wirth/18; Staudinger, *Wirtschaftspolitik*, p. 96. Hilferding and Brüning were close enough that they jointly approached Theodor Wolff in October 1930 with a confidential appeal to alter the editorial policies of the *Berliner Tageblatt* to avoid offending President Hindenburg; see Ernst Feder, *Heute sprach ich mit. . . . Tagebücher eines Berliner Publizisten 1926–1932*, ed. Cecile Lowenthal-Hensel and Arnold Paucker (Stuttgart, 1971), p. 273.
33 Staudinger, *Wirtschaftspolitik*, pp. 88–90.

Hilferding, and the chancellor's appointment calendar, which survives for the period from January 1931 to May 1932, records far more significant conversations with him (61) than with anyone else but Ludwig Kaas (86). Stegerwald and Schleicher come next (47 and 46 meetings), then Dietrich and Treviranus (39 and 38). The next four names on the list display a doubtless intentional symmetry: The chancellor consulted the industrialists Paul Silverberg and Hermann Bücher with the same frequency as the Social Democrats Breitscheid and Otto Braun (23–26 meetings each).[34] This pattern suggests a sustained effort to preserve the Great Coalition on an informal basis.

Thus Brüning developed a closely knit team of twelve men by the fall of 1930 – Bülow, Dietrich, Groener, Hilferding, Kaas, Luther, Pünder, Schäffer, Schleicher, Stegerwald, Trendelenburg, and Treviranus – with whom almost all important decisions were made. He also generated an unusual degree of personal loyalty among a wide variety of politicians and lobbyists who risked their careers to support his policies, and he eventually gained the trust of many foreign statesmen. Von Bülow wrote the German ambassador in Washington that Brüning was considered "the most impressive figure in German politics" throughout Europe. "This assessment is thoroughly justified, for not only has he drawn the cabinet as tightly together as is possible in this situation, he also constantly places his personal stamp on all domestic policies." Wirth later made the same point in less flattering terms when he called Brüning an "intellectual tyrant" in his dealings with the cabinet. Thus Brüning probably attained more personal influence over cabinet decisions and a greater role in formulating policy guidelines for each ministry than any chancellor since Bismarck. This influence highlights his exceptional intellect, reputation for honesty, and skill at persuading small groups, but it also implies of course that he bore unprecedented responsibility for policies that failed.[35]

The values of Brüning's inner circle are illuminated by the cases of two men who never gained inclusion, Paul Moldenhauer and Julius Curtius. Moldenhauer was considered highly gifted but of weak character; Pünder labeled him a "man without any deep *Weltanschauung*, who displays no real drive." When Moldenhauer informed the cabinet on 18 June 1930 that his party wanted him to resign, Brüning pressed him to reconsider, arguing that the cabinet could never assert its authority against the Reichstag delegations unless he defied the DVP. Moldenhauer responded that this would wreck his political career, but von Guérard declared sternly that "every minister must bear a measure of unpopularity."

34 Figures calculated from the "Tagesnotizen" in NL Pünder/43–44. The count is somewhat arbitrary because I have tried to exclude formal meetings with large groups and very brief encounters in favor of significant consultations with one person or a small group.
35 Bülow to Prittwitz, 20 January 1931, *Akten zur deutschen auswärtigen Politik, 1918–1945. Serie B: 1925–1933* (Göttingen, 1966–1983) (hereafter cited as *ADAP*), XVI:435; Wirth memoir, "Ereignisse und Gestalten von 1918–1933," question #22, p. 6, NL Wirth/18; Schwerin von Krosigk, *Es geschah in Deutschland*, pp. 133–34; Brecht, "Gedanken über Brünings Memoiren," pp. 627–29; Rudolf Morsey, *Brüning und Adenauer. Zwei deutsche Staatsmänner* (Düsseldorf, 1972), pp. 19–22; Mommsen, "Brünings Politik," pp. 18–22.

Moldenhauer then argued that he could better rally support for the chancellor in the DVP if he left the cabinet, but his unpublished memoirs nurture the suspicion that his primary concern was to avoid any action that might jeopardize his future earnings in the business world.[36] Curtius showed that he was made of sterner stuff when Moldenhauer resigned. After consulting the President, who formally requested him to remain foreign minister, he stoutly defended Brüning before the DVP central committee and declared emphatically that he would never resign unless Hindenburg requested it. This corporate lawyer had accepted a moral obligation to make decisions in office that might burn his bridges to the DVP and to former business colleagues, and Brüning and Hindenburg both applauded his sense of duty. Curtius had inherited all of Stresemann's enemies, unfortunately, while appearing second-rate to many of Stresemann's admirers. In this case questions about the man's ability hindered inclusion in Brüning's inner circle.[37]

Johann Viktor Bredt has offered striking testimony to the moral influence exerted by Brüning. This veteran of the Empire's Free Conservative Party always sought to follow the maxims of Bismarck and found Brüning a worthy successor of the Iron Chancellor when he joined the cabinet as justice minister. Bredt greatly admired Brüning's handling of cabinet meetings, the simplicity of his lifestyle, and his "incredible diligence." After the September elections of 1930, Bredt initially shared the anger of his Business Party colleagues against Brüning's covert cooperation with the SPD, but Brüning soon persuaded him to respect the Social Democrats' moderation. After Bredt was compelled to resign from office, he struggled tirelessly to rally his party behind Brüning, emphasizing the chancellor's skillful conduct of foreign policy. Largely because of Bredt's influence, the Business Party provided the government's margin of victory in all confidence votes after the DVP defected to the opposition in October 1931. Bredt even applauded Brüning's refusal to make concessions to the Business Party before these votes, noting that the chancellor "compelled our Reichstag delegation to pursue a pure policy of maintaining the state."[38]

In May 1931 Hans von Raumer echoed the hopes for a revival of civic virtue that animated Brüning's inner circle in a letter to his party chairman, Eduard Dingeldey. The industrial lobbyist protested the tendency within the DVP to

---

36 Pünder, *Politik*, entry of 28 May 1930, p. 52; *Kabinette Brüning*, I:209–14; Moldenhauer memoirs, *Quellen: Politik und Wirtschaft*, I:244–46; unpublished memoirs, NL Moldenhauer/3/2 and 4/2. In December 1929 Moldenhauer agonized over whether to join the cabinet because this would involve a substantial cut in pay, and he extracted a promise from I. G. Farben that he could return to his lucrative post on its supervisory board when he left government. After his resignation, Moldenhauer was shocked when Carl Duisberg refused to grant him more than a humble consultancy.

37 Meissner to Hindenburg, 27 June, and Hindenburg to Curtius, 27 June 1930, BAP R601/19721/vol. 46/115–17 (partly published in *Quellen: Politik und Wirtschaft*, I:263–64); DVP Zentralvorstand, 4 July 1930, BAK R45II/46/157–69; Curtius, *Sechs Jahre*, pp. 59–61, 69–72; Rödder, *Julius Curtius*, pp. 71–77.

38 Bredt, *Erinnerungen*, pp. 225–32, 253–66, 271–72, 287–90; compare Schumacher, *Mittelstandsfront*, pp. 144–83.

demand drastic reductions in welfare benefits before permitting any further reduction of government salaries. The two-hundred-year tradition of Prussian statecraft demanded that civil servants be the first to make material sacrifices in a crisis of the state, but they now displayed the selfishness usually attributed to the most militant elements in organized labor. Von Raumer linked this sad development with the spread of hedonism and juvenile delinquency:

> The disease of our age is the sentiment engendered by Marxism and materialism, which now dominates the widest circles of the German people, the outlook that sees the only purpose of life in living one's own life, and that ascribes value to ideals and institutions . . . only insofar as they help one to live one's own life. This sentiment is anarchic in its effects and must lead to the collapse of the state, because it replaces loyalty to the state with loyalty to interest groups. We must attempt to give the people a new view of life that sees the goal and purpose of life in service to the idea of the state, service to the community. That is the idea of old Prussia.

He concluded that the DVP must pursue this goal through partnership with Chancellor Brüning, the politician best qualified to revive the Prussian tradition.[39] Thus Brüning enjoyed great prestige among all who took seriously the patriotic maxims and edifying stories about Prussia that they had learned in school.

3.2. Brüning's Response to the Rise of National Socialism

Chancellor Brüning initially assumed that much time would be required to prepare the ground for any diplomatic offensive against the Treaty of Versailles. The reparations experts in the bureaucracy advocated a passive diplomatic posture until the business and farming interests in France, Great Britain, and the United States that were harmed by Germany's "export offensive" prodded their governments into the first initiative to revise the Young Plan. Most German officials did not expect such an initiative before the American presidential election in the fall of 1932. Brüning therefore concentrated on domestic problems during his first months in office, providing little guidance to German diplomats beyond vague exhortations to try harder to influence world public opinion.[40] The chancellor assumed that the Reichstag election campaign of 1930 would revolve around economic issues such as public works and cartel policy but noted with alarm to the cabinet on 20 August that the Nazis had brought foreign policy to the forefront of the political debate. Treviranus felt compelled to lay claim to the

---

39 Von Raumer to Dingeldey, 16 May 1931, NL Dingeldey/83/26–29.
40 Pünder to Curtius, 15 May, and Bülow to Ambassador Prittwitz, 5 May 1930, *ADAP*, XV:61, 91; Herbert von Dirksen, *Moscow, Tokyo, London: Twenty Years of German Foreign Policy* (Norman, Okla., 1952), pp. 101–02; Treviranus memorandum of 24 June 1930, *Kabinette Brüning*, I:232–35; conference of reparations experts, 15 November 1930, *Quellen: Politik und Wirtschaft*, I:465–68; Helbich, *Reparationen*, pp. 42–60; Knipping, *Ende der Locarno Ära*, pp. 162–66; Glashagen, "Reparationspolitik Brünings," pp. 107–17, 160–61.

Polish Corridor in his campaign rallies for the Conservative People's Party, announcing "the end of the Stresemann course" in foreign policy. Curtius demanded indignantly within the cabinet that Treviranus be muzzled, and the chancellor agreed. Brüning's campaign speeches consistently emphasized the need to avoid dangerous experiments in foreign policy.[41] He was compelled to reevaluate this position after the votes had been counted. To German politicians of all parties the evidence seemed overwhelming that the electorate had been swept by a tidal wave of indignation against France's stubborn defense of legal rights based on the Versailles Treaty. Most parties of the moderate right imitated Nazi foreign policy demands in the Reichstag session of October; the Communists outdid the Nazis by laying claim to the South Tyrol; and even the Free Unions denounced reparations as the main cause of Germany's unusually high level of unemployment. Thus Brüning had a democratic foundation for his belief that no German government could continue Stresemann's foreign policy completely unchanged.[42]

Brüning sought nevertheless to confine his modifications to style rather than substance. His first response to the election returns was to huddle with Kaas, Stegerwald, Bülow, Treviranus, and Pünder on the morning of 15 September. They dispatched Kaas to Geneva by airplane (then a highly unconventional form of travel) to persuade Curtius to adopt new rhetoric in the debates of the League of Nations. Curtius must not speak of a "policy of reconciliation" (*Verständigungspolitik*), Stresemann's favorite slogan, and he should cite the Nazi vote as evidence that the Western powers were destroying the credibility of German moderates.[43] The chancellor rejected any further change of course, however, because all diplomatic reports indicated unrelenting hostility abroad to the idea of a reparations moratorium and mounting fear that the German government would do something foolish to appease the Nazis. When the French foreign minister, Aristide Briand, complained about Curtius's new tone at Geneva, Brüning and Bülow transmitted soothing messages that the content of German foreign policy remained the same. Curtius took the same line at a tumultuous meeting of the Reichstag foreign affairs committee on 29 October and soon began again

---

41 *Kabinette Brüning*, 20 August and 3 September 1930, I:385–88, 408–14; "Im Westen nichts Neues" and "Brüning zur Aussenpolitik," *Der Deutsche*, 2 September 1930, #205; Curtius, *Sechs Jahre*, pp. 165–66; Rödder, *Curtius*, pp. 83–84.

42 ADGB Bundesausschuss, 12/13 October 1930, *Quellen: Gewerkschaften*, pp. 139–51, 157–59, 166–68; Winkler, *Katastrophe*, pp. 225–28; Schulz, *Von Brüning zu Hitler*, pp. 193–97, 318; memorandum for the chancellor by Hermann Pünder, 15 September 1930, *Kabinette Brüning*, I:425–27; Hans Schäffer memorandum, "Betrachtung zu den Wahlen für ausländische Geldgeber," 15 September 1930, NL Schäffer/29/186–87; editorial in *Zentralblatt der christlichen Gewerkschaften*, 1 October 1930, p. 290. For the growing mutual hostility displayed by public opinion in France and Germany since 1928/9, see Knipping, *Ende der Locarno Ära*, pp. 50–147; Jacobsen, *Locarno Diplomacy*, pp. 228–32, 353–59; and Haim Shamir, *Economic Crisis and French Foreign Policy 1930–1936* (Leiden, 1989), pp. 16–22. Contrast Hermann Graml, "Präsidialsystem und Aussenpolitik," *Vierteljahrshefte für Zeitgeschichte*, 21 (1973): 134–45, and Krüger, *Aussenpolitik*, pp. 516–23.

43 Bülow to Curtius, 15 September 1930, *ADAP*, XV:527; Pünder, *Politik*, 16 September 1930, pp. 59–60; Curtius, *Sechs Jahre*, pp. 170–72.

to speak of a "policy of reconciliation."[44] Brüning himself earnestly warned a meeting of the Reich Association of Industry in November that it would be a dangerous illusion to blame all of Germany's problems on reparations and counter-productive to adopt an aggressive diplomatic posture. "Here things are the opposite from the miracle at Jericho: if you blow too loud on the trumpets, the walls do not come tumbling down but grow stronger than ever. . . . To remain unpopular for months and even a whole year is better than to make the mistake again of raising this issue prematurely!" This speech won the approval of most industrialists but involved the chancellor in a painful debate with Fritz Thyssen, who demanded representation for "all nationalist elements" in the cabinet to achieve the immediate abolition of reparations.[45]

Brüning had already rejected numerous suggestions that he invite the Nazis to join his cabinet. The idea enjoyed little sympathy among colleagues in the Center Party, and the chancellor expressed his feelings openly among them. Heinrich Köhler provoked a rare display of temper on the afternoon of 15 September when he told Brüning that the best way to weaken Hitler's movement would be to saddle it with a share of government responsibility:

> Dr. Brüning, who had become ever more agitated during my remarks, now interrupted me and declared angrily: "No, never, under no circumstances. The National Socialist movement is a symptom of the fever of the German people that will soon disappear again. It has reached the top of its arc; it would be completely wrong to alter the composition of the Reich government on the basis of this temporary upsurge."[46]

Rudolf ten Hompel and Günther Gereke also gained the impression in these days that Brüning felt insurmountable repugnance at the thought of any coalition with the Nazis. Indeed, most Center Party leaders despised the Nazis as ignorant barbarians, an attitude reinforced by leading Catholic bishops who condemned the Nazi racial world-view as incompatible with Christianity. Apparently the only party colleague to support Köhler's idea at this juncture was the ultra-conservative Franz von Papen, who wrote Schleicher as an old colleague from the Prussian general staff to denounce efforts by Wirth and others to lay down the principle that the Nazis must never enter the government.[47]

44 Curtius memorandum of 19 September 1930, *ADAP*, XV:536–37; Bülow to Paris Embassy, 9 October 1930, *ADAP*, XVI:11–12; committee meeting of 29 October 1930, *Quellen: Politik und Wirtschaft*, I:452–53; Edward W. Bennett, *Germany and the Diplomacy of the Financial Crisis, 1931* (Cambridge, Mass., 1962), pp. 15–29; Knipping, *Ende der Locarno-Ära*, pp. 192–94; Rödder, *Curtius*, pp. 85–87.
45 RDI Hauptausschuss, 27 November 1930, "Veröffentlichungen des RDI," Nr. 55, in NL Silverberg/274/46–64 (partly published in *Quellen: Politik und Wirtschaft*, quotation on p. I:477); Neebe, *Grossindustrie*, pp. 85–87.
46 Köhler, *Lebenserinnerungen*, pp. 300–301.
47 Ten Hompel's unpublished memoirs, chapter 3, p. 39, NL ten Hompel/1; Gereke, *Königlich-preussischer Landrat*, pp. 166–67; Morsey, "Die Deutsche Zentrumspartei," pp. 297–98; Josef Becker, "Brüning, Prälat Kaas, und das Problem einer Regierungsbeteiligung der NSDAP, 1930–1932," *Historische Zeitschrift*, 196 (1963): 77–80; Aretz, *Katholische Arbeiterbewegung*, pp.

Brüning was influenced by his militantly antifascist colleagues in the Christian trade unions and Catholic Workers' Clubs, who had decided in 1923 that Italian Fascism posed a deadly threat to democracy and that Adolf Hitler was the most dangerous of Mussolini's German imitators. Brüning later recalled learning at the time of the Ruhr Struggle that Hitler was an egomaniac who did not really care about the fatherland at all; he had encouraged a neo-conservative friend, Edgar Jung, to visit Hitler in Munich with a request to support the government's campaign of passive resistance, but Jung found that the Nazi leader could think of nothing but the conquest of political power.[48] The organ of the Christian unions responded to the election returns of September 1930 by denouncing any suggestion that the Nazis participate in government:

> It must be recognized that such participation would mean the dismantling of the democratic state, especially since this corresponds with the wish of many delegates from the so-called bourgeois parties to restore the old authoritarian conditions. . . . And who can doubt that one of the first concerns of the German advocates of modern Italian statecraft would be to outlaw the trade unions, at least those unwilling to become organs of the new regime?

Adam Stegerwald, a member of the small group that conferred with Brüning just before his clash with Köhler, emphatically opposed any cooperation with the NSDAP and told party colleagues in January 1931 that Hitler had formed an unholy alliance with Ruhr industrialists to suppress the trade unions and slash wages by 20 percent. Brüning repeated this unfounded charge in his memoirs.[49]

Many conservative Protestants like Count Westarp and Max Habermann of the DHV also urged Brüning to seek a coalition with the Nazis in the fall of 1930. With them he could not afford angry outbursts but spoke instead in Bismarckian terms about the primacy of foreign policy. Until Germany achieved the decisive breakthrough toward abolishing reparations, Brüning argued, the government needed such a "national opposition" at its back; in opposition Hitler would state Germany's grievances with a vigor that no government could imitate, and fear of a Nazi takeover would encourage foreigners to grant concessions to

---

49–52; May, *Kaas*, III:212–13; Klaus Scholder, *The Churches and the Third Reich*, 2 vols. (London, 1987), I:132–35; episcopal guidelines on National Socialism from the fall of 1930, in Hans Müller, ed., *Katholische Kirche und Nationalsozialismus. Dokumente 1930–1933* (Munich, 1963), pp. 13–23; Papen to Schleicher, 24 September 1930, quoted in Petzold, *Franz von Papen*, pp. 59–60.

48 Brüning, *Memoiren*, p. 99; Patch, *Christian Trade Unions*, pp. 194–96; Aretz, *Katholische Arbeiterbewegung*, pp. 45–52; anonymous critique of "Die Hitlerbewegung," in *Der Deutsche*, 28 January 1923, #23. For Jung's dim view of Hitler ever since 1923, see Larry Eugene Jones, "The Limits of Collaboration: Edgar Jung, Herbert von Bose, and the Origins of the Conservative Resistance to Hitler, 1933–1934," in Larry Jones and James Retallack, eds., *Between Reform, Reaction, and Resistance: Studies in the History of German Conservatism from 1789 to 1945* (Providence and Oxford, 1993), pp. 471–74.

49 *Zentralblatt der christlichen Gewerkschaften*, 1 October 1930, p. 291; *Zentrumsprotokolle*, 12 January 1931, p. 504; Brüning, *Memoiren*, pp. 234–35; Patch, *Christian Trade Unions*, p. 206.

the present government. Brüning told Count Westarp on 2 October that the preparations for his diplomatic offensive would probably require three years, during which time there was no alternative to cooperation between the government and the SPD. In effect Brüning was formulating Otto Braun's case for a "Great Coalition of all reasonable persons" in the terms best suited to influence conservatives, although he also believed what he said about foreign policy, having concluded that the nationalistic agitation of the DNVP had played a major role in the diplomatic successes of Stresemann.[50] Historians must not be misled by the distortions in Brüning's memoirs into concluding that he supported the plan developed by some Ruhr industrialists and the Stahlhelm in October 1930 to promote a coalition of the Nazi Party, Center, and DNVP to dismantle welfare programs and achieve authoritarian constitutional reforms. Chancellor Brüning regarded the backers of this plan as his enemies, the men who had thwarted all efforts to revive the Central Association of November 1918 and sought to turn Hindenburg against him. Indeed, Habermann actually sought to thwart this plan when he urged Brüning to confer with Hitler; the DHV had long campaigned to strengthen the "left wing" of the Nazi Party and resist efforts by the "social reactionaries" in the DNVP and Ruhr industry to influence it.[51]

Habermann and Treviranus did persuade Brüning to explore Hitler's attitude in a personal meeting, but the chancellor insisted on the utmost secrecy – even Pünder was bypassed – to prevent Hitler from gaining prestige. His intermediary was Albert Krebs, a middle-level DHV functionary and veteran Nazi activist who edited the party's newspaper in Hamburg. On 19 September, five days after the election, Habermann dispatched Krebs to Berlin, where Treviranus told him that Brüning wanted to talk to Hitler. Treviranus emphasized that no coalition would be proposed; the chancellor just sought an exchange of ideas on how best to liberate Germany from the Versailles Treaty. Krebs was instructed in an elaborate conspiratorial system of cover names, mail drops, and secret telephone numbers; then he traveled to Munich to convey Brüning's invitation along with a DHV plan to fund disability insurance for Nazi Party members, intended by Habermann to create a material bond between the Nazis and political moderates. After some hesitation, Hitler agreed both to confer with the chancellor and to enter a limited financial partnership with the DHV.[52] Despite the careful

---

50 Westarp memorandum of October 1930, *Quellen: Politik und Wirtschaft*, I:443–44; Habermann memoir, "Der DHV im Kampf um das Reich," DHV Archive, pp. 72–73; Bredt, *Erinnerungen*, p. 229; Schulz, *Von Brüning zu Hitler*, pp. 172–74; Brüning, "Die Vereinigten Staaten und Europa," speech of 2 June 1954, *Reden*, pp. 284–85.

51 See Berghahn, *Stahlhelm*, pp. 154–63; Turner, *Big Business*, pp. 124–26; Haniel to Reusch, 16 October, and von Gilsa to Reusch, 30 October 1930, *Quellen: Politik und Wirtschaft*, I:419–20, 457–58; Patch, *Christian Trade Unions*, pp. 196–205; and Larry Eugene Jones, "Between the Fronts: The German National Union of Commercial Employees 1928 to 1933," *Journal of Modern History*, 48 (1976): 462–82. Contrast Grübler, *Spitzenverbände*, pp. 219–25, and Neebe, *Grossindustrie*, pp. 78–80.

52 Krebs diary, entries of 19–22 September 1930, NL Krebs/1/61–62; William S. Allen, ed., *The Infancy of Nazism: The Memoirs of ex-Gauleiter Albert Krebs, 1923–1933* (New York, 1976), pp. 168–74. Pünder apparently learned of the coming talk only on 30 September and was told that Hitler had requested it (*Politik in der Reichskanzlei*, p. 62).

language of the invitation, Hitler rushed to Berlin in great excitement, expecting to help form a new government. He intended to demand control of the Prussian premiership and the Reich ministries of defense and the interior. Brüning kept the Nazi leader waiting for two weeks, however, until his negotiations for "objective cooperation" with the SPD achieved their first breakthrough. Only when the chancellor knew that he did not need Hitler's support did he agree to a meeting on 5 October.[53]

Hitler and his lieutenants Wilhelm Frick and Gregor Strasser met the chancellor in the apartment of Treviranus. Brüning later recalled offering a frank explanation of his plans to lay the fiscal and economic foundation for a diplomatic offensive against the Versailles Treaty. The preparations would require at least eighteen months, during which time the Nazis must remain in opposition. Once the diplomatic offensive began, Brüning would be prepared to discuss coalitions between the Center and Nazi parties in some state governments. After Germany had achieved the right to rearm and the abolition of reparations in two or three years, the Nazis might want to enter the Reich cabinet, which might then seek a two-thirds majority in the Reichstag to amend the constitution, perhaps in the direction of monarchy. Would Hitler be interested in confidential contacts with the government to coordinate the form of political opposition most useful to German foreign policy? "I hope that I can appeal to you as an old front-line soldier," Brüning concluded, "just like my friends and me, for whom as old soldiers it is irrelevant whether the final success will be linked with our names." In reply Hitler demanded an immediate moratorium on reparations and delivered an hour-long monologue about his plans to "annihilate" all of Germany's enemies, first the Marxists and reactionaries at home, then France and Russia. He promised to avoid ad hominem attacks on the chancellor and President but would not moderate his opposition to the government unless granted at least three cabinet seats, a request that Brüning refused. Brüning's account of this conversation in his memoirs has been widely cited as proof of his reactionary goals and authoritarian values, but at the time he and Hitler said nothing about monarchism or altering the constitution when they summarized this meeting for their closest associates.[54] Even the conversation reported in the memoirs, moreover, amounts to little more than a request for immediate political concessions in exchange for vague speculation about future developments.

Brüning and Hitler agreed to confer again if the SPD decided to oppose the government, but they parted with little inclination to cooperate. Brüning reported to Hindenburg that the Nazis insisted on an immediate reparations moratorium "despite full knowledge of the catastrophic consequences of their

---

53 Goebbels, *Tagebücher*, entries of 22/3 September 1930, I:606–07; report by the monarchist agent Magnus von Levetzow on his conversations with Hitler and Göring, 3 October 1930, in Granier, *Magnus von Levetzow*, pp. 278–79; Schulz, *Von Brüning zu Hitler*, pp. 172–79.
54 Brüning, *Memoiren*, pp. 191–96. Compare Levetzow's account of a similar diatribe by Hitler on 29 September 1930, in Granier, *Levetzow*, pp. 276–78; Pünder, *Politik*, entries of 5–7 October 1930, pp. 64–65; Goebbels, *Tagebücher*, 6 October 1930, p. 614; Treviranus, *Ende von Weimar*, pp. 161–62; and Rödder, "Dichtung und Wahrheit," pp. 96–99.

suggestion." The chancellor and President agreed that they must expect the sharpest opposition from the Nazis and that the attitude of the Social Democrats was far more constructive. Treviranus spread the word among Brüning's conservative supporters that Hitler had no interest in a coalition because he desired complete freedom for irresponsible agitation. Brüning later recalled that Hitler impressed him as a "cheap imitation of Mussolini" (*Klichée Mussolini*), interested in nothing but the conquest of power.[55] Hitler found Brüning rather more impressive, perhaps even intimidating. At first he boasted to Goebbels that he had made a tremendous impression on the chancellor, but in the following weeks he concluded that Brüning was the chief obstacle to his own ambition.[56] Hitler and Hermann Göring praised Brüning's personal character in private, exempting him from the charge that the leaders of the Weimar Republic were all fools or scoundrels. Gregor Strasser later told Krebs that Hitler "was so strongly taken by the appearance and behavior of the Reich chancellor that he was only able to free himself from a feeling of inferiority toward Brüning by forming a hate complex against him." Krebs found that Brüning eventually attained mythic stature among functionaries at Munich party headquarters as a powerful and cunning opponent alongside "the Jews, the Jesuits, the Freemasons."[57]

Fortunately for Brüning, neither Hindenburg nor the defense ministry sympathized as yet with the idea of including Nazis in the cabinet. Groener and Schleicher had decided in 1929 to classify the NSDAP as a "subversive" organization like the Communist Party, which meant that no party member could be employed by the military in any capacity. President Hindenburg shared this view and told Brüning after the September election that he would never summon the Nazis to form a government because they would violate the constitution.[58] Fears of Nazi subversion mounted after three young army lieutenants in the Ulm garrison were arrested in September 1930 for spreading Nazi propaganda among their comrades. Justice Minister Bredt argued that they should quietly receive a dishonorable discharge because a "monster trial" would burn all bridges to the right. Groener and Interior Minister Wirth insisted, however, that the young hotheads be prosecuted for treason in a public trial in Leipzig, and Hindenburg agreed that drastic action was needed to restore military discipline. The interior ministry dispatched its top official to Leipzig to refute the testimony of the star

---

55 Pünder, *Politik*, 7 October 1930, p. 65; Pünder memorandum of 8 October 1930, *Kabinette Brüning*, I:510–12; Bracher, *Auflösung*, p. 330; Brüning, manuscript memoirs, p. 52, HUG FP 93.4.

56 Goebbels, *Tagebücher*, 6 October 1930 and 18 January 1931, I:614, II:9.

57 Ibid., 21 February and 29 March 1931, II:24–25, 40–41; Levetzow's reports to Fürst v. Donnersmarck on remarks by Göring and Hitler, 28 August and 20 November 1931, in Granier, *Levetzow*, pp. 297–99, 312–13; Krebs, *Infancy of Nazism*, p. 170.

58 Defense ministry circulars of 22 January and 16 April 1930, and conference of Reich and state interior ministries of 28/29 April 1930, in Ilse Maurer and Udo Wengst, eds., *Staat und NSDAP 1930–1932. Quellen zur Ära Brüning* (Düsseldorf, 1977), pp. 3–5, 8–50 (hereafter cited as *Quellen: Staat und NSDAP*); Bavarian Ambassador Preger to Held, 19 September 1930, *Quellen: Politik und Wirtschaft*, I:389; Brüning, *Memoiren*, pp. 188–89; Hürter, *Wilhelm Groener*, pp. 284–86.

witness for the defense, Adolf Hitler, that his party employed only legal methods in its struggle for power, and on 4 October the defendants were convicted and sentenced to eighteen months in prison.[59] Schleicher explained to divisional commanders that the NSDAP included many genuine patriots, but that Hitler lied when he claimed to employ only legal methods. The Nazi economic program resembled the Communist, and Hitler did not seek a share of responsibility but only boundless freedom to agitate. The Center Party, he concluded, could never be persuaded to form a coalition with the Nazis anyway, so it was pointless to explore this option.[60] The last statement is significant because Schleicher took great pains to collect information about Brüning's intentions.

Brüning and the defense ministry also took a firm line against the antirepublican right in October 1930 with the appointment as Reichswehr commander of General Kurt von Hammerstein-Equord, a friend of Schleicher who was considered by most knowledgeable observers to be the strongest supporter of the Weimar constitution among the generals.[61] The former crown prince invited Hammerstein to a hunting trip soon after his promotion but was shocked by the republican tenor of the general's dinner conversation. Hammerstein denounced the Hugenberg press for inciting treason and proclaimed that "we will not tolerate any effort by the lunatics to plunge Germany into riots and civil war." Dedicated monarchists concluded that Hammerstein was a closet red who advocated a military dictatorship in alliance with the SPD against the right.[62] The Brüning cabinet also opposed monarchism in December 1930 when it decided that it must commemorate the 60th anniversary of the founding of the Reich after learning that President Hindenburg had already accepted an invitation to a ceremony planned by veterans' groups. Brüning insisted that the government ceremony "must of course avoid at all costs any monarchist overtones; the celebration must simply commemorate the unification of the German nation."[63]

The Nazi lieutenants tried in Leipzig enjoyed great sympathy in the army, however, and pressure from the officer corps compelled the defense ministry to redefine its priorities. The Hugenberg press inspired many soldiers to denounce

59 Bredt, *Erinnerungen*, pp. 250–52; cabinet meeting of 25 September 1930, *Kabinette Brüning*, I:447–49; defense ministry circular of 6 October 1930, *Quellen: Staat und NSDAP*, pp. 159–60; Meissner to Schleicher, 7 October, and reply of 8 October 1930, BAP R601/Reel 112/vol. 763.1/19–20; Carsten, *Reichswehr*, pp. 315–19; Gerhard Schulz, *Aufstieg des Nationalsozialismus. Krise und Revolution in Deutschland* (Frankfurt a.M., 1975), pp. 588–97.

60 "Befehlshaberbesprechung," 25 October 1930, in Thilo Vogelsang, ed., "Dokumentation: Neue Dokumente zur Geschichte der Reichswehr, 1930–1933," *Vierteljahrshefte für Zeitgeschichte*, 2 (1954): 400–408.

61 Carsten, *Reichswehr*, pp. 325–28; Brüning to Kunrat Hammerstein, 23 September 1946, p. 1, HUG FP 93.10/Box 14/Hammerstein; *Zentrumsprotokolle*, remarks by Brüning on 12 December 1930, pp. 499–500; Pünder to Zechlin, 19 September 1929, NL Pünder/20/127–29; Severing, *Lebensweg*, II:378.

62 Otto Schmidt-Hannover to Schleicher, 8 November, and reply of 12 November 1930, NL Schleicher/59/5–6; Schleicher and Hammerstein to Müldner von Müllnheim, 1 December 1930 (source of quotation), NL Schleicher/42/59; Levetzow to Fürst v. Donnersmarck, 28 August 1931, in Granier, *Levetzow*, pp. 302–04; Schwerin von Krosigk, *Es geschah in Deutschland*, pp. 112–13.

63 *Kabinette Brüning*, 17 December 1930, I:743–44.

the "leftist course" of Groener and Schleicher, and old complaints bubbled to the surface that the army was being run by a clique of staff officers who weakly tolerated the efforts by the Prussian police to obstruct covert mobilization programs. Old comrades in arms and the leadership of the DNVP conveyed these complaints directly to President Hindenburg, and Groener soon noted with alarm that his subordinates had lost faith in his determination to achieve rearmament.[64] The defense minister therefore prodded the cabinet at the end of October to insist openly on Germany's right to rearm, and General Hammerstein told it that the army could not tolerate continued enforcement of the Versailles Treaty for more than one more year at most because it robbed Germany of even "the most primitive measure of national security." Thus the army pressured Brüning to place rearmament at the top of his agenda.[65]

Groener and Schleicher also retreated from the classification of the NSDAP as a "subversive" organization after the Leipzig trial. The defense minister cited Brüning's decision to confer with Hitler, which the chancellor had tried so hard to keep secret, to persuade Interior Minister Wirth that the old policy of treating Nazis like Communists could no longer be sustained. Wirth opposed any change of this policy, but no police agencies could discover hard evidence that the Nazis planned a putsch. Hitler skillfully avoided any call to overthrow the government, and the Prussian interior minister, Carl Severing, eventually acknowledged that his efforts to prosecute Goebbels for treason had been based on misquotations in the republican press.[66] Citing the disastrous failure of Bismarck's Anti-Socialist Law, Schleicher and Groener exhorted Brüning to avoid conflict with the apparent patriots in the NSDAP unless conclusive evidence emerged that Hitler was lying when he promised to employ only legal methods in the struggle for power. On 30 October the chancellor followed their wishes by instructing Wirth to resume payment of police subsidies to the state of Brunswick, which had hired Nazis as policemen after Nazis entered the state cabinet.[67] Groener clashed with Wirth again when he sought authorization to

---

64 Carsten, *Reichswehr*, pp. 319–25; Oberleutnant Stieff to his wife, 7 October 1930, in Vogelsang, *Reichswehr*, p. 419; Generalleutnant a.D. von Below to President Hindenburg, 7 October, Admiral von Schröder to Hindenburg, 9 October, and Hugenberg to Hindenburg, 9 October 1930, in BAP R601/Reel 112/vol. 763.1/57–61; General Heye to Groener, 13 October 1930, *Quellen: Staat und NSDAP*, pp. 160–62; memorandum by Major Theisen of 14 October and Groener's circular letter of 25 October 1930, and General Heinrici to Groener-Geyer, 29 March 1953, in Groener-Geyer, *General Groener*, pp. 397–99, 272–74; commanders' conference of 25 October 1930, in Vogelsang, ed., "Neue Dokumente," pp. 400–408.

65 *Kabinette Brüning*, 30 October 1930, I:591–93.

66 Wirth to the Oberreichsanwalt, 15 August 1930, with memorandum on "Das hochverräterische Unternehmen der NSDAP," BAP R15.01/25790/128–98; report on the Thuringian Nazi Party by Regierungspräsident Freyseng, 12 September, and confidential report of 18 September 1930 on a Hitler rally in Munich, BAP R15.01/25790/498–99, 508; Groener to Wirth, 15 October, and reply of 21 October 1930, *Quellen: Staat und NSDAP*, pp. 162–65; Severing to Wirth, 1 December 1930, BAP R15.01/25791/136–38.

67 *Kabinette Brüning*, meeting of 30 October 1930, I:584–87; Pünder, *Politik*, 21–24 December 1930, pp. 82–83; Schulz, *Von Brüning zu Hitler*, pp. 140–60; Hürter, *Wilhelm Groener*, pp. 287–90.

hire Nazis as civilian employees at military installations and train SA members for "frontier defense" in the eastern provinces. On 19 December Schleicher told the cabinet that the frontier defense program could not survive without Nazi volunteers, and Brüning declared that "the Reich government must avoid at all costs employing the same false methods against the National Socialists that were utilized against the Social Democrats in the prewar era." The cabinet granted the defense ministry's request, and Schleicher eventually brought the good news to the new SA commander, Ernst Röhm, in person.[68] Schleicher also began at this time to undermine Wirth and Curtius by arguing that Groener could coordinate the policies of the army and police much better if he also became interior minister, and that Brüning himself would make a superb foreign minister.[69]

Groener's feud with Wirth resulted in large part from his desire to prepare the German people for the restoration of conscription. The defense minister had sought ever since 1928 to persuade the government to revive patriotism among the younger generation by cracking down on atheist propaganda, pornography, journalists who revealed military secrets, and the performance of pacifist works by famous authors like Bertolt Brecht and Kurt Tucholsky that urged draft dodging in time of war. Groener considered the magazine founded by Wirth, *Die Deutsche Republik*, a prime offender in this regard and pressured the interior minister into dissolving all ties with it in November 1930. Brüning and the Christian clergy sympathized with Groener's views, but the chancellor and interior ministry opposed any of the legal restrictions on freedom of speech suggested by the defense ministry.[70] Groener and Schleicher hoped after the September elections that the popularity of Hitler's campaign against "cultural Bolshevism," a slogan sometimes used by Groener as well, would persuade all government agencies to promote the "militarization of the populace" (*Wehrhaftmachung der Bevölkerung*) through stricter censorship and financial support for athletic associations and shooting clubs. Their most cherished goal was to incorporate all the paramilitary leagues from the Nazi SA to the republican Reichsbanner (which was closely linked to the SPD) into a state-sponsored militia. Severing noted sadly that the defense ministry displayed far greater energy in promoting the "spirit of Potsdam" than did any other government agency in promoting the "spirit of Weimar."[71]

68 Groener to Brüning, 10 November 1930, Schleicher to Pünder, 11 December, and Ernst Röhm to Schleicher, 24 March 1931, and reply in *Quellen: Staat und NSDAP*, pp. 169–72, 189–90; *Kabinette Brüning*, meeting of 19 December 1930, I:751–54.

69 Pünder, *Politik*, 8 December 1930, pp. 79–80; Bracher, *Auflösung*, p. 340.

70 Hürter, *Wilhelm Groener*, pp. 294–304. See also Groener to Gleich, 24 March 1930, NL Schleicher/35/68; "Aufzeichnung über wehrfeindliche Tätigkeit pazifisticher Kreise," sent by Schleicher to State Secretary Zweigert in July 1930, BAP R15.01/13129.4/144–61; the numerous complaints by Groener to the chancellery and interior ministry about pacifist propaganda in BAK R43I/688; and Brüning to S.H. Cross, 22 July 1942, HUG FP 93.4.5.

71 Commanders' conference of 25 October 1930, in Vogelsang, ed., "Neue Dokumente," pp. 405–06; Hürter, *Wilhelm Groener*, pp. 291–92; Severing, *Lebensweg*, II:164, 280–81.

Wirth defended the constitutional rights of German writers but did not put up a struggle when Groener demanded a ban on the Hollywood film version of *All Quiet on the Western Front*. The Nazis employed stink bombs and sneeze powder to disrupt the first public screening in Berlin on 5 December, and President Hindenburg himself intervened unsuccessfully with Otto Braun to seek a ban on the film by the Prussian police. On 11 December the national board of film censors granted a request by five other state governments, a request quietly endorsed by the Reich cabinet, to ban further screenings on the grounds that the movie contained hateful caricatures of German soldiers. This ban caused dismay and indignation among Brüning's sympathizers in the SPD, Great Britain, and the United States, and it aroused mixed emotions within the Center Party. Brüning nimbly defended the decision to party colleagues on pacifist grounds; the film actually made war more likely, he argued, by aggravating international tensions.[72] Brüning then noted disturbing limitations on his own influence when his chief of staff appealed to Groener to drop a treason case against the newspaper *Tempo* to facilitate detente between the government and the Ullstein press. Groener refused, confessing fear of Nazi attacks if he appeared weak.[73] Thus Brüning felt compelled to make concessions to the defense ministry that muddled the distinction between the government and the "national opposition."

Brüning nevertheless developed a consistent though subtle antifascist strategy, which he explained most clearly to his party colleagues on 12 December 1930. He warned that the world economic crisis would last another two years at least. The Nazis could be weakened if brought into the government, but that would cause "panic" and remove them as a counter-weight to the Communists, who were more dangerous because better organized to launch an insurrection. If one did not bring the Nazis into government, however, then nothing could reduce their popularity "as long as the [economic] crisis lasts and there are no successes in foreign policy." Therefore it would be counter-productive to attack them; one should persevere with the existing form of semi-parliamentary government based on quiet consultation with the SPD and give Curtius time to pursue diplomatic victories. "If they try anything, strike swift and hard, but otherwise no police chicanery. Whenever I negotiate with National Socialists, they should always get the impression that I do not reject them in principle but cannot for the time being accept them into the government."[74] At a Center Party rally

---

72 Groener to Brüning, 25 July 1930, and cabinet meeting of 9 December, *Kabinette Brüning*, I:343–45, 691–93; Severing, *Lebensweg*, II:266–67; Otto Braun, *Von Weimar zu Hitler*, pp. 314–15; Frederic Sackett to Henry Stimson, 17 December 1930, in United States Department of State, *Papers Relating to the Foreign Relations of the United States* (hereafter cited as *FRUS*) *1931*, II:309–14; *Zentrumsprotokolle*, remarks by Brüning, 11 December 1930, p. 500; Pünder, *Politik*, 14 December 1930, p. 81; Modris Eksteins, "War, Memory, and Politics: The Fate of the Film *All Quiet on the Western Front*," *Central European History*, 13 (1980): 60–82.

73 Pünder to Groener, 8 January 1931, BAK R43I/688/221–22; for background see Modris Eksteins, *The Limits of Reason: The German Democratic Press and the Collapse of Weimar Democracy* (Oxford, 1975), pp. 195–98, 213–18, 233–36.

74 *Zentrumsprotokolle*, pp. 500–503.

soon thereafter, a Nazi heckler provoked Ludwig Kaas into a rare display of emotion:

> I would advise the National Socialists to take a vacation from politics, but without any return ticket. This is the only way you can serve the German people. If our sense of responsibility did not restrain us, we would make way for the National Socialists so that the German people could finally recognize their bloodthirsty ignorance. The National Socialists have said nothing about how one can achieve the diplomatic liberation of the German people, they just scream and complain. They adopt heroic poses and ridicule those of us who stand in the political front lines. . . . We care about the contents of the skull, but you only care about its shape.

Kaas's sharp tone was applauded in the liberal press and encouraged DVP leaders to hope that the Nazi wave had crested.[75] Usually, however, Brüning and Kaas avoided such frontal attacks as inexpedient.

Several officials in the Prussian and Reich interior ministries later reproached Brüning for hindering their efforts to prosecute leading Nazis for treason, and it is true that the chancellor sometimes vetoed the publication of data collected by police officials on the violent actions and revolutionary utterances of Hitler's followers. Prussian officials were often guilty of exaggeration in these reports, however, for example by quoting firebrands already expelled from the NSDAP, and they sometimes displayed confusion about the limits of free speech. The veteran Social Democrat who served as Berlin's chief of police actually urged prosecution of Nazi leaders for treason with a memorandum showing that some of them advocated a centrally planned economy. Officials in the Reich interior ministry pointed out drily that it was not illegal to advocate socialism.[76] Otto Braun, Carl Severing, and most senior leaders of the SPD agreed with Brüning that the KPD posed a greater threat of insurrection than did the Nazi Party, and that the latter group must be combated primarily through political rather than police methods. Brüning's critics doubtless under-estimated the danger of confirming Nazi legends about collusion between the "Weimar system" and foreign powers against all true patriots. Hitler himself predicted confidently to his lieutenants that persecution by the police would only strengthen their movement.[77] Brüning's cautious strategy for containing the Nazi threat generally proved effective until the President withdrew his support. It did have the distasteful result of making the chancellor reluctant to express solidarity with

75 Quotation from *Berliner Tageblatt*, 5 January 1931, #7; see also "Zentrum und Nationalsozialismus," *Kölnische Volkszeitung*, 6 January 1931, #9, and Weizsäcker's report of 20 February 1931 on his conversations with Dingeldey, *Weizsäcker-Papiere*, p. 425.

76 Orlow, *Weimar Prussia 1925–1933*, pp. 185–92; Prussian interior ministry memoranda of May and August 1930, *Quellen: Staat und NSDAP*, pp. 51–81, 96–155; 129-page memorandum by *Polizeipräsident* Karl Zörgiebel, "Zusammenstellung von Material über wirtschaftsgefährdende Tendenzen der N.S.D.A.P. sowie ihre Stellung zu den Grundbegriffen des Privateigentums," 5 September 1930, and attached correspondence in BAP RIM/25790/355–488.

77 Schulz, *Von Brüning zu Hitler*, pp. 155–60, 276–82; Winkler, *Katastrophe*, pp. 275–77; confidential report on Hitler's remarks to SA leaders on 15/16 September 1931, sent by the Munich police to the Reich interior ministry on 7 October, BAP R15.01/25792/394–97.

the victims of racial prejudice. Brüning often spoke in general terms of the need to respect the legal rights and religious beliefs of all fellow citizens, but he refused to receive leaders of Jewish organizations or to address the topic of anti-Semitism directly. In private he sometimes lashed out at his sharpest critics in the Prussian bureaucracy as a "Zionist clique," although he cultivated friendly ties with many assimilationist Jews.[78]

Brüning took Nazi radicalism more seriously after he toured the eastern provinces in the first two weeks of January 1931. He had decided to appeal to East Elbian farmers directly after several frustrating meetings with their lobbyists in Berlin; he would announce a modest expansion of the Eastern Aid program and seek to persuade them that they benefited from political stability in the form of lower interest rates. President Hindenburg, rejoicing at the prospect of reconciliation between the government and Junkerdom, lent Brüning his own fur coat from the Great War for the trip.[79] The chancellor soon discovered, however, that economic conditions in the provinces were worse than he had imagined and the process of radicalization further advanced. Hostile crowds confronted him at every stop, even in his old Reichstag district in Silesia. At first his police escort assumed that they were Communists, but most turned out to be Nazis. In Breslau a mob of 40,000 hurled stones at the official motorcade, and none of the local notables dared to oppose the troublemakers. Brüning foresaw that the spread of such rowdyism to the countryside doomed even Hugenberg's brand of nationalism, not to speak of more moderate forms of conservatism. He later recalled lying awake at night on this trip, pondering whether the critics of the Freiherr vom Stein had been right to oppose his plans to spread local self-government from the western provinces of Prussia to the eastern, since East Elbia still did not seem "ripe for democracy." Not even the name of Hindenburg, the savior of East Prussia in August 1914, could influence these crowds: "The Hindenburg myth, which still lived in the west and south of Germany, was already dead in the east." What would happen when the President's term expired in 1932? Brüning returned to Berlin on 12 January, sickly and depressed, and told his party colleagues that all political moderates must rally together against the extremists.[80]

---

78 See Pünder's dialogue with the Zionist leader Kurt Blumenfeld, 30 March 1931, *Kabinette Brüning*, II:1002–03; Brüning's remarks in *Zentrumsprotokolle*, 12 December 1930, p. 502; Brüning to Wilhelm Sollmann, 29 September 1940, in Knapp, ed., "Dokumentation: Brüning im Exil," pp. 108–09; Brüning to Professor S.H. Cross, 22 July 1932, HUG FP 93.4.5; and Müller, *Brüning Papers*, p. 94. See also Hamburger, "Betrachtungen über Heinrich Brünings Memoiren," pp. 33–34, and the misleading indictment of Brüning as an anti-Semite in Jochmann, "Brünings Deflationspolitik," pp. 103, 109–11.

79 Chancellor's reception for the Green Front, 17 December 1930, *Kabinette Brüning*, I:748–49; Brüning, *Memoiren*, pp. 241–43.

80 Brüning, *Memoiren*, pp. 242–44 (source of quotations); *Zentrumsprotokolle*, 12 January 1931, p. 505; Brüning's personal appointment book, entries of 5–14 January 1931, in Müller, *Brüning Papers*, p. 215; Brüning's Reichstag speech of 5 February 1931, *Verhandlungen des Reichstags*, 444/705–07.

Brüning was just beginning to understand the political consequences of rising unemployment. Nationwide a record 4.76 million workers had registered for jobless benefits by January 1931, as opposed to three million when he took office, and even this statistic understated the problem because working-class wives and teenagers living at home often found themselves purged from the jobless rolls by officials who felt that each family deserved only one job. More and more of the jobless, finding their national unemployment insurance benefits exhausted, landed in the far less generous welfare programs financed by local governments for the chronically unemployed, which usually demanded an embarrassing means test and sometimes imposed harsh requirements for compulsory labor. Malnutrition among the children of the jobless, juvenile delinquency among unemployed youth, and rising suicide rates had become glaring social problems, and the growing lines of hopeless men outside labor exchanges in every city contributed to an atmosphere of crisis that benefited the radical parties enormously.[81] Just after his return from East Elbia, Brüning instructed the labor ministry to convene a blue-ribbon panel to study the problem of unemployment. On 31 January the public learned that this panel would be chaired by the former labor minister Heinrich Brauns and composed of ten officials and economists, ranging in political affiliation from the SPD to the DNVP. Its deliberations, unfortunately, would require two months at least.[82] For the time being Brüning felt that he could combat unemployment only by restoring an atmosphere of political normalcy, so he launched a campaign to win a majority in favor of passing a budget in the normal parliamentary fashion during the Reichstag session scheduled to begin on 3 February. He hoped to lower interest rates and restore investor confidence by squelching all rumors that the government would resort to "dictatorship."[83]

Brüning first prepared for the Reichstag session by improving his relations with the SPD and DVP. He commissioned Pünder in late December to approach the SPD to discuss four possible amendments to the Reichstag's rules of order designed to restore parliamentary decorum – to suspend the Reichstag delegate's immunity from legal prosecution between sessions of parliament, to require that any proposal for new expenditure specify the method of financing, to prohibit multiple motions of no confidence if the government defeated one, and to authorize punitive action, including the suspension of legal immunity, against any Reichstag delegate who insulted a colleague and refused to apologize. The first and fourth proposals were motivated by the outrageous behavior of Nazi and Communist parliamentarians; the NSDAP in particular had abused parliamentary immunity by naming Reichstag delegates as nominal editors of most party

---

81 See Winkler, *Katastrophe*, pp. 19–59, 288–89, and Heidrun Homburg, "Vom Arbeitslosen zum Zwangsarbeiter. Arbeitslosenpolitik und Fraktionierung der Arbeiterschaft in Deutschland 1930–1933," *Archiv für Sozialgeschichte*, 25 (1985): 251–98.
82 Grübler, *Spitzenverbände*, p. 354.
83 See Brüning's Reichstag speech of 5 February 1931, *Verhandlungen des Reichstags*, 444/678–81.

newspapers so as to avoid actions for libel. The SPD objected to these two suggestions, however, for going too far, so Brüning quietly dropped them. Following this compromise, a substantial parliamentary majority approved the second and third proposals on 9 February 1931. The Nazi and DNVP delegations protested this blow against the "freedom of the Reichstag" with a walkout, but these were sensible reforms and the only legal restrictions on the powers of the Reichstag that Chancellor Brüning ever proposed; indeed, the rule about specifying the method of funding had already been proposed by the Social Democrat Hilferding as finance minister in the spring of 1929.[84]

Brüning meanwhile cultivated personal ties with the new chairman of the DVP, Eduard Dingeldey. Elected to replace the ailing Ernst Scholz in November 1930, this eloquent young lawyer supported the government's program but feared a wave of defections from his party to the NSDAP unless he could persuade Brüning to ally with Hitler. Dingeldey prophesied to party colleagues that Brüning would be compelled to abandon his sound policies unless he sought the support of the right instead of the left; the crucial lesson of the September elections was that "we must compel National Socialism to renounce agitation in favor of working for the state."[85] Sensing an indecisive streak in the man, Brüning sent Dingeldey a flattering appeal for close personal cooperation, and for seven months the DVP chairman entered the small circle of politicians with direct access to the chancellor. As the Reichstag convened, Dingeldey approached Brüning to demand that any shortfall in government revenue be covered by reduced expenditure, not tax increases or borrowing, and the chancellor agreed. By this time it was clear that the Nazis sought above all to force new Reichstag elections, which the DVP feared, and this reinforced Dingeldey's loyalty to the moderate camp.[86]

Brüning also prepared for the Reichstag session by launching another appeal for social partnership between big business and the trade unions. He declared at a rally of the Christian unions on 25 January that management and labor must decide jointly where wages still needed to be reduced to restore the competitiveness of German industry on the world market, and where work hours could be shortened to create more jobs. Excessive action in either direction would harm the economy, and the bureaucracy was not sufficiently well informed to resolve

---

84 Brüning to Pünder, 27 December 1930, and meeting of 2 February 1931, *Kabinette Brüning*, I:767–68, 839–42; Winkler, *Katastrophe*, pp. 288–89; Schulz, *Von Brüning zu Hitler*, pp. 282–83. See also p. 97, n. 84 above, but contrast Mommsen, *Rise and Fall*, pp. 359–60. In his *Memoiren*, pp. 255–56, Brüning states that these measures satisfied his most important objections to the "excesses" of parliamentary government, and that all of his concerns would have disappeared with one more amendment to the rules of order to restrict confidence votes to the annual debate over the budget. This last proposal would have represented a major restriction on parliamentary power, but there is no contemporary evidence that Chancellor Brüning ever sought it.

85 Dingeldey speech of 26 October 1930 (source of quotation), NL Dingeldey/53/24–26; Dingeldey to Ernst Scholz, 28 October 1930, NL Dingeldey/31/11–12; Jones, *Liberalism*, pp. 404–06.

86 Brüning to Dingeldey, 1 December, and reply of 4 December 1930, NL Dingeldey/32/35–36; Pünder to Dingeldey, 1 December, and reply of 2 December 1930, NL Dingeldey/33/28–29; *Zentrumsprotokolle*, 3–5 February 1931, pp. 508–09; Dingeldey memorandum, 4 February 1931, NL Dingeldey/36/107.

such delicate questions.[87] Hermann Bücher of Germany's General Electric Corporation and the management of I. G. Farben supported Brüning by urging business colleagues to endorse the forty-hour week demanded by the Free Unions, but coal and steel executives pressured the RDI to demand instead that state labor arbitration be abolished so that wages could be slashed by 25 percent. Stegerwald and Brüning were dismayed when RDI leaders presented this demand in two audiences at the end of January; the labor minister replied that such action would drive the SPD into opposition and lead to "dictatorship by the radical right."[88] The United Steelworks then poisoned the atmosphere by announcing that its plant at Ruhrort-Meiderich would shut down unless its workers agreed to modify their existing labor contract with a wage reduction of 20 percent. Two-thirds of the employees adhered to union discipline by rejecting this ultimatum on 11 February, the plant did shut down, and the business press blamed the trade unions for rising unemployment. On 20 February Stegerwald appealed directly to industrial leaders to revive the Central Association of November 1918, but they responded with hostile questions about the government's reluctance to slash welfare benefits and wages.[89] Brüning himself brought Fritz Thyssen, Albert Vögler, and Ernst Poensgen together with Christian union leaders for a secret meeting in the chancellery a week later that lasted over six hours. He later recalled that they were on the verge of agreement to revive the Central Association as midnight approached, when his nemesis Thyssen stood up to denounce the Christian trade unions for having betrayed the fatherland at every decisive moment in recent history. Brüning felt compelled thereafter to agree with labor leaders that many industrialists had foolishly pinned their hopes on the collapse of the trade unions.[90]

The issue of agrarian protectionism posed the greatest threat to the government's effort to secure a Reichstag majority, and it also divided the cabinet. The distress of the eastern provinces persuaded Brüning and most cabinet members that some further initiative was necessary, but the Green Front alienated them and outraged the business community by demanding that Germany be sealed off from all imported food.[91] Brüning sought to extricate himself from this crossfire

---

87 *Zentralblatt der christlichen Gewerkschaften*, 1 February 1931, p. 38.
88 Reception of 29 January 1931, *Kabinette Brüning*, I:822–23 (source of quotation); Reusch to Blank, 28 January, replies of 29 and 31 January, and Poensgen memorandum of 2 February 1931, *Quellen: Politik und Wirtschaft*, I:537–8, 543–47; Grübler, *Spitzenverbände*, pp. 346–51.
89 Patch, *Christian Trade Unions*, pp. 170–71; Winkler, *Katastrophe*, pp. 73–75; Stegerwald's speech to RDI Hauptausschuss, 20 February 1931, NL Stegerwald/007/vol. 1931:I/#869.
90 "Tagesnotiz," 26 February 1931, NL Pünder/43/236; Brüning, manuscript memoirs, pp. 72–73, HUG FP 93.4 (which is more specific than the published *Memoiren*, pp. 239–40). In *Memoiren*, p. 234, Brüning later qualified the charge that many businessmen hoped for the destruction of the trade unions as applying "not so much to the managers and owners of large enterprises as to smaller businessmen and lobbyists who had succumbed to the Nazi psychology."
91 Chancellery critique of agrarian proposals, 19 January 1931, *Kabinette Brüning*, I:789–93; Schleicher to Treviranus, 19 January 1931, NL Schleicher/55/26–28; Schleicher to Brüning and Schleicher to Knebel-Döberitz, 24 February 1931, NL Schleicher/54/69–70; Bülow to Prittwitz, 20 January 1931, *ADAP*, XVI:436; RDI circular, 29 January 1931, *Quellen: Politik und Wirtschaft*, I:538–42.

by exhorting agrarians to convert their less fertile land from grain production to forest or pasture. He eventually agreed to allow the cabinet to consider a wide range of tariff increases but warned that there would be no emergency decree for agriculture; the Green Front must scale back its demands enough to win a Reichstag majority.[92] Schiele provoked a stormy debate when he presented his tariff bill to the cabinet on 17 February. Stegerwald argued that these measures would transfer another two billion marks in national income from other classes to German farmers, infuriate the working class, cause a disastrous decline in exports, and undermine the campaign against reparations; he threatened to resign if they were implemented. Trendelenburg supported him, but the ministers of finance and foreign affairs declared that they could accept higher duties on meat and livestock. Schiele replied that farmers required protection on dairy products as well, and he even questioned Trendelenburg's patriotism. Brüning adjourned the quarrel by persuading the cabinet to seek authorization from the Reichstag to increase tariffs on a wide variety of foodstuffs, while it agreed internally that no tariff would be imposed on dairy products until Schiele reformed the farmers' cooperatives to reduce administrative overhead.[93]

Brüning's most difficult problem with the Reichstag was to persuade the SPD to accept this tariff authorization bill. In exchange, that party's leaders appealed to the chancellor to give them an "external sign of success" by canceling the planned construction of a second armored cruiser. Brüning replied that Groener had been promised a second ship by Chancellor Müller and would resign if construction was delayed further.[94] On 17 March an angry SPD deputation notified Brüning that it would propose an income tax surcharge on the floor of the Reichstag. The chancellor agreed that this was their right but demanded that the Reichstag adjourn itself until October as soon as it had passed the budget, explaining that the diplomatic initiatives required to undermine the popularity of the Nazis could never succeed if subject to parliamentary scrutiny. Hilferding appealed for at least a two-week session in June, but Brüning refused because "no Reichstag majority can be obtained for the work that lies ahead."[95] The chancellor and Center Party finally offered the SPD some material concessions by agreeing that tariff increases would be rescinded automatically if the cost of living rose, and that either the Reichstag or the Reichsrat could rescind them (the first draft required a vote by both houses). These concessions were significant enough to turn the agrarians in the Center Party against the bill, but

92 *Kabinette Brüning*, chancellor's receptions of 27, 29, and 30 January 1931, I:806–09, 814–21, 827–32; *Zentrumsprotokolle*, 5 February 1931, pp. 509–10.

93 *Kabinette Brüning*, meetings of 17–23 February 1931, I:874–76, 882–96, 905–12; Pünder, *Politik*, 25 February 1931, p. 90; Tilman Koops, "Zielkonflikte der Agrar- und Wirtschaftspolitik in der Ära Brüning," in Hans Mommsen, Dietmar Petzina, and Bernd Weisbrod, eds., *Industrielles System und politische Entwicklung in der Weimarer Republik* (Athenäum ed., Düsseldorf, 1977), pp. 860–64.

94 Winkler, *Katastrophe*, pp. 289–91; Harsch, *Social Democracy*, pp. 131–33; Hürter, *Wilhelm Groener*, pp. 156–58; *Zentrumsprotokolle*, 5–13 March 1931, pp. 519–23; Brüning, *Memoiren*, pp. 259–60, Pünder, *Politik*, entries of 25 February and 9 March 1931, pp. 90–91 (source of quotation).

95 Reception of 17 March 1931, *Kabinette Brüning*, II:955–62.

Stegerwald rammed approval through his parliamentary delegation in the chancellor's name. In a series of parliamentary votes on 20–25 March, the Social Democrats then allowed the armored cruiser to pass by abstaining and actively supported all other cabinet measures, including the amended tariff authorization bill. The SPD did pass its income tax surcharge, but the Reichsrat followed the cabinet's wishes by vetoing it, and Dingeldey was satisfied that Brüning had fulfilled his promise to prevent tax increases. On 26 March the Reichstag adjourned itself until October.[96]

An air of normalcy began to return when, for the first time in years, the cabinet secured parliamentary approval of a budget before the start of a new fiscal year. The government followed up this success on 28 March with an emergency decree to expand the powers of the police, drafted by the Reich interior ministry in close consultation with Brüning and Prussian Interior Minister Severing. It authorized the police to ban the wearing of uniforms by political associations and to dissolve rallies where speakers urged illegal actions or maliciously insulted government leaders or religious bodies. Joseph Wirth placed special emphasis on the protection of organized religion, including Judaism, against hostile propaganda. Both the Nazi and Communist parties announced that they would comply with the decree, but they bellowed that the Weimar constitution had been scrapped.[97] This decree was enforced most vigorously in Prussia and Bavaria and most frequently against Communists; Severing shared Brüning's concern about creating martyrs on the right and sternly rebuked police officials who harassed the Stahlhelm. In the next three months 1,105 individuals were convicted of violating this decree and sentenced to fines or short jail terms; of these roughly twice as many were Communists as Nazis.[98] Even this bias against the KPD weakened the Nazis, however, by depriving them of one of their most popular arguments, that only they could defend Germany against the reds. On 1 April the Thuringian DVP mustered the courage to topple Wilhelm Frick as prime minister, forming a new state government without Nazis, and many observers concluded that the Nazi wave had crested. Joseph Goebbels felt that the decree of 28 March caused "the worst crisis that the Party has had to go through." He paid the chancellor the highest compliment in a diary entry on 22 April: "Brüning, our most dangerous enemy."[99]

---

96 Chancellor's reception for SPD leaders, 18 March 1931, *Kabinette Brüning*, II:965–68; *Zentrums-protokolle*, 21–24 March 1931, pp. 524–26; Dingeldey to von Gilsa, 26 March 1931, NL Dingeldey/69/34; Winkler, *Katastrophe*, pp. 292–95.

97 Cabinet meeting of 9 March 1931, *Kabinette Brüning*, II:932–34; decree provisions and response on 29 March by the DNVP and NSDAP, *Ursachen und Folgen*, VIII:154–57; Wirth to state interior ministers and Wirth to the leaders of the Evangelical, Catholic, and Jewish churches, 28 March 1931, BAP R15.01/25877/1–4; KPD circular of 30 March 1931, BAP R15.01/25877/321–29.

98 See Severing's instructions to the Prussian police of 31 March and 17 April 1931, BAP R15.01/25877/58–64, and Wirth's circular to state interior ministers of 29 August 1931, with tables on prosecutions, in BAP R15.01/25877.1/98–109.

99 Goebbels, *Tagebücher*, 29–31 March and 22 April 1931, II:40–42, 54; Pünder, *Politik*, 1 April 1931, pp. 93–94; Winkler, *Katastrophe*, pp. 309–12; Schulze, *Otto Braun*, pp. 352–54.

Brüning sought to exploit the confusion in the Nazi Party by secretly encouraging the "Stennes Revolt" of April 1931, a challenge to Hitler's authority in the SA. Walther Stennes, a former officer in the Prussian gendarmerie and in the "Black Reichswehr" of 1923, now commanded the regional organization of the SA for northeastern Germany. For months he had been wrangling about finances and jurisdiction with Goebbels as the civilian *Gauleiter* of Berlin and with the new national commander of the SA in Munich, Ernst Röhm. After obtaining Hitler's permission, Röhm and Goebbels proclaimed Stennes deposed for insubordination on 1 April. Supporters of Stennes then briefly occupied the Berlin party headquarters and declared that they would launch their own movement. Goebbels and Hitler denounced Stennes as a wild-eyed revolutionary who advocated violent insurrection, and soon they accused him of being a paid *agent provocateur* who sought to lure unwary comrades into defying the presidential decree of 28 March so that the government could ban the whole Nazi movement. Most non-Nazi newspapers dismissed the latter charge but accepted the former, depicting Stennes as the leader of dangerous revolutionaries in the SA who had lost patience with Hitler's commitment to legality. Goebbels acknowledged privately, however, that the real cause of the conflict was a series of gross errors in the treatment of the Stormtroopers by party headquarters in Munich.[100] Stennes himself denied indignantly that he had ever urged defiance of the authorities. Speaking in the name of the "soldierly and proletarian elements" in the Nazi Party, he instead denounced the incompetence and corruption in Hitler's entourage, wasteful expenditures on the lavish new party headquarters in Munich, and Hitler's abandonment of any socialist economic program in the quest for financial support from big business. Stennes founded a small newspaper of his own, but his words were drowned out by the enormous Nazi propaganda machine.[101]

Brüning decided in the utmost secrecy to support the Stennes revolt. Bülow confided to Hans Schäffer that the foreign office had fomented this uprising on instructions from Brüning in order to wreck the Nazi movement, and that Stennes received money and encouragement to lead a secession when his people wanted to submit to Hitler. Hermann Bücher also confided to business associates that he had subsidized Stennes, and this action too probably took place at the chancellor's request. Years later Brüning himself testified that Stennes had

---

100 See the collection of press clippings and police intelligence reports, "Zwistigkeiten in der NSDAP im Apr. 1931," BAP R15.01/26073; Goebbels, *Tagebücher*, 28 March–9 April 1931, II:40–46; Orlow, *Nazi Party 1919–1933*, pp. 212–20; and Richard Bessel, *Political Violence and the Rise of Nazism: The Storm Troopers in Eastern Germany 1925–1934* (New Haven and London, 1984), pp. 54–66.
101 See Standartenführer Krach (a supporter of Stennes), "Betrachtung zu den Ereignissen innerhalb der N.S.D.A.P. vom 1. April 1931," 22 April 1931, BAP R15.01/26071.b/207–16; "Stennes Anklage gegen Hitler," *Vossische Zeitung*, 7 April 1931, #162; "Hitler–Stennes," *Der Deutsche*, 8 April 1931, #81; "Der Nazikrach vor Gericht," *Vorwärts*, 8 April 1931, #162; and the inaugural issue of Stennes's *Arbeiter – Bauern – Soldaten*, 9 April 1931, BAP R15.01/26073/92.

infiltrated the Free Corps in 1919 as an agent of the Prussian police and maintained lasting ties with Prussian State Secretary Weismann.[102] Brüning expected idealistic patriots to sympathize with Stennes. He persuaded his friend Habermann, for example, to take a more negative view of the Nazi movement by arguing that Hitler now resembled Hugenberg in his demand for unconditional obedience. "The NSDAP is becoming a new version of the DNVP," Brüning declared, "but without its parliamentary experience and technical competence."[103] Unfortunately, the chancellor neglected the importance of public relations in this affair. Some supporters of Stennes strengthened Hitler's case with wild statements about their "revolutionary" aims, and Brüning failed to assure a favorable depiction of the dissidents even in the organs of the Center Party.[104] Far from weakening the Nazi movement – only a few hundred Stormtroopers followed Stennes out of the party – the purge of this "revolutionary" persuaded many influential journalists, army officers, and judges that Hitler was truly dedicated to legality. Wilhelm Groener felt strengthened in his view that the NSDAP was no longer subversive, and two important court verdicts of 1931 referred directly to the Stennes affair to deny that civil servants could be dismissed for belonging to it.[105]

While fomenting schism in the Nazi Party, Brüning showed where his true sympathies lay after the death of Hermann Müller on 20 March. In a moving eulogy before the Reichstag, Brüning lauded the Social Democrat's unsurpassed patriotism and devotion to the public good, emphatically defending his decision as foreign minister in 1919 to sign the Versailles Treaty. Müller's party colleagues found this speech a great comfort against the slanders which they endured from the right. Brüning himself was reminded that the SPD still represented a great popular force when he placed a wreath on Müller's coffin and joined the funeral procession; tens of thousands of Social Democrats marched under the gaze of hundreds of thousands of mourners in the largest demonstration that Berlin had seen in years. Much to Brüning's embarrassment, President Hindenburg refused to participate because the SPD planned to carry red flags in the parade. Groener persuaded him at the last minute, however, to appear on his balcony dressed

102 Brüning to Stennes, 11 August 1949, *Briefe*, II:193; Schäffer diary, conversation with Bülow, 17 April 1931, NL Schäffer/10/121–22; Turner, *Big Business*, pp. 141–42. Brüning conferred with Bücher tête-à-tête on 7 and 11 February and 31 March 1931, and he later wrote Bücher's widow that he had employed the industrialist on a variety of sensitive missions; see the "Tagesnotizen" in NL Pünder/43, and Brüning to Dorothea Bücher, 27 August 1951, HUG FP 93.10/Box 2/Brie-Bürger.

103 Krebs diary, conversation with Habermann, 7 April 1931, NL Krebs/1/118; see also Krebs to Gregor Strasser, 9 April, and Rudolf Hess to Krebs, 16 April 1931, NL Krebs/7/238–40.

104 See "Der Weg in den Sumpf," *Arbeiter – Bauern – Soldaten*, 15 April 1931 (BAP R15.01/26073/131); "Das Ende der SA-Revolte," *Kölnische Zeitung*, 8 April 1931, #189; and "Der Krach," *Germania*, 8 April 1931, #160.

105 Carsten, *Reichswehr*, pp. 332–35; Schulz, *Aufstieg der NSDAP*, pp. 636–37; Groener to Gleich, 26 April 1931, in Groener-Geyer, *Groener*, pp. 279–80; summary of court verdicts compiled on 25 May 1932, BAP R15.01/25794/79.

in black and raise his top hat as the coffin rolled by.[106] Something like the "Great Coalition of all reasonable persons" advocated by Otto Braun appeared to exist.

Unfortunately, the picture of a revival of parliamentary government was deceptive. Even while the Reichstag debated the budget, the finance ministry collected evidence of another disastrous decline in tax receipts. On 6 March Dietrich, Hans Schäffer, and Luther came to Brüning in a highly agitated state to report that the Reich faced a deficit of RM 425 million in the next three months alone. They demanded an immediate emergency decree to impose sweeping new austerity measures and tax increases. Brüning replied that he could not issue such a decree until May at the earliest because a decent interval must pass after the Reichstag adjourned – and nobody even suggested consulting parliament about the real problems that faced the treasury. The chancellor also refused to impose any new austerity measures without a simultaneous diplomatic initiative against reparations: "The German people can bear no further sacrifices in the financial area without decisive steps in the reparations question.... Cutting back again and again, without reparations reform, that will tear our poor nation to pieces." Thus Brüning felt compelled because of domestic political divisions to depart from his passive and soothing foreign policy.[107] On 27 March the Brauns Commission completed the first part of its report on unemployment but could suggest no new remedies. Brauns hoped to see 400,000 jobless workers employed in public works but could suggest no method of financing other than a foreign loan. This report did nothing to dispel the fatalistic belief inside and outside government that Germany had no power to alter the unemployment rate on its own.[108]

3.3. Germany Takes the Diplomatic Initiative

Brüning had actually discussed the need for greater activism in foreign policy with his national security advisers ever since December 1930, when the economic outlook darkened. He had originally planned to build a trade surplus as the best way to pressure the Western powers to revise the Young Plan, and Germany did achieve impressive surpluses of 1.6 billion marks in 1930 and 2.9 billion in 1931. This surplus came primarily at the expense of France and Great Britain, moreover, which enhanced its political value. In later years Brüning pointed to this fact as evidence for the success of his master plan, and this exaggerated claim to

---

106 Brüning's speech of 21 March 1931, *Verhandlungen des Reichstags*, 445/1855–56; Brüning, *Memoiren*, pp. 260–61; Severing, *Lebensweg*, II:282; Winkler, *Katastrophe*, pp. 296–97.

107 Conference of 6 March 1931, *Kabinette Brüning*, II:925–28; Schäffer diary, 6 March 1931, NL Schäffer/10/70–75; Pünder, *Politik*, 9 March 1931, pp. 92–93; Rödder, *Curtius*, pp. 237–38.

108 Cabinet meeting of 27 March 1931, *Kabinette Brüning*, II:986–94; Grübler, *Spitzenverbände*, pp. 361–71; Balderston, *German Economic Crisis*, pp. 296–300; Winkler, *Katastrophe*, pp. 314–16.

foresight might well give the impression that he deliberately threw millions of Germans out of work for the sake of foreign policy.[109] In fact his original plan was to increase the volume of exports by lowering Germany's price niveau, to create jobs in export industries while undermining reparations. By December 1930, however, it was obvious that the volume of exports was not growing; it merely shrank less rapidly than that of imports. Germany's trade surplus resulted primarily from Schiele's drastic form of agrarian protectionism, which did not figure in Brüning's original plans. He had never intended for Germany to have the highest unemployment rate in Europe, nor for the German people to suffer a major decline in the quality of its nutrition as more and more families found themselves unable to afford meat and imported produce. But this was the situation he faced at year's end.[110]

The Nazi electoral success had modified the rhetoric of German foreign policy, but the disheartening economic data collected at year's end modified the substance. On 15 December Brüning assembled Curtius, Dietrich, Bülow, Schäffer, and Luther in his apartment to discuss the need for a new strategy. The chancellor insisted that "the first discussion of the reparations question must come now. Domestic politics will compel us to do something. Even if we succeed in February in getting the Reichstag to dissolve itself until November, if we have not made substantial progress by then, this government and perhaps a great deal more will blow up." Curtius then suggested a new approach:

> If the whole world becomes calm, then it would be hard to raise the issue of reparations. Therefore [we should] take some political initiative alongside reparations. Disarmament and the eastern question [i.e., the Polish border] would be suitable. They could be given an economic rationale. Can we not solve the reparations problem by raising the issue of disarmament? We could also inject the question of war guilt in order to create sympathy in America.

Brüning endorsed this idea, hoping that President Hoover would forgive the war debts owed America to facilitate the abolition of reparations if he could achieve progress toward his cherished goal of world disarmament.[111] On 19 December

---

109 Helbich, *Reparationen*, pp. 45–49; Shamir, *Economic Crisis*, pp. 93–97; Glashagen, "Reparationspolitik Brünings," pp. 149–56; statistical appendices on German trade in Jürgen Schiemann, *Die deutsche Währung in der Weltwirtschaftskrise 1929–1933* (Bonn and Stuttgart, 1980), pp. 306–13; Hans Schäffer to Helbich, 17 October 1960, NL Schäffer/46/102; Luther, *Vor dem Abgrund*, pp. 100–106, 131–41; Mommsen, "Brünings Politik," pp. 24–31.

110 See Horst Sanmann, "Daten und Alternativen," pp. 112–19; Gottfried Plumpe, "Wirtschaftspolitik in der Weltwirtschaftskrise. Realität und Alternativen," *Geschichte und Gesellschaft*, 11 (1985): 329–42; Schiemann, *Deutsche Währung*, pp. 155–58; Knipping, *Ende der Locarno-Ära*, pp. 192–98; and Bennett, *Financial Crisis*, pp. 18–20.

111 Schäffer diary, 15 December 1930, *Quellen: Politik und Wirtschaft*, I:512–14; foreign office memorandum of 31 December 1930, *ADAP*, XVI:325, n. 2. Brüning, *Memoiren*, pp. 193–94, recalls describing this plan to Hitler on 5 October 1930, but the other sources suggest that it was a new idea in December. On Hoover's enthusiasm for disarmament, see Bennett, *German Rearmament*, pp. 139–42.

Brüning suggested to U.S. Ambassador Frederic Sackett that Hoover should convene an international conference to discuss economic recovery, reparations, and disarmament. If Hoover displayed any interest, Brüning and Curtius thought of appealing to him to host a grand conference for heads of state to discuss an extension of the ban on offensive warfare in the Kellogg–Briand Pact of 1928; they anticipated that the subject of reparations would then arise of its own.[112]

Many senior officials felt that the new activism of Brüning and Curtius reflected wishful thinking. The diplomat Ernst von Weizsäcker offered his family the following tart observations:

> Our foreign office is much too nervous. Looking toward the man on the street is sometimes necessary (even in Italy, as my Italian colleagues assure me), but one must not look *only* toward the street, which has become the custom here. In domestic affairs Brüning does what he considers necessary, even if that is unpopular. As compensation they allow Curtius, who is struggling for his survival as minister (most do not give him more than a month) to perform acrobatic feats on the patriotic stage. C[urtius] has become so accustomed to this role that he considers himself one of the few true friends of the fatherland in the foreign office, perhaps the only one.[113]

Most officials with experience of reparations diplomacy believed that any request for a moratorium on the payment of reparations would be rejected by foreign governments and stampede private investors into disastrous withdrawals of their funds from Germany. Bülow expressed such skepticism that Pünder told him angrily to either keep silent or suggest a better plan.[114] On 12 January Brüning persuaded all his national security advisers to accept an invitation from the League of Nations to attend a World Disarmament Conference that would begin in Geneva in February 1932. He then exhorted them to coordinate all phases of fiscal policy, military planning, and diplomacy more closely. He encountered a "perplexed silence," however, when he concluded that it would be necessary to take some initiative concerning reparations by May 1931 at the latest; one official apparently muttered that this was "madness" (*Wahnsinn*). Brüning was angered by this "sometimes friendly, sometimes icy rejection by the leading officials of the ministries." Only the politicians Dietrich and Curtius were supportive. Hostile press leaks after the meeting made Brüning resolve never to discuss his goals frankly before such a large audience again.[115]

112 Chancellor's reception of 19 December 1930, *Kabinette Brüning*, I:755–58; memorandum of 30 December 1930, *ADAP*, XVI:324–25.
113 Letter of 26 December 1930, *Weizsäcker-Papiere*, p. 412.
114 Pünder to Bülow, 3 January 1931, *ADAP*, XVI:336–37; Bennett, *Financial Crisis*, pp. 35–36.
115 Brüning, *Memoiren*, pp. 228–29, with additional details in the manuscript memoirs, pp. 69–70 (the published version softens the expletive muttered by Karl Ritter from "*Wahnsinn*" to "*undenkbar*"). See also the bland official minutes of 12 January and Dietrich to Brüning, 17 January 1931, *Kabinette Brüning*, I:777–79, 787–89; the Schäffer diary, 6 January 1931, NL Schäffer/10/8; and Glashagen, "Reparationspolitik Brünings," pp. 317–19.

The new strategy of Curtius and Brüning certainly had flaws. They perceived correctly that Anglo–American public opinion was becoming hostile to the Versailles settlement on both moral and economic grounds. Indeed, Ambassador Sackett himself had displayed surprising enthusiasm for German irredentism when he toured the Polish Corridor in August, noting repeatedly that the border settlement of 1919 had obviously impoverished the whole region.[116] The British and U.S. governments were preoccupied with their own economic problems, however, and Brüning felt stymied when Sackett reported at the beginning of February that President Hoover was too busy to host an international conference. Thereafter the chancellor repeatedly instructed his associates to give the German people the impression that steps were being taken against reparations without doing anything to alarm foreign investors or governments. This was not a policy but merely the statement of a conundrum.[117] Another major flaw in the new strategy was Brüning's failure to consult the Reichswehr, which was not represented in the meeting of 15 December. After much argument between the foreign office and the general staff, Brüning and Curtius finally accepted on 18 March 1931 the military thesis that Germany's goal at the Disarmament Conference must be to secure recognition of its "parity of rights" with France. Brüning asked skeptically whether "parity of rights" really mattered given Germany's fiscal constraints, but Schleicher replied that military expenditure must increase by at least 15 percent in 1932, a stunning demand given the latest figures on tax receipts. Brüning persuaded the generals that Germany should conceal its real aims at the conference for as long as possible, confining itself in public to the innocuous demand that France disarm to German levels, but he would not be able to pose to foreign leaders indefinitely as an apostle of disarmament.[118] Without genuine progress toward disarmament, however, the new diplomatic strategy boiled down to the highly dubious thesis that Germany would be more likely to win concessions if it simultaneously raised as many different demands as possible.

Curtius and Bülow actually devoted most of their energy to achieving a customs union with Austria to redress yet a third grievance against Versailles. The idea of *Anschluss* enjoyed support by all German parties from the Nazis to the Communists. Chancellor Wirth had wisely laid down the principle in 1922 that this issue could not be raised until after the final abolition of reparations,

116 Regierungspräsident Budding to Brüning, 14 August 1930, *ADAP*, XV:454–55; Bernard V. Burke, *Ambassador Frederic Sackett and the Collapse of the Weimar Republic, 1930–1933: The United States and Hitler's Rise to Power* (Cambridge, 1994), pp. 68–70; Bennett, *Financial Crisis*, pp. 31–39, 132–33. For background see also Bennett, *German Rearmament*, pp. 100–109, and Martin Gilbert, *The Roots of Appeasement* (Oxford, 1966).

117 Bülow memorandum of 2 February and conference of 7 February 1931, *Kabinette Brüning*, I:778, 854–57; *Zentrumsprotokolle*, 5 February 1931, p. 510; Schäffer diary, conversation with Bülow, 3 March 1931, NL Schäffer/10/66–67.

118 Schönheinz to von Mackensen, 10 March 1931, *ADAP*, XVII:27–29; disarmament conference of 18 March 1931, *Kabinette Brüning*, II:962–64; Bennett, *German Rearmament*, pp. 52–55; Rödder, *Curtius*, pp. 143–49.

but the onset of the Great Depression made many Austrians eager for closer economic ties with Germany. In February 1930 Curtius had persuaded Chancellor Müller to prepare a draft treaty for a customs union in talks with the Austrian Chancellor Schober. Brüning displayed no interest in the idea when he took office, but Bülow's enthusiastic support for it encouraged Curtius to advocate his promotion to state secretary.[119] In August 1930 Bülow brought the record of Müller's talks with Schober to Chancellor Brüning and requested authorization to pursue this project. Brüning told him "to lay it on ice," sensing correctly that it might divert attention from reparations and arouse expectations among the German people that could not be fulfilled. By year's end, however, a steady stream of Austrian bankers and businessmen appeared at Brüning's office to proclaim that a customs union offered their only hope to avoid economic collapse, and Brüning began to fear press leaks about his opposition to the idea. He dropped that opposition by February 1931, after Curtius and Bülow argued that the idea of *Anschluss* would be forever discredited among Austrians if Germany failed to help them now. Curtius agreed to take sole responsibility for the initiative, even to the point of denying that he had informed the chancellor, so that Brüning would not be compromised if the project failed. Even cabinet colleagues and Austrian leaders were kept in the dark about Brüning's prior knowledge.[120] Brüning apparently never understood that Bülow deliberately sought with this maneuver to forestall what he considered a futile and dangerous initiative against reparations. The diplomat warned Hans Schäffer confidentially not to expect any revision of the Young Plan for five years because of this other project. Schäffer and Hans Luther knew that the customs union would provoke serious diplomatic opposition but welcomed it for diverting attention away from an initiative against reparations that might destroy Germany's credit abroad.[121]

Curtius and Hermann Pünder completed a draft treaty in Vienna in early March, and the German cabinet approved it on 18 March. Foreign governments were notified of the customs union without any warning three days later, as German diplomats argued implausibly that it would not compromise Austrian

119 F. G. Stambrook, "The German-Austrian Customs Union Project of 1931: A Study of German Methods and Motives," in Hans W. Gatzke, ed., *European Diplomacy between Two Wars* (Chicago, 1972), pp. 95–105; Anne Orde, "The Origins of the German-Austrian Customs Union Affair of 1931," *Central European History*, 13 (1980): 34–59; Bennett, *Financial Crisis*, pp. 41–44; Krüger, *Aussenpolitik*, pp. 530–32; Schulz, *Von Brüning zu Hitler*, pp. 300–303; chancellor's receptions for Schober, 22 and 24 February 1930, *Kabinett Müller II*, II:1480–95.

120 Brüning, "The Changing Background of Democracy," Page-Barbour lecture #2, pp. 8–10, HUG FP 93.45; Brüning to Treviranus, 20 November 1942 (source of quotation), HUG FP 93.10/Box 34/Treviranus (3); Brüning to Hans Berger, 27 March 1955, HUG FP 93.10/Box 3/Hans Berger; Brüning, *Memoiren*, pp. 263–64; Wirth to Curtius, 9 April 1931, NL Wirth/11; Schäffer diary, 18 June 1931, NL Schäffer/11/239–40; Luther, *Vor dem Abgrund*, pp. 161–62; Bennett, *Financial Crisis*, pp. 45–46; Rödder, *Curtius*, pp. 190–94.

121 Schäffer diary, 9 September 1930, 16 March and 17 April 1931, NL Schäffer/9/218, 10/94, and 10/110–18; Schäffer's note on a conversation with Luther, 17 March 1931, *Quellen: Politik und Wirtschaft*, I:565; Ambassador Rumbold's report on a conversation with Bülow, 6 May 1931, *DBFP*, II:45–46.

independence but simply represented a step toward the goal of European economic integration that France itself had long championed. Bülow privately confessed to the German ambassador in Paris that some government colleagues felt qualms of conscience about the whole affair, and indeed, the German rationale was unusually disingenuous even for the language of diplomacy. Curtius told the cabinet that "*Anschluss* is not yet feasible politically, but economically . . . it can be furthered decisively," and Dietrich applauded the plan as a major step toward the "further dissolution of the Treaty of Versailles."[122] Bülow's aims actually went even beyond *Anschluss*. He hoped that Czechoslovakia would be compelled to apply for membership in the customs union from fear of economic "encirclement," and that Czech participation would give Germany such a stranglehold on Polish commerce that the Poles would accept border revisions in exchange for economic aid. These calculations verged on megalomania.[123]

The Brüning cabinet insisted on pursuing the customs union even when it provoked a major diplomatic confrontation. French government leaders always assumed that this was a major step toward *Anschluss*, and they resolved to oppose it with all their resources. France demanded that Austria and Germany take no action until the League of Nations decided whether their agreement violated the prohibition against *Anschluss* in the Versailles Treaty, but Brüning denied that the League had any jurisdiction. When the British government seconded this request, Brüning conceded that France and Great Britain were free to obtain a legal opinion from the World Court, but he insisted that Germany and Austria were free to continue "technical preparations" during these proceedings.[124] The chancellor then authorized Bülow to visit President Hindenburg's vacation resort to underscore the importance of the customs union. It had originally been devised solely for its economic benefit, Bülow reported, but "has taken on a whole different aspect through the opposition of France and Czechoslovakia and has become the cardinal point of our entire foreign policy."[125]

This effort to defy France was thoroughly unrealistic because it possessed the only substantial gold reserves in Europe. By April 1931 the Austrians were inquiring confidentially whether the French government would grant them a loan, and on 11 May Austria's largest financial institution, the Credit-Anstalt, publicly announced its bankruptcy, appealing for foreign assistance. Brüning and

---

122 Stambrook, "Customs Union," pp. 110–15; Rödder, *Curtius*, pp. 194–97; Köpke memorandum of 21 February 1931, *ADAP*, XVI:571–74; Bülow to Hoesch, 17 March, and Curtius to Hoesch, 18 March 1931, *ADAP*, XVII:67–80; cabinet meetings of 16 and 18 March 1931, *Kabinette Brüning*, II:952–55, 969–71 (source of quotations).

123 Bülow to Prittwitz, 21 January 1931, and Bülow to Koch (Prague), 15 April 1931, *ADAP*, XVI:435–36, XVII:219–20; Schäffer diary, conversation with Bülow, 13 February 1931, NL Schäffer/10/54–55; Bennett, *Financial Crisis*, pp. 78–80. Compare Christoph Boyer, "Das deutsche Reich und die Tschechoslowakei im Zeichen der Weltwirtschaftskrise," *Vierteljahrshefte für Zeitgeschichte*, 39 (1991): 551–87.

124 Bennett, *Financial Crisis*, pp. 59–70; Tyrrell to Rumbold, 25 March 1931, *DBFP*, II:12–13; chancellor's reception for Rumbold, 25 March 1931, *Kabinette Brüning*, II:984–86; Curtius memorandum, 27 March 1931, *ADAP*, XVII:128–30.

125 Bülow memorandum, 15 April 1931, *ADAP*, XVII:217–18.

Trendelenburg immediately noted within the cabinet that Austrian support for the customs union was crumbling.[126] The German initiative succeeded only in humiliating Aristide Briand, Germany's best friend in Paris. For months the French foreign minister had sought to persuade his cabinet to grant Germany a substantial loan without political conditions. Unfortunately, he had recently cited the absence of *Anschluss* in a speech to the Chamber of Deputies to prove that the fears of his nationalist critics were groundless, so he appeared naive when news of the customs union broke. On 13 May he suffered a crushing defeat in the election for the French presidency, and Pünder noted ruefully that Briand's eclipse would aggravate international tensions. Brüning later confessed to the Austrian ambassador that he had blundered by not consulting Briand in advance about the customs union.[127]

The customs union project was a fiasco that distracted attention from the crucial issue of reparations, where Brüning stood closer to success than anyone realized. Germany's case that reparations harmed the entire world economy had gained influential support from the Bank of England, Wall Street, professional economists, and British industrialists. Ambassador Sackett had become an enthusiastic admirer of Brüning, and he often spoke with his British colleague, Sir Horace Rumbold, about the need for Western governments to combat the rise of Nazism by assisting the chancellor; this idea was also promoted in London by Major Archibald Church, a Labour MP and lobbyist for the electrotechnical industry. In early March Rumbold appealed to his foreign secretary, Arthur Henderson, to offer Brüning a gesture of support, since Germany might experience revolution if the unemployment rate did not decline soon. Rumbold suggested inviting the German chancellor to visit Prime Minister MacDonald's country house at Chequers for an informal exchange of views about disarmament, which would give Brüning added prestige at home. Church conveyed similar arguments directly to MacDonald, and Henderson issued the invitation on 14 March, which Brüning accepted for early June. Brüning had found a diplomatic opening at last.[128]

Preparations for Chequers were overshadowed by the German government's mounting cash-flow crisis. Brüning, Stegerwald, and Dietrich secretly agreed by 7 May on the central provisions of a second comprehensive "Emergency Decree to Preserve the Economy and Public Finances." Since the Reich confronted a

126 Shamir, *Economic Crisis*, pp. 8–10, 27–34; Bennett, *Financial Crisis*, pp. 59–74; cabinet meeting of 11 May and conference of 18 May 1931, *Kabinette Brüning*, II:1065–67, 1078–79.

127 Knipping, *Ende der Locarno-Ära*, pp. 202–17; Bennett, *Financial Crisis*, pp. 59–60; Geoffrey Warner, *Pierre Laval and the Eclipse of France* (New York, 1968), pp. 27–29; Hoesch to Curtius and Bülow, 15 April 1931, *ADAP*, XVII:222–23; Pünder, *Politik*, 14 May 1931, p. 97; Austrian Ambassador Frank to Foreign Minister Schober, 4 July 1931, Österreichisches Staatsarchiv/Archiv der Republik/NPA 10 (hereafter cited as OSA), Gesandtschaftsberichte Berlin/449–50.

128 Rumbold to Henderson, 4 and 6 March 1931, *DBFP*, I:573–81; Brüning to Hans Berger, 16 December 1949, HUG FP 93.10/Box 3/Hans Berger; Burke, *Frederic Sackett*, pp. 90–107, 119–21; Bennett, *Financial Crisis*, pp. 88–89; Glashagen, "Reparationspolitik Brünings," pp. 358–74, 455–57.

projected deficit of RM 746 million for the coming year, it would be necessary to reduce government salaries by another 4 to 8 percent, reduce welfare benefits substantially, and increase taxes on sugar and imported oil. Now the chancellor acknowledged that deflationary policies created a vicious circle, a point long emphasized by John Maynard Keynes, but he remained largely fatalistic: "The more salaries and wages are reduced, the more tax revenues sink. The more economy measures are adopted, the smaller become our public revenues. This circle can only be broken by lightening the burden of reparations, or by a stream of life-giving foreign capital." Brüning therefore decided that this decree should be issued as he left for Chequers, so that the domestic outcry would help him to launch a diplomatic campaign against reparations.[129] Brüning and his top advisers discussed all the old suggestions to help the unemployed by borrowing money for public works, drastic action against the cartels, or a shortened work week, but they perceived no prospect for success until reparations were suspended. The publication of the second and third portions of the Brauns Commission report on unemployment yielded no fresh ideas other than labor service brigades for jobless youth working outdoors at sub-minimum wages, an idea initially opposed by organized labor and big business alike.[130]

Brüning had no hope of lining up broad support for this painful decree, and there was nothing comparable to the extended public debate over the government's program in November 1930. Instead the chancellor visited Otto Braun on the morning of 8 May to give confidential notice of his intentions. Prussia's leader responded in what Pünder termed a "very harmonious" conversation that Brüning was on the right course but must go far enough in this decree so that further austerity measures would not be required for the rest of the year; the SPD could explain to its constituents the need for drastic action on one occasion but not two. Carl Severing was informed shortly thereafter and also expressed support; his only request was that the chancellor get the army to stop sending brass bands to perform at Stahlhelm rallies. The SPD Reichstag delegation then decided not to approach Brüning with any demands so that it could deny any role in the preparation of this bitter medicine.[131] State governments other than Prussia's were not consulted at all. Their leaders were merely summoned to Berlin to hear about the decree on the eve of publication, a procedure that marked the end of any serious effort to elevate the Reichsrat into the status of ersatz parliament.[132]

---

129 Meetings of 5, 7, and 11 May 1931, *Kabinette Brüning*, II:1043–59, 1062–63 (quotation on p. 1053).
130 Handels- und Industrie-Beiräte der Deutschen Zentrumspartei to Perlitius, Brüning, and Stegerwald, 23 April 1931, NL ten Hompel/20; Schäffer memorandum, "Zur Krisenfrage," 15 May 1931, NL Schäffer/30/143–49; Schäffer diary, 16–19 May 1931, NL Schäffer/10/161–67; cabinet meetings of 27–29 May 1931, *Kabinette Brüning*, II:1114–18, 1134–40; Grübler, *Spitzenverbände*, pp. 365–83; Winkler, *Katastrophe*, pp. 314–16; Schulz, *Von Brüning zu Hitler*, pp. 328–30.
131 Pünder memorandum of 8 May 1931, NL Pünder/137/182–83; Pünder memorandum of 18 May 1931, *Kabinette Brüning*, II:1080–81; Winkler, *Katastrophe*, pp. 323–24.
132 Chancellor's reception of 2 June 1931, *Kabinette Brüning*, II:1163–68; Besson, *Württemberg*, pp. 205–09; Mommsen, "Brünings Politik," pp. 35–36; Schulz, *Von Brüning zu Hitler*, pp. 362–63.

Brüning worried that new attacks from the right could influence the President. The Stahlhelm had launched a referendum campaign in February 1931 to force new state elections in Prussia that gained widespread support among moderate conservatives. At the end of April Hugenberg appealed to the Center Party to topple Otto Braun in the name of Christian morality, and Brüning's former friend Eduard Stadtler explained to the press that the chancellor was well intentioned but utterly indecisive – after many years of hesitation Brüning must choose once and for all between the left and right.[133] Pünder anxiously explained to Meissner for the President's benefit that Brüning refused to worry about partisan alignments and sought only to formulate realistic solutions to Germany's problems. He added the following defense of the Social Democrats:

> It is on the other hand correct, and deserves the highest praise, that the SPD has come more and more since the Reichstag election to offer its indirect support for the Brüning cabinet's calm and purely objective reforming labors. This is true in particular of the Prussian state government and Prime Minister Braun, who has supported the Brüning government with all his power even in very uncomfortable situations.

Pünder added that Brüning would not make overtures to the right unless the SPD sought to overturn his emergency decrees. Meissner replied that Brüning "could rest assured now as before that he had President Hindenburg behind him."[134]

Brüning had more difficulty retaining support from the DVP and big business. Pünder telephoned Ludwig Kastl on 12 May with confidential notice of the decree's basic features and received a promise that big business would support Brüning as long as he preserved a balanced budget. This assurance masked a fierce dispute, however, between moderates in the RDI and Ruhr industrialists who demanded that Brüning slash welfare outlay by a billion marks so that tax rates could be lowered.[135] Brüning dined privately with Dingeldey the next day to win his support, but the DVP Reichstag delegation then demanded that the cabinet avoid any reduction in government salaries. Dingeldey feared that the DVP would destroy itself if it defied the civil service lobby and Ruhr industrialists, and he felt compelled to support the Stahlhelm's referendum campaign against Otto Braun.[136] After being reassured about the President's support, however, Brüning offered no material concessions to the right.

---

133 Berghahn, *Der Stahlhelm*, pp. 164–75; Schulz, *Von Brüning zu Hitler*, pp. 353–56; "Das Rätselraten um Brüning," published in early May and reprinted in Eduard Stadtler, *Schafft es Brüning?* (Berlin, 1931), pp. 110–14.
134 Pünder memorandum of 9 May 1931, *Kabinette Brüning*, II:1059–62.
135 Pünder memorandum, 12 May 1931, NL Pünder/137/151; Grübler, *Spitzenverbände*, pp. 237–46; Blank to Reusch, 25 and 27 April and 20 May 1931, *Quellen: Politik und Wirtschaft*, I:613–14, 627–29.
136 Pünder Tagesnotiz, 13 May 1931, NL Pünder/43/183; Dingeldey to Brüning, 18 May 1931, *Quellen: Politik und Wirtschaft*, I:623–27; Hans von Raumer to Dingeldey, 16 May, and reply of 19 May 1931, NL Dingeldey/83/26–30; Curtius to Dingeldey, 17 April 1931, NL Dingeldey/67/6–7; Dingeldey's correspondence with Erich von Gilsa, February–May 1931, NL Dingeldey/69/8–44.

The chancellor did offer a few concessions to organized labor. He warned the cabinet that "we are injuring everyone and nowhere offer alluring economic prospects. Nowhere does the emergency decree exert a beneficial psychological influence. . . ."[137] Stegerwald insisted that something be done to appease the Free Unions. They had negotiated a joint declaration with the Christian unions to demand the end of reparations, which pleased Brüning greatly, but they refused to issue it when they heard rumors about the contents of the coming decree. On 30 May the Free Unions submitted detailed social policy demands to the chancellor as their conditions for joining the campaign against reparations, and Stegerwald embraced many of them.[138] The cabinet quickly agreed to concede a small "crisis tax" on the better paid categories of white-collar workers and 200 million marks' worth of public works, but Stegerwald provoked controversy with his third demand, authorization for the labor ministry to impose the forty-hour week on individual firms or whole branches of industry to stretch out job opportunities. Trendelenburg and Hans Luther protested that the cabinet needed to loosen government regulation of the economy, not tighten it. Stegerwald replied that "his ship was overloaded" with painful measures and that he might resign if the cabinet ignored his wishes. Brüning then intervened to grant the labor ministry these new powers with the understanding that no use would be made of them pending efforts to negotiate voluntary agreements to shorten the work week.[139] The chancellor agreed with Stegerwald that the government could survive only if organized labor received some kind of victory. He confided to Schäffer that the trade unions had reached the limit of their capacity to resist Communist agitation and might well decide that their survival required his fall so that they could go into flamboyant opposition against a reactionary government.[140]

After much agonizing, Brüning also decided that the Second Emergency Decree should be linked with a public declaration that the effort to pay reparations had brought Germany to the brink of economic collapse. Dietrich prodded the chancellor forward by telling the cabinet that Germany would have no choice but to declare a reparations moratorium soon after the Chequers conference, even though "we thereby take a step that resembles a declaration of war."[141]

---

137 Luther diary, 2 June 1931, published in *Vor dem Abgrund*, p. 166.
138 ADGB Bundesvorstand, 21 January and 29 May 1931, and trade union summit conference of 20 February 1931, *Quellen: Gewerkschaften*, pp. 230–33, 253–55, 306–10; ADGB Bundesvorstand to Brüning, 30 May 1931, *Quellen: Politik und Wirtschaft*, I:631–32.
139 Luther diary, 3 June 1931, *Quellen: Politik und Wirtschaft*, I:643–45 (source of quotation); Schäffer diary, 3 June 1931, NL Schäffer/11/182; meetings of 27 and 29 May and 3 June 1931, *Kabinette Brüning*, II:1114–16, 1131–40, 1171–74; Luther Tagesbericht, 1 June 1931, NL Luther/365/14–15.
140 Schäffer diary, 6–7 May 1931, NL Schäffer/10/140, 145. Compare Eisner, *Das Verhältnis der KPD zu den Gewerkschaften*, pp. 222–54; Winkler, *Katastrophe*, pp. 595–608; and Patch, *Christian Trade Unions*, pp. 170–76.
141 Luther diary, 30 May 1931, NL Luther/365/5–10 (partly published in *Quellen: Politik und Wirtschaft*, I:633–35); meeting of 3 June 1931, *Kabinette Brüning*, II:1178–81; Schäffer diary, 3 June 1931, NL Schäffer/11/182.

Brüning drafted this government declaration himself and then telephoned Berlin from London on the evening of 5 June to soften its terms to fit the mood of the British public. It was published the next morning, just hours before Brüning's talks with MacDonald began, and climaxed with the following assertion:

> The limit of the privations which we can impose on our people has been reached. The premises on which the Young Plan was based have proved to be erroneous as a result of the development undergone by the world. The Young Plan has failed to give the German people the relief which according to the intentions of all concerned it was meant to give and of which it at first held out promise. The Government realizes that the extremely precarious economic and financial situation of the Reich imperiously requires Germany's relief from unbearable reparation obligations. This is also a prerequisite for the economic recuperation of the world.[142]

This statement alarmed foreign bankers, and some observers have argued that it triggered Germany's subsequent Bank Crisis. Recent research suggests, however, that there was no great wave of foreign withdrawals in response to this declaration, that the run on the mark in July 1931 had deeper causes. Brüning's manifesto was probably an accurate prediction, not the cause of the banking crisis.[143]

Upon departing for Chequers, Brüning had the curtains of his railroad carriage lowered so that he would not see the angry protesters at the train stations along the route. In Hamburg he encountered Communist dockworkers who brandished their wrenches and screamed, "Down with the hunger dictator!" Brüning turned pale and disappeared into his cabin to study briefing books.[144] Thus it was a relief to arrive on British soil, especially now that the collapse of the Credit-Anstalt had made British leaders eager to discuss the impact of reparations on the international banking system. Brüning argued that Germany had reached the point where further efforts to pay reparations would probably result in economic collapse and a Nazi or Bolshevik revolution. Even if this did not happen, financing reparations and Germany's other foreign debts would require an annual trade surplus of five billion marks, which must involve a commercial policy ruinous to British exporters. Thus humanitarian feeling for Germany's unemployed, the desire to prevent the spread of totalitarianism, and British economic interests all demanded a moratorium on reparations. Brüning had been well briefed by an economist with excellent contacts in England, Moritz Julius Bonn, and the uproar at home in response to the Second Emergency Decree lent these arguments considerable weight. The German chancellor soon established

142 Schäffer diary, 5 June 1931, NL Schäffer/11/184; Brüning, *Memoiren*, pp. 278–79; cabinet meeting
     of 6 June 1931, *Kabinette Brüning*, II:1183; German manifesto translated in *FRUS 1931*, I:9–11.
143 See Harold James, "The Causes of the German Banking Crisis of 1931," *Economic History Review*,
     37 (1984): 68–87, and Balderston, *German Economic Crisis*, pp. 163–79. Contrast Born, *Bankenkrise*,
     pp. 68–71; Bennett, *Financial Crisis*, pp. 117–22; and Meister, *Grosse Depression*, pp. 224–26.
144 See Paul Schmidt, *Statist auf diplomatischer Bühne 1923–45* (Bonn, 1949), pp. 200–203.

rapport with MacDonald, who shared his earnest desire to reconcile Christian morality with political expediency. Brüning later recalled a private walk in the garden where MacDonald volunteered the surprising information that the Bank of England could hardly defend the British gold standard. Brüning predicted that Great Britain would find itself compelled to imitate most of the painful measures that Germany had already adopted; they represented the final reckoning of the costs of the Great War. He took advantage of the opening to link the troubles of both Germany and Great Britain to the Versailles Treaty, which had left France the only European power with substantial gold reserves.[145]

British financial experts then interrogated Brüning in the more formal session of 7 June. When they criticized Germany's provocative public manifesto, Brüning explained disarmingly that he had learned the importance of frankness after his mistakes with the Austrian customs union. Pressed for details about his budget, Brüning overwhelmed the conference with figures showing that Germany had eliminated all wasteful expenditure and pushed its tax rates up to the point of diminishing returns. He promised to take no action before the visit to Berlin in July by the U.S. Secretary of State, Henry Stimson, but warned that events might move quickly thereafter. Curtius overheard the Governor of the Bank of England, Montagu Norman, tell MacDonald that, in view of Brüning's frankness, if the German government "subsequently adopt unilateral measures, then nobody would have the right to reproach" it. Norman warned MacDonald, however, against any public declaration that he had discussed reparations with the Germans, since that would anger the French. The two delegations eventually agreed on a bland communiqué which concluded that "special stress was laid by the German Ministers on the difficulties of the existing position in Germany and the need for alleviation." Back home Brüning sought to portray this as a diplomatic victory, but the outcome did not seem impressive, and Brüning himself apparently considered the talks disappointing. He told the Austrian ambassador that Arthur Henderson and his permanent undersecretary, Robert Vansittart, were incorrigible francophiles.[146]

Brüning had achieved more than he realized. The chancellor's sober style of argument made an excellent impression on British government leaders, the Tory opposition, and newspaper editors alike. MacDonald repeated and endorsed all of Brüning's central arguments in a personal letter to Stimson, observing that "I found Doctor Bruening really very enlightening on these economic problems." MacDonald underscored the threat of a Communist or Nazi revolution in

145 Brüning, *Memoiren*, pp. 279–81; M. J. Bonn, "Aufzeichnung," sent to Hans Schäffer on 1 June 1931, and Schäffer to Bonn, 5 June 1931, NL Bonn/51; position paper for Chequers, *ADAP*, XVII:349–50; Schmidt, *Statist*, pp. 205–07; Bennett, *Financial Crisis*, pp. 123–27; Glashagen, "Reparationspolitik Brünings," pp. 506–08.

146 British summary of the conference, 7 June 1931, *DBFP*, II:71–77; Curtius memorandum of 10 June 1931, *ADAP*, XVII:408–09; Brüning, *Memoiren*, pp. 282–84; Brüning's remarks in *Zentrumsprotokolle*, 14 June 1931, p. 530; Wheeler-Bennett, *Knaves, Fools, and Heroes*, pp. 44–46; Ambassador Frank to Schober, 4 July 1931, ÖSA/Gesandtschaftsberichte Berlin/449.

Germany that might spread to other countries, and he even declared that French "hegemony" was just as great a threat to Europe as the rise of the totalitarian parties. "These men are facing a very awful situation," he concluded, "and anything which any of us can do to help them discreetly really ought to be done."[147] This letter reached Hoover when he had just concluded that the collapse of the Credit-Anstalt might send dominoes toppling all over Europe. At the beginning of June he had conferred with Sackett in Washington, who urged substantial revision of the Young Plan, and by 20 June Stimson and other advisers persuaded the American President to announce to the world a generous proposal for a one-year moratorium on all reparations and war debts. Thus Hoover renounced a major source of revenue for his own budget to promote worldwide economic recovery.[148]

By then Brüning had already confronted the most serious challenge to his government since July 1930. He returned to Germany on 10 June to encounter a fierce outcry against the Second Emergency Decree; Nazi demonstrators even stoned his railroad carriage. In Berlin Luther reported a second great run on the mark, of the same magnitude as that following the September elections. The Reichsbank had lost one billion marks in gold and foreign exchange since 26 May and now had only 1.5 billion left, and it was soon compelled to raise the discount rate from 5 to 7 percent.[149] On 11 June the impression that Brüning had failed at Chequers prompted the DVP to endorse the demand of the radical parties that the Reichstag convene immediately. Brüning told the cabinet that it must resign if that happened because a parliamentary session would wreck the budget. The crisis deepened the next day when the SPD Reichstag delegation issued an ultimatum to the cabinet: It too would vote to convene the Reichstag unless Brüning agreed either to raise the "crisis tax" substantially or to restore the eligibility of teenagers for unemployment insurance.[150]

Brüning confined himself to persuasion rather than material concessions as he sought to regain the support of the DVP. Luther and Hans Schäffer offered valuable support by telling business leaders that the monetary crisis resulted from the fear among investors that the irresponsible Reichstag would overturn the cabinet's sound fiscal policy. On 12 June Luther sternly declared to Dingeldey that he had been able to fend off utter financial panic only by issuing his personal guarantee to German bankers that the Reich budget was truly balanced; he would be compelled to withdraw this guarantee if the Reichstag decided to

---

147 MacDonald to Stimson, 8 June 1931, *FRUS 1931*, I:11–13; see also the summary of MacDonald's remarks to the American *chargé* in London, ibid., I:5–8, and Glashagen, "Reparationspolitik Brünings," pp. 523–26.

148 Bennett, *Financial Crisis*, pp. 134–65; Burke, *Frederic Sackett*, pp. 123–32; Godfrey Hodgson, *The Colonel: The Life and Wars of Henry Stimson, 1867–1950* (New York, 1990), pp. 193–203.

149 Brüning, *Memoiren*, pp. 285–86; Born, *Bankenkrise*, pp. 71–73; Schiemann, *Deutsche Währung*, pp. 142–44; Luther's "Tagesberichte," 13 and 15 June 1931, *Quellen: Politik und Wirtschaft*, I:663–65, 672–74.

150 Winkler, *Katastrophe*, pp. 342–45; cabinet meeting of 11 June 1931, *Kabinette Brüning*, II:1189–91; Schäffer diary, conversation with Pünder, 12 June 1931, NL Schäffer/11/212–13.

convene. Moved by these arguments, Paul Silverberg and Ludwig Kastl soon persuaded the Reich Association of Industry to proclaim its emphatic support for all provisions of the Second Emergency Decree. These declarations stunned Dingeldey and other DVP leaders.[151] Brüning himself approached Dingeldey during a long train ride from Cologne to Berlin on 13 June to promise that the government would declare a reparations moratorium before imposing any further restrictions on credit. The chancellor rejected Dingeldey's demand for the dismissal of Dietrich and Curtius, but he agreed to offer the vacant ministry of economics to the steel industrialist Albert Vögler. Vögler himself then materialized to present an ambitious plan to replace compulsory state labor arbitration with voluntary arbitration panels. Brüning promised to consider the idea but rejected it two days later after consulting Stegerwald, and Vögler then refused to join the cabinet. Now the chancellor's bargain with Dingeldey was reduced to a vague agreement to promote some "loosening" of both collective labor contracts and cartel agreements, and to consider personnel changes that would create a cabinet "with the greatest authority imaginable" when serious negotiations over reparations began.[152] Dingeldey felt compelled to return to the government camp nevertheless, in part because of threats by pro-Brüning moderates to secede from the DVP.[153] On 16 June he persuaded his Reichstag delegation to oppose convening the Reichstag, even though Ruhr lobbyists observed accurately that Brüning had not really promised him anything. This decision helped Brüning to win a majority that day on the Reichstag's Council of Elders. Dingeldey boasted to party colleagues that he had dealt a mortal blow to the "incompetent" Dietrich and "compelled" Brüning to alter his policies, but these claims merely alienated Brüning's friends without impressing his enemies.[154]

Brüning made somewhat more substantial concessions to his critics in organized labor. Union leaders approached him on 15 June to declare that they could not live with two central provisions of the Second Emergency Decree, the elimination of teenagers from unemployment insurance and the reduction in wages paid municipal blue-collar workers to the lower rates paid workers employed by

---

151 Luther diary, 11 June 1931, NL Luther/425/67–70; Luther memoranda of 12 June and Silverberg speech to RDI Hauptausschuss, 19 June 1931, *Quellen: Politik und Wirtschaft*, I:655–58, 696–705; Schäffer memorandum of 16 June 1931, NL Schäffer/30/193–99; Silverberg to Reusch, 26 June 1931, NL Silverberg/274/106–08.

152 Dingeldey memoranda of 13 and 15 June 1931, and Dingeldey to Brüning, 15 June 1931 (source of quotation), *Quellen: Politik und Wirtschaft*, I:666–69, 677–79; cabinet meeting of 15 June 1931, *Kabinette Brüning*, II:1191–94; Luther diary, 15 June 1931, NL Luther/425/73–74.

153 See Wilhelm Kalle to Dingeldey, 13 June 1931, *Quellen: Politik und Wirtschaft*, I:669–70; Kalle's telegrams of 14 June 1931, NL Dingeldey/75/10–11; and Otto Thiel to Dingeldey, 18 June 1931, NL Dingeldey/92/21–26.

154 Meeting of DVP Reichstag delegation, 16 June 1931, *Quellen: Politik und Wirtschaft*, I:681–83; DVP resolution of 16 June 1931, NL Dingeldey/36/69–70; Schäffer diary, conversation with Dietrich, 18 June 1931, NL Schäffer/11/247–48; Dingeldey circular to DVP functionaries, 25 June 1931, NL Dingeldey/101/35–36; Helmuth Albrecht to Dingeldey, 28 June 1931, NL Dingeldey/36/67–68; Remscheid to Dingeldey, 11 July 1931, NL Dingeldey/46/46–47; von Gilsa to Dingeldey, 16 July 1931, NL Dingeldey/69/49–50.

the Reich. After Bernhard Otte of the Christian unions endorsed the argument that these provisions would drive union members into the arms of the Communists, the chancellor promised to revise them within two or three months. The SPD then agreed to oppose convening the Reichstag, but Hilferding insisted that the Reichstag budget committee at least should meet. Brüning decided that this too would wreck the budget and again threatened to resign.[155] On 16 June the whole cabinet agreed to resign if the budget committee convened. Groener observed that this would mean "the end of parliamentarism," and Meissner assured the cabinet that President Hindenburg would reappoint Brüning to form a new minority government. Brüning later recalled threatening the Social Democrats at this juncture with the prospect of martial law, so he had apparently agreed with Groener to dissolve the Reichstag and postpone new elections indefinitely if that seemed the only alternative to rule by Hitler and Hugenberg.[156] Brüning continued nevertheless to rely primarily on the pursuit of material compromise with the SPD. He approached the Social Democrats again later that day to promise that he would instruct the authorities to continue granting unemployment insurance benefits to needy teenagers and would convene the budget committee in August to negotiate further concessions. His only explicit threat was the old one that, if he fell, the Prussian Center would topple Otto Braun. An overwhelming majority of the SPD Reichstag delegation then decided to defer to the chancellor and oppose convening even the budget committee. Pünder noted in his diary that hardly anyone understood how close Germany had come to civil war.[157]

The parties that supported Brüning on 16 June heaved a great sigh of relief four days later when they heard of the Hoover Moratorium, for which Brüning deserved some credit. Germany now paid a price, however, for its efforts to isolate France diplomatically. President Hoover failed to consult French leaders before his announcement, and they insisted on Franco–American negotiations to establish guarantees that the Young Plan would return in full force after the economic crisis passed. France did not accept the moratorium until 6 July, after Hoover agreed that Germany would continue to pay reparations, which would be returned to it in the form of loans. The run on the mark had ended briefly in mid-June but resumed during these frustrating negotiations, and Brüning had some reason to blame French stubbornness for hindering economic recovery.[158]

155 ADGB Bundesvorstand, 10–17 June 1931, *Quellen: Gewerkschaften*, pp. 312–28; chancellor's receptions for trade union and SPD leaders, 15 June 1931, *Kabinette Brüning*, II:1194–98, 1205–06.
156 Brüning, *Memoiren*, pp. 286–89; cabinet meeting of 16 June 1931, *Kabinette Brüning*, II:1212–14; Luther Tagesbericht, 16 June 1931, *Quellen: Politik und Wirtschaft*, I:683–86.
157 Winkler, *Katastrophe*, pp. 351–52; Luther Tagesbericht, 16 June 1931, *Quellen: Politik und Wirtschaft*, I:683–86; ADGB Bundesvorstand, 17 June 1931, *Quellen: Gewerkschaften*, pp. 328–29; Pünder, *Politik*, 16 June 1931, p. 100.
158 Luther Tagesberichte, 22–23 June 1931, *Quellen: Politik und Wirtschaft*, I:721–23; Brüning to Herbert Hoover, 24 August 1954, HUG FP 93.10/Box 15/Herbert Hoover; Bennett, *Financial Crisis*, pp. 166–76; Barry Eichengreen, *Golden Fetters: The Gold Standard and the Great Depression, 1919–1939* (New York and Oxford, 1992), pp. 270–78; Rödder, *Curtius*, pp. 249–52.

Brüning did make one conciliatory gesture toward France in a radio address of 23 June, suggesting a Franco–German conference à la Chequers as soon as France accepted the Hoover Moratorium. "I am convinced," the chancellor declared, "that a really well-balanced and fruitful cooperation among the peoples of Europe . . . will only seem secure on the day that in the souls of the two great neighboring nations the past will have been overcome and their joint vision directed toward the future. . . ." This effort to imitate the rhetoric of Stresemann made an excellent impression on Western governments and German Social Democrats alike.[159] Brüning flatly rejected any substantive concessions to France, however. When Ambassador Sackett demanded at the beginning of July that Germany not build its second armored cruiser, to allay suspicions that the savings from the Hoover Moratorium would promote rearmament, Brüning replied that this project was dear to the heart of President Hindenburg. When Sackett renewed the demand, Brüning replied that major Berlin banks were on the verge of collapse and that the army might be called upon at any moment to put down mass uprisings. "Even though this is principally a naval question," Brüning confessed, "the younger army officers in particular would view this as so great a renunciation of the interests of the armed forces of Germany that the loyalty of the army would be heavily jeopardized." Brüning would only offer a confidential promise not to seek funds for a third armored cruiser in 1932.[160] Brüning would not even renounce the doomed customs union with Austria, and the sight of Austrian leaders groveling before French gold had an unfortunate psychological impact in Berlin. Brüning and most of his advisers became obsessed with resisting the temptation to sacrifice Germany's "right" to demand revisions of the Versailles Treaty because of financial pressure.[161]

German banks experienced a dangerous crescendo of withdrawals on 6–8 July despite the ratification of the Hoover Moratorium. Foreign short-term credits to Germany had declined from 15.5 billion marks in July 1930 to 13 billion in July 1931, and the Reichsbank's reserves of gold and foreign exchange now dipped below 40 percent of German money in circulation, the level defined by the Reichsbank law of 1924 and the Hague Accord of March 1930 as the minimum necessary to defend the gold standard. Technically, France had the right to request authorization from the World Court to apply military sanctions against Germany.[162] Hans Luther therefore undertook a dramatic flight to London and Paris on 9/10 July to appeal for aid from their central banks. Montagu Norman confessed that he had no money to lend, however, and the

---

159 Brüning's speech translated in *FRUS 1931*, I:51–54; Brüning, *Memoiren*, pp. 294–96; Winkler, *Katastrophe*, pp. 359–61.

160 Sackett to State Department, 2 July 1931, *FRUS 1931*, I:130–31 (source of quotation); chancellor's receptions for Sackett on 30 June, 2 and 5 July 1931, *Kabinette Brüning*, II:1256–59, 1272–74, 1289–91; Bennett, *Financial Crisis*, pp. 183–99; Burke, *Frederic Sackett*, pp. 135–41.

161 See Bennett, *Financial Crisis*, pp. 295–301; Brüning's remarks in *Zentrumsprotokolle*, 14 June 1931, pp. 530–31; Brüning, *Memoiren*, pp. 308–09, 326; and the reparations conference of 19 June 1931, *ADAP*, XVII:454–60.

162 Born, *Bankenkrise*, pp. 91–97; Schiemann, *Deutsche Währung*, pp. 167–72; James, "Causes of the Banking Crisis," pp. 71–80; Balderston, *German Economic Crisis*, pp. 159–73.

French bankers referred Luther to Finance Minister Flandin. He declared that "just as there must be a moratorium on payments, so also must there be a moratorium on Germany's demands against France," including the construction of armored cruisers, the customs union with Austria, and any revision of the Polish border. Thus Luther's only achievement was to confirm the cabinet's fear of "blackmail" by France.[163] The failure of this mission compelled the government to proclaim a bank holiday on 14/15 July, after which the banks were reopened on a limited basis just to pay out wages and salaries while the government contemplated major reforms. The Reichsbank increased the discount rate to 10 percent on 16 July and a stunning 15 percent two weeks later, which brought lending to a virtual halt. Brüning considered Luther's plane trip a "fiasco" that merely conveyed a sense of desperation to foreign investors (indeed, Montagu Norman referred to Luther as a "crying old woman" after their meeting). Many industrialists clamored for Luther's dismissal, and the chancellor was compelled thereafter to accept primary responsibility for dealing with the Bank Crisis.[164]

This run on the mark probably began with the flight of German capital, and the real cause was almost undoubtedly the poor liquidity of many German banks and the spontaneous growth of fears among investors at home and abroad about their solvency.[165] Brüning blamed it, however, on signals to French investors by the French government, designed to wreck the customs union with Austria. Near the end of a marathon cabinet session on 13 July, he depicted the whole crisis as a titanic contest of wills with France, which Germany could win if it avoided any renunciation of its "political rights." France was plunging all of eastern Europe and even Great Britain into chaos through its refusal to lend its gold reserves to other countries without humiliating conditions. If Germany held firm, France would be forced to grant it an unconditional loan or else forfeit all sympathy abroad. When Hans Schäffer replied with an earnest appeal for cooperation among all the statesmen of Europe, Brüning began to suspect him of francophilia.[166] Bülow, Dietrich, and especially Luther encouraged Brüning's unfortunate tendency to interpret the Bank Crisis as a continuation of the Great

163 Luther, *Vor dem Abgrund*, pp. 185–86; Luther memorandum of 10 July 1931, *Quellen: Politik und Wirtschaft*, I:740–44; meeting of 11 July 1931, *Kabinette Brüning*, II:1324–26; James, *Reichsbank*, pp. 158–60.

164 Born, *Bankenkrise*, pp. 85–115; tables on the discount rate in Balderston, *German Economic Crisis*, pp. 146–50; Brüning, *Memoiren*, pp. 306–07; James, *Reichsbank*, pp. 158–60 (source of Norman quotation); Dingeldey to Brüning, 15 July 1931, NL Dingeldey/36/61–62; Pünder, *Politik*, pp. 165–66; von Gilsa to Reusch, 25 July 1931, *Quellen: Politik und Wirtschaft*, I:792–93.

165 See James, "Causes of the German Banking Crisis," pp. 76–81; James, *German Slump*, pp. 295–304; and Balderston, *German Economic Crisis*, pp. 163–73.

166 Schäffer diary, 13 July 1931, NL Schäffer/11/364–65; Brüning, *Memoiren*, pp. 307–09; Brüning to the Duchess of Atholl, 23 September 1936, *Briefe*, I:129–30; Brüning to Otto Friedrich, 7 January 1958, in Müller, *Brüning Papers*, p. 182; Schwerin von Krosigk, *Staatsbankrott*, p. 75; Shamir, *Economic Crisis*, pp. 44–47. Note that France contributed a mere 5% of total foreign credits to Germany in 1930, vs. 39% from the United States, 18% from the Netherlands, 15% from Great Britain, and 13% from Switzerland (Born, *Bankenkrise*, p. 18).

War by other means, with a new opportunity to win the Anglo–Saxon powers over to Germany's side. Luther actually told government colleagues that the Hoover Moratorium inaugurated a historic phase for Europe comparable to that begun when Prussia terminated its alliance with Napoleon in December 1812, "namely that of mental liberation from French political plans." Military action had no place under modern conditions, of course, but "the metaphor naturally implies the need for a new Vienna Congress, and nobody can tell whether a new Waterloo must come first, perhaps even with a modern equivalent of the exclamation [by the Duke of Wellington], 'I wish it were night, or that the Prussians would come!'"[167] Such fantasies did not promote constructive thinking about financial problems.

Pünder and Hans Schäffer noted that Great Britain lacked the resources to offer Germany assistance, no matter how good the chancellor's rapport with British leaders might be. When the prospects for reopening German banks appeared darkest on 14 July, they insisted therefore on a new approach to France. Ambassador Hoesch was instructed to inquire whether Pierre Laval, the new French premier, would welcome a visit from Brüning. Laval must be warned that the German government could make no "concrete political concessions" for a loan, but it might promise confidentially to drop the Austrian customs union if the World Court ruled against it, to include the second armored cruiser among the topics of discussion at the World Disarmament Conference, and not to pursue any revision of its eastern border for three years.[168] Hoesch transmitted a wildly optimistic reply the next day, while a run on the British pound impelled Ramsay MacDonald to appeal for an immediate financial conference in London. Brüning agreed to visit Paris that weekend with a small delegation for a "French Chequers" and then proceed to formal negotiations in London with a major corps of experts.[169]

Brüning displayed weak nerves at this juncture by seeking to distance himself from Jewish advisers. He had become suspicious of Schäffer's friendships with Berlin bankers and eagerness for an understanding with France, so he decided to take the eminently Prussian Count Schwerin von Krosigk to Paris as his financial adviser. Schäffer would naturally head the large corps of experts in London, but Brüning expressed concern that his plan to include Carl Melchior in that delegation would encourage Nazi propaganda against the influence of Jewish financiers. Pünder explained to Schäffer apologetically that Hermann Dietrich "often says things against the Jews" to the chancellor. Schäffer got Melchior reinstated after an outburst of righteous indignation in Dietrich's

---

167 Luther diary, 18 September 1931, NL Luther/366/59. Compare the remarks by Dietrich and Luther in the Schäffer diary, 20 June 1931, *Quellen: Politik und Wirtschaft*, I:717–18, and by Bülow in the cabinet meeting of 13 July, *Kabinette Brüning*, II:1354–55.

168 Bülow to Hoesch, 14 July 1931, *ADAP*, XVIII:71–72; Pünder, *Politik*, chronicle compiled on 10 August 1931, pp. 163–64; Wandel, *Schäffer*, pp. 206–08.

169 Bülow memorandum, 16 July 1931, *ADAP*, XVIII:87–90; Pünder, *Politik*, pp. 167–69; Bennett, *Financial Crisis*, pp. 245–58.

office: "I pounded on the desk and declared that I would not accept the exclusion of a highly respected man solely on the basis of his faith, which is also my faith." Brüning's impulse to defer to Nazi sensibilities was deplorable, of course, and there was no foundation for his charge many years later that Schäffer regularly leaked the details of cabinet discussions to French contacts.[170] The chancellor was probably correct, however, that Schäffer and his banker friends under-estimated the political risk of accepting a French loan on terms that implied recognition of the legitimacy of the Treaty of Versailles. Two master tacticians on the far right, Joseph Goebbels and Reinhold Quaatz, both prophesied gleefully in their diaries that Brüning would make such a deal in Paris, which would cause his fall when the Reichstag convened.[171]

Brüning, Curtius, Bülow, and Schwerin von Krosigk assembled at the Friedrichstrasse station for the train trip to Paris on the evening of 17 July. The crowd was friendly for once, cheering even, but the German leaders were distressed when Treviranus arrived in great excitement to convey reports of French troop movements near the border. Treviranus believed that military sanctions were imminent, but Brüning discounted the rumors. The small German delegation then spent the night on the train swapping war stories as they sipped wine, but Brüning often lost track of the conversation because of the powerful feelings awakened by the sight of railroad stations where he had debarked as a soldier.[172]

In Paris Laval and Finance Minister Flandin confirmed Brüning's fears by imposing extensive conditions for a loan to Germany, both economic and political. French investors would demand impressive collateral for any bond issue, they explained, such as the impounding of German tariff revenues, as well as the proclamation of a "political moratorium" against any demand for the revision of existing treaties. No German official was prepared to consider such a bargain. Flandin even threatened not to attend the London Conference unless Germany agreed to these terms in advance, but Laval persuaded him to go without preconditions. The German delegates ascribed this decision to the good impression made by Brüning, who avoided polemics and calmly explained why the German economy needed a new loan so urgently that there was no time to discuss complex political issues. Near the end of the conference Brüning remarked to Laval in French that it was the tragedy of all efforts at Franco–German rapprochement that the French always demanded as a precondition what could only be the result of the process: "Personally,

170 Schäffer diary, 17 July 1931, NL Schäffer/12/381–82; Brüning, *Memoiren*, p. 326; Schwerin von Krosigk, *Staatsbankrott*, pp. 74–75; Schwerin von Krosigk interview of 24 April 1952, pp. 1–3, IfZ/ZS 145/Schwerin von Krosigk; Staudinger, *Wirtschaftspolitik*, pp. 103–06; Wandel, *Schäffer*, pp. 208–09; Brüning to Pünder, June 1947, NL Pünder/613/205–06; Müller, *Brüning Papers*, pp. 87–94, 176, 192–93.
171 Goebbels, *Tagebücher*, 17 July 1931, II:90; Quaatz, *Tagebuch*, 17 July 1931, pp. 139–40.
172 *New York Times*, 18 July 1931, p. 6; Schwerin von Krosigk, *Staatsbankrott*, pp. 75–76; interview of 24 April 1952, pp. 2–3, IfZ/ZS 145/Schwerin von Krosigk; Brüning, *Memoiren*, pp. 326–27.

it makes me very sad."[173] Brüning did establish cordial personal relations with Laval, who like Brüning had risen to power as a politician uniquely qualified to mediate between trade unionists and conservative nationalists. They understood each other perfectly when Brüning explained that he would be toppled if he offered political concessions in exchange for a loan, and Laval replied that he would be toppled if he did not demand them. Brüning later recalled that they avoided misunderstandings thereafter with regular telephone calls in the middle of the night to distinguish in advance between serious government pronouncements and those intended only for domestic political consumption.[174]

On 20 July the statesmen in Paris crossed the channel for five days of formal negotiations in London that brought little result. When urged to endorse the "political moratorium" demanded by the French, Curtius told the British delegation "that he and Chancellor Brüning had done their best to fight against their own public opinion. There was no statesman in Germany less afraid than Dr. Brüning, but Dr. Brüning and he both knew that they had reached the limit beyond which they could not go. . . ." Schäffer warned French contacts that their demands might lead not just to Brüning's fall, but to his assassination and an enduring dictatorship by the radical right.[175] The London Conference could agree only to exhort foreign lenders to freeze their existing credits to Germany and to establish an international committee of experts to study Germany's financial situation. Brüning's only victory was to ensure that this panel would be appointed by the heads of the central banks, who were more sympathetic than government leaders to Germany's problems. He took greatest pride in winning over the American delegation after an exchange of war stories with Henry Stimson. They found that they had briefly confronted each other in Picardy in 1918, and Stimson admired the gallantry of the German troops. At the end of the conference the U.S. Secretary of State promised Brüning solemnly to do everything in his power to save "the Germany of Dr. Brüning" from the "other Germany" of militarists and demagogues. Their friendship blossomed when Stimson visited Berlin a few days later.[176] The United States had

173 Schwerin von Krosigk, *Staatsbankrott*, pp. 77–79 (source of quotation); Schmidt, *Statist auf diplomatischer Bühne*, pp. 218–19; Schwerin von Krosigk memorandum of 18 July 1931, *Kabinette Brüning*, II:1390–93; memoranda by Hoesch and Bülow, *ADAP*, XVIII:115–26; British memorandum of 19 July 1931, *DBFP*, II:212–17; Shamir, *Economic Crisis*, pp. 67–69; Rödder, *Curtius*, pp. 256–58.
174 Curtius memorandum, 25 July 1931, *ADAP*, XVIII:147–50; Austrian Ambassador Frank's report on a conversation with Curtius, 28 July 1931, ÖSA/Gesandtschaftsberichte Berlin/477–78; Brüning, *Memoiren*, pp. 328–36; Brüning to René de Chambrun, 3 January 1950, in Treviranus, *Exil*, pp. 129–30; Warner, *Pierre Laval*, pp. 17–43.
175 Arthur Henderson memorandum of 21 July 1931, *DBFP*, II:221; Schäffer memorandum of 24 July 1931, NL Schäffer/31/241–43.
176 Brüning, *Memoiren*, pp. 339–42, 413 (source of quotation); Hindenburg's reception for Stimson, 27 July 1931, *Kabinette Brüning*, II:1430–33; Schwerin von Krosigk, *Staatsbankrott*, pp. 79–80; Schmidt, *Statist*, pp. 223–24; Bennett, *Financial Crisis*, pp. 274–79; Burke, *Frederic Sackett*, pp. 145–46.

Brüning and Foreign Minister Curtius bid farewell to U.S. Secretary of State Henry Stimson after his visit to Berlin in July 1931. (Bundesarchiv Koblenz 102-12114A)

already done its utmost for Germany with the Hoover Moratorium, however; only France could offer further assistance.

Brüning later reflected that the London Conference signaled a tragic failure by the statesmen of the industrialized world to cooperate in the face of economic crisis. Thereafter the impulse to seek national economic advantage at the expense of one's neighbors became irresistible. The American Smoot–Hawley tariffs had encouraged a trade war. France enacted modest tariff increases in the spring of 1931 and a rigorous system of import quotas that fall, and even Great Britain abandoned free trade in favor of the system of Imperial Preference. The countries with massive gold reserves, France and the United States, made no effort to use them to revive world trade, and Great Britain's decision to abandon the gold standard in September 1931 eventually sparked a destructive round of competitive devaluations. It was not so much the Great Depression itself that discredited democracy in so many countries, Brüning concluded, as the fact that "nearly all the democratic governments hoped to solve the crisis only from their own selfish national point of view by methods which were bound to increase the economic crisis in the world and prolong its duration." Brüning's indictment was thoroughly justified, but he failed to acknowledge that Germany shared responsibility for this deplorable state of affairs because of Schiele's food tariffs and the effort to defy France over the Austrian customs union.[177]

---

177 Page-Barbour lecture #1 (January 1939), pp. 13–16, HUG FP 93.45 (source of quotation); Brüning to Treviranus, 20 November 1942, HUG FP 93.10/Box 34/Treviranus (3). Compare Kindleberger, *World in Depression*, pp. 142–67, 288–305; Shamir, *Economic Crisis*, pp. 99–115; and Eichengreen, *Golden Fetters*, pp. 285–310.

4

Economics and Politics in the Shadow of the Bank Crisis

The Bank Crisis of July 1931 compelled the Brüning cabinet to reexamine its policy of deflation, but it eventually reaffirmed and intensified that policy with its fourth "Emergency Decree to Secure the Economy and Public Finances" of December 1931. Historians agree that this was the most critical phase in the formulation of Brüning's economic policy, but they remain deeply divided as to the determinants of his course. Economic historians sympathetic to Brüning have developed sophisticated arguments that treaty obligations, conditions on financial markets, and the peculiar features of the German economy left the government almost no maneuvering room.[1] Critics of Brüning either have argued that he was ignorant of recent developments in economics,[2] or else they discern a conscious decision to subordinate the goal of economic recovery to a political agenda. Members of this last school emphasize Brüning's preoccupation with foreign policy[3] and/or allege that he "instrumentalized" the economic crisis for the sake of authoritarian political reforms.[4] A sound analysis must seek to incorporate all these arguments except the very last. Volatile financial markets and popular fears of inflation did impose narrow limits on the government's freedom to maneuver, but subjective intellectual limitations also warped Brüning's analysis. Reparations were a real economic problem, but by January 1932 Brüning doubtless placed too much emphasis on foreign policy. The accusation that he instrumentalized the economic crisis for domestic political purposes is misleading, however.

---

1 For good summaries of the debate, see Kruedener, ed., *Economic Crisis and Political Collapse*, and Kershaw, ed., *Weimar: Why Did German Democracy Fail?*
2 See, for example, Kroll, *Von der Weltwirtschaftskrise zur Staatskonjunktur*; Sanmann, "Daten und Alternativen;" and Jochmann, "Brüning's Deflationspolitik."
3 For example, Plumpe, "Wirtschaftspolitik in der Weltwirtschaftskrise," and Rainer Meister, *Die grosse Depression*.
4 See Mommsen, "Heinrich Brünings Politik als Reichskanzler"; Peter-Christian Witt, "Finanzpolitik als Verfassungs- und Gesellschaftspolitik. Überlegungen zur Finanzpolitik des Deutschen Reiches in den Jahren 1930 bis 1932," *Geschichte und Gesellschaft*, 8 (1982): 386–414; and Büttner, "Politische Alternativen."

4.1. The Reorganization of the Banking System

Hermann Dietrich was the first cabinet member to raise fundamental objections to the policy of deflation. In mid-May of 1931 he concluded that the austerity measures planned for the Second Emergency Decree would merely accelerate the process of economic contraction, and he urged the chancellor to stimulate the economy through public works instead. Brüning expressed sympathy with the idea but insisted that the budget must balance, which left Dietrich unable to propose anything more attractive than an increase in the sales tax to finance public works.[5] After consulting the economist M. J. Bonn, Hans Schäffer opposed Dietrich in a memorandum arguing that the government must not increase public borrowing because it competed for scarce loan funds with private enterprise. "In view of the overall credit situation in Germany, balancing the budget must have priority over all other tasks." Brüning's reliance on spending cuts to balance the budget was the only rational policy, Schäffer concluded, because they harmed the economy less than tax increases would. The economic crisis would soon end as the costs of production sank low enough to restore business profitability. These arguments neatly summarized orthodox liberal opinion and persuaded the cabinet to persevere with its course of fiscal austerity in the Second Emergency Decree of June 1931.[6]

The Bank Crisis soon discredited Schäffer's premise that recovery was imminent. Despite Brüning's occasional efforts to blame that crisis on France (see Section 3.3), it had domestic origins in the reckless lending practices and low liquidity of many German banks. The first clear sign of danger came with the collapse of Nordwolle, a major textile manufacturer in Bremen whose chief executive officers, the brothers Lahusen, had gambled heavily on wool futures and concealed enormous losses from their own supervisory board, taking out new loans that they could never repay. Their foremost creditor was the Danatbank (Darmstädter- und Nationalbank), headed by Jakob Goldschmidt. He apparently received a detailed report on these problems in early May 1931, but he too kept the secret.[7] Only in late June did Reichsbank inspectors learn some of the truth, and Hans Luther delivered an alarming report to the cabinet on 1 July. The Danatbank, he noted, had itself speculated heavily in the funding of municipal debt; if it failed, municipal savings and loans all over the Rhineland would be jeopardized, and foreign investors would almost undoubtedly panic. Brüning's

---

5 Schäffer diary, conversations with Pünder on 16 May and Dietrich on 19 May 1931, NL Schäffer/10/161–62, 166–67; see also Schwerin von Krosigk, *Staatsbankrott*, pp. 63–64, and Wilhelm Grotkopp, *Die grosse Krise. Lehren aus der Überwindung der Wirtschaftskrise 1929/32* (Düsseldorf, 1954), pp. 75–76.

6 Schäffer diary, 8 and 15 May 1931, NL Schäffer/10/146, 160; Schäffer, "Zur Krisenfrage," 15 May 1931, NL Schäffer/30/143–49.

7 See Gerald Feldman, "Jakob Goldschmidt, the History of the Banking Crisis of 1931, and the Problem of Freedom of Manoeuvre in the Weimar Economy," in Christoph Buchheim et al., eds., *Zerrissene Zwischenkriegszeit. Wirtschaftshistorische Beiträge. Knut Borchardt zum 65. Geburtstag* (Baden-Baden, 1994), pp. 323–25.

first response was to demand rigorous prosecution of the parties responsible, but the cabinet decided to lend Nordwolle 50 million marks secretly.[8] That plan was revealed as inadequate, however, by the crescendo of withdrawals from all German banks on 6–8 July. Luther responded by negotiating directly with prominent industrialists to form a "guarantee syndicate" by Germany's largest corporations to assume responsibility for at least $500 million in foreign debt. On 8 July he secured cabinet approval for this plan by promising that it would exert an enormous psychological impact on financial markets, comparable to that of the new currency that he had introduced as finance minister in 1923/4. Pünder then telegraphed the text of this complex emergency decree to President Hindenburg at Neudeck in East Prussia – where, much to his annoyance, there was nobody who could explain it to him – so that he could sign a copy while the three responsible ministers counter-signed the original in Berlin. The decree's publication did nothing, however, to slow the run on the mark.[9] Luther next responded with his futile visit to London and Paris (discussed above), the failure of which compelled Brüning to take charge of the problem.

Brüning was dismayed by the egotistical behavior of the Berlin bankers and feared that their competitive instincts might wreck the whole system of private enterprise. On 1 July Jakob Wassermann of the mammoth Deutsche Bank assured Luther that the Berlin bankers' private association for mutual aid would assist any bank with liquidity problems. He withdrew this offer the next day, however, and declared that, to be fair to the competition, the government must not guarantee the deposits of any bank without placing it in receivership. Instead of cooperating, the bankers exchanged recriminations that made depositors even more nervous. Goldschmidt had risen from obscurity to great wealth and fame as the most aggressive promoter of industrial mergers in the banking community, and several top officials of the Deutsche Bank sought to blame the crisis on his unorthodox practices. When the Danatbank warned the cabinet on Saturday, 11 July, that it would be unable to open its doors the following Monday, Brüning consulted all the leading bankers of Berlin, but they failed to make suggestions and proved maddeningly evasive when questioned about their balance sheets. When Wassermann declared that the crisis could be mastered easily with the liquidation of the Danatbank, Brüning concluded that he cared only about destroying a business rival, not the health of the economy. Other shrewd observers shared this suspicion, but Brüning later allowed the charming Goldschmidt to distort his memory of these events during years of shared exile in America –

8 Born, *Die deutsche Bankenkrise*, pp. 75–80; Harold James, "Causes of the German Banking Crisis," pp. 78–79; Luther Tagesbericht, 13 June 1930, *Quellen: Politik und Wirtschaft*, I:663–64; Schäffer diary, 1 July 1931, NL Schäffer/11/288–89; cabinet meetings of 1–4 July 1931, *Kabinette Brüning*, II:1264–68, 1278–84; Brüning, *Memoiren*, p. 302.
9 Luther, *Vor dem Abgrund*, pp. 180–81; Pünder, *Politik*, chronicle of the Bank Crisis compiled on 10 August 1931, pp. 155–56; meetings of 6–8 July 1931, *Kabinette Brüning*, II:1292–94, 1301–02, 1306–09; Dorpalen, *Hindenburg*, p. 227.

most notably when he concluded that Wassermann had sought as a Zionist to ruin Goldschmidt because he was a good German patriot as well as a Jew.[10] Brüning's suspicions at the time were nurtured by the Deutsche Bank's willingness to grant Ludwig Kaas repeated loans without security for the Center Party's bankrupt publishing house in Cologne. These transactions would not stand up well to public scrutiny, and the chancellor feared that the bankers sought to gain a hold over him.[11]

The cabinet decided on the night of 11/12 July to guarantee the deposits of the Danatbank, but not to advance credit without achieving a corresponding measure of control. Hans Schäffer suggested (like his friends among the bankers) that this crisis should be blamed on reparations, but Brüning insisted angrily that the collapse of Nordwolle and the Danatbank resulted from unethical business practices; he concluded that "there must be guarantees against any repetition of such deeds."[12] On Sunday, 12 July, Wassermann warned the cabinet that the Dresdener Bank was also failing, but its directors indignantly denied this when summoned by the chancellor. Brüning sternly warned that they should expect no help later if they were not honest now, but they insisted that there was no danger. The cabinet then decided that only the Danatbank should stay closed on Monday, while the Reich issued a guarantee of its deposits.[13] Most banks experienced a sharp increase of withdrawals on Monday, however, so the government declared a general bank holiday for Tuesday and Wednesday while it formulated half a dozen emergency decrees. Brüning became furious when the leaders of the Dresdner Bank returned with abject apologies to confess that they had misled him to protect their firm's reputation; they too needed a government guarantee for their depositors. On 16 July the banks were reopened on a limited basis to pay out wages and salaries; the Reichsbank gained control over all transactions involving foreign exchange and raised interest rates drastically while the cabinet pondered further structural reforms. The brothers Lahusen were arrested the next day, and Nordwolle declared bankruptcy after Meissner informed the cabinet that President Hindenburg refused to sign any decree to help these miscreants.[14]

After the London Conference of 20–24 July failed to offer meaningful solu-

---

10 Luther, *Vor dem Abgrund*, pp. 180–81; cabinet meeting of 11 July 1931, *Kabinette Brüning*, II:1324–33; Schäffer diary, 8 August 1931, NL Schäffer/13/587–88, and 20 November 1931, published in Wandel, *Schäffer*, p. 327; Deutsche Bank memorandum for the Reich chancellery, 1 October 1931, in *Quellen: Politik und Wirtschaft*, I:849–52; Brüning, *Memoiren*, pp. 312–14; Brüning to Carl Goetz, 13 November 1952, reply of 21 November, and Brüning to Goetz, 17 December 1952, HUG FP 93.10/Box 12/Carl Goetz; Brüning to Theodore Beste, 22 December 1956, HUG FP 93.10/Box 4/Theodore Beste; Feldman, "Jakob Goldschmidt," pp. 309–22.
11 Brüning, *Memoiren*, pp. 445–47; Henning Köhler, "Das Verhältnis von Reichsregierung und Grossbanken 1931," in Mommsen, Petzina, and Weisbrod, eds., *Industrielles System*, pp. 871–74.
12 *Kabinette Brüning*, II:1327–28.
13 Schäffer diary, 12 July 1931, NL Schäffer/11/358–59; Schäffer memorandum of August 1931, *Quellen: Politik und Wirtschaft*, I:828–29; Luther, *Vor dem Abgrund*, pp. 192–93.
14 Cabinet meetings of 15 and 20 July 1931, *Kabinette Brüning*, II:1364–66, 1394–98; Schäffer memorandum of August 1931, *Quellen: Politik und Wirtschaft*, I:830–33.

tions for any of the problems of the international banking system, Brüning returned to Berlin resolved to take vigorous action himself. The cabinet decided to advance RM 52.5 million to a consortium of industrialists who would purchase the Danatbank, and to pump RM 300 million directly into the larger Dresdner Bank in exchange for 75 percent ownership by the Reich. Brüning feared "an upsurge of public opinion in favor of nationalizing the entire banking system," which he sought to forestall by demanding that all directors of both banks submit their resignations.[15] The leaders of the Danatbank agreed, but the chancellor had a stormy meeting on 1 August with the directors of the Dresdner Bank, who protested that his plan to announce their resignations would have a "catastrophic" effect on financial markets. Schäffer noted in his diary that Brüning became "frightfully angry," issued his press release, and instructed aides to explore options for the criminal prosecution of recalcitrant bankers. That same day the cabinet imposed new controls on foreign exchange that were backed up by the threat of imprisonment for ten years at hard labor. A new Guarantee and Acceptance Bank was also established, authorized to upgrade bills of exchange with only two signatures into the three-signature paper eligible for discounting at the Reichsbank. Thereafter the Reichsbank enjoyed more freedom to expand the money supply because it could choose to finance a wider variety of business transactions. All banks opened for unrestricted business on 5 August, as deposits and withdrawals returned to normal levels.[16]

At the end of July Brüning invited several prominent businessmen and economists to join the cabinet's discussions of bank reform, alongside the Social Democrats Hilferding and Otto Braun. A consensus soon emerged that deflation had entered a vicious circle as the expectation of lower prices slowed the circulation of money. The chancellor secured general agreement, however, with his fatalistic conclusion that "it is difficult for Germany to improve matters amid a world crisis. The process of contraction will continue until [world market] prices rise again. Before that there can be no improvement."[17] Some industrialists did advance innovative suggestions to ameliorate the process of deflation by creating a form of supplemental currency to compensate for the withdrawal of foreign credits. Hermann Warmbold, an expert on chemical fertilizers and I. G. Farben executive, suggested a new issue of "stockpile notes" (*Lagerscheine*) to grant farmers and other small producers cash advances based on the value of their unsold products. Paul Silverberg supported him by declaring that "one can combat a serious deflation only with measures that look like inflation," but this would be a temporary and controlled inflation. Brüning termed this a suggestion worthy of study.[18]

15 Cabinet meetings of 28–30 July 1931, *Kabinette Brüning*, II:1438–43, 1457–66 (quotation on p. 1462); Schäffer chronicle, *Quellen: Politik und Wirtschaft*, I:835–36; Born, *Bankenkrise*, pp. 125–30.
16 Cabinet meeting of 1 August 1931 and excerpt from Schäffer diary, *Kabinette Brüning*, II:1500; Brüning, *Memoiren*, pp. 349–51; Born, *Bankenkrise*, pp. 116–23; James, *German Slump*, pp. 314–22.
17 *Kabinette Brüning*, 31 July 1931, II:1483–87.
18 Schäffer diary, 3 August 1931, NL Schäffer/13/544–46; *Kabinette Brüning*, II:1509–10.

Brüning promptly commissioned Stegerwald to discuss this plan for "stock-pile notes" with the economic experts they trusted most in the Center Party. Stegerwald expressed sympathy for the idea, but Centrist businessmen and labor leaders rejected it as inflationary, observing that the NSDAP was the only political party to advocate a supplemental currency. The Centrist press then began to denounce schemes by the special interests to relieve themselves of debt by engineering a second hyper-inflation in alliance with the Nazis, and possibly with the connivance of Finance Minister Dietrich. Brüning has been accused of manipulating the popular fear of inflation, but in this case at least that fear was clearly an elemental force that prevented him from pursuing an idea which he found attractive.[19] Only after the Center Party raised this hue and cry did Brüning tell the cabinet that "considerations of foreign policy will make it difficult to avoid deflation in the near future."[20]

Even industrialists with constructive ideas for monetary policy placed far more emphasis on the need for drastic wage reductions. Paul Reusch and seven other captains of industry had just sent Brüning a formal indictment of the "welfare state" (*Versorgungsstaat*) as the cause of the depression. They demanded *Reichsreform* to lower administrative costs, the abolition of unemployment insurance, central control over municipal spending, and above all freedom for employers facing bankruptcy to undercut the wage levels guaranteed in collective labor contracts. When Albert Vögler presented these arguments to the cabinet, Brüning replied sharply that further wage reductions were out of the question.[21] Even Brüning's ally Hermann Bücher of the German General Electric Corporation urged him to abolish state labor arbitration, while the Center Party's Business Advisory Council declared that all legal protection should be suspended for 25 percent of the wage guaranteed by collective labor contracts. Vögler soon demanded the abolition of collective bargaining itself so that factory owners could negotiate wage reductions of up to 40 percent with the personnel of each plant. Brüning and Stegerwald were appalled by these proposals.[22]

---

19 Wilhelm Fonk to Rudolf ten Hompel, 6 and 12 August 1931, Fonk memorandum on a meeting with Stegerwald, 21 August 1931, and Fonk to Stegerwald, 22 August 1931, NL ten Hompel/32; petition to the government by the Reichsverband der Katholischen Arbeitervereine and reply by Stegerwald, *Westdeutsche Arbeiterzeitung*, 8 August 1931, p. 187; editorial by Bernhard Letterhaus, *Westdeutsche Arbeiterzeitung*, 15 August 1931, p. 194; "Ist das wahr?" *Deutsche Bodensee-Zeitung*, 21 August 1931, #190 (clipping in NL Dietrich/249/214). These sources support the conclusions of Knut Borchardt, "Das Gewicht der Inflationsangst in den wirtschaftspolitischen Entscheidungsprozessen während der Weltwirtschaftskrise," in Feldman, ed., *Nachwirkungen der Inflation*, pp. 233–60. Contrast Plumpe, "Wirtschaftspolitik," pp. 351–56, and Jochmann, "Brünings Deflationspolitik," pp. 111–12.

20 Wirtschaftsausschuss, 22 August 1931, *Kabinette Brüning*, II:1606.

21 Paul Reusch et al. to the chancellor, 30 July 1931, and cabinet meeting of 31 July, *Kabinette Brüning*, II:1470–77, 1489–91.

22 Schäffer diary, 3 August 1931, NL Schäffer/13/543–44; Vögler to Trendelenburg, 27 August 1931, NL Pünder/142/264; Wilhelm Fonk memorandum for Stegerwald, 12 August 1931, NL ten Hompel/32; ten Hompel to Brüning, 7 September 1931, and reminiscences in "Hatte Schacht recht?" pp. 20–23, NL ten Hompel/1; League of Christian Trade Unions circulars of 12 and 20 August 1931, BAK Kleine Erwerbung 461/3/92–97; Bernd Weisbrod, "Industrial Crisis Strategy in the Great Depression," in Kruedener, ed., *Economic Crisis*, pp. 51–55.

Brüning displayed more sympathy for a proposal by Hermann Schmitz of I. G. Farben to revive the planned economy of the Great War. Foreign lending would never resume, Schmitz told the cabinet, without institutional guarantees against the foolish misdirection of German investment during the 1920s: "In these difficult circumstances a certain degree of planned economy cannot be avoided, an economic central authority with commissars granted extensive powers. The situation is similar to that of August 1914 and demands similar measures." This idea received enthusiastic support from Hilferding, who urged the government to retain ownership of the two failed banks as the first step toward direct supervision of all major investment decisions. At first Brüning rejected any talk of a "planned economy," but Hilferding nevertheless floated his proposal in the press.[23] By mid-August Brüning was persuaded that "our banking system has developed in a completely false direction over the last ten years. Everything has been viewed from the perspective of Berlin." The banks had invested enormous sums in the largest industrial enterprises, ignoring smaller factories that often achieved the best rates of growth. The chancellor therefore canceled his agreement to sell the Danatbank to industrialists, insisting that the Reich control both it and the Dresdner Bank directly, and he filled the supervisory boards of both banks with obscure provincial businessmen free of the Berliner's assumption that bigger meant better. Schäffer thought that Brüning was elevating second-raters on the advice of political cronies, but the leaders of the Free Unions applauded his course.[24] Brüning was influenced by the report of the parliamentary commission chaired by his party colleague Clemens Lammers which had investigated the structure of the German economy in 1927–9, the *Enquête-Ausschuss*. It had concluded that the major investment banks displayed a harmful bias in favor of the largest firms in the most stagnant branches of industry – coal, iron, steel, and textiles – firms strengthened artificially by protective tariffs and cartel agreements, firms so large that bankers assumed they would never be permitted to go under. Brüning probably exaggerated the importance of this economic problem, but his actions also had the shrewd political aim of refuting Communist charges that he was the agent of finance capital.[25]

The chancellor also concluded that the obstreperous political behavior of the Ruhr industrialists resulted from colossal investment blunders. The cabinet had almost dissolved the Rhenish–Westphalian Coal Syndicate in May 1931 after

23 Cabinet meeting, 31 July 1931, *Kabinette Brüning*, II:1488, 1495–96; Hilferding, "Probleme der Kreditkrise," *Die Gesellschaft*, 8 (1931): 235–36.

24 Schäffer diary, 8 and 14 August 1931, NL Schäffer/13/586, 623–24; cabinet meetings of 14–18 August, *Kabinette Brüning*, II:1554–57 (source of quotation), 1582–89; ADGB Bundesausschuss, 10 August 1931, *Quellen: Gewerkschaften*, p. 374.

25 See James, *German Slump*, pp. 114–54; James, "Economic Reasons," pp. 35–37; Feldman, "Industrialists, Bankers, and the Problem of Unemployment," pp. 88–93; and Balderston, *German Economic Crisis*, pp. 50–81. Compare the KPD circular of 23 June 1931, in *Quellen: Generallinie*, pp. 352–55, and Ernst Thälmann's speech of 24 July 1931, in Weber, ed., *Der Deutsche Kommunismus*, pp. 152–54.

Trendelenburg blamed it for "misguided investments exceeding those of public enterprise," and Brüning observed that the engineers made all the key decisions without consulting the salesmen. The syndicate was then renewed temporarily but threatened with suppression if it did not lower coal prices substantially.[26] Brüning considered the United Steelworks even more badly mismanaged. He had learned that the new technology adopted by it in the 1920s with massive bank loans made it more vulnerable to recession by causing a steep increase in the unit costs of production as the volume of output declined. Brüning later recalled extracting a confession from steel industrialists early in 1931 that their modernized plants could never make a profit unless they operated at more than 54 percent of maximum capacity, while they had operated at only 60 to 65 percent in the best of times. They had assumed expanding demand for steel and now sought "to compensate for their false investment decisions at the cost of the workers through ever more drastic wage reductions." Capacity utilization in the United Steelworks had in fact sunk to 52 percent in 1930 and 36 percent in 1931, a level at which profitability could not be restored even with starvation wages.[27] When the steel barons approached the chancellor on 18 August to appeal for more government financing for exports to the Soviet Union, Brüning replied sternly that no government could save them from the consequences of their mistakes. He later recalled deciding at this time that the United Steelworks must be broken up into its component firms to restore a "healthy order of magnitude in the enterprises of banking and industry." Thus Brüning had come to agree with the economic historians who today criticize him most sharply about the basic cause of the unusual severity of the depression in Germany: not "excessive" wages but the proliferation of cartels, syndicates, and trusts.[28]

Brüning's outlook was influenced by the groundswell of anticapitalist sentiment in response to the Bank Crisis that even affected his closest associates. On 16 August the chancellor devoted an afternoon to discuss the Bank Crisis with his friend Friedrich Dessauer, who had opened the columns of the Frankfurt organ of the Center Party to advocates of a "Christian socialism." Dessauer exhorted Brüning to crack the whip in all his dealings with business leaders, testifying from personal experience "that they are more deeply mired in egotism than anyone would believe, that they are meek and open to suggestions in the hour of need but immediately revert to their bourgeois possessiveness as soon as they feel the ground under their feet again. You must maintain your power over

---

26 Cabinet meeting, 29 May 1931, *Kabinette Brüning*, II:1131–37; Tschirbs, *Tarifpolitik*, pp. 403–06.

27 Brüning, manuscript memoirs, p. 73, HUG FP 93.4; see also Brüning's speech of 2 June 1954 in *Reden*, pp. 305–06, and Weisbrod, *Schwerindustrie*, pp. 52–92, 480–81.

28 Chancellor's reception of 18 August 1931, *Kabinette Brüning*, II:1577–80; rebuttal in Vögler to Trendelenburg, 27 August 1931, NL Pünder/142/256–74; Brüning to Wilhelm Sollmann, 1 February 1945, IfZ/F206/64–66 (source of quotation). Compare Krohn, "'Ökonomische Zwangslagen,'" pp. 415–26, and Carl-Ludwig Holtfrerich, "Was the Policy of Deflation in Germany Unavoidable?," in Kruedener, ed., *Economic Crisis*, pp. 71–79.

them for a long time."[29] After consulting Stegerwald, the leaders of the Christian trade unions declared publicly that the Bank Crisis revealed "the more or less complete failure of private enterprise. . . . The lovely formula of the free play of market forces has already been destroyed by the monopolies." Heinrich Imbusch eventually launched a militant campaign to nationalize the coal mines in January 1932 after Stegerwald intimated that the cabinet might entertain this suggestion once it had put Germany's fiscal house in order.[30] Populist appeals to either smash the trusts or nationalize them also became prominent in the rallies of the State Party, the Christian Social People's Service, and the Young German Order, appeals often linked with calls to subdivide the bankrupt estates of East Elbia into peasant homesteads.[31] Brüning responded to this groundswell of sentiment with numerous speeches on the "abuses of capitalism." He denied any plan to abolish private enterprise but emphasized that the government might be compelled to dissolve all cartels and syndicates and to steer the investment decisions of the big banks in order to save it. His position resembled that of moderate Social Democrats.[32]

Indeed, Brüning struggled to reform the banking system in a way that would gain the SPD's support when the Reichstag convened in October. Carl Cremer, Brüning's former ally in the DVP and a legal consultant for the United Steelworks, complained sharply to Dingeldey that the chancellor should not allow the Reichstag to meet at all: "In this situation policies adopted out of concern for the Reichstag can only be those that satisfy the Social Democrats, in other words, half-measures or outright mistakes."[33] Cremer saw this fear confirmed when the cabinet created a new bank oversight office, following Hilferding's advice to grant it broad powers and place it under the control of the cabinet instead of the Reichsbank. When Luther protested, Brüning explained that "something dramatic must occur, right away, before the Reichstag convenes."[34] An emergency decree of 19 September created a "Reich Commissar for Banking," authorized "to inspect the balance sheets and records of the banks in order to influence bank

---

29 Pünder Tagesnotiz, 16 August 1931, NL Pünder/43/84; Dessauer to Brüning, 26 August 1931, NL Dessauer/10 (source of quotation); Franz Focke, *Sozialismus aus christlicher Verantwortung. Die Idee eines christlichen Sozialismus in der katholisch-sozialen Bewegung und in der CDU* (Wuppertal, 1978), pp. 162–65.

30 *Zentralblatt der christlichen Gewerkschaften*, 1 August 1931, pp. 227–28; Patch, *Christian Trade Unions*, pp. 176–81; Schäfer, *Heinrich Imbusch*, pp. 237–41.

31 Speech by Dietrich, Staatspartei Gesamtvorstand, 15 August 1931, *Quellen: Linksliberalismus*, pp. 653–54; Wilhelm Simpfendörfer's open letter to Brüning, 31 August, and speech by Gustav Hülser at the CSVD party congress of 18–21 September 1931, *Der christliche Volksdienst* (Stuttgart), 5 September 1931, p. 1, and 3 October 1931, p. 3; Hornung, *Jungdeutscher Orden*, pp. 111–20.

32 See Brüning's remarks in *Zentrumsprotokolle*, 25 August 1931, pp. 535–37; UPI interview of 26 August 1931, *Schulthess' Europäischer Geschichtskalender 1931*, pp. 189–90; Reichstag speech of 13 October 1931, *Verhandlungen des Reichstags*, 446/2070–76; speech of 5 November 1931, in Brüning, *Reden*, p. 80; and Winkler, *Katastrophe*, pp. 370–73.

33 Cremer to Dingeldey, 18 and 20 August 1931, NL Dingeldey/101/54–57.

34 Cabinet meetings of 18 and 29 August 1931, *Kabinette Brüning*, II:1582–89, 1619–23; Luther Tagesbericht, 5 September 1931, NL Luther/366/16–17.

policies from the standpoint of the German economy as a whole." The decree also created special tribunals to hand down summary justice against those accused of fraud, tax evasion, or illegal speculation in foreign currency. Brüning told the cabinet that President Hindenburg himself demanded such action to combat the appalling decline in civic spirit revealed by the recent scandals. Schäffer and Dietrich were dismayed by the prospect of miscarriages of justice, but Dietrich confessed to his aide that he dared not protest because Brüning would suspect that he had something to hide.[35] Brüning justified this action to the leaders of the Reich Association of Industry with a stern lecture on the dubious practices of Nordwolle, the Danatbank, and the United Steelworks. He warned that there must be a few "exemplary executions" of large industrial firms to prevent bankers from assuming that they were the safest risks; if the abuses of capitalism were not reformed, the clamor for an expansion of state enterprise would become irresistible. Carl Duisberg and Ludwig Kastl came away from this meeting still convinced that Brüning was irreplaceable, but even they reproached the chancellor for making businessmen his scapegoats. Paul Reusch decided that Brüning must be toppled.[36]

Brüning did sympathize with one of Reusch's demands, that the fiscal autonomy of municipal governments be restricted. Brüning, Dietrich, and Hans Luther had long blamed the budget woes of many cities on salaries far higher than those paid comparable officials of the Reich and on reckless borrowing in the boom years to construct new libraries, swimming pools, and city halls. On 28 July Brüning told the cabinet that there must be no bailout of the municipal savings and loans without drastic action by city governments: "The mayors must first confess that they have committed errors and go before the populace with a clear plan. . . . Everything that has been done wrong must be altered at a single blow." The chancellor explained to party colleagues that "people have lost grasp of the value of money. The municipalities in particular have lived only for the day and thereby largely caused the crisis of the banks."[37] On 5 August the Reich government decreed that mayors must obtain approval from their state governments before taking out any foreign loan, and the chancellor decided to go further when the cabinet learned two weeks later that many cities were on the verge of default.[38] On 24 August the cabinet issued an emergency decree empowering

35 Born, *Bankenkrise*, pp. 153–62; Luther Tagesbericht, 12 September 1931, NL Luther/366/37–39; cabinet meeting of 19 September 1931, *Kabinette Brüning*, II:1706–11; Schäffer diary, 19 September 1931, NL Schäffer/14/802–04.

36 Chancellor's reception for industrialists, 18 September 1931, *Kabinette Brüning*, II:1700–1705; Schäffer diary, 18 September 1931, NL Schäffer/14/793–96; Kastl to Brüning, 2 October 1931, NL Pünder/140/3–7; Neebe, *Grossindustrie*, pp. 99–101.

37 Brüning, "Arbeit der Zentrumspartei," pp. 377–87; Schäffer diary, 28 July 1931, NL Schäffer/12/471–72; *Zentrumsprotokolle*, 25 August 1931, p. 536; Ursula Büttner, *Hamburg in der Staats- und Wirtschaftskrise 1928–1931* (Hamburg, 1982), pp. 165–67.

38 Cabinet meetings of 5 and 16/17 August 1931, *Kabinette Brüning*, II:1516–18, 1564–76; chancellor's reception for mayors, 10 August 1931, *Quellen: Politik und Wirtschaft*, II:873–81; Schäffer diary, 14–17 August 1931, NL Schäffer/13/624–25, 649–54.

state governments "to adopt all measures necessary to balance the budgets of the states and municipalities in the form of decrees." This "Dietramszell Emergency Decree" (named after the vacation resort where Hindenburg signed it) delegated sweeping presidential decree powers to the states. Past court rulings had implied that Article 48 did not authorize the Reich to lower municipal salaries by decree, but Brüning encouraged the state governments to test these legal waters, and they were eager to proceed. On this issue Brüning adopted Carl Schmitt's daring interpretation of the scope of Article 48 against the views of more cautious jurists. Otto Braun and other state leaders soon claimed sweeping powers under this charter to slash municipal salaries, eliminate government offices, raise tax rates, and borrow money without parliamentary approval, even when this was forbidden by state constitutions.[39]

The Dietramszell Emergency Decree caused an avalanche of spending reductions by local government agencies in the fall of 1931 that closed many theaters, drastically reduced hours in libraries and museums, terminated some public health programs, and halted many construction projects. Municipal governments and the opposition parties filed over a dozen lawsuits against these measures, but Germany's supreme court ruled in December that any state decree which served the purpose of balancing budgets, and hence of terminating the fiscal "state of emergency," was constitutional under Article 48.[40] Brüning later recalled that he sought to compel state and local governments to assume so much responsibility for unpopular decisions that they would return within a year to implore the Reich to take direct control of their budgets. He termed the Dietramszell Decree "the most decisive reform of the state since the Weimar constitution and a return to the best traditions of the Prussian administration 100 years ago." His pride seems misplaced, for the ultimate result of this policy was to undermine the power of local governments to resist the creation of a totalitarian dictatorship after their elected councils became impotent and their chief executives unpopular. Bavaria's Prime Minister Held wrote Brüning prophetically that, although everyone who knew the chancellor trusted him to use these powers with great discretion, nobody could guarantee that a future government would not abuse them: "Every attempt then to combat such an abuse would be doomed to failure in both

39 Deutscher Städtetag circular, 29 August 1931, *Quellen: Politik und Wirtschaft*, II:926–28; conference between Severing and State Secretary Zweigert, 7 September 1931, BAP R15.01/13121/63–65; conferences between Brüning and Otto Braun of 10 September 1931, NL Schäffer/14/757–64, and 11 September 1931, *Kabinette Brüning*, II:1673–79; Schulz, *Von Brüning zu Hitler*, pp. 477–79; Wolfgang März, "'. . . nach rückwärts als Aufhebung, nach vorwärts als Sperre.' Eine verfassungsgeschichtliche Miniatur zum Recht des Ausnahmezustands im Bundesstaat der Weimarer Republik," in Jürgen Heideking et al., eds., *Wege in die Zeitgeschichte. Festschrift zum 65. Geburtstag von Gerhard Schulz* (Berlin and New York, 1989), pp. 110–14.
40 März, "Verfassungsgeschichtliche Miniatur," pp. 115–22; Bavarian ambassador's memorandum of 19 August 1931, *Quellen: Politik und Wirtschaft*, II:912–15; Besson, *Württemberg*, pp. 177–78, 209–11; Klaus Schaap, *Die Endphase der Weimarer Republik im Freistaat Oldenburg, 1928–1933* (Düsseldorf, 1978), pp. 162–69; Volker Wunderlich, *Arbeiterbewegung und Selbstverwaltung. KPD und Kommunalpolitik in der Weimarer Republik* (Wuppertal, 1980), pp. 236–46; Horst Matzerath, *Nationalsozialismus und kommunale Selbstverwaltung* (Stuttgart and Berlin, 1970), pp. 21–32.

political and judicial terms, if such a government could show that it was only doing that which had earlier been declared permissible under the Weimar constitution."[41]

Despite these disastrous long-term consequences, it is difficult to see what practical alternative Brüning had to the Dietramszell Decree. No banker would lend to German cities by August 1931, and Hans Schäffer insisted that any increase of subsidies to them would bankrupt the national treasury. Most economists at the time agreed with Brüning that the municipalities had borrowed excessively in the 1920s and hampered economic recovery by keeping interest rates unduly high. Foreign bankers often raised this point as the Reichsbank anxiously sought to negotiate the "Standstill Agreement" limiting their freedom to withdraw deposits from Germany that had been urged by the London Conference in July. As Brüning told a deputation of mayors on 10 August, "further credits to Germany depend on very powerful restrictions in the cities' freedom of movement. . . . There must be severe legal barriers, which appear primitive to outsiders, in order to show that similar developments are impossible in the future." A weak Standstill Agreement was concluded on 19 August, but its success would depend on continuing cooperation by foreign bankers.[42] As with the issue of monarchism, Brüning's memoirs are unreliable when they depict this decree as the first step in an elaborate plan to centralize government power. Indeed, the passage describing this supposed plan is linked with a daydream about a restored monarchy and written in confused language that suggests a failure of memory to distinguish between wishes and actual events (the memoirist fails to use the subjunctive for counter-factual statements about what would have happened if he had remained in office until August 1932). The contemporary sources indicate that the Dietramszell Decree was an ad hoc solution to an overwhelming practical problem, and Chancellor Brüning, as we shall see, rejected all further proposals to weaken state and local government after the pressure from foreign bankers eased.[43]

The Dietramszell Decree had unfortunate personal consequences for Brüning. As chancellor he often cited the city of Cologne as a prime example of fiscal irresponsibility, and its mayor, Konrad Adenauer, was compelled to surrender control over his budget to a Prussian state commissar as the condition for reopening local savings and loans. Adenauer firmly believed, however, that some financial risks were justified in the effort to provide valuable facilities and services to the public, and that the Reich had an obligation to help the cities cope

---

41 Brüning, *Memoiren*, pp. 371–72; Held to Brüning, 20 February 1932, in Schönhoven, *BVP*, p. 269; Mommsen, "Staat und Bürokratie," pp. 104–20; Matzerath, *Kommunale Selbstverwaltung*, pp. 61–104.
42 Chancellor's reception, 10 August 1931, *Quellen: Politik und Wirtschaft*, II:879–80; Knut Borchardt, "A Decade of Debate about Brüning's Economic Policy," in Kruedener, ed., *Economic Crisis*, pp. 114–16, 128–34; James, *German Slump*, pp. 86–109. Contrast Witt, "Finanzpolitik," pp. 397–401.
43 Contrast Mommsen, "Brüning's Politik," p. 33, and Heimers, *Unitarismus*, pp. 309–10, which attach great weight to Brüning, *Memoiren*, pp. 371–73.

with rising welfare costs. His unhappy experiences in 1931 helped to persuade him in later years that Brüning's Prussian statecraft had no constructive role to play in the Federal Republic of Germany.[44]

4.2. The Formation of Brüning's Second Cabinet

As indicated by his handling of the Bank Crisis, Brüning's top priority in domestic politics in August 1931 was to prevent further growth by the Communist Party. The chancellor confided to Max Habermann that only by retaining the support of the Social Democrats could he neutralize Communist agitation among the unemployed, which posed the greatest threat to public order in the coming winter.[45] On 1 August Brüning solemnly promised Theodor Leipart of the Free Unions to regulate the selfish bankers rigorously and never to form a cabinet with Hugenberg or the Nazis. The chancellor then struggled to fulfill his June promise to the SPD to alleviate the worst hardships in the Second Emergency Decree; the cabinet scraped together RM 100 million to restore some cuts in jobless benefits and canceled the requirement that wages for blue-collar municipal workers must be adjusted to match those of workers employed by the Reich. That provision would have caused wage reductions of as much as 25 percent in some regions, but instead Stegerwald mediated a voluntary agreement between the municipalities and their workers for a modest reduction of 4 percent across the board. These decisions enhanced the prestige of the SPD and exposed the government to attacks for subservience to organized labor. Even the Cologne organ of the Center Party protested that "the power of the trade unions has proved itself stronger than the authority of the emergency decree."[46]

Brüning was compelled to abandon this focus on the grievances of the unemployed by the first crisis in his relations with President Hindenburg. The field marshal admired Brüning's technical skill in handling the Bank Crisis but feared that his own personal authority was being invoked too often on behalf of controversial decrees that he only partly understood. Yearning for the formation of a rightist parliamentary majority that would relieve him of this responsibility,

---

44 Morsey, *Brüning und Adenauer*, pp. 23–26, 39–41; Hans-Peter Schwarz, *Adenauer. Der Aufstieg: 1876–1952* (Stuttgart, 1986), pp. 317–26; Josef Hofmann, *Erinnerungen*, pp. 49–51; Brüning to Otto Friedrich, 30 August 1954, HUG FP 93.4.5/Folder 2, and 18 June 1956, HUG FP 93.4.5/Folder 1.

45 As Habermann told Krebs, who conveyed a warning to the Nazi leadership not to expect any overtures from Brüning; see the Krebs diary, 20 August 1931, NL Krebs/1/154, and Krebs to Rudolf Hess, 21 August 1931, NL Krebs/7/252–53. Compare Quaatz, *Tagebuch*, conversation with Brüning on 27 August 1931, pp. 143–45.

46 Leipart memorandum on an audience with Brüning, 1 August, and ADGB Bundesausschuss, 10 August 1931, *Quellen: Gewerkschaften*, pp. 370–74; *Zentralblatt der christlichen Gewerkschaften*, 1 September 1931, pp. 271–72; cabinet meeting of 14 August 1931, and chancellor's receptions for SPD leaders of 19 August and 1 and 7 September 1931, *Kabinette Brüning*, II:1560–62, 1591–98, 1642–51, 1660–62; *Kölnische Volkszeitung*, 25 August 1931, #400B (source of quotation); Rudolf ten Hompel to Brüning, 7 September 1931, in ten Hompel's unpublished memoirs, chapter 3, pp. 20–23, NL ten Hompel/1; Winkler, *Katastrophe*, pp. 416–18.

Hindenburg agreed to receive Alfred Hugenberg on 1 August in a disturbing departure from his earlier policy of refusing to confer with leaders of the opposition parties. The President appealed to the DNVP chairman to support Brüning, but Hugenberg emphasized that the fall of Otto Braun and a "sharp dividing line versus the SPD" remained the preconditions for rapprochement between Brüning and the right. Meissner informed Pünder afterward that Hugenberg had for the first time made a favorable impression on the President, who wanted Brüning to confer with the leader of the DNVP himself.[47]

Among the President's closest advisers, Defense Minister Groener always displayed the most sympathy for Brüning, but the widower's influence declined after he married his housekeeper in October 1930. A healthy baby appeared six months later, and Oskar von Hindenburg's wife, the President's official hostess, decided that the Groeners were not suitable for polite society. After several painful snubs, the defense minister confided to his oldest friend in April 1931 that he had lost interest in politics and turned over most of his duties to Schleicher; it was becoming ever more difficult to avoid arguments with the eighty-four-year-old Hindenburg "because he clings to his outmoded opinions from the earliest Prussian era." By the summer of 1931 Schleicher had assumed most of the burden of explaining Brüning's measures to the President in simple language replete with military terms, and he began to distance himself from the chancellor by labeling him a "procrastinator" (*Zauderer*). In later years Brüning traced his eventual rupture with the general back to Schleicher's fear that Groener had lost influence through his remarriage, and that Brüning could not retain Hindenburg's support without Groener's aid.[48]

Schleicher had long advised Hindenburg that Otto Braun should be toppled on grounds of national security, and he secretly encouraged the Stahlhelm in December 1930 to launch its referendum campaign to require new state elections in Prussia. By the spring of 1931 the Nazis, Communists, DNVP, DVP, and several splinter parties supported this referendum, and friends of the President questioned Brüning's patriotism when he spoke out against it.[49] The Stahlhelm

---

47 Meissner to Pünder, 1 August 1931, in Matthias and Morsey, eds., *Ende der Parteien*, p. 623 (source of quotation); Quaatz, *Tagebuch*, 15 July and 9 August 1931, pp. 139, 142; Meissner's summary of the President's efforts from 1925 through 1 August 1931 to involve the DNVP in government, BAP R601/19721/vol. 46/253–55; Meissner, *Staatssekretär*, pp. 212–13; Dorpalen, *Hindenburg*, pp. 226–33. In April 1931 Hindenburg had informed rightist leaders seeking an audience that the Reichstag was the only proper forum for opposition parties to raise their complaints (see Meissner to Pünder, 14 April 1931, NL Pünder/633/16–18).

48 Eschenburg, "Die Rolle der Persönlichkeit," pp. 265–69; Groener to Gleich, 26 April 1931, in Groener-Geyer, *Groener*, p. 279 (source of quotation); Groener to Schleicher, 23 August 1931, NL Schleicher/21/89–92; Plehwe, *Schleicher*, pp. 138–39; Brüning, manuscript memoirs, p. 314, HUG FP 93.4; Brüning to Graf Brünneck, 19 August 1949, HUG FP 93.10/Box 5/Manfred von Brünneck; Brüning to Otto Gessler, 31 January 1955, in Gessler, *Reichswehrpolitik*, p. 508.

49 Levetzow memorandum of 18 December 1930, in Granier, *Levetzow*, p. 290; commentary by Schleicher and Noeldechen on a petition to Hindenburg from Graf Garnier-Turawa, 4 January 1931, NL Schleicher/54/48–59; Dorpalen, *Hindenburg*, pp. 229–31; Berghahn, *Stahlhelm*, pp. 162–78; Ishida, *Jungkonservative*, pp. 164–67.

showered the Reich cabinet and President with complaints that the Prussian police interfered with its campaign, and Hindenburg concluded in June, contrary to the statistical evidence, that Severing and Otto Braun treated the right more harshly than the left. He demanded that Brüning take action against this alleged bias, but Brüning defended the conduct of Severing, and the Prussian interior minister appeased Hindenburg temporarily by banning a Communist sports festival.[50] Hindenburg renewed his protests in sharper form, however, after the Prussian government ordered all newspapers to carry an official polemic against the Stahlhelm just before the final referendum vote on 9 August. Now Brüning too became angry because the Prussian manifesto denounced "fascism" while he paid a state visit to Mussolini in Rome. The Italian dictator promised Brüning vigorous support for the campaign to abolish reparations, and his foreign minister assured Curtius that Italian Fascists really had nothing in common with German Nazis. Brüning found Mussolini a charming host and was anxious that Otto Braun not lump him together with Hitler. The chancellor therefore agreed with Hindenburg to decree that state governments must obtain the approval of the Reich before issuing compulsory press releases in future. This rebuke to Braun nearly overshadowed his victory in the referendum, which gained the support of only 37 percent of those eligible to vote.[51]

Otto Braun sought rapprochement with Brüning by embracing the idea of *Reichsreform*. In June 1931 Hans Luther had urged the chancellor to include Braun and Severing in a "cabinet of national concentration" to rally popular support for the final struggle to abolish reparations. Luther hoped that the DVP would support a revival of the Great Coalition if the government pursued a heroic foreign policy and *Reichsreform*. Brüning liked the idea, but Braun reported opposition by his party colleagues.[52] Braun himself revived Luther's proposal after the onset of the Bank Crisis because of Prussia's budget woes and the fear that his parliamentary majority would not survive the state elections due next spring. At the end of July he therefore commissioned plans to merge the interior, finance, and justice ministries of Prussia and the Reich, following the recommendations made in 1929/30 by a committee of experts appointed by the federal and state governments to which Brüning himself had belonged. According to this plan, the Prussian provinces would gain enhanced autonomy

---

50 "Appell an Hindenburg und Brüning," *Berliner Lokal-Anzeiger*, 1 April 1931, #100; Stahlhelm to Chancellor Brüning, 13 April 1931, BAP R15.01/25877/342–48; Meissner to Oskar von Hindenburg, 28 and 29 June 1931, *Quellen: Politik und Wirtschaft*, I:724–27; cabinet meetings of 29 and 30 June 1931, *Kabinette Brüning*, II:1244–54; Hindenburg to the Crown Prince, 11 July 1931, NL Schleicher/21/68–69; Severing, *Lebensweg*, II:288–90; Winkler, *Katastrophe*, pp. 364–66.

51 Prussian government declaration of 6 August 1931, *Ursachen und Folgen*, VIII:355–57; protest telegram from Dingeldey to Pünder, 6 August 1931, and Reich interior ministry memorandum of 7 August, BAP R15.01/25877.1/51–52; cabinet meetings of 7 and 10 August 1931, *Kabinette Brüning*, II:1539–42, 1546–52; Curtius memoranda of 9 August 1931, *ADAP*, XVIII:243–47; Brüning, *Memoiren*, pp. 354–57; Winkler, *Katastrophe*, pp. 389–90.

52 Luther diary, 17 June 1931, *Quellen: Politik und Wirtschaft*, I:690–91; Schäffer diary, 21 June 1931, NL Schäffer/11/260–61.

as the central Prussian government turned over many of its functions to the Reich. Braun published a newspaper editorial on 11 August advocating *Reichs-reform*, and when Brüning made no immediate response, he left Berlin for a hunting trip, muttering to his aides that the chancellor should see how he fared without Braun's help for a change.[53] Pünder and Hans Schäffer then conferred with Prussian colleagues to finalize the plan for *Reichsreform*, and Joseph Wirth also supported the project, having drafted a similar plan in May. Brüning's left-leaning supporters worried about opposition from Schleicher but felt confident that the chancellor would embrace their proposals as a boon to the campaign against reparations, since foreign bankers kept demanding such reforms.[54] Prussia's Finance Minister Höpker-Aschoff, who feared chaos after the next state elections, jeopardized his career by publishing their controversial plan on 23 August. Unfortunately, the BVP interpreted it as a plot to impose Prussian hegemony over southern Germany; the Center Party press was unenthusiastic; and the DNVP eagerly defended the historic dignity of Prussia, which must be restored to the spirit of Frederick William I, not parceled up.[55]

In mid-August Brüning and Ludwig Kaas apparently approached Breitscheid and Otto Wels to inquire in utmost confidence about a closer alliance with the SPD in the coming winter, to be cemented by the appointment of Braun and/or Severing to the Reich cabinet. Pünder withdrew the offer before the SPD could reach a decision, however, and its leaders deduced that Schleicher had vetoed the project.[56] The general did not need to intervene so crudely, however, because Brüning had become alarmed by rumors that the President was falling under the influence of Hugenberg during his vacation in remote Dietramszell. Erwin Planck reported from the chancellery to Schleicher (who was on his honeymoon) that it should be easy to turn Brüning against any alliance with the SPD because he was so anxious to shore up his position with Hindenburg. Schleicher sent Brüning a friendly assurance of continued support, and the chancellor replied

---

53 Schulz, *Von Brüning zu Hitler*, pp. 429–38; Schulze, *Otto Braun*, pp. 694–96; Rumbold's report on a conversation with Weismann, 20 August 1931, *DBFP*, II:251–53. For background on the *Verfas-sungsausschuss der Länderkonferenz*, to which Brüning was appointed by the Reich cabinet in early 1928 as an expert on fiscal policy, see Arnold Brecht, *Kraft des Geistes*, pp. 62–64, 71–93, and Gerhard Schulz, *Die Periode der Konsolidierung und der Revision des Bismarckschen Reichsaufbaus 1919–1930. Zwischen Demokratie und Diktatur, Band I*, 2nd ed. (Berlin and New York, 1987), pp. 564–606.

54 Schäffer diary, 14–16 August 1931, NL Schäffer/13/622–23, 645; Wirth to Brüning, 15 May 1931, and 11-page draft "Gesetz über die Reichsreform," 22 May 1931, NL Wirth/75 (also in BAK R43I/1882).

55 Staatspartei Gesamtvorstand, 15 August 1931, *Quellen: Linksliberalismus*, pp. 659–60; Schulze, *Otto Braun*, pp. 698–99; Schönhoven, *BVP*, p. 262; "Ein Entwurf zur Reichsreform," *Tremonia*, 21 August 1931, #231; Winterfeld speech of 19 September 1931, "Unsere Partei," 1 October 1931 (NL Hugenberg/87/230–41); press clippings in NL Wirth/75.

56 See Severing's account (which does not give a date) in *Lebensweg*, II:303–04, and the similar report by Heinrich von Gleichen in the Schäffer diary, 25 November 1932, NL Schäffer/23/1006. Compare Erwin Planck to Schleicher, 18 August 1931, in Vogelsang, *Reichswehr*, pp. 428–29.

with almost pathetic gratitude.[57] On 24 August Brüning decided not to pursue
Reichsreform after meeting Generals Hammerstein and Schleicher in the resort
of Wildbad, on his way to a Center Party conference in Stuttgart. During a
relaxed afternoon that featured a hike through the woods, Brüning promised not
to expand the cabinet leftward, while Schleicher and Hammerstein pledged their
continued support for his centrist course. Schleicher dispatched a senior officer
to Dietramszell to assure the President that the army supported the cabinet with
undiminished enthusiasm, and Brüning publicly opposed any "political experiments" in Stuttgart the next day. To his host Eugen Bolz, Brüning emphasized
his constitutional scruples; no two-thirds majority could be found in the
Reichstag for *Reichsreform*, but he considered it highly improper to invoke Article
48 for this purpose.[58] Planck reported gleefully to Schleicher on 26 August that
"Pünder's Prussian coup is finally dead." Pünder sniffed after Brüning's fall that
everything might have turned out differently if only the chancellor had listened
to him instead of to Planck.[59]

   With this assurance of military support, Brüning and Kaas agreed on 27
August to the meeting with Hugenberg desired by the President. Brüning sought
to shift the focus of the meeting away from Hugenberg's demand to form rightist cabinets in Prussia and the Reich, toward a proposal floated by Count Westarp
to spare Germany a divisive presidential election by mustering a two-thirds
majority in the Reichstag to prolong Hindenburg's term. Brüning told
Hugenberg that the DNVP should for its own sake avoid entering the government until the economic crisis bottomed out, which would not occur until the
summer of 1932 at the earliest. Indeed, unpopular austerity measures would be
necessary for another year after that, and the formation of a rightist government
would have disastrous consequences for foreign policy if it came before the final
abolition of reparations and the conclusion of the World Disarmament Conference. Brüning declared himself willing to advise the President and Center Party
to support a rightist cabinet then, but first he must know whether the DNVP
would help maintain Hindenburg in office. Hugenberg replied that he could give
no answer without consulting Hitler, and the conference ended with sharp disagreement over Hugenberg's new plan for a moratorium on the servicing of all
kinds of foreign debts. Hugenberg felt that Kaas sympathized with his arguments, but that Brüning as an old trade unionist was full of resentment against

---

57 Brüning, "Ein Brief," in *Reden*, pp. 233–34; Planck to Schleicher, 11 and 18 August 1931, in
   Vogelsang, *Reichswehr*, pp. 427–29; Brüning to Schleicher, 21 August 1931, NL Schleicher/76/160.
58 Schleicher to Groener, 28 August 1931, published in Gordon Craig, ed., "Briefe Schleichers an
   Groener," *Die Welt als Geschichte*, 11 (1951): 129; *Zentrumsprotokolle*, 25 August 1931, pp. 537–40;
   Brüning, *Memoiren*, pp. 373–74; affidavit by General von der Bussche-Ippenburg, 25 January 1952,
   in Werner Conze, ed., "Dokumentation: Zum Sturz Brünings," *Vierteljahrshefte für Zeitgeschichte*,
   1 (1953): 267; Schulze, *Otto Braun*, pp. 698–99.
59 Planck to Schleicher, 26 August 1931, NL Schleicher/21/98–99; Pünder, *Politik*, 13 August 1932,
   pp. 138–39.

big business.[60] Some observers have concluded from Brüning's account of this conversation in his memoirs that he intended to burden the democratic parties with the responsibility for all unpopular decisions and then leave Hitler and Hugenberg to benefit from his victories. The DNVP chairman gained a very different impression at the time, however, and reported to Hindenburg's friend Oldenburg-Januschau that the chancellor ignored the President's wishes by offering the right nothing more than occasional briefings on foreign policy.[61] Hugenberg redoubled his efforts to reach agreement with Hitler on a joint presidential candidate and to organize unity rallies for all rightist organizations. He told DNVP activists that, if Brüning really did seek to lay the foundation for a "great turn toward the right," then "the proper moment would be now." He alleged, however, that Brüning was a hypocrite who had adopted "Marxist" economic principles and sought to "destroy Prussia."[62]

President Hindenburg prodded Brüning for a detailed report on his conference with Hugenberg and became angry when it was delayed. The chancellor deputized Kaas to write the report, but his account failed to emphasize the crucial point that the DNVP leader refused to endorse Hindenburg's retention in office. Meissner's aide Doehle then obtained Hugenberg's version of the conversation for the President and reported to Brüning at the end of August that Hindenburg was on the verge of letting him drop. Brüning was stunned and could never explain this sudden withdrawal of trust to his own satisfaction.[63] At times he suspected that the Vatican had undermined him by informing Hindenburg that it favored the admission of the rightist parties into the Reich cabinet. Brüning had quarreled with Cardinal Pacelli, the Vatican secretary of state, during his visit to Rome on 8 August. He later recalled that Pacelli had pressed him to form a coalition with the right to facilitate the negotiation of a Reich concordat with the Vatican that would bring German law into conformity with canon law. "The Social Democrats in Germany are not religious," Brüning recalled replying, "but they are tolerant, while I am convinced that the Nazis are neither religious nor tolerant." Brüning's memoirs probably exaggerate Pacelli's sympathy for the Nazis,[64] but the main problem with this version of history is

60 Brüning, *Memoiren*, pp. 375–78; Quaatz, *Tagebuch*, 27–28 August 1931, pp. 143–47; Bracher, *Auflösung*, pp. 392–95.
61 Hugenberg to Oldenburg-Januschau, 29 August 1931, in Quaatz, *Tagebuch*, pp. 149–53; contrast Mommsen, "Brünings Politik," pp. 39–41.
62 Hugenberg speech of 20 September 1931, "Unsere Partei," 1 October 1931 (NL Hugenberg/87/234–37); Schmidt-Hannover, *Umdenken*, pp. 271–76; Leopold, *Alfred Hugenberg*, pp. 97–101; Schulz, *Von Brüning zu Hitler*, pp. 494–96.
63 Brüning, *Memoiren*, pp. 379–85; Brüning to Manfred von Brünneck, 17 March 1955, HUG FP 93.10/Box 5/Manfred von Brünneck; Quaatz, *Tagebuch*, conversation with Doehle on 31 August 1931, p. 149.
64 Brüning, *Memoiren*, pp. 358–59 (source of quotation); Brüning to Johannes Maier-Hultschin, 4 February 1946, HUG FP 93.10/Box 22/Johannes Maier (3); Brüning to Josef Hedit, undated, and Brüning to Heinrich Krone, 16 November 1960, in Müller, *Brüning Papers*, pp. 189–92. Brüning's recollections have been criticized in "Brüning contra Pacelli," in Ludwig Volk, *Katholische Kirche*

the premise that Hindenburg cared about the Vatican's attitude. The Lutheran President detested any effort by the Catholic clergy to meddle in politics, and most German Protestants felt new admiration for Brüning when rumors spread that he had quarreled with Pacelli.[65]

At times Brüning suspected, somewhat more plausibly, that Hindenburg had become impatient for rearmament and believed that only a rightist cabinet would pursue this goal vigorously. Hindenburg usually sought to restrain the generals, but he may have been influenced by the aggressive Werner von Blomberg, who gained new opportunities to socialize with the President after his transfer to the East Prussian divisional command in 1929. Wirth later recalled a private conversation in the fall of 1930 when Hindenburg blurted out that "I still hope to teach France a lesson. Give me 24 army corps and you'll see!"[66] At times Brüning blamed his enemies among the Berlin bankers, and at times he thought that Hugenberg, who was also vacationing in Upper Bavaria, had influenced the President directly. Hugenberg's confidant Otto Schmidt-Hannover did in fact spend a day with the President on 4 September but later recalled that Hindenburg was still loyal to his chancellor.[67] The real causes of the sudden chill between Brüning and Hindenburg thus remain somewhat obscure, but the chancellor had obviously exaggerated the strength of his personal bond with the President from the outset.

Brüning's difficulties multiplied when Austria formally renounced any customs union with Germany on 3 September 1931. Now the public learned that the cabinet's one overt initiative to undermine the Versailles order had ended in failure, and protests from the DVP soon compelled Foreign Minister Curtius to submit his resignation.[68] Brüning later recalled that Schleicher demanded sweeping personnel changes in the cabinet on 6 September in the direction of "an extreme German Nationalist tendency." Hindenburg seconded this demand when Brüning reported to him a week later. Brüning replied that it would be folly to jeopardize his Reichstag majority without firm guarantees that the right would support Hindenburg's reelection, and he urged the President to take Hitler's measure in a personal meeting. Hindenburg replied that he did not want

und Nationalsozialismus. Ausgewählte Aufsätze (Mainz, 1987), pp. 315–20; Ludwig Volk, *Das Reichs-konkordat vom 20. Juli 1933* (Mainz, 1972), pp. 46–49; Morsey, *Zur Entstehung*, pp. 45–47; and May, *Ludwig Kaas*, II:482–94.

65 See Josef Hofmann, *Erinnerungen*, pp. 62–63, and Count Westarp to Walther Rademacher, 2 December 1931, NL Westarp. When Westarp told Hindenburg in March 1929 that Ludwig Kaas might make a good foreign minister, the President retorted, "But I'm not going to make a Richelieu." See Jonas, *Volkskonservativen*, p. 186.

66 Brüning, "Ein Brief," in *Reden*, pp. 232–34; Brüning to Maier-Hultschin, 4 February 1946, HUG FP 93.10/Box 22/Johannes Maier (3); Dorpalen, *Hindenburg*, pp. 248–49, 427–29; Hans-Otto Meissner, *Junge Jahre im Reichspräsidentenpalais*, pp. 214–15; Wirth's handwritten memorandum of 28 August 1940, NL Wirth/135.

67 Brüning, "Ein Brief," in *Reden*, pp. 234–37; Dorpalen, *Hindenburg*, pp. 231–33; Schmidt-Hannover, *Umdenken*, p. 277.

68 Dingeldey to Curtius, 4 September 1931, *Quellen: Politik und Wirtschaft*, II:941–43; Rödder, *Julius Curtius*, pp. 214–22, 264–70.

to serve another term and refused to deal with "this Austrian corporal." The President urged the dismissal of Wirth as well as Curtius, the appointment of new ministers of economics, justice, and transport congenial to the DNVP, and perhaps the replacement of Dietrich and Stegerwald as well. Such a cabinet had no chance to win toleration by the Reichstag, but Hindenburg also declared that he would never break his oath to the constitution; Brüning felt that he demanded "the squaring of the circle."[69] Brüning arranged a secret meeting with his old professor, Martin Spahn, and poured out his heart in an effort to seek detente with the DNVP, but Hugenberg merely sharpened his attacks.[70] The Pan-German League also organized a letter-writing campaign among landowners and retired generals as an overture to the major rally for the "National Opposition" that Hugenberg planned to hold at Bad Harzburg on 11 October. When Brüning reported to the President at the end of September, Hindenburg mournfully pointed to a stack of correspondence "from the best men in the German Reich" demanding the chancellor's dismissal. Brüning sensed that Hindenburg would be relieved if he volunteered to resign. He later recalled choosing this moment to suggest for the first time that a monarchy might eventually be restored in some form, but this failed to lift the President's spirits.[71]

Big business had meanwhile launched a vigorous campaign to abolish state labor arbitration. Great Britain's surprising decision to abandon the gold standard on 21 September encouraged this campaign because it wiped out the competitive advantage achieved by earlier deflation in Germany. The chancellor and his labor minister now found it more difficult to refute the arguments of the Ruhr coal mine operators in particular, who demanded wage reductions of 12 percent and threatened widespread closings. When Christian trade unionists urged Stegerwald to reject any wage cuts, he replied on 23 September that such a policy would cause a "cabinet crisis and the transfer of political power to Hitler and Hugenberg."[72] Trendelenburg urged the cabinet the next day to require the renegotiation of all collective labor contracts by the end of the year, because the trade unions must be compelled to share responsibility for lowering wages enough to reduce unemployment. Stegerwald replied that he would never allow such a declaration of "open season" on workers, but Dingeldey promptly raised similar demands at a DVP rally in Hamburg.[73] On 29 September the eleven major busi-

69 Brüning, *Memoiren*, pp. 385–88. Compare Groener to Gleich, 20/21 September 1931, *Quellen: Politik und Wirtschaft*, II:984, and Quaatz, *Tagebuch*, memorandum on a conversation with Meissner, 23 September 1931, p. 155.

70 Brüning to J. Borchmeyer, 26 July 1951, in Müller, *Brüning Papers*, p. 175; Brüning to Otto Schmidt-Hannover, 25 May 1954, HUG FP 93.10/Box 30/Otto Schmidt-Hannover.

71 Brüning, *Memoiren*, pp. 417–18; Levetzow to Fürst v. Donnersmarck, 28 August 1931, in Granier, *Levetzow*, pp. 299–300; "Brief an den Reichspräsident," 5 September 1931, in *Deutsche Zeitung*, 26 September 1931 (BAP R601/19721/vol. 46/158).

72 Zechen-Verband to Stegerwald, 14 September 1931, BAK R43I/2178/306–15; Stegerwald-Brüning conference of 22 September, *Kabinette Brüning*, II:1718–20; Stegerwald to Jakob Kaiser, 23 September 1931, NL Stegerwald/014/Nachtragsband/#17.

73 Schäffer diary, 24 September 1931, NL Schäffer/14/829–31; Jones, *German Liberalism*, p. 429.

ness associations sent the chancellor an open letter that identified socialism as the cause of the economic crisis and untrammeled free enterprise as the only cure. Brüning's sympathizers removed any explicit criticism of the current government from the letter, and Pünder sought to persuade the press that the business leaders intended to support the chancellor's reforms. The manifesto demanded the abolition of state labor arbitration, however, and howls of protest from organized labor soon compelled Brüning to distance himself from this program. The impression spread that big business had withdrawn its support from the government.[74]

Fortunately for Brüning, the President and defense ministry took no position on these demands, although Hindenburg urged the chancellor to recruit at least one prominent industrialist for the cabinet to counteract the impression that he was losing ground on the right.[75] Schleicher did exploit the crisis, however, to urge Brüning to abandon his constitutional scruples and dissolve the Reichstag indefinitely. Brüning later recalled that the general urged a *Staatsstreich* (coup d'état) as the cabinet's only chance to survive when he conferred with the chancellor and Kaas on 24 September. Brüning replied that it would be "a crime" to violate the constitution when he still enjoyed the confidence of a Reichstag majority, but Schleicher reported (a bit prematurely) that the DVP had just decided to topple him. Stunned, Brüning murmured that the government must still try to get along with the Reichstag somehow, and he turned to Kaas for support. His party chairman apparently encouraged Schleicher's worst tendencies, however, with a subtle discourse on natural law concluding that universal principles of equity sometimes justified the violation of written constitutions.[76]

Even Brüning's closest supporters were losing patience with constitutional government. Hermann Dietrich offered at the beginning of October to join a "cabinet of martial law" if allowed to purge the uncooperative governing boards of the Reichsbank and national railway, and Treviranus could not understand why Brüning insisted on allowing the Reichstag to convene.[77] Stegerwald too lost patience after Groener and Meissner warned the cabinet that the courts might reject an emergency decree to lower government pensions on the grounds that this would violate tenure rights guaranteed by an article of the constitution not listed as suspendable in Article 48, Paragraph 2. If such necessary measures

---

74 Neebe, *Grossindustrie*, pp. 100–102; business petition of 29 September and Pünder to Zechlin, 30 September 1931, *Kabinette Brüning*, II:1764–69; "Tagesnotiz" of 30 September 1931, NL Pünder/43/33; ADGB Bundesausschuss, 2 October 1931, *Quellen: Gewerkschaften*, pp. 397–400; Brüning, *Memoiren*, p. 419.

75 Remarks by Brüning, *Zentrumsprotokolle*, 12 October 1931, p. 545. Schleicher endorsed some "loosening of collective labor contracts" in August 1931, but Groener sympathized with Stegerwald's resistance to such demands; see Vogelsang, *Reichswehr*, pp. 426–27, and Groener to Gleich, 20/21 September 1931, *Quellen: Politik und Wirtschaft*, II:984.

76 Brüning, *Memoiren*, pp. 399–400; Morsey, *Untergang*, pp. 25–26.

77 Schäffer diary, 1–2 October 1931, NL Schäffer/14/871–73; Blank to Reusch, 1 October 1931, *Quellen: Politik und Wirtschaft*, II:1011–13.

could not be carried out on the basis of Article 48, the labor minister declared, then they must be based on "the state's right to self-defense." Stegerwald acknowledged that such action entailed the "danger of dictatorship" but concluded that "the time has come when the government must choose between the constitution and the state and the people."[78] Of course Brüning received similar advice from the leaders of Fascist Italy. Planck told Hans Schäffer that Brüning had become depressed after his visit to Rome by the contrast between himself and the dynamic, grandiloquent Mussolini: "Since then he keeps feeling that they have a natural Caesar. He is being made into one artificially by circumstances."[79] But Brüning was also urged to establish "dictatorship" by many respected political moderates, such as Eduard Hamm of the German Congress of Chambers of Commerce and the retired defense minister, Otto Gessler. Even Otto Braun in effect urged "dictatorship" by suggesting that *Reichsreform* was so important that it should be implemented by presidential decree if a two-thirds majority could not be found in the Reichstag. Thus Brüning faced great pressure from many quarters to abandon the Weimar constitution at least temporarily.[80]

Brüning therefore displayed real commitment to the rule of law when he decided to accept only a modest streamlining of his cabinet. He averted crisis in the Ruhr by arranging a government subsidy for its coal mines. On 30 September an emergency decree prepared at the chancellor's initiative imposed wage reductions there of 7 percent, which were made almost painless by the suspension of the miners' unemployment insurance dues.[81] Brüning then shored up his position in the Reichstag by scaling back the third "Emergency Decree to Secure the Economy and Public Finances" planned for the beginning of October. It did shorten the period of eligibility for unemployment insurance benefits, but Brüning rejected the further austerity measures urged by Schäffer. He also persuaded Meissner and Groener to accept the popular demand to lower the ceiling on government pensions from 80 to 75 percent of the retiree's former salary. When the courts agreed that the constitution protected the real, not the nominal value of pensions, there was little to arouse controversy in the Third Emergency Decree promulgated on 6 October.[82]

78 *Kabinette Brüning*, 2 October 1931, II:1787; compare the debate of 24 September, II:1734–35, and Kurz, "Artikel 48," pp. 405–06.
79 Schäffer diary, 18 August 1931, NL Schäffer/13/665; compare Brüning, *Memoiren*, pp. 355–56, and Josef Hofmann, *Erinnerungen*, p. 62.
80 Ten Hompel memoirs, chapter 3, pp. 39–40, NL ten Hompel/1; Pünder memorandum of 21 September 1931 on a conversation with Hamm, *Kabinette Brüning*, II:986–88; Gessler to Rudolf Pechel, 18 March and 13 August 1947, in Gessler, *Reichswehrpolitik*, pp. 509–10; Brüning to Ernst-Günther Prühs, 19 February 1950, in Müller, *Brüning Papers*, pp. 194–96; Schulz, *Von Brüning zu Hitler*, pp. 406–08, 429–38; Schulze, *Otto Braun*, p. 696.
81 Pünder's Tagesnotizen, 24–26 September 1931, NL Pünder/43/38–40; cabinet meeting of 30 September 1931, *Kabinette Brüning*, II:1772–75; Winkler, *Katastrophe*, pp. 418–20; Tschirbs, *Tarifpolitik*, pp. 412–19; Bähr, *Staatliche Schlichtung*, pp. 321–24.
82 Schäffer diary, 29 September and 2 October 1931, NL Schäffer/14/861–63, 875–88; Luther Tagesbericht, 2 October 1931, NL Luther/366/135–37; cabinet meetings of 3–5 October 1931, *Kabinette Brüning*, II:1802–12; Schulz, *Von Brüning zu Hitler*, pp. 542–47.

Brüning sought to clear the air with Hindenburg on 5 October by offering his resignation. He promised to advise the Center Party to tolerate a rightist cabinet if Hugenberg and Hitler promised to reelect Hindenburg as President, but Treviranus spread the word that the Center Party would be outraged if Brüning fell. Brüning also reminded Groener of his old promise that Hindenburg would never abandon him, while Treviranus notified industrial lobbyists that "the future decisions of the chancellor will naturally depend in large measure on who participates in the rally at Bad Harzburg." This blatant threat helped to persuade almost all prominent industrialists to decline Hugenberg's invitation, and the impression that big business had turned against the government was neutralized.[83] When Groener and Schleicher accompanied Brüning loyally for a presidential audience on 7 October, Hindenburg agreed to accept a minor cabinet shuffle: Brüning would become foreign minister as well as chancellor, while his party colleagues Wirth and von Guérard would resign so that the cabinet would not have a Catholic majority. Curtius bid the cabinet farewell with a selfless appeal that it do everything possible to keep Brüning in power because of the extraordinary confidence he enjoyed among foreign leaders.[84]

Brüning then dampened Hindenburg's enthusiasm for the right by arranging Hitler's first presidential audience on 10 October, the eve of the Harzburg rally. First the chancellor himself conferred with the Nazi leader, suggesting as he had with Hugenberg that a new rightist cabinet might be formed in a year or two if Hitler committed himself now to retaining Hindenburg as President. Hitler replied that he must first consult Hugenberg and was then ushered into the President's office. After listening to one of Hitler's hour-long monologues, Hindenburg complained sharply about the rude behavior of Nazi agitators. As Brüning had anticipated, the President found the Nazi leader uncouth and told aides afterward that he was obviously unqualified for high office.[85] This audience also helped to spoil the atmosphere at Harzburg the next day, when Hitler refused to attend a unity banquet or review the marching of anyone but his own Stormtroopers. Schmidt-Hannover observed that the presidential audience had transformed the normally ingratiating Hitler into "a mixture of a prima donna and Napoleon." Hitler had apparently concluded that he could gain power without any help from Hugenberg. Thereafter the leaders of the Stahlhelm publicly attacked Hitler for his violations of soldierly etiquette, spoiling the

83 Brüning, *Memoiren*, pp. 421–23; Blank to Reusch, 1 and 5 October 1931, and Blank to Springorum, 5 October 1931 (source of quotation), *Quellen: Politik und Wirtschaft*, II:1011–12, 1017–19; Turner, *Big Business*, pp. 167–71.

84 Brüning, *Memoiren*, pp. 423–24; cabinet meeting of 7 October 1931, *Kabinette Brüning*, II:1815–17; remarks by Brüning, *Zentrumsprotokolle*, 12 October 1931, pp. 544–45; Brüning to Magnus von Braun, 7 February 1951, HUG FP 93.10/Box 2/Brach-Breucker.

85 Brüning, *Memoiren*, pp. 391–92, emphasizes the cordiality of these meetings, but contrast Brüning's interview of September 1945, p. 4, HUG FP 93.10/Box 16/Interview; Brüning to J. Borchmeyer, 26 July 1951, in Müller, *Brüning Papers*, p. 174; Levetzow to Fürst v. Donnersmarck, 14 October 1931 (recounting Hitler's version of the audience), in Granier, *Levetzow*, pp. 310–11; and Dorpalen, *Hindenburg*, pp. 241–42.

image of unity on the right that Hugenberg sought to project.[86] Brüning had some reason to congratulate himself on a successful gambit but later confided to Pünder that Hitler's presidential audience had been a mistake because it encouraged many army officers and judges to regard the Nazi leader as a legitimate contender for power.[87]

Brüning arranged a truce in his party's press polemics with the NSDAP after this meeting with Hitler, but he was neither optimistic about this courtship nor prepared to offer significant concessions. The chancellor told party colleagues that there was little chance of "a union of forces in a broad front" because "the right wants to seize the rudder now that things cannot get any worse." He advised them to oppose the formation of a rightist cabinet, and they all agreed.[88] Addressing the Reichstag on 16 October, Brüning reproached the Nazis for undermining national unity on the eve of decisive negotiations over reparations:

> When I see that one side of this House – no matter how patriotic these men are, even though they want the best, just as the men on the other side do – always proclaims the struggle against the other side as the first precondition for any successful policy, then I can only conclude that it is just not possible to achieve that political expression of our national community [*Volksgemeinschaft*] which we really need at all costs in this historic moment. (Bravo! in the middle.) Let me add that one maxim has guided all our work in these weeks and months: I consider it impossible to find any course that will get us through this hard winter if it immediately arouses a hostile and united front among workers.

Hans Schäffer found this speech completely honest, "very passionate and impressive," and ideal for arousing a guilty conscience among the DVP delegates who were tempted to side with the Harzburg Front.[89]

Brüning had begun the search for new ministers congenial to the President on 2 October by offering the ministry of justice to the former DVP chairman Ernst Scholz, but he declined when Dingeldey objected.[90] Brüning next invited Gessler, who had friendly relations with Hindenburg, to become interior minister, and Gessler came to Berlin on 8 October to argue that the Reichstag should be dissolved indefinitely while the government launched an all-out struggle against the radical parties. Brüning sent him to the President, curious himself as to whether Hindenburg sympathized with the idea of a *Staatsstreich*, and was

---

86 Quaatz, *Tagebuch*, 18–29 October 1931, pp. 156–60; Levetzow to Fürst v. Donnersmarck, 14 October 1931, in Granier, *Levetzow*, pp. 308–09; Schmidt-Hannover, *Umdenken*, pp. 280–85; Theodor Duesterberg, *Der Stahlhelm und Hitler* (Wolfenbüttel and Hanover, 1949), pp. 15–33; Leopold, *Alfred Hugenberg*, pp. 101–04; Orlow, *Nazi Party*, pp. 234–36; Schulz, *Von Brüning zu Hitler*, pp. 555–60.
87 Pünder, *Politik*, 6 March 1932, p. 116.
88 *Zentrumsprotokolle*, meetings of 12–14 October 1931, pp. 542–44, 548–49; contrast Becker, "Brüning, Prälat Kaas," pp. 89–93.
89 *Verhandlungen des Reichstags*, 446/2194–95; Schäffer diary, 16 October 1931, NL Schäffer/14/926.
90 Brüning, *Memoiren*, p. 420; Scholz to Brüning, 9 October 1931, *Kabinette Brüning*, II:1822.

much relieved when the field marshal rejected Gessler's plan emphatically. Erwin Planck then suggested that Groener add the interior ministry to his responsibilities, and when Brüning agreed, Schleicher became enthusiastic again in support of the chancellor. Groener accepted this double yoke in exchange for Brüning's promise to support efforts to unite all the paramilitary leagues in some kind of state-sponsored militia.[91] Brüning also offered the ministry of transport to Hermann Schmitz of I. G. Farben but beat a hasty retreat when he heard a rumor that Schmitz was guilty of tax fraud. He then offered the ministries of transport and economics to Silverberg and Albert Vögler, but they declined when he refused to promise them any change of social policy. Brüning eventually decided to move Treviranus to the transport ministry but could secure the services only of Hermann Warmbold for economics, a business executive with some interesting ideas but no significant following. The chancellor angered Vögler by spreading a malicious report that he could not join the cabinet because the United Steelworks was on the verge of bankruptcy.[92]

The result of these maneuvers was a further contraction in the cabinet's base of support, not the rightward expansion desired by Hindenburg. The President signaled his displeasure by refusing Brüning's request to declare in advance that there would be no new elections if the Reichstag voted to topple him; worse still, Meissner informed rightist leaders that the President had taken this crucial decision out of the chancellor's hands.[93] Brüning's only new recruit of any stature was Hans von Schlange-Schöningen, the former head of the DNVP in Pomerania, who agreed on 9 October to replace Treviranus as Reich Commissar for Eastern Aid if he received the authority to develop a more generous program.[94] Brüning also hoped to impress Hindenburg with the creation of an Economic Advisory Council to seek consensus over economic policy under the President's chairmanship. Brüning secured the participation of several prominent agrarians in the DNVP and the industrial trio of Silverberg, Vögler, and Schmitz, alongside the leaders of the Free Unions and other notables. The chancellor told Christian trade unionists that this council was needed as a "safety valve" for the "overheated steam engine" of the German state; it should tie the hands of so many interest groups that he could not be toppled while its deliberations proceeded.[95]

---

91 Brüning, *Memoiren*, p. 426; Brüning to Gessler, 31 January 1955, and Gessler to Rudolf Pechel, 18 March and 13 August 1947, in Gessler, *Reichswehrpolitik*, pp. 508–10; Brüning to Ullmann, 23 September 1947, NL Ullmann/6/263–65; Hürter, *Groener*, pp. 308–09.

92 Brüning, *Memoiren*, pp. 425–26; Brüning to Hans von Raumer, 18 July 1957, HUG FP 93.4.5; Silverberg to Krupp, 12 October 1931, *Quellen: Politik und Wirtschaft*, II:1035–38; Turner, *Big Business*, pp. 166–67; Neebe, *Grossindustrie*, pp. 103–06.

93 Pünder memorandum, 9 October 1931, *Kabinette Brüning*, II:1817–18; Quaatz, *Tagebuch*, 15 October 1931, p. 156.

94 Hans Schlange-Schöningen, *Am Tage danach* (Hamburg, 1946), pp. 43–52; Schulz, *Von Brüning zu Hitler*, pp. 591–98.

95 Cabinet meeting, 10 October 1931, *Kabinette Brüning*, III:1823–25; Fahrenbach to Jakob Kaiser, 10 October 1931, NL Kaiser/220; Pünder, *Politik*, 1 November 1931, pp. 105–06; Brüning, *Memoiren*, p. 394. The *Wirtschaftsbeirat* was an attenuated version of a plan presented to Hindenburg on 5

As the Reichstag convened, Brüning sought popularity and deflected attention from his strained relations with Hindenburg by emphasizing his quarrel with the Ruhr industrialists. After the leaders of the Christian miners' and textile workers' unions warned him emphatically that they would accept no measure to allow employers to undercut wages bound by collective labor contract, the chancellor took a firm stand against the demands of heavy industry. Brüning told party colleagues that the cabinet shuffle resulted from "the struggle to abolish state labor arbitration and collective bargaining. People want to destroy the trade unions, and he was reproached for having been a trade unionist. . . ." He won their applause by pledging to accept no revision of collective bargaining that was not based on genuine consensus between management and labor, and in the Reichstag he launched yet another appeal to revive the Central Association of November 1918.[96] The chancellor paid the price for this stance when the DVP Reichstag delegation decided on 10 October to support a motion of no confidence against him, although Dingeldey granted Brüning's supporters permission to vote their conscience.[97] The SPD backed Brüning more firmly than ever. In September it expelled six of his left-wing Marxist critics from its Reichstag delegation, and the government's handling of the Bank Crisis and opposition to the Harzburg Front left only two delegates opposed to the policy of toleration by October. Thus Brüning succeeded in retaining the support of the SPD against the increasingly vitriolic agitation of the Communists.[98] To the surprise of many, the Business Party also announced support for the government. The chancellor had arranged modest financial assistance for a bank linked with the party, and Brüning may have swayed Business Party leaders with the implied threat that corrupt dealings by that bank might be revealed. Johann Viktor Bredt has insisted, however, that he rallied his delegation for a statesmanlike course after meetings with rightist leaders showed that they had no constructive alternative to Brüning's policies. Dingeldey and 20 DVP delegates opposed Brüning in the confidence vote of 16 October, but five party colleagues backed the government while four absented themselves; with the Business Party's support, Brüning won by a comfortable margin of 295 to 270. The Reichstag then adjourned itself until February 1932.[99]

October by the ex-chancellor Wilhelm Cuno for "a sort of crown council" to formulate economic policy, to be composed mostly of industrialists; see Neebe, *Grossindustrie*, pp. 103–04.

96 Christian miners' union Hauptvorstand meeting of 10 October 1931, p. 4, NL Imbusch/2; Heinrich Fahrenbrach to Jakob Kaiser, 10 October 1931, NL Kaiser/220; *Zentrumsprotokolle*, 12 October 1931, pp. 545–48 (source of quotation); speeches of 13 and 16 October 1931, *Verhandlungen des Reichstags*, 446/2077, 2193–94; Dessauer to Brüning, 8 October 1931, NL Dessauer/10.

97 Jones, *German Liberalism*, pp. 429–30; Dingeldey to Otto Thiel, 24 October 1931, NL Dingeldey/92/33–35; Dingeldey to Frank Glatzel, 24 October 1931, NL Dingeldey/53/98–100.

98 Keil, *Erlebnisse*, II:405–06; Winkler, *Katastrophe*, pp. 400–406, 423–35; Schaefer, *SPD*, pp. 167–71; Harsch, *Social Democracy*, pp. 145–48; KPD circulars of 12 September and 7 October 1931, *Quellen: Generallinie*, pp. 386–91, 402–04.

99 Bredt, *Erinnerungen*, pp. 271–73; Brüning, *Memoiren*, pp. 443–44; Schumacher, *Mittelstandsfront*, pp. 177–80; Jones, *German Liberalism*, pp. 430–33.

Some of Brüning's supporters interpreted his second cabinet as a new form of "presidential government," a clean break with the parliamentary heritage, but the chancellor's speeches continued to emphasize that the Reichstag enjoyed the power to rescind emergency decrees and that he would restore parliamentary government intact as soon as the economic crisis passed. He later ridiculed the notion of "presidential government" as an invention of romantic intellectuals with no political experience, such as Hans Zehrer, who had badly misled Schleicher. The President, Brüning later reflected, had become a problem by the fall of 1931 because rule by decree encouraged him to claim "a dominant position versus the Reich government and the Reichstag that was never desired by the fathers of the constitution.... My mission and my only chance for success was to preserve at great pains an equilibrium between the sinking power of the parliament and the rising power of the Reich President."[100]

Brüning felt compelled, however, to keep his disagreements with the President a secret even from his closest colleagues. Joseph Wirth accepted his dismissal from the cabinet with good grace but found Brüning curiously deaf when he warned that the Hindenburg family had become intolerant of Roman Catholics and dangerously impatient for rearmament. The former chancellor prophesied that Hindenburg's reactionary friends would interfere more and more with government policy until Brüning had no choice but to resign: "In the back room of the Reich chancellery is a bottle from which you will drink. It is filled with gall. We have all taken a drink from it, but for you is reserved the most bitter drink of all." Treviranus also noted by November 1931 that Hindenburg no longer considered Brüning Germany's savior, but the chancellor assured him and Wirth that he retained the President's complete confidence, breaking off discussion.[101] Brüning believed that Hindenburg was indispensable as the only man sure to defeat any candidate of the right in the presidential elections due next spring. The chancellor hoped that the bitter disagreements between Nationalists and Nazis over economic and social policy made it obvious to any rational observer that the "Harzburg Front" could never offer a viable alternative to the existing government. He also hoped that the President's most influential advisers, Meissner, Schleicher, and Oskar von Hindenburg, remained so jealous of each other that they could not unite against him.[102]

After winning the Reichstag's vote of confidence, Brüning took up the cause

---

100 *Zentrumsprotokolle*, 25 August 1931, p. 537; speech of 5 November 1931, in Brüning, *Reden*, p. 73; Brüning to Hans von Raumer, 10 September 1947, and to August Winkelmann, 28 January 1949, in *Briefe*, II:481–84; Brüning to Philipp Dessauer, 16 March 1956, in Müller, *Brüning Papers*, pp. 178–79 (source of quotation).

101 Wirth memoir, "Ereignisse und Gestalten von 1918–1933," question #21, p. 5 (source of quotation), question #22, pp. 6–7, and question #23, NL Wirth/18; Treviranus, *Ende von Weimar*, pp. 289–91.

102 Brüning, *Memoiren*, p. 467; Brüning to Graf Brünneck, 19 August 1949, HUG FP 93.10/Box 5/Manfred von Brünneck; Brüning to Graf Galen, 12 October 1948, pp. 5–6, HUG FP 93.10/Box 11/Franz Graf Galen; Brüning's speech of 16 October 1931, *Verhandlungen des Reichstags*, 446/2195.

of *Reichsreform* to strengthen the office of Reich chancellor. After Höpker-Aschoff announced that he would resign as Prussian finance minister, Brüning suggested to Otto Braun on 20 October that Dietrich unite the finance portfolios of Prussia and the Reich. Braun responded with a hearty invitation to merge their justice and agriculture ministries too, and he even offered in a private conversation to retire from public life and recommend Brüning as his successor. Brüning and Braun both recalled this later as a friendly gesture motivated solely by Braun's desire to avoid chaos after the next state elections, but the Reich did bring financial pressure to bear. Braun approached Brüning and Schäffer on 23 November to appeal for assistance in view of Prussia's imminent bankruptcy, but Schäffer would only arrange credits from the Reichsbank on the condition that Prussia support Brüning more energetically. This experience must have made retirement seem more attractive to Braun, who was nearing the point of physical and emotional collapse.[103] Brüning was thrilled by this offer because it would make him less dependent on Hindenburg:

> As Reich chancellor I could be dismissed by the President, but not as Prussian prime minister. Everything that happened in the summer of 1932, the breach of the constitution by the President and the Reich government, could have been avoided. Administrative and personnel reforms could have been accomplished quickly and without friction. Without altering the constitution, a *Reichsreform* could have been achieved that would actually have returned us to the principles of the Bismarckian constitution.

Press leaks to the effect that *Reichsreform* was merely a pretext to revive the Great Coalition spoiled the atmosphere, however, and when Brüning went to Hindenburg in late November to champion this plan, someone had already persuaded him to reject it. Hindenburg declared gruffly that he could not permit his chancellor to risk his health by assuming more burdens, and that he disliked any plan to reduce the historic dignity of the Prussian state. Brüning felt unable to persist without giving the impression of deplorable personal ambition.[104]

Brüning's memoirs demonstrate that he created problems for himself through clumsy handling of the field marshal. In May 1931 Brüning rode the train to Kiel with Hindenburg to attend the launching of Germany's new armored cruiser, and the President praised him exuberantly for securing parliamentary

---

103 Pünder to Weismann, 20 October 1931, NL Pünder/658/25–27; Brüning, *Memoiren*, pp. 246–47; Braun, *Von Weimar zu Hitler*, pp. 352–55; chancellor's reception for Braun and Klepper, 23 November 1931, *Kabinette Brüning*, III:2001–02; Schäffer diary, 23 November 1931, NL Schäffer/15/1072–74; Winkler, *Katastrophe*, pp. 475–79; Hagen Schulze, *Otto Braun*, pp. 700–704; Schulz, *Von Brüning zu Hitler*, pp. 581–89. Braun later recalled offering his post to Brüning on 3 November, while Brüning said the offer came at the end of the month.
104 Brüning, *Memoiren*, pp. 247–48. Compare Brüning to Wilhelm Sollmann, 29 September 1940, in Knapp, ed., "Dokumentation: Brüning im Exil," pp. 107–08; Brüning to Josef Deutz, 19 August 1949, HUG FP 93.10/Box 6/Dale-Deym; and Pünder to Walther Jänecke, 10 November 1932 (should be 1931), NL Pünder/180/96.

approval for the construction of a second. In reply, Brüning delivered an hour-long lecture on the five most important tasks of foreign and domestic policy in the months ahead; he felt obliged to explain his worries in exhaustive detail even though he noticed that Hindenburg had difficulty following his remarks.[105] When Brüning justified various measures as necessary to guarantee the President's reelection, Hindenburg obviously resented the implication that he was an ordinary politician greedy for office. When Brüning speculated that a monarchy might someday be restored in some form, he just reminded the field marshal of his broken oath to Wilhelm II. On 11 November, the anniversary of the armistice, Hindenburg confided to Brüning that he dreaded any campaign for reelection because it would dredge up all the most painful questions about his conduct in November 1918. He remained convinced nevertheless that the abdication of the kaiser had been necessary because the troops would have mutinied otherwise; his highest duty as a Prussian soldier was to save the life of his monarch. Hindenburg's view was actually quite sensible, but Brüning exclaimed that the front-line troops had been loyal to the throne – the mutineers had had no stomach for a fight, headquarters had lost its nerve. Hindenburg replied sadly that "I knew already in February 1918 that the war was lost, but I wanted to give Ludendorff one more chance." Brüning then left the room in a cold fury, seeking out Groener to denounce any commander-in-chief who asked 100,000 men to sacrifice their lives for an offensive that he did not think could succeed.[106]

Brüning gave further evidence of war trauma shortly thereafter when he ruminated with Hans Schäffer over a bottle of wine about the many comrades from the Great War who had never adjusted properly to civilian life. Brüning still maintained that the war would not have been lost if only the general staff had kept its nerve.

> Then he showed me a stack of photographs of the kaiser and his sons, of parades and audiences at court, which are being sold in mass quantities at a shop here on the Stresemannstrasse. He cannot bear to look at these things, they are so disgusting to him. . . . A friend sent him the pictures to show what really kindles the German people's enthusiasm. The German people have little talent for politics.

Schäffer protested that it was more a question of experience than talent.[107] Brüning obviously nurtured a terrible suspicion that the Imperial government had plunged Germany into an unnecessary war. The man who uttered these remarks would only favor a restoration of monarchy in moments of utter despair over Germany's political future.

105 Brüning, *Memoiren*, pp. 273–75.
106 Ibid., pp. 452–56; compare his earlier account as reported in Wheeler-Bennett, *Wooden Titan*, pp. 352–57.
107 Schäffer diary, 20 November 1931, published in Wandel, *Schäffer*, pp. 315–24.

4.3. The Decision to Persevere with Deflation

While Brüning was distracted by political problems, a thoughtful discussion of alternatives to deflation began within the ministerial bureaucracy. In August 1931 an earnest student of the writings of Keynes, Wilhelm Lautenbach of the economics ministry, formulated a plan to spend two to three billion marks for the construction of roads and railroads, to be financed jointly by the government and Reichsbank through some new form of "credit creation," a phrase that he soon changed to the more innocuous "short-term financing." Lautenbach argued that such a plan could not result in inflation while so many factors of production lay idle; it would accelerate the circulation of money so much that the Reichsbank could easily cover it by creating just RM 200–300 million in additional currency, and the Reich treasury would recoup much of the cost in the form of reduced jobless benefits and increased tax revenue. Lautenbach acknowledged, however, that his plan might well cause a loss of foreign exchange reserves, so the government must restrict imports. He also emphasized that the lopsided deflation of the past eighteen months, when some wages and prices experienced free fall while others proved rigid, had so distorted relative prices that the marketplace no longer transmitted useful signals as to where capital and labor would best be employed. Public works must therefore be combined with vigorous measures to reduce wages bound by collective labor contracts and prices bound by cartel agreements.[108] His economic analysis was sophisticated, but he demanded measures offensive to free traders, organized labor, and big business alike as corollaries to a proposal that aroused fears of inflation. German "Keynesians" in 1931/2 were influenced not by the famous ideas of the *General Theory* (not published until 1936, although outlined in articles in 1933) but by the *Treatise on Money* (published in October 1930) and Keynes's memoranda for the Macmillan Committee. At this stage Keynes was far more cautious, more preoccupied with international exchange rates and the "stickiness" of the costs of production in the recessions of the 1920s, than the Keynes of popular memory.[109]

Lautenbach acquired an influential ally when he approached Hans Schäffer on 26 August. His arguments reinforced powerful new impressions that Schäffer had gathered from reading Keynes, the Swedish economist Gustav Cassel, and the German Heinrich Rittershausen. Schäffer concluded that the "best economists" now considered deflation harmful; governments should seek

---

108 "Defizitpolitik?" memorandum of 24 August 1931 and revised version of 9 September, in Wilhelm Lautenbach, *Zins, Kredit und Produktion*, ed. Wolfgang Stützel (Tübingen, 1952), pp. 137–55.

109 See Lautenbach's lecture on Keynes of December 1931, in *Zins, Kredit und Produktion*, pp. 155–65; Knut Borchardt, "Zur Aufarbeitung der Vor- und Frühgeschichte des Keynesianismus in Deutschland. Zugleich ein Beitrag zur Position von W. Lautenbach," *Jahrbücher für Nationalökonomie und Statistik*, 197 (1982): 359–70; and Robert Skidelsky, *John Maynard Keynes. Volume II: The Economist as Savior, 1920–1937* (New York, 1994), pp. 314–401.

to stabilize or even raise price levels. Schäffer decided to embrace Lautenbach's plan a few days later when Dietrich told him that "further deflation will ruin everything."[110] The state secretary of finance then argued in a thoughtful memorandum that the government must stimulate industrial production by expanding the money supply enough to spend RM 2.5 billion on public works. He noted that economic recovery might jeopardize the diplomatic campaign against reparations but asked, "Is it responsible to reject on tactical grounds a correct and useful solution, beneficial to society and soothing for politics?"[111]

Schäffer encountered disappointment as he canvassed support for this plan. Hans Luther conceded that such a program might produce an ephemeral recovery, but it would also destroy the impetus for *Reichsreform*, he argued, and weaken support abroad for the abolition of reparations; when the apparent recovery petered out, genuine revival would prove more difficult than if the government had done nothing. The process of deflation remained "healthy despite all its pain" because it was still weeding out inefficient producers.[112] Schäffer's arguments nevertheless impelled Luther to consult one of the handful of "Keynesian" economists in Germany, the Kiel professor Gerhard Colm. Colm endorsed Lautenbach's idea but warned that timing was critical: "It all depends on whether our efforts to lower prices and the costs of production have already reached that low-point where business again becomes profitable." Any action to stimulate the economy might cause disaster if undertaken too soon, and only the statesman's intuition could determine when the time was ripe.[113] M. J. Bonn told Schäffer that the government must avoid any policy which appeared inflationary to the German people, and Trendelenburg declared that "stimulation can only help if we are already at the bottom. . . . I do not believe that we are that far yet."[114]

Luther agreed to give the ideas of Schäffer and Lautenbach a thorough airing before the "Friedrich List Society," a club promoting dialogue between academics and policy-makers. He brought sixteen distinguished economists, including most who had expressed views similar to Lautenbach's, to Berlin for a secret conference with a dozen senior officials on 16/17 September.[115] The meeting did not yield consensus on any alternative to the policy of the Reichsbank. Six participants supported Lautenbach's plan (Colm, Heimann, Lautenbach, Neisser, Rittershausen, and Röpke), but the majority remained skeptical. Edgar Salin agreed with "the younger scholars" that central banks should seek to prevent any

110 Schäffer diary, 26–31 August 1931, NL Schäffer/13/706–15, 727.
111 "Gedanken zur Krisenbekämpfung," 2 September 1931, *Quellen: Politik und Wirtschaft*, I:933–39.
112 Luther to Schäffer, 4 September 1931, *Quellen: Politik und Wirtschaft*, II:940.
113 Luther Tagesbericht, 7 September 1931, NL Luther/366/21–22; on Colm's background see Krohn, *Wirtschaftstheorien*, pp. 25–26.
114 Schäffer diary, 11–14 September 1931, NL Schäffer/14/768–76.
115 Knut Borchardt and Hans Otto Schötz, eds., *Wirtschaftspolitik in der Krise. Die (Geheim-) Konferenz der Friedrich List-Gesellschaft im September 1931 über Möglichkeiten und Folgen einer Kreditausweitung* (Baden-Baden, 1991), pp. 17–32; Luther Tagesbericht, 12 September 1931, *Quellen: Politik und Wirtschaft*, II:951–52.

further decline in price levels, but he argued that only France and the United States possessed the gold reserves necessary to inaugurate such a policy. Walter Eucken judged that Lautenbach's plan was very dangerous in an economy so closely bound to the world market as Germany's; the campaign to lower "sticky" wages and prices, which Lautenbach intended to link with public works, must be carried out first before risking any such experiment.[116] Rudolf Hilferding emerged as the most vigorous defender of the Reichsbank. After agonized reflection, he had recently conceded to Luther in a cabinet meeting "that the central bank cannot create money." He now argued with more conviction that both the U.S. Federal Reserve and the Bank of England had failed miserably to reverse economic trends by loosening credit. What the Reichsbank should do was to continue its quiet campaign to compensate for the withdrawal of foreign credits by relaxing the rules that governed the discounting of commercial bills of exchange. Nobody could say in advance how far this kind of monetary expansion could be pushed; the Reichsbank must simply grope its way forward, tightening the rules again if it noted any increase in prices or decline in the value of the mark versus foreign currencies.[117] Even the "Keynesian" minority distinguished between two phases of deflation, a necessary first phase in which inefficient producers were eliminated, and a destructive second phase, when economic recovery became possible but did not occur because of a collapse in investor confidence. If Germany had entered the second phase, they agreed, then the money supply should be expanded, but they offered no clear response to Luther's queries as to how policy-makers could distinguish one phase from the other.[118]

Luther closed the meeting of the List Society by declaring without contradiction that the participants agreed unanimously on two points: (1) that the German people's fear of inflation made it impossible to announce any dramatic program to expand the money supply, so that the government must act secretly if it ever decided to implement Lautenbach's plan, and (2) that the government must continue its campaign to lower wages bound by long-term collective labor contracts and prices bound by cartel agreements. The Reichsbank president felt vindicated by the best brains in the country.[119] Thereafter Schäffer too conceded that popular psychology tied the government's hands. When Bonn sent him a refutation of his memorandum of 2 September, the state secretary glumly replied:

---

116 *Konferenz der List-Gesellschaft*, pp. 40–42, 68–80, 131–36, 145–49; see also the summary of the discussion in the Schäffer diary, 16 September 1931, NL Schäffer/14/784a–784f. Meister, *Grosse Depression*, pp. 313–14, lists Salin and Eucken misleadingly as supporters of the Lautenbach plan.

117 Cabinet meeting of 29 August 1931, *Kabinette Brüning*, II:1622; *Konferenz der List-Gesellschaft*, pp. 80–90. For the convergence between Hilferding's Marxian and orthodox liberal analysis of the Great Depression, see Staudinger, *Wirtschaftspolitik*, pp. 87–89; Robert Gates, "German Socialism and the Crisis of 1929–33," *Central European History*, 7 (1974): 332–59; and Harold James, "Rudolf Hilferding," pp. 864–68.

118 *Konferenz der List-Gesellschaft*, pp. 131–32, 158–59.

119 *Konferenz der List-Gesellschaft*, pp. 300–304; Luther, *Vor dem Abgrund*, pp. 244–49; Luther Tagesbericht, 16/17 September 1931, NL Luther/366/47–48, 53–54.

Even if one could prove a hundred times over that a measure does not mean
inflation, if the majority of people regard it as inflation, then this opinion
has the same effect as if it really were inflation. If that must be feared, then
we have no alternative but to abandon the measure. . . . The mere fact that
you, honored professor – and, I must acknowledge, not you alone – regard
this plan as inflationary precludes its implementation. You need fear no
further rash action on my part. . . . But you must understand how hard it is
for someone in a responsible position to bear the sight of this crisis "burning
out" when he sees what burns up with it day by day.[120]

Some historians have argued that Schäffer abandoned the "Keynesian" camp
only under massive pressure from Brüning, but Schäffer himself later recalled
that he was genuinely persuaded by Trendelenburg's argument that it was impossible to "eliminate the economic crisis from within." Instead, one could only
hope "to achieve 'ignition' and accelerate the rise at the moment when the crisis
had burned itself out and the first signs of recovery emerged." This basic idea,
he added, had guided all of Brüning's economic policy.[121]

The idea of deficit spending for public works suffered further as its most powerful sympathizers, Dietrich and Stegerwald, became distracted with plans for
homesteading. By September 1931 both ministers displayed a cultural pessimism
that hampered the search for a plan to revive the economy. Dietrich hurled
himself into a campaign for the creation of shanty towns on the outskirts of
industrial cities, where the unemployed could receive plots of land to grow food
and the materials to build cottages lacking sewers, running water, or electricity.
Lautenbach and other "Keynesians" judged such plans a dangerous diversion
from the problem of stimulating industrial recovery, but Dietrich feared that
German industry would never provide jobs again for the millions of unemployed.[122] Stegerwald agitated for a massive increase in the number of peasant
homesteads in East Elbia, to be carved out of bankrupt estates. He told the
cabinet that, since the Great War, "the hegemony of the European states has
doubtless been lost forever because of the upsurge of the other quarters of the
globe. . . . The overheated flowering of German industry has driven too many
people into the cities. It will be necessary to bring more people into the countryside." But in fact there were few young proletarians willing or able to transform themselves into peasants.[123]

120 Schäffer diary, conversation with Ludwig Kastl, 21 September 1931, NL Schäffer/14/807;
    "Aufzeichnungen zur Denkschrift vom 2. September 1931," 15 October 1931, and Schäffer to
    Bonn, 26 October 1931, NL Bonn/52.
121 Schäffer to Luther, 22 April 1947 and 28 September 1961, NL Schäffer/44/4–9, 39–42; Schäffer
    to Wolfgang Helbich, 17 October 1960, NL Schäffer/46/102 (source of quotation). Contrast
    Jochmann, "Brünings Deflationspolitik," pp. 109–11; Büttner, "Politische Alternativen," pp.
    229–31; and Meister, *Grosse Depression*, pp. 302–03.
122 Dietrich to Brüning, 3 September 1931, NL Dietrich/307/87–88; Dietrich's "Programm zur
    Minderung der Arbeitslosigkeit durch Kleinsiedlerstellen," 7 September 1931, BAK
    R43I/1452/81–95; cabinet meetings of 7 and 21 September 1931, *Kabinette Brüning*, II:1664–66,
    1714–15; Schwerin von Krosigk, *Staatsbankrott*, pp. 87–88; Grotkopp, *Krise*, pp. 94–96, 104–09.
123 Cabinet meeting of 27 October 1931, *Kabinette Brüning*, III:1845; Schäffer diary, 27 October 1931,
    NL Schäffer/14/950; Schorr, *Stegerwald*, pp. 230–32.

Luther also appeased "Keynesians" within the government by quietly achieving a modest expansion of the money supply in the fall of 1931, prodded forward by public speeches in which Chancellor Brüning repeatedly emphasized the need for looser credit. The discount rate was cut from 10 to 8 percent on 2 September, 7 percent on 10 December, and 6 percent in March 1932. In July 1931 the Reichsbank quietly abandoned its rule that 40 percent of money in circulation must be covered by reserves of gold and foreign exchange. Through the operations of the Guarantee and Acceptance Bank and generous financing for exports to the Soviet Union, it actually increased the German money supply from RM 5.88 to RM 6.37 billion between August and December 1931 despite substantial ongoing losses of foreign credits. Its new credits to the Soviet Union alone probably created 150,000 jobs in export industries. Luther recalled later that a third of the bills of exchange held by the Reichsbank as collateral at the end of 1931 would have been unacceptable in normal times. The Reichsbank grew more cautious thereafter, but Luther and Brüning did have reason in later years to resent the accusation that they had aggravated the depression through tight credit.[124]

Brüning finally intervened directly in the debate over economic policy on 21 September, when the stunning news arrived that Great Britain had abandoned the gold standard. We now know (and Keynes argued at the time) that the British government had stumbled onto a policy that could stimulate industrial exports without the harmful side effects of deflation, and many historians argue that Brüning should have imitated this action.[125] Brüning, Dietrich, and Schäffer all initially considered this an act of desperation, however, that would ruin England's banks and insurance companies. The schism of the Labour Party and a short-lived naval mutiny created the impression that Great Britain was on the verge of anarchy.[126] After consulting a wide variety of experts, Brüning soon recognized that British export industries would achieve substantial gains to balance against these losses in the financial sector. All the experts agreed, however, that certain unique features of the British economy limited the risk of abandoning the gold standard. The British still owned assets overseas roughly equivalent to their total foreign debt, and most of their debts were denominated in sterling; German debts, on the other hand, were denominated in gold and would rise in value after any devaluation of the mark. Montagu Norman also confided to Luther that the Bank of England expected the vast gold reserves of India to cushion the fall of the pound because wealthy Indians would experience an immediate incentive to buy sterling. All the experts agreed, finally, that British

---

124 Calculations on the money supply in Harold James, "German Banking Crisis," pp. 85–86; James, *Reichsbank*, pp. 296–316; Balderston, *German Economic Crisis*, pp. 178–83; Borchardt, "A Decade of Debate," pp. 106–09, 119–20; Meister, *Grosse Depression*, pp. 236–37; Luther, *Vor dem Abgrund*, pp. 252–53; Brüning, *Memoiren*, pp. 349–51; Brüning to H. Heck, 12 November 1941, in Müller, *Brüning Papers*, p. 189.

125 See, for example, Charles Maier, "Die Nicht-Determiniertheit ökonomischer Modelle. Überlegungen zu Knut Borchardts These von der 'kranken Wirtschaft' der Weimarer Republik," *Geschichte und Gesellschaft*, 11 (1985): 275–94.

126 Schäffer diary, 21 September 1931, NL Schäffer/14/812; Brüning, *Memoiren*, pp. 366–69.

savers were unlikely to panic because they had never experienced hyper-inflation. By 2 October the Brüning cabinet therefore decided that Germany must adhere to the gold standard. Schäffer and Lautenbach not only endorsed this decision, they demanded further deflationary measures to counteract the British effort to conquer German export markets.[127]

In later years Brüning depicted himself as an advocate of devaluation whose hands were tied by the Young Plan, which obliged Germany to preserve the mark's value at 0.358 grams of fine gold. He later recalled (although Luther did not) a secret agreement with Luther in December 1930 to devalue the mark by 20 percent as soon as the Young Plan was nullified. He would have imitated the British in September 1931, "if I had not been warned at the moment by the French and, less emphatically, by the British Government that this would be considered a major violation of the Reparations Treaties which would seriously impede the final solution of the reparations problem."[128] This assertion seems greatly exaggerated. The French did oppose any effort to revise the Young Plan's provisions about the gold standard at the London Conference in July, but the British and American delegations sympathized with Brüning's request for more flexible regulations. Great Britain's departure from the gold standard then cost the Bank of France two billion francs on its deposits in London, which placed a great strain on Anglo–French relations and improved Germany's diplomatic position. Some British officials actually hoped that Germany would imitate their action, although they avoided offering advice, and Pierre Laval was quite conciliatory when he visited Berlin on 27 September. He did not utter threats but sought instead to promote economic cooperation and a united front against Bolshevism.[129] The documentary record strongly suggests that the German cabinet adhered to the gold standard on economic rather than diplomatic grounds, for reasons that seem fairly persuasive even in retrospect.

The cabinet's decision to preserve the gold standard made a new round of deflation all but inevitable to protect German export markets. Dietrich

---

127 Schäffer diary, 22 September 1931, NL Schäffer/14/813–18, and 23 September, *Quellen: Politik und Wirtschaft,* II:951–52; Luther, *Vor dem Abgrund,* p. 154; Austrian Ambassador Frank's reports on conversations with Luther and Schäffer, 23 and 25 September 1931, ÖSA/Gesandtschafts-berichte Berlin/506–09; remarks by Dietrich, Staatspartei Vorstand, 26 September 1931, *Quellen: Politik und Wirtschaft,* II:1001; cabinet meetings of 24 September and 2 October 1931, *Kabinette Brüning,* II:1723–26, 1782–83; Schiemann, *Deutsche Währung,* pp. 211–33; Knut Borchardt, "Germany's Exchange Rate Options during the Great Depression," in Borchardt, *Perspectives,* pp. 184–203; Borchardt, "Keynesianismus in Deutschland," pp. 367–69; Meister, *Grosse Depression,* pp. 249–52, 319–21.
128 Brüning, "Democratic Reorientation," Brookings Institute lecture of 6 March 1941, p. 9, HUG FP 93.45 (source of quotation); Brüning, *Memoiren,* pp. 221, 232; Brüning's memoranda of September 1934 and February 1940, *Briefe,* I:33–34, 514; Brüning to Hans Staudinger, 30 January 1941, HUG FP 93.4.5/folder 2.
129 Report on the London Conference, *DBFP,* II:444–51, 482–83; memoranda of 27 September 1931 on receptions for Laval by Brüning and Curtius, *Kabinette Brüning,* II:1745–51; Borchardt, "Exchange Rate Options," in *Perspectives,* pp. 194–97; Schiemann, *Deutsche Währung,* pp. 186–206; Shamir, *Economic Crisis,* pp. 75–77, 148–61; Rödder, *Curtius,* pp. 129–31.

announced to the cabinet on 2 October that he would renounce his opposition to deflation, "if we are resolved to take up the struggle across the board . . . , to tackle price levels, rents, salaries, social legislation, and interest rates simultaneously." This was the kernel of the Fourth Emergency Decree. Brüning declared that President Hindenburg should convene his Economic Advisory Council to seek voluntary agreements to lower interest rates, cartel prices, and wages; the government would intervene only if it failed.[130] By the time the council first met in late October, however, Brüning concluded glumly that the issues of interest rates, the gold standard, and Eastern Aid were too controversial to place on its agenda. He no longer hoped for genuine consensus, just a vague declaration of principles to help prepare public opinion for unprecedented forms of government intervention.[131]

The Economic Advisory Council failed to suggest any alternative to the government's deflationary policy. On 10 November Paul Silverberg did offer a bold plan to expand the money supply by two billion marks, but nobody seconded the proposal when Luther raised objections. Brüning himself appeared the next day to present the official view that Germany's economic recovery could not begin until price levels began to rise on world commodities markets. "All the theoreticians," Brüning declared, "are in agreement about that. But Germany has no power to alter the level of world prices." Even Economics Minister Warmbold, who had suggested the creation of "stockpile notes" in August, now condemned Silverberg's initiative as premature.[132] The Free Unions also opposed Silverberg. Peter Grassmann told the council's first session that workers suffered more than anyone from inflation, and Otto Suhr of the socialist white-collar unions termed Silverberg's plan an experiment too dangerous to attempt.[133] At the penultimate session of the council, Grassmann criticized the government for exerting more downward pressure on wages than on the cost of living, but he apologized to Brüning privately for this speech directed to the gallery. He also approached Luther in private to applaud his courageous defense of a sound currency: "You must persevere! In 40 or 50 years they will say, 'That was the man.'" Brüning became indignant when the Social Democratic press sought to create the impression that labor leaders on the council had mounted serious opposition to the government; *Vorwärts* even published remarks supposedly addressed by Grassmann to the council's final session that were never delivered. In essence the trade unionists on the council had supported the government's position.[134]

---

130 *Kabinette Brüning*, II:1784–96; compare the Schäffer diary, NL Schäffer/14/873–94, and Luther's Tagesbericht, NL Luther/366/135–37.
131 Meeting of 27 October 1931, *Kabinette Brüning*, III:1843–44.
132 Meetings of 10, 11, and 16 November 1931, *Kabinette Brüning*, III:1934–37, 1946–48, 1962–63.
133 Meetings of 29 October and 11 November 1931, *Kabinette Brüning*, III:1869, 1949–50.
134 Luther diary, 23 November 1931, NL Luther/425/10 (source of quotation); Schäffer diary, 22 November 1931, NL Schäffer/15/1068; chancellor's reception for SPD leaders, 23 November 1931, *Kabinette Brüning*, III:1999–2000; Winkler, *Katastrophe*, pp. 437–39.

The real decisions about economic policy occurred in the secret meetings of the cabinet. There the first sharp debate came when Luther sought to exploit the economic crisis for the sake of *Reichsreform*. Treviranus provoked the quarrel by declaring on 28 October that mortgage interest rates must be slashed in half to save German agriculture. Schäffer and Luther were horrified by the proposal, but Brüning supported it. Luther then observed that it might be possible to lower interest rates, but only after "a great and general action program is implemented that will restore the German people's confidence in itself and the world's in Germany, which must therefore include *Reichsreform*." Brüning replied that *Reichsreform* "would provoke resistance from so many quarters that orderly work by the government would become impossible."[135] Luther approached Stegerwald and Warmbold a week later with an offer to lower mortgage interest rates, "if the Reich takes direct control of executive power at least within the territory of the Prussian state." On 18 November he prophesied to the cabinet that chaos and martial law would result if it delayed *Reichsreform* further, but Brüning told him angrily to hold his tongue because such dire predictions would cause great turmoil if leaked to the press. The chancellor also reached final agreement with Bavaria at this time to redress its grievances against his earlier decrees.[136] Brüning's opposition to any further effort to weaken state and local governments after the Dietramszell Decree was one of the reasons why Schleicher labeled him a "procrastinator."

Schlange-Schöningen provoked a second controversy within the cabinet after he was sworn in as Reich Commissar for Eastern Aid on 9 November. Brüning welcomed him by persuading Otto Braun that Prussia should withdraw from the administration of the program, and he insisted that the cabinet do everything possible to prevent a further decline of agricultural production in East Elbia.[137] Like Treviranus, Schlange-Schöningen blamed high interest rates for the depression, and he offered a program for debt relief on 16 November that created a form of trusteeship in which foreclosure was banned and debt service had the last claim on farm income. As Luther observed caustically, a provision sheltering even works of art from foreclosure created the impression that Schlange sought "to rescue families, not farms." Luther feared that this decree undermined the very foundations of capitalism, and Dietrich warned that it would outrage public opinion, but it won cabinet approval on 17 November after Schlange promised Stegerwald that his trustees would turn over "hopelessly bankrupt" estates to agents of the labor ministry for subdivision into

---

135 Schäffer diary, 28 October 1931, NL Schäffer/14/956–7; Luther Tagesbericht, 28 October 1931, NL Luther/366/202–05 (source of Luther quotation); *Kabinette Brüning*, III:1855–59 (source of Brüning quotation).

136 Luther Tagesbericht, 7 November 1931, *Quellen: Politik und Wirtschaft*, II:1089–90; Luther diary, 18 November 1931, NL Luther/425/4–5; Schönhoven, *BVP*, pp. 264–67.

137 Cabinet meetings of 4–5 November 1931, *Kabinette Brüning*, III:1907–10, 1915–19; Schlange-Schöningen, *Am Tage danach*, pp. 49–55; Schulz, *Von Brüning zu Hitler*, pp. 591–98.

homesteads.[138] Thus the cabinet displayed renewed deference to the wishes of Hindenburg, which had not received this much consideration since May 1930. Three conservative agrarians nevertheless resigned from the Economic Advisory Council because the government refused to extend such debt relief west of the Elbe. Brüning persuaded the council to conclude its deliberations on 23 November by endorsing his policy in general terms, but this walkout dispelled any impression that he had forged real consensus.[139]

Hans Schäffer discovered another major constraint on government policy when he sought to trim the military budget. Schäffer told Brüning on 9 November that the treasury confronted obligations of RM 376 million at year's end for which there were no funds. The time had come for the desperate measure of doubling the national sales tax (*Umsatzsteuer*) to 2 percent, because this was the only tax that had not already reached the point of diminishing returns. Brüning implored Schäffer to devise some other solution.[140] Schäffer suggested to the cabinet on 24 November that his tax increase could be scaled back if the defense ministry accepted budget cuts similar to those imposed on every other government agency, but the chancellor quickly whispered to him that this was impossible. Schäffer concluded grimly that, "with regard to the budget, we already live under a military dictatorship." He threatened to resign unless granted either his tax increase or a guarantee that the Reichsbank would extend credit to cover any shortfall in the treasury's cash flow.[141]

Thus Schäffer placed Lautenbach's monetary ideas back on the agenda, but now the Reichsbank emerged as another constraint on the cabinet's decisions. Luther personally sympathized with Schäffer's request. On 29 November he exhorted his board of governors to approve a major reduction in the discount rate from 8 to 6.5 percent, to be announced simultaneously with the Fourth Emergency Decree. Most of his colleagues considered this reduction too large, however, and felt that the Reichsbank must defend its autonomy by acting only after the government program was implemented.[142] On 2 December Luther appealed to his vice-president Dreyse to devise some method to help Schäffer avoid a tax hike. Luther insisted that the money supply could be expanded sub-

138 Cabinet meetings of 16 and 17 November 1931, *Kabinette Brüning*, III:1964–67, 1974–79; Schäffer diary, 16 and 17 November 1931, NL Schäffer/15/1026–30; Heinrich Muth, "Agrarpolitik und Parteipolitik im Frühjahr 1932," in Hermens and Schieder, eds., *Staat, Wirtschaft und Politik*, pp. 319–27.

139 Brandes, Holtmeier, and von Oppen to the chancellor, 19 November 1931, *Kabinette Brüning*, III:1989–90; Blank to Reusch, 24 November 1931, *Quellen: Politik und Wirtschaft*, II:1112–14; Bracher, *Auflösung*, pp. 387–89.

140 Schäffer diary, 9 November 1931, NL Schäffer/15/996–98; *Kabinette Brüning*, III:1923; Schäffer to Dietrich, 19 November 1931, NL Schäffer/31/443–49.

141 Cabinet meeting of 24 November 1931, *Kabinette Brüning*, III:2005–06; Schäffer diary, 24 November 1931, NL Schäffer/15/1080–82; Schäffer memorandum for Dietrich, 26 November 1931, *Quellen: Politik und Wirtschaft*, II:1116–19 (source of quotation); Luther diary, 26 November 1931, NL Luther/425/11.

142 Luther diary, 29 November 1931, NL Luther/425/15–17.

stantially without any danger of inflation, if only the Reichsbank could do it in secret. He could not think of any technique to accomplish this, however, and Dreyse refused to help. In his personal diary Luther expressed despair over the narrow-minded orthodoxy of the bank governors, who sought to apply the "art of sailing" to a modern economy powered by a "steam engine." He revealed nothing of these disagreements to the cabinet, however, stoutly defending the collective policy of the Reichsbank leadership.[143]

Hemmed in by all these constraints, the triumvirate of Brüning, Dietrich, and Stegerwald decided by the end of November to focus on eliminating that distortion of relative prices which Lautenbach and all the experts in the List Society had identified as a crucial barrier to recovery. They would impose a 10 percent reduction in all cartel prices, return wages governed by collective labor contracts to the level of 10 January 1927, lower government salaries by 9 percent, impose comparable reductions of rents and railroad freight rates, and create a "Reich Price Commissar" to monitor retail markups and lower them where excessive.[144] They judged that the decree's wage provisions would reduce most wages by about 10 percent, deduct 15 percent in the few trades that had avoided cuts in the spring and summer of 1931, and leave unaffected the growing number of workers who lacked protection by a collective labor contract. When Luther demanded a global wage reduction of 20 percent, with additional cuts for workers who had fared unusually well in the past, Brüning replied that "a general reduction of wages cannot be sought, but rather a reduction of the great differentials and implementation of more elasticity in the system."[145] Thus the chancellor rejected the view of businessmen that economic recovery required lower real wages; he still sought instead to enhance opportunities for German exporters through balanced reductions of wages and prices.

The cabinet wrestled with the thorny issues of interest rates and the sales tax on 4/5 December. Stegerwald and Dietrich had been persuaded by Schäffer of the need for his tax hike, but they insisted in exchange that all interest rates on bonds and mortgages of 8 percent or higher be reduced by one-fourth. When Luther emphasized the practical difficulties, Stegerwald exclaimed that "we are conducting a dictatorship like Mussolini and Russia, and only in the question of interest rates do we dictate nothing. The world has never seen anything like this." His threat "to go on vacation" indefinitely

---

143 See the diary entries in NL Luther/425/17–21, 36, excerpts of which are published in Luther, *Vor dem Abgrund*, pp. 221–23, and *Quellen: Politik und Wirtschaft*, II:1135.

144 Cabinet meeting of 28 November 1931, *Kabinette Brüning*, III:2018–23; Luther diary, 28 November 1931, NL Luther/425/13–14; decree provisions published in *Ursachen und Folgen*, VIII:320–25.

145 Cabinet meeting of 9 November 1931, *Kabinette Brüning*, III:1928 (source of quotation); Luther diary, 18–19 November 1931, NL Luther/425/5–6; Luther Tagesbericht, 19 November 1931, *Quellen: Politik und Wirtschaft*, II:1104; Luther to Brüning, 20 November 1931, NL Pünder/142/86–95.

persuaded the cabinet to act.[146] Warmbold, Schiele, and Schlange-Schöningen continued to oppose the sales tax hike, however, and Brüning reported that they stood in agreement with the man he hoped to recruit as price commissar, Mayor Carl Goerdeler of Leipzig, the most prominent member of the DNVP to display independence from Hugenberg. Brüning declared fiercely that he must insist on the 2 percent sales tax, but that the Reichstag would never accept it unless the Reichsbank simultaneously lowered the discount rate by two points to 6 percent. He threatened to resign otherwise, proclaiming that "the discount rate and interest rates of the banks are wrecking the whole economy." Luther replied angrily that the Reichsbank could not be dictated to in this fashion, and Brüning apologized for his sharp tone, pleading exhaustion.[147]

Brüning's informal government coalition nearly collapsed as this decree took final shape. Goerdeler demanded the abolition of state labor arbitration as his price for taking office. Otto Wels threatened in public that the SPD would topple Brüning if he lowered wages further and failed to combat National Socialism more vigorously. The leaders of the Business Party, Christian Social People's Service, and State Party all howled in protest when they heard about the sales tax hike.[148] Luther tried to persuade his board of governors to lower the discount rate by two points after Schäffer warned him that all the politicians in the cabinet had become obsessed with this issue, but on 8 December it voted to go down by just one.[149] On his way to seek the President's approval for a decree which had thus lost its best hope for stimulating the economy, Brüning encountered Warmbold, who submitted his resignation. The chancellor delayed this step by promising to reopen the debate over monetary policy in February, but Warmbold removed his signature from the controversial decree. Brüning then obtained the President's signature but found him "very unfriendly," and Meissner later warned the cabinet that the President had signed this decree "with grave reservations." Hindenburg nevertheless gave Brüning one last gesture of active support by appealing personally to Goerdeler to become price commissar. So exhausted that he could barely stand, Brüning then hurled himself into the task of defending the decree at a news conference, then in a meeting

146 Cabinet meeting of 4 December 1931, *Kabinette Brüning*, III:2050–52; Schäffer diary, 4 December (source of quotation), NL Schäffer/16/1132–33; Luther Tagesbericht, 4 December, NL Luther/367/77–82; James, *Reichsbank*, pp. 298–301.

147 Cabinet meeting of 5 December 1931, *Kabinette Brüning*, III:2061–67; Schäffer diary, 4–5 December, NL Schäffer/16/1121–29, 1144–50 (source of quotation); Luther diary, NL Luther/425/24–25; Luther Tagesbericht, *Quellen: Politik und Wirtschaft*, II:1152–54.

148 Luther diary, 5 December 1931, NL Luther/425/26–27; Winkler, *Katastrophe*, pp. 456–57; Schaefer, *SPD*, pp. 174–75; chancellery note of 2 December 1931 on phone calls with Wilhelm Simpfendörfer, BAK R43I/1161/88; letters to Brüning of 5 December 1931 from Goerdeler, Jacob Mollath, and J. V. Bredt, NL Pünder/143/150–58; cabinet meeting of 6 December 1931, *Kabinette Brüning*, III:2069–70.

149 Luther diary, 6 and 7 December 1931, *Quellen: Politik und Wirtschaft*, II:1157–59, 1163–64; Luther diary, 8 December 1931, NL Luther/425/31–36; Schäffer diary, 8 December, NL Schäffer/16/1161–64.

with the business editors of the major dailies, and finally in a radio address to the nation.[150]

Brüning still sought earnestly to explain his decisions to the voters after the fact but did not test the waters of public opinion while formulating this decree. Between his disastrous eastern tour of January 1931 and February 1932, when the presidential election campaign began, the chancellor appeared in public only at the two brief sessions of the Reichstag and a few rallies of the Center Party and Christian trade unions. Believing that the crucial problems of reparations and bank reform could not be debated in public without risk of disastrous financial panics, he waged an ever sharper campaign against press leaks and paid little attention even to friendly journalists. Brüning later compared himself to Bismarck and Frederick the Great as a statesman compelled by Germany's miserable geopolitical situation to adopt risky diplomatic maneuvers that could never be explained in public.[151] The secrecy of cabinet deliberations encouraged wild rumors about what sacrifices might be demanded next and what new powers the cabinet might claim. The anxiety was greatest among those groups neglected in Brüning's efforts to promote consensus between management and organized labor. Shopkeepers found themselves excluded from the Economic Advisory Council, and they anticipated that the new price commissar would make their lives miserable. Civil servants had some reason to believe that the government blamed them unfairly for fiscal problems. Brüning's policies thus contributed to the unusual susceptibility of these groups to Nazi electoral propaganda in the year 1932.[152]

The response of big business and organized labor to the Fourth Emergency Decree suggested nevertheless that Brüning had arranged a scrupulously fair compromise between their conflicting demands. Liberal businessmen were disturbed by the decree's interference with contract rights, but the Reich Association of Industry adopted no clear stand, and its leaders privately acknowledged that the decree incorporated some of their suggestions. Only Brüning's old enemies, the Ruhr coal mine operators, denounced it as proof that the trade unions controlled the government; the leaders of the Ruhr steel industry conferred with the economics ministry in a more constructive spirit to guarantee

---

150 Brüning, *Memoiren*, pp. 478–79; Meissner quotation from cabinet meeting of 17 December 1931, *Kabinette Brüning*, III:2107.
151 See the Schäffer diary, 14 August and 10 November 1931, NL Schäffer/13/621 and 15/1007–09; von Batocki to Stegerwald, 4 July 1931, and Gertrud Bäumer to Hermann Dietrich, 6 July, in Heinrich Muth, ed., "Quellen zu Brüning," *Geschichte in Wissenschaft und Unterricht*, 64 (1963): pp. 233–36; cabinet meeting on press leaks, 4 November 1931, *Kabinette Brüning*, III: 1902–05; Brüning's remarks to a Center Party rally of 5 November 1931, *Reden*, pp. 67–68; and Brüning to Hermann Ullmann, 7 December 1955, NL Ullmann/6/42. In September 1931 Brüning even banned for a short time the newspaper that he had founded, *Der Deutsche*, for insulting the Soviet government (*Memoiren*, p. 381).
152 See Walther Jänecke to Pünder, 11 November 1931, NL Pünder/180/94–95; Josef Hofmann, *Erinnerungen*, pp. 63–64; Childers, *Nazi Voter*, pp. 211–42; Falter, *Hitlers Wähler*, pp. 242–56; Winkler, *Mittelstand*, pp. 144–46; and Mommsen, "Staat und Bürokratie," pp. 103–19.

that the campaign against domestic cartels did not jeopardize international agreements.[153] The press organs of the Christian trade unions and SPD initially attacked the Fourth Emergency Decree for tending to lower the real income of workers. The Christian unions soon implored their members to understand the government's difficulties, however, while the SPD acknowledged that Brüning had adopted many of its demands for government intervention in the economy since the Bank Crisis. Three influential Social Democrats, Breitscheid, Aufhäuser, and Hertz, sought on 9/10 December to persuade their Reichstag delegation to terminate the policy of toleration, but they found little support. Wilhelm Keil observed that nobody in the SPD had suggested an economic program with any better chance to promote recovery than Brüning's. Wels then wrote the chancellor to request a guarantee that the government would not impose further wage reductions until after a significant decline in the cost of living took place. When Brüning issued this promise in an open letter, the SPD dropped its opposition.[154] Thus Brüning retained credibility with both management and labor, a feat that may have required some pandering to their negative images of price-gouging retailers and overpaid, under-worked bureaucrats.

4.4. The Primacy of Foreign Policy

When Brüning justified the Fourth Emergency Decree to party colleagues with a lecture on world economic conditions, Heinrich Imbusch of the Christian miners' union replied bluntly that "it is useless to preach reason to people who are hungry."[155] This exchange highlighted Brüning's growing tendency to focus on foreign rather than domestic policy after the promulgation of the Fourth Emergency Decree. That decree represented an honest and thoughtful attempt to promote economic recovery, but it obviously did not succeed. The sales tax hike discouraged economic activity, and the forcible conversion of long-term interest rates probably discouraged investment further. German industry continued to lose export markets to British competitors, and the government counted a record 6.1 million unemployed workers by February 1932, a stunning 33 percent of the labor force, with further millions working part-time.[156] As this disheartening data accumulated, however, Brüning became absorbed in complex diplomatic calculations.

153 RDI circular, 11 December 1931, *Quellen: Politik und Wirtschaft*, II:1167–68; Bergbauverein "Stimmungsbericht" of 1 January 1932 (sent to the Labor Ministry by the RDI Fachgruppe Bergbau on 22 February), BAP/RAM/288/312–27; Trendelenburg's conference with Ernst Poensgen and J. W. Reichert, 10 December 1931, BAK R13I/405/288–33; Büttner, "Politische Alternativen," pp. 225–27.
154 Patch, *Christian Trade Unions*, pp. 175–76; Winkler, *Katastrophe*, pp. 457–61; Schaefer, *SPD*, pp. 173–79; Keil, *Erlebnisse*, II:407; Wels to Brüning, 12 December 1931, reply of same day, and chancellor's reception for union leaders, 14 December, *Kabinette Brüning*, III:2095–98.
155 *Zentrumsprotokolle*, 15 December 1931, p. 557.
156 See Meister, *Grosse Depression*, pp. 264–69; Schiemann, *Deutsche Währung*, pp. 180–84; Balderston, *German Economic Crisis*, pp. 319–23; and Schulz, *Von Brüning zu Hitler*, pp. 712–20.

When Brüning assumed responsibility for the foreign ministry in October 1931, he launched the diplomatic discussion of what should happen when the Hoover Moratorium expired by instructing his ambassador in Washington to exploit Wall Street's fear of default on Germany's commercial debt. President Hoover must be told that the German government's "most important task at this time is to save the system of private enterprise, preserve the currency, and service the private foreign debt. This goal currently absorbs all our powers," leaving nothing for reparations.[157] Hoover agreed with Pierre Laval, however, that Germany must formally request the Young Plan powers to assemble their financial experts in Basel to assess its capacity to resume the payment of reparations. Brüning's telephone diplomacy with Laval then secured agreement that the panel should be composed mostly of professional bankers. This was a victory for Germany, because while the French government insisted on the legal principle that private debts had nothing to do with state obligations, the bankers displayed more interest in the practical question raised by Brüning of how much total debt Germany could service.[158] The committee's final "Beneduce Report," published on 23 December, concluded not only that Germany could afford no reparations in the foreseeable future, but also that the "Standstill Agreement" of August 1931 must be strengthened, because another RM 1.2 billion in foreign credits had been withdrawn from Germany under its terms. Brüning was quite pleased by this result.[159]

Brüning was further encouraged to launch a diplomatic offensive when the Free Unions publicly demanded the complete abolition of reparations. They signed a joint declaration to this effect with the Christian unions on 4 December, and Theodor Leipart quarreled openly with Breitscheid over this issue at a public rally twelve days later. Brüning later recalled demanding that Leipart take this stand in exchange for the chancellor's open letter on wage policy. Thus the Free Unions took a major step toward the populist nationalism of the Christian unions. One of Leipart's colleagues advised him to imitate Brüning's successful tactic of deflecting political antagonisms onto foreign targets: "Just as Brüning justifies the emergency decrees with diplomatic arguments, so too can the trade unions defend their policy of toleration in the most effective and persuasive manner." After the unions took this stand, French Ambassador André François-Poncet reported to Paris that German public opinion was now unanimous in opposing any resumption of reparations.[160]

157 Brüning to German Embassy in Washington, 18 October (source of quotation), and Bülow to German Embassy, 31 October 1931, *ADAP*, XIX:11–15, 64–68.
158 Stimson to Ambassador Sackett, 27 October 1931, *FRUS 1931*, I:333–34; chancellor's reception for Sackett, 30 October 1931, *Kabinette Brüning*, III:1879–80; correspondence from 5–19 November 1931, *ADAP*, XIX:86–89, 98–99, 151–53; Shamir, *Economic Crisis*, pp. 75–77; Kent, *Spoils of War*, pp. 354–60.
159 "Beneduce Report," *DBFP*, II:495–514; Schulz, *Von Brüning zu Hitler*, pp. 674–77.
160 Winkler, *Katastrophe*, pp. 463–74; Harsch, *Social Democracy*, pp. 154–55; memorandum by Hans Arons of 19 December 1931, *Quellen: Gewerkschaften*, pp. 461–64 (source of quotation); Brüning, *Memoiren*, pp. 470–72; Michael Schneider, *Arbeitsbeschaffungsprogramm*, pp. 116–30; Keil, *Erleb-*

Brüning saw the last precondition for a diplomatic offensive fulfilled on 23 January 1932, when the Reichsbank agreed with foreign bankers that all foreign investors who wanted to withdraw their funds from Germany would have them paid into blocked accounts, which could be converted into foreign exchange only after the Reichsbank had satisfied all more urgent claims on that scarce commodity. This second and much stronger Standstill Agreement led to a drastic reduction in foreign withdrawals and eventually to default on much of Germany's foreign debt after Hitler came to power. Brüning later recalled it as his greatest diplomatic victory:

> For cognoscenti [*Eingeweihten*] we were over the hump. In half a year the Versailles Treaty would crumble to pieces. The 33 billion marks that foreigners had invested since 1924, which now could not be withdrawn at will, were a stronger weapon for us than a million soldiers. If the world did not concede our demands to abolish almost all provisions of the Versailles Treaty in the next half year, then we were now, as Kaas told the Reichstag in February, like Samson strong enough to tear down the pillars that supported the prosperity and order of the next generation. As always on the eve of great successes, however, it was necessary to allow nobody but the closest colleagues, who could keep silent as the grave, to know how far we had come and what weapons we possessed for the final struggle.

This Second Standstill Agreement did in fact expand the German government's maneuvering room dramatically.[161]

During these talks among the bankers, Brüning confronted the most difficult choice of his diplomatic career. At the end of December the British government issued invitations for an international reparations conference to begin in Lausanne on 18 January. François-Poncet warned Brüning, however, that his government could not discuss any permanent revision of the Young Plan until after it faced parliamentary elections in May.[162] After consulting many diplomats and bankers, Brüning and State Secretary von Bülow concluded that they could prolong the Hoover Moratorium by two or three years in an immediate conference but had an excellent chance to abolish reparations completely if they waited until June. They embraced the latter option because reparations might be restored if the world economy revived during a two-year moratorium.[163] On 9 January Brüning signaled that he would raise sweeping demands at the conference when he told the press that "Germany's situation obviously makes the

nisse, II:428–31; Hannes Heer, *Burgfrieden oder Klassenkampf? Zur Politik der sozialdemokratischen Gewerkschaften 1930–1933* (Neuwied and Berlin, 1971), pp. 39–52; Patch, *Christian Trade Unions*, pp. 207–09; Shamir, *Economic Crisis*, pp. 163–64.

161 Brüning, *Memoiren*, pp. 491–92; James, *Reichsbank*, pp. 218–36; Schuker, *American "Reparations" to Germany*, pp. 59–81.

162 Schäffer diary, 19 December 1931, *Quellen: Politik und Wirtschaft*, II:1189–92.

163 Reparations conference of 5 January and chancellor's reception for Ambassadors Hoesch, Schubert, and Neurath, 8 January 1932, *Kabinette Brüning*, III:2141–47, 2152–53; reparations conference of 7 January 1932, *ADAP*, XIX:384–86; Schäffer diary, 7 January 1932, NL Schäffer/17/34–48.

continuation of political payments impossible. It is equally obvious that every attempt to maintain such a system of political payments must cause disaster, not just for Germany but for the whole world." This statement caused outrage in Paris, and the French government rejected the invitation to Lausanne.[164] Only after a month of pleading by the British did the French agree to go to Lausanne in June. Brüning told Laval that only the permanent abolition of reparations could revive investor confidence, but as the French leader suspected, he actually feared that economic recovery was all too likely during a prolonged moratorium. Thus Brüning did seek in this case to "instrumentalize" the economic crisis for the sake of foreign policy.[165]

Brüning's decision to postpone the Lausanne Conference was sharply criticized by Hans Schäffer, Silverberg, and Hilferding. They did not believe that Germany could secure the abolition of reparations even in June, so they urged Brüning to seek detente and perhaps new French loans by agreeing promptly to resume the payment of reparations at a somewhat reduced level in two or three years. Several historians have also embraced this viewpoint, but President Hindenburg told Meissner bluntly that he would resign before signing any such agreement.[166] The French had made no loan offers to Germany since July, moreover, and Laval probably lost this policy option in October when his treasury too began to experience a dramatic shortfall in revenue. Brüning had good reason to believe that Germany could only hope for the time being to freeze existing foreign credits, not obtain new ones. When Germany did achieve diplomatic victory at Lausanne in June, just after Brüning's dismissal, Schäffer retracted all his criticisms and became a fervent admirer of Brüning's statecraft.[167]

Brüning's diplomatic gamble made him far more rigid on the subject of monetary policy. Although the chancellor had promised Warmbold to reopen this debate in February 1932, he became furious when the civil servant Ernst Wagemann publicly attacked the policy of deflation. A "Study Group for Credit Policy and the Money Supply" had recently been founded by a loose alliance of "economic reformers" who shared an admiration of Keynes, including Wladimir Woytinsky of the Free Unions, the economics department at the University of

---

164 Press release of 9 January 1932, *Quellen: Politik und Wirtschaft*, II:1204–06; Pünder, *Politik*, 11 January 1932, pp. 111–12; Shamir, *Economic Crisis*, pp. 163–65; Schulz, *Von Brüning zu Hitler*, pp. 687–92.

165 Brüning's correspondence with Ambassador Hoesch and conferences of German reparations experts, *ADAP*, XIX:442–45, 454–56, 514–20, 564–68; Warner, *Laval*, pp. 51–53; Kent, *Spoils of War*, pp. 361–65.

166 Schäffer diary, conversation with Bülow, 17 January, and with Luther and Hilferding, 27 January 1932, NL Schäffer/17/94, 126–29; Schäffer to Dietrich, 18 January 1932, NL Schäffer/32/14–24; Schwerin von Krosigk, *Staatsbankrott*, pp. 96–97; Quaatz, *Tagebuch*, conversation with Meissner and Hugenberg, 12 December 1931, p. 166; Schulz, *Von Brüning zu Hitler*, pp. 702–04; Winkler, *Katastrophe*, pp. 468–71, 578–79; Mommsen, "Brünings Politik," pp. 28–31; Plumpe, "Wirtschaftspolitik," p. 343.

167 Shamir, *Economic Crisis*, pp. 67–69; Borchardt, "Decade of Debate," pp. 114–16; Brüning's reception for François-Poncet, 4 November 1931, *Kabinette Brüning*, III:1912–14; Schäffer diary, 17 June and 9 July 1932, NL Schäffer/21/585, 653–54.

Kiel, and Wagemann, who headed the Reich Statistical Office and the Reich Institute for Research into the Business Cycle. They launched a public relations offensive in January by inviting Keynes to lecture in Berlin, while Woytinsky published a plan similar to Lautenbach's, and Wagemann published an even bolder plan to spend over three billion marks on public works. Keynes declined to attend their rally, however, after M. J. Bonn warned him that it was more a political than an academic exercise, so Wagemann agreed to address it instead.[168] Responding angrily to this announcement, Brüning and Luther denounced Wagemann to the press as an apostle of inflation, and they urged the cabinet to muzzle this critic, whose views enjoyed special weight because of his position. Within the cabinet only Warmbold defended Wagemann (who was his brother-in-law), but only Luther explicitly condemned his plan as inflationary. Brüning (whose remarks are preserved in three conflicting versions) may have conceded that Wagemann's plan could alleviate unemployment, at least temporarily, but he emphasized the political costs – organized labor would reject any further reduction of wages and welfare benefits if it sensed that there was an alternative to deflation, and the French would insist that Germany could afford to resume paying reparations. These remarks have recently been interpreted as proof that Brüning knew how to promote economic recovery but chose to prolong the German people's suffering in order to dismantle the welfare state.[169]

That conclusion would be misleading, however, because almost all senior government officials remained committed to Trendelenburg's doctrine that no scheme to promote industrial recovery could succeed until the world economic crisis had "bottomed out." Hans Schäffer firmly believed that Wagemann's plan was misguided; he exhorted Brüning and Luther to oppose it, and he reproached Wagemann sharply for arguments resembling "the form in which cure-alls for the human body and laundry detergent for its clothing are pressed on the broad public."[170] Most German economists, most newspapers, and all political parties from the SPD to the DNVP denounced the plans of Wagemann and Woytinsky, as did the leadership of the Reich Association of Industry. I. G. Farben anxiously

168 See Grotkopp, *Krise*, pp. 34–65; George Garvy, "Keynes and the Economic Activists of Pre-Hitler Germany," *Journal of Political Economy*, 83 (1975): 391–405; Büttner, "Politische Alternativen," pp. 245–46; and the Schäffer diary, conversation with Koch-Weser, 29 January 1932, NL Schäffer/17/147–48.
169 *Kabinette Brüning*, meeting of 28 January 1932, III:2241–42; Luther Tagesbericht, 28 January 1932, *Quellen: Politik und Wirtschaft*, II:1240–42; Schäffer diary, 28 January 1932, NL Schäffer/17/134; Mommsen, "Staat und Bürokratie," pp. 111–12; Büttner, "Politische Alternativen," pp. 232–33; Meister, *Grosse Depression*, pp. 348–50. According to Luther, Brüning condemned Wagemann's "completely misleading idea," which would give France the "mistaken impression" that Germany could help itself. In the official cabinet minutes, however, Brüning never quite says that Wagemann's economic arguments were mistaken, and Schäffer makes the chancellor sound rather cynical: "He [Brüning] had only driven the policy of deflation further because he needed it to lower the budgets [of federal, state, and local government] and social insurance benefits down to the only bearable level."
170 Schäffer to Wagemann, 28 January 1932, *Quellen: Politik und Wirtschaft*, II:1243–44; Schäffer diary, 29 January 1932, NL Schäffer/17/136.

disclaimed any corporate responsibility for Warmbold's ideas, while Hilferding and other SPD leaders joined leading industrialists to exhort Brüning and Luther to keep up the good fight for a sound currency. Wilhelm Fonk of the Center Party's Business Advisory Council told the chancellor that "he has been all over Germany in recent times, and people everywhere tell him the same thing, that any alteration of the currency would arouse the strongest objections."[171] On 12 February Trendelenburg convened a major conference of government experts to assess the Wagemann plan, in which Lautenbach played a leading role. All the participants agreed that the potential value of public works must be balanced against the great economic value of a permanent abolition of reparations, and by the end of the meeting they all endorsed Trendelenburg's thesis that the German government must wait until the world economic crisis bottomed out before attempting to finance public works through monetary expansion. The elderly Brüning still expressed this consensus view when he attacked Wagemann's ideas many years later.[172] As chancellor Brüning never made a conscious choice between economic recovery and a political agenda, because world market prices did not begin to rise until after he left office.

Brüning's strategy actually won endorsement from Keynes himself. The celebrated Cambridge economist delivered a lecture in Hamburg on 6 January 1932 and caused a mild stir by advising Germany to abandon the gold standard. Brüning received Keynes in Berlin shortly thereafter and found him unfamiliar with the provisions of the Young Plan that restricted German monetary policy, so Keynes became lodged in his memory as one of those impatient critics who ignored the diplomatic constraints on the German government.[173] In Hamburg, however, Keynes had displayed sympathy for Brüning's predicament. He opposed any government scheme to revive industrial production until financial markets had been stabilized, noting that the Bank Crisis of the previous summer could easily recur. Keynes also acknowledged that the German government could not abandon the gold standard until the Lausanne Conference had been successfully concluded. Like Schäffer and Hilferding, he did urge the German government to seek quick agreement at Lausanne by offering to resume the payment of reparations on a reduced scale after three years.[174] But in their Berlin meeting

171 Luther Tagesberichte, 29 January (source of quotation), 2 and 4 February 1932, NL Luther/368/242, 248, 267–69; Pünder to Thilo von Wilmowsky, 28 January 1932, NL Pünder/97/185–87; Grotkopp, *Krise*, pp. 54–70, 182–89; Michael Schneider, *Arbeitsbeschaffungsprogramm*, pp. 63–87, 108–30; Meister, *Grosse Depression*, pp. 344–51; Weisbrod, "Industrial Crisis Strategy," p. 61. Contrast Holtfrerich, "Was the Policy of Deflation Unavoidable?," in Kruedener, ed., *Economic Crisis*, and Büttner, "Politische Alternativen."

172 Economics ministry memorandum of 5 February and conference of 12 February 1932, *Kabinette Brüning*, III:2276–78, 2288–90; Brüning to Dr. Dräger, 30 August 1953, HUG FP 93.10/Box 7/Heinrich Dräger.

173 Brüning, *Memoiren*, p. 506; Grotkopp, *Krise*, pp. 202–03. Brüning later judged Keynes more favorably after reading Henry Harrod's biography; see Brüning to Jakob Goldschmidt, 31 October 1951, *Briefe*, II:285–86, and Brüning to Franz Greiser, 24 July 1953, HUG FP 93.10/Box 11/Grabein-Guttenberg.

174 "The Economic Prospects, 1932," in *The Collected Writings of John Maynard Keynes*, ed. Donald Moggridge et al. (Cambridge, 1972–1982), vol. 21, pp. 39–47.

Brüning persuaded Keynes to withdraw even this criticism. The German people, Keynes reported to an old friend after this visit, displayed "a unanimous and overwhelming determination to pay no reparations whatever. . . . Any German minister who was to make any statement inconsistent with this could not survive a week." The French, he concluded, must be made to understand that they could expect nothing more than a small token payment even after the immediate crisis had passed. The Lausanne Conference must therefore be postponed until June, when diplomatic isolation and rising unemployment would compel France to make a generous offer. Even though no German officials would say this in public, Keynes added, his conversations with "those whose views would be decisive" persuaded him "that Germany will depart from her present gold parity the moment that any suitable and convenient opportunity arises for doing so." Thus Keynes endorsed Brüning's pivotal decisions and offered some corroboration for Brüning's later recollection that he planned to devalue the mark by 20 percent after reparations were abolished.[175]

Even after noting the many constraints on government policy, it must be acknowledged that Brüning did not pay enough attention to the devastating psychological and political consequences of unemployment during his last months in office. He and his top advisers accepted one of Keynes's fundamental criticisms of neoclassical economics, that recovery from a recession might well require government action to create jobs, but they always believed that the initial downswing must be allowed to run its "natural" course. Brüning was inhibited from questioning this dubious premise by hopes for a great diplomatic victory when the world economic cycle hit bottom and by the same cultural pessimism already noted for Dietrich and Stegerwald. In November 1931 Brüning confided to Luther that he expected Germany's standard of living to sink to the level of Czechoslovakia's: "The aftermath of the Napoleonic Wars suggests that a new economic upturn can only be expected after twenty years. He does not say that in public so as not to rob the German people of all courage."[176] Brüning almost seemed to regard the Great Depression as a divine judgment on the high living of the 1920s, which somehow insulted the memory of the war dead. Holding that Germany could overcome its social and political crisis only through a revival of Prussian virtues, he could never give top priority to the search for prosperity.

175 Keynes to Walter Case, 21 January 1932, ibid., pp. 48–49; Brüning, *Memoiren*, p. 221.
176 Luther diary, 30 November 1931, NL Luther/425/17–18.

5

Brüning's Fall

Brüning was not entirely responsible for the exaggerated emphasis on foreign policy that characterized his last months in office. In the fall of 1931 the presidential entourage and officer corps became enamored of the idea that Germany could be saved only by a united front of conservatives, nationalists, and National Socialists. Brüning's memoirs have spread confusion about this point, but he sought consistently from December 1931 through May 1932 to demonstrate to the President and army command that the personal ambition and conflicting programs of Hugenberg and Hitler made such hopes illusory. He confronted growing suspicion, however, that his own ambition, Roman Catholicism, or trade union background was the real obstacle. A covert struggle between the chancellor and the presidential entourage underlay the public drama of the presidential elections in the spring of 1932, when Hindenburg apparently took a clear stand against the right and defeated it at the polls. This struggle caused paralysis in domestic politics, and Brüning had some reason to conclude that his only hope for success lay in foreign policy.[1]

5.1. Schleicher's Strategy for "Taming" the NSDAP

Hitler displayed new self-confidence in the fall of 1931 partly because of independent overtures to him by the leaders of the army, which Brüning initially authorized but soon lost any control over. In September 1931 Schleicher arranged for Hitler to meet General Hammerstein, and Schleicher himself received the Nazi leader twice in October. Hitler promised them to adopt only legal methods in his struggle for power and to respect the position of the Reichswehr and President as forces above politics. He also revealed his determination to subordinate all other budget priorities and political considerations to a program for massive rearmament. Hammerstein reportedly concluded with

---

1 Compare Bracher, *Auflösung*, pp. 385–92; Morsey, *Zur Entstehung*, pp. 50–53; Mommsen, "Brünings Politik," pp. 28–31; Kruedener, "Brüning's Policy of Deflation," in Kruedener, ed., *Economic Crisis*, pp. 86–91; and Schulz, *Von Brüning zu Hitler*, pp. 637, 651–52, 725–28.

relief that, "apart from the speed," Hitler wanted the same things as the army command. Schleicher and Groener came away with a dim view of Hitler's intellect but an exaggerated idea of his commitment to legality.[2] Hitler told his entourage that Schleicher would make him chancellor if he supported the reelection of Hindenburg, but the general apparently hoped to secure this office for Groener. Schleicher told Reinhold Quaatz on 20 October that Brüning was a "procrastinator [*cunctator*], not a leader for crisis situations," adding that Hindenburg had lost patience with the chancellor's failure to form a rightist cabinet. He also told Stahlhelm leaders on 29 October that Brüning made an excellent foreign minister but that Germany needed "a strong man with a military spirit for home affairs."[3] Schleicher, his closest aides later agreed, had concluded that Germany was experiencing a tidal wave of nationalist sentiment comparable to the socialist wave of 1918/19, which must be mastered through a process similar to the cooptation of the SPD then. He argued that "business knows very well that one should elect the loudest and most unpleasant stockholders to the board of directors." He also cited the British slogan, "Let Labour try!" Schleicher doubted that Brüning was willing or able to act on these maxims, and he probably decided by November 1931 that the chancellor must be toppled soon after the presidential elections if he did not agree to "tame" the Nazis by granting them a share of power.[4]

Schleicher pressured Brüning to alter course rightward by befriending the new French ambassador accredited in August 1931, André François-Poncet. Brüning disliked this conservative politician and former lobbyist for the French steel industry, who displayed unprecedented activism for an ambassador by promoting direct contacts between French and German industrialists and generals. For his part François-Poncet obviously sensed Brüning's hostility toward France and found him devious. After Brüning fell the ambassador termed him a "chauvinist" at heart, and he always attributed far more candor and cosmopolitanism to aristocrats like Schleicher.[5] In November 1931 François-Poncet sought out

2 Carsten, *Reichswehr*, pp. 332–34 (source of quotation); Vogelsang, *Reichswehr*, pp. 135–38; Meissner, *Staatssekretär*, pp. 194–95; Groener to Gleich, 1 November 1931, in Groener-Geyer, *Groener*, pp. 283–84; Otto Wagener, *Hitler aus nächster Nähe. Aufzeichnungen eines Vertrauten, 1929–1932*, ed. Henry A. Turner (Frankfurt a.M., 1978), pp. 368–70, 473–74; Treviranus, *Ende von Weimar*, pp. 288–92. Compare the account of a monologue in which Hitler offered an ecstatic vision of rearmament at no matter what the cost in Duesterberg, *Der Stahlhelm und Hitler*, p. 14.
3 Levetzow to Fürst v. Donnersmarck, 20 November 1931, reporting a conversation with Hitler, in Granier, *Levetzow*, pp. 313–17; Quaatz, *Tagebuch*, conversation with Meissner and Schleicher on 20 October 1931, pp. 157–58; Carsten, *Reichswehr*, p. 331.
4 See Eugen Ott, "Ein Bild des Generals Kurt von Schleicher," *Politische Studien*, 10 (1959): 367; depositions by Ferdinand Noeldechen and Hans Henning von Holtzendorff in Conze, ed., "Dokumentation: Zum Sturz Brünings," pp. 269–73 (source of quotations); Bracher, *Auflösung*, pp. 374–81; and Axel Schildt, *Militärdiktatur mit Massenbasis? Die Querfrontkonzeption der Reichswehrführung um General von Schleicher am Ende der Weimarer Republik* (Frankfurt a.M., 1981), pp. 52–53. Contrast Peter Hayes, "'A Question Mark with Epaulettes'?," pp. 44–45, and Plehwe, *Schleicher*, pp. 144–47.
5 Brüning, *Memoiren*, pp. 342, 469–72; Schäffer diary, conversation with François-Poncet, 15 February 1932, NL Schäffer/18/221–23; Wilhelm Regendanz to Schleicher, 16 June 1932, NL Schleicher/34/115; Harry Kessler, *Tagebuch*, dinner with François-Poncet on 1 July 1932, pp. 673–75

numerous politicians in Berlin to echo Schleicher's arguments about the need for a "dictatorship" ignoring the Reichstag, or else a coalition extending from the Center to the Nazi Party. Brüning was probably correct to allege in later years that Schleicher had inspired these declarations in an effort to show Brüning and the President that only a government incorporating the right would possess enough authority to make further diplomatic progress. François-Poncet's official dispatches in November about the tensions within the German government actually persuaded the French foreign office briefly that Brüning was about to fall and that it must seek an accommodation with Hitler.[6]

This alliance between Schleicher and the French ambassador seems puzzling, because the general's primary motive for advocating detente with the NSDAP was to facilitate rearmament. Schleicher and Groener believed that neither the existing "frontier defense" program in the eastern provinces nor their hopes for a "Swiss-style militia" had any future without the cooperation of Nazi leaders. With 250,000 members by December 1931, in sheer size the SA was surging ahead of the army's traditional partner in such programs, the Stahlhelm, and its membership was much younger on the average.[7] Thus Schleicher's plans entailed a threat of sorts to French national security, and Brüning eventually deduced that the industrial interests represented by François-Poncet must desire a new arms race.

Brüning's friend Max Habermann also championed Schleicher's "taming" strategy, as the DHV sought to strengthen those within the Nazi Party who opposed any collaboration with the "social reactionaries" in the Harzburg Front. Habermann editorialized in October 1931 that Hitler had far more in common with Brüning's effort to purge capitalism of its abuses than with Hugenberg's campaign to abolish welfare programs, more in common too with Brüning's skillful revisionist diplomacy than with Hugenberg's clumsy defiance of foreign powers. Gregor Strasser, the second-ranking Nazi leader, then entered a public exchange with Habermann in which he distanced himself from Hugenberg by endorsing trade unionism, state labor arbitration, and unemployment insurance. This exchange alarmed the proponents of cooperation with the NSDAP among Ruhr industrialists, who concluded that the Christian trade unions had gained

(source of quotation); Plehwe, *Kurt von Schleicher*, pp. 161–62; Annette Messemer, "André François-Poncet und Deutschland. Die Jahre zwischen den Kriegen," *Vierteljahrshefte für Zeitgeschichte*, 39 (1991): 505–20.

6 Schäffer diary, conversations with Dietrich on 5 November, Brüning on 7 November, Bülow on 23 November, and an official in the Paris embassy on 26 November 1931, NL Schäffer/15/981, 991, 1069–70, 1090–91; Luther Tagesbericht, conversation with François-Poncet, 17 November 1931, *Quellen: Politik und Wirtschaft*, II:1102–03; Harry Graf Kessler, *Tagebuch*, conversation with Eduard v. d. Heydt, 9 December 1931, pp. 652–53; Hans Staudinger to Brüning, 16 February 1941, HUG FP 93.4.5/folder 2; Staudinger, *Wirtschaftspolitik*, p. 58; Brüning to Wilhelm Breucker, 29 August 1955, and to Heinrich Lübke, 15 November 1960, in Müller, *Brüning Papers*, pp. 177, 192–93.

7 Groener to Brüning, September 1931, *Quellen: Staat und NSDAP*, pp. 197–98; affidavit of 7 February 1949 by Adam von Carlowitz, in Conze, ed., "Dokumentation: Sturz Brünings," p. 270; Vogelsang, *Reichswehr*, pp. 157–60; Hürter, *Groener*, pp. 291–93, 310–12; Peter Merkl, *The Making of a Stormtrooper* (Princeton, 1980), pp. 109–10, 179; Bessel, *Political Violence*, pp. 67–74.

significant influence over it.[8] In early November Habermann arranged audiences with both Brüning and Hitler. The chancellor explained politely that foreign policy considerations precluded any coalition with the Nazis for the time being.[9] Strasser then brought Habermann and the DHV chairman Hans Bechly to Munich on 6 November to see Hitler, who endorsed Strasser's declarations regarding social policy. The DHV leaders were dismayed by Hitler's rambling monologue, however, and when he left the room they told Strasser (as Habermann reported to Albert Krebs) that "Brüning was the last and only German politician who might still be able to control the force of Nazism and put it to work for Germany's future":

> After Brüning there was no one. The middle-class parties . . . were intellectually and numerically bankrupt. The Social Democrats still had most of their voting strength, . . . but they were as intellectually sterile in confronting the driving new ideas as the bourgeois parties were. Thus, sooner or later, unless the Army could be used against him under some pretext, Hitler would actually come to power legally. His opponents would be so weak that none of them would be able to prevent him from establishing a total dictatorship. . . . Such a dictatorship would be a catastrophe for Germany.

Strasser appeared to agree, but he warned Habermann that Hitler felt too strong to content himself with a mere share of power; such an offer might have been accepted in September 1930, but not now.[10]

Schleicher's taming strategy also gained some support within the Center Party, most notably from Franz von Papen. In September 1931 this conservative delegate to the Prussian Landtag brought the Center's wealthiest contributor, the industrialist Peter Klöckner, to urge Brüning to make a deal with the Nazis to prolong Hindenburg's term. In a much publicized speech on 2 October, Papen then demanded that Brüning establish "a dictatorship on a nationalist basis" that would break with parliamentarism completely and achieve a "sensible incorporation of the nationalist right and the National Socialists." Papen expected Brüning to seek his "toleration majority" in the Reichstag on the right instead of the left but never explained why he expected Hugenberg and Hitler to be any

---

8 Max Habermann, "Brüning and Hitler," *Deutsche Handels-Wacht*, 25 October 1931, republished in Werner Jochmann, ed., *Nationalsozialismus und Revolution. Ursprung und Geschichte der NSDAP in Hamburg, 1922–1933: Dokumente* (Frankfurt a.M., 1963), pp. 351–56; *Der Deutsche*, 1 November 1931, #254, and 11 November 1931, #261; Blank to Reusch, 12 October, and von Gilsa to Reusch, 3 November 1931, *Quellen: Politik und Wirtschaft*, II:1040–43, 1086–87; von Gilsa to Dingeldey, 3 November 1931, NL Dingeldey/69/67–68; Larry Jones, "Between the Fronts," pp. 476–77; Patch, *Christian Trade Unions*, pp. 196–205.

9 Habermann circular to DHV Gauvorsteher, 7 November 1931, DHV Archive, Hamburg.

10 Krebs, *Infancy of Nazism*, pp. 29–31 (source of quotation), 224–27, 236–37; Krebs diary, 20 October, 6 and 27 November, and 3 December 1931, NL Krebs/1/177, 185, 193–94; Karl Hahn, "Max Habermann und der 20. Juli," affidavit of 21 February 1946, DHV Archive. Otto Wagener also recalled later that Hitler rejected any genuine coalition by the fall of 1931, declaring that the NSDAP would inevitably win an absolute electoral majority if it refused to compromise its principles; see Wagener, *Hitler aus nächster Nähe*, pp. 309–10, 352, 368–70.

less likely than the leaders of the SPD to demand influence over government policy in exchange for their toleration. The Catholic industrialist Rudolf ten Hompel urged a similar course on Brüning, but the chancellor rejected their advice emphatically.[11] Party chairman Kaas always supported the chancellor in public, but Hugenberg and Schleicher both noted after August 1931 that Kaas displayed more sympathy for the right than did Brüning, and Stegerwald later confided to Hans Schäffer that Kaas had urged the chancellor unsuccessfully in the fall of 1931 to bring some Nazis into his cabinet. When the Center Party national committee met on 5/6 November, Kaas publicly expressed heartfelt regret that "the idea of union [*Sammelgedanke*] . . . is still not strong enough to incorporate those groups" which had not yet participated in government, a veiled reference to the NSDAP. Brüning curtly rejected any "political experiments," but only Stegerwald explicitly opposed any coalition with the Nazi Party.[12] Kaas then visited Cardinal Pacelli for extended consultations in the Vatican, and he apparently brought word back to Brüning in December that Pope Pius XI had reluctantly concluded that German Catholics should consider a temporary, tactical alliance with the Nazis to avoid dependence on the atheistic Social Democrats.[13]

Placed under such pressure, Brüning agonized over whether he too should pursue Schleicher's "taming" strategy. He arranged a series of clandestine meetings with an old acquaintance from the days of the Ruhr Struggle in 1923, the Free Corps veteran Paul Schulz, who was now Gregor Strasser's top aide. Brüning's memoirs later inflated these meetings into an effort to arrange a coalition government with the NSDAP for the coming spring, but far more believable is Brüning's recollection in private correspondence that he had merely sought accurate information about Hitler's intentions. Schulz himself later recalled that Brüning was mainly interested in impressing Hindenburg. Schleicher had complained to the President that the chancellor maintained no contact with Nazi leaders, but Brüning could refute this charge when he described his pipeline to Strasser.[14] Brüning and Strasser certainly did not have any close

11 Franz von Papen, *Der Wahrheit eine Gasse* (Munich, 1952), pp. 158–68; Jürgen A. Bach, *Franz von Papen in der Weimarer Republik. Aktivitäten in Politik und Presse 1918–1932* (Düsseldorf, 1977), pp. 181–84 (source of quotation); Rolfs, *The Sorcerer's Apprentice*, pp. 55–80; Papen to Schleicher, 21 May 1932, in Matthias and Morsey, eds., *Ende der Parteien*, p. 423; ten Hompel memoirs, chapter 3, pp. 38–39, NL ten Hompel/1.

12 Quaatz, *Tagebuch*, entries of 27 and 28 August and 20 October 1931, pp. 143–47, 157–58; Schäffer diary, conversation with Stegerwald, 6 August 1932, NL Schäffer/22/718–20; *Kölnische Volkszeitung*, 5 November 1931, #524B, and 6 November, #525. Compare Becker, "Brüning, Prälat Kaas," pp. 91–97, and May, *Ludwig Kaas*, III:222–24.

13 See Stewart A. Stehlin, *Weimar and the Vatican, 1919–1933: German-Vatican Diplomatic Relations in the Interwar Years* (Princeton, 1983), pp. 358–60; Morsey, "Deutsche Zentrumspartei," pp. 301–02; and Klaus Scholder, "Altes und Neues zur Vorgeschichte des Reichskonkordats," *Vierteljahrshefte für Zeitgeschichte*, 26 (1978): 560–61. Compare Köhler, *Lebenserinnerungen*, p. 287, and Wirth's memoir of August 1942, "Gespräche zweier deutscher Politiker am Vierwaldstädtersee," section I, question #11, NL Wirth/18.

14 Brüning, *Memoiren*, pp. 461–62; Stachura, *Gregor Strasser*, pp. 90–91, 102; Schulz memoir of 21 July 1951, and Brüning to Dr. Leutze, 6 December 1956, in Udo Kissenkoetter, *Gregor Strasser und die NSDAP* (Stuttgart, 1978), pp. 199–201, 204–05.

alliance at this juncture. When Strasser promised the bloody suppression of the KPD in a vitriolic speech on 5 December, he termed Brüning's fall his "most fervent wish." Brüning told his cabinet and the American ambassador that Strasser was one of the most dangerous Nazis and would be imprisoned if there were proper laws against inciting violence.[15]

Brüning did echo Schleicher's thinking during a tête-à-tête with Hans Schäffer on 20 November. The chancellor expressed loathing for the Nazis but noted that state elections in Hesse had just created the first potential majority for a coalition between the Nazi and Center parties. Such coalitions should be pursued on the state level, Brüning told Schäffer, to see whether the NSDAP could behave responsibly in the Reich government. "The great danger that must be avoided is that the Nazis will remain in opposition until the presidential election. Then it is quite possible that Hitler will be elected President in the second round" if the SPD failed to agree with the moderate parties on a single candidate. If the NSDAP entered a parliamentary coalition, on the other hand, it would disintegrate after three months. "People have no idea of the extent of the political confusion that prevails among them." Hitler himself "makes a powerful impression through his sincere belief in his cause, through his fanaticism and his mystical sense of vocation, but only for the first time, at most for the second. Thereafter one quickly senses how little stands behind it."[16] Schäffer warned Dietrich and Hans Luther after this conversation that Brüning, although he felt a "very powerful hatred" of National Socialism, apparently planned to adopt his most painful austerity measures in conjunction with the left "and then open a new account with the right."[17]

Yet Brüning actually turned against Schleicher's "taming" strategy in the next two weeks. As memoirist, Brüning later portrayed himself as an active supporter of coalition talks with the Nazis in Hesse, blaming their failure on an overly nervous reaction by party colleagues to the discovery by police on 25 November of the Boxheim Documents, contingency plans by the Hessian SA for a brutal response to any Communist uprising. In fact, Pünder discouraged the chairman of the Hessian Center in the chancellor's name from pursuing any new coalition two days before the discovery in Boxheim.[18] Brüning has been reproached sharply for ignoring the evidence discovered in Boxheim of treason by Nazi leaders, and the memoirist's tone encourages such charges, but the chancellor actually gave these documents the attention they deserved. The cabinet promptly

---

15 Cabinet minutes of 6 and 7 December 1931, *Kabinette Brüning*, III:2071, 2078; Burke, *Frederic Sackett*, p. 180. Treviranus, *Ende von Weimar*, p. 164, asserts that Brüning reached agreement with Strasser on the night of 1/2 December 1931 that Strasser would become chancellor as soon as he won the support of a majority within the Nazi Reichstag delegation for his moderate course. In fact, Brüning spent that night discussing with senior officials whether to prosecute Nazi leaders for treason (see below). Treviranus probably misdated Brüning's lengthy meeting with Strasser under very different circumstances in December 1932 (see Brüning, *Memoiren*, pp. 639–40).

16 Schäffer diary, 20 November 1931, published in Wandel, *Schäffer*, pp. 321–28.

17 Schäffer diary, 16 November 1931, NL Schäffer/15/1024–25; Luther diary, 2 December 1931, *Quellen: Politik und Wirtschaft*, II:1137; Mommsen, "Brünings Politik," pp. 37–41.

18 Brüning, *Memoiren*, pp. 463–68; Pünder, *Politik*, entries of 18–23 November 1931, pp. 107–09.

instructed the Reich's chief prosecuting attorney to open proceedings against their author, Werner Best, on a charge of high treason, and Brüning personally received Severing, Breitscheid, the just retired Interior Minister Wirth, Groener, and Schleicher for prolonged discussions of whether the government should take further action. Strasser publicly denounced Brüning for subservience to the Prussian state government because he allowed this prosecution to go forward.[19] The Boxheim Documents contained blood-curdling details about a system of martial law in which all weapons would be confiscated, all food rationed, money abolished, labor made compulsory, and disobedience to the authorities punished with death; but they also stated clearly that the Hessian SA contemplated such measures only if a Communist insurrection had destroyed the current legal order. Press speculation that the documents denied the legitimacy of the Weimar Republic or contemplated the execution of republican officials lacked any foundation, as did reports that Hitler knew of the plan. Despite thorough investigation, the Reich prosecuting attorney was eventually compelled to drop the case against Best for lack of evidence in September 1932.[20] Hitler moved swiftly to limit the damage, moreover, by dispatching Hermann Göring to assure the defense ministry and President that the Nazi leader remained committed to legality and would expel anyone who violated that policy from his party. Ernst Röhm prohibited any further contingency planning by district leaders of the SA, and the best confidential police intelligence supported Hitler's assertion that he had ordered all SA commanders to do nothing after a Communist uprising until they received an appeal from the republican authorities to help defend the state.[21] Thus the Boxheim Documents probably could not have led to criminal convictions no matter what Brüning did.

The Center Party did publicize the gruesome details of the Boxheim Documents, and the entire party leadership was appalled by the mentality displayed in them. The lead editorial of *Germania* concluded that "the crucial question goes beyond that of legality or illegality, the crucial question is whether the national leadership of the Nazi Party tolerates or even approves the discussion and preparation of such insane methods of government by important party leaders." It echoed the demand in the Social Democratic press that

---

19 Bracher, *Auflösung*, pp. 381–83; cabinet meeting of 28 November 1931, *Kabinette Brüning*, III:2022–23; Oberreichsanwalt Werner to Interior Minister Groener, 30 November 1931, BAP R15.01/25792/562; Pünder, "Tagesnotizen," 28 November–1 December 1931, NL Pünder/44/181–85; Gregor Strasser, "Allerlei Fragen um den 'Boxheimerhof,'" *Völkischer Beobachter*, 7 December 1931, #240/41.

20 Schulz, *Von Brüning zu Hitler*, pp. 604–08, expresses uncertainty about the actual contents of the documents, but see the photostatic copies in BAP R15.01/26140/246–53. See also the Reichsgericht decision of 12 October 1932 in BAP R15.01/26140/273–78.

21 Confidential report on Hitler's remarks to a national conference of SA leaders in Munich on 15/16 September 1931, forwarded by the Munich police to the Reich interior ministry on 7 October, BAP R15.01/25792/396–97; declaration by Göring, forwarded by the defense ministry to the interior ministry on 27 November 1931, BAP R15.01/25792/565–66; presidential reception for Göring, 11 December 1931, *Kabinette Brüning*, III:2091–93; Ernst Röhm circular to SA leaders, 9 December 1931, forwarded by the Munich police on 23 December, BAP R15.01/26140/254–55.

Best should be expelled from the NSDAP regardless of whether he could be convicted of any crime, a step that Hitler refused to take.[22] The Hessian Center Party publicly rejected most of the Nazi conditions for a coalition on 11 December. Brüning later recalled drafting this letter himself in a conciliatory tone designed to keep talks going, but the actual text demanded that the Hessian Nazis renounce any armed force and repudiate several planks in their campaign platform that were incompatible with the state constitution. The press of all stripes interpreted this letter as a sharp rebuff, the talks were broken off, and a minority cabinet of the Weimar Coalition retained power in Hesse throughout Brüning's tenure.[23]

Brüning backed away further from Schleicher's "taming" strategy as evidence mounted that it jeopardized the prospects for toleration of the Fourth Emergency Decree by the SPD. Wilhelm Groener noted a groundswell of indignation against the Nazis when he addressed state police officials in his new capacity as Reich interior minister on 17 November. He told them that the Communist Party alone posed a threat of insurrection, endorsing Hitler's argument that the Stormtroopers were the prime victims of political violence and deserved more police protection, but they replied sharply that Stormtroopers committed murder at least as often as Red Guards, and that Germany needed a ban on all wearing of uniforms by the paramilitary leagues. Groener's new aides in the interior ministry supported these arguments, and Groener soon decided to leave them all in their posts, dashing Schleicher's hopes for a purge of the staunchly republican officials in the rival bureaucracy.[24] The political risks of the taming strategy became clear after Brüning passed along to Breitscheid and Otto Wels the allegations by Schleicher that leftist officials in the Prussian interior ministry sought to incite the Nazis into acts of violence that would justify a ban on their party. Seething with indignation, the SPD leaders declared publicly that Brüning should fall if he did not do more to curb political violence, and similar protests came from the State Party. An embarrassed Brüning soon distanced himself from Schleicher's accusation.[25]

Stegerwald distanced the cabinet further from Schleicher's line when he gave Free Union leaders advance notice of the provisions of the Fourth Emergency

---

22 See the press clippings in BAP R15.01/25792, especially "Strengste Legalität," *Germania*, 27 November 1931, #509.
23 Brüning, *Memoiren*, p. 468; Hessian Nazi Party to the Hessian Center, 8 December 1931, and reply of 11 December, *Schulthess' Europäischer Geschichtskalender 1931*, pp. 265–69; Schön, *National-sozialismus in Hessen*, pp. 193–95; Schulz, *Von Brüning zu Hitler*, pp. 608–09.
24 Hitler to Groener, 14 November, conference with state interior ministers of 17 November, Groener to State Secretary Zweigert, 18 November 1931, and Oberregierungsrat Erbe to Dingeldey, 9 April 1932, in *Quellen: Staat und NSDAP*, pp. 213–29, 309–12; Vogelsang, *Reichswehr*, pp. 138–39; Hürter, *Groener*, pp. 313–18.
25 Vogelsang, *Reichswehr*, pp. 139–41; Winkler, *Katastrophe*, pp. 446–56; Staatspartei Vorstand, 12 November 1931, *Quellen: Linksliberalismus*, pp. 673–74; Weber to Brüning, 7 December 1931, *Kabinette Brüning*, III:2085–86; Severing to Brüning, 29 December 1931, and Pünder to Wilhelm Abegg, 5 January 1932, NL Pünder/97/279–80.

Decree on 5 December. Sensing their concern about rumors that Brüning sought a coalition with Hitler, he promised solemnly that nobody in the cabinet desired this. If the President ever decided to appoint a cabinet led by Nazis, Stegerwald declared, the leaders of the Center Party would consult their colleagues in the SPD to arrive at a joint decision as to "whether it is more practical to let the Nazis govern alone, or whether more harm could be averted if we go in with them."[26] Brüning himself became indignant when Hitler held a press conference for foreign reporters on 4 December to pose as the true representative of the German people. The chancellor vetoed a proposal by Severing to deport Hitler as an undesirable alien but concluded that heightened repression was now justified. Brüning told Hans Luther that he now regretted having authorized Schleicher to receive Hitler, "because the army no longer believes firmly in the state's determination to defend itself. He saw something like this before in 1918." The time had come to draw clear battle lines.[27]

Brüning therefore decided to link the Fourth Emergency Decree with a public attack on Nazi extremism. On 7 December the chancellor secured unanimous cabinet approval for new decree provisions to ban demonstrations in the Christmas holiday season and all wearing of uniforms to display membership in a political association. Brüning himself initiated this last proposal to satisfy the state governments; Groener swung behind the idea from indignation over the Boxheim Documents, and even Schleicher agreed that the SA must be taught a lesson. The extent to which the uniform ban was enforced against the right is unclear – some judges acquitted all non-Communists charged with wearing a uniform – and Schleicher promised that restrictions on the Stahlhelm would soon be eased after a personal appeal from the Crown Prince.[28] But the chancellor certainly adopted a firm tone in his radio address of 8 December, which included the following summary of Nazi methods:

> Although the party leader of the National Socialists has emphasized the legal methods and goals of his political plans, this stands in sharp contrast to the declarations of leaders who also think they have authority, which urge us to take up a senseless fratricidal struggle and a foolish foreign policy. If one declares that, having come to power by legal means, one will then break

26 Schäffer diary, dinner with Stegerwald, 5 December 1931, NL Schäffer/16/1146–47; compare Winkler, *Katastrophe*, pp. 459–60, and ADGB Bundesausschuss, 25 November 1931, *Quellen: Gewerkschaften*, pp. 427–33.

27 "Hitler an die Auslandspresse," *Vossische Zeitung*, 5 December 1931, #574; Severing, *Lebensweg*, II:316–17; Feder, *Heute sprach ich mit . . .* , 8 December 1931, p. 307; Brüning's remarks to Center Reichstag delegation, 15 December 1931, *Zentrumsprotokolle*, p. 556; Luther diary, 7 December 1931, NL Luther/425/29–30. Compare Pünder's memorandum of 14 December on a second disagreement with Severing after Hitler announced that he would hold a second press conference, *Quellen: Staat und NSDAP*, pp. 266–68.

28 Conference of 7 December 1931, *Kabinette Brüning*, III:2077–78; draft decree of 26 November and final decree provisions, BAP R15.01/25871/318–34; correspondence between the Crown Prince, Hammerstein, and Schleicher, 22–26 December 1931, NL Schleicher/21/120–30; Reichswehr command conference of 11/12 January 1932, in Vogelsang, ed., "Neue Dokumente," pp. 415–17; Schulz, *Von Brüning zu Hitler*, pp. 610–13; Hürter, *Groener*, pp. 319–21, 326.

the bounds of the law, that is not legality; it is even less so if at the same time plans for vengeance are being drafted and discussed by the inner circle. ... It is [also] unbearable for our country if reference is made to domestic political changes and the fluctuating mood of public opinion in order to create the impression abroad that there are divided fronts in Germany, that there is a government of tomorrow that can claim to speak for the German people.[29]

Göring pronounced himself shocked by this unprovoked attack, and the rumors that Brüning would form a coalition with Hitler ceased. Political moderates rejoiced over this speech, and the leaders of the SPD felt renewed confidence that Brüning was Germany's best hope to prevent a Nazi dictatorship. Schleicher later termed this speech the turning point which revealed that Brüning had no intention of expanding his cabinet rightward.[30]

Thereafter Brüning always sought to buy time for his semi-parliamentary government based on quiet consultations with the SPD until world economic recovery and diplomatic successes brought the electorate back to its senses. "In cultural matters an abyss separated me from Social Democracy," he later recalled. "But like Stresemann and many others I had reluctantly concluded that, when it was necessary to rescue the fatherland from imminent peril without brutally demanding more power in return, one could rely on the SPD much more than on the right of Hugenberg and the Pan-Germans."[31] After observing the response to his Fourth Emergency Decree, Brüning told party colleagues that "the conduct of the SPD deserves respect. They have kept to a statesmanlike course despite a variety of difficulties in their ranks. Much is possible with the SPD, but nothing against it." In February 1932 he explained to them his strategy to abolish reparations, achieve a relaxation of the treaty restrictions on German armaments, and then begin some sort of public works program. "If the government carries out its plans successfully," he concluded, "then the ghost of the National Socialist German Workers' Party will soon be laid to rest."[32] Thus Chancellor Brüning had no desire to expand his coalition rightward, but he could retain Hindenburg's support only if he appeared to pursue such expansion. By now Schleicher, Meissner, and Oskar von Hindenburg competed for the President's favor by volunteering to conduct their own inquiries whenever Brüning reported himself unable to reach agreement with the right. The effort of will necessary to persuade them all that he pursued a coalition which he really considered unobtainable and pernicious was so intense that it distorted Brüning's

---

29 *Quellen: Staat und NSDAP*, pp. 237–39.
30 Levetzow to Donnersmarck, 15 December 1931, on a conversation with Göring, in Granier, *Levetzow*, pp. 322–25; Luther diary, 9 December 1931, NL Luther/425/35; Schäffer diary, conversation with Hilferding, 12 December 1931, NL Schäffer/16/1175–76; Winkler, *Katastrophe*, pp. 461–63; Schleicher's letter of 14 June 1932 to an unnamed friend, in Vogelsang, *Reichswehr*, pp. 470–72.
31 Brüning, *Memoiren*, pp. 378–79; compare the Schäffer diary, 27 August 1931, NL Schäffer/13/713.
32 *Zentrumsprotokolle*, 15 December 1931 and 23 February 1932, pp. 556–57, 562.

memory of these events when he wrote his memoirs, which always make it appear that the chancellor acted as his President wanted him to act.[33]

Unfortunately for Brüning, a growing sense of urgency about rearmament made senior army officers more sympathetic toward the Nazis just when he decided to attack them. The League of Nations failed to respond when Japan conquered southern Manchuria in the fall of 1931, and German generals saw the old principle confirmed that national security depended entirely on armed might. A redeployment of the Red Army toward Siberia undermined the old premise that Germany could rely on Soviet assistance if attacked by Poland, and wild rumors of invasion circulated in Germany's eastern provinces.[34] On 3 December the general staff committed itself in utmost secrecy to a four-year "emergency armament" program that required an immediate 15 percent increase in the military budget, an additional RM 100 million per year at least. When Schleicher warned that the cabinet would never approve such a program under current fiscal conditions, the general staff replied that anything less would leave national security hopelessly compromised. Brüning angered these military planners by refusing to discuss any budget increase until after the Geneva Disarmament Conference that would convene in February 1932.[35] The army then designated as its chief delegate to Geneva Schleicher's old rival Blomberg. Brüning found this choice disturbing, but Schleicher assured him that Blomberg was being eased into retirement. It seems far more likely that the officer corps had signaled a loss of patience with Schleicher.[36] He nervously assured divisional commanders in early January that Brüning would exploit the probable failure of the Geneva Conference to claim unrestricted freedom to rearm. Hitler did eventually choose this course in October 1933, but as yet the foreign office firmly opposed such plans, and Brüning had certainly not endorsed them. Schleicher must have sensed that new political leadership would be required to fulfill this promise to the generals. The belief spreading within the officer corps that all political considerations must be subordinated to rearmament probably made a rift between Brüning and the President's most influential adviser inevitable.[37]

---

33 Compare Brüning, *Memoiren*, p. 467; Brüning to Graf Brünneck, 19 August 1949, HUG FP 93.10/Box 5/Manfred von Brünneck; Brüning to Graf Galen, 12 October 1948, pp. 5–6, HUG FP 93.10/Box 11/Franz Graf Galen; and Morsey, *Zur Entstehung*, pp. 50–53.

34 Brüning, "Ein Brief," in *Reden*, pp. 226–27; Brüning to Erwin Brettauer, 13 December 1956, *Briefe*, II:418–19; Post, *Civil-Military Fabric*, pp. 277–78, 295–301. For background, see Christopher Thorne, *The Limits of Foreign Policy: The West, the League and the Far Eastern Crisis of 1931–1933* (New York, 1973).

35 *Truppenamt* memoranda for Hammerstein of 3 and 18 December 1931, in Geyer, ed., "Das Zweite Rüstungsprogramm," pp. 138–50; Bennett, *German Rearmament*, pp. 57–62.

36 Brüning, *Memoiren*, pp. 492–93; Brüning to Graf Brünneck, 19 August 1949, HUG FP 93.10/Box 5/Manfred von Brünneck; Michael Geyer, *Aufrüstung oder Sicherheit. Die Reichswehr in der Krise der Machtpolitik 1924–1936* (Wiesbaden, 1980), pp. 255–60; Post, *Civil-Military Fabric*, pp. 152–56, 302–11.

37 Commanders' conference of 11 January 1932, in Vogelsang, ed., "Neue Dokumente," pp. 413–14; Bennett, *German Rearmament*, pp. 75–77, 499–508; Post, *Civil-Military Fabric*, pp. 311–21, 352–55; Salewski, "Zur deutschen Sicherheitspolitik," pp. 132–39.

5.2. The Reelection of the President

A few supporters suggested to Brüning that the eighty-four-year-old Hindenburg should be allowed to retire because of his age and erratic judgment. Stegerwald, Johann Viktor Bredt, and Fritz Schäffer of the BVP urged Brüning to run for President himself, but he replied sharply that a Roman Catholic had no chance of victory, that Hindenburg was the only candidate sure to defeat any nominee of the Harzburg Front. The chancellor implored them to say nothing more about this idea, because he would be dismissed at once if rumors of a Brüning candidacy reached the presidential palace.[38] The most experienced politicians in the SPD agreed with Brüning's logic, and Otto Braun gruffly vetoed an effort by Severing and Arnold Brecht to find a younger and more centrist candidate for the parties of the Weimar coalition. Braun, Otto Wels, and Paul Löbe all told party colleagues that Hindenburg was the only hope for the survival of the Weimar Republic.[39] In medical terms they were obviously taking a gamble, although Hindenburg did assure friends that he still felt vigorous. Brüning later recalled that he and Groener had secured authoritative doctors' opinions that Hindenburg would retain his faculties unimpaired for another two years at least.[40]

Hindenburg yearned to retire, however. As the year 1931 drew to a close, Brüning, Schleicher, and Otto Braun all implored the President to stand for reelection, but he complained bitterly about the attacks against him in the press and the endless negotiations of political life, which contrasted so unfavorably with the simple pattern of command and compliance in the army.[41] On 5 January 1932, Hindenburg told Brüning emphatically that he would remain in harness only on the condition that "the office must be laid in his hands as an accomplished fact, because he is not inclined or in a position to undertake a new election campaign." Thus it appeared that Hindenburg would agree to serve only if the Reichstag prolonged his term. Relying on optimistic reports from Pünder about Hitler's attitude, Brüning told Hindenburg that there was an excellent chance to secure the necessary two-thirds majority for this, and someone close to the chancellor promptly leaked the plan

---

38 Bredt, *Erinerrungen*, pp. 274–75; Josef Deutz to Brüning, 11 August 1949, and reply of 19 August, HUG FP 93.10/Box 6/Dale-Deym; Fritz Schäffer memoir of 13 April 1959 on a conversation with Ludwig Kaas, in Schwend, "Die Bayerische Volkspartei," pp. 459–60; Altendorfer, *Fritz Schäffer*, pp. 593–94.

39 Otto Braun to Karl Kautsky, 19 February 1932, in Erich Matthias, ed., "Dokumentation: Hindenburg zwischen den Fronten," *Vierteljahrshefte für Zeitgeschichte*, 8 (1960): 82–84; Severing, *Lebensweg*, II:314–15; Keil, *Erlebnisse*, II:434–35; Staudinger, *Wirtschaftspolitik*, pp. 95–96; Arnold Brecht, "Gedanken über Brünings Memoiren," pp. 613–15; May, *Ludwig Kaas*, III:153–54; Winkler, *Katastrophe*, pp. 480–81; Hagen Schulze, *Otto Braun*, pp. 716–20.

40 Brüning to Jakob Goldschmidt, 29 November 1945, HUG FP 93.10/Box 12/Jakob Goldschmidt; Brüning to Hans von Raumer, 18 September 1957, HUG FP 93.10/Box 26/Hans von Raumer; Gereke, *Königlich-preussischer Landrat*, pp. 175–76; Hindenburg to General von Mackensen, 9 February 1932, BAP R601/19712/vol. 21/6.

41 Dorpalen, *Hindenburg*, pp. 255–61; Braun, *Von Weimar zu Hitler*, pp. 368–69; Brüning, "The Essence of Democracy," Dartmouth College lecture #2, pp. 36–37, HUG FP 93.45.

to the press. Brüning commissioned Groener to open negotiations with Hitler the next day.[42]

Schleicher had already launched his own campaign to secure the Nazis' support for Hindenburg. Hermann Göring visited the President on 11 December to argue that "Brüning is too dependent on Social Democracy." The ex-fighter ace declared that his party would support Hindenburg's reelection, but only in exchange for the right to designate the chancellor, interior minister, and defense minister in the next cabinet. Hindenburg replied stiffly that he would never accept a chancellor or defense minister forced on him by the parties. Brüning nevertheless became so angry when he learned of this meeting that he threatened to resign if such contacts with opposition leaders were repeated.[43] Ignoring this protest, Schleicher inquired among contacts in the Stahlhelm and elsewhere whether the right would support Hindenburg if the "procrastinator" Brüning was replaced as chancellor by someone more decisive, perhaps Groener. In mid-December he also sought to facilitate agreement with the right by authorizing the induction of Nazis as regular soldiers, not just frontier defense volunteers, now that Hitler had "proved his commitment to legality." Schleicher's proposed directive was certain to offend the SPD because it equated the SA's Boxheim Documents with discussions in the republican Reichsbanner about ways to assist the police in case of an uprising by the totalitarian parties. Brüning persuaded him to delay action until Hitler had taken a definite stand on the presidential election.[44]

Groener found Hitler maddeningly evasive when they opened negotiations on 6 January, so the defense minister brought Schleicher and Brüning himself into these talks. The government leaders promptly granted one of Hitler's demands, that Prussia's state elections occur in April as required by law (the government had never intended to postpone them), but they rejected the further demand for new Reichstag elections as well, which were not required until 1934. Brüning was determined not to permit Reichstag elections until the painful sacrifices approved by the pro-government parties had brought tangible benefits. Sensing that Hitler was adamant on this point, he told Hans Schäffer on 9 January that these talks were doomed to failure.[45] The impasse quickly deteriorated into

---

42 Brüning, *Memoiren*, pp. 453–54; presidential reception of 5 January 1932, *Kabinette Brüning*, III:2139–40 (source of quotation); "1931/1932," in *Der Deutsche*, 5 January 1932, #3. Pünder later claimed to possess a written record of a conversation on 8 December 1931 in which Hitler declared unequivocally "that my 107 men in the Reichstag will vote for the law to prolong the term of the Reich President" (*Politik in der Reichskanzlei*, pp. 134–35).

43 Meissner memorandum of 12 December 1931, *Kabinette Brüning*, III:2091–93; conversation with Meissner on 12 December 1931, in Quaatz, *Tagebuch*, p. 166; Brüning, *Memoiren*, p. 467.

44 Conference with state officials in the Reich interior ministry, 14 December 1931, *Quellen: Staat und NSDAP*, pp. 261–65; Stahlhelm circular of 18 December 1931, *Quellen: Politik und Wirtschaft*, II:1188; Brüning, *Memoiren*, pp. 452, 494–96; Keil, *Erlebnisse*, II:434–35; Vogelsang, *Reichswehr*, pp. 141–42; Plehwe, *Schleicher*, pp. 152–54.

45 Pünder memorandum of 13 January 1932, *Kabinette Brüning*, III:2159–62; Pünder, *Politik*, 7 January 1932, pp. 110–11; Schäffer diary, 9 January 1932, NL Schäffer/17/58–60; Goebbels, *Tagebücher*, 5–10 January 1932, II:104–08; Dorpalen, *Hindenburg*, pp. 263–64; Bracher, *Auflösung*, pp. 395–96.

rupture the next day, when Hugenberg joined the talks. He peppered the chancellor with hostile questions about his policies and told Meissner that he could support the President only if Brüning was dismissed and new Reichstag elections held. Hugenberg announced the failure of the talks to the world on 11 January.[46]

Hitler skillfully shifted the blame for this rupture to Brüning. He sought out Meissner, Dingeldey, and others to complain about Brüning's cold manner and underhanded tactics; his most fervent wish was to nominate Hindenburg as the presidential candidate of the Harzburg Front, but Brüning sought to exploit the field marshal's name to obtain a parliamentary vote of confidence for himself. Even Pünder felt that Brüning must have been clumsy in his dealings with Hitler, and Meissner became so angry that he promised DNVP leaders on 11 January that the chancellor would be dismissed when he returned from the Lausanne reparations conference. Brüning would fail at Lausanne, Meissner predicted, which would justify a change in course. Reinhold Quaatz replied that Brüning might succeed there, in which case his position would become unassailable.[47] Hitler soon published a detailed memorandum reproaching the chancellor for an effort to violate the constitution. His legal arguments were ill-informed but embarrassing, and Hugenberg angered Meissner further by demonstrating that deliberate press leaks from the cabinet about these negotiations had exposed Hindenburg to public embarrassment. Pünder, Meissner, and Schleicher all blamed each other for the debacle.[48]

Meissner informed the cabinet haughtily on 13 January that Hindenburg would stand for reelection only if there was "no serious opposition candidate" except for that of the Communists.[49] Brüning and Schleicher then sought jointly to forestall any nominations by the rightist parties through an overture to Germany's leading associations of combat veterans, the Stahlhelm and the larger but less cohesive Kyffhäuserbund. Schleicher told their leaders, Franz Seldte, Theodor Duesterberg, and Rudolf von Horn, that Hindenburg would campaign if they "raised him on their shields" as a candidate above all parties. They supported the idea but encountered surprising opposition among their provincial affiliates, fueled by resentment against the ban on uniforms of 8 December. The

---

46 Pünder memorandum of 13 January and Hugenberg memorandum of 10 January 1932, *Quellen: Politik und Wirtschaft*, II:1210–11, 1215–16; Quaatz, *Tagebuch*, conversation with Meissner on 10 January 1932, pp. 170–71; open letter from Hugenberg to Brüning, 11 January 1932, *Ursachen und Folgen*, VIII:381–82 (compare the even more hostile rough draft in NL Hugenberg/36/34–42).

47 Pünder, *Politik*, 7 January 1932, pp. 110–11; memorandum on the negotiations of 8–14 January 1932, in Quaatz, *Tagebuch*, pp. 171–72; Count Westarp to Hiller von Gaertringen (on a conversation with Meissner), 14 January 1932, *Quellen: Politik und Wirtschaft*, II:1219–20; Dingeldey to B. Noltenius, 6 April 1932, NL Dingeldey/37/26–27; Dingeldey memorandum of 15 December 1932, in Vogelsang, *Reichswehr*, pp. 440–42; Meissner, *Staatssekretär*, pp. 216–17.

48 Hitler's memorandum for Brüning, 15 January, and reply of 23 January 1932, *Ursachen und Folgen*, VIII:383–89; Hugenberg to Meissner, 20 January 1932, and reply of 25 January, BAP R601/19712/vol. 19/25–28; Schäffer diary, 1 February 1932, *Quellen: Politik und Wirtschaft*, II:1260–61; Pünder, *Politik*, 12 February 1932, p. 113; Schulz, *Von Brüning zu Hitler*, pp. 710–11.

49 Pünder memorandum, 13 January 1932, *Quellen: Politik und Wirtschaft*, II:1211–12.

Stahlhelm in particular was torn between a sentimental attachment to its honorary member Hindenburg and the desire to preserve the imagined unity of the Harzburg Front. Thus began two weeks of absurd negotiations in which the Kyffhäuserbund refused to act without the support of the Stahlhelm, which refused to proceed without authorization from Hugenberg, who insisted on consulting Hitler, who avoided any clear stand while maneuvering to acquire German citizenship so that he could run himself.[50]

Brüning regained the support of the presidential entourage when Hitler's intentions became clear. After Schleicher reported on 23 January that he could reach no agreement with the Stahlhelm, Meissner suggested that Brüning offer his resignation to dispel the impression that he obstructed unity on the right. Meissner apparently hoped that the offer might be accepted, but Brüning agreed only "in order to persuade President von Hindenburg that Hitler was not willing to support Hindenburg's reelection even at the price of my resignation."[51] The atmosphere changed abruptly three days later, when Brüning conveyed to the President's top advisers a confidential report from Schlange-Schöningen that Hitler would run. The chancellor declared that Hindenburg was the only candidate who could defeat him. "What then would happen," Brüning concluded, "if Hitler became Reich President would be as bad as one can possibly imagine." Brüning renewed his offer to resign if that would persuade Hindenburg to run, but Groener insisted that he must retain office, and Schleicher agreed – doubtless because Brüning's contacts with the SPD were now essential for Hindenburg's reelection. Groener went straight to the President to declare that it was unthinkable for a Prussian general to dismiss his chief of staff on the eve of battle. Brüning conveyed his offer to resign to Hindenburg in person the next day but found it rejected with a gratifying display of emotion; Brüning told Pünder that Hindenburg answered tearfully, "My dear, good friend, you cannot do that to me."[52]

Groener proved better able than Schleicher to learn from this experience. The defense minister had supported Schleicher's taming strategy with praise for Hitler's selfless character and profound grasp of world-historical trends, but he abandoned this flirtation after learning that Hitler would run for President. Hitler was a "scheming politician" (*abgefeimte Politiker*) and the "idol of stupidity," Groener wrote his oldest friend, and "we must now do everything to secure

---

50 See Volker Berghahn, "Die Harzburger Front und die Kandidatur Hindenburgs für die Präsidentschaftswahlen 1932," *Vierteljahrshefte für Zeitgeschichte*, 13 (1965): 64–82; and Duesterberg, *Der Stahlhelm und Hitler*, p. 34.

51 Brüning's affidavit of 13 August 1948 for the trial of Schacht, NL Dietrich/200/35. Contrast Meissner's statements to Quaatz in his *Tagebuch*, 2 March 1932, p. 182, with those to Pünder on 27 January 1932, *Kabinette Brüning*, III:2227–28.

52 Pünder memorandum, 27 January 1932, *Kabinette Brüning*, III:2227–32 (source of quotations); Schäffer diary, conversation with Schleicher, 29 January 1932, *Quellen: Politik und Wirtschaft*, II:1248–49; Brüning, *Memoiren*, pp. 516–17.

the position of Brüning."[53] On 29 January Schleicher insisted nevertheless that the defense ministry lift the ban on hiring Nazis as soldiers. His directive still equated the Boxheim Documents with discussions in the Reichsbanner, and it caused an uproar when leaked to the press on 11 February. Groener revealed some estrangement from his top aide by assuring Reichsbanner leaders that he believed in their sincere desire to defend the constitution. Hermann Dietrich signaled his displeasure with Schleicher by blocking the disbursement of any government funds for "military sports" programs for German youth until after the presidential election, on the grounds that such funds might flow into Hitler's campaign coffers.[54]

The Reich chancellery had meanwhile encouraged the mayor of Berlin, Heinrich Sahm, to organize a committee to distribute petitions urging the President to stand for reelection. Sahm preserved Hindenburg from any connection with the political parties by inviting all major non-Communist newspapers to participate.[55] The mayor launched his public campaign on 1 February with an American slogan, proclaiming Hindenburg "the first in war, the first in peace, and the first in the hearts of his countrymen." His committee was dominated by moderate conservatives and national liberals, but it included some Christian trade unionists and two Social Democrats. Sahm invited Seldte and Duesterberg to join, but they declined after consulting Hugenberg, and their example deterred other notables such as Gustav Krupp. Cardinal Bertram of Breslau, the primate of the Catholic Church in northern Germany, withdrew his signature after noting that his south German counterpart, Cardinal Faulhaber of Munich, had declined to join. The DNVP, DVP, and Stahlhelm hoped that the leftist complexion of the Sahm Committee would cause Hindenburg to refuse to campaign until Brüning resigned.[56]

Brüning sought to prod Hindenburg into a decision by renewing his offer to resign on 6 February, just before he left to attend the opening session of the Geneva Disarmament Conference. Hindenburg again refused the offer; although he had not yet decided whether to run, the President declared, he had

---

53 Contrast Groener's address to divisional commanders, 11 January 1932, *Quellen: Staat und NSDAP*, pp. 271–72; Keil, *Erlebnisse*, II:434–35; and the Schäffer diary, 11 January 1932, NL Schäffer/17/61–62; with Groener's letters to Gleich of 24 January 1932 (*Quellen: Politik und Wirtschaft*, II:1229–30) and 26 January 1932 (*Quellen: Staat und NSDAP*, pp. 274–76).

54 Defense ministry circular of 29 January 1932 and Schleicher memorandum of 17 February, *Quellen: Staat und NSDAP*, pp. 276–79; Groener to Karl Höltermann, 23 February 1932, BAP R15.01/13117/81–82; Bennett, *German Rearmament*, pp. 71–74; Vogelsang, *Reichswehr*, pp. 157–62; Hürter, *Groener*, pp. 310–11.

55 Undated memorandum from late January by Kurt Neven Dumont of the *Kölnische Zeitung*, and Sahm circular to newspaper editors, 30 January 1932, in BAP R601/19712/vol. 19.1/86–92.

56 Dorpalen, *Hindenburg*, pp. 268–69; Berghahn, "Harzburger Front," pp. 68–69; Winkler, *Katastrophe*, pp. 480–84; Pünder to Thilo von Wilmowsky, 28 January, reply of 2 February, and Krupp to Sahm, 30 January 1932, NL Pünder/97/166–67, 184–87; Bertram to Sahm, 1 February 1932, and two telegrams from Faulhaber, 30 and 31 January 1932, NL Pünder/97/150–51; Dingeldey to Wilhelm Kalle, 5 February 1932, *Quellen: Politik und Wirtschaft*, III:1263–64.

decided to reject any political concessions to purchase the support of Hitler or Hugenberg.[57] This assurance seems disingenuous, because Schleicher offered Hugenberg major concessions in the President's name that very day. The general proposed appointing a new chancellor just after the Prussian state elections in April, preferably Groener or perhaps a conservative Catholic agrarian, with Brüning as foreign minister and Hugenberg as vice-chancellor in charge of economic policy. Yearning to become chancellor himself, the DNVP chairman brought the Nazis into these negotiations to eliminate any role for Brüning and Groener. When Hugenberg reported that Hitler demanded the right to appoint either the chancellor or the defense minister, Schleicher broke off the talks on 8 February. He told Brüning nothing more about them than that Hugenberg still demanded immediate Reichstag elections.[58]

There followed a comedy of misunderstanding when the Stahlhelm leaders visited Hindenburg on 10 February. Hugenberg had kept them in the dark about his recent meetings with Schleicher, so Seldte and Duesterberg reproached the President for making only the vaguest of promises to the right, which might never be fulfilled – a fair summary of their dealings with Brüning. Hindenburg, doubtless assuming that his listeners knew of Schleicher's offer, declared loftily that he had given them ample proof of his good intentions and must reject any further concessions. When Seldte and Duesterberg continued to express skepticism, Hindenburg pounded on the table and dismissed them. Schleicher hurled himself upon the combat veterans as they left the President's office to ask what more they could possibly demand after his offer to Hugenberg, about which they now learned for the first time. They declared themselves completely satisfied and implored Hugenberg to accept the plan that afternoon. Duesterberg noted correctly that "not since the revolution has the government made any such offers to the right." Hugenberg again insisted on the need to consult Hitler, however, and mobilized support for a hard line among the Stahlhelm's provincial leaders. On 12 February Schleicher even suggested that Seldte himself become chancellor, but Hugenberg persuaded the provincial leaders that this was merely a trap to detach them from their "allies" in the NSDAP.[59] The next day Hermann Göring conveyed a peremptory demand that all factions on the right support Hitler for President, and Hugenberg finally understood that the Nazis sought a dangerous "Hitler dictatorship." He then agreed with the Stahlhelm to support

57 Pünder memorandum, 6 February 1932, *Kabinette Brüning*, III:2280–81.
58 Schleicher memorandum of late February 1932, *Quellen: Politik und Wirtschaft*, II:1299–1300; Quaatz, *Tagebuch*, 8–9 February 1932, pp. 176–77; Pünder Tagesnotiz, 12 February 1932, NL Pünder/44/110; Berghahn, "Harzburger Front," pp. 70–71. For evidence of Hugenberg's personal ambition, see Bang to Hugenberg, 21 January 1932, and reply of 28 January, NL Hugenberg/36/9–12. Contrast Schulz, *Von Brüning zu Hitler*, p. 729, who argues that, since Hindenburg still wanted to retain Brüning as foreign minister, "there can be no question about his loyalty to Brüning at this juncture."
59 Memorandum by General Horn's aide Karwiese, mid-February 1932, *Quellen: Politik und Wirtschaft*, II:1280–83 (source of quotation); Quaatz, *Tagebuch*, 12 February 1932, pp. 177–78; Berghahn, "Harzburger Front," pp. 71–75.

Duesterberg on the first presidential ballot, hoping that Hindenburg would grant concessions for their support in the second round. Duesterberg promised in advance to throw his support to Hindenburg if the President appointed a new "cabinet of national concentration" and repealed the uniform ban of 8 December.[60] The DNVP and Stahlhelm had fallen between two stools, however; with shrewder tactics they might have toppled Brüning even before the presidential campaign began.

Hindenburg gradually lost interest in the attitude of the Stahlhelm as the Sahm Committee collected three million signatures in just two weeks. Count Westarp also presented a special petition by 430 conservative notables urging Hindenburg to run that apparently moved him more than the appeal by millions of ordinary voters. Westarp had encountered a number of surprising rejections from Ruhr industrialists and old war comrades of Hindenburg, which revealed a crisis of conscience among German conservatives, but he sought to conceal this from the President. Pledges of support also arrived from most organizations of the moderate right, such as the Christian Nationalist Peasants' Party, Christian Social People's Service, and the Young German Order.[61] Brüning strengthened his own position with his performance at Geneva on 6–10 February. The defense ministry and foreign office agreed that Germany should initially confine itself to the high-minded demand that its neighbors disarm, but they disagreed sharply over how much Germany should demand for itself after France refused.[62] In Geneva Brüning pleased both factions as he appealed simultaneously to German resentment against the Versailles Treaty and the swelling current of Anglo–American pacifism. He eloquently depicted the exposure of German cities to devastating air raids, the humiliation felt by German youth because they alone in the world did not have the right to bear arms, and the urgent need on grounds both of security and justice for Germany's neighbors to disarm. The British, American, and Italian delegations responded with demonstrative applause much louder than that accorded French speakers. General Hammerstein also applauded this performance in a briefing for divisional commanders, and he told the British ambassador that Brüning was "head and shoulders above any other statesman in the country." Brüning believed that it was Hindenburg's enthusiasm for his disarmament proposals that finally made him decide to

---

60 Stahlhelm circular, 24 February 1932, *Quellen: Politik und Wirtschaft*, II:1303–05; Duesterberg to Hindenburg, 11 February, and Meissner memorandum on a conversation with Bundeskanzler Wagner, 15 February 1932, BAP R601/19712/vol. 19/58–63; Quaatz, *Tagebuch*, 13–19 February 1932, pp. 178–80; Berghahn, "Harzburger Front," pp. 76–79.

61 Hindenburg to Friedrich von Berg-Markienen, 25 February 1932, in Matthias, ed., "Dokumentation: Hindenburg," pp. 78–79 (also in *Quellen: Politik und Wirtschaft*, II:1306–07); declarations of support from rightist organizations in BAP R601/19712/vol. 19 and 19:1; Dorpalen, *Hindenburg*, pp. 269–71; Larry Eugene Jones, "Hindenburg and the Conservative Dilemma in the 1932 Presidential Elections," *German Studies Review*, 20 (1997): 235–39.

62 Foreign office draft guidelines of 18 December 1931, defense ministry reply of 23 December, Frohwein memorandum of 7 January 1932, and Bülow to Frohwein, 7 January, *ADAP*, XIX:288–90, 315–16, 380–83, 387; cabinet meeting of 15 January 1932, *Kabinette Brüning*, III:2173–81; Bennett, *German Rearmament*, pp. 53–58.

campaign for reelection.[63] Brüning returned from Geneva in an agony of impatience and told the President that he was undermining his own authority through endless negotiations with the hopelessly divided right. When the Kyffhäuserbund offered to endorse him unconditionally, Hindenburg finally decided that he would not be perceived as the candidate of the left, so he announced on 15 February that he would accept Sahm's invitation "in order to spare myself from the reproach that I decided to abandon my post in a difficult time."[64]

Hindenburg nevertheless remained loyal to the ideal of unity on the right, and he sought to revive the influence of his aristocratic peers as the only men with the personal qualities needed to forge this unity. The President suggested to his old comrade from the Battle of Tannenberg, August von Mackensen, that Germany's real problem was the rise of plebeians to dominate all rightist organizations:

> I have always belonged inwardly to the *old* conservative party, even while seeking dutifully to behave in a nonpartisan manner as Reich President. The new right under its current leaders has estranged itself from me, for reasons that I won't go into for the sake of peace. It goes without saying that I wish this would change soon. The way things stand now causes me great pain, because some of my old comrades and friends misunderstand me. I hope that history will judge me differently![65]

Just after announcing that he would run, Hindenburg instructed Brüning to replace Groener as interior minister with an aristocratic landowner virtually unknown to the public, Oskar v. d. Osten-Warnitz. Baffled, Brüning persuaded the President with some difficulty that this nomination should not be pursued until after the next Reichstag session. Neither Schleicher nor the leaders of the DNVP considered Osten-Warnitz suitable for high office, so this incident shows that Hindenburg had begun to rely on advice from his oldest personal friends.[66] Hindenburg suffered greatly thereafter when Friedrich von Berg-Markienen was compelled to resign as "Marshal of the German Nobility" for publicly endorsing his candidacy, when prominent functionaries of the Kyffhäuserbund attacked General von Horn, and when monarchists raised questions about his treatment

63 Ibid., pp. 95–136; Brüning's NBC radio interview, 13 February 1932, and Geneva speech of 9 February, *Schulthess' Europäischer Geschichtskalender 1932*, pp. 23–24, 449–53; Hammerstein's briefing of 27 February 1932, in Vogelsang, ed., "Neue Dokumente," pp. 418–19; Ambassador Rumbold to Simon, 1 March 1932, *DBFP*, III:101–03; Brüning, *Memoiren*, p. 527.

64 Austrian Ambassador Frank to Buresch, 12 February 1932, reporting a conversation with Brüning, ÖSA/Gesandtschaftsberichte Berlin/592–93; Kyffhäuserbund memorandum of February 1932, *Quellen: Politik und Wirtschaft*, II:1279–85; Pünder memorandum of 15 February 1932, *Kabinette Brüning*, III:2294–96 (quotation on p. 2296); Hindenburg to General von Horn, 23 February 1932, BAP R601/19712/vol. 19.1/19–20.

65 Hindenburg to Mackensen, 9 February 1932, BAP R601/19712/vol. 21/6–7. For Hindenburg's attitude toward "meine Standesgenossen," compare Gessler, *Reichswehrpolitik*, pp. 343–44, and Wirth's memoir, "Ereignisse und Gestalten von 1918–1933," question #21, pp. 6–7, NL Wirth/18.

66 Pünder memorandum of 15 February 1932, *Kabinette Brüning*, III:2294; compare Quaatz, *Tagebuch*, 20–21 November 1931, p. 162.

of the kaiser in November 1918.[67] With Schleicher's help, he wrote a memorandum about his candidacy on 25 February to circulate to aristocratic friends. It praised Brüning's skill in foreign policy, noted his selfless offer to resign, and blamed the failure of the negotiations with the right on the personal ambition of Hugenberg and Hitler. "The Harzburg Front is now only a fiction," Hindenburg concluded, "or to be more precise, never really existed." But he emphasized that he would sacrifice Brüning if an opportunity emerged to forge unity on the right, and that he would resume these negotiations after the Prussian state elections in April.[68]

Brüning's strategy appeared successful when the Reichstag convened on 23 February to set the date for the presidential election. The roster of candidates was now clear: The KPD had long since nominated its leader, the ex-pugilist Ernst Thälmann; Goebbels had just announced to a monster rally in Berlin that Hitler would run; and the DNVP and Stahlhelm had quietly notified the press that they would support Duesterberg. Thus Hitler embraced the confrontation tactics urged by Joseph Goebbels despite warnings from Gregor Strasser that the NSDAP risked disaster if it challenged Germany's most revered authority figure directly (this quarrel within the Nazi leadership was the first real sign of an emerging alliance between Brüning and Strasser). When all factions of the Harzburg Front declared against Hindenburg, it became much easier for the SPD to announce support for the incumbent.[69] It is difficult to imagine any figure to the right of Brüning who could have integrated the Social Democrats into the Hindenburg front and any figure to his left who could have persuaded the field marshal to stand for election. Hitler might well have gained power already in the spring of 1932 but for Brüning.

Goebbels soon plunged the Reichstag into turmoil by referring to Hindenburg as the candidate of the "party of deserters" (i.e., the SPD). An uproar drowned out his remarks, and Goebbels was expelled from the session when he refused to withdraw them.[70] By now Brüning had secured formal authorization from Meissner, Schleicher, and Oskar von Hindenburg to declare that he had given the rightist parties every opportunity to form a government, but that their disunity and the Nazis' desire for one-party rule made this impossible. The chancellor regarded this as a major turning point in his troubled relations with the presidential entourage and strode to the Reichstag podium on 25 February with a new sense of freedom to attack the Nazis openly:

67 *Deutsches Adelblatt*, issues of 6 and 27 February 1932, BAP R601/19712/vol. 19/47–49; General von Einem to Hindenburg, 22 February 1932, BAP R601/19712/vol. 21/96–98; Hindenburg to General von Below, 12 March 1932, BAP R601/19712/vol. 21/161–62.

68 *Quellen: Politik und Wirtschaft*, II:1306–10. Compare Hindenburg to Oldenburg-Januschau, 17 and 22 February 1932, in Hubatsch, *Hindenburg und der Staat*, pp. 310–12; and the correspondence with Mackensen, Graf v. Arnim-Boitzenburg, General von Einem, Berg-Markienen, and Herr v. Eisenhart-Rothe in BAP R601/19712/vol. 21/78ff.

69 Goebbels, *Tagebücher*, 19 January–15 February 1932, II:111–28; Orlow, *Nazi Party*, pp. 244–49; Stachura, *Gregor Strasser*, pp. 94–97; Winkler, *Katastrophe*, pp. 511–13; Schaefer, *SPD*, pp. 179–89.

70 *Verhandlungen des Reichstags*, 446/2250.

You are always talking about the "system," sometimes you call it the Brüning system, sometimes the system of 9 November. . . . Gentlemen, don't you dare to connect me in any way with the 9th of November! . . . Where was I on the 9th of November? . . . Gentlemen, on 9 November I belonged to the army unit that formed the spearhead of the Winterfeldt Group for the suppression of the revolution. (Stormy, long lasting applause from the parties of the middle.)

This declaration that the chancellor of the Weimar Republic had sought with armed force to prevent its foundation highlighted the inner conflicts of the *Vernunftrepublikaner*, but it was also shrewd tactics; Brüning had developed a real talent for exposing the hypocrisy of the Nazis' patriotic rhetoric. Referring to a charge by the Baltic German Alfred Rosenberg that the policies of the Center Party were designed to strengthen France, Brüning declared that "I refuse to listen to such reproaches from a man who had not even discovered which fatherland he had at a time when I was fighting in the war to my very last breath." He rebutted countless Nazi interjections, maintained his composure when they screamed and crowded round the podium, and flawlessly resumed his reasoning when the tumult died down. This speech was recorded and frequently played on the radio; Pünder considered it the ideal overture for the presidential campaign.[71]

Brüning noticed that his remarks about the 9th of November encountered an icy reception from the SPD, so he quickly added to polite applause from the left that Germany's problems had not begun with the abdication of the kaiser but with "the political mistakes of the prewar period."[72] Otto Braun again sprang to Brüning's aid by criticizing his party colleagues' lukewarm endorsement of Hindenburg as the "lesser evil." Braun issued his own manifesto to praise the field marshal as "the embodiment of calm and reliability, of manly fidelity and a devoted sense of duty to the whole nation." Thus he helped to galvanize the SPD into playing a vigorous role in the election campaign. It held as many rallies as all the other pro-Hindenburg parties combined, and the Reichsbanner was the major force on the streets opposing the intimidation tactics of the SA.[73]

Meissner and Pünder persuaded an energetic former state secretary in the Reich chancellery, Franz Kempner, to manage the Hindenburg campaign. Kempner soon drafted a comprehensive plan to blanket Germany with propaganda at an initial cost of RM 567,000, eased Mayor Sahm out of the picture as someone too closely associated with the left liberal press, and formed a new "Hindenburg Committee" to coordinate the campaign efforts of nonsocialists. Social

71 Brüning, *Reden*, pp. 116–24 (source of quotations); Brüning, *Memoiren*, pp. 528–29; Meissner's rough draft for the chancellor's speech, sent to Pünder on 22 February 1932, BAK R43I/585/117–24; Pünder, *Politik*, 25 February 1932, pp. 114–15; Goebbels, *Tagebücher*, II:133; May, *Ludwig Kaas*, II:654–55.
72 Brüning, *Memoiren*, pp. 529–530; Brüning, *Reden*, p. 125; Winkler, *Katastrophe*, pp. 488–90.
73 Braun manifesto of 10 March 1932, *Ursachen und Folgen*, VIII:410–11; Winkler, *Katastrophe*, pp. 512–16.

Democrats were not invited to participate because Kempner wanted the two armies of Hindenburg's supporters to "march separately."[74] Brüning and Schleicher recruited a politician standing just to the right of the cabinet to chair the Hindenburg Committee, Günther Gereke of the Christian Nationalist Peasants' Party, and Carl Duisberg of I. G. Farben agreed to head the board of fundraisers. The committee decided at its founding meeting to concentrate on praise for Hindenburg's personal character, not defense of Brüning's policies, and Hindenburg was reassured to learn that it consisted almost exclusively of conservative men who had already supported him in 1925. Someone at the first meeting noted that the campaign might be hampered because the committee included no women, but his colleagues would agree only to found a ladies' auxiliary.[75]

Brüning hoped that the Hindenburg Committee would promote a grand alliance of all parties and interest groups that still supported the rule of law, but big business proved reluctant to play its part. I. G. Farben pledged a handsome 100,000 marks, and Finance Minister Dietrich spread the word that the government expected other firms to follow this example. The electro-technical industry offered just 50,000, however, and the largest banks just 10,000 each. The United Steelworks and Rhenish–Westphalian Coal Syndicate refused to participate in any significant way, although Gustav Krupp and Paul Silverberg pledged 10,000 marks each as individuals. Brüning alleged in his memoirs that the United Steelworks offered a paltry 5,000 marks to Hindenburg and 500,000 to Hitler. Duisberg's initial solicitation yielded a disappointing total of just RM 295,000, and Dietrich complained bitterly to Hans Schäffer that "the bourgeoisie is not prepared to make sacrifices for the preservation of its economic order." The only industrialist who surpassed expectations was Friedrich Flick, who was angling for a government bailout of his mining interests and eventually donated RM 450,000.[76]

Dietrich responded to this disappointment by soliciting contributions from public enterprise. The Reichsbank and postal ministry declined to participate, but the national railway donated 500,000 marks on 25 February, nearly twice as

74 Kempner to Meissner, 16 February, Sahm to Meissner, 16 February, and Meissner's press releases of 17–20 February 1932, in BAP R601/19712/vol. 19.1/126–32; Sahm memoirs in Vogelsang, *Reichswehr*, pp. 435–38; chancellery memorandum of 18 February 1932, *Kabinette Brüning*, III:2308–13.

75 Gereke, *Königlich-preussischer Landrat*, pp. 175–77; Hindenburgausschüsse conference of 22 February 1932, *Quellen: Politik und Wirtschaft*, II:1291–94; Hindenburg to von Berg-Markienen, 25 February 1932, in Matthias, ed., "Dokumentation: Hindenburg," pp. 80–81; Jones, "Hindenburg," pp. 239–40.

76 Helmuth Tammen, "Die I.G. Farbenindustrie Aktiengesellschaft (1925–1933)" (Ph.D. diss., Freie Universität Berlin, 1978), pp. 177–80; Turner, *German Big Business*, pp. 220–21, 254; Jones, "Hindenburg," pp. 240–42; Schäffer diary, 29 February and 2 March 1932 (source of quotation), NL Schäffer/18/285, 19/295; Kempner to Dietrich, 4 March 1932, NL Dietrich/226/96; Brüning, *Memoiren*, pp. 531–33. Brüning praised the captains of industry to Treviranus in 1949 for having raised 12 million marks for Hindenburg's campaign (Treviranus, *Ende von Weimar*, pp. 296–97), an incredible figure that may have masked Brüning's embarrassment over the diversion of public funds discussed below.

much as Duisberg could raise.[77] When the small discretionary funds of the chancellery and interior ministry had been exhausted, the cabinet decided to subsidize the Hindenburg campaign indirectly through the state of Prussia, whose constitution did not require a strict accounting for all expenditures. Carl Severing set the tone for the campaign by instructing police chiefs that "positive support for Hindenburg by all Prussian officials is essential. . . . The presidential election will determine the fate of the German people; it must bring the triumph of reason. Everything must be mobilized to guarantee the victory of Hindenburg in the first round."[78] When he discovered that the Prussian finance ministry could not fund electoral propaganda, Severing told the leaders of the Reich cabinet on 1 March that the "extraordinary situation" required "extraordinary methods." Brüning was pained by legal scruples, but Groener and Dietrich persuaded him to advance Severing RM 1.8 million for distribution to the parties of the Weimar coalition in Prussia. Some of this money had to be repaid in the form of curtailed Reich police subsidies, but more secret contributions followed. Gereke later recalled that Schleicher provided another million marks from the secret budget of the defense ministry. The Hugenberg press exaggerated when it alleged that eight million marks of the taxpayers' money had been diverted to the Hindenburg campaign, but it had gotten wind of a real scandal.[79] When Kempner was left with RM 500,000 in unpaid bills at the end of the campaign, he complained bitterly to Dietrich and Meissner that they had told him repeatedly to spare no expense, promised him that "the necessary funds must be and would be obtained," and now left him to face the creditors alone. The Papen government eventually paid these bills at Meissner's request in July 1932.[80]

The source of these campaign funds was an embarrassing secret, and even more scandalous was the diversion of some of this money to partisan causes. Gereke salted away half a million marks for his party's upcoming campaign in the Prussian state elections, telling himself that the goals of the "Hindenburg Front" logically implied the defeat of the Weimar Coalition in Prussia.[81] Some

---

77 Schäffer diary, 29 February 1932, NL Schäffer/18/285; note for Pünder on a report from Kempner, 25 February 1932, BAK R43I/585/134–35.

78 Brüning, *Memoiren*, p. 532; Severing's briefing for police officials, 29 February 1932, *Quellen: Staat und NSDAP*, pp. 282–87.

79 Severing, *Lebensweg*, II:319–25; Gereke, *Königlich-preussischer Landrat*, pp. 183–85; *Berliner Lokal-Anzeiger*, 10 March 1932, #118; *Deutsche Zeitung*, 12 March 1932, #61b. Duisberg later testified at the corruption trial of Günter Gereke under the Third Reich that he had raised "several hundred thousand marks" in legitimate contributions for Hindenburg, but that Kempner had disbursed hundreds of thousands more "from a source that he did not want to talk about." See the deposition of 11 April 1933, Landesarchiv Berlin, "Gereke Prozess," II:143–44 (thanks to Henry Turner for this information).

80 Kempner to Dietrich and Meissner, 9 May 1932, Meissner to State Secretary Zarden in the finance ministry, 20 June 1932, and reply of 16 July, BAP R601/19717/vol. 35/345–47, 354–55.

81 Affidavit by the Verband der Preussischen Landgemeinden, 17 March 1933, and testimony by Gereke of 23 March, Landesarchiv Berlin, "Gereke Prozess," I:1–14, 19; Gereke, *Landrat*, pp. 187–88, 240–48.

of the funds disbursed by Severing doubtless served the opposite goal. Even Brüning sometimes tried to bend the law to reward organizations loyal to Hindenburg. After the DHV sternly decided to expel all Nazi members who insulted the field marshal, the chancellor endorsed a request from Max Habermann for a postage discount of 30 percent for the DHV newsletter so that it could better explain this policy. When Postal Minister Schätzel noted that the law prohibited any discounts, Pünder replied that the chancellor was "very disappointed" – he knew the letter of the law but hoped that "you would view this matter within the context of greater political developments." Schätzel decided to forgive the DHV its packing costs, which were not bound by law, and thus achieve a modest discount of 10 percent.[82] Meanwhile the People's League for Catholic Germany, which was closely linked to the Center Party, faced imminent bankruptcy. One of its directors, Stegerwald, promised to secure the chancellor's approval for a scheme to sell to the Hindenburg Committee for 50,000 marks pamphlets that cost only 30,000 to produce.[83] Thus the attitude spread that the struggle against Hitler justified extraordinary methods. Brüning distanced himself as much as possible from the administration of campaign finances, but he was aware of serious abuses and dreaded their exposure.[84]

The Hindenburg Committee's tactical decision to distance the President from the chancellor meant little after Brüning emerged as the most energetic campaigner on Hindenburg's behalf. His Reichstag speech of 25 February set the tone for the campaign:

> One thing alone, besides my trust in a higher Power, has sustained me during the difficult tasks of the last two years and rekindled my hopes again and again, and that is the fact that I could serve a man like *President von Hindenburg*. . . . Don't think that you can even approach the stature of a *historic figure* like this, and do not forget one thing: Only the reelection of the President can make the world believe that the German people is still characterized by piety and by respect for its history, for tradition, and for the greatness of a man.[85]

Brüning spread this message tirelessly in mass rallies from Düsseldorf to Königsberg, abandoning the reserve about public appearances that he had displayed since January 1931. His speeches and the placards of the Hindenburg Committee lauded the President as the embodiment of "dignity, wisdom, tradition, and nonpartisanship," in contrast to Hitler's spirit of "hatred, fractiousness, and

82 Habermann to Pünder, 11 February, Pünder to Schätzel, 13 February, reply of 19 February, and Pünder to Schätzel, 22 February 1932, BAK R43I/585/79–82, 125–31; for background, see Larry Jones, "Between the Fronts," pp. 478–79.

83 Volksverein für das katholische Deutschland, Vorstandssitzung, 23 February 1932, NL Marx/274/23; for background, see Dirk Müller, *Arbeiter, Katholizismus, Staat,* pp. 135–39, and Klein, *Volksverein,* pp. 191–212, 278–79.

84 Brüning to Treviranus, 30 September 1955 and 9 July 1958, HUG FP 93.10/Box 34/G.R. Treviranus (2).

85 Brüning, *Reden,* p. 126.

inexperience." He sometimes offered heavy-handed advice to Hindenburg in the form of comparisons with Kaiser Wilhelm I, a modest man who had assembled the most talented cabinet possible and then given it a free hand. Usually, however, Brüning provided unqualified praise for the war hero and soul of honor who would uphold the constitution and guarantee fair treatment of every segment of the population. Brüning attracted large crowds, and many observers agreed that he displayed new skill and even passion as an orator in this campaign; his speeches also gave the public the impression of complete harmony between President and chancellor.[86] Brüning's rhetoric provoked sardonic smiles among Social Democrats, and he later acknowledged having cultivated a "Hindenburg myth" far removed from the truth about the man's modest capacities and timid character. Brüning remained convinced, however, that this myth was the most powerful psychological weapon in the moderates' arsenal.[87]

On the campaign trail, Brüning also refined his impulsive remarks to the Reichstag about the founding of the Weimar Republic into a thoughtful critique of the Nazis' pernicious myth about a "stab in the back":

> I must combat the tendency to date the time of suffering [*Elendsweg*] of the German people from the 9th of November. . . . No, I don't like to discuss the events before and just after the war; I don't see any service to our people in rancorous debates about the past. But one thing is certain: Catastrophic political mistakes were made before 1914, and military mistakes at the beginning of the war in 1914, which have imposed a heavy burden of fate on the German people in these years now and in our days and for decades to come.[88]

Thus Brüning did seek to establish that the old Imperial government was responsible for Germany's worst problems.

On 13 March Hindenburg came very close to the absolute majority needed for victory in the first round of voting with 49.6 percent; Hitler received 30 percent, Thälmann 13 percent, and Duesterberg 7 percent. A second round of voting was scheduled for 10 April in which a plurality would suffice, and Hindenburg's victory seemed inevitable. Duesterberg promptly withdrew from the race, and Hugenberg sought concessions from the President in exchange for an endorsement. The authority of the DNVP chairman was collapsing, however, and the Reichslandbund, Pan-German League, and many leading monarchists

---

86 See the placards in NL Pünder/98/83, 160; Brüning's Essen speech of 7 March 1932, *Essener Volkszeitung*, 8 March 1932, #68 (with press clippings in BAP R601/19717/vol. 35); Berlin speech of 11 March, *Ursachen und Folgen*, VIII:411–13; Ambassador Rumbold to Simon, 16 March 1932, *DBFP*, III:105–06; Wheeler-Bennett, *Knaves, Fools, and Heroes*, pp. 49–50; and Bracher, *Auflösung*, pp. 415–17. See also the "Anekdoten um Hindenburg," emphasizing the paternal solicitude that he displayed for Brüning, in *Der Deutsche*, 25 February 1932, #47.

87 Stampfer, *14 Jahre*, pp. 611–12; Brüning, "Ein Brief," in *Reden*, p. 228; Brüning to Hans von Raumer, 4 July 1954, HUG FP 93.10/Box 22/Hans von Raumer.

88 Verbatim transcript, Essen speech of 7 March 1932, *Essener Volkszeitung*, 8 March 1932, #68.

threw their support to Hitler.[89] The personal ambition of Crown Prince Wilhelm now posed the last threat to Hindenburg's reelection. Brüning had heard rumors that the Nazis would nominate the prince, so he arranged a meeting in February. "I hinted," Brüning later recalled, "that there might be a possibility later to introduce the monarchy by election of one of his sons as President, but that if he himself accepted candidacy under the Nazis every chance of the Hohenzollern family would be lost forever." Thus Chancellor Brüning may have contemplated the nomination of a Hohenzollern prince for the office of President, but only as a desperate last resort if Hindenburg died suddenly and there seemed no other way to prevent the election of Hitler.[90] After the first round of voting, however, Wilhelm's friends persuaded him that he could restore unity to the right by running for President himself, and Hitler pledged his support if Wilhelm could persuade Hindenburg to withdraw from the race. The prince wrote his father on 29 March to request permission but received a sharp rebuff from the ex-kaiser, who had persuaded himself in his lonely Dutch exile that Hitler would restore him to the throne if elected President. Prince Wilhelm therefore told the press on 3 April that he would vote for Hitler to uphold the ideals of the Harzburg Front, a gesture that angered Brüning but removed the immediate threat. Thus the only documented effort to restore the Hohenzollern to power during Brüning's chancellorship was undertaken by his worst enemies in an attempt to prevent the reelection of Hindenburg.[91]

Hindenburg preserved his distance from the cabinet throughout the campaign. His only speech to the nation, broadcast over the radio on 10 March, noted coolly that a number of provisions in the government's emergency decrees "could be improved," although he did soften Meissner's draft, which said that they were "not always correct or useful." His only defense of the government's record was to cite the Prussian army's field service manual, which taught all young lieutenants that "a mistake in the choice of methods is not as bad as the failure to take any action."[92] Hindenburg refused to address any public rallies. He did agree to frequent consultations with Gereke, to whom he expressed resentment that Brüning had made him dependent on the SPD, and he deliv-

89 Quaatz, *Tagebuch*, 14–25 March 1932, pp. 183–86; Berghahn, *Stahlhelm*, pp. 212–18; Jones, "Agrarian Splinter Parties," p. 221; Granier, *Levetzow*, pp. 170–72; Leopold, *Hugenberg*, pp. 110–12; Jones, "Hindenburg," pp. 242–48.

90 Brüning to Norman Ebbutt, 11 June 1946, in Müller, *Brüning Papers*, pp. 181–82. Compare Brüning, *Memoiren*, pp. 520–21; Kessler, *Tagebücher*, conversation with Brüning on 20 July 1935, p. 738; and Brüning to George Viereck, 26 April 1938, in Müller, *Brüning Papers*, pp. 201–02. The Crown Prince later told Erwin Planck that Brüning had "promised him the Regency [*Reichsverweserschaft*] at a later time," but Planck and Hans Schäffer agreed that Wilhelm was guilty of wishful thinking; see the Schäffer diary, 28 October 1932, NL Schäffer/23/945–46.

91 Friedrich Wilhelm, Prinz von Preussen, *Das Haus Hohenzollern 1918–1945* (Munich and Vienna, 1985), pp. 90–93; Granier, *Levetzow*, pp. 173–74, 339–40.

92 Speech published in Hubatsch, *Hindenburg*, pp. 316–19; drafts in BAP R601/19712/vol. 19/145–78.

ered soothing remarks to deputations of artisans, university students, and farmers.[93] In one of these meetings Hindenburg spoke with unusual frankness, expressing horror at the "moral civil war" that was tearing Germany to pieces. He defended the SPD against the charge that it was the "party of deserters," but he appeared most upset by reports of the mistreatment of ethnic Germans in eastern Europe:

> The preparations for civil war are complete. The hostile fronts are in place, and they hate each other more than the Versailles Treaty. Germany's irreconcilable enemies are waiting for this civil war. . . . They await our fraternal struggle as a pretext to attain the final goal that they could not attain in 1919: the destruction of the Reich. The challenge in Memel took place only because of the German divisions that make us incapable of bringing the assembled force of our nation to support our foreign policy. . . . To the Germans suffering under foreign and unjust rule I cry, "The fatherland has not abandoned you; we are merely powerless to oppose the violation of your legal rights as long as our internal feuds [*der deutsche Hader*] cripple us."[94]

These remarks suggest that Hindenburg sympathized with the army officers who were eager for rearmament.

On 10 April the President won the second round of voting with 53 percent to 37 for Hitler. Some of Hitler's added votes since March came at the expense of Ernst Thälmann, but most came from Duesterberg's camp; at least two-thirds of the supporters of the DNVP and Stahlhelm appear to have voted for Hitler. Hindenburg was appalled that so many conservatives actually preferred the corporal to the field marshal, and he held Brüning largely responsible.[95] Schleicher sought tirelessly during the campaign to undermine Brüning's reputation. The general told DVP leaders that the chancellor hindered economic recovery by refusing to slash welfare benefits, while he decried the "procrastinator" to Social Democrats for hesitating to launch a public works program. Dingeldey, who maintained very close contact with Schleicher, imposed strict party discipline in the Reichstag confidence vote of 26 February and expelled from the DVP two moderates who absented themselves rather than oppose Brüning, Curtius and Siegfried von Kardorff. He assured followers on the basis of information from Schleicher that the Brüning issue would not exist much longer to divide them, because Hindenburg would appoint a rightist cabinet with "full powers to implement its plans even without parliament" soon after 10 April.[96] The President told

---

93 Gereke, *Landrat*, pp. 181–82; Zechlin to Meissner, 19 February 1932, BAP R601/19717/vol. 35/87–88; Hindenburg's speech to artisans on 2 March and to students on 9 March 1932, BAP R601/19712/vol. 19/130–31, 141.

94 Reception for a deputation from the *Landgemeinden* led by Gereke, 5 April 1932, BAP R601/19712/vol. 19/209–11.

95 Jürgen W. Falter, "The Two Hindenburg Elections of 1925 and 1932: A Total Reversal of Voter Coalitions," *Central European History*, 23 (1990): 225–41; Hamilton, *Who Voted for Hitler?*, pp. 77–79, 113–14; Dorpalen, *Hindenburg*, pp. 292–99.

96 Quaatz, *Tagebuch*, conversation with Meissner on 2 March 1932, p. 182; Severing, *Lebensweg*, II:336; Dingeldey to Wilhelm Kalle, 5 February 1932, *Quellen: Politik und Wirtschaft*, II:1263–64;

Groener privately that "Brüning did not exactly correspond to his idea of a Reich chancellor," and when Otto Braun congratulated him on his reelection, he replied earnestly that he did not feel bound to the policies of the parties that had supported him.[97]

Brüning nevertheless regarded the presidential election as a decisive victory. When Oskar von Hindenburg conveyed polite thanks for Brüning's public defense of his father, the chancellor persuaded himself that he had won the "eternal gratitude of the house of Hindenburg." He felt that his policies had received an impressive electoral endorsement and that Hindenburg had a moral obligation to his voters not to carry out any sharp change of course.[98] Thus Brüning displayed wishful thinking about the attitude of the presidential entourage, but he was probably correct about the wishes of the electoral majority. Two small parties, the DVP and Christian Nationalist Peasants' Party, did combine support for Hindenburg with opposition to Brüning, but their position obviously bewildered the voters. Hitler and Goebbels focused their fire in this campaign directly on the Brüning cabinet and its emergency decrees. By early April every major Nazi rally featured a rebuttal of Brüning's accusation that the NSDAP favored inflation, and one of the most widely distributed Nazi pamphlets bore the title, "If you vote for Hindenburg, then you vote for Brüning." Indeed, for every political organization that retained a significant following, the decision on Hindenburg coincided with that on Brüning; in the minds of most voters, the two leaders were obviously linked. Brüning was probably correct to interpret this election result as an endorsement of his policy of constitutional government, patient revisionist diplomacy, and the impartial mediation of class conflict.[99]

5.3. The SA Ban

Mounting violence on the campaign trail persuaded Groener and Brüning that the SA must be outlawed, but General Schleicher resisted this policy. In late March Groener warned Schleicher that the state governments would ban the SA

Dingeldey to Kalle, 10 March 1932, NL Dingeldey/75/74 (source of quotation); Schäffer diary, conversation with Moldenhauer, 11 April 1932, NL Schäffer/20/443; Jones, *German Liberalism*, pp. 440–42.

97 Groener, "Chronologische Darstellung," memoir of October 1932 on the events leading to his resignation, in Vogelsang, *Reichswehr*, p. 456; Braun, *Von Weimar zu Hitler*, p. 373.

98 Oskar von Hindenburg to Brüning, 13 March 1932, BAK Kleine Erwerbung 828; Brüning to Dannie Heineman, 15 September 1937, p. 1, HUG FP 93.10/Box 14/D.N. Heineman; Brüning, *Memoiren*, pp. 532–37 (source of quotation).

99 See Bracher, *Auflösung*, p. 422; Childers, *Nazi Voter*, pp. 196–98 (source of quotation); Reuth, *Goebbels*, pp. 143–44; Hitler's campaign speeches, 2–9 April 1932, in *Hitler, Reden, Schriften, Anordnungen*, vol. 5, part 1, pp. 3–48; Gessner, *Agrarverbände*, pp. 258–62; Jones, "Agrarian Splinter Parties," pp. 219–22; Jones, *German Liberalism*, pp. 435–43; and Patch, *Christian Trade Unions*, pp. 209–12. See also the sharp criticism of Dingeldey's equivocal position by Adolf Hueck from the right and Richard Merton, Walther Rademacher, and Frank Glatzel from the left, NL Dingeldey/46/83, 36/4–14, 53/169–70.

if the Reich did not, but he replied with a furious denunciation of Carl Severing and the SPD:

> Your Excellency is supposed to be won over for a struggle against the right in the Prussian elections, to be stamped as a loyal ally of the socialists. Any means is justified to this end, including dark hints about frontier defense even to French journalists and explicit threats by the party leadership and Prussian interior ministry that they won't vote for Hindenburg on 10 April if you don't take up the struggle against the SA. . . . I am really looking forward to 11 April, when we can speak plain German to this pack of liars. . . . I am very glad that we have a counterweight [to the SPD] in the form of the Nazis, even though they are of course not our brothers and must be treated with the greatest of care. If they did not exist, it would be necessary to invent them.[100]

Groener briefly sought in Schleicher's spirit to defend the "patriotic elements" in the SA at a conference with state police officials on 5 April, but he encountered such emphatic opposition that he promised to ban the organization within two weeks after the presidential election. The chancellor and the foreign office were promptly informed of this secret agreement, and they both approved.[101]

In later years Brüning sometimes deplored Groener's SA ban as premature, depicting himself as a reluctant convert to the idea.[102] In fact, the chancellor had sought for weeks to intensify the struggle against the NSDAP. He displayed steadily mounting anger during the second round of the presidential campaign against the Nazis' disastrous search for scapegoats, which was driving Germany to the brink of civil war, and their strident propaganda against the "Weimar system." The only real "system," he declared in Baden, was the Nazi "system of the most reckless and irresponsible demagoguery." In Hamburg Brüning proclaimed that "they can't go on forever defaming and kicking the responsible majority of the people. They will force us one day to make revelations, and those will be documented revelations, after which it will only be possible to write the 'national' in National Socialist within quotation marks."[103] Thus Brüning alluded to an investigation that he had commissioned in early March into alleged financial ties between Hitler and foreign industrialists who desired an arms race. After wild reports from police informants indicated that the Nazis received massive

---

100 Groener to Schleicher, 23 March 1932, *Quellen: Staat und NSDAP*, pp. 300–301, and reply of 25 March, in Groener-Geyer, *Groener*, pp. 304–05. For background, see Zweigert to Wirth, 15 September 1931, BAP R15.01/13129.3/187; Severing to Groener, 13 November 1931, BAP R15.01/25792/519–20; Bavarian Prime Minister Held to Brüning, 15 March 1932, *Kabinette Brüning*, III:2368–69; and Vogelsang, *Reichswehr*, pp. 162–65.

101 See the two different records of the conference of 5 April in *Quellen: Staat und NSDAP*, pp. 304–09, and Vogelsang, *Reichswehr*, pp. 445–49; cabinet meeting of 1 April and Pünder to Brüning, 6 April 1932, *Kabinette Brüning*, III:2409–10, 2417–19; and Koepke to Bülow, 9 April 1932, *ADAP*, XX:98–99.

102 Brüning, *Memoiren*, pp. 538–40; Brüning, "Ein Brief," in *Reden*, pp. 229–30; Brüning to Ullmann, 23 September 1947, NL Ullmann/6/261–65.

103 "Der Wahlkampf," *Der Deutsche*, 6 April 1932, #80; "Vom Wahlkampf. Brüning warnt die Nationalsozialisten," *Der Deutsche*, 9 April 1932, #83.

subsidies from the Schneider works of Le Creusot, the Skoda works in Czecho-slovakia, and even French military intelligence, Brüning sought legal opinions on the feasibility of imprisoning Nazi leaders for treason.[104] His memory served him best when he later recalled having sought for months to persuade Hindenburg that the time would come for the forcible suppression of the Nazi movement just after his reelection. The blow must be carried out by Brüning himself, however, because the public knew that he abhorred violence and had sought to treat the Nazis fairly: "If anyone to the left or right of me were to deliver such a blow, he must fail because people would believe that partisanship or frivolity stood behind it."[105]

Brüning judged the time ripe for action in large part because the KPD had failed to grow despite catastrophic levels of unemployment. In September 1931 officials in the Reich interior ministry judged a Communist insurrection during the coming winter a real possibility, and Brüning could not ignore their argument that the state must avoid violent confrontation with the rightist paramilitary leagues under such circumstances.[106] The KPD actually suffered a decline, however, in the next six months. It won 13 percent of the national vote in September 1930 and in the first round of presidential voting, but Thälmann won only 10 percent in the second round when the votes really counted. In all three states that held elections both in the year 1931 and the spring of 1932, the Communist share dropped significantly, from 22 to 16 percent in Hamburg, 14 to 11 percent in Hesse, and 7.2 to 5.7 percent in Oldenburg. Although the KPD claimed a rapidly growing membership, income from dues declined sharply, and the number of active members in the paramilitary Communist Schutzbund plummeted from 46,000 in June 1931 to 11,782 in June 1932. Even the KPD leadership acknowledged that its struggle against fascism had often degenerated into "individual terror," that is, a series of blood feuds between rival gangs of young men and juveniles who displayed little interest in politics. Brüning deserved some of the credit for the weakening of the KPD, because his tough regulation of big business since the Bank Crisis discredited the party line that he pursued a "fascist course" and was the agent of finance capital.[107] By April 1932 the threat of Communist insurrection could safely be discounted.

104 Schäffer diary, 4 and 8 March 1932, NL Schäffer/19/318–19, 342–43; Pünder memorandum of 16 April 1932, *Kabinette Brüning*, III:2455–56; Brüning's interview of September 1945, pp. 1–3, HUG FP 93.10/Box 16/Interview.
105 Brüning to Dannie Heineman, 15 September 1937, pp. 2–3, HUG FP 93.10/Box 14/D.N. Heineman.
106 See the unsigned memorandum, "Über die Möglichkeit einer kommunistischen Revolution im kommenden Winter," 16 September 1931, BAP R15.01/13129.3/182–86.
107 See Falter et al., *Wahlen*, pp. 44–46, 94–100; Rosenhaft, *Beating the Fascists?*, pp. 49–52, 76–77, 95, 111–27, 209–13; Fischer, *German Communists*, pp. 122–61; Hermann Weber's introduction to *Quellen: Generallinie*, pp. XXXIV–LIII; and Ernst Thälmann, "Der faschistische Kurs der Brüning-Regierung," speech of 19 February 1932, in Weber, ed., *Der deutsche Kommunismus*, pp. 157–86.

When the chancellor returned to Berlin from the campaign trail on 10 April, Groener reported that the "psychological moment" had come to dissolve the SA. The old goal of creating "a great military sports league under Reich supervision" must be postponed because the excesses of the Brownshirts undermined the authority of the Reich. All parties from the SPD to the DNVP and all state governments but that of Brunswick (which included Nazis) desired the ban. Groener had also persuaded Generals Schleicher and Hammerstein to endorse his plan, but Schleicher had experienced a change of heart the day before, after receiving pleas from Dingeldey and Gereke that such a ban would ruin the prospects for the moderate right in the Prussian state elections. Now, with support from the President's representative Meissner, Schleicher urged Brüning to issue an ultimatum to Hitler with a term of one week in order to spare Hindenburg reproaches from the right. Groener opposed this idea, however, because it would make the government appear indecisive, and Brüning sided with him, expressing anger over his brushes with the SA at campaign rallies. The chancellor's arguments persuaded Meissner and left Schleicher isolated.[108]

Schleicher refused to accept this defeat. On 11/12 April he encouraged Oskar von Hindenburg to oppose the SA ban, informed divisional commanders of his negative attitude, and leaked the news to Nazi leaders as well. Brüning encountered a frigid atmosphere when he congratulated the President on his election victory and conveyed a pro forma offer by the cabinet to resign. The President declined the offer "for now" but noted that several ministers must be changed after the Prussian state elections, when "the separation from the Social Democrats must be carried out."[109] Oskar and Crown Prince Wilhelm felt that all true patriots would regard this ban as proof that the President had struck a dishonorable bargain with the Social Democrats to secure his reelection. Groener encountered the President's son on 12 April as he read a Bismarck biography, open to the chapter about Prussia's constitutional crisis of the 1860s. "The chancellor should read this book," Oskar declared, "and learn from it how to govern in such times." Groener and Brüning found the President hostile when they approached him a few hours later. They depicted the SA ban as essential for diplomatic progress at Geneva, adding that Prussia had tied their hands with the threat of independent action. After both men threatened to resign, Hindenburg approved the decree, but he obviously resented such pressure tactics.[110]

Promulgated on 13 April, the SA ban dealt an effective blow to the Nazi Party. In most states the police acted vigorously to close SA hostels and search party

---

108 Groener to Brüning, 10 April 1932, and cabinet meeting of 13 April, *Kabinette Brüning*, III:2426–29, 2433–34; Pünder memorandum, 30 May 1932, *Quellen: Staat und NSDAP*, pp. 322–26; Vogelsang, *Reichswehr*, pp. 167–72, 449–53; Hürter, *Groener*, pp. 340–45.

109 Pünder, *Politik*, 11 April 1932, p. 118 (source of quotation); Goebbels, *Tagebücher*, 11 April 1932, II:153–54; Brüning, *Memoiren*, pp. 540–42; Carsten, *Reichswehr*, pp. 342–45; Vogelsang, *Reichswehr*, pp. 175–77.

110 Groener, "Chronologische Darstellung," in Vogelsang, *Reichswehr*, pp. 453–54 (source of quotation); Crown Prince to Groener, 14 April 1932, *Quellen: Staat und NSDAP*, pp. 317–18; von Graevenitz to Pünder, 16 April 1932, NL Pünder/165/48–50; Brüning, *Memoiren*, pp. 543–44.

offices, although the Stormtroopers had been forewarned, and few weapons were discovered. Overruling objections from the Reich justice ministry, which displayed tender concern for property rights, Groener instructed the police to confiscate all SA equipment that was even remotely military in nature, including uniforms, insignia, banners, tents, field stoves, and trucks. Schleicher sent word to Nazi leaders that he was so upset by these developments that he contemplated resignation.[111] On 15 April the Reich interior ministry received a phone call from an indignant Goebbels, who complained that the Berlin police had left him stranded by confiscating the car driven by his uniformed chauffeur. When told that he must address himself to the Prussian interior ministry, which was in charge of implementing the ban, Goebbels spluttered that Germany had become a "nigger state, worse than Abyssinia." Hitler himself tore the receiver from Goebbels's hand to scream that he would tell all to the foreign press, that the German government had lost all claim to authority through such action: "He would not tolerate this any longer and rejected all responsibility for the consequences." The police eventually returned the car, but the image of a red-faced Hitler and Goebbels hailing a taxi as they contemplated a foolhardy putsch conveys some indication of the likely fate of the Nazi movement had Brüning remained in office for another year. Brüning had come to understand the affinity between fascist movements and the schoolyard bully whose aggressive impulse flares up at any sign of weakness, but who loses heart in the face of resolute opposition.[112]

Schleicher sabotaged the SA ban as Brüning departed again for Geneva by persuading General Hammerstein to give the President a hostile defense ministry dossier on the Reichsbanner. The file's summary declared that all the accusations used to justify the banning of the SA – that it illegally arrogated police functions, provided military training to members, and prepared a revolution (*Umsturz*) – applied in equal measure to the Reichsbanner. The file contained nothing more than old clippings from rightist newspapers, however, and a malicious commentary on the Reichsbanner training manual. Groener had long since investigated most of these charges and found them groundless.[113] Hindenburg nevertheless instructed Groener in an open letter on 16 April to study whether the SA ban should not be extended to other organizations, a gesture that revived

---

111 Groener's correspondence with the justice ministry and instructions to the police of 13 April 1932, BAP R15.01/25871/387–413; Goebbels, *Tagebücher*, 14 April 1932, II:154–55; Schulz, *Von Brüning zu Hitler*, p. 765; Hsi-Huey Liang, *The Berlin Police Force in the Weimar Republic* (Berkeley and Los Angeles, 1970), pp. 109–13; Orlow, *Nazi Party*, pp. 252–55; Pridham, *Nazi Movement in Bavaria*, pp. 272–73.

112 Interior ministry memorandum of 15 April 1932, NL Pünder/154/17; Brüning to Dannie Heineman, 15 September 1937, pp. 5–6, HUG FP 93.10/Box 14/D.N. Heineman. Goebbels twists the story to his own advantage in *Tagebücher*, II:155–56.

113 Vogelsang, *Reichswehr*, pp. 176–78; files on the "Anmassung militärischer Befugnisse des Reichsbanners Schwarz-Rot-Gold," BAP R15.01/13116 (November 1930–November 1931), 13117 (January–April 1932), and related correspondence in vol. 13118 (especially pp. 4–16, Groener to Severing, 13 January 1932, and reply of 19 January).

morale among Nazi leaders. Groener gave the Reichsbanner leadership opportunity to refute the army's accusations, and when Severing promised that the
Prussian police would never allow any private association to usurp any of its
functions, Groener considered the case closed.[114] Schleicher argued with some
justification that he was compelled to oppose the SA ban by the widespread sympathy for the Nazis within the officer corps, but he himself had undermined military discipline by fostering the impression that the ban served partisan leftist
goals. Groener considered Hammerstein's action a grave impropriety that
dragged the army back into "the political swamp." He feared that most generals
had foolishly decided to pin their hopes for rearmament on Hitler, and he sensed
that Schleicher, "my old friend, disciple, adopted son, my hope for the nation,"
had decided to betray him.[115]

In Geneva Brüning agonized for several hours on 16 April over his response
to the President's open letter but then took Groener's side. Hindenburg avoided
conflict by approving a new emergency decree (issued on 3 May) to define clear
guidelines that would apply equally to all paramilitary leagues.[116] Groener
assured himself of Brüning's support in a private meeting on 24 April, when
Brüning traveled from Geneva to a Prussian enclave in southwestern Germany
to cast his vote in the Prussian state elections. While they rode together back to
Geneva, Brüning pressed Groener to reveal at last the true story of the Great
War, and this conversation forms the dramatic climax of Brüning's memoirs
by completing the narrator's long-delayed process of disillusionment with the
war effort. Brüning was devastated to hear that the general staff had plunged
Germany into an unnecessary war through nervousness and incompetence, and
that Hindenburg was a weakling and ingrate. In October 1918 the field marshal
had tearfully promised eternal loyalty and gratitude if Groener agreed to become
quartermaster-general, but on 9 November Hindenburg decided without consulting him that the kaiser must abdicate, broke down in tears before he could
break the fatal news, and left Groener to take full responsibility. The same thing
happened in June 1919, when Hindenburg left Groener to take responsibility for
advising President Ebert to sign the Versailles Treaty. At this point Brüning
interrupted:

> Your Excellency, I understand the tragedy of your life. I do not want to
> sound bitter, but if you had told me any of these things in February 1930,
> then I would not have succumbed to the same appeal and the same tears of

114 Hindenburg to Groener, 16 April 1932, *Ursachen und Folgen*, VIII:464–65; Goebbels, *Tagebücher*,
   16 April 1932, II:156–57; Groener's correspondence with Reichsbanner leaders and Severing,
   20–26 April 1932, BAP R15.01/13117/31–40, 73, 88–94.
115 Schleicher to Groener, 13 April, and Groener to Schleicher, 29 November 1932 (source of last
   quotation), NL Groener, Reel 25, #224; Groener to Gleich, 25 April 1932, *Quellen: Politik und
   Wirtschaft*, II:1407–08; Groener to Richard Bahr, 22 May 1932, NL Groener, Reel 25, #231.
116 Tagesnotiz of 16 April 1932, NL Pünder/44/47; Pünder to Brüning, 18 April 1932, *Kabinette
   Brüning*, III:2456–58; Hindenburg memorandum of 26 April 1932, *Quellen: Politik und Wirtschaft*,
   II:1413–14; press release of 26 April and government decree of 3 May 1932, *Ursachen und Folgen*,
   VIII:467–68; cabinet meeting of 3 May 1932, *Kabinette Brüning*, III:2483–86.

the Reich President against my better judgment. My instincts were against him when he made his first appeal to me. Only your guarantee that you would see to it that the President stood behind me until success had been achieved persuaded me to accept the assignment.

Groener replied sadly that he might not be able to keep this promise because of Hindenburg's yearning for a rightist cabinet. "I now knew," Brüning concluded grimly, "that a policy based on a personality like Hindenburg's *must* inevitably fail. The only thing that could still save us was a decisive success at Geneva."[117]

The Prussian state elections dealt a major blow to the moderate parties and compelled Brüning to explore again the possibility of a coalition with the Nazis on the state level. The Center Party increased its share of the vote from 14 percent in 1928 to 15 percent, but the SPD plummeted from 29 to 21 percent, the State Party from 4.5 to 1.5 percent. The Nazis scored an impressive 36 percent, and with the KPD and DNVP, the sworn enemies of the constitution would command a solid majority when the new Landtag convened on 24 May. Just before the election, the parties of the Weimar Coalition had made it possible for Otto Braun to cling to power indefinitely by altering the Landtag's rules of order to require an absolute majority for the election of a new prime minister. Braun considered this maneuver antidemocratic, however, and advised the Prussian Center to create a parliamentary majority by forming a coalition with the NSDAP.[118] Schleicher and Groener also urged Brüning to help form a coalition with the Nazis in Prussia, and Meissner had advised Hindenburg for several weeks that this would be the litmus test of Brüning's sincerity about moving toward the right.[119] The chancellor insisted nevertheless that the Nazis must not be offered the Prussian premiership nor any alteration of Reich policy or the Reich cabinet. He had prepared for this day by drafting contingency plans with the old Prussian cabinet to transfer control of their police and court system to the Reich, and before the election he had assured Hermann Dietrich that the Reich would "take over Prussian affairs" if it turned out badly. At the beginning of May Brüning stipulated as the basis for coalition talks with the Prussian Nazis that a trustworthy conservative like Carl Goerdeler become prime minister and that a Reich commissar control the Prussian police. On 9 May the chancellor correctly informed his party colleagues that the Nazi leadership was deeply divided over this proposal, and they agreed to wait for Hitler and his lieutenants to make up their minds.[120]

117 Brüning, *Memoiren*, pp. 546–52 (source of quotations); Tagesnotiz, 24 April 1932, NL Pünder/44/39; Groener to Gleich, 25 April 1932, in Groener-Geyer, *Wilhelm Groener*, pp. 310–11. Brüning wrote Mona Anderson on 12 April 1938 that this conversation had destroyed his last remnants of faith in the generals (*Briefe*, I:193).

118 Falter et al., *Wahlen*, p. 101; Schulz, *Von Brüning zu Hitler*, pp. 770–75; Hagen Schulze, *Otto Braun*, pp. 725–29; Winkler, *Katastrophe*, pp. 547–49; Orlow, *Weimar Prussia 1925–1933*, pp. 208–10.

119 Groener to Gleich, 2 April 1932, in Vogelsang, *Reichswehr*, pp. 444–45; Meissner to Dr. Karl Hoppmann, 21 March 1932, BAP R601/Reel 4/vol. 22/144–45.

120 Schäffer diary, 7 April (source of quotation) and 27 April 1932, NL Schäffer/20/432–33, 513–14; Pünder to Brüning, 27 April 1932, *Kabinette Brüning*, III:2470–72; *Zentrumsprotokolle*, 9 May 1932, p. 567; Brüning's speech of 30 July 1932, in *Kölnische Volkszeitung*, 31 July 1932, #208; Brüning,

Brüning's approach to the Prussian question doubtless offered the best hope for involving the Nazis in a coalition where they could not do much harm, but Schleicher again undermined Brüning's plans. Gregor Strasser wanted to accept Brüning's offer, and even the militant Goebbels had become discouraged because of Hindenburg's reelection, the SA ban, and the prospect that he might be compelled to wait until 1934 for the next Reichstag elections. "We confront a difficult decision," Goebbels wrote in his diary on 26 April, whether to go "with the Center into government power or against the Center. Nothing can be accomplished through parliamentary methods against the Center, neither in Prussia nor the Reich. That must be pondered carefully." That same day, however, Nazi leaders received word from Schleicher that he advocated a simultaneous change of cabinets in both Prussia and the Reich. Hitler conferred with the general on 28 April and decided to suspend coalition talks with the Prussian Center.[121] Schleicher approached Brüning forthrightly on 2 May to discuss their differences. Like many other observers, including Stegerwald and Hans Schäffer, he argued that the coalition talks in Prussia would never succeed unless the Nazis were offered some concessions in the Reich cabinet as well. Brüning replied that he could not do this because of his promises to the SPD, so Schleicher asked whether he could at least agree to serve on as foreign minister in a right-of-center cabinet. Brüning later recalled answering with an offer to make Schleicher chancellor if granted another three months to conduct his diplomatic conferences without interference. He then sought to charm the general by referring to their shared experience as soldiers but apparently lost his self-control, exclaiming that staff officers like Schleicher had always demanded bold action in the war but lost their nerve when things looked bleak; only the men in the trenches had the courage needed to hold one's fire until the enemy came so close that he could not be missed. Brüning could not have chosen more offensive remarks.[122]

Brüning's critics in the presidential entourage hoped that the Reichstag would topple the chancellor. At the end of March rightist officials charged with oversight of the public debt sought to embarrass Brüning by refusing to authorize any more government borrowing on the basis of emergency decrees, and the cabinet was compelled to summon the Reichstag to request parliamentary authorization. Hugenberg prepared for this session by seeking to bribe the Business

Memoiren, pp. 569–71; Brüning to Ernst-Günther Prühs, 19 February 1950, in Müller, *Brüning Papers*, pp. 194–96; Hömig, *Das preussische Zentrum*, pp. 257–60; Winkler, *Katastrophe*, pp. 551–53; Orlow, *Nazi Party*, pp. 253–56. Prussia's Finance Minister Klepper suggested on 6 January 1932 that the Reich purchase the Prussian system of criminal justice to help balance the state budget, and Brüning supported the idea. Otto Braun initially rejected this proposal as "blackmail" but soon authorized contingency planning along these lines as a form of insurance against the election returns. See Schulze, *Otto Braun*, pp. 713–15, and the Schäffer diary, NL Schäffer/17/24–26, 115–16, and 18/164–66, 175–85.

121 Goebbels, *Tagebücher*, 23–29 April 1932, II:158–63; Quaatz, *Tagebuch*, 28 April 1932, p. 188.

122 Brüning, *Memoiren*, pp. 575–80; Pünder Tagesnotiz of 2 May 1932, NL Pünder/44/31. Compare the Schäffer diary, conversation with Stegerwald, 27 April 1932; Wheeler-Bennett, *Knaves, Fools, and Heroes*, pp. 51–52; and Treviranus, *Ende von Weimar*, p. 291.

Party, but he proved unable to raise the RM 200,000 that his intermediary named as the price for "a gain of 20" in the next confidence vote. Hitler and Schleicher did reach agreement, however, to topple first Groener and then Brüning, rescind the SA ban, and hold new Reichstag elections.[123] On the eve of the Reichstag session, President Hindenburg summoned Brüning on 9 May to demand the immediate formation of a Prussian coalition with the Nazis and declare that he would receive the party leaders to discuss the situation in the Reich. Brüning protested that this would undermine his authority, threatening to resign immediately, and Hindenburg grudgingly agreed to postpone his receptions until the end of the month.[124] Hindenburg's instinctive caution was reinforced when Brüning enjoyed a surprisingly favorable reception in the Reichstag on 11 May. The chancellor exhorted it "not to become soft in the last five minutes," depicting himself as a long-distance runner who was now "in the last hundred meters before the finish line" of the campaign to redress the grievances of Versailles. The stenographic record noted "long-lasting, stormy approval and applause," and the government preserved a majority of over two dozen the next day as it defeated the last motion of no confidence ever raised against it. This show of enthusiasm was somewhat cynical, because the parties of the moderate right anticipated that they would commit suicide if they provoked new elections. The vote nevertheless created a problem for the presidential entourage, because there was no precedent for dismissing a chancellor who enjoyed the Reichstag's confidence.[125]

Brüning's position weakened despite this victory when Groener was compelled to resign as defense minister. On 10 May Groener sought to defend the SA ban to the Reichstag, but he appeared ill and lost his train of thought when interrupted. He too retained the support of a parliamentary majority, but Count Westarp and Johann Viktor Bredt told Brüning that this speech was a disaster, that he must dismiss Groener to avoid being dragged down with him. When Hindenburg summoned Westarp for advice the next day, they agreed that Groener was no longer "fit for active duty" but that Brüning should retain office for the sake of foreign policy. Schleicher then forced the issue by threatening that he and Hammerstein would resign if Groener remained defense minister. Groener decided on 12 May to lay that office down and concentrate on the interior ministry, and Brüning felt obliged to endorse this decision by his loyal supporter, even though Hindenburg obviously wanted Groener to resign from both posts. The chancellor offered the defense ministry to Schleicher, but he replied

---

123 Schulz, *Von Brüning zu Hitler*, pp. 781–93; Schwerin von Krosigk, *Staatsbankrott*, pp. 100–101; Wilhelm Füssel (Dresden) to Hugenberg, 1 and 14 May 1932 (source of quotation), and reply of 18 May, NL Hugenberg/36/203–09; Goebbels, *Tagebücher*, 8 May 1932, II:165–66; Quaatz, *Tagebuch*, memorandum of 6 May 1932, p. 189.

124 Meissner memorandum, 9 May 1932, *Quellen: Politik und Wirtschaft*, II:1445–46; Pünder, *Politik*, 9 May 1932, pp. 118–19.

125 Brüning, *Reden*, pp. 143, 164; Pünder memorandum, 27 April 1932, *Kabinette Brüning*, III:2470–71; Schulz, *Von Brüning zu Hitler*, pp. 822–24.

evasively in their last interview on 17 May, and the press learned immediately that he had refused to join the cabinet. Some shrewd observers immediately termed this rebuff "the beginning of the end" for Brüning.[126] Schleicher and Hammerstein told army colleagues after Groener resigned that Brüning's survival in office depended on the prompt formation of a coalition with the Nazis in Prussia, but Schleicher himself made this impossible through his ongoing contacts with Hitler. The Nazi leader offered a pledge of loyalty on 19 May by expelling Albert Krebs from his party simply for publishing an editorial critical of Schleicher. "The NSDAP," Hitler reportedly boasted to his Prussian parliamentary delegation, "now has a coalition that is more important and more valuable than any parliamentary alliance, that is the coalition with the Reichswehr."[127]

5.4. Brüning's Race Against Time

Brüning pinned his hopes on a diplomatic breakthrough but did not perceive that he was on the verge of victory over reparations. Preliminary discussions about the Lausanne Conference indicated that France remained inflexible, and the United States offered no hint that it would forgive war debts to promote a settlement. Brüning and Bülow feared that this issue would not be resolved until after the U.S. presidential elections that fall; if Hoover was defeated, serious negotiations could not begin until the spring of 1933. Brüning therefore exhorted the cabinet to "hold out" for another year without any change in fiscal or economic policy. On 24 May he again proclaimed that he was "one hundred meters from the finish line" in a speech to the Reichsrat foreign policy committee, but the complicated scenario he described did not imply the abolition of reparations before March 1933.[128]

Hans Schäffer feared that the Reich would go bankrupt long before then. He resented Brüning's decision to postpone the Lausanne Conference from January to June and became angry when Dietrich and Brüning decided on political

---

126 Pünder, *Politik*, 10–18 May 1932, pp. 120–24; Pünder "Tagesnotiz," 17 May 1932, NL Pünder/44/16; Brüning, *Memoiren*, pp. 587–89; Oldenburg-Januschau to Wilhelm von Gayl, 21 May, and Westarp memorandum of 1 June 1932, *Quellen: Politik und Wirtschaft*, II:1469, 1514–15; Bredt, *Erinnerungen*, p. 278; Groener, "Chronologische Darstellung," in Vogelsang, *Reichswehr*, pp. 456–57; Vorstand der Staatspartei, 18 May 1932, *Quellen: Linksliberalismus*, pp. 711–12; Goebbels, *Tagebücher*, 10–12 May 1932, II:166–68; Hürter, *Groener*, pp. 349–51.

127 Vogelsang, *Reichswehr*, pp. 189, 196; Hammerstein's briefing for divisional commanders, 21 May 1932, in Vogelsang, ed., "Neue Dokumente," pp. 423–25; Goebbels, *Tagebücher*, 13–24 May 1932, II:169–72; Alvensleben to Schleicher, 20 May 1932, NL Schleicher/25/51; Krebs, *Infancy of Nazism*, pp. 188–89; chancellery intelligence report of 20 May 1932 (source of quotation), NL Pünder/45/71. Compare the published version of Hitler's remarks in *Hitler. Reden, Schriften, Anordnungen*, vol. 5, part 1, pp. 110–11.

128 Schäffer diary, 4 and 21 March 1932, Bülow to Neurath, 4 May 1932, and Brüning's speech of 24 May, *Quellen: Politik und Wirtschaft*, II:1316–17, 1347, 1436–37, 1472–78; Bülow to the foreign office, 18 April 1932, *ADAP*, XX:127–29; conference on reparations, 27 May 1932, *Kabinette Brüning*, III:2575–77.

grounds during the presidential campaign to reduce the beer tax and veto several small tax increases that he proposed.[129] When Brüning ordered him to deceive foreigners about his cash flow, Schäffer concluded that the chancellor displayed the same blind faith in willpower exhibited by General Ludendorff in the spring of 1918 and Chancellor Cuno in 1923, when the heads of government had set the German people tasks that exceeded its strength. On 19 March Schäffer implored Brüning to offer France political concessions in exchange for prompt agreement over reparations. Brüning ignored this letter, however, and continued to assure anxious colleagues that his financial wizard would keep the treasury afloat somehow. At the end of April Schäffer therefore resigned from office to persuade Brüning of the gravity of the situation, although he spared the chancellor any embarrassment by keeping this step secret as he left Berlin on vacation. Schäffer's decision has been interpreted as the result of "Keynesian" sympathies, but he explicitly urged the cabinet to forget about any public works program; instead, it should balance the budget at all costs while seeking prompt agreement over reparations.[130]

Brüning perceived his best opportunity for political salvation in the Geneva Disarmament Conference, which dealt with the issue closest to Hindenburg's heart. He thought that he achieved a breakthrough there on 26 April, when the U.S. Secretary of State, Henry Stimson, brought him and Bülow together with Prime Minister MacDonald at his cottage in Bessing. Brüning thought that they signaled acceptance for Groener's idea that a 100,000-man "Swiss-style militia" with very short terms of service should be created alongside the professional Reichswehr, which would allow Germany to create a pool of one million trained soldiers in a few years without a major increase in military spending. Brüning notified Hindenburg and the cabinet that he had achieved a diplomatic triumph but could reveal no details until France ratified the bargain.[131] Stimson and MacDonald remembered nothing, however, about a German militia after this conversation. They rejoiced because Brüning seemed to place all his emphasis on French disarmament; the only request on Germany's behalf noted by them was that the Reichswehr term of service be reduced from twelve years to six, which would not allow any rapid expansion of the pool of trained manpower. Brüning had either scaled back Groener's program drastically to win agreement or else phrased the crucial demand in language so exquisitely subtle that his listeners failed to

129 Schäffer diary, 24 and 25 February and 7 March 1932, NL Schäffer/18/272–73, 19/337–38; "Die Haushaltslage am 28. February 1932," NL Schäffer/32/75–86; cabinet meeting, 17 March 1932, *Kabinette Brüning*, III:2374–76.

130 Schäffer to Brüning, 19 March 1932, and diary entry of 26 April, *Quellen: Politik und Wirtschaft*, III:1342–45, 1412–13; Schäffer diary, 20–24 March and 2 May 1932, NL Schäffer/19/384–85, 402–07, and 20/527–32; Schwerin von Krosigk, *Staatsbankrott*, pp. 99–102; Wandel, *Schäffer*, pp. 224–28.

131 Bülow memorandum, 26 April 1932, and cabinet meeting of 2 May, *Kabinette Brüning*, III:2467–69, 2480–83; Brüning, *Memoiren*, pp. 554–62, 567–68; Schulz, *Von Brüning zu Hitler*, pp. 828–32.

notice it.[132] In later years Brüning denounced General Blomberg for deceptive reports to Hindenburg about the Geneva talks that unfairly questioned the chancellor's dedication to rearmament. To undermine Brüning's position, however, Blomberg would only have needed to tell the truth about the lack of progress.[133]

The depth of Chancellor Brüning's yearning for a diplomatic triumph was reflected in the tricks later played by his memory. In exile he insisted that his American friends had extracted French agreement to the plan for a "Swiss-style militia." On 30 May, just after Hindenburg demanded Brüning's resignation, U.S. Ambassador Sackett supposedly brought word that full agreement over German "equality of rights" could be achieved if Brüning returned to Geneva for a meeting with French leaders. Only Brüning could strike this bargain, because only he was trusted by Western governments. Brüning recounted this story again and again, sometimes concluding that Hindenburg had toppled him because he could not bear to see a Roman Catholic achieve such triumph, sometimes alleging that the French steel industry had brought him down to profit from a new arms race. Brüning accused Ambassador François-Poncet in particular, a former lobbyist for the steel industry, of helping to bring the Nazis to power by telling Hindenburg that France would be more likely to grant concessions to a rightist government.[134] These assertions seem wildly exaggerated. Whatever his differences with Brüning, François-Poncet sought to improve Franco–German relations, not foment an arms race. The French parliamentary elections of May 1932 produced a major swing to the left, moreover, that greatly strengthened the advocates of a reconciliation with Germany based on the abolition of reparations. Sackett did urge Brüning on 30 May to go to Geneva to meet the new French premier, Edouard Herriot, and when Brüning imparted the news of his impending resignation, Sackett decided not to deliver an informal letter to him from the American disarmament delegation. The American delegates had only written, however, to urge Brüning to counteract the disastrous impression on French public opinion made by the recent publication of Stresemann's irredentist private correspondence from the 1920s. This undelivered

132 Memorandum of 26 April and Hugh Gibson to State Department, 29 April 1932, *FRUS 1932*, I:108–14; Schmidt, *Statist auf diplomatischer Bühne*, pp. 236–37; Wilhelm Deist, "Brüning, Herriot und die Abrüstungsgespräche von Bessinge 1932," *Vierteljahrshefte für Zeitgeschichte*, 5 (1957): 265–72; Bennett, *German Rearmament*, pp. 149–58; Burke, *Frederic Sackett*, pp. 204–07. In September 1932 Bülow referred to the Bessing talks to support Germany's demand for "equality of rights" in armaments, but Stimson and MacDonald both denied emphatically that they had signaled acceptance for any German rearmament; see *DBFP*, IV:137, 195–96, 219.
133 Schulz, "Suche nach dem Schuldigen," pp. 671–74; Brüning to Graf Galen, 12 October 1948, in Müller, *Brüning Papers*, pp. 185–86.
134 Brüning, *Memoiren*, pp. 601–02; Brüning to John Foster Dulles, 5 December 1939, in Müller, *Brüning Papers*, pp. 180–81; Brüning, "The Statesman," pp. 112–15; Brüning, "Ein Brief," in *Reden*, pp. 242–45; Brüning to Ullmann, 23 September 1947, NL Ullmann/6/264–65; Brüning, *Briefe*, I:85, 369–71, 539–43, and II:24–29, 70–72, 104, 454–55.

letter was not, as Brüning later assumed, an announcement of any sort of diplomatic breakthrough.[135]

Brüning also asserted later, apparently without any foundation, that he had been about to secure Czech agreement to join a customs union with Germany and Austria when toppled.[136] He even claimed that he had almost persuaded Poland to return the Corridor. During his last weeks in office Brüning did converse with Polish representatives in Geneva, and he encouraged friends in German and Belgian industry to explore joint ventures with French colleagues to develop hydroelectric power along the Moselle River. The chancellor told Schwerin von Krosigk that the king of Belgium would soon propose a comprehensive plan to reconcile France and Germany, involving joint projects for industrial development, parity in armaments, the abolition of reparations, and the return to Germany of Danzig, West Prussia, and the Cameroons. King Albert was a critic of the Treaty of Versailles, but it is most unlikely that he ever intended to call for a revision of Poland's borders and unimaginable that France or Poland would have accepted such a plan. Brüning's memory nevertheless inflated this scheme into another virtual accomplishment that had been ruined by his fall.[137]

While the chancellor concentrated on diplomacy, the politicians in his cabinet cast about for some short-term program to alleviate economic distress. In February 1932 Dietrich and Stegerwald advocated substantial funding for public works in the budget for the coming fiscal year. Dietrich acknowledged, however, that public works could not be financed unless he relieved the pressure on the budget through painful reductions in entitlements, so he and Brüning agreed that discussion of this issue should be postponed until after the presidential election.[138] Stegerwald became alarmed, however, when the Free Unions scheduled a special Crisis Congress to discuss a bold plan to spend two billion marks on public works. The labor minister therefore developed his own plan to spend

135 Reports to Berlin by Ambassador Hoesch, 9, 13, and 31 May 1932, *ADAP*, XX:171–76, 181–82, 221–23; Josef Becker, "Probleme der Aussenpolitik Brünings," in Josef Becker and Klaus Hildebrand, eds., *Internationale Beziehungen in der Weltwirtschaftskrise 1929–1933* (Munich, 1980), pp. 268–78; Bennett, *German Rearmament*, pp. 158–61; Shamir, *Economic Crisis*, pp. 163–65; Burke, *Frederic Sackett*, pp. 216–23.

136 Contrast Brüning's memorandum of March 1938, *Briefe*, I:493–99, with his record of a noncommittal conversation with Benes on 26 April 1932, *ADAP*, XX:68–69, and Boyer, "Das Deutsche Reich und die Tschechoslowakei."

137 Schäffer diary, conversation with Schwerin von Krosigk, 19 April 1932, NL Schäffer/20/482–84; Pünder note of 23 April 1932, *Kabinette Brüning*, III:2465–67; Bülow to Brüning, 4 May 1932, *ADAP*, XX:161–63; Schwerin von Krosigk, *Staatsbankrott*, pp. 102–03; Brüning's conversation with Lord Lothian, June 1939, and Brüning to Wheeler-Bennett, 3 February 1940, *Briefe*, I:266–70, 307–09; Jacques Willequet, "Die Regierung König Alberts und die Wiederaufrüstung Deutschlands, 1932–1934," in Becker and Hildebrand, eds., *Internationale Beziehungen*, pp. 129–53.

138 Schäffer diary, entries of 12, 13, and 18 February 1932, NL Schäffer/18/199, 210–13, 242–44; Chefbesprechung, 20 February 1932, *Kabinette Brüning*, III:2318–22.

1.2 billion to employ 200,000 workers directly and perhaps 400,000 more indirectly, which he hoped to announce at the congress. "In this matter," Stegerwald wrote Pünder, "the dangers of the political situation appear so great to me that we must not shrink from methods of financing that would appear objectionable in other circumstances." The plan was leaked to the press on 7 March, and Economics Minister Warmbold rebuked Stegerwald sharply for diverging from established policy in a bid for popularity.[139]

Stegerwald told the cabinet that he did not want to attend the Crisis Congress on 13 April unless he could offer good news about public works, so Brüning agreed to appear himself. The chancellor begged off at the last minute, however, after Otto Braun advised him confidentially not to attend, so Stegerwald was compelled to enter the lion's den after all.[140] As he had feared, the senior officials in the ministries of economics and finance and all cabinet ministers but Dietrich insisted that he must not announce any program for public works. The time would not be ripe for this, they declared, until the world economic crisis "bottomed out" and reparations were abolished (two developments which they apparently assumed would occur simultaneously); even then the Reichsbank must act surreptitiously so as to maintain confidence in the mark.[141] Stegerwald could only win permission to make two promises to organized labor, that the subdivision of bankrupt East Elbian estates into small homesteads would accelerate, and that the government would stretch out job opportunities by imposing the forty-hour week on some branches of industry.[142] His speech proved as unpopular as he had feared. Stegerwald provoked emphatic contradiction when he declared that it was better to do nothing than to do something that might jeopardize the currency, even though Otto Braun endorsed this proposition in the name of the SPD leadership. The trade unionists seemed indifferent to the prospect of homesteads and applauded only his promise about the forty-hour week.[143]

The Crisis Congress did not generate much pressure on the cabinet to alter its priorities. The Free Unions formally endorsed the "Woytinsky–Tarnow–

139 Stegerwald to Pünder, 3 March 1932, and Fessler's note of 7 March, BAK R43I/2045/12–15; Schäffer diary, 4 March 1932, *Quellen: Politik und Wirtschaft*, II:1313–16, and 17 March 1932, NL Schäffer/19/371–72; memoranda by Schwerin von Krosigk, 14 March, and Hans Schäffer, 2 June 1932, NL Schäffer/32/120–30, 211; Henning Köhler, "Arbeitsbeschaffung, Siedlung und Reparationen," pp. 277–82.

140 Luther Tagesbericht, 18 March 1932, NL Luther/368/112; chancellery note of 21 March, invitation to Brüning of 1 April, acceptance of 6 April, and Brüning to ADGB Bundesvorstand, 13 April 1932, BAK R43I/2024/312–21; Pünder's Tagesnotiz, 12 April 1932, NL Pünder/44/51.

141 Interministerial conferences of 1 and 5 April 1932, BAK R43I/2045/26–31; note of 7 April and Chefbesprechung of 8 April 1932, *Kabinette Brüning*, III:2421–26; Luther Tagesbericht, 8 April 1932, *Quellen: Politik und Wirtschaft*, II:1368–69.

142 Cabinet meeting of 12 April 1932, *Kabinette Brüning*, III:2432–33; Schäffer diary, NL Schäffer/20/446–53; Luther's report in *Quellen: Politik und Wirtschaft*, II:1370–72; draft for chancellor's address to the Crisis Congress, BAK R43I/2024/323–27; Schlange-Schöningen, *Am Tage danach*, pp. 61–62.

143 Stegerwald's speech of 13 April 1932, *Quellen: Politik und Wirtschaft*, II:1374–79; Michael Schneider, *Arbeitsbeschaffungsprogramm*, pp. 90–98; Winkler, *Katastrophe*, pp. 538–41.

Baade Plan" to spend two billion marks on public works, but many union leaders acknowledged privately that this was merely a bargaining position, not a practical blueprint for action. After two private conferences with Hans Luther, Leipart told his colleagues that "the Reichsbank has already done a great deal to revive production" through liberal discounting of bills of exchange; a massive public works program might cause another bank crisis. The National Economic Council also endorsed public works but acknowledged that it might not be possible to finance more than a one-billion-mark program. Under the influence of Hilferding, the SPD Reichstag delegation continued to oppose any such program as probably inflationary and certainly a hindrance to Brüning's foreign policy.[144] The only prominent convert to the W–T–B Plan was Gregor Strasser, who praised the Free Unions in the Reichstag on 10 May for embracing ideas about "the creation of credit" first proposed by the Nazis. Brüning won vigorous applause from every party from the SPD to the DNVP with the following reply: "For reasons of both domestic and foreign policy, I for one must refuse most emphatically to do anything under any circumstances that could temporarily bring a small alleviation, but which could bring our currency into the gravest danger." Brüning promised that the government was drafting plans along the lines suggested by Strasser and the Free Unions, but he insisted that "public works can only drive the wheel up toward the top again after the low point of a crisis has already been overcome."[145]

Brüning and Luther did endorse public works if they could be financed in the conventional manner through a bond issue, and on 12 April Dietrich presented the cabinet a program costing 1.4 billion marks, two-thirds of it to be financed through tax-free government bonds. The defense ministry supported the idea, since rearmament was impossible without economic recovery, and Brüning won authorization from the Reichstag on 12 May to issue up to one billion marks' worth of tax-free bonds for public works. German bankers proved reluctant to subscribe to this issue, however, and Luther did not want to issue the government a cash advance on anticipated sales until the fate of reparations was determined. The cabinet therefore felt compelled to scale back Dietrich's plan drastically in late May. Its final draft for a Fifth Emergency Decree allocated only RM 135 million for public works and mostly contained painful austerity measures. There is no reason to doubt Brüning's later assertions that he was resolved to finance Dietrich's full program just after the final abolition of reparations – Schwerin von Krosigk, Leipart, Gereke, and the "economic

---

144 ADGB leadership conferences of 3 February-12 April 1932, *Quellen: Gewerkschaften*, pp. 478–79, 503–09, 525–28, quotation on p. 540; Reichswirtschaftsrat report of 12 March and Luther Tagesbericht, 8 April 1932, *Quellen: Politik und Wirtschaft*, II:1319–28, 1467–70; Staudinger, *Wirtschaftspolitik*, pp. 88–90; Michael Schneider, *Arbeitsbeschaffungsprogramm*, pp. 120–30; Gates, "German Socialism," pp. 342–53.

145 Strasser speech, *Verhandlungen des Reichstags*, 446/2512–21; Brüning's reply in *Reden*, pp. 150–51, 159; Grotkopp, *Krise*, pp. 29–31, 68–76; Winkler, *Katastrophe*, pp. 562, 637–39; Schneider, *Arbeitsbeschaffungsprogramm*, pp. 146–54.

reformer" Wilhelm Grotkopp have all supported this testimony – but it must be recalled that Brüning anticipated many months of negotiations over reparations.[146] The cabinet's only immediate achievement was to forge consensus among management, labor, and the paramilitary leagues in support of "Voluntary Labor Service" brigades in which young men would drain swamps or dig artificial lakes at subminimum wages, but the Reich could spare only 50 million marks for this program.[147]

Some of Brüning's advisers argued that, even if the government could not revive the economy, it could mollify public opinion by expropriating Germany's most unpopular capitalists in Ruhr heavy industry and East Elbian agriculture. Heinrich Imbusch of the Christian miners' union actually launched a campaign in January 1932 to nationalize heavy industry.[148] The chancellor privately assured industrialists that he sought to forestall nationalization, however, and he apparently collaborated with Paul Silverberg to prevent the Reichstag from debating Imbusch's bill during its May session.[149] Brüning and Dietrich did carry out a major stock transaction in early May that could have had momentous implications: They secretly purchased a controlling interest in the Gelsenkirchen Mining Company from Friedrich Flick at a cost of RM 100 million, four times the market price. Control of this company gave the Reich a one-sixth interest in the mammoth United Steelworks, and the government received further offers to sell from other major stockholders in that trust. Dietrich's last official act was to establish a method of payment designed to keep the transaction secret, but press reports in mid-June and an investigation by the Papen cabinet raised a storm of controversy. Brüning accepted responsibility for authorizing the purchase, although not the excessive price, and later recalled this action as part of a comprehensive plan to bust the trusts. Dietrich confessed privately to Schäffer, however, that Flick had stampeded him by threatening to sell to French investors, who might have gained access to embarrassing information about covert ties

---

146 Meister, *Grosse Depression*, pp. 379–92; Schildt, *Militärdiktatur*, pp. 88–89; Köhler, "Arbeitsbeschaffung," pp. 283–85; cabinet meetings of 13–19 May 1932, *Kabinette Brüning*, III:2506–10, 2516–17, 2528–42; summary of the planned emergency decree in *Kölnische Volkszeitung*, 22 May 1932, #141; Brüning, *Memoiren*, pp. 503–04, 572–75; Brüning to Paul Kretzschmar, 14 March 1952, in Müller, *Brüning Papers*, p. 191; Schwerin von Krosigk, *Staatsbankrott*, pp. 65–66; Leipart's remarks to the ADGB Bundesausschuss, 14 June 1932, *Quellen: Gewerkschaften*, p. 588; Gereke, *Landrat*, pp. 187–90; Grotkopp, *Krise*, pp. 74–75.

147 Cabinet meeting, 21 May 1932, *Kabinette Brüning*, III:2551–52; ADGB Bundesvorstand, 31 May 1932, *Quellen: Gewerkschaften*, pp. 574–75; Winkler, *Katastrophe*, pp. 410–11, 604–06, 718–20; Schneider, *Arbeitsbeschaffungsprogramm*, pp. 143–46.

148 See the advice by "Georg Risse" (actually Walter Dirks) in the *Deutsche Republik*, 28 November 1931 (vol. 6, #9), pp. 260–63; Fessler's chancellery memorandum of 1 February 1932, *Kabinette Brüning*, III:2252–53; Patch, *Christian Trade Unions*, pp. 176–81; and Schlange-Schöningen to Brüning, 15 May 1932, *Quellen: Politik und Wirtschaft*, II:1455–57. Dirks was an editor employed by Brüning's friend Dessauer at the *Rhein-Mainische Volkszeitung* (see Focke, *Sozialismus aus christlicher Verantwortung*, pp. 162–65).

149 Brüning's Reichstag speech of 11 May 1932, *Reden*, pp. 155–56; Kastl to Krupp, 14 May 1932, *Quellen: Politik und Wirtschaft*, II:1451–54; RDI Fachgruppe Bergbau to Silverberg, 7 May 1932, and reply by his secretary on 27 May, NL Silverberg/383/110–11.

between industry and the defense ministry. The Flick Affair probably resulted from the cabinet's determination not to strengthen the French bargaining position at Geneva and Lausanne, not any coherent plan for economic reform.[150]

Stegerwald's dogged efforts to fulfill his promises to the Free Unions had meanwhile antagonized Warmbold and Schlange-Schöningen, two ministers who retained sympathy in the presidential palace. On 20 April the labor minister submitted to the cabinet a plan to impose a ceiling forty work hours per week on the mining, chemical, paper, food, and construction industries. Stegerwald hoped that this decree would create 100,000 new jobs, but Warmbold denounced the plan for stifling free enterprise. All efforts to resolve this dispute by promoting voluntary agreements between management and labor failed miserably, as did efforts by labor ministry officials to seek consensus with their colleagues from the economics ministry.[151] On 6 May Warmbold announced his resignation. Brüning implored him not to explain his reasons to the press, but he insisted on declaring that he had already tried to resign in December because of opposition to the Fourth Emergency Decree; since then "the differences of opinion in questions of fundamental principle have become yet sharper." Brüning suspected that Warmbold was acting on instructions from Schleicher, and the Goebbels diary does portray this resignation as the first detonation in the series of mines laid by Hitler and Schleicher in Brüning's path.[152] Warmbold's announcement and press leaks about the cabinet's plan for a forty-hour week caused the Ruhr lobbyist Otto Hugo of the DVP to attack Brüning for the "open proclamation of a socialist policy," and the pro-business *Berliner Börsenzeitung* denounced the "Stegerwaldian spirit, i.e., the spirit of theoretical economic planners" as the primary cause of the Great Depression. These polemics must have strengthened the President's impression that Brüning was losing ground on the right.[153] Brüning requested Stegerwald to withdraw his work

---

150 Brüning to Pünder, 18 November 1947, NL Pünder/231/3–4; Brüning, "Democratic Reorientation," lecture of 6 March 1941, p. 7, HUG FP 93.45; Schäffer diary, 22 and 28 June and 5 July 1932, NL Schäffer/21/605, 620–21, 635–40; Gerhard Volkland, "Hintergründe und politische Auswirkungen der Gelsenkirchen-Affäre im Jahre 1932," *Zeitschrift für Geschichtswissenschaft*, 11 (1963): 289–318; Henning Köhler, "Zum Verhältnis Friedrich Flicks zur Reichsregierung am Ende der Weimarer Republik," in Mommsen, Weisbrod, and Petzina, eds., *Industrielles System*, pp. 878–83; Schulz, *Von Brüning zu Hitler*, pp. 896–99.

151 Patch, *Christian Trade Unions*, pp. 183–84; Stegerwald to cabinet, 20 April, and inter-ministerial conference of 28 April 1932, BAK R43I/1456/47–52 and 2043/100–102; minutes of a conference in the labor ministry on 29 April between the coal mine operators and the miners' unions, NL Silverberg/383/97–105; related documents on the labor ministry's negotiations with industrialists and the economics ministry, BAP/RAM/288/338–72.

152 Warmbold to Hindenburg, 28 April 1932, *Quellen: Politik und Wirtschaft*, II:1423–24; Warmbold's original letter, Pünder to Meissner, 4 May 1932, press release of 6 May (source of quotation), and Warmbold's more detailed rationale for the President, BAP R601/19721/vol. 46/241–49; Gerhard Ritter, *Carl Goerdeler und die deutsche Widerstandsbewegung* (Stuttgart, 1954), p. 52; Goebbels, *Tagebücher*, 4–6 May 1932, II:164–65.

153 Hugo to Dingeldey, 6 May 1932, *Quellen: Politik und Wirtschaft*, II:1438–39; *Berliner Börsenzeitung*, 14 May 1932, #224; "Wühlereien gegen Stegerwald," *Der Deutsche*, 29 May 1932, #124; Schorr, *Stegerwald*, pp. 241–44; Patch, *Christian Trade Unions*, pp. 183–84.

hours plan, and most ministers opposed it when the cabinet met on 23 May. Stegerwald refused to withdraw it, however, until he saw the final provisions of the next emergency decree regarding homesteads and public works. He agonized over the swelling deficit in the welfare funds administered by the labor ministry and was nearing the end of his willingness to accept further odium.[154]

Stegerwald's disaffection resulted in part from a campaign by Carl Goerdeler to slaughter some of the sacred cows of organized labor. After joining the cabinet as price commissar in December 1931, Goerdeler took great pains to persuade the business community of his commitment to free-market principles. He therefore clashed repeatedly with the labor minister, demanding for example that the law against night-time baking be repealed and that a means test be introduced for all unemployment insurance.[155] Goerdeler also floated an ambitious plan in January 1932 to transfer control of unemployment relief to the trade unions, arguing that their painful membership losses would compel them to accept this burden if the government promised to make union membership compulsory. Brüning was intrigued, but the SPD opposed the idea, and the Communists launched damaging attacks on "fascist" leanings in the Free Unions when they got wind of these discussions. Stegerwald concluded that any effort to implement this plan would drive the Social Democrats into opposition.[156] The Leipzig mayor nevertheless gained new self-confidence in March when Hindenburg personally requested him to remain in the cabinet even though he had completed his mission to lower all bound prices by at least 10 percent. In April he submitted directly to Hindenburg a highly ambitious plan, calling for *Reichsreform*, labor service brigades, public works, and the transfer of unemployment insurance to the trade unions, that was opposed by all other cabinet ministers.[157] Knowing that Brüning hoped to recruit him as economics minister when Warmbold resigned, Goerdeler renewed his push for a means test in the cabinet on 7 May, promising that it would save 120 million marks per year; Stegerwald replied that the real savings would be far less, not enough to justify the insult to workers. Brüning announced to the cabinet on 18 May that their Fifth Emergency Decree would retain insurance benefits for thirteen weeks after a layoff without any means test, but Goerdeler continued to attack this provision as too generous. Brüning later recalled Goerdeler as his chosen successor and loyal ally, but it

---

154 Blank to Reusch, 18 May 1932, *Quellen: Politik und Wirtschaft*, II:1460–61; cabinet meetings of 23 May 1932, *Kabinette Brüning*, III:2558–68. See also the report on strained relations with the labor minister in the Christian miners' union Hauptvorstand meeting of 30 April 1932, pp. 3–11, NL Imbusch/2, and Stegerwald's remarks in *Zentrumsprotokolle*, 12 May 1932, pp. 570–71.

155 See Goerdeler's speech to the RDI Kartell-Ausschuss, 16 December 1931, NL Silverberg/347/139–48; cabinet meetings of 21 January, 17 and 29 February 1932, *Kabinette Brüning*, III:2203–09, 2304–08, 2332–37; and the Schäffer diary, 18 February 1932, NL Schäffer/18/240–42.

156 Meeting of 25 January 1932, *Kabinette Brüning*, III:2220–25; Stegerwald's conference with Christian union leaders, 11 February 1932, BAK Kleine Erwerbung 461/7/24; Schäffer diary, 12 February 1932, NL Schäffer/18/203–06; Heer, *Burgfrieden oder Klassenkampf*, pp. 44–80.

157 Ritter, *Carl Goerdeler*, pp. 41–52.

seems doubtful whether a Chancellor Goerdeler would have pursued policies much different from those of Franz von Papen. Even Brüning later emphasized that he was too "dogmatic in his deflationary proposals."[158]

Meanwhile Stegerwald sought to fulfill his second promise to the Free Unions by submitting to the cabinet on 19 April a draft decree that authorized labor ministry officials to purchase "hopelessly bankrupt" estates in East Elbia at whatever price they considered fair and subdivide them for homesteaders. Schlange-Schöningen responded to Pünder that labor ministry officials knew nothing about agriculture. "I cannot make 25 percent of my fellow landowners walk the plank," he declared, "without being in a position to guarantee personally that my eastern homeland is placed on a healthy economic footing by genuine experts." Stegerwald told Brüning and Schäffer that Schlange's demand for jurisdiction would mean "surrender to the control of the big landowners. Such a development can only be obtained over his [Stegerwald's] political corpse."[159] Brüning sought anxiously to persuade Stegerwald that the cabinet could not survive unless foreclosures were controlled by a prominent agrarian, and the labor minister satisfied some of Schlange's objections with a revised draft for cabinet discussion on 20 May. The two men agreed that Schlange's agents would decide which estates to acquire and then turn them over to labor ministry officials for subdivision. Schlange still objected that Stegerwald's method for determining the purchase price was too arbitrary, and the cabinet agreed that the decree should be rewritten again. Schlange had looked forward to this cabinet meeting with dread; Stegerwald would doubtless gain the chancellor's support, he told his chief of staff, because the Catholic Church was determined "to conquer the Protestant East." The meeting's outcome was a pleasant surprise that revived his loyalty to Brüning.[160]

A copy of the labor ministry's alarming draft decree was leaked to the Reichslandbund on the same day it was discussed by the cabinet, and agrarian lobbyists denounced it as a "Bolshevik" scheme for "expropriation." On 24 May Wilhelm von Gayl and Count Kalckreuth forwarded the draft decree to President Hindenburg with sharp attacks on "this new descent into state socialism," and Meissner promptly invited Gayl to draft counter-proposals for him to convey to Hindenburg in Neudeck. The DNVP Reichstag delegation wrote Hindenburg

---

158 Luther Tagesberichte of 7 and 13 May 1932, and von Wilmowsky to Reusch, 20 May 1932, *Quellen: Politik und Wirtschaft*, II:1442–43, 1448–49, 1467; conferences of 18 May 1932, *Kabinette Brüning*, III:2527–34; Pünder, *Politik*, 18 May 1932, p. 124; Brüning, *Memoiren*, p. 600; Brüning to Gerhard Ritter, 11 July 1952 (source of quotation), HUG FP 93.10/Box 26/Gerhard Ritter; Brüning to Ewald Löser, 15 December 1955, *Briefe*, I:458–59.

159 Udo Wengst, "Schlange-Schöningen, Ostsiedlung und die Demission der Regierung Brüning," *Geschichte in Wissenschaft und Unterricht*, 30 (1979): 539–41 (source of quotations); Schulz, *Von Brüning zu Hitler*, pp. 802–17; Schäffer diary, conversation with Stegerwald, 22 March 1932, NL Schäffer/19/398; chancellery note of 19 April and conferences of 6 May 1932, *Kabinette Brüning*, III:2461, 2492–95.

160 Cabinet meeting, 20 May 1932, *Kabinette Brüning*, III:2544–49 (see esp. n. 8); Karl Passarge diary, 20 May 1932 (source of quotation), *Quellen: Politik und Wirtschaft*, II:1462–63; Brüning, *Memoiren*, pp. 583–84; Wengst, "Schlange-Schöningen," pp. 543–45.

the next day that he must convene the Reichstag and deny Brüning the authority to issue any more emergency decrees, and it too attacked the draft decree as
"Bolshevism" on 27 May.[161] Brüning was indignant over suffering such attacks
because of a draft that had been rejected, but the cabinet had in fact decided
to abandon the policy of subsidizing grain producers. The chancellor himself
warned a deputation of landowners on 14 May that 500,000 hectares of arable
land must be auctioned off to restore profitability by restricting grain output,
and Schlange-Schöningen estimated that between one-fourth and one-third of
the large estates of East Elbia could not survive.[162] Such a policy guaranteed
strident opposition from landowners regardless of the details of implementation.

None of these policy disputes actually determined Brüning's fate. For some
time, most probably, he had retained office only because Hindenburg felt that he
deserved the month of June at least to try his hand at Lausanne. In mid-May,
however, Schleicher, Meissner, and Oskar von Hindenburg were overtaken by a
sense of urgency, and a change in course long intended took place hastily, with
remarkably little preparation. Perhaps, as Brüning suspected, they feared that he
would triumph at Lausanne, but they probably feared even more that it would
soon become impossible to strike a bargain with the right because of the SA ban,
Stegerwald's campaign for the forty-hour week, and the cabinet's homesteading
plans. The longer they associated with Brüning, the more closely they became
identified with the "Weimar system" that must be overthrown.[163] Brüning
himself precipitated the final breach when he decided that rumors about his fall,
mostly spread by Schleicher, had become so pervasive as to discourage foreign
governments from negotiating with him. As Meissner left for Neudeck on 24
May to explain to the President the contents of the next emergency decree,
Brüning commissioned him to declare that the chancellor refused to take responsibility for these unpopular measures or to represent Germany at international
conferences unless Hindenburg made a visible gesture of support for the
cabinet.[164]

According to Meissner's memoirs, Hindenburg greeted him in Neudeck with
the observation "that he encountered a wave of discontent and distrust of the

---

161 RLB circular of 21 May 1932, BAP/RLB/54/54–60; Gayl to Hindenburg, 24 May, and Kalck-
     reuth to Hindenburg, 24 May 1932, *Quellen: Politik und Wirtschaft*, II:1486–96; DNVP Reichs-
     tagsfraktion (Wilhelm Koch) to Hindenburg, 25 May 1932, BAP R601/19721/vol. 47/7–8; Muth,
     "Agrarpolitik und Parteipolitik," pp. 335–57; Schulz, *Von Brüning zu Hitler*, pp. 845–49.
162 See Brüning to Major Baur, 12 July 1957, HUG FP 93.10/Box 3/Georg Baur; chancellor's recep-
     tion for the Reichsgrundbesitzerverband, 14 May 1932, *Kabinette Brüning*, III:2518–21; and Diet-
     rich's testimonial for Schlange, 6 May 1947, NL Dietrich/466/17–18.
163 Note that Meissner became almost hysterical during the presidential campaign over allegations
     that he belonged to the SPD; see his correspondence with Reinhold Quaatz and the Dresden local
     of the DNVP, 4–7 March 1932, BAP R601/Reel 4/vol. 22/91–102.
164 Pünder memorandum, 18 May 1932, *Kabinette Brüning*, III:2534–35; Pünder, *Politik*, 22–24 May
     1932, pp. 124–25; report from the German embassy in Paris, 25 May 1932, *Quellen: Politik und
     Wirtschaft*, II:1497; Brüning, *Memoiren*, pp. 590–93; Brüning to Jakob Goldschmidt, 29 Novem-
     ber 1945, HUG FP 93.10/Box 12/Jakob Goldschmidt; Brüning to Graf Galen, 12 October 1948,
     in Müller, *Brüning Papers*, pp. 185–86.

intentions of the Reich government everywhere in the countryside, and that he was pressed by all circles in East Prussia to call patriotic men friendly to agriculture into the government." The memoirist professed surprise over this development, but he had actually collaborated with Schleicher to bombard the President with petitions and newspaper editorials from the DNVP, NSDAP, and Reichslandbund. Schleicher reiterated his criticism of the "procrastinator" in lengthy telephone conversations with Oskar von Hindenburg, and on 25 May the general notified Goebbels that Brüning would be dismissed any day now and replaced by his aristocratic party colleague Franz von Papen. Schleicher later confided to Meissner that he had turned against Brüning because only a government supported by the NSDAP could promote rearmament vigorously. He told Schwerin von Krosigk that "Brüning accomplished nothing, he could not make a decision."[165] Hugenberg told party colleagues that Schleicher had given Brüning the final shove without any coherent plan or systematic preparation of political forces, merely because his differences with Brüning had gradually reached a point that he considered intolerable. Hugenberg felt that all parties would have been much better served if Schleicher had postponed this crisis until autumn.[166]

On 26 May Meissner returned to Berlin and announced to the press that President Hindenburg demanded a major revision of the section on homesteads in the Fifth Emergency Decree and better treatment of war invalids. Meissner reported privately to Brüning that Hindenburg might agree nevertheless to sign this decree, but only in exchange for a rightward extension of the cabinet, not through the addition of Nazis but with "people like Goerdeler and Schleicher." Hindenburg refused to keep Groener in the cabinet as interior minister and demanded that the Center Party immediately form a coalition with the Nazis in the state of Prussia. Brüning replied that it had proved most difficult to reach agreement in Prussia; these negotiations would require months, if they succeeded at all, and the Lausanne Conference required a clarification of conditions in the Reich long before then. Meissner's news plunged Brüning into depression. "He is much inclined," Pünder noted in his diary, "to resign completely, also as foreign minister, and leave matters to the right." Within a few weeks, oddly enough, Brüning was telling Treviranus that he had nearly achieved a coalition with the Nazis in Prussia when Hindenburg toppled him; thus his memory quickly distorted the past as he sought to justify himself against the reproaches of the presidential entourage.[167]

---

165 Meissner, *Staatssekretär*, pp. 222–25; Goebbels, *Tagebücher*, 25 May 1932, II:173–74; Quaatz, *Tagebuch*, 25 May 1932, p. 191; Schwerin von Krosigk's interview of 24 April 1952, pp. 3–4, IfZ/ZS 145/Schwerin von Krosigk; Plehwe, *Schleicher*, pp. 185–89; Schulz, *Von Brüning zu Hitler*, pp. 851–54.

166 DNVP Reichstag delegation, 3 June 1932, and pp. 3–4 of 5 December 1932, NL Spahn/175.

167 Meissner's press release of 26 May 1932, *Schulthess' Europäischer Geschichtskalender 1932*, p. 91; Meissner to Brüning, 26 May 1932, *Kabinette Brüning*, III:2574–75; Meissner memorandum of 10 June 1932, in Vogelsang, *Reichswehr*, pp. 463–64; Pünder, *Politik*, 26 May 1932, p. 126; Treviranus to Wilhelm Regendanz, 22 June 1932, NL Schleicher/22/43–44.

Martin Schiele and Schlange-Schöningen made extraordinary efforts to defend the cabinet's agricultural policy to the President, and Hindenburg was actually persuaded by Schiele that the cabinet had done everything possible to restore profitability to grain production.[168] The headstrong Schlange-Schöningen proved less helpful to Brüning. After much agonizing, he decided on 27 May to employ all his personal influence with the President to save the chancellor. That morning he wrote Hindenburg to refute the accusation that the government intended to "expropriate" anyone. When Meissner phoned to warn that Hindenburg still opposed the homesteading decree, Schlange dispatched a grandiloquent manifesto that climaxed with the following prophecy:

> The strong will to internal colonization reveals the nation's drive to help itself and regain health. This will cannot be satisfied with promises; land and opportunities for action must be created. It permeates – thank God for this sign of vitality – all the classes and parties of our nation. In it there is undoubtedly a further development of the ideas of the Freiherr vom Stein, who was also combated as a revolutionary after the collapse of 1806 by certain circles struck with blindness, but who nevertheless created the foundation for revival and the psychological preconditions for liberation. If certain elements among big landowners . . . refuse to recognize the signs of the time, then I fear that they are digging their own grave, and that a great storm will one day sweep them away.

This was an honest expression of the Brüning cabinet's ideals but a clumsy gesture. Hindenburg took offense at the stern lecture from a junior minister and observed to Meissner that Schlange was welcome to resign if he wanted to. Brüning later concluded that Schlange had unintentionally strengthened Hindenburg's fear of "Bolshevik" tendencies in the cabinet.[169]

On the eve of his decisive interview with the President on 29 May, Brüning was disheartened by reports that Oskar von Hindenburg now ridiculed him and Stegerwald as "the trade unionists." Brüning received several warnings that he would be dismissed and told his closest aides that his "antennae" said the game was lost. He nevertheless put on a brave front at a reception for the foreign press, proclaiming that he would devote more attention to the struggle against unemployment, and observers sympathetic to Brüning dismissed the rumors of a crisis as more idle clamor by the divided remnants of the Harzburg Front.[170] Despite

---

168 Graf Kalckreuth to Hindenburg, 12 May, Schiele to Meissner, 24 May, and Hindenburg to Kalckreuth, 29 May 1932, BAP R601/19721/vol. 47/10–19; chancellery memorandum of 28 May 1932, *Kabinette Brüning*, III:2582–83.

169 Schlange-Schöningen's correspondence of 26/27 May and Passarge diary entries, *Quellen: Politik und Wirtschaft*, II:1498–1506 (quotation on p. 1505); Meissner, *Staatssekretär*, pp. 226–27; Wengst, "Schlange-Schöningen," pp. 545–48; Schulz, *Von Brüning zu Hitler*, pp. 855–56; Brüning to Pünder, 18 November 1947, NL Pünder/231/4; Brüning to Major Baur, 20 January 1949, HUG FP 93.10/Box 3/Georg Baur.

170 Pünder, *Politik*, 28–29 May 1932, pp. 126–27; Schäffer diary, conversations with Bülow on 2 June 1932 and Luther on 5 June, NL Schäffer/21/546–47, 552–53; *Schulthess' Europäischer Geschichtskalender 1932*, chancellor's press conference of 28 May 1932, p. 92; "Die Reichsregierung und ihre Gegner," *Kölnische Volkszeitung*, 28 May 1932, #147; Bredt, *Erinnerungen*, pp. 278–79; Newton to Simon, 31 May 1932, *DBFP*, III:144–47.

all the warnings, Brüning experienced shock, disbelief, and rage when the blow actually fell. The chancellor opened his private audience by declaring that the cabinet would soon regain popularity through diplomatic victories, but this would be possible only if the President put an end to the "shadow government" (*Nebenregierung*) of his personal friends and relied on the cabinet for advice. Brüning promised to continue negotiations for a right-of-center coalition in Prussia under Goerdeler but made no other concession to Hindenburg's demands. The President replied that he had heard that Brüning was unwilling to form any coalition with the right. Hindenburg then announced two decisions that he had written down on a large sheet of paper to guide his memory: This "unpopular" cabinet would not be allowed to issue any more emergency decrees, nor could it change its personnel. Brüning said that the President evidently wanted him to resign, and Hindenburg agreed. "At long last," the President explained, "I must go toward the right; the newspapers and the whole nation demand it. But you have always refused." Brüning could not resist observing that Hindenburg's reputation might suffer from such treatment of his loyal cabinet, contrary to the wishes of those who had voted for him so recently. Hindenburg ignored these thrusts as he rose to conclude the interview, declaring that "my conscience requires me to part with you." Almost as an afterthought, he invited Brüning to remain foreign minister, but he could offer no explanation of who the next chancellor would be or what policy he might follow. Brüning replied that his conscience would not allow him to take responsibility for foreign policy under such circumstances.[171]

Berlin then experienced two days of confusion. Schleicher had offered the chancellorship to Franz von Papen on 28 May, but Papen hesitated when Ludwig Kaas fiercely threatened to expel him from the Center Party. Kaas had visited Papen at his estate in the Saarland in mid-May and reproached him for intriguing against Brüning, but Papen replied that all current difficulties stemmed from Brüning's refusal in November 1931 to heed their joint advice to create a presidential cabinet completely independent of the Reichstag. Papen transmitted a wildly optimistic account of this discussion to Schleicher, who apparently concluded from it that he could secure the toleration of a Reichstag majority from the Nazi to the Center parties for a cabinet with the Catholic Papen as its figurehead and himself as defense minister. In fact Kaas was entirely loyal to Brüning, and Schleicher's choice of Papen infuriated most Centrists, who regarded it as an attempt to split their party.[172] While Papen agonized, Hans Luther gained

---

171 Brüning, *Memoiren*, pp. 597–600; Pünder, *Politik*, 29 May 1932, pp. 128–29 (source of quotation, based on Brüning's report). Hindenburg offered Meissner a similar account; see Meissner's memorandum of 10 June 1932 in Vogelsang, *Reichswehr*, pp. 464–65, and Meissner, *Staatssekretär*, p. 227. Contrast Schulz, *Von Brüning zu Hitler*, pp. 857–61, 873, who argues that Hindenburg did not want Brüning to resign.

172 Petzold, *Franz von Papen*, pp. 60–61; Bach, *Franz von Papen*, pp. 185–90; May, *Ludwig Kaas*, III:165–73; Papen, *Wahrheit*, pp. 182–89; Papen to Schleicher, 21 May 1932, in Matthias and Morsey, eds., *Ende der Parteien*, p. 423; Pünder, *Politik*, 31 May 1932, pp. 131–32; Schlange-Schöningen, *Am Tage danach*, p. 77; Meissner, *Staatssekretär*, pp. 230–31; Brüning to Käthe Mönnig, 23 July 1952, HUG FP 93.10/Box 22/Käthe Mönnig.

audience with the President on 30 May to argue that the stability of the mark required the immediate promulgation of the Fifth Emergency Decree, and Hindenburg asked Brüning to remain in office long enough to implement it. Brüning indignantly rejected this attempt to saddle him with the responsibility for unpopular actions before dismissing him, and all his ministers agreed that the President's irresponsible conduct left them no choice but to resign. Brüning later recalled that his last statement to Hindenburg when he submitted his resignation was a stern warning that "any attempt to restore the monarchy by unconstitutional means would destroy the monarchy forever, and would force me to oppose him on constitutional grounds."[173]

Hindenburg won no applause as he conferred with party leaders on 30/31 May. Hitler confirmed the vague promise already issued to Schleicher of "fruitful cooperation" (*erspriessliche Zusammenarbeit*) with any cabinet that lifted the SA ban and ordered new Reichstag elections, but he refused to put anything in writing. Even Hugenberg warned the President not to trust the Nazi leader's word, and he advised party colleagues to have nothing to do with the next cabinet. Only Dingeldey actually endorsed Schleicher's strategy. The leaders of the Business Party implored Hindenburg not to allow new Reichstag elections, and all the other party leaders expressed bewilderment and regret over Brüning's fall. Meissner argued that the Reichstag was about to topple Brüning anyway, but politicians ranging from Breitscheid to Westarp denied this emphatically. They saw no justification for dismissing a chancellor who had recently won a vote of confidence, and they warned that the President's action would radicalize the working class and alienate foreign governments.[174] Westarp told Hindenburg that Brüning had done everything possible to move toward the right without driving the SPD into opposition, which no government could afford to do without ironclad guarantees of support from the Nazis. Hindenburg himself said little in these interviews, but Meissner replied that "the change was necessary in order to make possible a more firmly and clearly nationalist policy and to liberate the cabinet from the influence of the trade unions." After the audience Meissner pursued Westarp into the hallway to reiterate that Brüning's economic policy had been confused because "the influence of the trade unions and Stegerwald hindered thorough measures."[175]

The bewilderment over Hindenburg's conduct mounted when the obscure Franz von Papen (who held no office since losing his Landtag seat in April) finally accepted the chancellorship on 31 May. Brüning and many other experienced

---

173 Luther to Meissner, 30 May 1932, BAP R601/19721/vol. 47/30–31; cabinet meeting and Pünder memorandum of 30 May 1932, *Kabinette Brüning*, III:2585–88; Pünder, *Politik*, 30 May 1932, pp. 129–31; Quaatz, *Tagebuch*, 28–30 May 1932, pp. 191–92; Brüning to Norman Ebbutt, 11 June 1946 (source of quotation), in Müller, *Brüning Papers*, pp. 181–82.

174 Meissner's notes of 30–31 May 1932, in Hubatsch, *Hindenburg*, pp. 320–23; Quaatz memorandum of 1 June 1932, *Tagebuch*, pp. 192–93; DNVP Reichstag delegation, 3 June 1932, NL Spahn/175; Keil, *Erlebnisse*, II:446–48.

175 Westarp memorandum, 1 June 1932, *Quellen: Politik und Wirtschaft*, II:1519–21.

politicians tried to warn Schleicher that the Nazis would resume their violent intimidation tactics as soon as the SA ban was lifted and then go over into flamboyant opposition to the government as soon as Reichstag elections strengthened them further. Schleicher and Papen ignored such warnings, however, as they assembled a "cabinet of gentlemen" congenial to the President (seven of the ten ministers were noblemen). Most of the new ministers were not only reactionary in outlook but quite inexperienced as well, cavaliers who believed that their finesse and good breeding would enable them to clear all the hurdles before which Brüning had balked. Even François-Poncet, who was not Brüning's friend, reported gloomily to Paris that Germany now had a "nationalist government, supported by militaristic and reactionary elements, in place of a liberal cabinet, willingly tolerated" by parliament. Brüning was justified to label this "presidential" cabinet a grotesque caricature of his form of government.[176]

176 Schäffer diary, 2 June 1932, conversations with Dietrich and Pünder, NL Schäffer/21/543–44; Pünder, *Politik*, 7 June 1932, pp. 134–35; Staatspartei Vorstand, 12 June 1932, *Quellen: Politik und Wirtschaft*, II:1533–35; François-Poncet to Herriot, 12 July 1932, *Documents Diplomatiques Français, 1932–1939. Serie I*, (Paris, 1964-) (hereafter cited as *DDF*), I:18; Brüning, *Memoiren*, pp. 607–09; Brüning, "The Essence of Democracy," Dartmouth College lecture #2 of March 1937, pp. 33–35, HUG FP 93.45; Bracher, *Auflösung*, pp. 465–80; Schulz, *Von Brüning zu Hitler*, pp. 866–69; Dorpalen, *Hindenburg*, pp. 329–35; Winkler, *Weimar*, pp. 474–80.

6

The Destruction of the Rule of Law

On a rational level, Brüning knew after his dismissal that he should try to pre-serve some foundation for cooperation between the Center Party and the Presi-dent. When his cabinet last met, Wilhelm Groener rejoiced at the prospect of a public debate over Hindenburg's character and methods, but Brüning declared that "despite everything Hindenburg is the only rallying point that the people still have." He also advised Bülow, Schwerin von Krosigk, and Erwin Planck to accept office under Papen in order to preserve continuity in government policy.[1] Brüning was so angry with Hindenburg, however, that he could barely control himself, and this anger warped his judgment during the last months of the Weimar Republic.

6.1. The Failure of Presidential Government

Brüning suffered a physical collapse after his rupture with Hindenburg and required two days of bed rest. He felt that the President's farewell letter con-tained "the weakest expression of gratitude that had ever been conveyed to any minister in the history of Prussia and Germany." After rousing himself to pay the proper farewell visits to foreign embassies, he returned to find Oskar von Hindenburg in his official residence, preparing to move in the belongings of his family as the presidential palace underwent renovation. Brüning interpreted this simple misunderstanding as a calculated insult. When he heard that Oskar's wife told friends that "we are so glad to be rid of the plebeians at last," he resolved to break off all social relations with the Hindenburg family.[2] Brüning's rage infected his closest associates. Hermann Dietrich suffered a physical collapse lasting weeks, and Ludwig Kaas seethed with indignation during his interview with the President on 31 May. He then took to bed as well, despairing of

---

1 Schlange-Schöningen, *Am Tage danach*, p. 73 (source of quotation); Treviranus, *Ende von Weimar*, pp. 313–14; Brüning, *Memoiren*, p. 614; Pünder, *Politik*, 7 June 1932, pp. 134–35.
2 Manuscript memoirs, pp. 329–34, HUG FP 93.4; compare President Hindenburg to Brüning, 31 May 1932, *Ursachen und Folgen*, VIII:527, and Oskar von Hindenburg to Pünder, 18 June 1932, NL Pünder/6/137.

Germany's future. Only after two weeks did Brüning recover sufficiently to move out of the chancellery and into modest lodgings in St. Hedwig's Catholic Hospital, and he then found solace in an automobile tour of southern Germany with Friedrich Dessauer. He continued to suffer from acute insomnia, however, and Schleicher exploited this fact by telling journalists that people who could not sleep were useless in politics.[3]

Brüning's anger apparently reflected a powerful desire to regard Hindenburg as the father he had never known. These feelings erupted a few years later when Brüning explained to a friend how Hindenburg had misunderstood his duty as head of state:

> The head of state and the prime minister must agree on an objective and nonpartisan policy and course of action. In public the premier must struggle and, as Bismarck said, "descend into the mud." The head of state sends him into combat. He watches carefully over his minister's actions. If he fails, he encourages him; if he becomes too combative and tempestuous, he warns and restrains him. If people try to stab him in the back, he protects him. He must be a father to him and the country. He rejoices in the successes of his minister. He spurs him on if he encounters difficulties. He surrounds him alone with the atmosphere of absolute confidence. Only if he sees that the minister is seriously jeopardizing the national inheritance does he call [crossed out: "another of his sons"] someone else to save that inheritance.[4]

In the last sentence a deep emotional need received such naked expression that the writer became embarrassed. Brüning's anger therefore deepened when he learned that Hindenburg was unaffected by their rupture. The President won recruits for the Papen cabinet with the same tearful appeals not to abandon an old man in his hour of need that had won Brüning over in March 1930. When Pünder and Hans Schäffer appeared for their farewell audiences, he expressed polite regret that Brüning was so upset but could not understand why; after all, no cabinet could last forever. A few weeks later Hindenburg asked Pünder's successor, Erwin Planck, "Is the little guy [*der Kleine*] still mad at me?" Brüning had no reason to be, Hindenburg added: "He promised me back then to form a rightist cabinet quickly, but then he would not do it." Only now did Brüning perceive that the field marshal regarded nobody outside a few score families of the landed aristocracy as peers with whom concepts like friendship or personal loyalty had meaning.[5]

On 4 June the Papen cabinet formally announced the dissolution of the

---

3 Brüning, *Memoiren*, pp. 610, 624; manuscript memoirs, pp. 332–39; Pünder, *Politik*, 15 June 1932, p. 137; Dietrich to Höpker-Aschoff, 15 June 1932, NL Dietrich/223/63; May, *Ludwig Kaas*, II:660–61, and III:162, 172–73.

4 Brüning to Dannie Heineman, 15 September 1937, p. 4, HUG FP 93.10/Box 14/D.N. Heineman.

5 Schäffer diary, presidential audience of 8 June 1932, published in Wandel, *Schäffer*, pp. 328–29, and conversation with Erwin Planck, 6 July 1932 (source of quotation), NL Schäffer/21/647; Pünder, *Politik*, 15 June 1932, pp. 137–38; Dorpalen, *Hindenburg*, pp. 333–35; Gessler, *Reichswehrpolitik*, pp. 344–45.

Reichstag, scheduling new elections for the end of July. It also launched an inept campaign to influence public opinion with a shrill manifesto that depicted Brüning as a disastrous failure who had allowed the "welfare state," "state social-ism," "cultural Bolshevism," and atheism to bring Germany to its knees. Brüning later observed that "such things had not been seen in the last hundred years of Prussian and German history. The last remnants of chivalry [*ritterlicher Gesinnung*] in politics were finally destroyed. The Reich President and Reich government stooped to the level of Goebbels' demagoguery."[6] The former cabinet ministers replied with an honest defense of their fiscal policy but stretched the truth by declaring that they had completed all preparations to employ 600,000 people in public works. To Papen's claim to champion a "Chris-tian state" they replied that "the Christian conception of the state that we rep-resent regards it as our foremost duty to distribute unavoidable sacrifices in the most equitable way possible. The whole country must see to it that our efforts to this end are continued for the welfare of the whole nation and not the special interests of parties and small groups."[7]

Brüning advised party colleagues that he should play no role in the Reichstag election campaign so as to relieve them of the burden of defending his austerity measures. They sensed a popular backlash against the President, however, that could strengthen their party. Kaas encouraged Catholic journalists to label Papen a second "Ephialtes" (the ancient Greek who betrayed the Spartans' defensive position at Thermopylae to the Persian army), and the epithet achieved an impressive echo. On 8 June the Center Party executive committee decided to seek "revenge for Brüning" in this campaign, and the ex-chancellor soon became the party's most demanded public speaker. That same day Fritz Schäffer of the BVP told the press that Brüning's fall was "a sin" and "a disastrous failure of statecraft" that opened the door to a "one-party dictatorship by Hitler." Thus Brüning became more popular as victim of the President's caprice than he had been as head of government.[8] The ailing Kaas appealed to Brüning to take over as party chairman but was persuaded to retain office on condition that Brüning and Joseph Joos would do most of the actual work of running the party. Brüning held no party office other than his Reichstag mandate, but activists in the Center Party and BVP looked to him as their "leader" when Kaas left Germany in late June for extended convalescent leave.[9] Outrage over the appointment of Papen was not confined to Catholic voters. Communism suddenly revived in popular-

6 Government manifesto in *Quellen: Wirtschaft und Politik*, II:1524–25; Brüning, manuscript memoirs, p. 332, HUG FP 93.4.

7 Declaration by the former cabinet, 6 June 1932, *Quellen: Politik und Wirtschaft*, II:1525–27; Trevi-ranus, *Ende von Weimar*, pp. 333–34; Brüning, *Memoiren*, p. 612. Compare pp. 261–62 above.

8 Brüning, *Memoiren*, pp. 615–16; *Zentrumsprotokolle*, 1 June 1932, pp. 572–75; Morsey, "Deutsche Zentrumspartei," pp. 306–13; Detlef Junker, *Die Deutsche Zentrumspartei und Hitler. Ein Beitrag zur Problematik des politischen Katholizismus in Deutschland* (Stuttgart, 1969), pp. 72–73; Altendorfer, *Fritz Schäffer*, pp. 601–05. See also Hofmann, *Erinnerungen*, p. 64; Heinrich Köhler, *Lebenserinnerungen*, p. 308; and the description of a Cologne campaign rally in *Kölnische Volkszeitung*, 4 July 1932, #184.

9 May, *Ludwig Kaas*, II:660–61; Morsey, *Untergang*, pp. 25–31; Schwend, "BVP," pp. 462–64; Fritz Schäffer memoir, "So ward ein grosses Reich zerstört," p. 68, NL Fritz Schäffer/55.

Brüning alongside the founder of the Center Party, Ludwig Windhorst, in a campaign poster from July 1932. The caption: "One will unites us: Justice and bread for everyone in the national state. Vote for List 4, the Center." (Bundesarchiv Koblenz 2/23/16)

ity after months of decline, and the leaders of the SPD and KPD experienced unprecedented pressure from below to form a united front against this "fascist" government. Joseph Goebbels concluded within a few days of Papen's appointment that his party must break with this chancellor soon to retain popularity.[10]

10 Henryk Skrzypczak, "Kanzlerwechsel und Einheitsfront. Abwehrreaktionen der Arbeiterbewegung auf die Machtübergabe an Franz von Papen," *Internationale wissenschaftliche Korrespondenz zur Geschichte der Arbeiterbewegung*, 18 (1982): 482–99; Bahne, *KPD*, pp. 23–30; Winkler, *Katastrophe*, pp. 614–26; Goebbels, *Tagebücher*, 2–5 June 1932, II:178–80.

The new government confirmed many popular fears with its first major emergency decree on 14 June. Papen mostly implemented the austerity measures planned by Brüning, but he dropped any support for peasant homesteads in East Elbia and virtually abolished the system of unemployment insurance by decreeing that all who lost their jobs would become subject to a means test after just six weeks (instead of thirteen weeks in Brüning's version). The leaders of the Free and Christian trade unions, Center Party, and SPD all agreed that this decree represented a drastic departure from Brüning's effort to divide material burdens fairly. The new cabinet's popularity sank further when it rescinded the SA ban two days later, causing an immediate upsurge in political violence.[11] These developments plunged Brüning into depression as he perceived the disastrous consequences of his fall. Hans Schäffer and Treviranus were both dismayed to find the ex-chancellor obsessed with Hindenburg's "betrayal" and full of wild theories about who had conspired to turn the President against him. They sought to rekindle his interest in Germany's future by arguing that the time might soon return for a close alliance among the Center Party, Reichswehr, and President, but Brüning merely expressed his contempt for the new cabinet by alleging that Schleicher intended to make the Crown Prince the next head of state. Brüning termed Prince Wilhelm "a very erratic and therefore unreliable man" and observed that "the Hohenzollern family in general must be getting degenerate [*muss überhaupt schwer belastet sein*], otherwise they would not be feuding so."[12]

On the campaign trail Brüning cautiously advocated a revival of parliamentary influence:

> The goal must be to avoid under any circumstances in the coming years a return of the abuses and exaggerations of parliamentarism and of the democratic system which we sometimes had in the years before 1930. It will be just as necessary, however, to activate a reasonable parliament again and thereby guarantee that the free will of a free people has the necessary influence on the development of the nation. . . . Even government with emergency decrees requires that one take account of other opinions or have discussions to ensure that such decrees are not rejected by the Reichstag.

Brüning endorsed most of the austerity measures in Papen's decree but insisted that landless sons of peasants from the west and south had the right to partition the bankrupt estates of East Elbia. He also rejected Papen's insinuations that no true Christian would cooperate with the SPD: "We took the course of strengthening the sense of responsibility [for the state] wherever it was present." Brüning

---

11 Winkler, *Katastrophe*, pp. 626–28; Altendorfer, *Fritz Schäffer*, pp. 612–21; Pünder, *Politik*, 15 June 1932, pp. 137–38; *Zentrumsprotokolle*, 22 June 1932, p. 577; *Zentralblatt der christlichen Gewerkschaften*, 1 July 1932, pp. 169–70, 175; ADGB Bundesausschuss, 9/10 September 1932, *Quellen: Gewerkschaften*, pp. 676–82.

12 Schäffer diary, conversations with Brüning, 7 and 30 June 1932, NL Schäffer/21/564–72, 624–27 (quotation on p. 567); Treviranus to Wilhelm Regendanz, 22 June 1932, NL Schleicher/22/43–44.

scrupulously avoided any attack on the President, but supporters like Stegerwald, Joos, Hermann Dietrich, and Fritz Schäffer proclaimed that a passive and gullible Hindenburg had fallen under the sway of the most reactionary and selfish industrialists and East Elbian landowners.[13]

The new cabinet acquired no popularity even when reparations were finally abolished. After three weeks of negotiations at Lausanne, France agreed on 8 July to cancel reparations in exchange for a promise by Germany to pay three billion marks after three years. That promise was never kept, but it aroused concern in Germany at the time. Brüning had intended to make any final payment contingent on a loan to Germany of an equivalent sum, and he reproached the new cabinet with some reason for departing from his policy never to do anything which indicated that Germany had the economic capacity to pay reparations. Finance Minister Schwerin von Krosigk sought, for example, to break the deadlock in Lausanne by offering to support a French plan for financial assistance to the countries of the Danube basin, but Premier Herriot exclaimed: "Then I must have misunderstood before when the German delegation declared that it could pay nothing!"[14] Papen himself made a dramatic offer, against the advice of his aides, of a military alliance with France to be sealed by an exchange of general staff officers, a proposal that outraged the British and aroused French distrust. He then offered a final payment of three billion marks after three years in exchange for French recognition of Germany's "parity of rights" in armaments, but Herriot again seized on this as admission of Germany's capacity to pay. Papen made a bad personal impression on the French delegation despite his graceful French and connection through marriage to French nobility, and Germany was soon compelled to offer the final payment in exchange for nothing. Papen's delegation was pelted with rotten eggs when it returned to Berlin. The nationalist press denounced the Lausanne accord as hopelessly inadequate, while moderate papers gave Brüning the credit for it. Brüning himself was tempted to denounce the pact, but Hans Schäffer persuaded him to embrace it instead as the fruit of his own diplomacy, a view propagated by Schäffer in his influential new position as general manager of the Ullstein press.[15]

13 Brüning's speech to a rally in Cologne, *Kölnische Volkszeitung*, 4 July 1932, #184; remarks by Dietrich to State Party leaders, 12 June 1932, *Quellen: Politik und Wirtschaft*, II:1533–35; Dietrich's circular to party colleagues in Baden, 23 July 1932, NL Dietrich/223/237–38; speeches by Stegerwald and Joos in Deutsche Zentrumspartei, "Um den sozialen Volksstaat. Die christliche Arbeiterschaft im Wahlkampf 1932" (proceedings of a rally in Essen on 29 June 1932), pp. 16–22, 28–30; Altendorfer, *Fritz Schäffer*, pp. 601–05.

14 Schmidt, *Statist auf diplomatischer Bühne*, pp. 243–44 (source of quotation); Brüning's speech of 11 July 1932, *Kölnische Volkszeitung*, 14 July 1932, #191; Brüning to Hans Berger, 21 January 1951, HUG FP 93.10/Box 3/Hans Berger; Schulz, *Von Brüning zu Hitler*, pp. 907–16.

15 Brüning, *Memoiren*, pp. 616–17; Kessler, *Tagebücher*, conversation with François-Poncet, 1 July 1932, pp. 673–74; survey of the German press in François-Poncet to Herriot, 12 July 1932, *DDF*, I:17–21; Schäffer diary, conversation with Brüning, 9 July 1932, NL Schäffer/21/653–54; Rolfs, *Sorcerer's Apprentice*, pp. 105–26; Bennett, *German Rearmament*, pp. 176–78; Kent, *Spoils of War*, pp. 368–72.

The appointment of Papen also isolated Germany at the Geneva Disarmament Conference. The French, British, American, and Soviet governments all expressed grave concern over the triumph of "militarism" in Berlin. Americans in particular recalled Papen's clumsy efforts to sabotage their munitions industry as military attaché in Washington during the Great War, and Ambassador Sackett decided immediately after Brüning's fall that the United States could do nothing more to help Germany now that it was ruled by Junkers and generals. Against the advice of the foreign office, Schleicher nevertheless decided in July to drop the pose of supporting worldwide disarmament at Geneva and to demand instead military parity for Germany. The German delegation promptly forfeited all sympathy from the British and Americans.[16]

Papen and his interior minister, Wilhelm von Gayl, decided soon after the Lausanne Conference to seek prestige by deposing the Prussian state government. Otto Braun had left Germany for convalescent leave after the heartbreaking loss of his parliamentary majority, and his cabinet was open to discussion of a voluntary transfer of police power to a nonpartisan Reich commissar, as foreseen in Brüning's old contingency plans. Papen decided instead to blame Carl Severing for the political violence unleashed by the SA, remove the Prussian cabinet by force on 20 July, and purge all Social Democrats from the Prussian bureaucracy. Brüning was outraged by this misuse of Article 48 against a state government that had always done its best to preserve order. His campaign rally in Munich the next day became a protest rally with the leaders of the Bavarian People's Party against this effort to impose "dictatorship" on the states. Brüning praised Severing in particular as "a man who has devoted fourteen years of his life to struggle against Communism and for the state like hardly anyone else." He nevertheless implored friends in organized labor not to proclaim a general strike but instead to challenge Papen in the courts. The SPD and trade unions were too demoralized to take any bold action, but as Brüning feared, Papen's blow against Prussia had a catastrophic impact on class tensions and drove a wedge between the three south German governments and Berlin.[17]

The Reichstag elections at the end of July revealed the gulf separating the government from public opinion. The Nazi Party gained a disheartening 37 percent of the vote. The Center/BVP share increased slightly to 16 percent, an impressive achievement under the circumstances, but the only other party to gain was the KPD with 15 percent; the SPD and DNVP suffered moderate losses, while all other groups shrank to insignificance. These returns created an ago-

16 German ambassadors' reports of 31 May–6 June 1932, *ADAP*, XX:221–23, 245–48; reports to Sir John Simon of 31 May–4 June 1932, *DBFP*, III:144–48, 151–52; Burke, *Frederic Sackett*, pp. 225–35; Bennett, *German Rearmament*, pp. 170–207; Schulz, *Von Brüning zu Hitler*, pp. 901–06, 915–16.

17 Speeches by Brüning and Fritz Schäffer in *Kölnische Volkszeitung*, 22 July 1932, #199 (source of quotation); Brüning, *Memoiren*, pp. 618–20; Schäffer memorandum of 20 July 1932, NL Schäffer/32/231–36, and conversations with Brüning and Erwin Planck, 22 and 28 July and 28 October 1932, NL Schäffer/21/677–80, 694, and 23/946–48; Winkler, *Katastrophe*, pp. 646–80; Schulz, *Von Brüning zu Hitler*, pp. 918–33; Harsch, *Social Democracy*, pp. 190–202; Hömig, *Das preussische Zentrum*, pp. 265–73; Besson, *Württemberg*, pp. 274–94; Heimars, *Unitarismus*, pp. 314–22.

nizing dilemma for the Center Party because the Nazis and Communists together commanded a parliamentary majority; the only way this Reichstag could function would be through cooperation between Nazis and Centrists.[18] Brüning later observed that the "senseless Reichstag dissolution of June 1932" was the crucial turning point in the collapse of the Weimar Republic, because it exposed the moderate parties to an impossible election campaign when they had no successes to show for all the painful sacrifices that they had accepted. He went through life telling himself that democracy could have been saved if only he had remained in office until August, because "then all the successes would have been visible and undeniable, and the wild agitation would have had no foundation. The experiment would have led to complete success, not just for the emergency at that moment but for Germany's future political development."[19] He exaggerated, no doubt, but the results of the Lausanne Conference would have appeared far more significant to the voters if Brüning had remained in office and launched Dietrich's billion-mark program for public works. The Nazis would also have mobilized less support if the SA ban had remained in effect.

Brüning decided soon after the election to seek to revive parliamentary government by making Hitler the chancellor of a cabinet bound to a formal coalition between the Center and Nazi parties. Hitler must not be authorized to issue presidential emergency decrees, he insisted, and reliable non-Nazis must control the defense ministry and Prussian police. Brüning quickly persuaded all leaders of the Center Party and BVP to support this plan and conveyed the suggestion to Otto Meissner by 4 August. Brüning agreed to postpone any overture to the Nazis, however, when emissaries of Papen appealed for the cabinet to be given a chance to negotiate with them first.[20] Thus Brüning again created a dilemma for the Nazi leadership, as he had in April with his terms for a coalition in Prussia. Goebbels reflected again in his diary that his party's only chance for any share of power might be to accept the straitjacket of a parliamentary coalition with the wily Centrists. Once again, however, Schleicher approached Hitler with a more attractive offer, suggesting on 6 August that Hitler form a "presidential" cabinet authorized to issue emergency decrees, with Gregor Strasser as interior minister of both Prussia and the Reich. Schleicher trusted that he could discipline the Nazis as defense minister, but the jubilant Nazi leadership considered this a sure

18 See Childers, *Nazi Voter*, pp. 202–09; Falter, *Hitlers Wähler*, pp. 139–46, 186–93, 211–30; and Bracher, *Auflösung*, pp. 529–36.
19 Brüning to Hans von Raumer, 1 May 1947, HUG FP 93.10/Box 26/Hans von Raumer; Brüning to Kurt Kluge, 8 November 1947, in Müller, *Brüning Papers*, pp. 190–91. Compare his campaign speech in *Kölnische Volkszeitung*, 4 July 1932, #184.
20 Brüning, *Memoiren*, p. 621; Quaatz, *Tagebuch*, conversation with Meissner, 4 August 1932, p. 199; Werner Best's report on a conversation with Fritz Bockius of the Hessian Center on 6 August 1932, in Schulz, *Von Brüning zu Hitler*, p. 945; Schäffer diary, conversation with Brüning, 11 August 1932, NL Schäffer/22/737–38; Brüning's remarks to Ambassador Rumbold, reported on 14 June 1933, *DBFP*, V:353; Fritz Schäffer memoir, "So ward ein grosses Reich zerstört," pp. 64–65, NL Fritz Schäffer/55; Junker, *Zentrumspartei*, pp. 78–86; Morsey, *Untergang*, pp. 56–58; Altendorfer, *Fritz Schäffer*, pp. 648–52.

formula for the total conquest of power. Fortunately, President Hindenburg vetoed Schleicher's plan, refusing to consider the man he called "the corporal" for the chancellorship on any terms.[21]

Franz von Papen now sought to consolidate his hold on the chancellorship by setting an ambush for Hitler. On 13 August he lured the Nazi leader into unguarded praise of Mussolini's violent methods in a private conversation and then ushered him into a brief audience with the President. Hitler asked politely to be appointed chancellor, and Hindenburg politely declined, but Papen merged the contents of these conversations into a press release modeled on Bismarck's Ems Despatch. The public was informed that Hitler had stormed into the President's office to demand "total power over the state," a violent one-party dictatorship, and encountered an angry rebuff.[22] This press release could have been the signal for a counter-offensive against the Nazis similar to that issued by Brüning with the SA ban, but now there were no political parties, state governments, or trade unions ready to follow the chancellor in a struggle against the extremists. The leaders of the Center Party, for example, did not know whom to believe when Nazi colleagues told them that "the reactionaries" had defamed Hitler to prevent the formation of a parliamentary majority; Stegerwald actually found Hitler more credible than Papen.[23] Seeking to consolidate his hold on the chancellorship, Papen had effectively sabotaged Schleicher's detente with the Nazis but did not have any other policy to put in its place.

Brüning forged ahead with his effort to achieve parliamentary cooperation with the NSDAP. He conferred with Kaas and Fritz Schäffer in Munich on 14 August, and they authorized him to meet with Gregor Strasser in Tübingen three days later. Now Brüning and Strasser did become allies, as Brüning promised the Center Party's support if Strasser could persuade Hitler to head a parliamentary cabinet with Schleicher as defense minister and another non-Nazi, perhaps Carl Goerdeler, as Reich commissar in Prussia. Strasser arranged a follow-up meeting a week later where Hitler agreed to delay any confidence motion against Papen and seemed to accept Brüning's other conditions for a partnership. The ex-chancellor therefore commissioned his party colleagues

---

21 Goebbels, *Tagebücher*, 1–7 August 1932, II:211–17; Quaatz, *Tagebuch*, 10 August 1932, pp. 200–201; Dorpalen, *Hindenburg*, pp. 349–51. Some memoirists later reported that Hindenburg spoke in private of Hitler as the "Austrian corporal" or "Bohemian corporal," but Oskar insisted that his father had only referred to "the corporal": See Henry Turner, *Hitler's Thirty Days to Power: January 1933* (Reading, Mass., 1996), pp. 12, 194.

22 Presidential reception and press release, 13 August 1932, and cabinet meeting of 15 August, *Akten der Reichskanzlei. Das Kabinett von Papen*, ed. Karl-Heinz Minuth, 2 vols. (Boppard am Rhein, 1989), I:391–92, 398–99; Dorpalen, *Hindenburg*, pp. 349–57; Pünder, *Politik*, conversation with Planck on 17 August 1932, pp. 140–41; Goebbels, *Tagebücher*, 12–13 August 1932, II:223–25. Planck told Hans Schäffer on 22 August (NL Schäffer/22/783) that Hitler had aroused Papen's disgust by demanding a violent campaign to "annihilate" the Marxists. When Papen replied that such methods were impossible in a *Kulturstaat*, that even Mussolini had consolidated his rule with little bloodshed, Hitler exclaimed that Mussolini had killed 5,000 Marxists but kept this fact secret.

23 Hitler to Meissner and Planck, 13 August 1932, and Planck's reply of 14 August, *Kabinett von Papen*, I:393–97; *Zentrumsprotokolle*, meetings of 29 August and 12 September 1932, pp. 581–87.

Dessauer, Thomas Esser, Joos, and Eugen Bolz to seek agreement on a joint economic and social program with the Nazi Reichstag delegation, and the Nazis behaved with perfect decorum when the Reichstag convened on 30 August. Centrists helped to elect Hermann Göring president of the Reichstag in accord with the tradition that this office should go to the largest delegation, and the Reichstag adjourned itself until 12 September so that the coalition talks could proceed. In later years Brüning sometimes argued that he had never sought to make Hitler chancellor, that these talks merely sought to deflect the Nazis from introducing a motion to impeach Hindenburg, but the other sources suggest that the whole Center Party leadership did hope at least briefly for the success of these negotiations.[24]

Brüning's plan entailed grave risks, however, and he soon backed away from it. Papen was doubtless correct to tell his cabinet that Hitler should not become head of government under any conditions, because this generalissimo of a private army would soon evade any supervision if granted legal authority as Reich chancellor.[25] Unfortunately, Papen later forgot this truth. Hitler probably never intended to form a genuine coalition with the Center, just to exert pressure on the presidential entourage. During these coalition talks he ordered the SA to intensify its street violence in an effort to make Germany ungovernable, and while insisting on the utmost secrecy for any discussion of a parliamentary coalition, on 23 August he publicly declared his solidarity with three Stormtroopers from Potempa who had been sentenced to death for an especially brutal killing. Hitler's dominant impulse was to rely on intimidation in the struggle for power.[26] Rudolf Hilferding sternly warned colleagues in the SPD and Center Party that the Nazis would never revive parliamentary government, and he even urged toleration for Papen as the only way to prevent a Hitler dictatorship.[27] These arguments soon made an impression on Brüning, especially when Hilferding warned that the Centrists working on the coalition platform had succumbed to the influence of their Nazi counterparts. His party colleagues, Brüning later recalled, had all but agreed to support a motion to impeach Hindenburg that might well have won a two-thirds majority and opened the door to Hitler's election as President. On 31 August Brüning therefore sent word to Papen through Carl Goerdeler that he had redirected his efforts toward per-

---

24 Brüning, *Memoiren*, pp. 622–25; *Zentrumsprotokolle*, 29 August 1932, pp. 583–84; Pünder, *Politik*, 31 August 1932, p. 144; Schäffer diary, 1 September 1932, NL Schäffer/22/825–27; Morsey, *Untergang*, pp. 61–64; Junker, *Zentrumspartei*, pp. 96–106; Altendorfer, *Fritz Schäffer*, pp. 654–58; Sailer, *Eugen Bolz*, pp. 95–96, 182–83. Contrast Brüning to Maier-Hultschin, 26 March 1947, HUG FP 93.10/Box 22/Johannes Maier (3); Brüning to Otto Schmidt-Hannover, 20 October 1948, Box 30/Otto Schmidt-Hannover; and Brüning to Joseph Joos, 23 December 1948, Box 16/Joos.

25 *Kabinett von Papen*, meeting of 15 August 1932, I:400.

26 Goebbels, *Tagebücher*, 25–29 August 1932, II:230–33; Paul Schulz memoir of 21 July 1951, in Kissenkoetter, *Gregor Strasser*, p. 202; Schulz, *Von Brüning zu Hitler*, pp. 966–71; Fest, *Hitler*, pp. 473–78.

27 Winkler, *Katastrophe*, pp. 722–25; Keil, *Erlebnisse*, II:455–59.

suading the Nazis to adjourn the Reichstag for six months to give the presidential cabinet "a fair chance" (he used the English phrase) to revive the economy.[28]

Brüning failed, however, to prevent a dangerous collision between the government and the Reichstag. When the ex-chancellor learned that Papen had won the President's authorization to hold new elections as often as necessary to crush any parliamentary opposition, he dispatched Max Habermann to the defense ministry on 7 September to warn that Hindenburg might be impeached if he violated the spirit of the constitution in this fashion. Brüning persuaded himself that Papen would heed this warning and avoid confrontation, so he ignored the chancellor's scheduled speech at the Reichstag session of 12 September to dine with Hans Schäffer, an uncharacteristically frivolous act. While Germany stumbled into a new political crisis, they engaged in a remarkably optimistic discussion of the long-term evolution of social democracy away from Marxist dogma.[29] In Brüning's absence the KPD secured unanimous approval for a change in the scheduled order of business to allow an immediate vote on a motion of no confidence. Not even the DNVP was willing to lift a finger to spare Papen this embarrassment. Göring then ignored the chancellor's arrival to begin the confidence vote. A livid Papen threw his insurance policy, a presidential decree dissolving parliament, onto the speaker's podium and stalked out of the chamber as his government lost by the humiliating margin of 512 to 42.[30] Schleicher urged the cabinet to postpone new elections indefinitely, and Hindenburg had authorized such action, but a second warning from Brüning that the President might be impeached persuaded Papen that the time was not ripe to violate the constitution. Elections were scheduled for 6 November.[31]

Brüning soon noted signs of demoralization in his party as it entered the fourth national election campaign of the year. His semi-clandestine negotiations with Nazi leaders spread confusion among grass-roots activists in the Center Party and BVP, who experienced the Nazis as violent thugs disrupting all rallies by opponents, not amusingly inexperienced colleagues on parliamentary committees. These activists were compelled to organize a "Popular Front" (*Volksfront*) militia for self-defense (modeled on the "Iron Front" of the SPD and Free Unions), and they felt that any negotiations with Nazis conflicted with the goal

---

28 Brüning, *Memoiren*, pp. 625–26; *Kabinett von Papen*, meeting of 31 August 1932, I:481 (source of quotation); Schäffer diary, 1 September 1932, NL Schäffer/22/826–27; Vogelsang, *Reichswehr*, pp. 270–74. Compare Wirth's memoir, "Ereignisse und Gestalten von 1918–1933," question #25, and the strangely optimistic reports on their negotiations with Hitler by Eugen Bolz and Joseph Joos in Besson, *Württemberg*, pp. 302–03, and *Zentrumsprotokolle*, 12 September 1932, p. 586.

29 Brüning, *Memoiren*, pp. 626–28; Brüning to Maier-Hultschin, 26 March 1947, HUG FP 93.10/Box 22/Johannes Maier (3); Pünder, *Politik*, 31 August 1932, p. 144; *Zentrumsprotokolle*, 12 September 1932, pp. 585–89; Schäffer diary, 12–15 September 1932, NL Schäffer/22/851–53, 861–62; Vogelsang, *Reichswehr*, p. 276; Schulz, *Von Brüning zu Hitler*, pp. 963–74.

30 Dorpalen, *Hindenburg*, pp. 358–64; Brüning, *Memoiren*, pp. 628–29; *Zentrumsprotokolle*, 12–13 September 1932, pp. 589–92; Goebbels, *Tagebücher*, 12 September 1932, II:241–42; Quaatz, *Tagebuch*, 12 September 1932, p. 203.

31 *Kabinett von Papen*, meetings of 30 August and 14 September 1932, I:477–78, and II:578–83.

of restoring constitutional government.[32] Papen's measures also polarized the Catholic parties along class lines. Many bourgeois Catholics sympathized with Papen and applauded a decree of 4 September that corporations would be forgiven a portion of their tax obligations in future years if they invested now to create jobs. Even Brüning agreed that this measure was constructive, although he predicted that Papen's disastrous political tactics would negate the economic benefit.[33] Papen outraged organized labor, however, with a decree the next day authorizing employers to undercut wages bound by collective bargaining if they hired new workers. Numerous rallies of both the Free and Christian trade unions denounced this "reactionary" and "plutocratic" government for seeking to abolish the Weimar constitution and restore the Wilhelmian class hierarchy.[34]

Center Party leaders were most upset by the numerous speeches in which Chancellor Papen argued that the recent papal encyclical *Quadragesimo anno* exhorted all good Catholics to reject the "regime of the political parties" and search for a "corporatist" alternative to parliamentary democracy. Brüning therefore appealed to Ludwig Kaas to return to Germany, because only "he as a Roman prelate could declare authoritatively to the Catholic portion of the nation that this [Papen's] practice had nothing in common with the ideal" of social harmony proclaimed by the Vatican. Kaas agreed and criticized Papen vigorously on the campaign trail, earning widespread applause for the proposal that a modified presidential cabinet without Papen should be given a fixed term for undisturbed work on Germany's economic problems. These speeches helped to limit Center Party losses to less than one percentage point on 6 November; the Nazi voting share dropped significantly from 37 to 33 percent, and voter turnout declined for the first time since 1928, evidence that the nation's political fever was breaking. Only the KPD and DNVP registered gains, however, so it would be more difficult than ever to form a majority coalition in the new Reichstag.[35] The resurgence of the Communist Party, which Brüning had

---

32 Morsey, "Deutsche Zentrumspartei," pp. 302–03; Aretz, *Katholische Arbeiterbewegung*, pp. 49–70; Stump, *Düsseldorf*, pp. 89–93; Kühr, *Essen*, pp. 69–73, 104–11, 283–93; Kaufmann, *Münster*, pp. 154–60; Pridham, *Nazi Movement in Bavaria*, pp. 156–60, 270–76, 301–02; Klaus Schönhoven, "Zwischen Anpassung und Ausschaltung: Die Bayerische Volkspartei in der Endphase der Weimarer Republik 1932/33," *Historische Zeitschrift*, 224 (1977): 340–78.

33 Grotkopp, *Die grosse Krise*, pp. 112–17; Pünder, *Politik*, conversation with Brüning on 18 September 1932, pp. 146–47; Hackelsberger to ten Hompel, 8 August 1932, NL ten Hompel/21; ten Hompel to Papen, 9 September 1932, NL ten Hompel/23; ten Hompel to Father Muckermann, 11 October 1932, NL ten Hompel/24; Brüning, *Memoiren*, p. 629; Morsey, *Untergang*, pp. 63–67; Schwarz, *Adenauer*, pp. 335–36.

34 Winkler, *Katastrophe*, pp. 726–30; ADGB Bundesausschuss, 9–10 September 1932, *Quellen: Gewerkschaften*, pp. 676–83; *Verhandlungen des 13. Kongresses der christlichen Gewerkschaften, 18.–20. September 1932* (Berlin, 1932), pp. 66–68, 97, 123–24, 145–46, 177–83, 224–30, 269–70; circular from Jakob Kaiser to Volksfront district leaders, 5 October 1932, KAB Archiv; *Zentralblatt der christlichen Gewerkschaften*, 1 November 1932, pp. 283–84.

35 Brüning, *Memoiren*, p. 630 (source of quotation); Sailer, *Eugen Bolz*, pp. 162–68; May, *Ludwig Kaas*, III:249–51; Morsey, "Deutsche Zentrumspartei," pp. 324–28; Childers, *Nazi Voter*, pp. 206–11. For background, see pp. 88–89 above.

combated so effectively, benefited the Nazis by reviving the worst anxieties of the propertied.

Brüning sought anxiously during this campaign to revive the President's concern about the constitutionality of government actions. Since August Papen and Gayl had publicly canvassed support for a "New State" without Article 54 of the Weimar constitution (which required that cabinets enjoy the confidence of the Reichstag), and with a corporatist upper house and some restrictions on voting rights. They hoped to cap these reforms by restoring a monarchy, and they advised Hindenburg that Article 48 and the "right of the state to defend itself" authorized him to do almost anything he considered necessary, even amend the constitution by decree.[36] The President therefore displayed no concern when the supreme court condemned many of Papen's measures during and after the Prussian coup. On 25 October the court condemned as unconstitutional the creation of a new Prussian cabinet and the purge of civil servants, confirming the right of the old cabinet to represent Prussia in the Reichsrat. None of Brüning's measures had ever encountered such judicial criticism, which gravely undermined the government's claim to defend the rule of law, but Hindenburg ignored a personal appeal from Otto Braun to enforce this verdict.[37] Appalled by this attitude, Brüning proclaimed on the campaign trail that "the Center Party must be a constitutional party, or it will be nothing." He even termed the Weimar constitution a "holy empire" (*sacrum imperium*), exploiting on its behalf the nostalgia among German Catholics for the Holy Roman Empire. He sought to appease the President by quietly canvassing support for a permanent merger of the offices of Reich chancellor and Prussian prime minister, and he apparently suggested some restriction on the Reichstag's power to initiate confidence motions, but he always defended Article 54 and the existing suffrage law. The neo-conservative Heinrich von Gleichen told Hans Schäffer on 25 November that Brüning's eloquent arguments had persuaded him that these two features of the present system should be retained no matter what. Hindenburg displayed no interest in Brüning's suggestions, however, and Papen instructed his cabinet after the election to draft sweeping amendments to the constitution without regard for the question of whether they could win a qualified Reichstag majority.[38]

36 Bracher, *Auflösung*, pp. 471–79; Schulz, *Von Brüning zu Hitler*, pp. 996–99; Dorpalen, *Hindenburg*, pp. 357–64; Kurz, "Artikel 48," pp. 408–12; Schwerin von Krosigk, *Staatsbankrott*, pp. 145–47; defense ministry memorandum of 29 August 1932 in Vogelsang, *Reichswehr*, pp. 480–81; Quaatz to Hugenberg, 25 October 1932, in Quaatz, *Tagebuch*, p. 206.

37 Gerhard Schulz, "'Preussenschlag' oder Staatsstreich? Neues zum 20. Juli 1932," *Der Staat*, 17 (1978): 553–81; Winkler, *Katastrophe*, pp. 761–65; conference of Hindenburg, Braun, and Papen, 29 October 1932, *Kabinett von Papen*, II:831–34.

38 "Das Sacrum Imperium der Verfassung," Breslau campaign speech in *Kölnische Volkszeitung*, 5 November 1932, #305; Brüning, *Memoiren*, pp. 631–32; Keil, *Erlebnisse*, II:468–70; Schäffer diary, 25 November 1932, NL Schäffer/23/1006–09; cabinet meeting of 9 November 1932, *Kabinett von Papen*, II:906; Schulz, *Von Brüning zu Hitler*, pp. 1005–08. Compare Klaus Breuning, *Die Vision des Reiches. Deutscher Katholizismus zwischen Demokratie und Diktatur (1929–1934)* (Munich, 1969), and Wirth to Breitscheid, 14 November 1932, NL Wirth/9. See also the records of a discussion group

General Schleicher had become alarmed by the wave of laborite protests against the government, and he insisted on 17 November that Papen offer his resignation so that the President could seek a broader base of support. Hindenburg first offered to appoint Hitler chancellor of a parliamentary cabinet if he could find a Reichstag majority, but the offer was withdrawn when Hitler demanded the same decree powers granted Brüning and Papen.[39] On 24 November Hindenburg commissioned Ludwig Kaas to make a last effort to form a majority coalition. Kaas suggested that Brüning was better qualified, but Meissner interjected that this was impossible out of consideration for the President – as Brüning observed later, everyone who had participated in the decision to topple him closed ranks thereafter to deny him access to Hindenburg. Kaas reported the next day that no majority coalition could be formed; the President could improve the situation only by dismissing Papen, because any other chancellor would find it easier to make peace with the Reichstag. Brüning became more specific when Meissner sought him out for confidential advice: Of the men who enjoyed the President's confidence, only Schleicher had any chance to pacify organized labor while securing some form of Nazi participation in or toleration of the government. Brüning noted that he personally refused to speak with Schleicher, but there was nobody else for the job.[40]

Papen expected a renewal of his mandate when the effort to form a majority coalition failed, and he urged the President on 1 December to dissolve the Reichstag and postpone elections indefinitely, while the government drafted a new constitution to be implemented through plebiscite or perhaps simply by presidential decree. Hindenburg was supportive, but the next day Schleicher rallied the cabinet against the plan after his aide described the frightening results of a war game conducted by the general staff to determine the likely consequences of "a general strike by everyone," that is, by the trade unions, Communists, and SA. All but one of the ministers declared that Papen must be replaced by Schleicher. Hindenburg sadly accepted this recommendation but voiced suspicion of Schleicher's motives; he now felt victimized by the same pressure tactics that Schleicher had used earlier against Hermann Müller and Brüning, when dubious national security arguments promoted a change of cabinet.[41]

on constitutional reform that included several of Brüning's friends, in Gerhard Schulz, ed., "Dokumentation: Sand gegen den Wind. Letzter Versuch zur Beratung einer Reform der Weimarer Reichsverfassung im Frühjahr 1933," *Vierteljahrshefte für Zeitgeschichte*, 44 (1996): 295–319.

39 Dorpalen, *Hindenburg*, pp. 376–83; Schildt, *Militärdiktatur*, pp. 91–96; cabinet meeting of 17 November 1932, and presidential receptions and Hitler-Meissner correspondence of 19–24 November, *Kabinett von Papen*, II:956–60, 984–1000.

40 Presidential receptions of 24/25 November 1932, *Kabinett von Papen*, II:1003–04, 1024–25; Brüning, *Memoiren*, pp. 635–36, 653–54. Compare Regendanz to Schleicher, 30 October 1932, NL Schleicher/22/231–32.

41 Eugen Ott memorandum of 2 December 1932 and commentary in Vogelsang, *Reichswehr*, pp. 327–29, 484–85 (source of quotation); meeting of 2 December 1932, *Kabinett von Papen*, II:1035–38; Schwerin von Krosigk, *Staatsbankrott*, pp. 149–52; Quaatz, *Tagebuch*, 27 November–2 December 1932, pp. 214–16; Papen, *Wahrheit*, pp. 243–52, 276–79; Bracher, *Auflösung*, pp. 586–92; Dorpalen, *Hindenburg*, pp. 384–96.

Brüning welcomed the formation of the Schleicher cabinet as proof that President Hindenburg "wanted to return to the basic principles of my policy." The Center Party helped to delay any vote of confidence, and Schleicher allowed the Reichstag to repeal Papen's unpopular wage decree of 5 September. Thus Schleicher did seek to imitate Brüning's impartial mediation of class conflict.[42] The general still did not share Brüning's respect for the constitution, however. For months he had courted trade union leaders by promising to support public works, and he made a favorable impression on Theodor Leipart and Heinrich Imbusch. This courtship encouraged the neo-conservative publicist Hans Zehrer to prophesy the emergence of a new form of government based on a "trade union axis," that is, an alliance of the army, trade unions, and paramilitary leagues that would supplant the discredited political parties. Schleicher does not appear to have made any serious effort to pursue this goal, but he probably hoped to win enough credibility among labor leaders that they would not be inclined to launch a general strike if he decided to violate the constitution temporarily. The general asked Rudolf Breitscheid just before he became chancellor how the SPD would respond if Hindenburg dissolved the Reichstag and did not hold elections for six months. If the government promised to restore the constitution intact thereafter, "would Social Democracy immediately take to the barricades?" Breitscheid replied coldly that "Social Democracy would oppose such a breach of the constitution with all its power." Schleicher apparently hoped that his contacts with union leaders might help to neutralize such opposition by the SPD, but his viewpoint merely antagonized the defenders of the Weimar constitution without going nearly far enough to satisfy its foes, who were determined to abolish forever the "regime of the parties."[43]

Schleicher's first priority as chancellor was to win toleration from the Nazi Party in cooperation with Gregor Strasser. On 29 November Schleicher and Strasser jointly invited Hitler to come to Berlin and discuss the possibility of Nazi participation in a Schleicher cabinet, but he refused. On 4 December Schleicher apparently offered to appoint Strasser as Prussian prime minister and a member of the Reich cabinet, and the general told several associates that if

42 Brüning, "Ein Brief," in *Reden*, pp. 250–52 (source of quotation); *Zentrumsprotokolle*, 5 December 1932, pp. 603–04; cabinet meetings of 7 and 14 December 1932, *Akten der Reichskanzlei. Das Kabinett von Schleicher*, ed. Anton Bolecki (Boppard am Rhein, 1986), pp. 23–24, 99–101; remarks by Hugenberg in DNVP Reichstagsfraktion, 5 December 1932, pp. 5–6, NL Spahn/175; Bracher, *Auflösung*, pp. 592–603; Turner, *Big Business*, pp. 302–09.

43 Breitscheid memorandum of 28 November 1932, pp. 2–3, ADGB-Restakten, NB 112 (photocopies in the DGB Archive, Düsseldorf); Schleicher's reception for Leipart and Eggert, 28 November 1932, *Quellen: Gewerkschaften*, pp. 766–70; Hugenberg's remarks in DNVP Reichstagsfraktion, 5 December 1932, pp. 7–8, NL Spahn/175; Bendersky, *Carl Schmitt*, pp. 74–119; Patch, *Christian Trade Unions*, pp. 212–15; Heinrich Muth, "Schleicher und die Gewerkschaften 1932. Ein Quellenproblem," *Vierteljahrshefte für Zeitgeschichte*, 29 (1981): 189–215; Winkler, *Katastrophe*, pp. 713–20, 734–54, 793–816; Schildt, *Militärdiktatur*, pp. 139–70; Fritzsche, *Politische Romantik*, pp. 267–92; Turner, *Thirty Days*, pp. 21–24; Hans Mommsen, "Government without Parties: Conservative Plans for Constitutional Revision at the End of the Weimar Republic," in Jones and Retallack, eds., *Between Reform, Reaction, and Resistance*, pp. 347–73.

Hitler vetoed this arrangement, then Strasser was prepared to break with him and lead at least sixty moderate Reichstag delegates out of the NSDAP. Strasser sought anxiously to win Hitler's permission, however, and when Hitler insisted on an all-or-nothing strategy, Strasser abruptly resigned from all his party offices on 8 December and left Germany on vacation. This action came as a great shock to Brüning, who concluded that Schleicher had foolishly encouraged Strasser to play the same role played earlier by Treviranus in the DNVP. Even against Hugenberg this gambit had failed, Brüning noted, and to repeat such an operation on the Nazi Party reflected disastrous ignorance of Hitler's role as charismatic leader. Schleicher was not as obtuse as Brüning feared and doubtless raised the specter of a party schism only to pressure Hitler into accepting a role as junior partner in the government. The general's tactics spread much confusion about his real aims, however; even such a close associate as Meissner labeled his courtship of Strasser "a bad imitation of the Treviranus affair."[44]

Schleicher clung for weeks to the hope that Strasser could persuade Hitler to authorize the entry of some Nazis into the existing cabinet. Brüning soon learned, however, just how weak the new chancellor's position was. Strasser sought Brüning out in Freudenstadt on 28 December to warn that Franz von Papen had just arranged a secret meeting with Hitler for early January to forge an alliance against their mutual enemy Schleicher. Papen had inflicted a grievous wound on his successor by informing Nazi leaders that Hindenburg no longer trusted Schleicher, and he offered his services as mediator between Hitler and Hindenburg just when Nazi fortunes seemed to be collapsing. Brüning advised Strasser to warn Schleicher at once, and then to make peace with Hitler and resume the struggle for a moderate line within the Nazi leadership. This plan was doomed, however, after the vengeful Papen actually conferred with Hitler in Cologne on 4 January. The two men could not yet agree on who should succeed Schleicher, but this overture from the President's friend revived Hitler's faith that his all-or-nothing strategy was succeeding.[45]

Strasser did reestablish contact with Schleicher, who urged his cabinet on 16 January to add him, Hugenberg, and some liaison officer with the Center Party to its ranks. Schleicher argued that this cabinet shuffle would have a favorable impact on public opinion, which could be translated into an electoral majority if

---

44 Goebbels, *Tagebücher*, 1–8 December 1932, II:287–98; Brüning, *Memoiren*, pp. 633–35; Brüning to Ullmann, 13 March 1954, NL Ullmann/6/56; quotation from Moldenhauer to Dingeldey, 25 January 1933, NL Dingeldey/78/5; Kissenkoetter, *Gregor Strasser*, pp. 162–72, 202–04; Peter Hayes, "Question Mark," pp. 55–60; Turner, *Thirty Days*, pp. 23–29. For other reports that Schleicher sought to engineer a schism of the NSDAP, see François-Poncet to Herriot, 29 November 1932, reporting a conversation with Schleicher and Meissner, *DDF*, II:88–90; Quaatz, *Tagebuch*, conversations with Meissner on 30 November and 16 December 1932, pp. 215–18; Otto Braun, *Von Weimar zu Hitler*, pp. 273–75; Schwerin von Krosigk, *Es geschah in Deutschland*, pp. 117–18; Papen, *Wahrheit*, p. 244; and Hjalmar Schacht, *Confessions of "The Old Wizard": The Autobiography of Hjalmar Horace Greeley Schacht*, trans. Diana Pyke (Cambridge, Mass., 1955), pp. 273–74.

45 Brüning, *Memoiren*, pp. 639–41; Heinrich Muth, "Das 'Kölner Gespräch' am 4. Januar 1933," *Geschichte in Wissenschaft und Unterricht*, 37 (1986): 463–80, 529–41; Turner, *Thirty Days*, pp. 38–46.

the cabinet acted vigorously to create jobs and peasant homesteads. It would be necessary, however, to dissolve the Reichstag and postpone new elections until autumn so that government measures could have a visible economic impact. This plan may have had some merit under the grim circumstances, but Schleicher clung to strange illusions. That very day Hitler whipped an imposing Nazi Party rally into furious denunciations of Strasser, and the mild-mannered pharmacist withdrew from political life completely.[46] Schleicher could not even retain the support of the DNVP as the Reichslandbund renewed its campaign against "agricultural Bolshevism." Alfred Hugenberg believed that his highest priority must be to prevent the Center Party and Heinrich Brüning from regaining their position "at the tip of the scales" in a parliamentary coalition with the Nazis, so he opened negotiations with Hitler on 17 January. At first he shrewdly demanded firm guarantees that the Nazis would not control the defense ministry or Prussian police, but he became angry when Meissner told him three days later that the chancellor could not keep his promise to give Hugenberg the portfolios of both economics and agriculture because of objections from the other parties. The DNVP chairman therefore announced in public that his party would oppose the government when the Reichstag convened, even though he had not received any assurance that Hitler would agree to a coalition on bearable terms.[47]

Even at this late date, Brüning helped to secure an offer from the Reichstag council of elders to give Schleicher a breathing space until the end of March at least. The Strasser affair made the Nazi leadership nervous enough to agree to prolong the Reichstag's voluntary adjournment for another two months. Brüning lined up a majority for this plan at the council meeting of 20 January but warned the chancellor that the Center Party would consider any "compulsory adjournment a violation of the constitution, because a genuine state of emergency does not exist." Schleicher obstinately instructed his officials to prepare a legal rationale for a compulsory adjournment, however, and notified the council of elders that he wanted a swift resolution of the crisis. It decided to convene the Reichstag on 31 January.[48] The leaders of the SPD, BVP, and Center Party despaired when they compared notes at the end of the day and found that Schleicher had given them contradictory accounts of his plans. Nobody could understand what he hoped to accomplish. That very night, Brüning later

---

46 Cabinet meeting of 16 January 1933, *Kabinett von Schleicher*, pp. 230–36; reports by Max Reiner of 10 and 13 January 1933 on confidential press briefings by Schleicher, NL Schäffer/33/16–24; Brüning, *Memoiren*, pp. 642–43; Stachura, *Strasser*, pp. 117–19; Turner, *Thirty Days*, pp. 66–68, 84–91.

47 Hugenberg to Hitler, 28 December 1932, NL Hugenberg/37/29–31; Quaatz, *Tagebuch*, 17–20 January 1933, pp. 223–24; Goebbels, *Tagebücher*, 18 January 1933, II:341; DNVP circular to provincial affiliates, 19 January 1932, *Ursachen und Folgen*, VIII:748–49; DNVP Reichstag delegation resolution of 21 January 1933, *Kabinett von Schleicher*, pp. 282–83; Larry Eugene Jones, "'The Greatest Stupidity of My Life': Alfred Hugenberg and the Formation of the Hitler Cabinet, January 1933," *Journal of Contemporary History*, 27 (1992): 70–73.

48 Cabinet meeting of 16 January 1933 and subsequent legal opinions, *Kabinett von Schleicher*, pp. 230–32, 238–43, 267–69; *Zentrumsprotokolle*, 20 January 1933, pp. 606–08 (source of quotation); Goebbels, *Tagebücher*, 19–20 January 1933, II:343; Turner, *Thirty Days*, pp. 104–07.

recalled, a distraught Erwin Planck sought him out to confess that Schleicher's decision had rested on false premises; Oskar von Hindenburg had promised Schleicher backing from the President, but he had just defected to the camp of Papen and Hitler. Brüning's memory seems quite accurate, because Meissner did tell Hugenberg on 21 January that the President had just been persuaded to appoint Hitler chancellor even without a parliamentary majority, "if the cabinet is supported by the Stahlhelm, Landbund, and industry, if, that is, it can be regarded as a cabinet of the entire nationalist movement, so that it would be impossible for one party to coerce the others." Schleicher hoped to remain defense minister, Meissner noted, but Hitler objected to that solution, and the President had been persuaded that Schleicher's services were not essential.[49]

On 23 January Schleicher requested authorization from the President to dissolve the Reichstag and postpone new elections for several months. Hindenburg replied that he could accept responsibility for such a grave breach of the constitution (which he had approved when proposed earlier by Papen) only if Schleicher secured declarations of support from a broad array of party leaders.[50] When the leaders of the Center Party met to discuss Schleicher's request, Brüning insisted that they not even discuss whether a temporary violation of the constitution might be justified; the Center Party's historic mission, he declared, was "to defend the foundations of the rule of law and constitutional government." Party chairman Kaas then rebuffed Schleicher:

> Whoever looks back on the history of our domestic political development since the fall of the Brüning cabinet and evaluates it objectively must arrive at the conclusion that there can be no talk of a genuine state emergency, but at most an emergency of a system of government that has made so many mistakes . . . as to create its own difficult situation today. No breach of the constitution can extricate us from these difficulties, but only the earnest and systematic return to methods which fully exploit the possibilities within the constitution for the creation of viable government combinations. . . . Illegality from above will foster illegality from below to an extent that is incalculable.

This was an accurate summary of the disastrous consequences of Brüning's dismissal but offered no constructive suggestions for the moment.[51] Schleicher's plan enjoyed a few sympathizers in the SPD, but the general lost any chance for that party's support at the beginning of January when he rejected Otto Braun's

---

49 Brüning, *Memoiren*, pp. 643–45; Brüning to Friedrich Stampfer, 16 December 1946, HUG FP 93.10/Box 32/Friedrich Stampfer; Brüning to Graf Brünneck, 19 August 1949, HUG FP 93.10/Box 5/Manfred von Brünneck; Quaatz, *Tagebuch*, conversation with Hugenberg and Meissner, 21 January 1933, pp. 224–25 (source of quotation); Goebbels, *Tagebücher*, 14–22 January 1933, II:337–46; Papen, *Wahrheit*, pp. 259–66; Turner, *Thirty Days*, pp. 111–17.

50 Presidential audience of 23 January 1933, *Kabinett von Schleicher*, pp. 284–85; Turner, *Thirty Days*, pp. 118–23.

51 *Zentrumsprotokolle*, 26 January 1933, pp. 608–09; Kaas to Schleicher, 26 January 1933, *Kabinett von Schleicher*, pp. 304–05; Morsey, *Untergang*, pp. 84–85.

request to reinstate the lawful cabinet of the state of Prussia. On 26 January the SPD rejected any compulsory adjournment as a *Staatsstreich* (coup d'état), and Braun declared that anyone who advocated such a plan should be prosecuted for treason. Schleicher made a feeble effort to gain the support of the Free Unions, but no labor leader wanted to jeopardize long established political ties for his sake. Thus the leaders of the Center Party and Social Democracy both insisted on scrupulous adherence to Article 25 of the constitution in a situation where this suggested that Hindenburg should appoint Hitler chancellor as the only politician with any chance to win a majority in new elections.[52]

As word spread that Schleicher was doomed, Social Democrats and bourgeois moderates feared most that Hindenburg would reappoint his sentimental favorite Papen to lead a "cabinet of struggle" supported only by the DNVP. Schleicher himself planted newspaper stories to appear on the morning of 28 January that the appointment of Papen would lead to civil war, and then he offered his resignation to Hindenburg with a plea to make Hitler chancellor with a reliable non-Nazi (meaning himself) as minister of defense.[53] Brüning lay ill with severe bronchitis, but he reluctantly endorsed Hitler's appointment when colleagues came to visit; he feared above all that a second Papen cabinet would goad Schleicher into a putsch or the trade unions into a general strike. Fritz Schäffer of the BVP approached Brüning and Kaas on 28 January to express concern about rumors that their personal animus against Papen hindered a resolution of the crisis, and they apparently authorized him to tell Papen that the Center would agree to join a parliamentary coalition with the Nazi Party and DNVP. Papen held that it was too late for such a solution because Hitler insisted on a "presidential" cabinet with decree powers. He made use of Schäffer's offer, however, to give Hindenburg the soothing impression that he and Hitler were engaged in the formation of a "parliamentary" cabinet that would secure a comfortable majority in the Reichstag by granting the ministry of justice to a representative of the Catholic parties.[54] On 30 January Hindenburg was finally persuaded by Papen, Meissner, and his son Oskar to make "the corporal" the head of a cabinet in which three Nazis would supposedly be controlled by eight conservatives, with Papen as vice-chancellor and Hugenberg as minister of economics and agricul-

---

52 Chancellor's reception for Free Union leaders, 26 January 1933, and Otto Braun to Schleicher, 28 January, *Kabinett von Schleicher*, pp. 300–03, 311–12; Winkler, *Katastrophe*, pp. 846–50; Schulze, *Otto Braun*, pp. 773–76; Schulz, *Von Brüning zu Hitler*, pp. 1046–49.

53 *Zentrumsprotokolle*, 27 January 1933, pp. 610–11; cabinet meeting and presidential reception of 28 January 1933, *Kabinett von Schleicher*, pp. 306–11, 316–19; Papen, *Wahrheit*, pp. 267–68; Turner, *Thirty Days*, pp. 128–33; Winkler, *Katastrophe*, pp. 853–55.

54 Morsey, *Untergang*, pp. 86–95; Turner, *Thirty Days*, pp. 140–42, 150–52; Altendorfer, *Fritz Schäffer*, pp. 686–88; Brüning, *Memoiren*, pp. 646–47; Rumbold to Sir John Simon, 28 January 1933, giving Meissner's assessment of Brüning's attitude, *DBFP*, IV:390–92; Brüning to Theodore Draper, 6 November 1947, HUG FP 93.10/Box 7/Theodore Draper; Papen, *Wahrheit*, pp. 270–71. After 1945 Fritz Schäffer sometimes maintained that Brüning had volunteered to serve as foreign minister under Papen in a last-ditch effort to exclude the Nazis from power, but Papen and Brüning both recalled, far more plausibly, that the whole maneuver had been aimed against Papen, not Hitler. See the polemical exchange in *Die Welt*, 19 September 1952, #218, and 29 September, #226.

ture. Papen had jettisoned all the safeguards demanded by Brüning and Hugenberg in his anxiety to reach agreement. Göring gained control of the Prussian police; the greatest admirer of Hitler among the generals, Werner von Blomberg, became minister of defense; and Hitler and Papen had an understanding that the Nazi leader would be authorized to hold new elections and issue presidential emergency decrees during the election campaign. Despite the obvious flaws in these arrangements, not the army command, the trade unions, nor the moderate parties saw any reason to protest this development so long as Hitler scheduled new elections within sixty days of any dissolution of the Reichstag. As Brüning feared, plans for the use of force were being discussed in both the defense ministry and trade union leadership in case Papen was appointed chancellor. News of the Hitler cabinet brought a strange sense of relief, however, and none of Germany's leading politicians could suggest any practical alternative to this experiment.[55] This stunning failure of imagination and will among Germany's political elite resulted from the fact that the forces opposed to Hitler had dissolved into a bitter war of each against all since Brüning's fall.

6.2. The Triumph of Totalitarianism

When Brüning later contemplated the chain of events leading to Hitler's appointment as chancellor, he felt that there had been an utter collapse of moral values in the presidential entourage. Personal vanity, he thought, had made Oskar von Hindenburg implacably hostile to him. During the war Brüning had been ordered to write a harsh critique of the military performance of the field marshal's son for the general staff, and someone apparently found the document in the national archive and showed it to the Hindenburgs early in 1932. Oskar was also greedy, Brüning alleged, and sought government aid from Treviranus in October 1931 to purchase land to expand the family estate at Neudeck. Brüning vetoed the arrangement, but Hitler did make such a gift after coming to power. Oskar was further vulnerable to Nazi blackmail, Brüning suspected, because of improper grants of Eastern Aid (*Osthilfe*) loans to his landowning friends.[56] Brüning considered Otto Meissner a fairly conscientious civil servant, but he had long heard distressing rumors about Meissner's friendship with Curt Sobernheim of the Commerzbank. Gregor Strasser told Brüning that the

---

55 Schwerin von Krosigk diary, 29–30 January 1933, *Kabinett von Schleicher*, pp. 320–23; Quaatz, *Tagebuch*, 27–29 January 1933, pp. 227–29; Goebbels, *Tagebücher*, 28–31 January 1933, II:352–59; Papen, *Wahrheit*, pp. 269–75; SPD-ADGB leadership conferences of 30 January and 5 February 1933, in *Quellen: Gewerkschaften*, pp. 823–38; Turner, *Thirty Days*, pp. 142–60; Jones, "Greatest Stupidity," pp. 73–77; Vogelsang, *Reichswehr*, pp. 288–89; Schulz, *Von Brüning zu Hitler*, pp. 1046–49; Winkler, *Katastrophe*, pp. 855–64.

56 Brüning, *Memoiren*, pp. 393–95; Treviranus, *Ende von Weimar*, pp. 154–55; Brüning's interview of September 1945 with American prosecutors, pp. 4–7, HUG FP 93.10/Box 16/Interview; Brüning to Schmidt-Hannover, 20 October 1948, p. 3, HUG FP 93.10/Box 30/Otto Schmidt-Hannover; Brüning to Graf Brünneck, 19 January 1955, HUG FP 93.10/Box 5/Manfred von Brünneck; Brüning to Hans von Raumer, 18 July 1957, HUG FP 93.4.5.

Nazis had obtained proof of a long history of risk-free investments based on confidential information from cabinet meetings, made by Sobernheim in the name of Frau Meissner. Brüning deduced that Papen and Göring must have collected enough evidence by January 1933 to threaten Meissner with prison if he did not help to persuade the President to appoint Hitler chancellor. Meissner was also vulnerable, Brüning thought, because he had illegally diverted campaign contributions for the presidential election to a slush fund to influence the press.[57] Brüning felt that Franz von Papen had such limited intellectual capacity that he could not be held fully accountable, but that he had often acted from malice and not just ignorance. "I did not then know," Brüning observed in the first draft of his memoirs about the year 1932, "that Papen had practiced treason against the Center Party for years and actually based his political career on it."[58]

Brüning sometimes went beyond such attacks on individuals to indict Germany's conservative elites as a group. Most senior army officers, he felt, had fallen under the sway of right-wing ideologues who taught that Germany's problems could be solved only through autarchy and massive rearmament. Only Schleicher deserved respect as one who, despite "Machiavellian" methods, always tried to prevent a Nazi dictatorship. President Hindenburg himself was honest but hopelessly timid; he suddenly withdrew support from both Brüning and Schleicher, in a sense from Papen as well, at the moment when they recognized the necessity of vigorous action against the SA. This timidity was no mere personal failing but reflected the grim fact that European armies were reliable only against insurrectionary movements of the left and not the right, because of the officers' social background. The root cause of all these problems was the fact that the DNVP and Reichslandbund had long since fallen under the sway of men who placed the brutal defense of material interests ahead of any conservative principles. Many corrupt landowners, bankers, and industrialists believed that only a Nazi seizure of power could save them from criminal prosecution. In both May and December of 1932, Brüning alleged, the Nazi movement stood on the brink of disintegration when Hitler was rescued at the last moment by overtures from the presidential entourage and conservative leaders, extended for purely selfish reasons.[59] Many of these accusations are unverifiable, and Brüning chose

---

57 Brüning, *Memoiren*, pp. 522–23, 591–92; Brüning's interview of September 1945, pp. 7–9, HUG FP 93.10/Box 16/Interview; Brüning to Hermann Ullmann, 7 February 1948, NL Ullmann/6/254; Brüning to Graf Brünneck, 19 August 1949, HUG FP 93.10/Box 5/Manfred von Brünneck; Brüning to Treviranus, 30 September 1955 and 9 July 1958, HUG FP 93.10/Box 34/G.R. Treviranus (2); Brüning to Hans von Raumer, 25 February 1958, HUG FP 93.10/Box 26/Hans von Raumer; Müller, *Brüning Papers*, pp. 102–04, 187–88. Compare the similar report about Meissner, based on information from Robert Weismann, in Staudinger, *Wirtschaftspolitik*, pp. 113–14.

58 Manuscript memoirs, pp. 330, 338, 342, HUG FP 93.4; Brüning to Draper, 6 November 1947, HUG FP 93.10/Box 7/Theodore Draper.

59 Brüning, *Memoiren*, pp. 376–78, 435–36, 449–50; Brüning to Dannie Heineman, 15 September 1937, pp. 1–5, HUG FP 93.10/Box 14/D.N. Heineman; Brüning to Theodor Draper, 11 July 1947, HUG FP 93.10/Box 7/Theodore Draper; Brüning to Graf Galen, 12 October 1948, pp. 1–4, HUG FP 93.10/Box 11/Franz Graf Galen; Brüning to Johannes Dettmer, 13 August 1950, HUG FP 93.10/Box 6/Dale-Deym; Brüning to Graf Brünneck, 19 June 1952, HUG FP 93.10/Box 5/Manfred von Brünneck.

on both legal and political grounds not to publish most of them. This lifelong admirer of conservatism has nevertheless offered powerful testimony that responsibility for the dissolution of the Weimar Republic rested squarely on the shoulders of its conservative elites.

In February 1933 Brüning nevertheless initially resembled most other bourgeois politicians by clinging to the hope that politics would continue more or less as usual. Chancellor Hitler seemed quite reasonable in his first discussions with Center Party leaders. He renounced the "policy of bayonets" advocated by the DNVP in favor of a government "bound to the people." He wanted to include the Center Party in his cabinet, Hitler declared, but confronted resistance from the bigoted Protestants around Hindenburg. Even such an experienced observer as Stegerwald concluded that "Hitler knows that dictatorship is impossible, but Hugenberg is of the opposite opinion." Kaas could not decide whether to volunteer the services of a party colleague as minister of justice, but Brüning apparently supported this idea from his sickbed. The Center Party focused its criticism of the new "cabinet of contradictions" on the "reactionary" Hugenberg and persisted in this line even after Hitler blamed it for denying him a parliamentary majority, dissolved the Reichstag, and scheduled elections for 5 March.[60]

Brüning urged his friends in government to retain office and obstruct dangerous or criminal policies from within the system. State Secretary von Bülow had already consulted him in June 1932, when Nazi emissaries first intimated that Hitler wanted to retain his diplomatic services for the Third Reich. Brüning and Bülow agreed that, if Hitler came to power, it would be his patriotic duty to remain in office unless Germany's new masters insisted on a foreign policy contrary to the national interest; by exercising the threat to resign, he might be able to dissuade the Nazis from foolish adventures. Two weeks after Hitler's appointment, Brüning encountered Schwerin von Krosigk and promised to defend his decision to remain finance minister. Brüning warned, however, that the point might come when no man of honor could remain in this government, and the count later regretted that he had not listened more carefully. Bülow actually drafted a letter of resignation in May 1933 to protest the official boycott of Jewish shops, but Brüning persuaded him not to submit it on the grounds that "one does not leave one's country in the lurch because it has a bad government."[61]

---

60 *Zentrumsprotokolle*, 31 January and 2 February 1933, pp. 612–13, 616 (source of quotations); Morsey, *Untergang*, pp. 95–105; May, *Ludwig Kaas*, III:292–304. In his memoirs Brüning described vain exhortations to the dilatory Kaas to participate in the new cabinet, and Blomberg told military colleagues at the time that the Center Party would have joined if Brüning had been healthy, but Brüning later wrote Schmidt-Hannover that he had prevented any party colleague from joining. See Brüning, *Memoiren*, pp. 647–48; commanders' conference of 3 February 1933, in Vogelsang, ed., "Neue Dokumente," pp. 432–33; and Brüning to Schmidt-Hannover, 20 October 1948, p. 3, HUG FP 93.10/Box 30/Otto Schmidt-Hannover.

61 Memorandum by Laboulaye on a conversation with Bülow, 20 June 1932, *DDF*, I:106; Brüning, *Memoiren*, p. 650; Brüning to Eugen Klee, 11 December 1946, and to Peter Pfeiffer, 29 January 1947, *Briefe*, I:453–55; Schwerin von Krosigk, *Staatsbankrott*, pp. 174–79, and *Es geschah in Deutschland*, pp. 307–10; Krüger and Hahn, "Bülows Loyalitätskonflikt," pp. 409–10 (source of quotation).

Brüning began to understand the true gravity of the situation when he talked with Schleicher on 11 February. Brüning telephoned with condolences after Schleicher's dismissal, and the two men restored a sense of comradeship as fellow victims of Hindenburg's caprice when the general visited him. Schleicher warned that Hitler had already made an excellent impression on most generals by promising massive rearmament, and that Blomberg would never stand up to the Nazis. Schleicher perceived, Brüning later recalled, that the only chance to prevent a totalitarian dictatorship was to persuade Hindenburg and General Hammerstein to proclaim martial law, arrest Hitler and Göring, and suppress the SA. Those who wished to encourage such action must wait for the DNVP and presidential entourage to become disillusioned with the Nazis, but they must act before the officer corps became enamored of Hitler's program for rearmament and territorial expansion.[62]

Brüning gained further insight into the grim facts of political life through reports from the campaign trail about unprecedented acts of intimidation. Terrorism gained official sanction in late February when Göring deputized Nazi Stormtroopers as auxiliary Prussian police, while a presidential emergency decree sharpened restrictions on the press and authorized the detention of anyone considered a threat to public order. Most moderate politicians clung nevertheless to the hope that Germany was experiencing random acts of violence by overly enthusiastic followers of Hitler, and that any group would be safe if it repudiated all "Marxist" influences.[63] Brüning displayed exceptional courage by publicly accusing the new chancellor of responsibility for a systematic campaign to destroy the rule of law. Article 48, he noted, was now abused to justify any arbitrary exercise of power, and Hitler's only achievement in office had been to replace scores of professional civil servants with personal cronies. Brüning's party colleagues long remembered his passionate defense of the *Rechtsstaat* in this campaign as the only thing that distinguished civilization from barbarism.[64] Brüning was especially vehement in his criticism of the violent persecution of the Social Democrats. When a police officer interrupted his Gelsenkirchen speech of 26 February to warn that the meeting would be dispersed if he continued to criticize government measures, Brüning exclaimed that he could not be forbidden at least to repeat what he had said last year at Hindenburg's cam-

---

62 Brüning, *Memoiren*, pp. 647–50; Brüning, "Ein Brief," in *Reden*, pp. 259–61. Compare Kessler, *Tagebücher*, conversation with Hilferding on 27 February 1933, p. 709; Schäffer diary, conversation with Schleicher, 29 March 1933, NL Schäffer/24/27–31; and Hanshenning von Holtzendorff, "Die Politik des Generals von Schleicher gegenüber der NSDAP, 1930–1933," affidavit of 22 June 1946, NL Schleicher/98/13–15.

63 Karl Dietrich Bracher, *Stufen der Machtergreifung* (Ullstein reprint: Frankfurt a.M., 1983), pp. 108–37; Morsey, *Untergang*, pp. 106–08; Aretz, *Katholische Arbeiterbewegung*, pp. 72–75; Besson, *Württemberg*, pp. 342–52; Jones, *German Liberalism*, pp. 466–71.

64 Würzburg and Breslau campaign speeches in *Kölnische Volkszeitung*, 21 February 1933, #52, and 26 February, #57; Brüning, *Memoiren*, pp. 650–52; Friedrich Muckermann, *Im Kampf zwischen zwei Epochen. Lebenserinnerungen*, ed. Nikolaus Junk (Mainz, 1973), pp. 543–44; Josef Hofmann, *Erinnerungen*, p. 175; Alphons Nobel, "Der letzte demokratische Kanzler," in Vernekohl, ed., *Heinrich Brüning*, p. 154.

paign rallies, when he lauded the President as the "guardian of the constitution and the father of the poor and oppressed." He had intended to withdraw from public life but now saw that he still had a mission "to see to it that those who elected the Reich President are not oppressed by those who combated and defamed him." Brüning's rally in Essen climaxed with the declaration that the Center Party and he personally could never tolerate any effort to deprive the Social Democrats of the equal protection of the law after they had proved over so many years that they were "loyal to the constitution and to the fatherland." Brüning's attitude compared favorably with that of Joseph Wirth and Heinrich Imbusch, who blamed the victims of this persecution for having failed to purge their party of Marxist influence in the past. Even the leaders of the Free Unions did everything they could to distance themselves from the unfortunate SPD.[65]

After a courageous campaign, the SPD and Center Party preserved their shares of the national vote almost intact on 5 March. The Nazis fell short of an absolute majority with 44 percent, but the DNVP won 8 percent, so there was no need for Hitler to expand his coalition as long as the President and DNVP continued to sail in his wake. After the election many Catholic agrarians, industrialists, and civil servants demanded support for Hitler's "government of national concentration," so Kaas swallowed his pride and approached Vice-Chancellor Papen on 6 March with an apology for past attacks and a plea for cooperation among all good Catholics to defend the vital interests of the Church.[66] Some such tactical retreat was inevitable, but Brüning soon decided that Kaas and Cardinal Pacelli went much too far by encouraging Catholics to believe that there was nothing immoral about the Third Reich. Brüning (or his posthumous editors) chose to leave his sharpest criticism of Pacelli unpublished:

> All successes [Pacelli believed] could only be attained by papal diplomacy. The system of concordats led him and the Vatican to despise democracy and the parliamentary system. . . . Rigid governments, rigid centralization, and rigid treaties were supposed to introduce an era of stable order, an era of peace and quiet.

Brüning's published memoirs nevertheless aroused fierce controversy by alleging that Kaas secured the Center Party's approval of Hitler's Enabling Act of 23 March, which destroyed all semblance of constitutional government,

---

65 Brüning speeches in *Kölnische Volkszeitung*, 26 and 27 February and 2 March 1933, nos. 57, 58, and 61; speech by Imbusch to a closed meeting of Christian miners ("Gewerkverein Generalversammlung"), 12 March 1932, NL Imbusch/1; Hofmann, *Erinnerungen*, p. 69; May, *Ludwig Kaas*, III:307–33; Theodor Leipart to Wilhelm Keil, 3 March 1933, in *Quellen: Gewerkschaften*, pp. 853–54; Hans Mommsen, "Die deutschen Gewerkschaften zwischen Anpassung und Widerstand 1930–1944," in Heinz Oskar Vetter, ed., *Vom Sozialistengesetz zur Mitbestimmung. Zum 100. Geburtstag von Hans Böckler* (Cologne, 1975), pp. 281–90.

66 May, *Ludwig Kaas*, III:325–27; Morsey, *Untergang*, pp. 116–21; Brüning, *Memoiren*, pp. 663–64.

in exchange for a worthless promise by Hitler to negotiate a concordat with the Vatican.[67]

Brüning was probably correct in most of his assertions about March 1933, although he failed to acknowledge the extent to which Church leaders became suspicious of the Third Reich thereafter. At the first cabinet meeting after the election, Hitler announced that he would seek a two-thirds majority in the Reichstag for an Enabling Act that would give the cabinet virtually unlimited legislative powers. The major obstacle was the Center Party, and Hitler declared that its voters could not be won over until the new regime achieved an understanding with the Vatican. He had probably decided already to seek a concordat modeled on the Lateran Treaties of 1929, which Hitler had long praised as one of Mussolini's greatest achievements. Little is known about the contacts between Kaas and government leaders during the next two weeks, but Kaas did place editorials in the Centrist press reminding German Catholics that Mussolini and the Vatican had worked out their differences.[68]

Brüning prepared for the Reichstag session by reaching agreement with Hugenberg on amendments to the Enabling Act designed to protect civil liberties and require formal approval by the President for every cabinet decree. Brüning found that Hugenberg shared his concern for the rule of law, but they failed to establish contact with Hindenburg, who displayed a curious detachment from current events. The DNVP chairman then suffered a humiliating repudiation by his own Reichstag delegation on 20 March, when Eduard Stadtler proposed that the DNVP should merge with the Nazi Party. Hugenberg implored his party colleagues to continue to support an independent existence for the DNVP and Center Party – he gladly acknowledged that the SPD was doomed – but he felt compelled to drop any talk of an ultimatum to Hitler.[69] Hugenberg's retreat was enough in itself to doom Brüning's plan, but the memoirist recalled with the most pain that even Kaas lost interest in it as he conferred with Hitler and Papen:

67 Brüning, manuscript memoirs, pp. 351–52, HUG FP 93.4, and *Memoiren*, pp. 630–31, 656–74; Volk, *Reichskonkordat*, pp. 60–84; "Die unverzeihlichen Sünden des Prälaten Kaas," in Volk, *Katholische Kirche*, pp. 321–27; Morsey, *Untergang*, pp. 125–96; Scholder, *Churches*, I:240–53, 383–400; Konrad Repgen, "Über die Entstehung der Reichskonkordats-Offerte im Frühjahr 1933 und die Bedeutung des Reichskonkordats," *Vierteljahrshefte für Zeitgeschichte*, 26 (1978): 499–534; Klaus Scholder, "Altes und Neues zur Vorgeschichte des Reichskonkordats. Erwiderung auf Konrad Repgen," *Vierteljahrshefte für Zeitgeschichte*, 26 (1978): 535–70; May, *Ludwig Kaas*, III:368–83, 407–09; Konrad Repgen, ed., "Dokumentation: Zur Vatikanischen Strategie beim Reichskonkordat," *Vierteljahrshefte für Zeitgeschichte*, 31 (1983): 506–35.

68 Scholder, *Churches*, I:240–41; Repgen, "Entstehung der Reichskonkordats-Offerte," pp. 524–29; Scholder, "Altes und Neues," pp. 543–51; Bracher, *Stufen der Machtergreifung*, pp. 217–25; May, *Ludwig Kaas*, III:326–27. Hitler told the cabinet on 14 July 1933 that a Reich Concordat had been his goal ever since he took office; see Alphons Kupper, ed., *Staatliche Akten über die Reichskonkordatsverhandlungen 1933* (Mainz, 1969), pp. 236–37.

69 Brüning, *Memoiren*, pp. 652–55; Brüning, "Ein Brief," in *Reden*, pp. 258–59; Brüning to Schmidt-Hannover, 25 May 1954, HUG FP 93.10/Box 30/Otto Schmidt-Hannover; DNVP Reichstagsfraktion, 20 March 1933, pp. 11–18, NL Spahn/175; Quaatz, *Tagebuch*, 11–22 March 1933, pp. 240–44; Dorpalen, *Hindenburg*, pp. 450–63; Clemens, *Martin Spahn*, pp. 201–04.

Kaas's resistance became weaker as Hitler spoke of a concordat and Papen assured him that one was as good as guaranteed. Because of his whole background, it was natural and understandable that this was the question that interested Kaas most. Ever since 1920 he had always wanted to help formulate a Reich concordat. For him as a prelate, secure relations between the Vatican and the German Reich represented a decisive issue, which all other issues must be coordinated with, if not subordinated to. Hitler and Papen must have noticed how the growing prospects for a concordat preoccupied Kaas more and more.

Brüning was certainly correct that Kaas and Pacelli had long dedicated themselves to securing formal recognition by the German government of the new code of canon law adopted by the Vatican in 1917, and that this project had absorbed more and more of Kaas's time and energy since 1929.[70]

Brüning and Kaas began to quarrel in earnest on 18/19 March in the Cologne apartment of Bernhard Letterhaus. Letterhaus reported to friends that an astonishing confrontation erupted when Brüning demanded opposition to the Enabling Act on the grounds that "the regime of the Nazis can no longer be reconciled with the law." Kaas rejected this view and eventually "pounded on the table with the words, 'Am I the leader of the party, or who?'" The debate continued as the Center Reichstag delegation assembled in Berlin on 20 March. Kaas warned his colleagues that "a fundamental reorientation toward the religious side" was unavoidable now that they had lost much of their freedom of political action.[71] Kaas hoped to extract promises from Hitler that would make the act acceptable, but Brüning insisted that the man's word meant nothing. Brüning confided to Hans Schäffer that he could never support the Enabling Act, "because he could not bear to see how those people who had elected the Reich President on his recommendation are being mistreated and tortured under that man's rule." He apparently made no effort to publicize his reservations, however, and only one Centrist newspaper, Dessauer's *Rhein-Mainische Volkszeitung*, dared to criticize the proposed law.[72]

On Sunday morning, 21 March, the newly elected Reichstag delegates assembled in the old Garrison Church of Potsdam to witness the first great ceremony organized by Joseph Goebbels as propaganda minister. For Brüning this "Day of Potsdam" was a nightmare, the ultimate perversion of his ideals. He felt like a condemned man being led to the scaffold during the drive to the ceremony. Once there he was appalled to hear President Hindenburg issue the following appeal:

70 Brüning, *Memoiren*, p. 656; May, *Ludwig Kaas*, II:482–94, 649–53; Morsey, *Untergang*, pp. 27–31.

71 Carl Bachem memorandum of 22 April 1933, in Matthias and Morsey, eds., *Ende der Parteien*, pp. 434–35; *Zentrumsprotokolle*, 20 March 1933, p. 623.

72 Schäffer diary, 20 March 1933, NL Schäffer/24/23–24; Vernekohl, "Ein Staatsmann aus Westfalen," in Vernekohl, ed., *Heinrich Brüning*, p. 123; Morsey, *Untergang*, p. 125.

The place where we are assembled today summons us to look back on old Prussia, which became great through fear of God, dutiful work, never failing courage, and devoted love of the fatherland, and which united the German tribes on this basis. May the old spirit of this place inspire today's generation, may it free us from selfishness and partisan quarrels, may it bring us together in a national revival and spiritual renewal for the sake of a united, free, proud Germany!

After Hitler briefly explained the program of the new "cabinet of national concentration," the chancellor and President laid wreaths on the tombs of Frederick William I and Frederick the Great, greeted a cheering throng outside the church, shook hands with the Crown Prince and other dignitaries from the Wilhelmian Empire, and reviewed formidable columns of soldiers, Nazi Stormtroopers, Stahlhelm veterans, and the Prussian police. Brüning perceived a disgusting "intoxication" (*Rausch*) in this ceremony and could not believe his eyes when Hindenburg wiped away a tear on the podium. "How," he asked himself, "can a man whose voters were being dragged into concentration camps and SA cellars allow himself to be celebrated by those who were responsible?"[73]

Discussions within the Center Reichstag delegation after the ceremony nevertheless indicated widespread support for the Enabling Act. For most party colleagues, Brüning acknowledged, this attitude had nothing to do with thoughts of a concordat. The industrialist Albert Hackelsberger led a small group of optimists who expected to play a major role in the Third Reich if they reached agreement with Hitler quickly, and a much larger group of pessimists held that defiance would merely goad the Nazis into wholesale violence against the SPD and trade unions. On 22/23 March Kaas told the delegation that it would be pointless to demand amendments to the bill because neither the DNVP nor Hindenburg objected to its terms. Hitler nevertheless offered impressive oral assurances, Kaas declared, about the authority of the President, the rights of the Catholic Church, and the treatment of Catholic civil servants, and the Center should vote for the Enabling Act if Hitler agreed to put these promises into writing. Brüning replied that he would never vote for the act, terming it "the most monstrous resolution ever demanded of a parliament," and the decision of the delegation remained uncertain.[74] Hitler's Reichstag speech of 23 March then improved the atmosphere, however, by making rhetorical concessions to many of Kaas's demands. Hitler clearly pledged to respect the existing concordats between the Vatican and German state governments, to preserve confessional schools unchanged, and "to cultivate and further develop our friendly relations

73 See Bracher, *Stufen der Machtergreifung*, pp. 202–13; Hindenburg's speech in *Ursachen und Folgen*, IX:133–34; Brüning, *Memoiren*, p. 657; and Clara Siebert's memoir in Josef Becker, ed., "Dokumentation: Zentrum und Ermächtigungsgesetz 1933," *Vierteljahrshefte für Zeitgeschichte*, 9 (1961): 208.

74 *Zentrumsprotokolle*, 22–23 March 1923, pp. 624–31 (quotation on p. 631); Brüning, *Memoiren*, pp. 657–58; Wirth memoir, "Ereignisse und Gestalten von 1918–1933," question #29, p. 1; May, *Ludwig Kaas*, III:346–57; Morsey, *Untergang*, pp. 130–34.

with the Holy See." Brüning later recalled that Kaas described this last promise as "the greatest success that had been achieved in any country for the last ten years" in the realm of church–state relations.[75]

After this speech Kaas urged his delegation to support the Enabling Act with the observation that German history had entered a new era. A straw vote revealed that only 14 of the 74 delegates supported Brüning's position, including Wirth, Bolz, Joos, Dessauer, Stegerwald, Imbusch, and Jakob Kaiser. Kaas appealed to the minority to vote with the majority, expressing concern for their personal safety, but for some time they would not agree. Brüning spoke of laying down his Reichstag mandate. Wirth offered to join him in this gesture and broke into tears as he recalled the hopeful days of 1919. Brüning again emphasized his responsibility for the fate of millions of Social Democrats, and then he left the caucus to prowl the back corridors of the half-burned Reichstag building, seeking advice from the handful of delegates in other parties whom he still trusted. He contemplated secession from the Center Party and had received pledges of support from Catholic laborites, but Karl Ulitzka, the veteran leader of the Silesian Center, persuaded him that such action would destroy any hope for unified Catholic resistance to religious persecution. Brüning also told himself that the Enabling Act might possibly improve the legal situation, since Papen assured everyone that he would be empowered to veto cabinet decrees as the President's representative. Wirth and Brüning eventually dropped their opposition and joined their colleagues for the humiliating march through crowds of jeering Stormtroopers to the Kroll Opera House, where the Centrists voted unanimously in favor of the government. Otto Wels of the SPD was left in sole possession of the historic role that Brüning desperately wanted to share as he defied the dictator, led a united delegation in voting No, and guaranteed his party a moral claim to play a leading role again after this wave of barbarism had passed.[76] Thereafter Brüning always regarded opposition to the Enabling Act as the litmus test of which veterans of the Center Party truly deserved to play a role in politics again after the Nazi regime fell. He remained friendly with Hermann Dietrich and Theodor Heuss of the State Party but could never agree with them in later years about who had advised whom to vote for this law. Brüning was wracked with guilt about his vote but told himself again and again that his decision had saved the lives of many Social Democrats.[77]

75 Brüning, *Memoiren*, p. 656; Kaas's letter to Hitler is juxtaposed with Hitler's speech in Matthias and Morsey, eds., *Ende der Parteien*, pp. 429–31.

76 *Zentrumsprotokolle*, 23 March 1933, pp. 631–32; Brüning, *Memoiren*, pp. 658–60; Brüning to Maier-Hultschin, 26 March 1947, HUG FP 93.10/Box 22/Johannes Maier (3); Siebert memoir in Becker, ed., "Zentrum und Ermächtigungsgesetz," pp. 209–10; Wirth memoir, "Ereignisse und Gestalten von 1918–1933," question #29, pp. 1–2, and question #30; Letterhaus to Graf Galen, 27 March 1933, and Carl Bachem's memorandum of 28 April, in Matthias and Morsey, eds., *Ende der Parteien*, pp. 433–35; Aretz, *Katholische Arbeiterbewegung*, pp. 77–78; Morsey, *Untergang*, pp. 138–41; Sailer, *Eugen Bolz*, pp. 186–88; Bracher, *Stufen der Machtergreifung*, pp. 227–36.

77 Brüning, *Memoiren*, p. 658; Brüning's political testament of 25 May 1935, in *Briefe*, I:464–65; Brüning to Treviranus, 14 July 1952, HUG FP 93.10/Box 34/G.R. Treviranus (2); Brüning to Gustav Olef, 10 July 1958, HUG FP 93.10/Box 23/Gustav Olef; Jakob Kaiser memorandum of 25

Kaas left for Rome the day after this vote in order, as he later explained, "to continue on the course adopted by me in the Reichstag on 23 March by reporting on the situation created by the chancellor's government declaration and to explore the possibilities for a comprehensive understanding between Church and State." The most plausible interpretation of this abrupt departure is that he had already agreed with Papen to promote a Reich concordat, and Brüning actually applauded his decision not to allow the bungling Papen to conduct these negotiations alone.[78] Brüning saw his fears about the Vatican's attitude confirmed, however, when the German episcopate rescinded its condemnation of National Socialism a few days later. Archbishop Conrad Gröber of Freiburg and the papal nuncio, Cesare Orsenigo, had both embraced Papen's line that German Catholics must rally behind Hitler as the only alternative to Communism. Most German bishops denied this premise, but on 10 March the Pope himself told Cardinal Faulhaber in Rome that Hitler deserved credit as the first head of any secular government to condemn Communism forthrightly. Thus it became obvious that the Vatican desired a change of course.[79] On 28 March Faulhaber and Cardinal Bertram therefore published the following pastoral guidelines on National Socialism:

> It should now be acknowledged that public and solemn declarations have been issued by the highest representative of the Reich government, who is also the authoritative leader of that movement, which recognize the inviolability of the Catholic faith and the unalterable tasks and rights of the Church. . . . The episcopate therefore expresses its confidence that its earlier general bans and warnings need no longer be regarded as necessary. . . . For Catholic Christians to whom the voice of their Church is holy, there is no need at the present time for a special reminder that they must be loyal to the lawful authorities and fulfill their civic duties conscientiously, rejecting any illegal or subversive activities.

This declaration pleased both the Vatican and Hitler, but the few Centrist politicians shown the draft in advance had termed it a formula for disaster. They warned that it would be interpreted as a capitulation and cripple the Center Party by implying that the bishops did not even consider it preferable to the NSDAP.

April 1958 on a conversation with Theodor Heuss, NL Kaiser/246; Saldern, *Hermann Dietrich*, pp. 198–99; Morsey, "Zentrumspartei und Zentrumspolitiker im rückblickenden Urteil Heinrich Brünings," pp. 57–59.
78 Kaas to Diego von Bergen, 19 November 1935, in Kupper, ed., *Staatliche Akten*, pp. 495–96 (source of quotation); Scholder, *Churches*, I:246–50; Scholder, "Altes und Neues," pp. 551–54; Brüning to Maier-Hultschin, 29 April 1958, HUG FP 93.10/Box 21/Johannes Maier (1). Contrast Volk, *Reichskonkordat*, pp. 83–84, and Repgen, "Reichskonkordats-Offerte," pp. 515–22.
79 Conrad Gröber, "Meine Mitarbeit am deutschen Konkordat," memoir of 1947, in Ludwig Volk, ed., *Kirchliche Akten über die Reichskonkordatsverhandlungen 1933* (Mainz, 1969), pp. 306–13; Faulhaber's notes on his papal audience and report to Bavarian bishops of 20 April 1933, in Ludwig Volk, ed., *Akten Kardinal Michael von Faulhabers. Band I: 1917–1934* (Mainz, 1975), pp. 660–62, 714–15; Brüning to Hermann Josef Schmitt, 12 May 1959, *Briefe*, II:468–69; Scholder, *Churches*, I:242–43.

Their advice was ignored, but Bertram and Faulhaber themselves soon noted with anguish that their declaration resulted in a loss of prestige for the episcopate and a sense of abandonment among Catholic victims of persecution.[80]

Kaas further encouraged the impression of a genuine reconciliation between Catholicism and the Third Reich when he returned to Berlin at the beginning of April. After conferring with Hitler, he published an editorial praising the chancellor's Reichstag speech of 23 March as the logical development of the "idea of union" (*Sammelgedanke*) championed by Kaas ever since November 1931. Germany found itself in a momentous "evolutionary process" in which the "undeniably excessive formal freedoms" of the Weimar Republic would inevitably be supplanted by "an austere and temporarily no doubt excessive state discipline" over all walks of life. The Center Party felt obliged to participate actively in this transformation, to join the government parties as "sowers of the future." Kaas's rhetoric now resembled that of Papen, who had just founded a "League of the Cross and Eagle" to supplant the Center Party as a "nonpartisan" defender of Catholic interests.[81] Kaas met the vice-chancellor on a train to Rome on 8 April, and in the next ten days they and Pacelli hammered out the terms of a draft treaty to submit to Hitler. Kaas rejoiced inordinately when the dictator accepted a treaty provision, authorizing priests to perform "emergency marriages" without a civil license, that had been rejected by all previous cabinets of the Weimar Republic. A ray of hope shot through the Vatican that, as Kaas argued in an analysis of the Lateran Treaties published in September 1933, "the 'authoritarian state' must be better able than any other to understand the premises of the authoritarian Church."[82]

When Kaas decided to stay in Rome until the concordat was ratified, an overwhelming majority of the Center Party executive committee and Reichstag delegation elected Brüning as party chairman on 6 May. He proclaimed a stubborn resolve to defend the *Rechtsstaat* in alliance with the DNVP, the only other party that retained any freedom of action. A spirit of resistance flickered up at this meeting, although Brüning sensed that they were only fighting to salvage their personal honor, not to determine Germany's fate.[83] He now began to propagate

---

80 Pastoral guidelines in Hans Müller, ed., *Katholische Kirche*, pp. 76–78; Brüning, *Memoiren*, pp. 663–64; Faulhaber's report to Bavarian bishops, 20 April 1933, in Volk, ed., *Akten Faulhabers*, pp. 714–16; notes on the Fulda Bishops' Conference of 30–31 May 1933, in Volk, ed., *Kirchliche Akten*, pp. 55–58; Volk, *Reichskonkordat*, pp. 68–80, 88; Scholder, *Churches*, I:250–53; Morsey, *Untergang*, pp. 154–57.

81 "Der Weg des Zentrums," *Kölnische Volkszeitung*, 5 April 1933, reprinted in Becker, ed., "Zentrum und Ermächtigungsgesetz," pp. 195, 202–07; Breuning, *Vision des Reichs*, pp. 180–92; Sailer, *Eugen Bolz*, pp. 162–68.

82 Kaas diary, 7–18 April 1933, and Kaas to Bergen, 19 November 1935, in Kupper, ed., *Staatliche Akten*, pp. 12–17, 495–96; Ludwig Kaas, "Der Konkordatstyp des faschistischen Italien," *Zeitschrift für ausländisches öffentliches Recht und Völkerrecht*, 3 (1933): 517; Scholder, "Altes und Neues," pp. 554–59. Contrast Repgen, "Reichskonkordats-Offerte," pp. 508–10, 517–20.

83 Report to Center Party activists, 6 May 1933, in Matthias and Morsey, eds., *Ende der Parteien*, pp. 435–38; Brüning, *Memoiren*, pp. 664–69; May, *Ludwig Kaas*, III:374–81; Morsey, *Untergang*, pp. 176–79; Muckermann, *Im Kampf*, pp. 544–45.

a restoration of monarchy in order to rally Germany's conservative elites against the Nazis. Brüning's colleagues in the BVP had sought unsuccessfully in March to restore the Wittelsbach dynasty in order to prevent the Nazi takeover of Bavaria, and Hindenburg had nurtured further speculation along these lines by insisting that Hitler receive an agent of the House of Hohenzollern to explain his intentions. Brüning told British Ambassador Rumbold in June that "only the restoration of what he called a moderate monarchy, by which he meant a constitutional monarchy, could save Germany from prolonged unrest and trouble. Such a monarchy would make for stability and would be a guarantee against foreign adventures." Rumbold noted that monarchism had become generally accepted among opponents of the Nazis, even Social Democrats.[84] Brüning had obviously concluded that only the prospect of restoration could neutralize the impression on the officer corps made by Hitler's promise of lavish spending for rearmament.

Vatican diplomats had meanwhile balked when Hitler demanded a prohibition of political activity by the clergy similar to that contained in Mussolini's Lateran Treaties. Pacelli insisted that such a ban was appropriate only in predominantly Catholic countries, and the Vatican resisted firmly on this point until the dissolution of the trade unions, SPD, and by 27 June even the DNVP made it obvious that political parties had no future in Germany. Thus Brüning was unfair to accuse Pacelli of betraying the Center Party.[85] In June the Vatican received many reports from Germany about vicious persecution of Catholic priests and Church-affiliated organizations. Papen maintained that these problems resulted from Brüning's obstinate refusal to dissolve the Center Party, but Cardinal Bertram warned the Vatican emphatically not to trust Papen's judgment. Brüning's arguments helped to persuade many Church dignitaries that Hitler would break his word, and they began to debate the concordat in terms of the best tactics to prepare for the wave of religious persecution that lay ahead.[86] Pacelli and Kaas finalized the treaty terms with Papen on 2 July, by which time they had ample reason to consider the Center Party an empty husk that could legitimately be abandoned in exchange for guarantees of autonomy for Church-affiliated organizations. Joos was outraged, however, when Kaas telephoned him from Rome that day and exclaimed in surprise, "What, you have not dissolved yourselves yet?" This question was burned into the memory of the party loyalists around Brüning as an imperious demand that the Center Party

---

84 Rumbold to Simon, 14 June 1933, *DBFP*, IV:351–54; Schönhoven, "Zwischen Anpassung und Ausschaltung," pp. 366–70; Friedrich Wilhelm, *Haus Hohenzollern*, pp. 119–23.

85 Brüning, manuscript memoirs, pp. 351–52, HUG FP 93.4; Brüning, *Memoiren*, pp. 670–72; Volk, *Reichskonkordat*, pp. 121–23, 181–84. Brüning sent word to Rumbold at the end of June 1933 that he would dissolve his party because the "Cardinal Secretary of State was hostile to existence of the Centre Party in its present form" (*DBFP*, V:383).

86 Faulhaber's memorandum on a conversation with Papen, 10 June, Bertram to Pacelli, 23 June, and memorandum by Pater Leiber, 29 June 1933, in Volk, ed., *Kirchliche Akten*, pp. 61–63, 67–68, 88–89; notes on the Fulda Bishops' Conference, 29 August 1933, in Bernhard Stasiewski, ed., *Akten deutscher Bischöfe über die Lage der Kirche 1933–1945. Band I: 1933–34* (Mainz, 1968), pp. 366–67; Repgen, ed., "Dokumentation: Zur Vatikanischen Strategie," pp. 530–35.

immolate itself to promote the success of Vatican diplomacy.[87] After numerous Centrist politicians threatened to defect to the NSDAP, Brüning finally agreed three days later to dissolve the party. He noted bitterly that no German bishop conveyed any thanks, either in public or private, for its sixty-three years of service in defense of Catholic interests.[88]

Brüning continued to lobby Church dignitaries against ratification of the concordat but was overruled at the end of August, and the final signing took place on 10 September.[89] During these weeks he read aloud to small groups of supporters from hospital reports on the Jewish and Social Democratic victims of the sadistic Stormtroopers, and he told them that Hitler's ultimate aim was to destroy the Christian churches. The Jesuit Friedrich Muckermann has testified eloquently that Brüning shook him out of his moral lethargy, shattering the premise that nothing could be seriously wrong with the Third Reich if the Vatican negotiated with it. Brüning had no concrete ideas about what form resistance should take but warned that the struggle against the Nazis required a willingness to risk everything: "Easy compromises were no longer possible, it demanded total commitment by the entire personality."[90] Thus Brüning fostered the outlook that eventually led many of his friends to risk their lives in the resistance movement. He also planted seeds of resistance when he introduced the courageous Free trade unionist Wilhelm Leuschner to Carl Goerdeler and encouraged Jakob Kaiser and other Christian trade unionists to discuss with Leuschner the creation of a unified labor federation in the future. Irmgard von Willisen, the widow of Brüning's closest friend in the officer corps, became his agent to maintain contact with Schleicher and the handful of senior officers who opposed the Nazis, including Generals Hammerstein and Bredow.[91]

Brüning refused, however, to do anything that might harm Germany's reputation abroad. When aggressive speeches by Papen threatened to forge a united front against Germany at the Geneva Disarmament Conference, Brüning approached Hitler on 16 May to help formulate a soothing declaration and then employed his influence with the SPD to secure unanimous approval of the chancellor's speech in the Reichstag.[92] Brüning was mortified in mid-August when *Le Temps* revealed that he advised the Pope not to sign the concordat. The Nazi

---

87 Brüning, *Memoiren*, pp. 673–74; Morsey, *Untergang*, pp. 194–96; Repgen, "Reichskonkordats-Offerte," pp. 529–33; Scholder, *Churches*, I:398–400; Muckermann, *Im Kampf*, pp. 458–59; memorandum by Hermann-Josef Schmitt on a visit to Pacelli in February 1934, in Volk, ed., *Kirchliche Akten*, pp. 304–05.
88 Morsey, *Untergang*, pp. 198–221; Volk, *Reichskonkordat*, pp. 181–84; Brüning, *Memoiren*, p. 673; Muckermann, *Im Kampf*, pp. 443–44.
89 Minutes of the Fulda Bishops' Conference of 29 August 1933, in Stasiewski, ed., *Akten deutscher Bischöfe*, pp. 366–67; Gröber's memoir in Volk, ed., *Kirchliche Akten*, pp. 326–30.
90 Muckermann, *Im Kampf*, pp. 457–58, 547–50.
91 Brüning to Theodore Draper, November 1947, and diary entry of 8 November 1934, *Briefe*, I:26–27, 41; Brüning to Maier-Hultschin, 13 March 1946, HUG FP 93.10/Box 22/Johannes Maier (3); Brüning to Kunrat Hammerstein, 23 September 1946, pp. 5–6, HUG FP 93.10/Box 14/Hammerstein; Ritter, *Carl Goerdeler*, pp. 122–24, 285–88; Focke, *Sozialismus aus christlicher Verantwortung*, pp. 175–81.
92 Brüning, *Memoiren*, pp. 669–70; Winkler, *Katastrophe*, pp. 932–34.

press denounced him for sacrificing the national interest to his personal ambition, and he felt compelled to declare publicly that he would never do anything to jeopardize the new government's chances for diplomatic success. With British diplomats, Brüning avoided criticism of Germany's President or chancellor and declared his willingness to support Hitler if he returned to a moderate and lawful policy. Thus a rigid code of patriotism governed all his exchanges with foreigners.[93] Joseph Wirth went even further than Brüning in this regard. Denounced as a leftist in the Nazi press, he fled Germany in fear of his life after passage of the Enabling Act, but he placed a favorable interpretation on recent events among foreign acquaintances in Rome and Vienna and sent the German authorities detailed reports on his observations there. "No matter what we think about politics," Wirth wrote his friend Heinrich Köhler, "we are loyal to our country and seek with all our powers to improve its position."[94]

In the fall of 1933 Brüning became disoriented by the nervous strain of constant police surveillance and the difficulty of visualizing any personal future. In October St. Hedwig's Hospital received threats for providing him shelter, and a senior Gestapo detective warned that he might be interned. Brüning therefore began to change his lodgings every two or three days, seeking refuge with a network of admirers from all walks of life who regarded him as Germany's greatest statesman. Evading Gestapo surveillance became his primary occupation. By the spring of 1934, Muckermann later recalled, the normally courageous Brüning resembled "a hunted animal, constantly startled and already exhausted, just waiting for the final bullet." Police harassment of his friends, renewed warnings that he would be imprisoned or even killed, and the onset of a heart ailment induced Brüning to allow Muckermann's brother to drive him across the Dutch border on 21 May 1934. Thus he began a new life in exile, with no worldly belongings except for the contents of a few suitcases.[95]

Brüning fled Germany in the midst of a major political crisis that dashed his hopes for a military coup against Hitler. He and Treviranus took heart early in 1934 from the escalating quarrel between the SA and other elements of the new regime; they assumed that Papen, Schleicher, and Gregor Strasser still had a good chance to persuade the army to seize power in the President's name. Brüning advised Schleicher to restore personal ties with Oskar von Hindenburg but found to his dismay that Schleicher seemed to pin his hopes instead on the corrupt Ernst Röhm, who was detested by most generals. Schleicher also engaged in conversations with Ambassador François-Poncet that exposed him to

93 Kupper, ed., *Staatliche Akten*, p. 235, n. 2; Ambassador Rumbold to Simon, 14 June 1933, *DBFP*, V:353–54; Phipps to Simon, 21 March 1934, *DBFP*, VI:572–73; Bracher, *Stufen der Machtergreifung*, pp. 283–84.

94 Wirth to Christine Teusch, 1 and 19 May 1933, NL Wirth/41; Wirth to Heinrich Köhler, 6 May 1933, NL Wirth/23.

95 Phipps to Sir John Simon, 11 November 1933 and 21 March 1934, *DBFP*, VI:33, 572; Muckermann, *Im Kampf*, pp. 569–70; Brüning, *Memoiren*, pp. 678–79; Treviranus, *Ende von Weimar*, pp. 397–98; Hermann Muckermann, "Wie Heinrich Brüning am 21. Mai 1934 Deutschland verliess," *Deutsche Rundschau*, 71, #8 (August 1948): 112–17; Müller, *Brüning Papers*, pp. 34–36.

the charge of conspiring with foreign powers. Papen proved incapable, moreover, of coordinating his actions with Schleicher. He hoped to restore a monarchy when Hindenburg died but relied primarily on appeals to Hitler's conscience, although his staff eventually persuaded him to deliver a bold public attack on the lawless elements in the Nazi Party in Marburg on 17 June. Brüning later recalled that Papen's chief speechwriter, Edgar Jung, showed him a copy of the speech in advance; Brüning admired its contents but implored Jung not to allow its delivery until the army had agreed to act. Papen blundered ahead anyway on his own, and as Brüning feared, the Marburg speech helped to give Hitler the warning needed to launch a massive preemptive strike. In the "Blood Purge" of 29/30 June, SS executioners shot several dozen SA leaders and scores of other victims, including Schleicher and his wife, Gregor Strasser, and Jung and two other aides of Papen. Most generals were so relieved by the elimination of the military pretensions of the SA that they raised no protest and even provided logistical support to the assassins. President Hindenburg accepted the story that all the victims had been engaged in a plot to assassinate Hitler, and Papen meekly agreed to pave the way for *Anschluss* as ambassador to Austria.[96] Brüning was stupefied by this display of cynicism, asking himself how army officers could associate with murderers. When he recalled a speech by a Conservative politician that he had admired in his youth, he could only reflect: "What have the conservative elements come to!"[97]

6.3. Brüning in Exile

Foreign admirers made Brüning's transition to exile fairly comfortable in material terms. Henricus Poels, a leader of the Dutch Catholic social movement, and Erwin Brettauer, a Swiss banker, issued standing invitations to reside with them and some financial assistance. Major Archibald Church, the former Labour MP who had promoted reconciliation with Germany, obtained a British visa for Brüning in June 1934 and lodged him in London with business colleagues, Ian and Mona Anderson. Brüning soon revived friendships with British leaders of the effort to abolish reparations in 1931/2, such as Montagu Norman and John Wheeler-Bennett, and he was free to travel from one pleasant household to another in England, the Netherlands, and the Swiss resort of Melide.[98] Brüning

---

96 Brüning to Theodore Draper, 6 November 1947, HUG FP 93.10/Box 7/Theodore Draper; Brüning, *Briefe*, I:25–28; Phipps to Sir John Simon, 21 March 1934, on a conversation with Treviranus and Brüning, and 2 July 1934, on a conversation with François-Poncet, *DBFP*, VI:571–74, 781; Wheeler-Bennett, *Knaves, Fools, and Heroes*, pp. 87–88; Treviranus, *Exil*, pp. 15–29; Papen, *Wahrheit*, pp. 343–63; Larry Jones, "Limits of Collaboration," pp. 475–97; Petzold, *Franz von Papen*, pp. 208–23; von Plehwe, *Kurt von Schleicher*, pp. 288–300; Wolfgang Sauer, *Die Mobilmachung der Gewalt* (Ullstein reprint: Frankfurt a.M., 1974), pp. 291–364.

97 Diary entry of 24 December 1934 (source of quotation), *Briefe*, I:53; Kessler, *Tagebücher*, conversation with Brüning on 22 August 1935, pp. 745–46.

98 Treviranus, *Für Deutschland im Exil*, pp. 26–37; Brüning, *Briefe*, I:21–24; Frank Müller, *Brüning Papers*, p. 37.

was also introduced to Winston Churchill in September 1934 and found his forceful personality a great tonic. Brüning admired Churchill's campaign to build a strong air force to deter German aggression and sought out his company repeatedly in the following years as the only British politician courageous enough to stand up to Hitler. He was also captivated by Churchill's thesis that the Allies had made a disastrous mistake in 1918 by abolishing the German monarchy.[99]

Exile is always painful, especially for those dedicated to serving "the nation," and most of all for one who knew that his failure in office had led to catastrophe. Brüning wanted desperately to defend his record and dictated detailed memoirs of his chancellorship in England and Switzerland from August 1934 to March 1935. He decided not to publish them, however, because sensational accounts by other émigrés encouraged public opinion in Great Britain and America to condemn all of German political history before the Nazi seizure of power as authoritarian and morally corrupt. Brüning agonized over the likely impact if he published what he knew or suspected about the senility of President Hindenburg, the financial corruption in his entourage, and the "Machiavellism" of Schleicher, and he decided "to keep silent for Germany." Only through a voluminous private correspondence did he seek to clarify who were the real villains of recent German history.[100] Brüning wrote his most loyal supporters in Germany that he could serve his country in future only "as a quiet adviser and perhaps a mediator" with foreign governments. He feared that he could never return to public office, even if the Third Reich fell, because Nazi propaganda had discredited all leaders of the Weimar Republic in the eyes of young Germans.[101]

Brüning's career as self-appointed lobbyist for the fatherland got off to a shaky start in June 1934 when Prime Minister MacDonald and Robert Vansittart of the Foreign Office invited him to explain the bewildering developments in Germany. Brüning warned them against the Nazis' aggressive tendencies but argued that the German army would oppose any war; the generals understood that they could never win a second world war and supported rearmament only because experience showed that Germany could achieve no diplomatic success without it. The British government could foment a putsch if it assured the generals that a monarchist regime would attain the redress of Germany's legitimate grievances. Great Britain should offer them the return of the Polish Corridor, permission for Germany to form a customs union with Austria, and a substan-

---

99 Brüning, *Briefe*, I:29–31, 147–49, 184–88, 210–11; Treviranus, *Exil*, pp. 51–56; Patch, "Brüning's Recollections of Monarchism."

100 Morsey, *Zur Entstehung*, pp. 10–12, 22–24, 29–32; Morsey, "Zur Problematik einer Briefedition," pp. 89–94; Müller, *Brüning Papers*, pp. 113–30.

101 Brüning's political testament of 25 May 1935, and Brüning to Hans Schäffer, February 1936, *Briefe*, I:105–06, 464–65; Rudolf Morsey, "Emigration und Nachkriegsplanung. Vorschläge und Vorstellungen Heinrich Brünings über den Neuaufbau in Deutschland," in Lothar Albertin and Werner Link, eds., *Politische Parteien auf dem Weg zur parlamentarischen Demokratie in Deutschland* (Düsseldorf, 1981), pp. 228–29.

tial loan; in return the new German government could be expected to sign a disarmament treaty along the lines suggested by Brüning at Bessing in April 1932 and rejoin the League of Nations. Brüning almost spoke as if he were still in power. Vansittart, who distrusted Prussian militarism as much as National Socialism, concluded that the German national character had become so perverted that even the scholarly Brüning, whose record in office he admired, was now more interested in territorial aggrandizement than in toppling a criminal regime.[102]

Similar questions about Brüning's priorities soon led to a painful rupture with Major Church. In October 1934 Church suggested that Brüning issue a public statement urging residents of the Saarland to vote against reincorporation into Germany in the upcoming League of Nations plebiscite, but Brüning replied that he would rather die than inflict such a blow to the Fatherland. This issue had already caused painful disputes between veterans of the Christian trade unions; a provincial leader of the Christian miners' union in Saarbrücken had volunteered his services to Adolf Hitler as the leader of the pro-German referendum campaign, while Heinrich Imbusch devoted himself to the campaign for a negative vote organized by the remnants of the SPD and KPD. Brüning was obviously appalled by Imbusch's conduct. Major Church continued to raise the subject, however, even after the pro-German side won 91 percent of the vote in January 1935, so Brüning cut off all personal relations. He resolved to tell all his friends in future and stipulate as a condition for accepting any academic post that he could never issue public statements harmful to German national interests.[103]

Brüning explored an academic career to enlighten the Anglo–American public about the liberal and democratic strains in German history. Catholic admirers brought him to teach at the Immaculate Conception Seminary on Long Island in the fall of 1935, and he began to deliver public lectures to a wide variety of groups throughout New England. In the fall of 1936, Harvard University hired him to teach international relations part-time, and for the next three years he divided his time equally between England and America. Brüning opened his first Boston lecture in 1935 by declaring that he would rather expose himself to vilification than reveal any facts that might harm Germany.[104] Brüning wrote his fellow exile Hans Schäffer that it made him physically ill to maintain this silence

---

102 Brüning memorandum of 14 June 1934, *Briefe*, I:23–24; Vansittart memorandum of 7 April 1934, *DBFP*, VI:975–90; Sir Robert Vansittart, *The Mist Procession* (London, 1958), pp. 418–20, 478.

103 Brüning to Mona Anderson, 28 October and 15 November 1934, and diary entry of 8 February 1935, *Briefe*, I:36, 42, 60; Patch, *Christian Trade Unions*, pp. 224–25; Schäfer, *Heinrich Imbusch*, pp. 257–72.

104 Treviranus, *Exil*, p. 88; George Shuster, "Dr. Brüning's Sojourn in the United States (1935–1945)," in Hermens and Schieder, eds., *Staat, Wirtschaft und Politik*, pp. 450–52; Brüning to Mona Anderson, February 1936, and to Albert Ickler, 8 December 1937, *Briefe*, I:109–11, 159–60. For Brüning's efforts to demonstrate that the German people had always placed as high a value on liberty as the English, see Brüning's Boston University lecture of 1 November 1943, HUG FP 93.45, and Brüning to Dorothy Thompson, 20 April 1943, *Briefe*, I:521–24.

when he contemplated the awful mistreatment of the Social Democrats by the Nazis, but the most he would do was to declare in the *New York Times* of 29 January 1936 that he could never support the Third Reich as long as it violated the principles of freedom of conscience and equal protection of the law for all citizens. This statement did not go nearly far enough in the eyes of many other émigrés, and Brüning ignored all invitations to join émigré organizations.[105]

Brüning gained some notoriety in America by supporting George Shuster's lonely campaign in the journal *Commonweal* to persuade Catholics that they should not support Franco in the Spanish Civil War. Brüning argued that the constitutions of both the Weimar Republic and Spain's Second Republic had performed a valuable service to Catholicism, because they abolished archaic Church privileges but retained adequate provision for religious instruction in the public schools. This stance helped Brüning to win acceptance by some leftist émigrés as a supporter of an anti-fascist "popular front."[106] Brüning feared that the Catholic Church had lost its popular foundation irretrievably by failing to oppose the spread of fascism, and in private he denounced those clerics like Archbishop Gröber who supported Hitler as a shield against Bolshevism. Brüning applauded the firmly anti-Nazi encyclical issued by Pope Pius XI in March 1937, *Mit brennender Sorge*, but thought it came at least a year too late. He saw his worst fears of authoritarian tendencies in the Church hierarchy confirmed with Cardinal Pacelli's election as Pope Pius XII in 1939. Brüning was not reconciled with Vatican policy until the reign of Pope John XXIII, whose ecumenicism and respect for the laity revived his hopes for the future of the Catholic Church.[107]

Brüning also sought to nurture the kind of resistance movement in the German army that he had pretended to Ramsay MacDonald already existed. From 1934 to 1939 he communicated with the general staff through Carl Goerdeler, Irmgard von Willisen, and the diplomat Adam von Trott zu Solz, who all enjoyed freedom to travel abroad. A small band of loyal followers from the Center Party, led by Bernhard Letterhaus, met Brüning in Holland once or twice a year and forged some military contacts themselves, and the ex-chancellor arranged meetings in Switzerland with General von Vietinghoff-Scheel in March 1935 and a young captain from military intelligence in January 1936. Through all these intermediaries, Brüning sought to persuade the generals Beck, Fritsch, Rundstedt, and Falkenhausen of the urgent necessity on moral,

---

105 Brüning to Schäffer, February 1936, *Briefe*, I:106–07; Morsey, "Emigration und Nachkriegsplanung," pp. 224–25; Joachim Radkau, *Die deutsche Emigration in den USA: Ihr Einfluss auf die amerikanische Europapolitik 1933–1945* (Düsseldorf, 1971), pp. 184–88.

106 See Shuster, "Brüning's Sojourn," pp. 459–60; Brüning's Detroit lecture of 7 December 1941, pp. 1–3, HUG FP 93.45; and Radkau, *Deutsche Emigration*, p. 185 and n. 1135.

107 Brüning, *Briefe*, I:120–23, 137–38, 209, and II:461; Shuster, "Brüning's Sojourn," p. 458; Treviranus, *Exil*, pp. 199–200; Morsey, "Zur Problematik einer Briefedition," p. 76.

political, and economic grounds of toppling Hitler.[108] Brüning wrote a detailed program for them in August 1935 after Willisen brought word that the general staff hoped to persuade Hitler to purge "the radicals" from the Nazi Party. Hitler must be removed as well, Brüning insisted, and the army should then hold elections for a constitutional convention, with suffrage restricted to war veterans and the widows and orphans of war veterans. This assembly should be encouraged to restore a hereditary monarchy "in principle" (without naming a monarch), to create a lower house of parliament based on indirect elections, and to grant veto power over the budget to an upper house including leaders of the trade unions and economic associations, representatives of the provinces, and life peers appointed by the Crown. This plan resembled Chancellor Papen's ideas for a "New State" and may well have influenced the constitutional plans drafted by the Kreisau Circle during the Second World War.[109] We should not deduce anything about Brüning's intentions while chancellor, however, from this desperate effort to prod the monarchist generals into action. After they failed to prevent the Second World War, Brüning never again suggested any sort of restoration.

When Hitler gained further prestige by remilitarizing the Rhineland in March 1936, Brüning wrote his friends in Germany that successes in foreign policy could be applauded only if they promoted a peaceful world order, and that Hitler revealed grievous shortcomings as a statesman by resorting constantly to the threat of force.[110] Again and again, however, Brüning learned that success legitimized almost any policy in the eyes of a great many German officers and civil servants. All of his informants, Brüning confided to his diary in December 1934, "confirm my old experience that the army has no political ideas." In subsequent crises the generals always became alarmed when it seemed that Hitler was about to launch a mad gamble, but their opposition evaporated when the gamble paid off. Hitler's triumph at the Munich Conference of 1938 dealt a crushing blow to efforts by the small group of idealists in the conservative Resistance to recruit support among more pragmatic colleagues. After Hitler's final success without war, the annexation of Prague in March 1939, Helmuth James von Moltke informed Brüning that resistance in the army had collapsed

---

108 See Hugo Stehkämper, "Protest, Opposition und Widerstand im Umkreis der Zentrumspartei," in Jürgen Schmädeke and Peter Steinbach, eds., *Der Widerstand gegen den Nationalsozialismus* (Munich and Zürich, 1985), pp. 890–910; Müller, *Brüning Papers*, pp. 39–40; Brüning, *Briefe*, I:63, 82, 103–04; and Brüning to Maier-Hultschin, 13 March 1946, HUG FP 93.10/Box 22/Johannes Maier (3).

109 Diary entry of 19 August and memorandum for "Friedrich" (i.e., the general staff), 18 August 1935, *Briefe*, I:82, 466–82. Compare Goerdeler's memorandum of 26 March 1943 in Ritter, *Carl Goerdeler*, pp. 577–95; Hans Mommsen, "Social Views and Constitutional Plans of the Resistance," in Hermann Graml et al., *The German Resistance to Hitler* (Berkeley and Los Angeles, 1970); and Ger van Roon, "Staatsvorstellungen des Kreisauer Kreises," in Schmädeke and Steinbach, eds., *Widerstand*.

110 "Für die Freunde," 19 September 1936, *Briefe*, I:127–28.

altogether. Brüning's gloomy private reflections support the views of those historians who argue that Germany's conservative elites remained basically loyal to
Hitler as long as there seemed to be good prospects for the success of his foreign
policy.[111]

Thus Brüning engaged in wishful thinking and perhaps even deception when
he declared repeatedly to British and American contacts that the German army
was led by resolute anti-fascists who would take bold action as soon as they
received assurances about German national security. Brüning made slight varia-
tions on his original proposal to Ramsay MacDonald to Vansittart on several later
occasions, to journalists and newspaper publishers, to the retired Henry Stimson
and the assistant U.S. Secretary of State, George Messersmith, to President
Roosevelt himself in January 1938, to Sir John Simon, to Churchill during the
Sudeten Crisis, and in the summer of 1939 to Lord Halifax and Vansittart's successor, Alexander Cadogan. Brüning offered them the sound advice to rearm
quickly, since Hitler would escalate his demands at any sign of weakness, but
then he plunged them into confusion by urging a bargain with German military
conspirators. He always mentioned the Polish Corridor as the minimum reward
that the generals would deserve for toppling Hitler, and he sometimes demanded
the borders of 1914, even Alsace-Lorraine. None of his listeners considered such
a bargain legitimate or feasible.[112]

When the Second World War broke out, Brüning felt like a spectator to a play
by Euripides, who foresaw a tragic fate long in advance but could do nothing
to alter the behavior of the protagonists.[113] In London he had helped Carl
Goerdeler, the driving force in the conservative Resistance, to establish contact
with numerous politicians and diplomats, but mounting suspicion of "Prussian
militarism" caused them all to rebuff Goerdeler's advances during his last visit
in May 1939. Brüning hoped to meet Goerdeler again in August to convey
another urgent appeal to the generals for Hitler's removal, but Goerdeler was
detained in Ankara by illness, and Brüning embarked on one of the last passen-
ger liners to depart for New York before the outbreak of war. He angrily blamed
the failure of the generals to act on the spinelessness of British foreign policy,
but in a more lucid moment he recognized that his mediating efforts had become
futile after the *Reichskristallnacht*, the horrendous night of anti-Jewish violence

---

111 Brüning, *Briefe*, I:52 (source of quotation), 119–20, 181–83, 250–51; Brüning to Treviranus, 16
November 1937, in Treviranus, *Exil*, p. 46; Peter Hoffmann, *The History of the German Resistance
1933–1945* (Cambridge, Mass., 1977), pp. 18–112; Klemens von Klemperer, *German Resistance
against Hitler: The Search for Allies Abroad, 1938–1945* (Oxford, 1992), pp. 105–12; "German
Society and the Resistance to Hitler," in Mommsen, *From Weimar to Auschwitz*; Klaus-Jürgen
Müller, "Zur Struktur und Eigenart der nationalkonservativen Opposition bis 1938," in
Schmädecke and Steinbach, eds., *Widerstand*, pp. 329–44.

112 See *Briefe*, I:70, 94, 111–13, 117–18, 143, 168–74, 184–88, 198–99, 206–14, 230–33, 261–65,
280–84; Treviranus, *Exil*, pp. 175–76; and Stephen A. Schuker, "Ambivalent Exile: Heinrich
Brüning and America's Good War," in Christoph Buchheim et al., eds., *Zerrissene Zwischenkriegszeit*, pp. 352–54.

113 Brüning to Mona Anderson, 24 November 1938 and 27 June 1940, *Briefe*, I:220, 316–17.

in November 1938 that destroyed sympathy for Germany abroad.[114] Back at Harvard, Brüning received a visit from Trott zu Solz, who had been dispatched by Ernst von Weizsäcker at the foreign office to explore possibilities for a peaceful resolution of the "Phony War" with Great Britain and France. Brüning traveled to Washington on 11/12 November 1939, conferred with Messersmith, and again gained audience with President Roosevelt; he passed along Trott's message with a strong endorsement of the man's character but confessed uncertainty about Weizsäcker's intentions. Brüning gained a friendly hearing for Trott in the State Department, but here too the German visitor encountered mounting suspicion of Prussian militarism. Even Trott acknowledged, moreover, that the generals would not act against Hitler until Germany began to suffer defeats on the battlefield.[115]

Catastrophe for Europe coincided with the attainment of personal security for Brüning, who became the Littauer Professor of Government at Harvard's new School of Public Administration in September 1939. He devoted a large portion of his salary and all his influence to the assistance of German refugees; working with the Unitarians and the American Friends Service Committee, he helped to bring numerous Social Democrats and other victims of Nazi persecution to America. Brüning sought desperately to arrange Hilferding's passage to America after the fall of France and was plunged into depression by news of his friend's death in a Gestapo cell. He maintained his public silence about the Hitler regime, however, condemning émigrés like Wirth who supported Allied propaganda or discussed the formation of a government-in-exile. By 1943 Wirth dreamed of a return to power in the train of conquering armies and made preparations to form a provisional government with Social Democrats who shared his Swiss exile. Brüning regarded this as a form of "exile neurosis" that he was determined to avoid.[116]

Brüning became a highly controversial figure after the invasion of the Soviet Union and America's entry into the war. He continued to lobby privately for an arrangement with the German army as a substitute for the policy of unconditional surrender, and his academic lectures emphasized the similarity between the "totalitarian" Communists and Nazis. Brüning made a very bad impression, even on friends like Wheeler-Bennett, when he seemed to echo Nazi arguments that the West must ally with Germany against the Soviet menace. British observers, leftist German émigrés, and many colleagues on the Harvard faculty

---

114 Klemperer, *German Resistance*, pp. 92–95, 112–17; Ritter, *Carl Goerdeler*, pp. 198–231; Treviranus, *Exil*, p. 69; Brüning, *Briefe*, I:214–18, 250–51, 280–84; Brüning to Hermann Pünder, June 1947, NL Pünder/613/200–204.

115 Klemperer, *German Resistance*, pp. 56, 182–85; Brüning to Messersmith, 30 November and 22 December 1939, *Briefe*, I:296–300.

116 Knapp, ed., "Dokumentation: Brüning im Exil," pp. 95–115; Schulze, ed., "Dokumentation: Rückblick auf Weimar," pp. 148–53; Brüning, *Briefe*, I:318–23, 336–43, 378–79; Morsey, "Emigration und Nachkriegsplanung," pp. 228–30; Klemperer, *German Resistance*, pp. 59–60, 163–67, 221.

concluded that he sought to disrupt the Grand Alliance. In 1943 the émigré Bernhard Menne published a malicious exposé that depicted Brüning as a monarchist counter-revolutionary who had killed off German democracy, flirted with Hitler, and shared the basic goals of Nazi foreign policy despite some disagreement about methods. The retired Vansittart publicly endorsed Menne's thesis, declaring that Brüning must not have any influence over Germany's future. Brüning shrugged off such attacks by "Communist fellow travelers," but he felt so isolated at Harvard that he submitted his resignation (which was rejected). He was disheartened by the spread of the view that the German "national character" had for centuries been characterized by authoritarianism, and he feared that this "war hysteria" would lead to irresistible pressure for the dismemberment of Germany.[117]

The appointment of Brüning's old friend Henry Stimson as Secretary of War in 1940 nevertheless preserved access for him to senior American officials, and he offered them excellent advice in October 1944 on how to revive democracy in a conquered Germany. He warned that a bombed-out people, who had been taught for twelve years to revile all political parties and liberal institutions, would find it impossible to hold prompt elections for a constitutional convention. Political thinking and action must be revived at the lowest level of municipal self-government; only after three to five years would it be feasible to hold national elections. The future German constitution should be simpler than that of Weimar, which had undermined parliamentary government with redundant guarantees of democracy – the popular referendum and the powerful presidency. The best collaborators for democratization could be found among former trade unionists, moderate Social Democrats, and the idealistic Catholics and Protestants who had drawn together under Gestapo persecution. The services of most older judges and civil servants could safely be retained because they had remained aloof from the NSDAP. The occupation authorities should not try to revive all the political parties of the Weimar Republic but rather simplify the party spectrum, and Prussia should be broken up into several smaller states. When asked if he favored the restoration of a monarchy, Brüning replied that the time for that had long since passed. His memorandum reads like a blueprint for U.S. occupation policy, and the occupiers granted important posts to almost every individual recommended by Brüning as a reliable anti-fascist, including Hermann Dietrich, Schlange-Schöningen, Stegerwald, Pünder, Adenauer, Jakob Kaiser, and Karl Arnold.[118]

117 Brüning, *Briefe*, I:392–93, 408–09, 416–19, 515–18; Bernhard Menne, *The Case of Dr. Bruening* (London and New York, n.d.); Treviranus, *Exil*, pp. 158–60, 173–76; Shuster, "Brüning's Sojourn," pp. 463–65; Lothar Kettenacker, "Der nationalkonservative Widerstand aus angelsächsischer Sicht," in Schmädecke and Steinbach, eds., *Widerstand*, pp. 712–31; Schucker, "Ambivalent Exile," pp. 331–35; Radkau, *Deutsche Emigration*, pp. 189–92.
118 Memorandum of October 1944 for DeWitt Poole of the Office of Strategic Services, *Briefe*, I:525–38; Brüning's interview of September 1945 with American officers, pp. 27–28, HUG FP 93.10/Box 16/Interview; Morsey, "Emigration und Nachkriegsplanung," pp. 230–33; Müller, *Brüning Papers*, pp. 41–42.

Brüning could not rejoice over the return to public life by some of his friends because so many others had died. The destruction of German cities by saturation bombing plunged him into chronic depression. He took heart from the heroism of the Stauffenberg plot to assassinate Hitler, but its failure led to the execution of Letterhaus, Habermann, Goerdeler, and dozens more of the friends upon whom Brüning had pinned his hopes for the revival of democracy.[119] Brüning's depression turned to anger after the decisions of the Potsdam Conference, which he considered the product of racial prejudice. The cession of Germany's fertile eastern provinces to Poland (including Brüning's old Reichstag district of Breslau) persuaded him that millions of Germans were doomed to starve. He sternly lectured Americans that they were unintentionally continuing the Nazi policy of genocide. Stimson sought Brüning out upon his return from Potsdam to report that he had been dismayed by the sight of bombed-out cities and excluded from important diplomatic meetings, and Brüning created from this encounter a legend that his friend had resigned from the American delegation and cabinet to protest the outrageous treatment of Germany.[120]

Brüning was further outraged by the unprecedented decision to form an International Military Tribunal to try Germans accused of war crimes and crimes against humanity. When two American officers requested background information for the prosecution in September 1945, Brüning exclaimed that "you can intern me, or you can shoot me, but you will not be able to force me to participate in the procedure of the War Criminal Trial, which will become a unilateral action against the German people, to shield from investigation the war crimes of some other European nations, especially the Russians." This trial might destroy "the last moral and natural law principles in international law." Stalin was the worst aggressor, and the proceedings would harm the effort to de-Nazify Germany. "People shot by foreigners are always martyrs." After this outburst Brüning offered an account of the Nazi seizure of power that minimized any wrongdoing even by men whom he actually considered quite culpable, such as Franz von Papen and Oskar von Hindenburg. His interviewers concluded indignantly that "Bruening is a violent reactionary and is 100 percent pro-German," and that his disagreements with the Nazis involved only domestic, not

---

119 Brüning to Edmund Stinnes, 14 July 1941, to Mona Anderson, 7 June and 15 October 1945, and to Freya von Moltke, 10 August 1946, *Briefe*, I:366, 431–32, 440, 448–52; Brüning to Hermann Ullmann, 13 July 1946, NL Ullmann/6/281–82; Shuster, "Brüning's Sojourn," pp. 460–66; Treviranus, *Exil*, pp. 149–50, 159–65; Aretz, *Katholische Arbeiterbewegung*, pp. 150–237; Ritter, *Carl Goerdeler*, pp. 336–438; Elfriede Nebgen, *Jakob Kaiser. Der Widerstandskämpfer* (Stuttgart and Berlin, 1967).

120 Brüning, "The Statesman," pp. 104–05; memoir of September 1945, *Briefe*, I:432–33; Brüning to Treviranus, 10 January 1956, HUG FP 93.10/Box 34/G.R. Treviranus (3); Treviranus, *Exil*, p. 180; Morsey, "Emigration und Nachkriegsplanung," pp. 236–37. Stimson had never been a member of the delegation to Potsdam, attending solely as an observer, and his only known disagreement with Truman involved his proposal to share A-bomb technology with the Soviet Union. He resigned from the cabinet after the conference because of a heart attack; see Hodgson, *Henry Stimson*, pp. 274–362.

foreign policy. They rejected as preposterous everything that he tried to tell them about German history.[121]

Such experiences inspired Brüning with contempt for the U.S. political system. Even before the outbreak of war, Brüning had criticized the decay of American democracy in terms suggesting a regression to the old views of Martin Spahn from 1913.[122] After the war he became even more harsh. Brüning initially credited President Roosevelt with skillful vagueness at the Yalta Conference and a plan to resist Soviet demands more firmly thereafter, which Truman had failed to understand. He eventually decided, however, that FDR had undermined the rule of law at home and subordinated foreign policy to the vagaries of public opinion, that he had proved "a much greater catastrophe for the world than Hindenburg."[123] Brüning's anger persisted even after the United States provided generous assistance to Germany under the Marshall Plan. The ex-chancellor nevertheless gave himself much credit for that plan because of the advice on European economic problems that he had submitted to key American officials and his conversations with elder statesmen such as Herbert Hoover.[124]

The shocking revelations about the Holocaust undermined Brüning's resolve to denounce the mistreatment of the German people. Before the war Brüning had shrewdly advised Jewish leaders in America to do everything they could to promote emigration from Nazi Germany, because Hitler was capable of anything. He nevertheless refused to believe the first reports of genocide. As George Shuster later recalled, "that Germans – even when they were Nazis – could actually pile millions of men, women and children into gas-ovens was a fact that he came eventually to accept, but it left a wound in his spirit which could never again be healed."[125] Brüning felt great admiration for the chief rabbi of Berlin, Leo Baeck, who had synthesized Judaism with "Prussia" and avoided any hatred of Germany despite his sufferings in Theresienstadt. In private correspondence he nevertheless sought defensively to minimize the dimensions and uniqueness of the Holocaust, and at times he even blamed the victim by recalling every

---

121 See Claire Nix's transcript in HUG FP 93.10/Box 16/Interview (Brüning quotations from pp. 13–13a), and the memorandum of 1 October 1945 by Captain Samuel Conkling and Lt. Morton Rome, published in Schucker, "Ambivalent Exile," pp. 338–42.

122 See Brüning to Raymond Buell, 14 April 1939, HUG FP 93.10/Box 2/Brie-Bürger.

123 Brüning to Ulrich Biel, 24 April 1946, to Theodor Heuss, 12 June 1951, and to Hans von Raumer, 4 July 1954 (source of quotation), in *Briefe*, II:32–33, 273–75, 356.

124 Memorandum for Senator Robert Taft, February 1947, and Brüning to Averell Harriman, 3 July 1947, *Briefe*, II:75–79, 89–91; Brüning to Michael Gibson, 14 February 1955, HUG FP 93.10/Box 12/Hugh Gibson; Rudolf Morsey, "Brünings Kritik am politischen Wiederaufbau in Deutschland, 1949–1955," in Joseph Listl and Herbert Schambeck, eds., *Demokratie in Anfechtung und Bewährung* (Berlin, 1982), pp. 285, 295; Müller, *Brüning Papers*, pp. 55–56. Hoover (who led a humanitarian relief mission to Germany early in 1947) and Secretary of Commerce Harriman were key figures in formulating the Marshall Plan, and they did echo Brüning's economic arguments; see John Gimbel, *The Origins of the Marshall Plan* (Stanford, 1976).

125 Brüning memoir, "Lage der Juden in Deutschland," outlining his contacts in 1933–38 with Leo Baeck, Jacob Landau, Felix Frankfurter, and Felix Warburg, *Briefe*, I:162–64; Shuster, "Brüning's Sojourn," p. 460.

rumor that Zionist bankers had contributed financially to the rise of the NSDAP. Brüning wrote a German friend in January 1949 that she must not expect genuine support for Germany from the American government any time soon:

> True, attitudes toward Germany among many foreigners have become favorable much more quickly than I expected at the end of the war. But there has been no such change among those who *determine* policy *in the final analysis* [emphasis in original]. The November night in 1938, when all the Jews in Germany were arrested, has not been forgotten. No people, with the exception of a few great individuals, is capable of such powerful hatred as the Jewish people; its influence is still very great, especially here. One cannot expect everyone to be as wise and charitable as Professor Baeck.

This lapse into racial stereotyping and grotesque exaggeration of Jewish power illustrate the deterioration of Brüning's judgment in exile.[126]

Brüning did exert a positive influence on postwar developments by promoting the formation of the Christian Democratic Union (CDU). A few German politicians sought after 1945 to revive a "Center Party" specifically for Catholics, but Brüning wrote dozens of German friends to argue that Catholics and Protestants were no longer divided by any serious political issues. The forward-looking Essen Program of the Christian trade unions in 1920 and the bitter experience of the Nazi dictatorship all demanded the formation of an "interconfessional, socially progressive party, conservative in tempo." Brüning also contributed to the emergence of stable leadership within the CDU by praising Konrad Adenauer as the party's outstanding politician and the only serious candidate to become the first chancellor of the Federal Republic. Brüning pressed home these arguments in personal meetings when the U.S. government finally permitted him to visit Germany in August 1948, and his attitude was publicized in countless CDU campaign posters. His influence helped to condemn the revived Center Party to marginality, and the founders of the CDU reciprocated by defending Chancellor Brüning's record.[127]

Brüning displayed a more equivocal attitude toward the other great act of political consolidation after 1945, the founding of a unified German labor

---

126 Brüning to Hans Peters, 18 May 1948, and to Leo Baeck, 13 May 1953, *Briefe*, II:126, 329–30; Brüning to Frau Dr. Mönnig, 19 January 1949 (source of quotation), HUG FP 93.10/Box 22/Käthe Mönnig; Brüning's interview of September 1945, pp. 3, 28, HUG FP 93.10/Box 16/Interview; Brüning to Joos, 23 December 1948, HUG FP 93.10/Box 16/Joos; Müller, *Brüning Papers*, pp. 44–46.

127 Quotation from Brüning to Franz Meinow, 16 October 1945, *Briefe*, I:440–41 (see also I:434–36 and II:18–19, 22–23, 37–38, 93, 142–47, 155, 159–68, 195–202, 207); Brüning to Wilhelm Sollmann, 20 August 1946, in Knapp, ed., "Brüning im Exil," pp. 116–20; Leo Schwering, "Stegerwalds und Brünings Vorstellungen über Parteireform und Parteiensystem," in Hermens and Schieder, eds., *Staat, Wirtschaft und Politik*, pp. 23–40; Morsey, "Brünings Kritik am Wiederaufbau," pp. 285–90; Morsey, "Zentrumspartei und Zentrumspolitiker," pp. 54, 62–66; Ute Schmidt, *Zentrum oder CDU. Politischer Katholizismus zwischen Tradition und Anpassung* (Opladen, 1987); Maria Mitchell, "Materialism and Secularism: CDU Politicians and National Socialism, 1945–1949," *Journal of Modern History*, 67 (1995): 294–95.

federation, which adopted the name of the Christian-nationalist umbrella organization that he had served in the 1920s, the Deutsche Gewerkschaftsbund. He claimed credit for the last-minute effort by the labor leaders of the Weimar Republic to merge their unions voluntarily after Hitler's appointment as chancellor, but he feared that anticlericalism and Marxism had revived during the war among the Social Democrats who dominated the new federation. Brüning advised former associates in the Christian unions to keep alive the threat of secession to exert pressure on their socialist colleagues, but he also made it easier for the new unions to preserve their unity by exhorting the CDU to achieve consensus with the SPD over social and economic policy. Brüning vigorously supported the laborite demand for *Mitbestimmung* in particular, that is, a powerful voice for workers in the boards of directors of major industrial corporations. By 1953 he recognized that there was no longer any chance to revive independent Christian trade unions, and he opposed the abortive effort to do so by a small group of Catholic laborites and bishops in the mid-1950s.[128]

The Parliamentary Council that drafted the Fundamental Law of the Federal Republic in 1948/9 followed advice long offered by Brüning when it embraced a simplified version of parliamentary government without the popular referendum or a powerful presidency. Brüning had offered this advice directly to the German people in an open letter on the causes of his fall from power that was published by Rudolf Pechel in 1947.[129] Brüning does not seem to have exerted any direct influence on the drafting of the Fundamental Law, however, nor did he display interest in the issues of states' rights that dominated the debates of the Parliamentary Council. He actually opposed one feature of the new constitution that might be considered the logical culmination of his own efforts to strengthen the position of the cabinet, the "constructive vote of no confidence" that requires a parliamentary majority to agree on a new chancellor before toppling the old. Brüning observed tartly to Alphons Nobel that this provision was a great mistake, that chancellors should defend their policies in parliament and resign if they could not win a vote of confidence, because "struggle and risk are the essence of politics." The ex-chancellor displayed a quiet faith in the German electorate that contrasted sharply with the dominant tendency on the Parliamentary Council to blame the demise of the Weimar Republic on "mass

---

128 Brüning to Wilhelm Sollmann, 17 June 1943, IfZ/F206/55, and 20 August 1946, in Knapp, ed., "Brüning im Exil," p. 118; Brüning to Hans Bechly, 28 May 1948, HUG FP 93.10/Box 3/ Hans Bechly; correspondence with Alphons Nobel from 1950–54 in HUG FP 93.10/Box 23/Alphons Nobel; Brüning, *Briefe*, II:163, 189–90, 220, 260, 291–92, 297, 385–86; Patch, *Christian Trade Unions*, pp. 216–35; Wolfgang Schroeder, *Katholizismus und Einheitsgewerkschaft. Der Streit um den DGB und der Niedergang des Sozialkatholizismus in der Bundesrepublik bis 1960* (Bonn, 1992).

129 See Brüning, "Ein Brief," in *Reden*, pp. 266–67 (first published in *Deutsche Rundschau*, vol. 70, #7).

democracy" and seek powerful government institutions that would be impervious to any return of radical voting behavior.[130]

Brüning's great ambition was to mold German foreign policy as a respected elder statesman. In the spring of 1949 he advised CDU leaders that the Federal Republic must pursue a nonaligned foreign policy to promote national reunification, but Adenauer decided after profound reflection that it must align itself with the West, contain Soviet expansionism, and achieve economic recovery before seeking reunification.[131] Thereafter Brüning criticized Adenauer repeatedly in private as a gullible idealist who failed to understand that France regarded NATO and European economic integration as new instruments to achieve Cardinal Richelieu's old dream of hegemony. NATO was irrelevant to German national interests because it planned to defend Europe on the Rhine, not the Elbe. Germany must avoid any economic or military commitment to the West unless it received "full sovereignty"; until then it should open negotiations about national reunification with the Soviet Union. This disagreement took on personal rancor when Brüning heard that Adenauer spitefully told American occupation officials that he had always seen a Prussian general's cap in the antechamber when visiting Chancellor Brüning's office.[132] A personal meeting in June 1950 went badly after Adenauer asked pointedly when Brüning intended to leave Germany again. For the eminently practical Adenauer, Brüning's actions seemed explicable only as part of a campaign to supplant him as CDU chairman. Brüning was annoyed by this ascription of selfish motives and outraged when Adenauer offered him a government pension in August 1951. Concluding that the current chancellor was a provincial Rhinelander, Brüning sympathized with the SPD's campaign to revive a sense of solidarity with the lost eastern provinces. Brüning especially resented Adenauer's decision to follow the advice of the francophile Hans Schäffer – called to Bonn as a special consultant despite his Swedish citizenship – regarding the Schuman Plan for economic integration. Brüning had maintained friendly ties with Schäffer during the first years of exile but concluded during the war that Schäffer claimed the credit for all of his achievements. Now he launched vicious and unfounded attacks on his former

---

130 Brüning to Alphons Nobel, 15 February 1951, *Briefe*, II:264. Compare Peter Merkl, *The Origin of the West German Republic* (Westport, Conn., 1982), pp. 80–84, 175–77, and Hans Mommsen, "Der lange Schatten der untergehenden Republik. Zur Kontinuität politischer Denkhaltungen von der späten Weimarer zur frühen Bundesrepublik," in Karl Dietrich Bracher et al., eds., *Die Weimarer Republik 1918–1933. Politik – Wirtschaft – Gesellschaft* (Düsseldorf, 1987), pp. 552–86.

131 Brüning's letters to Pechel, Robert Pferdmenges, Käthe Mönnig, Otto Friedrich, Hermann Pünder, and Adenauer, April-May 1949, *Briefe*, II:183–88; Morsey, *Brüning und Adenauer*, pp. 27–32; Schwarz, *Adenauer*, pp. 427–66.

132 Brüning's letters of January 1950-January 1951 to Theodor Steltzer, Manfred von Brünneck, Helene Weber, Pünder, and Kaiser, *Briefe*, II:215–16, 229–30, 237–38, 239–46, 255–57; Brüning to Pünder, 25 October 1950, NL Pünder/613/58–59; Müller, *Brüning Papers*, pp. 50–54.

colleague's patriotism and honesty in private letters (although his memoirs retained a highly favorable portrait). Schäffer did everything he could to maintain friendship with Brüning and labored skillfully to enhance the ex-chancellor's reputation among historians.[133]

Brüning decided to accept appointment as professor of political science at the University of Cologne in the fall of 1952 and return to Germany for good. He declined the offer of a CDU mandate in the Bundestag election of 1953, but Adenauer had some cause to regard him as a rival. He continued to attack Adenauer's foreign policy in private, and Jakob Kaiser echoed Brüning's views within the cabinet as minister in charge of relations with East Germany. In April 1954 Kaiser invited Brüning to join the steering committee of a new pressure group outside the CDU, "Indivisible Germany: A People's Movement for Reunification." Brüning promised support behind the scenes but refused to sign any public declaration for fear of Adenauer's wrath. The other former chancellor, Joseph Wirth, publicly denounced the Schuman Plan and even launched a new political party in 1953 to agitate for a neutralist foreign policy, which was rumored to accept Soviet financing. Brüning considered this action quixotic but respected Wirth's motives.[134] Thus it was natural for Adenauer to become alarmed in June 1954, when Brüning first expressed his view of foreign policy in a public lecture attended by representatives of the national press. Brüning praised Rathenau and Stresemann as exemplary statesmen who knew how to balance between West and East; the treaties of Rapallo, Locarno, and Berlin had sought brilliantly "to take advantage of Germany's geopolitical situation to stabilize the balance of power in Europe and thus preserve peace." Now Bonn pursued "a purely dogmatic foreign policy," however, ignoring the possibility of a thaw in relations with the Soviet Union. Germany could never be reunified if Adenauer insisted on joining NATO and the European Economic Community. "It is perfectly understandable," Brüning concluded, "that both France and the United States press for West Germany to remain dependent somehow on the Western world. But nobody would or could argue that the peace of Europe and of the world will thereby become more secure than it has been."[135]

---

133 Brüning to Otto Friedrich, 30 August 1954, pp. 1–4, HUG FP 93.4.5/Folder 2; Brüning to A. H. Berning, 30 December 1951 and 11 July 1952, and to Kurt Kluge, 2 August 1952, *Briefe*, II:291, 311–15; Morsey, *Brüning und Adenauer*, pp. 39–41; Morsey, "Brünings Kritik am Wiederaufbau," pp. 291–94; Schwarz, *Adenauer*, pp. 642–44, 710–27; Schulz, "Suche nach dem Schuldigen," pp. 679–85; Müller, *Brüning Papers*, pp. 87–95; Wandel, *Hans Schäffer*, pp. 228–31, 276.

134 Kaiser to Brüning, 7 April 1954, HUG FP 93.10/Box 18/Jakob Kaiser, and reply of 17 April in *Briefe*, II:349; Brüning to Josef Ersing, 8 July 1953, *Briefe*, II:333; Wirth's circular to Bundestag members, 1 January 1952, and Brüning to Wirth, 20 September 1954, NL Wirth/10; Morsey, "Brünings Kritik am Wiederaufbau," pp. 296–97; Focke, *Sozialismus*, pp. 261–300; Erich Kosthorst, *Jakob Kaiser. Bundesminister für gesamtdeutsche Fragen, 1949–1957* (Stuttgart, 1972).

135 "Die Vereinigten Staaten und Europa. Rede im Rhein-Ruhr-Klub Düsseldorf am 2. Juni 1954," in Brüning, *Reden*, pp. 294–98.

This speech included some thoughtful reflections on the dangers of the Cold War, but Adenauer orchestrated a devastating press campaign to depict it in the worst possible light. Numerous editorials charged that Brüning was blinded to contemporary realities by an anachronistic drive to make Germany a Great Power again, that he sought revenge for the defeat of 1945 just as he had for the defeat of 1918. Adenauer himself called a press conference to compare Brüning to the maverick Wirth, expressing anguish that such elder statesmen would seek "from *ressentiment* or the desire for profit . . . to harm the vital interests of the German people in such a fashion."[136] Brüning was astonished to find himself subjected to an "artillery barrage" of criticism as a chauvinist for a speech intended as a plea to avert World War III. When his last surviving relative, his sister Maria, died shortly thereafter, Brüning returned to America in 1955 to live out his days in Norwich, Vermont. He compared Adenauer to Schleicher as a clever but unscrupulous tactician, and to Hindenburg as "the second tragedy caused by aging [*Alterstragik*] that I have experienced."[137] Adenauer's attacks on this speech were somewhat unfair, but his victory in this debate had positive results. By now the Catholic majority in the CDU condemned "Prussianism" as another form of that "materialism" and "secularism" that had undermined Christian morality and paved the way for Hitler. Adenauer viewed the Rhineland as the heart of a German civilization far older and more urbane than that of Brandenburg, and this attitude certainly contributed something to Germany's reconciliation with France and the success of the Common Market. Under the circumstances of the 1950s, the German people were fortunate to find a chancellor who combined a wealth of political experience with lifelong distrust of the Prussian tradition.[138]

After his final rupture with Adenauer, Brüning lapsed into a peculiar nostalgia. As Germany entered an era of unprecedented stability and prosperity, he insisted that the Weimar Republic was far superior to the Federal in its constitution, dedicated civil servants, and dignified members of parliament. The Weimar Republic was still permeated by a tradition of service to the state that had been destroyed by the Third Reich and the Second World War.[139] Brüning became increasingly pessimistic in his American retirement. "Tradition" seemed dead both in Europe and America; the younger generation

---

136 See Rudolf Morsey, "Brünings Kritik an Adenauers Westpolitik. Vorgeschichte und Folgen seines Düsseldorfer Vortrags vom 2. Juni 1954," in Manfred Funke et al., eds., *Demokratie und Diktatur. Festschrift für Karl Dietrich Bracher* (Düsseldorf, 1987), pp. 349–64 (quotation on p. 356).

137 Brüning to Dr. Goldschmidt, HUG FP 93.10/Box 12/Theo Goldschmidt; Brüning to Otto Friedrich, 30 August 1954, pp. 7, 10–12, HUG FP 93.4.5/Folder 2; Brüning to Gustav Olef, 10 July 1958, p. 5 (source of quotation), HUG FP 93.10/Box 23/Gustav Olef.

138 See Gordon A. Craig, *From Bismarck to Adenauer: Aspects of German Statecraft*, rev. ed. (New York, 1965); Schwarz, *Adenauer*, pp. 87–101; and Mitchell, "Materialism and Secularism," pp. 283–94.

139 Brüning to Otto Friedrich, 30 August 1954, pp. 5–6, HUG FP 93.4.5/Folder 2; *Briefe*, II:264–65, 326, 335, 433–35.

sought nothing but material gain and sensual gratification. Brüning wrote Katharina von Kardorff that "every people goes under if it does not have a national goal for which it is prepared to make every personal and material sacrifice. . . ." He confided to Hans von Raumer that "this is why I can live no longer in the homeland. If one is not prepared to make every sacrifice for a national goal, then that leads inevitably to a softening and demoralization in every area of life." The only political development in the 1950s to rouse Brüning's enthusiasm was the foundation of the Fifth Republic in France; he regarded Charles de Gaulle as a successful imitator of his own doomed effort to restore a healthy balance between the legislative and executive powers.[140]

Brüning apparently despaired of completing his memoirs soon after his return to America and stopped all work on them in 1958, leaving several manuscripts whose contents overlapped.[141] He perceived that his first draft of 1934/5 had been unfair to some associates, to Schleicher in particular, who confronted grave problems that Brüning had not understood at the time. Unfortunately, that draft was written when he could remember the events of his chancellorship in vivid detail and possessed some valuable documents smuggled out of Germany, including personal letters from Hindenburg, that were later destroyed in a V-1 attack on London. As he sought to become more objective, his memory was fading badly, and Brüning found that his account grew ever less accurate in detail as he strove for greater truth. Equally frustrating was the fact that he could never establish just who had poisoned Hindenburg's mind against him, the question that he regarded as decisive for explaining the dissolution of the Weimar Republic.[142] On the deepest level Brüning was doubtless paralyzed by ambivalence toward the political mission that he had embraced in his youth, to revive the Prussian tradition. He tried after 1945 to establish or deepen relations with a number of aristocratic landowners and former leaders of the DNVP, providing even former enemies like Hugenberg with generous testimonials for their de-Nazification hearings. He sought to absolve the Junkers of any collective responsibility for his fall, arguing that only a tiny minority of the genuine nobility had turned against him, and he encouraged the Protestants in the CDU to defend Prussia's legacy against attacks by Rhenish and Bavarian Catholics. Brüning wrote Count Manfred von Brünneck that "what I want is to remind people of the good era of the Prussian state and of the bearers of its genuine tradition,"

---

140 Brüning to Katharina von Kardorff-Oheimb, 13 May 1957, and to Gustav Olef, 31 December 1959, *Briefe*, II:427, 459–60; Brüning to Hans von Raumer, 18 July 1957, pp. 2–3, HUG FP 93.4.5.

141 Morsey, *Zur Entstehung*, pp. 22–24, 29–32; Müller, *Brüning Papers*, pp. 138–40.

142 Brüning, *Memoiren*, pp. 11–12; Brüning to Ullmann, 13 July 1946, NL Ullmann/6/280–82; Brüning to Pünder, 4 May 1954, and Brüning to Josef Baumhoff, 27 December 1955, NL Pünder/613/5–6, 28–29; Brüning to Graf Brünneck, 17 March 1955, HUG FP 93.10/Box 5/Manfred von Brünneck; Brüning to Wolfgang Mommsen, 10 March 1956, in Müller, *Brüning Papers*, pp. 193–94; Brüning to Hans von Raumer, 18 July 1957, HUG FP 93.4.5; Schulz, "Suche nach dem Schuldigen."

the landed nobility. Brüning could not bring himself, however, to follow the count's advice to suppress all criticism of Hindenburg in order to win the younger generation's admiration for an exemplar of the "old Prussian virtues." Nor could he refrain from observing that the landed nobility had done much to destroy itself through its agitation against "agrarian Bolshevism" in May 1932 and its selfish conduct under Papen.[143] Brüning obviously feared that the Prussian tradition upon which he had always pinned his hopes was largely imaginary.

143 Graf Brünneck to Brüning, 20 March 1949, and reply of 19 August, HUG FP 93.10/Box 5/Manfred von Brünneck; Brüning to Graf Galen, 14 August 1949, HUG FP 93.10/Box 11/Franz Graf Galen; Müller, *Brüning Papers*, pp. 155–60; Mitchell, "Materialism and Secularism," pp. 303–06.

Conclusion

A great deal of justified skepticism has been expressed about the argument by some historians in recent years that Germans should adopt a "more balanced" view of the Third Reich in order to recover a sense of national identity.[1] This argument can be made much more effectively, however, regarding the Brüning era. Despite the peculiar distortions in his memoirs, Brüning should not be linked any longer with antidemocratic projects that he actually opposed as chancellor. It is not healthy for the ongoing political debate in Germany or elsewhere if historians of the Weimar Republic persuade their readers that support for parliamentary democracy was confined to the SPD, that a well-intentioned government can achieve full employment regardless of world economic conditions, or that Brüning's shortcomings suffice to explain the growing appeal of the totalitarian parties to the German electorate in 1930–2.

Despite all the attacks on the "Hunger Chancellor" by Communists, Brüning did not seek to resolve Germany's economic crisis at the expense of the working class. This is not to deny, of course, that the millions of unemployed workers suffered greatly, and Brüning did base some of his initial policy decisions on the dubious premise that German wages had risen too quickly from 1927 to 1929. The chancellor abandoned this explanation of the economic crisis by December 1930, however, and opposed any effort to lower real wages thereafter; his wage policy merely sought to avoid distortions of relative prices by encouraging all categories of nominal wages to adjust to the downward trend in the cost of living. The cumulative impact of his decisions was to leave the real value of wages and welfare benefits virtually unchanged. Careful analysis of the Reich budget under Brüning also reveals no effort to redistribute national income through fiscal policy. Martin Schiele's agrarian protectionism did restrict access to meat and imported fruit for working-class families, but Brüning accepted this program

---

1 See Richard J. Evans, *In Hitler's Shadow: West German Historians and the Attempt to Escape from the Nazi Past* (New York, 1989); Charles Maier, *The Unmasterable Past: History, Holocaust, and German National Identity* (Cambridge, Mass., 1988); and *"Historikerstreit." Die Dokumentation der Kontroverse um die Einzigartigkeit der nationalsozialistischen Judenvernichtung* (Munich, 1987).

only because of massive pressure by Hindenburg and firmly resisted new protectionist measures after March 1931. He also preserved intact all the principles of the welfare state developed in the 1920s, including compulsory state labor arbitration and unemployment insurance, even when that position drove the DVP into opposition. Workers' wages represented 56.7 percent of national income in 1929 and 57.0 percent in 1932; only after Hitler came to power did that proportion decline.[2] Brüning made every effort to distribute the costs of the Great Depression fairly.

Of course the question of whether sacrifices were distributed fairly may well be less important than the question of whether they could have been avoided. This book cannot claim to resolve conclusively the debate over the extent of Brüning's maneuvering room in economic policy, but it seems most probable that no German government could have achieved a dramatic reduction of the unemployment rate in this period. Consensus now prevails among economic historians that there was no alternative to Brüning's austerity policy before July 1931. The picture becomes less clear thereafter, because thoughtful alternatives to the policy of deflation were proposed, and the Reichsbank gained more freedom of action after the Bank Crisis with the imposition of some controls over foreign exchange. Those controls remained ineffective, however, until the Second Standstill Agreement of January 1932; until then Germany remained vulnerable to painful losses of foreign exchange. The cabinet's crucial decisions to adhere to the gold standard and persevere with deflation in the Fourth Emergency Decree of December 1931 were probably unavoidable.

Brüning achieved his greatest maneuvering room in January 1932. After the Second Standstill Agreement he could have reached quick agreement with France on a temporary extension of the Hoover Moratorium and then launched at least a modest jobs program. With an energetic effort, he might have raised 1 to 1.5 billion marks for public works, as proposed by Dietrich, Stegerwald, and the National Economic Council. Such a program would not have had a great impact on the unemployment rate according to today's macroeconomic models, which suggest 2 to 3 billion marks as the minimum expenditure required to accelerate the velocity of the circulation of money, but it might have restored some measure of confidence in the future among private investors and unemployed youth. Instead Brüning undertook a gamble with the postponement of the Lausanne Conference until June, hoping that the benefit from the complete abolition of reparations then would justify the risk of virtually ignoring the problem of unemployment for another five months. This was his most dubious decision. In general, however, Brüning correctly sensed that the basic trend of the

---

2 Ludwig Preller, *Sozialpolitik in der Weimarer Republik* (Athenäum reprint, Düsseldorf, 1978), pp. 399–473; James, *German Slump*, pp. 192–209, 220–38, 415–16; Winkler, *Katastrophe*, pp. 23–45, 81–85; Witt, "Finanzpolitik als Verfassungs- und Gesellschaftspolitik," pp. 401–10. Witt does suggest that Brüning's pressure on municipal governments to reduce their outlay was an effort to weaken the working class, since city budgets tended to redistribute income from rich to poor, but he does not specify what alternative Brüning had to this policy; contrast James, *German Slump*, pp. 87–108.

twentieth century has been toward the emergence of world markets that cannot be regulated effectively by any single government. Governments of industrial nations today are far more favorably placed than Brüning's with regard to secure credit, reliable statistics on economic performance, and institutions to regulate banks and stock exchanges, and yet international agreement among the advanced industrial nations is usually required before effective action can be taken to promote economic growth. Brüning accurately perceived the vital importance of such international cooperation, but many of his "Keynesian" critics exaggerate the significance of the nation-state for economics.[3]

President Hindenburg made it difficult for historians to judge whether Brüning calculated well with his gamble of January 1932, because he replaced Brüning prematurely with a chancellor so reactionary and inept that no success at Lausanne could improve the political situation. Whatever his shortcomings, Brüning rallied an absolute electoral majority against Hitler and Thälmann in the presidential elections, and he was coping with the Nazi menace through vigorous enforcement of the SA ban at the time of his dismissal. Against the totalitarian parties in May 1932, Chancellor Brüning retained the support of the republican Reichsbanner, the trade unions, all state governments, the Catholic episcopate, and a majority in a Reichstag that did not need to face elections until September 1934. All of these assets were squandered in June and July through a series of catastrophic mistakes by Kurt von Schleicher, Otto Meissner, Oskar von Hindenburg, and Franz von Papen. They justified their decisions as necessary to prevent the conquest of power by the totalitarian parties, but their judgment was badly warped by authoritarian values. Their definition of the "national interest" and "public opinion" granted far too much weight to generals and agrarians committed to goals that could not win electoral approval in a democratic system: a costly arms buildup and massive subsidies for grain producers whose costs of production far exceeded world market prices. Their worst mistake was the gratuitous assault on the SPD in the Prussian coup of July 1932, which fatally divided the opponents of fascism. As Brüning later argued, the "tragedy of Weimar" lay in Hindenburg's obstinate refusal to acknowledge that the SPD had become a responsible and patriotic party.[4]

Despite the widespread tendency to depict Brüning as the foe of parliamentary democracy, as chancellor he vigorously opposed any effort to blame Germany's problems on the Weimar constitution. He rejected every suggestion for some kind of "dictatorship" incompatible with the terms of Article 48, and none of his emergency decrees was condemned by the courts. Interior Minister Wirth did pursue a reform of the suffrage law, hoping to discourage the proliferation of small parties through restrictions on proportional representation, but

---

3 See Brüning's Page-Barbour Lecture #1 of January 1939, pp. 13–16, HUG FP 93.45; Kindleberger, *World in Depression*, pp. 288–305; Donald McCloskey, *If You're So Smart: The Narrative of Economic Expertise* (Chicago, 1990); and Harold James, "Gab es eine Alternative zur Wirtschaftspolitik Brünings?"
4 This was the theme of Brüning's first series of Harvard lectures in 1936 (see *Briefe*, I:111).

Brüning vetoed the project in March 1931 because it had no chance to win approval in the Reichstag. In October 1931 interior ministry officials actually prepared an emergency decree to abolish proportional representation, but Brüning again vetoed the idea.[5] He dedicated himself to the principle that the exercise of emergency powers could be justified only if the government avoided any effort to change the rules of the political game, to redistribute political power between left and right, or to redistribute wealth between the classes. The contrast between his record and Papen's in this regard offers a vital lesson to all architects of new democracies who feel compelled to incorporate something like Article 48 into their constitutions.

Brüning has often and with some justice been compared unfavorably to Franklin Delano Roosevelt, who displayed far more skill at persuading ordinary people that the government cared about their problems, even though his record at promoting economic recovery was not very impressive.[6] Brüning's strength as a politician certainly did not lie in public relations, and he neglected his duty to explain his policies to the public through much of the year 1931. The comparison to FDR is somewhat misleading, however, because the German electorate was so deeply divided into three major blocs with conflicting premises and values: class-conscious workers, practicing Roman Catholics, and the "Protestant bourgeois" bloc. All German politicians and parties were closely tied to one of these blocs and distrusted by the other two; even the master propagandists of the Nazi Party generated little appeal outside the third bloc.[7] The speeches of Chancellor Brüning straddled the deepest chasms in German society, because he sought as a Catholic to rally conservative Protestants and moderate Social Democrats in defense of constitutional government. Even Joseph Wirth, the best orator in the Center Party, discovered that this was an almost impossible task. Most of his speeches as interior minister sought to build bridges of understanding with conservative Protestants, but he found that they always misinterpreted and rejected his remarks.[8] Brüning's appeal to the Prussian tradition struck the only emotional chord that resonated among all three blocs, which could all celebrate the development of the *Rechtsstaat*, the emancipation of the serfs by Karl vom Stein, and the achievement of national unity under Bismarck.

Brüning did contribute to the radicalization of civil servants and shopkeepers by excluding their representatives from access to the formulation of policy, but he had good reason to believe that they would not engage in con-

---

5 Friedrich Schäfer, "Zur Frage des Wahlrechts in der Weimarer Republik," in Hermens and Schieder, eds., *Staat, Wirtschaft und Politik*, pp. 131–35; "Die Überwindung des Radikalismus," memorandum by Dr. Teipel for Wirth and Zweigert, 22 October 1931, NL Wirth/75.

6 See, for example, Hans Luther (who served as ambassador to the U.S. in 1933), *Vor dem Abgrund*, pp. 121–26.

7 See W. Phillips Shively, "Party Identification, Party Choice, and Voting Stability: The Weimar Case," *American Political Science Review*, 66 (1972): 1203–25; and Falter, *Hitlers Wähler*, pp. 51–53, 110–17, 169–93.

8 See Wirth to Otto Meissner, 31 March 1931, BAP R15.01/13121/48, and his undated reply to the letter by Wilhelm Hoegner of 20 August 1942, NL Wirth/18.

structive discussions. The German League of Civil Servants campaigned stri-
dently against any reduction in the nominal level of salaries and pensions,
because the Weimar Republic had failed to develop mechanisms to arbitrate labor
disputes in the public sector. Reductions of a similar magnitude to Brüning's
took place with little debate in Great Britain because of the creation of such
mechanisms in the 1920s.[9] Within the *Mittelstand* (petite bourgeoisie) the
problem had even deeper roots, because Wilhelmian governments had long
sought to promote social stability by protecting shopkeepers and artisans against
the threat of bankruptcy. Brüning had little chance to persuade them to accept
the conclusion of most economists, big businessmen, and labor leaders that there
must be thousands of bankruptcies in the small-business sector before the
German economy could revive. The record of the farmers' organizations suggests that interest groups committed to a program that defied the logic of the
world market could not be appeased during the Great Depression even if government leaders consulted them incessantly and provided lavish subsidies.
Brüning was no doubt correct to believe that the best chance to consolidate a
social foundation for parliamentary democracy was to promote consensus
between management and labor in the industrial sector. No chancellor could have
worked harder than he to promote such consensus – through formal summit conferences in June and November 1930, dozens of private approaches to the leaders
of big business and organized labor, his choice of expert advisers in the aftermath of the Bank Crisis, and the President's Economic Advisory Council in the
fall of 1931. Although the efforts to revive the Central Association of November 1918 failed because of mounting class tensions, Brüning did promote informal consensus and retained the support of the most influential leaders of both
the Free Unions and the Reich Association of Industry at the time of his fall.[10]

Brüning does deserve criticism for francophobia. He believed the worst of the
French government and may have missed an opportunity for valuable financial
aid when he allowed the project for a customs union with Austria to proceed.
Throughout his political career Brüning encouraged unity among Germans by
focusing attention on France's alleged pursuit of hegemony in Europe. This was
not a cold-blooded strategy; indeed, the trauma of the Great War played a surprisingly important role in the deliberations of the Brüning cabinet. The chancellor misinterpreted complex developments on financial markets in July 1931 as
the result of a French "offensive" against Germany, criticized Hindenburg to
his face in November 1931 for a loss of nerve in 1918, and erupted against
Schleicher with all the fury of the men stuck in the mud against the armchair
strategists of the general staff. At critical moments Chancellor Brüning sometimes reverted to the dichotomous thinking, which divides the world into

9 See Andreas Kunz, "Arbeitsbeziehungen und Arbeitskonflikte im öffentlichen Sektor. Deutschland
    und Grossbritannien im Vergleich," *Geschichte und Gesellschaft*, 12 (1986): 37–62.
10 See Wengst, "Unternehmerverbände und Gewerkschaften"; Tschirbs, *Tarifpolitik im Ruhrbergbau*,
    pp. 369–440; and James, *German Slump*, pp. 179–91, 226–45. Contrast Neebe, "Unternehmerver-
    bände und Gewerkschaften," pp. 312–17.

comrades and enemies, characteristic of so many combat veterans of the Great War.[11] After fleeing Germany he ranked France's stubborn defense of treaty rights that lacked any moral foundation high on the list of causes of the failure of German democracy. This attitude was shared by many fellow émigrés, even left-wing republicans such as Otto Braun, Joseph Wirth, and Friedrich Dessauer; it was a common defense mechanism among German politicians who agonized over their failure to prevent Hitler's triumph.[12]

Brüning was definitely constructive, on the other hand, in his thinking about the political role of the Catholic Church. Ever since his student days he championed ecumenicism, and he always supported the steps toward separation of church and state in the Weimar constitution. His articulation of "Prussian" values sought to focus attention on moral principles shared by Catholics and Protestants. Throughout his career Brüning pointed the way toward successful accommodation by pious Catholics to a world in which religious pluralism and a large degree of secularization are inevitable. The history of the Federal Republic supports Brüning's contention, expressed already in the Essen Program of 1920, that the Catholic Church hierarchy could best preserve its moral influence through support for cooperation with Protestants in a Christian democratic party where the clergy does not play an active role. He was misguided, however, to insinuate that the Vatican bore responsibility for his fall as chancellor or the dissolution of the Center Party in 1933. Cardinal Pacelli probably did suggest privately to Center Party leaders in 1931 that they should form a coalition with the Nazis (a suggestion made by many conservative Protestants), but there is no evidence that the Vatican undermined Brüning's position in the Reichstag or with President Hindenburg.

The final question about Brüning is whether his conception of statecraft retains anything of enduring value. We cannot simply dismiss his effort to revive civic virtue with a superior smile. Much unhappy experience in recent years suggests that enlightened self-interest may not be an adequate foundation for politics, that any truly successful policy must involve an effort to promote a sense of community and mutual obligation among the citizens. Brüning's particular concept of civic virtue was already distinctly old-fashioned by 1930, however. To some extent his "Prussian" values reflected the attitude of an older generation fighting a hopeless rear-guard action against jazz music, automobiles, and erotic experimentation by the younger generation. Brüning also displayed little understanding for the desire of many women for greater self-fulfillment. Leftist women's organizations launched Germany's first major campaign to legalize abortion in 1930/1, and even church-going women who rejected this demand agreed that the Great Depression had caused unprecedented suffering

---

11 See Paul Fussell, *The Great War and Modern Memory* (New York and London, 1975).
12 See Brüning to Raymond Buell, 21 September 1939, HUG FP 93.10/Box 2/Brie-Bürger; Brüning's second Page-Barbour Lecture of January 1939, p. 7, HUG FP 93.45; Braun, *Von Weimar zu Hitler*, p. 5; Dessauer to Wirth, 1 November 1939, NL Wirth/22; Wirth's Paris lecture of 8 February 1936, NL Wirth/9; and Wirth to Dessauer, 24 October 1945, NL Wirth/12.

for pregnant women and young mothers. Brüning's only known response was to implore liberal newspaper editors friendly to the government to avoid any mention of abortion so as not to offend President Hindenburg.[13] Brüning always supported the "family wage" with bonuses for family fathers, and he felt that married women did not really have a right to work. His government sought to deny them unemployment benefits and encouraged the Reichstag to pass a law in May 1932 requiring government agencies to dismiss married women employees if a man or single woman could be found to take their place. Thus Brüning may have encouraged many women to conclude that the Weimar Republic offered no attractive alternative to the frank traditionalism of the Nazis.[14]

The shortcomings of the old cult of Prussia are revealed by its exploitation under the Third Reich. Christian Graf von Krockow has warned shrewdly against the tendency to glorify Frederick the Great despite his growing isolation from all affectionate human contact during his years on the throne. Krockow contrasts the king's most influential maxim – "it is not necessary that I live, but it is necessary that I do my duty" – with the decision by his North American contemporaries to define "the pursuit of happiness" by individuals as the noblest purpose of the political community. Frederick at least knew that he was unhappy, that he had sacrificed something valuable in his career of conquest and public service, but his later admirers often lacked this degree of self-awareness:

> In our country an ideology triumphed in our century that no longer even felt the sacrifice of humanity but rather transformed it into the highest, most heroic quality. Finally happiness itself was proclaimed to be the opportunity to sacrifice oneself, as Ernst Jünger, spokesman of the *Zeitgeist*, proclaimed in 1932: "The highest happiness of man lies in being sacrificed, and the highest art of command lies in showing goals that are worthy of sacrifice."

Many of Chancellor Brüning's associates echoed Jünger at least faintly, and President Hindenburg actually told a visitor in December 1932 that "one must so revere the fatherland as to forget oneself completely."[15] Goebbels's "Day of Potsdam" was a hideous perversion of Brüning's Prussian ideal, but as chancel-

---

13 Atina Grossmann, "Abortion and Economic Crisis: The 1931 Campaign Against Paragraph 218," in Renate Bridenthal, Atina Grossmann, and Marion Kaplan, eds., *When Biology Became Destiny: Women in Weimar and Nazi Germany* (New York, 1984), pp. 66–86; Ernst Feder, *Heute sprach ich mit . . .*, entry of 11 October 1930, p. 273.

14 See Michael Schneider, *Christliche Gewerkschaften*, pp. 273–75, 545–48; Luther diary, conversation with Brüning on 7 December 1931, *Quellen: Politik und Wirtschaft*, II:1164; Gertrud Hanna to Frieda Wunderlich, 26 January 1933, *Quellen: Gewerkschaften*, pp. 812–14; Dörte Winkler, "Frauenarbeit versus Frauenideologie. Probleme der weiblichen Erwerbstätigkeit in Deutschland 1930–1945," *Archiv für Sozialgeschichte*, 17 (1977): 99–126; Heinrich Winkler, *Katastrophe*, pp. 56–59; and Renate Bridenthal and Claudia Koonz, "Beyond *Kinder, Küche, Kirche*: Weimar Women in Politics and Work," in Bridenthal, Grossmann, and Kaplan, eds., *When Biology Became Destiny*, pp. 33–65.

15 "Das Pflicht und das Glück," in Christian Graf von Krockow, *Preussen. Eine Bilanz* (Stuttgart, 1992), pp. 16–17; Hubatsch, *Hindenburg*, pp. 145–46.

lor he had done little to inoculate German youth against such propaganda. The history of the Second World War shows how successful the Nazis were at harnessing old concepts of Prussian duty to serve their new kind of totalitarian dictatorship.

Even the most idealistic versions of the Prussian tradition remain dangerously insular. Politicians approaching the twenty-first century should seek to make their citizens feel comfortable in the kind of multiethnic and multilingual society that flourishes in the global marketplace. The Great Elector set a noble precedent for this effort when he embraced the French Huguenot refugees after the revocation of the Edict of Nantes; this policy, often ignored by later admirers of Prussian statecraft, probably benefited the country more than the conquest of Silesia. In general, however, the "Prussian tradition" implies no moral vision broader than the transmutation of Prussian patriotism into German nationalism. An antagonistic relationship with neighboring peoples provides its central rationale for civic duty. Germans, like Americans after the end of the Cold War, obviously need some other rationale in future.

The best politicians will nevertheless always endeavor somehow to discharge the same two obligations felt so keenly by Heinrich Brüning, to uphold the rule of law regardless of partisan advantage, and to articulate the basic moral values that bind the political community together. Americans in particular cannot afford to ignore the following warning issued by Brüning at the University of Virginia on the eve of the Second World War:

> If the problems and the dangers for democracy become overwhelming, it will not be the constitution which saves democracy; it will depend only on one factor, whether the nation in its majority has not lost the appreciation that democracy can only live if it is based on higher and more exacting ethical principles than any other form of government. Democracy does not only give rights; it sets a higher task for every citizen from the moral point of view than any other form of government. . . . Every form of government must be based upon fundamental ethical principles which cannot be changed under any conditions. . . . In the last instance, there is no other safeguard; and if a nation has lost its understanding of this point, one day it will not escape the ruthless hand of a dictator.[16]

Despite his often expressed admiration for British mores and institutions, Brüning's view of civic virtue was shaped by a tradition that goes back to Rousseau (the subject of his master's thesis at Strasbourg) and Thomas Jefferson. This tradition has been widely discredited in Germany because of the experience of the 1920s, when the antidemocratic right always sought to link parliamentary democracy with moral corruption, and the 1930s, when the Nazis inundated the German people with perverted appeals for self-sacrifice. French and American history suggest nevertheless that a lively debate between

---

16 Page-Barbour Lecture #3 (unpaginated), HUG FP 93.45.

those who emphasize civic virtue as the basis of the political community and those who emphasize enlightened self-interest is an essential element of democratic political culture. Accepting Heinrich Brüning as a well-intentioned although sometimes misguided defender of parliamentary democracy could help to revive such debate in Germany.

Bibliography

Archival Sources

ARCHIV FÜR CHRISTLICH-DEMOKRATISCHE POLITIK, St. Augustin (archive of the Christian Democratic Union)
> Adam Stegerwald Papers, Nachlass (NL) Stegerwald

BUNDESARCHIV, Koblenz (German National Archive, cited as BAK)
Records of organizations
> Deutsche Demokratische Partei (German Democratic Party): R 45 III
> Deutsche Volkspartei (German People's Party): R 45 II
> Gesamtverband der christlichen Gewerkschaften Deutschlands (League of Christian Trade Unions): Kleine Erwerbung 461
> Reichskanzlei (Reich chancellery): R 43 I
> Verein deutscher Eisen- und Stahlindustrieller (Association of German Iron and Steel Industrialists): R 13 I
Personal papers
> Friedrich Baltrusch: Kleine Erwerbung 855
> Moritz Julius Bonn: NL Bonn
> Heinrich Brüning (photocopies of a few documents that Brüning took with him when he left Germany in 1934): Kleine Erwerbung 828
> Hermann Dietrich: NL Dietrich
> Eduard Dingeldey: NL Dingeldey
> Rudolf ten Hompel: NL ten Hompel
> Alfred Hugenberg: NL Hugenberg
> Jakob Kaiser: NL Kaiser
> Albert Krebs: NL Krebs
> Walther Lambach: NL Lambach
> Hans Luther: NL Luther
> Paul Moldenhauer: NL Moldenhauer
> Rudolf Pechel: NL Pechel
> Hermann Pünder: NL Pünder
> Fritz Schäffer: NL Fritz Schäffer
> Martin Spahn: NL Spahn

Paul Silverberg: NL Silverberg
Hermann Ullmann: NL Ullmann
Joseph Wirth: NL Wirth

BUNDESARCHIV, ABTEILUNG POTSDAM (Potsdam branch of the German National
Archive, cited as BAP)
Files consulted in 1979 under the German Democratic Republic
    Deutschnationale Volkspartei (German Nationalist People's Party): DNVP
    Reichsarbeitsministerium (Reich Labor Ministry): RAM
    Reichslandbund (Reich Agrarian League): RLB
Files consulted in 1995
    Präsidialkanzlei der Weimarer Republik (Office of the Reich President): R 601
    Reichsministerium des Innern (Reich Interior Ministry): R 15.01

BUNDESARCHIV-MILITÄRARCHIV, Freiburg (the National Military Archive)
    Kurt von Schleicher Papers, NL Schleicher

COLOGNE STADTARCHIV (Municipal Archive)
    Wilhelm Marx Papers, NL Marx

DGB ARCHIVE, Deutscher Gewerkschaftsbund, Düsseldorf (the headquarters of today's
German Labor Federation)
    Der Deutsche, 1921–33 (the only complete run of the daily newspaper founded
        by Brüning)
    Heinrich Imbusch Papers, NL Imbusch

DHV ARCHIVE, Deutscher Handels- und Industrieangestellten-Verband, Hamburg (the
headquarters of the successor organization of the German Nationalist Union of
Commercial Employees)
    Max Habermann memoirs, "Der DHV im Kampf um das Reich" (written in
        1934)
    Habermann's circular letters to DHV district leaders

HARVARD UNIVERSITY ARCHIVE (cited as HUG): THE BRÜNING PAPERS
    General correspondence from the years 1934–60: FP 93.10
    Journals, manuscripts, and personal papers: FP 93.35
    Lectures in America: FP 93.45
    Manuscript memoirs, dictated in 1934/5: FP 93.4
    Papers relating to the memoirs: FP 93.4.5

INSTITUT FÜR ZEITGESCHICHTE, Munich (Institute for Contemporary History, cited
as IfZ)
    Brüning letters to Wilhelm Sollmann from the 1940s: F206
    Wilhelm Groener papers (microfilm): NL Groener
    Hans Schäffer, daily diary and papers: NL Schäffer
    Lutz Graf Schwerin von Krosigk interview by Dr. Freiherr von Siegler, 24 April
        1952, Neufassung: ZS 145/Schwerin von Krosigk

KOMMISSION FÜR ZEITGESCHICHTE, Bonn
 Friedrich Dessauer Papers, NL Dessauer

ÖSTERREICHISCHES STAATSARCHIV/Archiv der Republik/NPA 10, Vienna (Austrian
State Archive, cited as ÖSA)
 Gesandschaftsberichte Berlin (reports from the Austrian ambassador to
 Germany, 1931/2)

GUSTAV STRESEMANN PAPERS, microfilmed by the U.S. National Archive: NL
Stresemann

KUNO VON WESTARP PAPERS, Schloss Gaertringen (consulted in 1978/9 with the
assistance of Friedrich Freiherr Hiller v. Gaertringen): NL Westarp

Published Memoirs, Diaries, Correspondence, and Polemics

Braun, Otto. *Von Weimar zu Hitler*. 2nd ed. New York, 1940.
Brecht, Arnold. "Gedanken über Brünings Memoiren." *Politische Vierteljahresschrift*, 12
 (1971): 607–40.
 Mit der Kraft des Geistes. Lebenserinnerungen 1927–67. Stuttgart, 1967.
Bredt, Johann Viktor. *Erinnerungen und Dokumente von Johann Victor Bredt, 1914 bis 1933*.
 Ed. Martin Schumacher. Düsseldorf, 1970.
Brüning, Heinrich. "Die Arbeit der Zentrumspartei auf finanzpolitischem Gebiete."
 In Karl Anton Schulte, ed., *Nationale Arbeit. Das Zentrum und sein Wirken in der
 deutschen Republik*. Leipzig, 1929.
 "Dokumentation: Heinrich Brüning im Exil. Briefe an Wilhelm Sollmann, 1940–
 1946." Ed. Thomas Knapp. *Vierteljahrshefte für Zeitgeschichte*, 22 (1974): 93–
 120.
 "Ein Brief." *Deutsche Rundschau*, 70, #7 (1947): 1–22 (cited by the pagination in
 Brüning, *Reden und Aufsätze*).
 Heinrich Brüning. Briefe und Gespräche 1934–1945. Ed. Claire Nix. Stuttgart, 1974
 (cited as "*Briefe*, I").
 Heinrich Brüning. Briefe 1946–1960. Ed. Claire Nix. Stuttgart, 1974 (cited as "*Briefe*,
 II").
 Heinrich Brüning. Reden und Aufsätze eines deutschen Staatsmanns. Ed. Wilhelm
 Vernekohl. Münster, 1968.
 Memoiren 1918–1934. Ed. Claire Nix and Theoderich Kampmann. Stuttgart,
 1970.
 "The Statesman," lecture of April 1946. *The Works of the Mind*. Chicago, 1947.
 "Welt-Finanzwesen." *Deutsche Arbeit*, 7 (1922): 111–14.
 "Der Wiederaufbau des deutschen Finanzwesens." *Jahrbuch der christlichen Ge-
 werkschaften für 1921*. Cologne, n.d. [1920]. Pp. 82–107.
Curtius, Julius. *Sechs Jahre Minister der Deutschen Republik*. Heidelberg, 1948.
Dirksen, Herbert von. *Moscow, Tokyo, London: Twenty Years of German Foreign Policy*.
 Norman, Okla., 1952.
Duesterberg, Theodor. *Der Stahlhelm und Hitler*. Wolfenbüttel and Hanover, 1949.
Feder, Ernst. *Heute sprach ich mit . . . Tagebücher eines Berliner Publizisten 1926–1932*. Ed.
 Cecile Lowenthal-Hensel and Arnold Paucker. Stuttgart, 1971.

Gereke, Günther. *Ich war königlich-preussischer Landrat.* Ed. Eberhard Czichon. East Berlin, n.d. [1970].

Gessler, Otto. *Reichswehrpolitik in der Weimarer Zeit.* Ed. Kurt Sendtner. Stuttgart, 1958.

Goebbels, Joseph. *Die Tagebücher von Joseph Goebbels. Sämtliche Fragmente: Teil I.* 4 vols. Ed. Elke Fröhlich. Munich, 1987.

Hamburger, Ernest. "Betrachtungen über Heinrich Brünings Memoiren." *Internationale wissenschaftliche Korrespondenz zur Geschichte der Arbeiterbeweung*, 8, #15 (1972): 18–39.

Hitler, Adolf. *Hitler. Reden, Schriften, Anordnungen.* Vol. 3, part 3 (January-September 1930), ed. Christian Hartmann. Munich, 1995. Vol. 5, part 1 (April-September 1932), ed. Klaus Lankheit. Munich, 1996.

Hoffmann, Josef. *Journalist in Republik, Diktatur und Besatzungszeit. Erinnerungen 1916–1947.* Ed. Rudolf Morsey. Mainz, 1977.

Kaas, Ludwig. "Der Konkordatstyp des faschistischen Italiens." *Zeitschrift für ausländisches öffentliches Recht und Völkerrecht*, 3 (1933): 488–522.

Keil, Wilhelm. *Erlebnisse eines Sozialdemokraten.* 2 vols. Stuttgart, 1948.

Kessler, Harry Graf. *Tagebücher 1918–1937.* 4th ed. Frankfurt a.M., 1979.

Keynes, John Maynard. *The Collected Writings of John Maynard Keynes.* Ed. Donald Moggridge et al. Cambridge, 1972–1982.

Köhler, Heinrich. *Lebenserinnerungen des Politikers und Staatsmannes 1878–1949.* Ed. Josef Becker. Stuttgart, 1964.

Krebs, Albert. *The Infancy of Nazism: The Memoirs of ex-Gauleiter Albert Krebs, 1923–1933.* Ed. William S. Allen. New York, 1976 (translation of *Tendenzen und Gestalten der NSDAP. Erinnerungen an die Frühzeit der Partei*, Stuttgart, 1959).

Lautenbach, Wilhelm. *Zins, Kredit und Produktion.* Ed. Wolfgang Stützel. Tübingen, 1952.

Luther, Hans. *Vor dem Abgrund, 1930–1933. Reichsbankpräsident in Krisenzeiten.* Berlin, 1964.

Meinecke, Friedrich. *The Age of German Liberation 1795–1815.* Ed. Peter Paret. Berkeley and Los Angeles, 1977.

Werke. 9 vols. Ed. Hans Herzfeld, Carl Hinrichs, and Walther Hofer. Darmstadt, Munich, and Stuttgart, 1957–1979.

Meissner, Hans-Otto. *Junge Jahre im Reichspräsidentenpalais. Erinnerungen an Ebert und Hindenburg 1919–1934.* Munich, 1988.

Meissner, Otto. *Staatssekretär unter Ebert – Hindenburg – Hitler.* Hamburg, 1950.

Muckermann, Friedrich. *Im Kampf zwischen zwei Epochen. Lebenserinnerungen.* Ed. Nikolaus Junk. Mainz, 1973.

Muckermann, Hermann. "Wie Heinrich Brüning am 21. Mai 1934 Deutschland verliess." *Deutsche Rundschau*, 71, #8 (1948): 112–17.

Ott, Eugen. "Ein Bild des Generals Kurt von Schleicher." *Politische Studien*, 10 (1959): 360–71.

Papen, Franz von. *Der Wahrheit eine Gasse.* Munich, 1952.

Pünder, Hermann. *Politik in der Reichskanzlei. Aufzeichnungen aus den Jahren 1929–1932.* Ed. Thilo Vogelsang. Stuttgart, 1961.

Quaatz, Reinhold. *Die Deutschnationalen und die Zerstörung der Weimarer Republik. Aus dem Tagebuch von Reinhold Quaatz 1928–1933.* Ed. Hermann Weiss and Paul Hoser. Munich, 1989.

Schäffer, Hans. "Dokumentation: Erinnerungen Hans Schäffers an Ernst Trendelenburg." Ed. Erna Danzl. *Vierteljahrshefte für Zeitgeschichte*, 25 (1977): 865–88.

Schlange-Schöningen, Hans. *Am Tage danach.* Hamburg, 1946.

Schmidt, Paul. *Statist auf diplomatischer Bühne 1923–45.* Bonn, 1949.

Schmidt-Hannover, Otto. *Umdenken oder Anarchie. Männer – Schicksale – Lehren.*
Göttingen, 1959.

Schwerin von Krosigk, Lutz Graf. *Es geschah in Deutschland. Menschenbilder unseres
Jahrhunderts.* Tübingen and Stuttgart, 1951.

 Staatsbankrott. Die Geschichte der Finanzpolitik des Deutschen Reiches von 1920 bis 1945.
Göttingen, 1974.

Severing, Carl. *Mein Lebensweg.* 2 vols. Cologne, 1950.

Shuster, George. "Dr. Brüning's Sojourn in the United States (1935–1945)." In Ferdinand Hermens and Theodor Schieder, eds., *Staat, Wirtschaft und Politik in der
Weimarer Republik.* Berlin, 1967.

Spahn, Martin. "Was ist Demokratie?" *Hochland*, 11, #1 (1913): 68–87.

Stadtler, Eduard. *Werksgemeinschaft als soziologisches Problem.* Berlin, 1926.

 Schafft es Brüning?. Berlin, 1931.

Stampfer, Friedrich. *Die ersten vierzehn Jahre der Deutschen Republik.* Offenbach a.M.,
1947.

Staudinger, Hans. *Wirtschaftspolitik im Weimarer Staat. Lebenserinnerungen eines politischen Beamten im Reich und in Preussen, 1889 bis 1934.* Ed. Hagen Schulze. Bonn,
1982.

Treviranus, Gottfried. *Das Ende von Weimar. Heinrich Brüning und seine Zeit.* Düsseldorf
and Vienna, 1968.

 Für Deutschland im Exil. Düsseldorf, 1973.

 "Zur Rolle und zur Person Kurt von Schleichers." In Hermens and Schieder, eds.,
Staat, Wirtschaft und Politik.

Ullmann, Hermann. "Das Essener Programm, November 1920." *Deutsche Rundschau*, 76
(1950): 897–903.

 Publizist in der Zeitenwende. Munich, 1965.

Vansittart, Robert. *The Mist Procession.* London, 1958.

Vernekohl, Wilhelm, ed. *Heinrich Brüning. Ein deutscher Staatsmann im Urteil der Zeit.*
Münster, 1961.

Weizsäcker, Ernst von. *Die Weizsäcker-Papiere 1900–1932.* Ed. Leonidas Hill. Berlin,
Frankfurt a.M., and Vienna, 1982.

Wagener, Otto. *Hitler aus nächster Nähe. Aufzeichnungen eines Vertrauten, 1929–1932.* Ed.
Henry A. Turner, Jr. Frankfurt a.M., 1978.

Wheeler-Bennett, John. "The End of the Weimar Republic." *Foreign Affairs*, 50 (January
1972): 351–71.

 Knaves, Fools and Heroes: Europe between the Wars. New York, 1975.

Other Published Primary Sources

Akten der Reichskanzlei der Weimarer Republik (cabinet minutes and related documents):
 Die Kabinette Marx III und IV, 1926–28. 2 vols. Ed. Günter Abramowski. Boppard am
Rhein, 1988.

 Das Kabinett Müller II, 1928–30. 2 vols. Ed. Martin Vogt. Boppard am Rhein, 1970.

 Die Kabinette Brüning I und II, 1930–32. 3 vols. Ed. Tilman Koops. Boppard am Rhein,
1982–90.

Das Kabinett von Papen, 1932. 2 vols. Ed. Karl-Heinz Minuth. Boppard am Rhein, 1989.

Das Kabinett von Schleicher, 1932/3. Ed. Anton Bolecki. Boppard am Rhein, 1986.

Akten zur deutschen auswärtigen Politik, 1918–1945. Serie B: 1925–1933, vols. 12–21. Göttingen, 1966–1983 (cited as *ADAP*).

Becker, Josef, ed. "Dokumentation: Zentrum und Ermächtigungsgesetz 1933." *Vierteljahrshefte für Zeitgeschichte,* 9 (1961): 195–210.

——— ed. "Dokumentation: Zur Politik der Wehrmachtabteilung in der Regierungskrise 1926/7." *Vierteljahrshefte für Zeitgeschichte,* 14 (1966): 69–78.

Borchardt, Knut, and Hans Otto Schötz, eds. *Wirtschaftspolitik in der Krise. Die (Geheim-) Konferenz der Friedrich List-Gesellschaft im September 1931 über Möglichkeiten und Folgen einer Kreditausweitung.* Baden-Baden, 1991.

Conze, Werner, ed. "Dokumentation: Zum Sturz Brünings." *Vierteljahrshefte für Zeitgeschichte,* 1 (1953): 261–88.

Deutscher Reichstag. *Stenographische Berichte der Verhandlungen des Deutschen Reichstags.* Berlin, 1920–1933.

Documents on British Foreign Policy, 1919–1939: Series II, vols. 1–6. London, 1946–1957 (cited as *DBFP*).

Documents Diplomatiques Français, 1932–1939. Première série (1932–1935), vols. 1–2. Paris, 1964–66 (cited as *DDF*).

Foreign Relations of the United States, 1930–1932. Washington, D.C., 1945–1948 (cited as *FRUS*).

Gesamtverband der christlichen Gewerkschaften Deutschlands (League of Christian Trade Unions)

25 Jahre christlicher Gewerkschaftsbewegung. Festschrift, Berlin, 1924.

Niederschrift der Verhandlungen des 10. Kongresses der christlichen Gewerkschaften Deutschlands, November 1920. Cologne, 1920.

Niederschrift der Verhandlungen des 11. Kongresses der christlichen Gewerkschaften Deutschlands, April 1926. Berlin, 1926.

Niederschrift der Verhandlungen des 12. Kongresses der christlichen Gewerkschaften Deutschlands, September 1929. Berlin, 1929.

Niederschrift der Verhandlungen des 13. Kongresses der christlichen Gewerkschaften Deutschlands, September 1932. Berlin, 1932.

Zentralblatt der christlichen Gewerkschaften (weekly journal).

Gessner, Dieter, ed. "Dokumentation: 'Grüne Front' oder 'Harzburger Front.'" *Vierteljahrshefte für Zeitgeschichte,* 29 (1981): 110–23.

Geyer, Michael, ed. "Dokumentation. Das Zweite Rüstungsprogramm (1930–34)." *Militärgeschichtliche Mitteilungen,* 16 (1975): 125–72.

Hubatsch, Walther. *Hindenburg und der Staat. Aus den Papieren des Generalfeldmarschalls und Reichspräsidenten von 1878 bis 1934.* Göttingen, 1966.

Kupper, Alfons, ed. *Staatliche Akten über die Reichskonkordatsverhandlungen 1933.* Mainz, 1969.

Matthias, Erich, ed. "Dokumentation: Hindenburg zwischen den Fronten. Zur Vorgeschichte der Reichspräsidentenwahlen von 1932." *Vierteljahrshefte für Zeitgeschichte,* 8 (1960): 75–84.

Morsey, Rudolf, ed. "Neue Quellen zur Vorgeschichte der Reichskanzlerschaft Brünings." In Hermens and Schieder, eds., *Staat, Wirtschaft und Politik.*

ed. *Die Protokolle der Reichstagsfraktion und des Fraktionsvorstands der Deutschen Zentrumspartei 1926–1933.* Mainz, 1969 (cited as *Zentrumsprotokolle*).

Müller, Hans, ed. *Katholische Kirche und Nationalsozialismus. Dokumente 1930–1933.* München, 1963.

Muth, Heinrich, ed. "Quellen zu Brüning." *Geschichte in Wissenschaft und Unterricht,* 64 (1963): 221–36.

Quellen zur Geschichte der deutschen Gewerkschaftsbewegung im 20. Jahrhundert. Band 4: Die Gewerkschaften in der Endphase der Republik, 1930–1933. Ed. Peter Jahn. Cologne, 1988 (cited as *Quellen: Gewerkschaften*).

Quellen zur Geschichte des Parlamentarismus und der Politischen Parteien (Sources for the History of Parliamentarism and of the Political Parties).

　Albertin, Lothar, and Konstanze Wegner, eds. *Linksliberalismus in der Weimarer Republik. Die Führungsgremien der Deutschen Demokratischen Partei und der Deutschen Staatspartei 1918–1933.* Düsseldorf, 1980 (cited as *Quellen: Linksliberalismus*).

　Maurer, Ilse, and Udo Wengst, eds. *Politik und Wirtschaft in der Krise, 1930–1932. Quellen zur Ära Brüning.* 2 vols. Düsseldorf, 1980 (cited as *Quellen: Politik und Wirtschaft*).

　eds. *Staat und NSDAP 1930–1932. Quellen zur Ära Brüning.* Düsseldorf, 1977 (cited as *Quellen: Staat und NSDAP*).

　Weber, Hermann, ed. *Die Generallinie. Rundschreiben des Zentralkomitees der KPD an die Bezirke 1929–1933.* Düsseldorf, 1981 (cited as *Quellen: Generallinie*).

Repgen, Konrad, ed. "Dokumentation. Zur Vatikanischen Strategie beim Reichskonkordat." *Vierteljahrshefte für Zeitgeschichte,* 31 (1983): 506–35.

Schulthess' Europäischer Geschichtskalender für die Jahre 1930–1932, vols. 71–73. Ed. Ulrich Thürauf. Munich, 1931–33.

Schulz, Gerhard, ed. "Dokumentation: Sand gegen den Wind. Letzter Versuch zur Beratung einer Reform der Weimarer Reichsverfassung im Frühjahr 1933." *Vierteljahrshefte für Zeitgeschichte,* 44 (1996): 295–319.

Schulze, Hagen, ed. "Dokumentation: Rückblick auf Weimar. Ein Briefwechsel zwischen Otto Braun und Joseph Wirth im Exil." *Vierteljahrshefte für Zeitgeschichte,* 26 (1978): 144–85.

Stasiewski, Bernhard, ed. *Akten deutscher Bischöfe über die Lage der Kirche 1933–1945. Band I: 1933–34.* Mainz, 1968.

Ursachen und Folgen. Vom deutschen Zusammenbruch 1918 und 1945 bis zur staatlichen Neuordnung Deutschlands in der Gegenwart. Eine Urkunden- und Dokumentensammlung zur Zeitgeschichte. 9 vols. Ed. Herbert Michaelis and Ernst Schraepler. Berlin, n.d. [1958].

Vogelsang, Thilo, ed. "Dokumentation: Neue Dokumente zur Geschichte der Reichswehr, 1930–1933." *Vierteljahrshefte für Zeitgeschichte,* 2 (1954): 397–436.

Volk, Ludwig, ed. *Akten Kardinal Michael von Faulhabers. Band I: 1917–1934.* Mainz, 1975.

　ed. *Kirchliche Akten über die Reichskonkordatsverhandlungen 1933.* Mainz, 1969.

Weber, Hermann, ed. *Der deutsche Kommunismus. Dokumente.* Cologne and Berlin, 1963.

Secondary Sources

Allen, William S. *The Nazi Seizure of Power: The Experience of a Single German Town 1922–1945.* Rev. ed. New York, 1984.

Altendorfer, Otto. *Fritz Schäffer als Politiker der Bayerischen Volkspartei 1888–1945*. 2 vols. Munich, 1993.

Aretz, Jürgen. *Katholische Arbeiterbewegung und Nationalsozialismus. Der Verband katholischer Arbeiter- und Knappenvereine Westdeutschlands, 1923–1945*. Mainz, 1978.

Bach, Jürgen A. *Franz von Papen in der Weimarer Republik. Aktivitäten in Politik und Presse 1918–1932*. Düsseldorf, 1977.

Bähr, Johannes. *Staatliche Schlichtung in der Weimarer Republik. Tarifpolitik, Korporatismus und industrieller Konflikt zwischen Inflation und Deflation 1919–1932*. Berlin, 1989.

Bahne, Siegfried. *Die KPD und das Ende von Weimar. Das Scheitern einer Politik, 1932–1935*. Frankfurt a.M. and New York, 1976.

Balderston, Theo. "The Beginning of the Depression in Germany, 1927–30: Investment and the Capital Market." *Economic History Review*, Second Series, 36 (1983): 395–415.

    The Origins and Course of the German Economic Crisis, November 1923 to May 1932. Berlin, 1993.

    "The Origins of Economic Instability in Germany 1924–1930: Market Forces versus Economic Policy." *Vierteljahresschrift für Sozial- und Wirtschaftsgeschichte*, 69 (1982): 488–514.

Becker, Josef. "Brüning, Prälat Kaas und das Problem einer Regierungsbeteiligung der NSDAP, 1930–1932." *Historische Zeitschrift*, 196 (1963): 74–111.

    "Heinrich Brüning in den Krisenjahren der Weimarer Republik." *Geschichte in Wissenschaft und Unterricht*, 17 (1966): 201–19.

    "Heinrich Brüning und das Scheitern der konservativen Alternative." *Aus Politik und Zeitgeschichte*, 80 (31 May 1980): 3–17.

    "Joseph Wirth und die Krise des Zentrums während des IV. Kabinetts Marx (1927/8)." *Zeitschrift für die Geschichte des Oberrheins*, 109 (1961): 361–482.

Becker, Josef, and Klaus Hildebrand, eds. *Internationale Beziehungen in der Weltwirtschaftskrise 1929–1933*. Munich, 1980.

Beer, Rüdiger Robert. *Heinrich Brüning*. 4th ed. Berlin, 1931.

Bendersky, Joseph. *Carl Schmitt: Theorist for the Reich*. Princeton, 1983.

Bennett, Edward W. *German Rearmament and the West, 1932–1933*. Princeton, 1979.

    Germany and the Diplomacy of the Financial Crisis, 1931. Cambridge, Mass., 1962.

Berghahn, Volker. "Die Harzburger Front und die Kandidatur Hindenburgs für die Präsidentschaftswahlen 1932." *Vierteljahrshefte für Zeitgeschichte*, 13 (1965): 64–82.

    Der Stahlhelm. Bund der Frontsoldaten, 1918–1935. Düsseldorf, 1966.

    "Das Volksbegehren gegen den Young-Plan und die Ursprünge des Präsidialregimes, 1928–30." In Dirk Stegman et al., eds., *Industrielle Gesellschaft und politisches System. Festschrift für Fritz Fischer*. Bonn, 1978.

Besson, Waldemar. *Württemberg und die deutsche Staatskrise 1928–1933. Eine Studie zur Auflösung der Weimarer Republik*. Stuttgart, 1959.

Böhnke, Wilfried. *Die NSDAP im Ruhrgebiet 1920–1933*. Bonn–Bad Godesberg, 1974.

Boldt, Hans. "Der Artikel 48 der deutschen Reichsverfassung." In Michael Stürmer, ed., *Die Weimarer Republik. Belagerte Civitas*. 2nd ed. Königstein/Ts., 1985.

Borchardt, Knut. "A Decade of Debate about Brüning's Economic Policy." In Jürgen Baron von Kruedener, ed., *Economic Crisis and Political Collapse: The Weimar Republic 1924–1933*. New York, Oxford, and Munich, 1990.

"Das Gewicht der Inflationsangst in den wirtschaftspolitischen Entscheidungs-prozessen während der Weltwirtschaftskrise." In Gerald Feldman, ed., *Die Nach-wirkungen der Inflation auf die deutsche Geschichte 1924–1933*. Munich, 1985.

"Noch einmal: Alternativen zu Brünings Wirtschaftspolitik?" *Historische Zeitschrift*, 237 (1983): 67–83.

Perspectives on Modern German Economic History and Policy. Transl. Peter Lambert. Cambridge, 1991. English translation of *Wachstum, Krisen, Handlungsspielräume der Wirtschaftspolitik. Studien zur Wirtschaftsgeschichte des 19. und 20. Jahrhunderts*. Göttingen, 1982.

"Zur Aufarbeitung der Vor- und Frühgeschichte des Keynesianismus in Deutschland. Zugleich ein Beitrag zur Position von W. Lautenbach." *Jahrbücher für Natio-nalökonomie und Statistik*, 197 (1982): 359–70.

Born, Karl Erich. *Die deutsche Bankenkrise 1931. Finanzen und Politik*. Munich, 1967.

Boyer, Christoph. "Das deutsche Reich und die Tschechoslowakei im Zeichen der Weltwirtschaftskrise." *Vierteljahrshefte für Zeitgeschichte*, 39 (1991): 551–87.

Bracher, Karl Dietrich. *Die Auflösung der Weimarer Republik. Eine Studie zum Problem des Machtverfalls in der Demokratie*. 5th ed. Villingen, Schwarzwald, 1971.

"Brünings unpolitische Politik und die Auflösung der Weimarer Republik." *Viertel-jahrshefte für Zeitgeschichte*, 19 (1971): 113–23.

Stufen der Machtergreifung. Ullstein reprint. Frankfurt a.M., 1983 (originally published as Part I of Karl Dietrich Bracher, Wolfgang Sauer, and Gerhard Schulz, *Die natio-nalsozialistische Machtergreifung* (Cologne and Opladen, 1960)).

Breuning, Klaus. *Die Vision des Reiches. Deutscher Katholizismus zwischen Demokratie und Diktatur (1929–1934)*. Munich, 1969.

Bridenthal, Renate, Atina Grossmann, and Marion Kaplan, eds. *When Biology Became Destiny: Women in Weimar and Nazi Germany*. New York, 1984.

Brose, Eric Dorn. *Christian Labor and the Politics of Frustration in Imperial Germany*. Washington, D.C., 1985.

Buchheim, Christoph, Michael Hutter, and Harold James, eds. *Zerrissene Zwi-schenkriegszeit. Wirtschaftshistorische Beiträge. Knut Borchardt zum 65. Geburtstag*. Baden-Baden, 1994.

Büttner, Ursula. *Hamburg in der Staats- und Wirtschaftskrise 1928–1931*. Hamburg, 1982.

"Politische Alternativen zum Brüningschen Deflationskurs." *Vierteljahrshefte für Zeitgeschichte*, 37 (1989): 209–51.

Burke, Bernard. *Ambassador Frederic Sackett and the Collapse of the Weimar Republic, 1930–1933: The United States and Hitler's Rise to Power*. Cambridge, 1994.

Busshoff, Heinrich. "Berufsständisches Gedankengut zu Beginn der 30er Jahre in Österreich und Deutschland." *Zeitschrift für Politik*, 13 (1966): 451–63.

Carsten, Francis L. *The Reichswehr in Politics 1918–1933*. Oxford, 1966.

Childers, Thomas. *The Nazi Voter: The Social Foundations of Fascism in Germany, 1919–1933*. Chapel Hill and London, 1983.

Clemens, Gabriele. *Martin Spahn und der Rechtskatholizismus in der Weimarer Republik*. Mainz, 1983.

Conze, Werner. "Die Krise des Parteienstaates in Deutschland 1929/30." *Historische Zeitschrift*, 178 (1954): 47–83.

"Die politischen Entscheidungen in Deutschland, 1929–1933." In Werner Conze and Hans Raupach, eds., *Die Staats- und Wirtschaftskrise des Deutschen Reichs 1929–1933*. Stuttgart, 1967.

"Die Reichsverfassungsreform als Ziel der Politik Brünings." *Der Staat*, 11 (1972): 209–17.

Craig, Gordon A. *From Bismarck to Adenauer: Aspects of German Statecraft*. Rev. ed. New York, 1965.

Dahrendorf, Ralf. *Society and Democracy in Germany*. New York, 1967.

Deist, Wilhelm. "Brüning, Herriot und die Abrüstungsgespräche von Bessinge 1932." *Vierteljahrshefte für Zeitgeschichte*, 5 (1957): 265–72.

Diner, Dan. "Constitutional Theory and 'State of Emergency' in the Weimar Republic: The Case of Carl Schmitt." *Tel Aviver Jahrbuch für deutsche Geschichte*, 17 (1988): 303–21.

Döhn, Lothar. *Politik und Interesse. Die Interessenstruktur der Deutschen Volkspartei.* Meisenheim am Glan, 1970.

Dörr, Manfred. "Die Deutschnationale Volkspartei 1925–1928." Ph.D. diss. University of Marburg, 1964.

Dorpalen, Andreas. *Hindenburg and the Weimar Republic*. Princeton, 1964.

Eichengreen, Barry. *Golden Fetters: The Gold Standard and the Great Depression, 1919–1939.* New York and Oxford, 1992.

Eisner, Freya. *Das Verhältnis der KPD zu den Gewerkschaften in der Weimarer Republik.* Frankfurt a.M., 1977.

Eksteins, Modris. *The Limits of Reason: The German Democratic Press and the Collapse of Weimar Democracy.* Oxford, 1975.

"War, Memory, and Politics: The Fate of the Film *All Quiet on the Western Front*." *Central European History*, 13 (1980): 60–82.

Eschenburg, Theodor. "Die Rolle der Persönlichkeit in der Krise der Weimarer Republik: Hindenburg, Brüning, Groener, Schleicher." In Theodor Eschenburg, *Republik von Weimar*. Munich, 1984. Translation in Hajo Holborn, ed. *Republic to Reich.* New York, 1972.

Falter, Jürgen W. *Hitlers Wähler*. Munich, 1991.

"The Two Hindenburg Elections of 1925 and 1932: A Total Reversal of Voter Coalitions." *Central European History*, 23 (1990): 225–41.

"Unemployment and the Radicalization of the German Electorate 1928–1933." In Peter Stachura, ed., *Unemployment and the Great Depression in Weimar Germany.* London, 1986.

Falter, Jürgen, Thomas Lindenberger, and Siegfried Schumann. *Wahlen und Abstimmungen in der Weimarer Republik*. Munich, 1986.

Feldman, Gerald. *The Great Disorder: Politics, Economics, and Society in the German Inflation, 1914–1924.* New York and Oxford, 1993.

"Industrialists, Bankers, and the Problem of Unemployment in the Weimar Republic." *Central European History*, 25 (1992): 76–96.

"Jakob Goldschmidt, the History of the Banking Crisis of 1931, and the Problem of Freedom of Manoeuvre in the Weimar Economy." In Christoph Buchheim et al., eds., *Zerrissene Zwischenkriegszeit.*

"The Weimar Republic: A Problem of Modernization?" *Archiv für Sozialgeschichte*, 26 (1986): 1–26.

ed. *Die Nachwirkungen der Inflation auf die deutsche Geschichte, 1924–1933.* Munich, 1985.

Feldman, Gerald, and Irmgard Steinisch. "Notwendigkeit und Grenzen sozialstaatlicher Intervention. Eine vergleichende Fallstudie des Ruhreisenstreits in Deutschland und des Generalstreiks in England." *Archiv für Sozialgeschichte*, 20 (1980): 57–117.

Fest, Joachim. *Hitler. Eine Biographie*. Frankfurt a.M., 1973.

Fischer, Conan. *The German Communists and the Rise of Nazism*. New York, 1991.

  Stormtroopers: A Social, Economic and Ideological Analysis, 1929–35. London, 1983.

Focke, Franz. *Sozialismus aus christlicher Verantwortung. Die Idee eines christlichen Sozialismus in der katholisch-sozialen Bewegung und in der CDU*. Wuppertal, 1978.

Friedenthal, Elisabeth. "Volksbegehren und Volksentscheid über den Young-Plan und die Deutschnationale Sezession." Ph.D. diss. University of Tübingen, 1957.

Fritzsche, Klaus. *Politische Romantik und Gegenrevolution. Fluchtwege in der Krise der bürgerlichen Gesellschaft: Das Beispiel des "Tat"-Kreises*. Frankfurt a.M., 1976.

Garvy, George. "Keynes and the Economic Activists of Pre-Hitler Germany." *Journal of Political Economy*, 83 (1975): 391–405.

Gates, Robert. "German Socialism and the Crisis of 1929–33." *Central European History*, 7 (1974): 332–59.

Gessner, Dieter. *Agrarverbände in der Weimarer Republik. Wirtschaftliche und soziale Voraussetzungen agrarkonservativer Politik vor 1933*. Düsseldorf, 1976.

Geyer, Michael. *Aufrüstung oder Sicherheit. Die Reichswehr in der Krise der Machtpolitik 1924–1936*. Wiesbaden, 1980.

Gies, Horst. "NSDAP und landwirtschaftliche Organisationen in der Endphase der Weimarer Republik." *Vierteljahrshefte für Zeitgeschichte*, 15 (1967): 341–76. Translation in Henry A. Turner, ed. *Nazism and the Third Reich*. New York, 1972.

Glashagen, Winfried. "Die Reparationspolitik Heinrich Brünings 1930–1932." Ph.D. diss. 2 vols. University of Bonn, 1980.

Graml, Hermann. "Präsidialsystem und Aussenpolitik." *Vierteljahrshefte für Zeitgeschichte*, 21 (1973): 134–45.

Granier, Gerhard. *Magnus von Levetzow: Seeoffizier, Monarchist und Wegbereiter Hitlers. Lebensweg und ausgewählte Dokumente*. Boppard am Rhein, 1982.

Grawert, Rolf, et al., eds. *Offene Staatlichkeit. Festschrift für Ernst-Wolfgang Böckenförde zum 65. Geburtstag*. Berlin, 1995.

Grill, Johnpeter Horst. *The Nazi Movement in Baden, 1920–1945*. Chapel Hill and London, 1983.

Grimm, Dieter. "Verfassungserfüllung – Verfassungsbewahrung – Verfassungsauflösung. Positionen der Staatsrechtslehre in der Staatskrise der Weimarer Republik." In Heinrich August Winkler, ed., *Die deutsche Staatskrise 1930–1933*. Munich, 1992.

Groener-Geyer, Dorothea. *General Groener, Soldat und Staatsmann*. Frankfurt a.M., 1955.

Grotkopp, Wilhelm. *Die grosse Krise. Lehren aus der Überwindung der Wirtschaftskrise 1929/32*. Düsseldorf, 1954.

Grübler, Michael. *Die Spitzenverbände der Wirtschaft und das erste Kabinett Brüning*. Düsseldorf, 1982.

Hamel, Iris. *Völkischer Verband und nationale Gewerkschaft. Der Deutschnationale Handlungsgehilfen-Verband 1893–1933*. Frankfurt a.M., 1967.

Hamilton, Richard. *Who Voted for Hitler?* Princeton, 1982.

Harsch, Donna. *German Social Democracy and the Rise of Nazism*. Chapel Hill and London, 1993.

Hartwich, Hans-Hermann. *Arbeitsmarkt, Verbände und Staat 1918–1933. Die öffentliche Bindung unternehmerischer Funktionen in der Weimarer Republik*. Berlin, 1967.

Hayes, Peter. " 'A Queston Mark with Epaulettes'? Kurt von Schleicher and Weimar Politics." *Journal of Modern History*, 52 (1980): 35–65.

Heer, Hannes. *Burgfrieden oder Klassenkampf? Zur Politik der sozialdemokratischen Gewerkschaften 1930–1933.* Neuwied and Berlin, 1971.

Heideking, Jürgen, Gerhard Hufnagel, and Franz Knipping, eds. *Wege in die Zeitgeschichte. Festschrift zum 65. Geburtstag von Gerhard Schulz.* Berlin and New York, 1989.

Heimers, Manfred Peter. *Unitarismus und süddeutsches Selbstbewusstsein. Weimarer Koalition und SPD in Baden in der Reichsreformdiskussion 1918–1933.* Düsseldorf, 1992.

Heitzer, Horstwalter. *Der Volksverein für das katholische Deutschland im Kaiserreich 1890–1918.* Mainz, 1979.

Helbich, Wolfgang. *Die Reparationen in der Ära Brüning. Zur Bedeutung des Young-Plans für die deutsche Politik 1930 bis 1932.* Berlin, 1962.

Hermans, Ferdinand A., and Theodor Schieder, eds. *Staat, Wirtschaft und Politik in der Weimarer Republik. Festschrift für Heinrich Brüning.* Berlin, 1967.

Hertz-Eichenrode, Dieter. *Wirtschaftskrise und Arbeitsbeschaffung. Konjunkturpolitik 1925/1926 und die Grundlagen der Krisenpolitik Brünings.* Frankfurt a.M. and New York, 1982.

Hiller von Gaertringen, Friedrich Freiherr. "Zur Beurteilung des 'Monarchismus' in der Weimarer Republik." In Gotthard Jasper, ed., *Tradition und Reform in der deutschen Politik.* Frankfurt a.M., 1976.

Hodgson, Godfrey. *The Colonel: The Life and Wars of Henry Stimson, 1867–1950.* New York, 1990.

Hömig, Herbert. *Das preussische Zentrum in der Weimarer Republik.* Mainz, 1979.

Hoepke, Klaus-Peter. *Die deutsche Rechte und der italienische Faschismus.* Düsseldorf, 1968.

Hohenzollern, Prince Friedrich Wilhelm von. *Das Haus Hohenzollern 1918–1945.* Munich and Vienna, 1985.

Holtfrerich, Carl-Ludwig. *Alternativen zu Brünings Wirtschaftspolitik in der Weltwirtschaftskrise*, Wiesbaden, 1982.

"Was the Policy of Deflation in Germany Unavoidable?" In Jürgen Baron von Kruedener, ed., *Economic Crisis and Political Collapse.*

"Zu hohe Löhne in der Weimarer Republik? Bemerkungen zur Borchardt-These." *Geschichte und Gesellschaft*, 10 (1984): 122–41.

Hornung, Klaus. *Der Jungdeutsche Orden.* Düsseldorf, 1958.

Hürter, Johannes. *Wilhelm Groener. Reichswehrminister am Ende der Weimarer Republik (1928–1932).* Munich, 1993.

Ishida, Yuji. *Jungkonservative in der Weimarer Republik. Der Ring-Kreis 1928–1933.* Frankfurt a.M., 1988.

Jacobsen, Jon. *Locarno Diplomacy: Germany and the West 1925–1929.* Princeton, 1972.

James, Harold. "The Causes of the German Banking Crisis of 1931." *Economic History Review*, 37 (1984): 68–87.

"Economic Reasons for the Collapse of the Weimar Republic." In Ian Kershaw, ed., *Weimar: Why Did German Democracy Fail?* New York, 1990.

"Gab es eine Alternative zur Wirtschaftspolitik Brünings?" *Vierteljahresschrift für Sozial- und Wirtschaftsgeschichte*, 70 (1983): 523–41.

The German Slump: Politics and Economics 1924–1936. Oxford, 1986.

The Reichsbank and Public Finance in Germany, 1924–1933. Frankfurt a.M., 1985.

"Rudolf Hilferding and the Application of the Political Economy of the Second International." *Historical Journal*, 24 (1981): 847–69.

Jarausch, Konrad. *Students, Society, and Politics in Imperial Germany: The Rise of Academic Illiberalism.* Princeton, 1982.

Jasper, Gotthard, ed. *Tradition und Reform in der deutschen Politik. Gedenkschrift für Waldemar Besson.* Frankfurt a.M., 1976.

Jochmann, Werner. "Brüning's Deflationspolitik und der Untergang der Weimarer Republik." In Dirk Stegmann et al., eds., *Industrielle Gesellschaft und politisches System.* Bonn, 1978.

Jonas, Erasmus. *Die Volkskonservativen 1928–1933. Entwicklung, Struktur, Standort und staatspolitische Zielsetzung.* Düsseldorf, 1965.

Jones, Larry Eugene. "Adam Stegerwald und die Krise des deutschen Parteiensystems." *Vierteljahrshefte für Zeitgeschichte,* 27 (1979): 1–29.

"Between the Fronts: The German National Union of Commercial Employees 1928 to 1933." *Journal of Modern History,* 48 (1976): 462–82.

"Crisis and Realignment: Agrarian Splinter Parties in the Late Weimar Republic, 1928–1933." In Robert G. Moeller, ed., *Peasants and Lords in Modern Germany.* London, 1985.

German Liberalism and the Dissolution of the Weimar Party System, 1918–1933. Chapel Hill and London, 1988.

"'The Greatest Stupidity of My Life': Alfred Hugenberg and the Formation of the Hitler Cabinet, January 1933." *Journal of Contemporary History,* 27 (1992): 63–87.

"Hindenburg and the Conservative Dilemma in the 1932 Presidential Elections." *German Studies Review,* 20 (1997): 235–59.

"In the Shadow of Stabilization: German Liberalism and the Legitimacy Crisis of the Weimar Party System, 1924–1930." In Gerald Feldman, ed., *Die Nachwirkungen der Inflation.*

"The Limits of Collaboration: Edgar Jung, Herbert von Bose, and the Origins of the Conservative Resistance to Hitler, 1933–1934." In Larry Eugene Jones and James Retallack, eds., *Between Reform, Reaction, and Resistance.*

"Sammlung oder Zersplitterung? Die Bestrebungen zur Bildung einer neuen Mittelpartei in der Endphase der Weimarer Republik 1930–1933." *Vierteljahrshefte für Zeitgeschichte,* 25 (1977): 265–304.

Jones, Larry Eugene, and James Retallack, eds. *Between Reform, Reaction, and Resistance: Studies in the History of German Conservatism from 1789 to 1945.* Providence and Oxford, 1993.

Junker, Detlef. *Die Deutsche Zentrumspartei und Hitler. Ein Beitrag zur Problematik des politischen Katholizismus in Deutschland.* Stuttgart, 1969.

Kater, Michael H. *The Nazi Party: A Social Profile of Members and Leaders, 1919–1945.* Cambridge, Mass., 1983.

Kaufmann, Doris. *Katholisches Milieu in Münster 1928–1933.* Düsseldorf, 1984.

Kent, Bruce. *The Spoils of War: The Politics, Economics, and Diplomacy of Reparations.* Oxford, 1989.

Kershaw, Ian, ed. *Weimar: Why Did German Democracy Fail?* New York, 1990.

Kindleberger, Charles. *The World in Depression, 1929–1939.* Rev. ed. Berkeley and Los Angeles, 1986.

Kissenkoetter, Udo. *Gregor Strasser und die NSDAP.* Stuttgart, 1978.

Klein, Gotthard. *Der Volksverein für das katholische Deutschland, 1890–1933. Geschichte, Bedeutung, Untergang.* Paderborn and Munich, 1996.

Klemperer, Klemens von. *German Resistance against Hitler: The Search for Allies Abroad, 1938–1945.* Oxford, 1992.

Germany's New Conservatism: Its History and Dilemma in the Twentieth Century. Princeton, 1968.

Klueting, Harm. "'Vernunftrepublikanismus' und 'Vertrauensdiktatur': Friedrich Meinecke in der Weimarer Republik." *Historische Zeitschrift,* 242 (1986): 70–98.

Knipping, Franz. *Deutschland, Frankreich und das Ende der Locarno Ära, 1928–1931.* Munich, 1987.

Köhler, Henning. "Arbeitsbeschaffung, Siedlung und Reparationen in der Schlussphase der Regierung Brüning." *Vierteljahrshefte für Zeitgeschichte,* 17 (1969): 267–307.

Kohler, Eric D. "The Successful German Center-Left: Joseph Hess and the Prussian Center Party, 1908–32." *Central European History,* 23 (1990): 313–48.

Koops, Tilman. "Heinrich Brünings 'Politische Erfahrungen' (Zum ersten Teil der Memoiren)." *Geschichte in Wissenschaft und Unterricht,* 24 (1973): 197–221.

Koshar, Rudy. *Social Life, Local Politics, and Nazism: Marburg, 1880–1935.* Chapel Hill and London, 1986.

Krockow, Christian Graf von. *Preussen. Eine Bilanz.* Stuttgart, 1992.

Krohn, Claus-Dieter. "'Ökonomische Zwangslagen' und das Scheitern der Weimarer Republik. Zu Knut Borchardt's Analyse der deutschen Wirtschaft in den zwanziger Jahren." *Geschichte und Gesellschaft,* 8 (1982): 415–26.

Stabilisierung und ökonomische Interessen. Die Finanzpolitik des Deutschen Reiches 1923–1927. Düsseldorf, 1974.

Wirtschaftstheorien als politische Interessen. Die akademische Nationalökonomie in Deutschland, 1918–1933. Frankfurt a.M., 1981.

Kroll, Gerhard. *Von der Weltwirtschaftskrise zur Staatskonjunktur.* Berlin, 1959.

Kruedener, Jürgen Baron von, ed. *Economic Crisis and Political Collapse: The Weimar Republic 1924–1933.* New York and Oxford, 1990.

Krüger, Peter. *Die Aussenpolitik der Republik von Weimar.* Darmstadt, 1985.

Krüger, Peter, and Erich Hahn. "Der Loyalitätskonflikt des Staatssekretärs Bernhard Wilhelm von Bülow im Frühjahr 1933." *Vierteljahrshefte für Zeitgeschichte,* 20 (1972): 376–410.

Kühr, Herbert. *Parteien und Wahlen im Stadt- und Landkreis Essen in der Zeit der Weimarer Republik.* Düsseldorf, 1973.

Kunz, Andreas. "Arbeitsbeziehungen und Arbeitskonflikte im öffentlichen Sektor. Deutschland und Grossbritannien im Vergleich." *Geschichte und Gesellschaft,* 12 (1986): 37–62.

Kurz, Achim. "Zur Interpretation des Artikels 48 Abs. 2 WRV 1930–33." In Rolf Grawert et al., eds., *Offene Staatlichkeit.*

Lebovics, Herman. *Social Conservatism and the Middle Classes in Germany, 1914–1933.* Princeton, 1969.

Leopold, John A. *Alfred Hugenberg: The Radical Nationalist Campaign against the Weimar Republic.* New Haven and London, 1977.

Liang, Hsi-Huey. *The Berlin Police Force in the Weimar Republic.* Berkeley and Los Angeles, 1970.

Lohe, Eilert. *Heinrich Brüning. Offizier – Staatsmann – Gelehrter.* Göttingen, 1969.

Luthardt, Wolfgang, ed. *Sozialdemokratische Arbeiterbewegung und Weimarer Republik, 1927–1933.* 2 vols. Frankfurt a.M., 1978.

Maier, Charles S. "Die Nicht-Determiniertheit ökonomischer Modelle. Überlegungen zu Knut Borchardts These von der 'kranken Wirtschaft' der Weimarer Republik." *Geschichte und Gesellschaft*, 11 (1985): 275–94.

Recasting Bourgeois Europe: Stabilization in France, Germany, and Italy in the Decade after World War I. Princeton, 1975.

"The Two Postwar Eras and the Conditions for Stability in Twentieth-Century Europe." In Charles S. Maier, *In Search of Stability: Explorations in Historical Political Economy.* Cambridge, 1987.

Matthias, Erich, and Rudolf Morsey, eds. *Das Ende der Parteien 1933. Darstellungen und Dokumente.* Düsseldorf, 1960.

Matzerath, Horst. *Nationalsozialismus und kommunale Selbstverwaltung.* Stuttgart and Berlin, 1970.

Maurer, Ilse. *Reichsfinanzen und Grosse Koalition. Zur Geschichte des Reichskabinetts Müller (1928–1930).* Bern and Frankfurt a.M., 1973.

May, George. *Ludwig Kaas. Der Priester, der Politiker und der Gelehrte aus der Schule von Ulrich Stutz.* 3 vols. Amsterdam, 1981.

Meister, Rainer. *Die grosse Depression. Zwangslagen und Handlungsspielräume der Wirtschafts- und Finanzpolitik in Deutschland 1929–1932.* Regensburg, 1991.

Merkl, Peter H. *The Making of a Stormtrooper.* Princeton, 1980.

The Origin of the West German Republic. 1963. Reprint. Westport, Conn., 1982.

Mitchell, Maria. "Materialism and Secularism: CDU Politicians and National Socialism, 1945–1949." *Journal of Modern History*, 67 (1995): 278–308.

Mommsen, Hans. "Betrachtungen zu den Memoiren Heinrich Brünings." *Jahrbuch für die Geschichte Mittel- und Ostdeutschlands*, 22 (1973): 270–80.

"Die deutschen Gewerkschaften zwischen Anpassung und Widerstand 1930–1944." In Heinz Oskar Vetter, ed., *Vom Sozialistengesetz zur Mitbestimmung.* Cologne, 1975.

From Weimar to Auschwitz: Essays in German History. Cambridge, 1991.

"Government without Parties: Conservative Plans for Constitutional Revision at the End of the Weimar Republic." In Larry Eugene Jones and James Retallack, eds., *Between Reform, Reaction, and Resistance.*

"Heinrich Brünings Politik als Reichskanzler. Das Scheitern eines politischen Alleinganges." In Karl Holl, ed., *Wirtschaftskrise und liberale Demokratie.* Göttingen, 1978.

"Der lange Schatten der untergehenden Republik. Zur Kontinuität politischer Denkhaltungen von der späten Weimarer zur frühen Bundesrepublik." In Karl Dietrich Bracher et al., eds., *Die Weimarer Republik 1918–1933.* Düsseldorf, 1987.

The Rise and Fall of Weimar Democracy. Transl. Elborg Forster and Larry Eugene Jones. Chapel Hill and London, 1996.

"Social Views and Constitutional Plans of the Resistance." In Hermann Graml et al., *The German Resistance to Hitler.* Berkeley and Los Angeles, 1970.

"Staat und Bürokratie in der Ära Brüning." In Gotthard Jasper, ed., *Tradition und Reform in der deutschen Politik.*

"Die Stellung der Beamtenschaft in Reich, Ländern und Gemeinden in der Ära Brüning." *Vierteljahrshefte für Zeitgeschichte*, 21 (1973): 151–65.

Mommsen, Hans, Dietmar Petzina, and Bernd Weisbrod, eds. *Industrielles System und politische Entwicklung in der Weimarer Republik.* Athenäum reprint. 2 vols. Düsseldorf, 1977.

Morsey, Rudolf. *Brüning und Adenauer. Zwei deutsche Staatsmänner.* Düsseldorf, 1972.
"Brünings Kritik am politischen Wiederaufbau in Deutschland, 1949–1955." In Joseph Listl and Herbert Schambeck, eds., *Demokratie in Anfechtung und Bewährung. Festschrift für Johannes Broermann.* Berlin, 1982.
"Brünings Kritik an Adenauers Westpolitik. Vorgeschichte und Folgen seines Düsseldorfer Vortrags vom 2. Juni 1954." In Manfred Funke et al., eds., *Demokratie und Diktatur. Festschrift für Karl Dietrich Bracher.* Düsseldorf, 1987.
"Brünings Kritik an der Reichsfinanzpolitik 1919–1929." In Erich Hassinger et al., eds., *Geschichte, Wirtschaft, Gesellschaft. Festschrift für Clemens Bauer.* Berlin, 1974.
"Brünings politische Weltanschauung vor 1918." In Gerhard A. Ritter, ed., *Gesellschaft, Parlament und Regierung.* Düsseldorf, 1974.
"Die Deutsche Zentrumspartei." In Erich Matthias and Rudolf Morsey, eds., *Das Ende der Parteien 1933.*
"Die deutschen Katholiken und der Nationalstaat zwischen Kulturkampf und dem ersten Weltkrieg." *Historisches Jahrbuch,* 90 (1970): 31–64.
"Emigration und Nachkriegsplanung. Vorschläge und Vorstellungen Heinrich Brünings über den Neuaufbau in Deutschland." In Lothar Albertin and Werner Link, eds., *Politische Parteien auf dem Weg zur parlamentarischen Demokratie in Deutschland.* Düsseldorf, 1981.
Der Untergang des politischen Katholizismus. Die Zentrumspartei zwischen christlichem Selbstverständnis und 'Nationaler Erhebung' 1932/33. Stuttgart and Zürich, 1977.
"Zentrumspartei und Zentrumspolitiker im rückblickenden Urteil Heinrich Brünings." In Jürgen Heideking et al., eds., *Wege in die Zeitgeschichte.*
Zur Entstehung, Authentizität und Kritik von Brünings "Memoiren 1918–1934." Opladen, 1975.
"Zur Problematik einer zeitgeschichtlichen Briefedition." *Historische Zeitschrift,* 221 (1975): 69–95.
Müller, Dirk. *Arbeiter, Katholizismus, Staat. Der Volksverein für das katholische Deutschland und die katholischen Arbeiterorganisationen in der Weimarer Republik.* Bonn, 1996.
Müller, Frank. *Die "Brüning Papers." Der letzte Zentrumskanzler im Spiegel seiner Selbstzeugnisse.* Frankfurt a.M., 1993.
Muth, Heinrich. "Agrarpolitik und Parteipolitik im Frühjahr 1932." In Ferdinand A. Hermens and Theodor Schieder, eds., *Staat, Wirtschaft und Politik.*
"Das 'Kölner Gespräch' am 4. Januar 1933." *Geschichte in Wissenschaft und Unterricht,* 37 (1986): 463–80, 529–41.
"Schleicher und die Gewerkschaften 1932. Ein Quellenproblem." *Vierteljahrshefte für Zeitgeschichte,* 29 (1981): 189–215.
Neebe, Reinhard. *Grossindustrie, Staat und NSDAP 1930–1933. Paul Silverberg und der Reichsverband der Deutschen Industrie in der Krise der Weimarer Republik.* Göttingen, 1981.
"Unternehmerverbände und Gewerkschaften in den Jahren der Grossen Krise, 1929–33." *Geschichte und Gesellschaft,* 9 (1983): 302–30.
Nobel, Alphons. *Brüning.* Leipzig, 1932.
Opitz, Günter. *Der Christlich-soziale Volksdienst. Versuch einer protestantischen Partei in der Weimarer Republik.* Düsseldorf, 1969.
Orde, Anne. "The Origins of the German-Austrian Customs Union Affair of 1931." *Central European History,* 13 (1980): 34–59.
Orlow, Dietrich. *The History of the Nazi Party 1919–1933.* Pittsburgh, 1969.

Weimar Prussia 1918–1925: The Unlikely Rock of Democracy. Pittsburgh, 1986.

Weimar Prussia 1925–1933: The Illusion of Strength. Pittsburgh, 1991.

Patch, William L., Jr. *Christian Trade Unions in the Weimar Republic: The Failure of "Corporate Pluralism."* New Haven and London, 1985.

"Class Prejudice and the Failure of the Weimar Republic." *German Studies Review*, 12 (1989): 35–54.

"Heinrich Brüning's Recollections of Monarchism: The Birth of a Red Herring." *Journal of Modern History* (forthcoming June 1998).

Petzold, Joachim. *Franz von Papen. Ein deutsches Verhängnis.* Munich and Berlin, 1995.

Plehwe, Friedrich-Karl von. *Reichskanzler Kurt von Schleicher. Weimars letzte Chance gegen Hitler.* Esslingen, 1983.

Plesse, Sigurd. *Die nationalsozialistische Machtergreifung im Oberharz. Clausthal-Zellerfeld 1929–1933.* Clausthal-Zellerfeld, 1970.

Plum, Günter. *Gesellschaftsstruktur und politisches Bewusstsein in einer katholischen Region 1928–1933. Untersuchung am Beispiel des Regierungsbezirks Aachen.* Stuttgart, 1972.

Plumpe, Gottfried. "Wirtschaftspolitik in der Weltwirtschaftskrise. Realität und Alternativen." *Geschichte und Gesellschaft*, 11 (1985): 326–57.

Pois, Robert. *Friedrich Meinecke and German Politics in the Twentieth Century.* Berkeley and Los Angeles, 1972.

Post, Gaines, Jr. *The Civil-Military Fabric of Weimar Foreign Policy.* Princeton, 1973.

Preller, Ludwig. *Sozialpolitik in der Weimarer Republik.* 1949. Athenäum reprint. Düsseldorf, 1978.

Pridham, Geoffrey. *Hitler's Rise to Power: The Nazi Movement in Bavaria, 1923–1933.* New York, 1973.

Radkau, Joachim. *Die deutsche Emigration in den USA. Ihr Einfluss auf die amerikanische Europapolitik 1933–1945.* Düsseldorf, 1971.

Reimann, Viktor. *Goebbels.* Garden City, N.Y., 1976.

Repgen, Konrad. "Über die Entstehung der Reichskonkordats-Offerte im Frühjahr 1933 und die Bedeutung des Reichskonkordats." *Vierteljahrshefte für Zeitgeschichte*, 26 (1978): 499–534.

Reuth, Ralf Georg. *Goebbels.* San Diego and New York, 1994.

Richter, Ludwig. "Das präsidiale Notverordnungsrecht in den ersten Jahren der Weimarer Republik. Friedrich Ebert und die Anwendung des Artikels 48 der Weimarer Reichsverfassung." In Eberhard Kolb, ed., *Friedrich Ebert als Reichspräsident. Amtsführung und Amtsverständnis.* Munich, 1997.

Ritschl, Albrecht. "Zu hohe Löhne in der Weimarer Republik? Eine Auseinandersetzung mit Holtfrerichs Berechnungen zur Lohnposition der Arbeiterschaft 1925–1932." *Geschichte und Gesellschaft*, 16 (1990): 375–402.

Ritter, Emil. *Die katholisch-soziale Bewegung Deutschlands im neunzehnten Jahrhundert und der Volksverein.* Cologne, 1954.

Ritter, Gerhard. *Carl Goerdeler und die deutsche Widerstandsbewegung.* Stuttgart, 1954. Abridged edition published in English as *The German Resistance: Carl Goerdeler's Struggle against Tyranny.* New York, 1958.

Rödder, Andreas. "Dichtung und Wahrheit. Der Quellenwert von Heinrich Brünings Memoiren und seine Kanzlerschaft." *Historische Zeitschrift*, 265 (1997): 77–116.

Stresemanns Erbe. Julius Curtius und die deutsche Aussenpolitik 1929–1931. Paderborn and Munich, 1996.

Rolfs, Richard. *The Sorcerer's Apprentice: The Life of Franz von Papen.* Lanham, Md., 1996.

Rosenhaft, Eve. *Beating the Fascists? The German Communists and Political Violence 1929–1933.* Cambridge, 1983.

Ross, Ronald. *Beleaguered Tower: The Dilemma of Political Catholicism in Wilhelmine Germany.* Notre Dame, 1976.

Ruppert, Karsten. *Im Dienst am Staat von Weimar. Das Zentrum als regierende Partei in der Weimarer Demokratie 1923–1930.* Düsseldorf, 1992.

Sailer, Joachim. *Eugen Bolz und die Krise des politischen Katholizismus in der Weimarer Republik.* Tübingen, 1994.

Saldern, Adelheid von. *Hermann Dietrich. Ein Staatsmann der Weimarer Republik.* Boppard am Rhein, 1966.

Salewski, Michael. "Zur deutschen Sicherheitspolitik in der Spätezeit der Weimarer Republik." *Vierteljahrshefte für Zeitgeschichte,* 22 (1974): 121–47.

Sanmann, Horst. "Daten und Alternativen der deutschen Wirtschafts- und Finanzpolitik in der Ära Brüning." *Hamburger Jahrbuch für Wirtschafts- und Gesellschaftspolitik,* 10 (1965): 109–40.

Sauer, Wolfgang. *Die Mobilmachung der Gewalt.* Ullstein reprint. Frankfurt a.M., 1974 (originally published as Part III of Karl Dietrich Bracher, Wolfgang Sauer, and Gerhard Schulz, *Die nationalsozialistische Machtergreifung* (Cologne and Opladen, 1960)).

Schaap, Klaus. *Die Endphase der Weimarer Republik im Freistaat Oldenburg, 1928–1933.* Düsseldorf, 1978.

Schäfer, Michael. *Heinrich Imbusch. Christlicher Gewerkschaftsführer und Widerstandskämpfer.* Munich, 1990.

Schaefer, Rainer. *SPD in der Ära Brüning: Tolerierung oder Mobilisierung? Handlungsspielräume und Strategien sozialdemokratischer Politik 1930–1932.* Frankfurt a.M., 1990.

Scheuner, Ulrich. "Die Anwendung des Art. 48 der Weimarer Reichsverfassung unter den Präsidentschaften von Ebert und Hindenburg." In Ferdinand A. Hermens and Theodor Schieder, eds., *Staat, Wirtschaft und Politik.*

Schiemann, Jürgen. *Die deutsche Währung in der Weltwirtschaftskrise 1929–1933.* Bonn and Stuttgart, 1980.

Schiffer, Reinhard. *Elemente direkter Demokratie im Weimarer Regierungssystem.* Düsseldorf, 1971.

Schiffmann, Dieter. "Die Freien Gewerkschaften und das Scheitern der Regierung Müller 1930." In Erich Matthias and Klaus Schönhoven, eds., *Solidarität und Menschenwürde. Etappen der deutschen Gewerkschaftsgeschichte von den Anfängen bis zur Gegenwart.* Bonn, 1984.

Schildt, Axel. *Militärdiktatur mit Massenbasis? Die Querfrontkonzeption der Reichswehrführung um General von Schleicher am Ende der Weimarer Republik.* Frankfurt a.M., 1981.

Schmädeke, Jürgen, and Peter Steinbach, eds. *Der Widerstand gegen den Nationalsozialismus. Die deutsche Gesellschaft und der Widerstand gegen Hitler.* Munich and Zürich, 1985.

Schmidt, Ute. *Zentrum oder CDU. Politischer Katholizismus zwischen Tradition und Anpassung.* Opladen, 1987.

Schneider, Michael. *Das Arbeitsbeschaffungsprogramm des ADGB. Zur gewerkschaftlichen Politik in der Endphase der Weimarer Republik.* Bonn–Bad Godesberg, 1975.

Die Christlichen Gewerkschaften 1894–1933. Bonn, 1982.

Schneider, Werner. *Die Deutsche Demokratische Partei in der Weimarer Republik, 1924–1930.* Munich, 1978.

Schön, Eberhart. *Die Entstehung des Nationalsozialismus in Hessen.* Meisenheim am Glan, 1972.

Schönhoven, Klaus. *Die Bayerische Volkspartei 1924–1932.* Düsseldorf, 1972.

"Zwischen Anpassung und Ausschaltung. Die Bayerische Volkspartei in der Endphase der Weimarer Republik 1932/33." *Historische Zeitschrift*, 224 (1977): 340–78.

Scholder, Klaus. "Altes und Neues zur Vorgeschichte des Reichskonkordats. Erwiderung auf Konrad Repgen." *Vierteljahrshefte für Zeitgeschichte*, 26 (1978): 535–70.

The Churches and the Third Reich. 2 vols. London, 1987.

Schorr, Helmut. *Adam Stegerwald. Politiker der ersten deutschen Republik.* Recklinghausen, 1966.

Schuker, Stephen A. "Ambivalent Exile: Heinrich Brüning and America's Good War." In Christoph Buchheim et al., eds., *Zerrissene Zwischenkriegszeit.*

American "Reparations" to Germany, 1919–1933: Implications for the Third-World Debt Crisis. Princeton, 1988.

Schulz, Gerhard. *Aufstieg des Nationalsozialismus. Krise und Revolution in Deutschland.* Frankfurt a.M., 1975.

"'Preussenschlag' oder Staatsstreich? Neues zum 20. Juli 1932." *Der Staat*, 17 (1978): 553–81.

"Reparationen und Krisenprobleme nach dem Wahlsieg der NSDAP 1930. Betrachtungen zur Regierung Brüning." *Vierteljahrschrift für Sozial- und Wirtschaftsgeschichte*, 67 (1980): 200–22.

"Die Suche nach dem Schuldigen. Heinrich Brüning und seine Demission als Reichskanzler." In Karl Dietrich Bracher et al., eds., *Staat und Parteien. Festschrift für Rudolf Morsey zum 65. Geburtstag.* Berlin, 1992.

Zwischen Demokratie und Diktatur. Verfassungspolitik und Reichsreform in der Weimarer Republik. Vol. 1: *Die Periode der Konsolidierung*; vol. 2: *Deutschland am Vorabend der grossen Krise.* 2nd ed. Berlin and New York, 1987. Vol. 3: *Von Brüning zu Hitler.* Berlin and New York, 1992.

Schulze, Hagen. *Otto Braun, oder Preussens demokratische Sendung.* Frankfurt a.M., 1977.

Schumacher, Martin. *Mittelstandsfront und Republik. Die Wirtschaftspartei – Reichspartei des deutschen Mittelstandes 1919–1933.* Düsseldorf, 1972.

Schwarz, Hans-Peter. *Adenauer. Der Aufstieg: 1876–1952.* Stuttgart, 1986.

Schwend, Karl. "Die Bayerische Volkspartei." In Erich Matthias and Rudolf Morsey, eds., *Das Ende der Parteien 1933.*

Shamir, Haim. *Economic Crisis and French Foreign Policy 1930–1936.* Leiden, 1989.

Shively, W. Phillips. "Party Identification, Party Choice, and Voting Stability: The Weimar Case." *American Political Science Review*, 66 (1972): 1203–25.

Skrzypczak, Henryk. "Kanzlerwechsel und Einheitsfront. Abwehrreaktionen der Arbeiterbewegung auf die Machtübergabe an Franz von Papen." *Internationale wissenschaftliche Korrespondenz zur Geschichte der Arbeiterbewegung*, 18 (1982): 482–99.

Sperber, Jonathan. *Popular Catholicism in Nineteenth-Century Germany.* Princeton, 1984.

Stachura, Peter. *Gregor Strasser and the Rise of Nazism.* London, 1983.

Stambrook, F. G. "The German-Austrian Customs Union Project of 1931: A Study of German Methods and Motives." In Hans W. Gatzke, ed., *European Diplomacy Between two Wars.* Chicago, 1972.

Stegmann, Dirk, B.-J. Wendt, and P. C. Witt, eds. *Industrielle Gesellschaft und politisches System. Festschrift für Fritz Fischer.* Bonn, 1978.

Stehlin, Stewart A. *Weimar and the Vatican, 1919–1933: German–Vatican Diplomatic Relations in the Interwar Years.* Princeton, 1983.

Stürmer, Michael. *Koalition und Opposition in der Weimarer Republik 1924–1928.* Düsseldorf, 1967.

ed. *Die Weimarer Republik. Belagerte Civitas.* 2nd ed. Königstein/Ts., 1985.

Stump, Wolfgang. *Geschichte und Organisation der Zentrumspartei in Düsseldorf, 1917–1933.* Düsseldorf, 1971.

Tschirbs, Rudolf. *Tarifpolitik im Ruhrbergbau 1918–1933.* Berlin and New York, 1986.

Turner, Henry Ashby, Jr. *German Big Business and the Rise of Hitler.* New York and Oxford, 1985.

Hitler's Thirty Days to Power: January 1933. Reading, Mass., 1996.

"The *Ruhrlade*: Secret Cabinet of Heavy Industry in the Weimar Republic." *Central European History*, 3 (1970): 195–228.

Stresemann and the Politics of the Weimar Republic. Princeton, 1963.

Vogelsang, Thilo. *Reichswehr, Staat und NSDAP. Beiträge zur deutschen Geschichte 1930–1932.* Stuttgart, 1962.

Volk, Ludwig. *Katholische Kirche und Nationalsozialismus. Ausgewählte Aufsätze.* Mainz, 1987.

Das Reichskonkordat vom 20. Juli 1933. Mainz, 1972.

Voth, Hans-Joachim. "Wages, Investment, and the Fate of the Weimar Republic: A Long-term Perspective." *German History*, 11 (1993): 265–92.

Wachtling, Oswald. *Joseph Joos. Journalist, Arbeiterführer, Zentrumspolitiker.* Mainz, 1974.

Wandel, Eckhard. *Hans Schäffer. Steuermann in wirtschaftlichen und politischen Krisen.* Stuttgart, 1974.

Warner, Geoffrey. *Pierre Laval and the Eclipse of France.* New York, 1968.

Weber, Hermann. *Die Wandlung des deutschen Kommunismus. Die Stalinisierung der KPD in der Weimarer Republik.* 2 vols. Frankfurt a.M., 1969.

Weisbrod, Bernd. "Die Befreiung von den 'Tariffesseln.' Deflationspolitik als Krisenstrategie der Unternehmer in der Ära Brüning." *Geschichte und Gesellschaft*, 11 (1985): 295–325.

"Economic Power and Political Stability Reconsidered: Heavy Industry in Weimar Germany." *Social History*, 4 (1979): 241–63.

"Industrial Crisis Strategy in the Great Depression." In Jürgen Baron von Kruedener, ed., *Economic Crisis and Political Collapse.*

Schwerindustrie in der Weimarer Republik. Interessenpolitik zwischen Stabilisierung und Krise. Wuppertal, 1978.

Wengst, Udo. "Schlange-Schöningen, Ostsiedlung und die Demission der Regierung Brüning." *Geschichte in Wissenschaft und Unterricht*, 30 (1979): 538–51.

"Unternehmerverbände und Gewerkschaften in Deutschland im Jahre 1930." *Vierteljahrshefte für Zeitgeschichte*, 25 (1977): 99–119.

Wheeler-Bennett, John. *Wooden Titan: Hindenburg in Twenty Years of German History 1914–1934.* New York, 1936.

Winkler, Dörte. "Frauenarbeit versus Frauenideologie. Probleme der weiblichen Erwerbstätigkeit in Deutschland 1930–1945." *Archiv für Sozialgeschichte*, 17 (1977): 99–126.

Winkler, Heinrich August. *Arbeiter und Arbeiterbewegung in der Weimarer Republik*. Vol.
2: *1924 bis 1930: Der Schein der Normalität*. 2nd ed. Berlin and Bonn, 1988. Vol. 3:
1930 bis 1933: Der Weg in die Katastrophe. Berlin and Bonn, 1987.

"From Social Protectionism to National Socialism: The German Small-Business
Movement in Comparative Perspective." *Journal of Modern History*, 48 (1976):
1–18.

*Mittelstand, Demokratie und Nationalsozialismus. Die politische Entwicklung von
Handwerk und Kleinhandel in der Weimarer Republik*. Cologne, 1972.

Weimar 1918–1933. Die Geschichte der ersten deutschen Demokratie. Munich, 1993.

ed. *Die deutsche Staatskrise 1930–1933*. Munich, 1992.

Wisser, Thomas. "Die Diktaturmassnahmen im Juli 1930 – Autoritäre Umwandlung der
Demokratie?" In Rolf Grawert et al., eds., *Offene Staatlichkeit*.

Witt, Peter-Christian. "Finanzpolitik als Verfassungs- und Gesellschaftspolitik. Überlegungen zur Finanzpolitik des Deutschen Reiches in den Jahren 1930 bis 1932."
Geschichte und Gesellschaft, 8 (1982): 386–414.

Wohl, Robert. *The Generation of 1914*. Cambridge, Mass., 1979.

Wolffsohn, Michael. *Industrie und Handwerk im Konflikt mit staatlicher Wirtschaftspolitik?
Studien zur Politik der Arbeitsbeschaffung in Deutschland 1930–1934*. Berlin, 1977.

Index